FIVE THOUSAND AMERICAN FAMILIES— PATTERNS OF ECONOMIC PROGRESS

VOLUME IX

Analyses of the First Twelve Years of the Panel Study of Income Dynamics

Edited by Martha S. Hill, Daniel H. Hill, and James N. Morgan

With Contributions by Sue A. Augustyniak, Richard D. Coe, Mary Corcoran, Linda P. Datcher, Greg J. Duncan, Scott Grosse, Daniel H. Hill, Martha S. Hill, Saul D. Hoffman, Renata Imbruglia, Abigail MacKenzie, James N. Morgan, Sandra J. Newman, and Michael Ponza

This Project Has Been Supported by the Office of the Assistant Secretary for Planning, the Department of Health and Human Services, and by the National Science Foundation

ISR

(Michigan. University.)
SURVEY RESEARCH CENTER
INSTITUTE FOR SOCIAL RESEARCH
THE UNIVERSITY OF MICHIGAN

Permission is hereby granted for the quotation of this
publication without prior specific permission for purposes
of criticism, review, or evaluation, subject only to the
"fair use" provisions of the Resolution on Permissions of
the Association of American University Presses, including
citation of the source.

Five Thousand American Families—Patterns of Economic Progress, Volume IX
Library of Congress CatalogsCard No. 74-62002
ISBN 0-87944-267-0

Published by the Institute for Social Research,
The University of Michigan, Ann Arbor, Michigan

Published 1981
Printed in the United States of America

CONTENTS

INTRODUCTION

This volume of findings from the Panel Study of Income Dynamics departs in format from previous volumes in the series. In addition to chapters addressing a central theme and chapters reporting other in-depth analyses, we have included a sequence of chapters either addressing methodological issues or providing brief descriptions of the data. While this format results in a less cohesive final product than that of some of our earlier volumes, it does allow us to expand our coverage of topics in an attempt to accommodate the interests of a more diverse audience. Chapters in the first part of the volume have the common goal of using the panel nature of the data to further our understanding of the dynamics of important family economic processes and conditions. The first four chapters analyze the dynamics of economic status, wages, poverty status, and welfare use. Intergenerational status transmission, an inherently dynamic subject, is analyzed in the fifth chapter. The sixth chapter, which concludes the section, is an analysis of changes in economic status associated with retirement.

Each of the investigations in this first section draws heavily on the literature, both to describe the present state of knowledge and methods and to determine where the application of panel data may result in a real breakthrough in understanding. The degree of guidance provided by the theories in the literature varies from topic to topic. The human capital and segmented labor market theories, for instance, have provided Saul Hoffman and Greg Duncan with numerous testable hypotheses for their analysis of the dynamics of wage change in Chapter 2, while poverty hypotheses have very few implications for the dynamics of poverty investigated by Martha Hill in Chapter 3.

The second part of this volume presents the findings from five different analyses, related primarily by the fact that they have utilized the Panel Study data. These chapters represent in-depth analyses of topics ranging from the effect of wage expectations on men's labor supply to race/sex differences in the effects of background on achievement. These chapters differ from those in the first section either because they do not address the dynamics of economic processes or because the process investigated, while still important, is related less directly to the determination of family economic well being.

The chapters in the last section of the volume contain analyses of three methodological subjects and four mostly descriptive analyses of data from the Panel Study. The methodological chapters address some of the fundamental economic advantages of panel data, the consistency of reports of wages, and the sampling design effects of the Panel Study. The descriptive chapters predominantly concentrate on trends that are of particular current relevance-- trends in child care arrangements, in residential property taxes, and in the characteristics of housing demand. Also included in this section is a brief chapter describing tests of wage trade-off hypotheses present in the economic literature. Our annual report of outside research using the Panel Study data appears in the final chapter. The twelfth wave (1979) questionnaire is reproduced as an appendix.

As in several of the preceding volumes in this series, Linda Stafford has again contributed in editing the volume. In addition, the volume has benefited by the suggestions of the following reviewers:

Reviewers Outside The University of Michigan

Ronald P. Abeles, National Institute on Aging
John M. Abowd, University of Chicago
Emily S. Andrews, Social Security Administration
Orley Ashenfelter, Princeton University
Wendy Baldwin, National Institute of Child Health and Human Development
Mary Jo Bane, Harvard University
Michael Borus, Center for Human Resource Research, Ohio State University
Kenneth Boulding, University of Colorado
Charles Brown, University of Maryland
Gary Chamberlain, University of Wisconsin
Andrew Cherlin, Johns Hopkins University
Tom Daymont, Ohio State University
Otis Dudley Duncan, University of Arizona
David L. Featherman, University of Wisconsin
Robert Ferber, University of Illinois
Alan Fox, Social Security Administration
Paul Glick, U. S. Department of Commerce (Census)
Arthur Goldberger, University of Wisconsin
Jacob Goodman, University of Virginia
Karl Gregory, Oakland University, Rochester, Mich.
Eric A. Hanushek, University of Rochester
John C. Hause, State University of New York, Stony Brook
Saul Hoffman, University of Delaware
Christopher S. Jencks, Northwestern University
Dick Lamanna, University of Notre Dame
Selig Lesnoy, Social Security Administration
Sar A. Levitan, George Washington University
Frank Levy, University of California, Berkeley
E. Scott Maynes, Cornell University
James Medoff, Harvard University

Jacob Mincer, Columbia University
Kirsten Moore, Urban Institute
Gilbert Nestel, Ohio State University
Michael Olneck, University of Wisconsin
Valerie Oppenheimer, University of California
Herbert S. Parnes, Rutgers University
Joe Pleck, Wellesley College
Mary Powers, Fordham University
Harriet Presser, College Park, Maryland
D. Lee Rainwater, Harvard University
Mary Rowe, Massachusetts Institute of Technology
J.C.R. Rowley, Ontario, Canada
Isabel Sawhill, Urban Institute
Bradley R. Schiller, American University
T. Paul Schultz, Yale University
Ethel Shanas, University of Illinois
Paul Taubman, Pennsylvania University
L.D. Taylor, University of Arizona
Timothy Smeeding, U.S. Department of Commerce (Census)
Clair Vickery, University of California
Heather Weiss, Cornell University
Robert J. Willis, State University of New York, Stony Brook
Michael Wiseman, University of California

University of Michigan Reviewers

Bob Axelrod
Elizabeth Douvan
Duane Alwin
Ren Farley
Deborah Freedman
David Goldberg
Al Hermalin
James House
George Johnson
Harold Johnson
Tom Juster
Eva Mueller
Anders Klevmarken
Glen Loury
Frank Stafford
Arnold Tannenbaum
Arland Thornton

Chapter 1

PERSISTENCE AND CHANGE IN ECONOMIC STATUS
AND THE ROLE OF CHANGING FAMILY COMPOSITION

Greg J. Duncan and James N. Morgan

INTRODUCTION

The Panel Study of Income Dynamics was begun in 1968, in the midst of the war on poverty, with a desire to do more than just count the casualties. Many observers were suggesting that there was a vicious cycle of poverty--a cumulative process involving psychological or sociological forces or cultural or environmental factors by which the poor stayed poor and the rich got richer. In such a situation, the obvious questions to be addressed by our study were what attitudes and behavior patterns appeared to facilitate climbing out of poverty, which ones caused people to fall into poverty or to stay there and whether different patterns emerged at the middle and upper ends of the income distribution.

Prior evidence on these questions came from single sample surveys or case studies. Case studies have produced exciting hypotheses, but the history of quantitative social science is that the most interesting hypotheses from case studies, as well as those deduced from single motive theories, commonly turn out to be either wrong or quantitatively unimportant. Moreover, the analytic payoff from static cross-sectional data is quite limited. Typically, these kinds of data show that the poor have "worse" attitudes--meaning that they are not highly motivated, lack a strong sense of personal efficacy, and are less oriented toward the future. But this evidence does not suggest conclusively that the attitudes caused the economic outcome. The attitudes may well have resulted from economic misfortune, or both attitudes and economic well-being may have been affected simultaneously by something else.

Inferring processes from outcomes and motivations from processes has always been a difficult and uncertain procedure. Whether we are concerned about wrong attitudes producing poverty, or about prejudicial discrimination according to race or sex or age, cross-sectional data are a weak source. Even if we think we have eliminated most of the competing alternative explanations, we don't know how

1

the process works, and, even if we could reconstruct some of the process by retrospect, the motives and purposes of the individual actors still would be obscure. Without that, it is difficult to design remedies.

Hence, the original design of the Panel Study called for measurement of a number of attitudes and behavior patterns in a representative sample of families, and for reinterviewing annually the heads of families that contained individuals from the original sample of families. After the fifth year of the study, it was clear that the wealth of findings could not be disseminated just through working papers, so we published the first two of the annual series of volumes called <u>Five Thousand American Families: Patterns of Economic Progress</u>, along with volumes of documentation to facilitate wider use of the data for secondary analysis. The main findings were already apparent by that time:

1. Initial attitudes and behavior patterns had little to do with subsequent economic progress, at least in the 1968-1972 period. If anything, the attitudes seemed to result from rather than cause economic change. Improved economic circumstances looked far more randomly distributed than anyone had expected. This finding held not only at the lower end of the income distribution, but at other levels as well.

2. On the other hand, there was far more change in family composition and it had far more effect on the economic status of individuals than most stereotypes implied. While some changes in family are expected, planned, or even inevitable, others are discretionary. The implication of this finding was that people may have more control over their economic status through decisions about marriage, divorce, or procreation, doubling up and undoubling than they do by seeking a better job or more work or investing more in their own human capital. In Volume IV we analyzed the factors associated with changes in family composition, and in Volume V we published a quantitative decomposition of change in status associated with changes in hours and earnings as against changes in family composition.

3. Finally, we found that there was not only far more year-to-year change in economic status than anyone had thought, but that there were substantial demographic differences between the very small group of families who were persistently poor and the much larger group who were only temporarily poor during any one year. (See the chapter in Volume VI by Richard Coe and the Coe and Martha Hill chapters in the present volume.) Specialists in welfare had known for a long time that the turnover on welfare rolls was too high to fit the stereotype of a culture of poverty, but those who believed in the stereotype

could always argue that the same people were reappearing on other rolls or other places. Our data indicate far less persistent dependency than has been commonly believed.

The policy implications of such a finding go far beyond the revision of theory. Federal revenue sharing rules and many other policies that are based on annual counts of the poor allocate too much assistance to areas where many people are poor temporarily and too little to areas with more persistent poverty. The misallocation is particularly wasteful if the help is intended to provide longer-term solutions, like education subsidies or job training, rather than temporary emergency help, like unemployment compensation.

This chapter looks again--but for a more recent, longer, and more inflationary period, 1971-1978--at how attitudes and behavior patterns, changes in family composition, and labor force events affect the extent of turnover and change in the economic status of individuals. The individual is used as the unit of observation in these analyses with family income or family income relative to needs as the primary measure of well-being. Particularly in light of the amount of change in family composition, it becomes increasingly difficult over longer periods to identify which individuals comprise "the same family." However, if we restrict the analysis to unchanged families, we are introducing potential selection bias. So long as we remember that larger families appear several times, the individual is a better unit of counting and family status is a better measure of well-being. We facilitate the interpretation by looking separately at family "heads," wives, young children and older children, defined by their situation in 1972.[1]

AN OVERVIEW OF CHANGE IN ECONOMIC STATUS

A common way of illustrating the changing economic positions of a population is with transition tables. Tables 1.1 and 1.2 compare the family economic position of our sample of individuals at two points in time--in 1971 and in 1978--using two measures of economic status--total family money income and family income relative to needs. Family income is the sum of pretax labor, transfer, and asset income of all family members. Family income/needs is calculated by

---

[1]Interviews conducted in the spring of year t gather annual income and needs information for the calendar year t-1. In this analysis, the point in time information on family status and attitudes was gathered in the 1972 interview but the income and needs information began in 1971. The household head is defined to be the husband in husband-wife families.

dividing family income by a poverty-level needs standard based on information on the number, age, and sex of family members. Income/needs is thus a ratio rather than a dollar amount; a value of two, for example, would indicate that a family's income was twice as high as its poverty-level needs.

Table 1.1

FAMILY INCOME MOBILITY TABLE, 1971-1978
(For all sample individuals.)

Family Income Quintile in 1971	Family Income Quintile in 1978					
	Lowest	Fourth	Third	Second	Highest	All
Lowest	5.4%	2.0%	1.3%	1.0%	0.3%	10.0%
Fourth	3.4	5.3	4.6	2.4	1.4	17.1
Third	1.9	4.1	6.6	6.6	2.9	22.1
Second	0.9	2.3	4.5	7.8	7.8	23.3
Highest	1.0	1.9	2.9	5.8	15.9	27.5
All	12.6%	15.6%	19.9%	23.6%	28.3%	100.0%

Tau B=.450

Number of observations: 12,456

Rather than using actual dollar amounts, Tables 1.1 and 1.2 are based on quintiles, formed by ranking all families according to income and income/needs and then dividing them into five equal groups. In 1971, the bottom one-fifth of all families received incomes below $4,200, while the top one-fifth received at least $16,000. These are the family income levels used to denote the lowest and highest family income quintiles in 1971. By 1978, inflation and real income growth had pushed the lowest and highest quintile break points to about $6,700 and $27,500, respectively.

The use of quintiles assumes that economic status is a relative rather than an absolute concept. One's position is maintained only if real income goes up (or down) as much as the average percentage increase of everyone else. Later in this chapter, we examine the proportions of families who stay ahead of inflation (and find that more than half manage to do that). The entries in Tables 1.1 and 1.2 show the fraction of all sample individuals falling into the various

Table 1.2

FAMILY INCOME/NEEDS MOBILITY TABLE, 1971-1978
(For all sample individuals.)

Family Income/Needs Quintile in 1971	Family Income/Needs Quintile in 1978					
	Lowest	Fourth	Third	Second	Highest	All
Lowest	9.7%	4.2%	2.4%	1.1%	0.7%	18.1%
Fourth	3.8	6.5	5.6	3.3	1.3	20.5%
Third	1.7	5.0	7.7	5.6	3.4	23.4
Second	0.8	2.5	4.7	5.8	5.9	19.7
Highest	0.6	1.1	2.3	4.2	10.1	18.1
All	16.6%	19.3%	22.7%	20.0%	21.4%	100.0%

Tau B=.460

Number of observations: 12,456

combinations of quintile positions during the two years. For example, the entry in the first row and column in Table 1.1 indicates that 5.4 percent of the population were in families with incomes below $4,200 in 1971 and below $6,700 in 1978.[2] The "All" column on the right end of the table shows that one-tenth of the entire sample were in families with incomes in the bottom quintile in 1971, so the fraction of those who stayed at the bottom was a little over one-half (5.4/10.0) of those who began there.[3] Of course some of those moving out of the bottom quintile didn't go very far, but over one-quarter (2.6/10.0) moved into the top three quintiles.

---

[2]Strictly speaking, the 5.4 percent figure is an estimate of the fraction of the population in the bottom fifth at both points in time. All estimates given in this chapter are calculated with a set of weights that adjust for differential sampling fractions in the original sample and for differential nonresponse since the first year.

[3]It may seem contradictory to find that fewer than one-fifth of the population were in families with incomes in the bottom one-fifth of the family income distribution. This results from the use of families to denote quintiles and individuals to produce the numbers in Table 1.1 and 1.2. Low income families were smaller than high income families, hence a smaller proportion of individuals were in low-income families.

There was only slightly less family income mobility at the top of the income distribution than at the bottom. Of all individuals in families with incomes high enough to place them in the top fifth of the income distribution in 1971, nearly three-fifths (15.9/27.5) stayed in the top quintile, while almost one-fifth (5.8/27.5) fell into the bottom three quintiles. In all, about two-fifths of the sample retained their family income quintile positions, about two-fifths moved one quintile position in either direction, and the remaining one-fifth moved at least two quintile positions.

Family income position is determined by the number and success of earners in the family, plus receipts of transfer and asset income. Family income/needs adjusts family income for family size and would be expected to produce mobility patterns different from those of income alone if changes in family size did not accompany, on average, corresponding changes in family income. Certain family composition changes decrease both needs and income (as when a child leaves home), others increase both needs and income (as when a single individual marries an income earner), while still others may increase needs and decrease income (as when the birth of a child causes the mother to reduce her market work). The net effects of these changes, however, are to produce a picture of family income/ needs mobility, shown in Table 1.2, that is quite similar to that of family income alone. Similar proportions of individuals remained in the same income/ needs quintile or changed one or more quintile positions. Mobility patterns out of the bottom and top quintiles were quite similar as well. It is only when patterns of change in economic status for various demographic subgroups of the population are examined that differences appear.

Patterns of Change for Population Subgroups

We have discovered that changes in family composition are sufficiently frequent and dramatic in their effects that a coherent analysis of changes in economic status must use the individual rather than the family as the unit of analysis. By the seventh year of our study (1974), fewer than one-third of the families in the sample had the same composition as in the first year and over one-third were headed by someone who had not been the head of the "same" family seven years before. While the incomes of new families formed by divorce or by children leaving home could be compared to the income of the intact or parental families at an earlier point in time, it is easier to follow individuals classified by their relationship to the head of the household in which they resided in a given year. In the following analysis of changes in economic status, which uses the interviewing year 1972 as a base,[4] we distinguish the following groups of individuals: male heads of households; female heads of household; wives; older children (15-29 years old), and younger children (1-14 years old).[5] Note that many individuals did not retain their initial status (wives may have become divorced and become heads of their own households, children may have split off and become heads of their own households, and so on), but the classification is unique at one point in time.

Family Income Mobility

Table 1.3 documents the extent of change in family income for the entire sample taken together and for the five subgroup defined above. Patterns were generally similar across the five groups except for the older children, who suffered a substantial drop in family income when they left their parental households. Women who began the period as wives did a little worse, on average, due primarily to those among them who became divorced or widowed.

Dramatic changes in income were experienced by a substantial minority of the population. When the family incomes between 1971 and 1978 were compared (and the 1971 incomes were inflated up to 1978 price levels), about one-seventh of the sample individuals were found to live in households in which real incomes fell by more than $10,000, while one-fifth lived in households in which family incomes increased by $10,000 or more. Large decreases were much more common among older children who were likely to split off and end up depending upon their own incomes rather than those of their parents. Decreases were less common among women who headed their own families, but only because many of them began the period with family incomes below $10,000 and, by definition, could not experience that much of an income loss. Women who were initially wives were somewhat more likely to experience large losses than were their husbands, confirming that family composition changes like divorce have more of a detrimental effect on the wives. Large income increases were much less frequent among the older children and somewhat less frequent among the female heads of households.

---

[4]Interviews conducted in the spring of 1972 gathered information on 1971 calendar-year incomes and needs. Throughout this chapter, individuals are classified by their relationship to the 1972 household head, and the first income report is for the 1971 calendar year.

[5]These five subgroups make up about 97.5 percent of the entire sample; the excluded individuals include adult children (30 years of age and older), grandchildren, brothers and sisters of the head, and more distant relatives. Couples living together but not legally married are treated as husband and wife.

Table 1.3

DISTRIBUTION OF CHANGES AND GROWTH IN REAL FAMILY INCOME, 1971-1978
(For various groups of sample individuals.)

	All	Male Household Heads in 1972	Female Household Heads in 1972	Wives in 1972	Children Age 15-19 in 1972	Children Age 1-14 in 1972
Change in Real Family Income, 1971-1978						
Fell by more than $10,000	14%	10%	6%	13%	34%	11%
Increased by more than $10,000	20	20	16	19	11	24
Quintile Position						
Did not change	41	43	45	43	29	42
Changed by one	39	42	31	41	37	39
Changed by more than one	20	15	24	17	34	20
Association (Tau B) between 1971 and 1978 Decile position	.450	.506	.378	.492	.250	.462
Growth in Family Income						
Average annual growth rate	-.002	.007	.012	-.005	-.049	.010
Kept up with inflation	54	56	53	51	35	62
Grew by more than 5 percent per year	27	25	32	23	20	32
Number of observations	12,456	2509	1156	2379	1876	4536

An examination of income quintile position shows a similar story. The pattern, shown in Table 1.1, of no change in the position of two-fifths of the sample, change of one position for another two-fifths, and more dramatic change for the remaining one-fifth held up across all of the sample subgroups except the older children and, to a lesser extent, female heads of households. Relative family income position was much less stable for the older children. Women who headed households were more likely to have either very stable or very unstable family incomes.

A final beginning- and end-year comparison of family income mobility was indicated by the overall association (Tau-B) between 1971 and 1978 family income position. Not surprisingly, income position was least stable for the older children and somewhat less stable for the female heads of households.

Comparisons of economic status at two points in time (1971 and 1978 in this case) do not make use of the income information in the intervening years and are sensitive to error or unusual circumstances at those two points in time. A different and, in most cases, preferred measure of change in economic status is an average annual growth rate. We calculated such a measure by fitting a regression line to the eight observations on family income for each individual in the sample. Each family income observation was inflated to 1978 price levels using the Consumer Price Index and then transformed by the natural logarithm function.[6] We use these growth rate calculations in two ways--as an interval measure of income growth and as a dichotomous measure of whether family income kept up with inflation. The inflation measure is constructed by merely noting whether the real income growth rate was positive.

Selective results for the mean and dispersion of annual growth in family income are given in the last three rows of Table 1.3. For the average individual, family incomes did not quite grow fast enough to keep up with inflation: the average annual growth rate for the entire sample was -0.2 percent per year. Translated into dollars, such a growth rate would reduce a $20,000 family income to about $19,720 in seven years. As might be expected, income

---

[6]The regression function is $\ln Y_t = \beta_0 + \beta_1 T_t$ where Y_t is family income in the t-th year and T_t is the deviation of the t-th year from the mid-point of the period. That is, $T_{1971}=-3.5$, $T_{1972}=-2.5,\ldots,$ $T_{1978}=3.5$. The slope of the regression, β_1 measures the change in the dependent variable associated with a unit change in the independent variable:

$$\beta_1 = \frac{d\ln Y}{dT} = \frac{d\ln Y}{dY}\frac{dY}{dT} = \frac{dY}{Y}/dT$$

dY/Y is the percentage change in family income, and β_1 is the annual growth rate.

growth rates were considerably more negative for the older children, many of whom split off and lost their parents´ incomes, and were slightly more negative for the wives. The other four groups did better, with growth rates in the neighborhood of one percent. (A one-percent annual growth rate would increase a $20,000 income to about $21,450 in seven years.)

Despite the turbulent economic conditions of the 1970s, with high inflation rates and a severe recession, slightly more than one-half of the sample lived in families in which incomes kept up with inflation during the 1971 to 1978 period. This fact will undoubtedly surprise many readers, but there are many reasons why this is the case. First, many people misperceive their success in keeping incomes rising with inflation. As Juster (1979) has pointed out, inflation is a continuous process, visible each week at the grocery store or at the gasoline station, while income increases occur very infrequently, often just once a year. Second, aggregate statistics indicate that per capita personal income almost kept pace with inflation; its real growth between 1971 and 1978 was negative but very small (-.15 percent). Whether most families keep up with inflation depends upon the distribution of individual family growth rates around the average. It is quite possible to have no real growth, on average, with a small proportion of families with large income losses (as around retirement) and a large proportion of families with modest but positive real income growth. Over time, new low-income families are always being formed, and older higher-income families are dying off. Moderate income increases can be very widespread even though aggregate income per capita stays constant. We examine the events that affect a family´s chances of keeping up with inflation later in this chapter, but for now it is sufficient to note that about 55 percent of the sample individuals were in families with incomes that did indeed keep up. As with the other measures of family income change, older children were the least likely to have kept up--only about one-third of them did. At least half of the individuals in each of the other groups coped successfully with inflation.

As a final measure of success, we can see what fraction of the various groups lived in families with real incomes that exhibited substantial growth. A 5 percent real growth will increase a $20,000 income over seven years by about 40 percent, to $28,150. Overall, more than one-quarter of the sample individuals were in families in which real incomes grew by at least 5 percent per year. Again, older children were considerably less likely to be in this group, while younger children and women who were initially single heads of households were somewhat more likely to be in it.

Family Income/Needs Mobility

Many of the family composition changes that produce dramatic income losses also produce compensating losses in the number of individuals dependent upon that lowered income. The case of children leaving home is the clearest example of this when the new family of the splitoff contains fewer members than the parental family. Divorces also produce a drop in needs that is usually much greater for the husbands than for the wives if there are children to be cared for.

These compensating changes in family needs produce a much more favorable picture of the fraction of individuals with positive growth in income/needs. The bottom half of Table 1.4 shows that the average growth rate in income relative to needs was 3.4 percent--a rate sufficient to bring a family just at the poverty line in 1971 more than 25 percent above it by 1978. These average growth rates differed much less across the sample subgroups than did the growth rates of incomes before the adjustment for family needs. In fact, the older children who had the lowest average family income growth rates had the highest average growth in family income/needs ratios. Consistent with this picture of higher income/ needs growth rates is the finding that more than two-thirds of all sample individuals were in families with real growth in income/needs, and about two-fifths lived in families in which these annual growth rates exceeded five percent.

Although the income/needs growth rates were quite different from and higher than growth rates for family income alone, the extent of relative change in the two measures was quite similar. Similar fractions of the sample remained in the same income and income/needs quintiles, and similar fractions moved one or more quintile positions. This generalization holds up quite well across all subgroups of sample individuals. So although real income/needs growth rates were generally higher and more uniform than growth rates of income alone, the extent of relative movement in economic position was quite similar for the two measures.

EFFECTS OF FAMILY COMPOSITION CHANGES

In our earliest analysis of change in family economic fortunes we tried to ignore the effects of family composition changes by restricting our analysis to families headed by the same individual. It become apparent that this procedure left out a large segment of the population; by the seventh year over one-fifth of the sample lived in families that were headed by someone different than in the

Table 1.4

DISTRIBUTION OF CHANGES AND GROWTH IN REAL FAMILY INCOME/NEEDS, 1971-1978
(For various groups of sample individuals.)

	All	Male Household Heads in 1971	Female Household Heads in 1972	Wives in 1972	Children Age 15-29 in 1972	Children Age 1-14 in 1972
Change in Real Family Income/Needs, Quintile Position						
Did not change	40%	41%	43%	40%	29%	42%
Changed by one	39	40	35	41	39	40
Changed by more than one	21	19	22	19	32	18
Association (Tau-B) between 1971 and 1978 Decile position	.47	.47	.46	.48	.30	.51
Growth in Family Income/Needs						
Average annual growth rate	.034	.034	.036	.026	.042	.035
Growth in income/needs kept up with inflation	69%	70%	69%	66%	71%	71%
Grew by more than 5 percent per year	42	41	39	38	52	42
Number of observations	12,456	2509	1156	2379	1876	4536

first year.[7] Furthermore, family composition changes often had devastating effects on economic status, especially for women. One of the most dramatic statistics to come out of our earlier work was that one-third of the initially married women living in families with incomes above the poverty line who became divorced and did not remarry were in poverty by the seventh year of the study (Volume IV, p. 5).

We have not attempted here to duplicate the careful look at the relationship between changes in family composition and economic status that filled much of our fourth volume of findings. But in Table 1.5, we have updated the principal findings by keeping our classification of sample individuals according to their relationship to the household heads in 1972 and looking within each group at the results of various kinds of major family composition changes.

There are three measures of change in family income: (1) the difference between 1978 family income and 1971 family income inflated to 1978 price levels; (2) whether the real growth in family income kept up with inflation during the 1971-1978 period; and (3) the real annual growth rate. The latter two measures were calculated for the income/needs measure of family economic status as well. To assess whether the associations between family composition change and status change are caused by a spurious correlation with some other factor (such as age), we also calculated adjusted family income and income/needs growth rates, obtained from regressions that included age and several other demographic variables.[8] An example of why the regression adjustments may be useful is found in assessing the impact of becoming widowed. Family income grows much less rapidly, if at all, for elderly couples than for couples just starting out. Since becoming widowed is much more likely to occur among older couples, part of the unadjusted comparison of income growth rates of women who became widows to others who did not is really just an age effect that has nothing to do with becoming widowed. A regression that controls for initial age will adjust for these age-related growth rate differentials and give a better estimate of the "pure" effect of becoming widowed.

---

[7]This statistic may seem to conflict with the earlier one that one-third of families had changed heads during the first seven years of the study. The two figures are consistent because one is for families and the other is for individuals. Newly formed families, on average, contain fewer individuals than intact families.

[8]Variables included in each regression are listed at the bottom of Table 1.5.

Table 1.5 (page 1 of 3)
EFFECTS OF FAMILY COMPOSITION CHANGES ON CHANGES IN ECONOMIC STATUS
(For various groups of sample individuals.)

Subgroup and Change	Percentage of Group	Family Income				Family Income/Needs			Number of Observations
		1978 Minus 1971	Beat Inflation?	Annual Growth Rate		Beat Inflation?	Annual Growth Rate		
				Unadjusted	Adjusted		Unadjusted	Adjusted	
Male Household Heads in 1972									2509
Remained unmarried	7.0%	$1717	.500	.007	.011	.692	.032%	.040	
Remained married	81.3	2717	.574	.008	.008	.705	.033	.032	
Divorced, separated, or widowed	7.4	-2094	.366	-.032	-.028	.674	.030	.038	
Married	4.3	8787	.705	.063	.040	.631	.055	.044	
Eta^2		.020	.017	.037		.001	.003		
$Beta^2$					.021			.002	
Wives in 1972									2379
Remained married	84.8	3086	.573	.010	.007	.707	.034	.033	
Widowed	7.8	-5267	.110	-.092	-.054	.460	-.011	.012	
Divorced/separated	7.1	-7385	.184	-.089	-.094	.357	-.031	-.033	
Eta^2		.061	.094	.166		.052	.016		
$Beta^2$					.115			.047	
Female Household Heads in 1972									1156
Remained unmarried	80.8%	$864	.446	-.014	-.009	.645	.020	.024	
Married	18.6	15,357	.886	.126	.100	.865	.107	.090	
Eta^2		.337	.344	.196		.037	.113		
$Beta^2$					.119			.066	

Table 1.5 (page 2 of 3)

Subgroup and Change	Percentage of Group	Family Income				Family Income/Needs			Number of Observations
		1978 Minus 1971	Beat Inflation?	Annual Growth Rate Unadjusted	Annual Growth Rate Adjusted	Beat Inflation?	Annual Growth Rate Unadjusted	Annual Growth Rate Adjusted	
Children 15-29 Years Old in 1972									
Remained children	21.9%	$3250	.577	.010	.008	.845	.065	.061	1860
Splitoff, unmarried	27.1	-15,712	.128	-.135	-.137	.533	-.006	-.008	
Splitoff, married	50.5	-5091	.377	-.028	-.026	.748	.058	.060	
Eta^2		.154	.110	.179		.065	.069		
Beta^2					.186			.076	
Children, 1-14 Years Old in 1972									
Splitoff	9.0%	$-9002	.166	-.095	-.092	.599	.014	.009	4536
Female head remained unmarried	7.4	1088	.535	-.002	-.001	.610	.019	.019	
Female head married	2.0	10521	.863	.097	.094	.746	.083	.089	
Parents stayed married	68.1	6995	.743	.033	.033	.781	.047	.047	
Parents divorced	5.3	-6602	.150	-.084	-.087	.281	-.043	-.038	
Others	8.3	2651	.432	-.018	-.017	.556	.014	.016	
Eta^2		.158	.191	.243		.082	.091		
Beta^2					.236			.089	

16

Table 1.5 (page 3 of 3)

Note: The "adjusted" column means are adjusted by
regression for the effects of the following variables:

Group	Head's Education	Wife's Education	Head's Age	Wife's Age	Race	Sex	Child's Age
Male Heads	X		X		X		
Wives		X		X	X		
Female heads	X		X		X		
Older children	X				X	X	X
Young Children	X		X		X		

"Percentage of Group" numbers may not add to 100.0 due to small excluded groups. All income
figures have been adjusted to 1978 price levels using the CPI.

Regression-adjusted estimates of the effects of family composition change are given in the "Adjusted" columns of Table 1.5 for the two annual growth rate measures. Also included in that table are summary measures (Eta^2, $Beta^2$) of the explanatory power of the family composition change.[9]

Adult Men

The family economic status was much less dependent upon family composition change for the adult men in the sample than for any other group. Becoming unmarried (through divorce, separation, or widowhood) or married accounted for at most four percent of the variation in family income change and much less of the variation in change in family income relative to needs. Marriage did increase real family income for the initially unmarried men by an average of nearly $9,000, and divorce or widowhood lowered it for the initially married men by an average of about $2000,[10] but these changes were not very important when compared to the variety of changes experienced by the adult men who remained in their 1972 marital status. Men earn most of the money income in most families, so changes in other family members or their earnings tend to have relatively small effects.

Adult Women

In contrast to the findings for adult men, the economic status of adult women was quite strongly affected by the loss of a spouse through separation or death or by marriage or remarriage. Initial wives who became divorced or separated had a drop in real family income amounting to more than $10,000 and were 30 percent less likely than women who remained married throughout the period to have either their income or income/needs keep up with inflation.[11] The annual economic growth rates for divorced women were negative for both measures of

---

[9] Eta^2 shows the fraction of variance of the change measure accounted for by the family composition change variables. For the "adjusted" columns, the number shown is $Beta^2$, which is the regression-adjusted fraction of variance explained. If family composition was uncorrelated with other predictor variables, $Eta^2 = Beta^2$.

[10] These income figures have not been reduced by alimony or child support payments. In Volume IV, we reported that alimony and child support payments reduced the real family income (in 1967 dollars) of divorced men by an additional $775.

[11] Calculations of family incomes for divorced women include alimony and child support payments. The small group of women who divorced and remarried are included in the "remained married" group; they fared better than those who stayed married (Hoffman and Holmes, 1976).

economic status; their family income fell at an annual rate of nearly
nine percent in real terms. Furthermore, these detrimental effects cannot be
attributed to spurious correlations with demographic characteristics like
education level or age. Many factors contribute to the serious economic
consequences of divorce: married women have less regular labor force
participation patterns and cannot command earnings levels that are as high as
their exhusbands´; children usually go with the mother after a divorce,
increasing the needs level of her new family and reducing her chances of having a
full-time paid job; and alimony and child support payments are inadequate in
maintaining her previous standard of living.

Women who became widowed also did worse, but the economic effects were not
as strong as with divorce. Furthermore, some of the apparent economic loss is
really an effect of age rather that the spouse´s death. The adjusted growth
rates in family income for the wives who became widowed were negative. However,
family needs decreased with the death of the spouse, so the adjusted growth rates
in income relative to needs for the women in this group were actually positive,
although not as large as the adjusted growth rates for the women who remained
married.

Marriage was associated with a dramatic increase in the economic status of
the initially unmarried female household heads. Relative to those who remained
unmarried, female heads who married enjoyed family income increases averaging
$16,000, a doubled chance of keeping up with inflation, and an adjusted family
income growth rate that was 10 percentage points higher. Marriage added to the
needs standard as well as to income, so the growth in income/needs was not as
large as for income alone, but it was still impressive.

Children

The economic status of older children in the sample was clearly dependent
upon decisions regarding marriage and splitting off from the parental households.
Changes in family income were much more dramatic than changes in income adjusted
for needs since both income and needs fell after the child left home. Relative
to those children who remained in their parental households, children who left
and married experienced a decrease in family income and a lower (but still
positive) growth in income/needs. Children who left home and remained unmarried
did much worse, with a large drop in income and a small negative income/needs
growth rate. Thus, decisions about marriage were as important for the older

children as they were for the adults who began the period as household heads or wives.

The younger children (age 1-14 in 1972) had little control over the economic fortunes of the families in which they lived, yet family composition changes explained more of the changes in economic status for these individuals than for any other group. Some were old enough by 1978 to split off and form their own households. As with older aged children, those who left suffered a decline in family income but little change in income adjusted for family needs. Most of the rest were in stable, two-parent families which, on average, did quite well. The real incomes of these stable families grew by about $7,000 between 1971 and 1978, or by about 3.3 percent per year. Real income/needs grew even faster (4.7 percent) and three-quarters of the children in families which managed to keep up with inflation.[12]

Children living in families where the parents became divorced or separated by the end of the period present a very different picture. Family incomes for them fell by $6,602, or by over 8 percent annually.[13] Their income relative to needs fell by half that amount. Although these children constituted only about 5 percent of the entire group of children, their economic vulnerability to the effects of marital disruption is striking.

The fortunes of the remaining groups of children mirrored the experience of their elders. For instance, those living in families with an initially unmarried mother who married did very well, especially when compared to those living in similar families with no marriage.

THE ROLE OF INITIAL CHARACTERISTICS AND INTERVENING EVENTS

Although family composition changes are surprisingly frequent and powerful in their economic effects, they account for, at most, one-tenth of the variation in the growth of family income and family income/needs. What accounts for the remainder? The social sciences are not without some hypotheses on this question. One possible set of explanations centers around the initial attitudes and skills of the family members. Achievement motivation is thought to lead to the taking of calculated risks and improved chances of success (Atkinson, 1958, 1966, 1974).

---

[12]It would be incorrect to say that three-quarters of the families kept up, since the child, not the family, is the analysis unit. Each family, in effect, is weighted by the number of children in it.

[13]Family income figures include alimony and child support payments.

A greater sense of efficacy--a sense that one's own actions matter--or an orientation toward the future may also enhance the chances for improvement (Andrisani, 1977; Duncan and Morgan, forthcoming 1981). Cognitive ability and skills acquired by education or on-the-job training could also play a role. Fortunately, the Panel Study was designed to test many of these hypotheses and the data contain numerous measures of potentially important attitudes and skills.

A second set of explanations for improvement center around certain types of events--both voluntary and otherwise--that may occur. Voluntary changes in residence, job, or labor force status may differentiate those who have kept up with inflation from those who have not. Involuntary events such as unemployment or health disability may also play a role.

Rather than attempting to develop a formal model of the ways in which attitudes, skills, and events affect family well-being, we instead estimate a simple recursive descriptive model, illustrated in Figure 1.1. The dependent variables of interest are a set of measures of change in economic status-- absolute changes and growth in rates of wages, family income, and income/needs. Predictor variables fall into two groups--initial characteristics and events. Events were measured after the initial characteristics and act as intervening variables in this model, helping to account for the effects of initial characteristics on changes in status. The effects of the events were estimated in regressions that included initial characteristics as control variables. The effects of initial characteristics on changes in economic status, on the other hand, came from regressions that did not include the event measures. This was done so that an estimate of the total effect of the initial characteristic could be obtained. To illustrate why this was necessary, let us suppose that achievement motivation leads to higher rates of growth in family income by facilitating voluntary, beneficial job changes. If measures of job changes were included in the regression, then the estimated importance of motivation itself would be attenuated. A regression that includes only initial characteristics would show the total effect of motivation. Important total effects can later be decomposed into direct effects that operate independently of the events and indirect effects operating through them.

Our regression analysis of changes in family economic status was confined to three groups of sample individuals--(1) male household heads who worked continuously (at least 500 hours per year) during the 1971-1978 period; (2) all male household heads regardless of labor force status; and (3) all women who were female heads of households in 1972. The subgroup of working men was treated

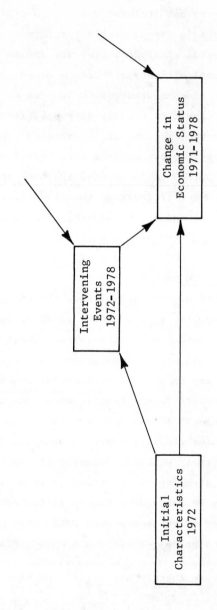

Figure 1.1

A FRAMEWORK FOR THE ANALYSIS OF INITIAL ATTITUDES
AND SKILLS, EVENTS, AND ECONOMIC OUTCOMES

separately so that dramatic changes in labor force status (such as retirement)
would not interfere with the investigation of the potentially more subtle effects
of initial characteristics on changes in earnings and family status. Women who
were initially married were not included in this analysis since no measures of
attitudes or cognitive skills are available for them.

The measures of initial characteristics are common to all three groups and
include a sense of personal efficacy and future orientation, an index of undue
risk avoidance, an index of connectedness to sources of information or help, a
"test score" measure of cognitive ability developed from the Wechsler-Bellvue
test, an index of achievement motivation,[14] years of education, and age. The age
measure consists of three dichotomous (one-zero) variables, corresponding to
membership in the under 30, 45 to 59, and 60 and over age groups. The 30 to 44
age group was omitted, so coefficients on the other three show the extent to
which the adjusted earnings and income growth rates of those in these groups
differ from those for 30 to 44-year-old people.

Households Headed by Men Who Worked

Initial Characteristics. Table 1.6 shows the estimated effects of these
initial characteristics on the annual growth rates of hourly earnings, annual
earnings, total family income, and family income relative to needs.[15] Although
hourly earnings are the most appropriate measure of earnings capacity, the
initial characteristics may operate through decisions about work hours, labor
force participation of others in the family, asset and transfer income, or even
family size and composition. All in all, this set of progressively more complex
measures of economic status provides numerous opportunities for the initial
characteristics to show their effects. Results for an even more comprehensive
set of outcome measures are given in Appendix Table A1.1. Absolute changes in
all but the income/needs measures of economic status are included there, along
with dichotomous measures of whether growth rates kept up with inflation. The
instability of hourly and annual earnings are also included as outcome measures,

---

[14]For details of the test score and motivation measure see Veroff (1971) and
Appendix F of Morgan et al. (1974, Volume I).

[15]Self-employed workers are included in this analysis. In calculating the
labor income of the self-employed, an attempt was made to divide total income
into labor and capital components. The procedure is detailed in the
documentation volumes. Annual growth rates are defined in Footnote 6. Table
gives regression coefficients and their standard errors so the size of effect is
clear.

to check to see whether some characteristics that lead to high growth may also lead to less stability.[16]

With the exception of age, education, and risk avoidance, virtually none of the initial characteristics had significant effects on any of the growth measures.[17] Age differences were the most striking, with younger people enjoying much higher growth rates in earnings and family income. Relative to those in the 30 to 44 age group, those under age 30 had growth rates that were 2 percent higher for hourly earnings, 4 percent higher for annual earnings, and 1.3 percent higher for family income.[18] Readers uncomfortable with the interpretation of these growth rate differences may want to refer to Table A1.1 for the alternative growth measures. In terms of one's chances of keeping up with inflation, for example, Table A1.1 shows that the very young had a nearly 10 percent higher chance of keeping their hourly wage rates growing faster than inflation, a 20 percent higher chance of keeping annual real earnings growth, and a statistically insignificant higher chance of enjoying family income increases that kept up with inflation. Counteracting these positive age effects were the facts that earnings were generally less stable for the young families who were most likely to be expanding in size, thus having more as well as larger mouths to feed as their incomes increased. Growth in income/needs for this youngest group was actually lower than for the 30-44 year olds.

Growth rates for the two older age groups were generally much lower than for the reference group—of 30-44 year olds. Compared to the latter group, the 45-60 year old men were less able to keep wage rates, annual earnings, and family incomes rising faster than inflation by margins of 6 percent, 10 percent, and 20 percent, respectively. As children left home, the 45-60 year olds were heading families with declining needs, so the growth in income/needs for this

---

[16]For evidence that high earnings go with stability rather than compensating for instability, see the Grosse and Morgan chapter in this volume and Morgan (1980).

[17]Table 1.6 shows only those coefficients that exceed their standard errors. The standard errors and significance tests are based on the assumptions of simple random sampling. The design effects associated with a clustered stratified sample such as the Panel Study's will result in true standard errors that are larger than those reported here.

[18]Translated into dollars, a 2.2 percent higher growth rate will add $1.65 more to a $10 per hour wage rate in seven years, while a 4.1 percent higher growth rate in annual earnings will add nearly $6,500 more to a $20,000 salary.

Table 1.6

EFFECTS OF BACKGROUND VARIABLES ON GROWTH IN ECONOMIC STATUS 1971–1978[a]
(For all male household heads who worked 500 hours or more 1971–1978.)

	Annual Growth Rate			
	Hourly Earnings	Annual Earnings	Total Family Income	Family Income / Needs
Efficacy	.001 (.001)	.001 (.001)	b	b
Future orientation	b	b	b	−.001 (.001)
Risk avoidance	−.003* (.001)	−.005** (.001)	−.003** (.001)	−.004** (.001)
Connectedness	−.002+ (.001)	b	b	−.001 (.001)
Test score	−.001 (.001)	b	−.002* (.001)	−.002+ (.001)
Achievement motivation	b	b	b	.001 (.001)
Education (in years)	.001 (.001)	.002* (.001)	.002** (.001)	.001* (.001)
Whether black	b	b	.007 (.007)	b
Age (in 1972)				
<30	.022** (.004)	.040** (.005)	.013** (.004)	−.010* (.004)
45–59	−.009* (.004)	−.017** (.005)	−.025** (.004)	b
60 or older	−.043** (.011)	−.072** (.013)	−.039** (.010)	−.031** (.011)
R^2	.052	.112	.077	.018

Number of observations: 1764

+ Significant at .10 level.
* Significant at .05 level.
** Significant at .01 level.
a All dollar amounts in 1978 prices.
b Variable included in regression but t-ratio less than 1.0.
(Standard errors of regression coefficients are in parentheses.)

group did not differ significantly from that of the 30-45 year old reference group.

The oldest group did much worse on all of the growth measures. This finding should be treated with some caution since the sample was restricted to continuous labor force participants. The individuals in the "60 or older" group would have passed their normal retirement age by the seventh year, and the fact that they had continued to work beyond it may have been in response to an unusually unfavorable economic event. Certainly those who retired experienced a more severe decline in income.

Additional years of formal education at the start appeared to promote faster growth in economic status, especially for the more comprehensive measures of status.[19] Although education had no significant effect on wage rate growth, it did have a significant positive effect on the growth rates of annual earnings, family income, and family needs. These results are not surprising since evidence suggests that more education is linked to less unemployment, an increased likelihood of having a working wife, increased savings, and smaller family size.

The only other variable with consistently significant effects was the index of undue risk avoidance, which was constructed from information on seat belt use, medical and automobile insurance coverage, and cigarette smoking. Persons who avoided unnecessary risks had lower growth rates, perhaps because they were also less willing to take the calculated risks (such as job changes) that are necessary to get ahead. Compensating for this lower growth was the fact that earnings were more stable for the risk averse.

The "connectedness" measure assumed that information and even help in getting a better job might come from friends and acquaintances. It added points for reading newspapers, going to church, bars, PTA meetings, or other organizations, belonging to a labor union, knowing many neighbors by name, and having relatives nearby. It did not help, nor did being white or black.

The negative evidence on such attitudes as achievement motivation, efficacy, and future orientation is impressive. None had coefficients for any of the growth rate measures that were statistically significant at even the 10 percent level. Nor did this picture change much with the additional growth measures

---

[19]Note that this education effect is adjusted for differences in cognitive ability as measured by the "test score" variable.

included in Table A1.1. Once again, our finding that those attitudes do not seem to matter much in a causal way is confirmed on these more recent data.[20]

Events. Although initial characteristics other than age and education are poor discriminators of subsequent success, we may still be able to identify strategies, institutional factors, and involuntary events that help or hinder some families, regardless of their initial characteristics. The list of job, residence, and family-related events is large enough to fill two tables, 1.7 and 1.8.

Table 1.7 contains job and locational variables.[21] Few of the job and residential mobility variables had consistent effects for all of the outcome measures and yet nearly all had important effects on at least one or two. Table 1.7 shows the estimated effects of those variables on annual growth rates and on the chances of beating inflation, while Appendix Table A1.2 shows similar results for the absolute changes and instability, along with the means and standard deviations for all of the measures.

With regard to labor market outcomes, the union status variables are of considerable interest. Historically, the ability of unions to win wage increases larger than those of non-union workers has been limited to periods of recession (Rees, 1977). This may appear surprising to the lay reader and is due, undoubtedly, to the fact that the wage increases of all union members in wage-setting industries find their way onto the front pages of newspapers. Increases for non-union workers are rarely published. In past periods of inflation, union contracts actually appeared to have locked their members into increases that were smaller than the market was willing to pay. As a consequence, non-union wage gains were larger during periods of economic growth and inflation. But the seventies brought inflation and recession at the same time, along with more diligent attempts on the part of firms and workers to protect themselves against inflation. The evidence in Table 1.7 suggest that union members were more successful at coping with inflation than were non-union workers. One-fifth of the men in this sample belonged to unions at both the beginning and end of the period, and they enjoyed a 1.2 percent higher annual wage rate growth than men who remained non-union (as well as a 10 percent higher likelihood of keeping real

---

[20]See Duncan and Morgan (forthcoming, 1981).

[21]Recall that the effects of these event measures are calculated in a multiple regression that includes the initial characteristics.

Table 1.7

EFFECTS OF JOB AND RESIDENTIAL MOBILITY VARIABLES ON CHANGES IN ECONOMIC STATUS[a]
(For all male household heads who worked 500 hours or more, 1971–1978.)

	Hourly Earnings		Annual Earnings		Total Family Income		Family Income/Needs	
	Annual Growth Rate (%)	Beat Inflation?	Annual Growth Rate (%)	Beat Inflation?	Annual Growth Rate (%)	Beat Inflation?	Annual Growth Rate (%)	Beat Inflation?
Number of residential moves	.004** (.001)	b	.005** (.002)	.009 (.009)	.004** (.001)	.016+ (.009)	.005** (.001)	.011 (.007)
Number of voluntary job changes	.002 (.002)	b	.003 (.002)	b	.005** (.002)	.014 (.012)	.005** (.002)	.016 (.010)
Number of involuntary job changes	-.008** (.003)	-.056** (.017)	-.009** (.003)	-.050** (.017)	-.007** (.002)	-.041* (.016)	-.007** (.002)	-.036** (.014)
Number of years unemployed more than one month	-.004* (.002)	-.021+ (.011)	-.003+ (.002)	b	b	b	b	-.010 (.009)
Change in ln city size	.008** (.001)	.019+ (.010)	.008** (.002)	.027** (.010)	.005** (.001)	.015+ (.009)	.006** (.001)	.018* (.008)
Regional change: Stayed South	b	.028 (.027)	b	b	-.005 (.004)	b	-.005 (.004)	b
Left South	b	b	b	b	b	b	b	.176* (.083)
Went South	b	-.095 (.078)	.026** (.013)	b	b	b	b	-.092 (.063)
Union status change: Stayed union	.012** (.005)	.104** (.032)	.011* (.005)	.049 (.032)	.005 (.004)	.058+ (.030)	.007 (.004)	.113** (.025)
Left union	-.014* (.006)	-.077+ (.042)	-.012+ (.007)	-.095* (.042)	-.006 (.006)	-.085* (.040)	b	b
Became union	.022** (.007)	.117* (.049)	.015+ (.008)	b	.008 (.006)	b	.009 (.007)	.068 (.039)
Disability: always disabled	b	b	b	b	-.099** (.034)	b	-.072* (.035)	b
Became disabled	.021+ (.011)	b	b	b	b	b	b	b
R^2 (adjusted)	.090	.052	.143	.079	.170	.119	.148	.132

Number of observations: 1764. *Significant at .05 level. **Significant at .01 level.
+Significant at .10 level.
a All dollar amounts in 1978 prices.
b Variable included in regression but t-ratio less than 1.0.
Note: All regression coefficients have been adjusted for the effects of background and family change variables.

wage growth positive).[22]   Furthermore, union wages appeared to be more stable.
The gains to union workers in terms of annual earnings were only slightly less
impressive.[23]

The wage premium attached to union members is usually estimated to be in the
15-20 percent range (Rees), so, not surprisingly, our data show that joining a
union increased wage rate growth relative to those who remained non-union, while
leaving union work decreased it.

Involuntary job changes and unemployment had consistently negative effects
on earnings growth that went far beyond mere loss of work hours. The hourly wage
rate measure adjusts for work hours and the fact that past job loss leads to
lower hourly wage growth means that earnings capacity was affected by the loss.
Interpretation of this result is difficult, however, since it may have been that
the unmeasured characteristics of the workers losing their jobs contributed to
the lower wage growth as well. Interestingly, involuntary job losses appear to
have been more important than the amount of unemployment itself. After adjusting
for the effects of job loss, extensive periods of unemployment (a month or more)
affect hourly earnings but do not appear to have affected the likelihood of
keeping annual earnings growing faster than inflation, nor do they seem to have
differentiated those with higher growth rates in family income. Perhaps some
workers insist on a better job, waiting through more unemployment to get it.[24]

Several of the locational variables had some significant effects on changes
in economic status. Voluntary residential mobility was associated with higher
growth rates for all economic status measures, and moving to a larger city also
helped. The direction of causation of the former is questionable while the
latter result might disappear if the higher costs of urban living were taken into
account, and both could be results rather than causes.

Table 1.8 shows the estimated effects of: labor force participation changes
among wives; marital decisions of husbands; and additions and subtractions of

---

[22]The mean values for the independent variables are given in Table A1.2. A
1.2 percent higher annual growth rate will increase a $10 per hour salary by 80
cents per hour more over seven years.

[23]The fact that the coefficient on the "Stayed Union" variable was
statistically insignificant for the measure of whether annual earnings kept up
with inflation but remained strong for the annual earnings growth rate indicates
that the union variable differentiates among those with very high or very low
growth rates rather than affecting those in the middle.

[24]There may be some selectivity bias operating to underestimate the effects
of job losses, if some leave the labor force and are not in the analysis.

children to and from family size. The movement of married women into and out of the labor force was associated with substantial changes in family income and income/needs. Families in which the wife began working during the seven-year period had a $3,250 higher average family income, a 2.5 percent higher family income growth rate, and a 15 percent higher likelihood of keeping incomes up with inflation, compared to families in which the wives were out of the labor force at both the beginning and end of the period.[25] Families in which wives dropped out of the labor force had comparably lower family income growth rates, smaller income changes, and a reduced likelihood of keeping family incomes rising with inflation.

Changes in the marital status of the family head made fewer significant differences, a result consistent with our finding that family composition changes did not matter very much for adult men.

The departure of children from the parental home reduced needs and produced increases in income/needs growth rates, while the birth of children did just the reverse. Since births may affect family status by causing mothers to drop out of the labor force, the regression was re-estimated leaving out the wife´s labor force changes in order to estimate a total effect for births. The results, shown at the bottom of Table 1.8, indicate that each additional birth was associated with a .6 percent lower family income growth rate, a $1,724 lower family income, and a 6 percent lower likelihood of keeping up with inflation. The results for the income/needs variable were even stronger.

All Households

Households headed by men who worked continuously during the 1971 to 1978 period made up only about half of all households.[26] The rest were evenly divided into households headed by women and households headed by men who spent some time out of the labor force. We estimated our model for all male heads of households as of 1972 and for female heads of households in 1972 as well, restricting our status measures to family income and income/needs and restricting the predictor

---

[25]It is tempting to overinterpret these numbers as well. If wives begin to work in response to a fall in family income due, say, to unemployment of the husband, then these figures underestimate the actual average contribution of the wife to family income.

[26]As with many statements about families over time, this requires a more precise restatement: of all individuals who headed families in 1972 and remained in the sample until 1979, 52 percent were men who worked at least 500 hours each year from 1971 to 1978.

Table 1.8

EFFECTS OF FAMILY VARIABLES ON CHANGES IN ECONOMIC STATUS[a]
(For all male household heads who worked 500 hours or more, 1971-1978.)

	Total Family Income			Family Income/Needs	
	Annual Growth Rate (%)	1978 Minus 1971 ($)	Beat Infla-tion?	Annual Growth Rate (%)	Beat Infla-tion?
Labor Force Status of Wife					
Wife stayed working	b	b	b	.004 (.004)	.071** (.024)
Wife quit working	-.028** (.005)	-4684** (1004)	-.221** (.036)	-.023** (.005)	-.219** (.031)
Wife started working	.025** (.004)	3259** (861)	.146** (.031)	.022** (.004)	.070** (.027)
Marital Status of Head					
Head stayed married	b	b	b	-.018* (.008)	-.105* (.049)
Head got unmarried	-.024* (.010)	-3150 (1965)	-.090 (.071)	b	.071 (.061)
Head got married	.019+ (.010)	2107 (2084)	b	-.016 (.011)	-.239** (.064)
Number of births	b	-1073* (522)	-.026 (.019)	-.012** (.003)	-.091** (.016)
Number of Years Kids Left Home	-.002 (.002)	b	b	.017** (.002)	.062** (.010)
Number of Births (Omitting change in wife's labor force status)	-.006* (.003)	-1724** (517)	-.058** (.019)	-.016** (.003)	-.121** (.016)
R^2 (adjusted)	.170	.099	.119	.148	.132

Number of observations: 1764
+ Significant at .10 level.
* Significant at .05 level.
** Significant at .01 level.
a All dollar amounts in 1978 prices.
b Variable included in regression but t-ratio less than 1.0.

Note: All regression coefficients have been adjusted for the effects of background and job and residential mobility variables.

variables to initial characteristics and changes in family composition and in labor force status. The results for the initial characteristics, shown in Table 1.9 and 1.10, continued to show age and some education effects, few effects of attitudes, and a strong race effect for the female-headed families.

Age effects on family income growth were quite strong, especially among the younger women, who did much better than the 30-45 year old reference group of women, and among the older men, who did much worse than the 30-45 year old reference group of men. The group of female household heads in their twenties included women with strong commitments to careers who had either not considered or had delayed marriage. Many were married, however, thereby increasing family income and income/needs. Compared to the 30-45 year old female heads, they had family income growth rates that were 9 percent higher, family income increases that were $6200 more and a 24 percent higher likelihood of keeping family income rising faster than inflation. Income/needs growth was also higher for those young women, but not as much as for income alone.

Families headed by an elderly man (age 60 or older in 1972) did much worse than younger families. Relative to the families headed by 30-45 year old men, these older families had a 40 percent lower chance of keeping their incomes up with inflation and a 30 percent lower chance of keeping income/needs ahead of it. This overstates the disadvantages somewhat, since taxes and work-related expenses were lower for the elderly, but the differences in age-related family income growth was too large to be explained away by such adjustments. Retirement, of course, accounted for much of the decline.

As with the working men only, few of the attitudes and behavior patterns had statistically significant effects and some of these operated in the wrong direction (more positive attitudes leading to lower growth rates). The undue risk avoidance index continued to have negative effects for these men, but there was also some evidence that the achievement motivation index may have played a minor role. That motivation appeared to matter for this entire group of male household heads but not for the subset of those who worked continuously suggests that it may have operated through decisions about retirement and entry into the labor force. The evidence on the effects of motivation on retirement, however, is not very compelling. (See Chapter 6).

As with the group of men who worked continuously, additional years of formal education appeared to be associated with above average increases in both income and income/needs for female as well as male household heads.

Table 1.9

EFFECTS OF BACKGROUND VARIABLES ON CHANGES IN ECONOMIC STATUS 1971-1978[a]
(For all male household heads in 1972.)

| | Total Family Income | | | Family Income/Needs | | Mean Value (Standard Deviation) of Variable |
	Annual Growth Rate (%)	1978 Minus 1971 ($)	Beat Inflation	Annual Growth Rate (%)	Beat Inflation	
Efficacy	b	215 (146)	.011* (.006)	b	b	4.38 (1.85)
Future Orientation	b	b	b	b	b	2.88 (1.99)
Risk Avoidance	-.002* (.001)	-552** (179)	-.017* (.007)	-.003** (.001)	.018** (.007)	5.26 (1.60)
Connectedness	-.001 (.001)	b	b	-.002+ (.001)	-.007 (.006)	6.16 (1.57)
Test Score	b	b	b	b	b	9.78 (2.21)
Achievement Motivation	.001+ (.001)	b	.004 (.004)	.002** (.001)	.007+ (.004)	9.15 (2.69)
Education (in years)	.001* (.001)	249** (94)	.006 (.004)	.001+ (.001)	.008* (.003)	11.77 (3.45)
Whether Black	b	b	b	b	b	.079 (.270)
Age (in 1972)						
<30	.016** (.004)	b	.035 (.026)	-.007+ (.004)	-.055* (.024)	.240 (.427)
45-59	-.042** (.004)	-7130** (69)	-.257** (.025)	-.021** (.004)	-.058* (.024)	.271 (.445)
60 or older	.056** (.005)	-8798** (786)	-.386** (.030)	.056** (.005)	-.296** (-.029)	.181 (.385)
R^2 (adjusted)	.143	.117	.136	.080	.067	
Mean (Standard Deviation)	.007 (.082)	2550 (12992)	.559 (.497)	.034 (.080)	.699 (.459)	

Number of Observations: 2509
+ Significant at .10 level.
* Significant at .05 level.
** Significant at .01 level.
a All dollar amounts in 1978 prices.
b Variable included in regression but t-ratio less than 1.0.

Table 1.10

EFFECTS OF BACKGROUND VARIABLES ON CHANGES IN ECONOMIC STATUS, 1971–1978[a]
(For all female household heads in 1972.)

	Total Family Income			Family Income/Needs		Mean Value (Standard Deviation) of Variable
	Annual Growth Rate (%)	1978 Minus 1971 ($)	Beat Infla-tion	Annual Growth Rate (%)	Beat Infla-tion	
Efficacy	−.003 (.002)	−232 (167)	−.013 (.008)	−.003+ (.002)	b	3.50 (1.95)
Future orientation	b	b	b	b	b	2.33 (1.85)
Risk avoidance	b	458+ (239)	b	b	b	4.96 (1.49)
Connectedness	−.002 (.002)	b	b	−.003+ (.002)	−.022* (.009)	5.72 (1.62)
Test score	−.003+ (.002)	−438** (157)	b	−.003* (.002)	−.018* (.007)	9.25 (2.32)
Achievement motivation	.002 (.001)	134 (124)	.012* (.006)	b	b	7.84 (2.66)
Education (in years)	.002+ (.001)	230* (113)	b	.002* (.001)	b	10.92 (3.59)
Whether black	−.015 (.010)	−2434** (866)	−.087* (.041)	−.014+ (.008)	−.099* (.040)	.169 (.374)
Age (in 1972)						
<30	.091** (.011)	6216** (947)	.241** (.045)	.051** (.009)	.070 (.044)	.208 (.406)
45–59	−.036** (.010)	−3947** (924)	−.140** (.044)	−.010 (.009)	b	.247 (.432)
60 or older	−.023* (.011)	−4425** (945)	−.140** (.045)	−.022* (.009)	−.099* (.043)	.352 (.478)
R^2 (adjusted)	.160	.164	.101	.098	.027	
Mean (Standard Deviation)	.012 (.123)	2169 (10872)	.529 (.499)	.036 (.101)	.688 (.464)	

Number of Observations: 1156
+ Significant at .10 level.
* Significant at .05 level.
** Significant at .01 level.
a All dollar amounts in 1978 prices.
b Variable included in regression but t-ratio less than 1.0.

Racial differences in income growth rates for men were small and generally insignificant. Among the women, however, blacks did considerably worse than whites. The likelihood of either family income or income relative to needs keeping up with inflation was about 10 percent lower for black than nonblack female household heads and real income changes were nearly $2,500 less for them. More analysis on racial differences appears in Chapter 2 of this volume (Table 1.11).

Events. The roles of changes in family composition, changes in labor force status, and growth in economic status are presented in Table 1.10 for the male household heads and in Table 1.12 for the female household heads. As in the two prior tables, the numbers on these tables show the regression-adjusted changes in growth rates, in absolute change, and in the likelihood of beating inflation associated with the predictor variables. The results shown on these tables have been adjusted by regression for the effects of initial characteristics.

As a general summary, these two tables show that labor force decisions had a powerful effect on income growth for the male household heads but not for females, while marital changes affected the economic fortunes of the families of the female heads but not the males. Consider first the changes associated with entry into and exit from the labor force. Some of the economic effects of exits were offset by the receipt of Social Security and private pension income (primarily those who retired), and some of the improvement from labor force entry were counteracted by losses of other income sources such as welfare. Relative to the group that was out of the labor force in both 1971 and 1978, however, the net effect of labor force exit on families headed by men was to lower income and income/needs growth rates by over 6 percent, to have real incomes decline by $7,500, and to lower by 30 percent the likelihood of keeping either income or income/needs growing faster than inflation. For female family heads, the effects of labor market exit were much smaller although still significant, presumably because they earned less in the first place and had less to lose if they dropped out of the labor force. In addition, they had a better chance of offsetting the loss in income by the receipt of transfer income such as AFDC.

Labor force entry had the expected positive effects on income growth, and these effects were generally larger (in absolute value) than were the effects of exit. Very few of the male household heads (2 percent) entered the labor force during the period, but the gains for those who did were large. Equally impressive were the economic benefits for women entrants. Relative to those remaining out of the labor force, both groups of entrants enjoyed 9 percent

Table 1.11

EFFECTS OF CHANGES IN FAMILY STATUS AND LABOR FORCE STATUS
ON ECONOMIC STATUS 1971-1978[a]

(For all male household heads in 1972.)

	Total Family Income			Family Income/Needs		Mean Value (Standard Deviation of Variable)
	Annual Growth Rate (%)	1978 Minus 1971 ($)	Beat Inflation	Annual Growth Rate (%)	Beat Inflation	
Labor Force Status of Head:						
Head stayed working	b	1612 (1115)	b	b	b	.752 (.432)
Head quit working	-.066** (.006)	-7528** (1053)	-.293** (.040)	-.063** (.006)	-.343** (.038)	.139 (.346)
Head started working	.086** (.011)	8006** (1855)	.236** (.071)	.080** (.011)	.182** (.066)	.021 (.145)
Marital Status of Head:						
Stayed married	b	b	.054 (.038)	-.008 (.006)	b	.813 (.390)
Got unmarried	-.024** (.008)	-1386 (1262)	b	b	.071 (.045)	.074 (.262)
Got married	.019* (.009)	2088 (1472)	b	b	-.193** (.052)	.043 (.202)
Labor Force Status of Wife:						
Wife stayed working	b	b	b	.005 (.004)	.064** (.023)	.216 (.411)
Wife quit working	-.027** (.004)	-4662** (748)	-.167** (.029)	-.023** (.004)	-.187** (.027)	.139 (.346)
Wife started working	.029** (.004)	4054** (716)	.152** (.027)	.024** (.004)	.091** (.026)	.161 (.368)
Number of births	-.004 (.003)	-803+ (439)	-.029+ (.017)	-.016** (.003)	-.091** (.016)	.296 (.639)
Number of years kids left home	-.004* (.002)	-307 (259)	b	.015** (.002)	.062** (.009)	.592 (1.007)
R² (adjusted)	.297	.215	.218	.259	.202	
Mean (Standard Deviation)	.007 (.082)	2550 (12992)	.559 (.497)	.034 (.080)	.699 (.459)	

Number of Observations: 2509
+ Significant at .10 level.
* Significant at .05 level.
** Significant at .01 level.
a All dollar amounts in 1978 prices.
b Variable included in regression but t-ratio less than 1.0.

Table 1.12

EFFECTS OF CHANGE IN FAMILY COMPOSITION AND LABOR FORCE STATUS
ON PROGRESS--CONTROLLING FOR BACKGROUND[a]

(For all female household heads in 1972.)

	Total Family Income			Family Income/Needs		Mean Value (Standard Deviation) of Variable
	Annual Growth Rate (%)	1978 Minus 1971 ($)	Beat Inflation	Annual Growth Rate (%)	Beat Inflation	
Labor Force Status of Head:						
Stayed working	.014 (.009)	1055 (772)	.106** (.040)	.010 (.008)	.160** (.040)	.384 (.487)
Quit working	-.045** (.009)	-1888** (771)	-.158** (.041)	-.048** (.008)	-.186** (.040)	.198 (.398)
Started working	.078** (.013)	2138+ (1108)	.192** (.058)	.667** (.012)	.220** (.057)	.078 (.267)
Marital Status:						
Got married	.123** (.009)	15442** (772)	.385** (.040)	.078** (.008)	.233** (.040)	.186 (.389)
Number of births	b	-1288+ (750)	b	b	b	.121 (.405)
Number of years kids left home	-.031** (.004)	-1078** (317)	-.093** (.017)	b	b	.475 (.922)
R^2 (adjusted)	.340	.383	.201	.218	.108	
Mean (Standard Deviation)	.012 (.123)	2169 (10872)	.529 (.499)	.036 (.101)	.688 (.464)	

Number of Observations: 2509
+ Significant at .10 level.
* Significant at .05 level.
** Significant at .01 level.
a All dollar amounts in 1978 prices.
b Variable included in regression but t-ratio less than 1.0.

higher growth rates in both family income and income/needs and a 20 percent
higher likelihood of keeping both of those status measures growing faster than
inflation. The only difference in effects was for the absolute change in family
income associated with entry; it was nearly four times higher for the men than
the women.

When the continuous labor force participants were compared with those who
were out of the labor force at both the beginning and end of the seven-year
interval, we found no differences among the men but substantial differences
favoring the participants among women. These results reflect the role of non-
labor income sources (such as Social Security, private pensions, welfare income,
and asset income) in keeping family incomes and income/needs growing.
Apparently, the sources available for the non-working men were growing just as
fast as labor incomes. For women, labor incomes grew considerably faster than
transfers.

Changes in the wife's labor force status affected the economic status of the
families of all male household heads in very similar ways to their effects on
continuously working male household heads. Family income changed by $4,000-
$5,000, income growth rates changed by about 3 percent, and income/needs growth
rates changed by over 2 percent. All of these changes were statistically
significant, although not nearly as powerful as changes in the head's labor force
status.

The effects of change in marital status on income growth were consistent
with our earlier findings that women were much more affected by these changes
than were the men. Female heads of households who married ended up with $15,000
higher family incomes on average than did female heads who remained unmarried, a
40 percent higher likelihood of keeping their income up with inflation, and a
23 percent higher likelihood of keeping their income/needs up with inflation.
For men, marriage or remarriage resulted in very small increases in income and a
substantially reduced likelihood of keeping income/needs growing faster than
inflation.

The arrival and departure of children had economic consequences that depended
upon the sex of the household head and the measure of economic status. Births
had virtually no effect on the economic status of female headed families, but for
male headed families they resulted in somewhat smaller growth of family income
and substantially slower growth of family income relative to needs. This result
was sensible since births add to needs and may reduce the labor force activity of
the mother.

The departure of other children certainly reduces family needs but it may reduce family income as well.[27] In families headed by men, the income loss appeared to be smaller than the reduction in needs, and the net affect on growth in income/needs was positive. Each additional departure was associated with a 6 percent higher likelihood of keeping income/needs ahead of inflation. Among female headed households, the reverse was true: family income fell by an amount equal to needs and the net effect on growth in income/needs was nil.

SUMMARY

Despite the shift to a period with higher levels of unemployment and more rapid increases in prices, we find many of the same patterns that we reported on earlier. Substantial mobility and change in economic status was evident through several different measures, and changes in family composition and labor force participation accounted for a substantial amount of that change.

A reassessment of the role of background factors, including attitudes and motivation, "events" such as moving and changing jobs, and changes in family composition and labor force participation again reaffirms the absence of any substantial evidence that attitudes or background measures, except for age, affect changes in economic well-being. However, changes in household composition and labor market events do affect well-being.

Table 1.13 summarizes which of all the background factors and events were most important in accounting for whether family income/needs kept up with inflation. We selected income/needs as a measure of economic status for this recapitulation because it is the most comprehensive measure of well-being, taking account of changes both in income and composition of the family. Some events affect the two in opposite directions, as when a working child leaves home, so it may be misleading to look at income alone. Furthermore, we are interested here in the explanatory power of background and events, which depends upon their ability to produce differences in income/needs changes and on the frequency with which they occur. Table 1.13 includes only factors which have partial correlations greater than .1. The partial correlations are shown in the middle column of numbers. The first column shows how each factor affects the probabilities of keeping up. A partial correlation measures the effect of including a variable in a regression where all the other variables have already

---

[27]The income of all family workers, regardless of whether they were used by the family to help defray expenses, was included in measure of total family money income.

Table 1.13

SUMMARY TABLE OF EVENTS THAT AFFECT A FAMILY'S
CHANCES OF KEEPING UP WITH INFLATION
(For various groups of sample individuals.)

	Effect on Likelihood of Keeping Income/ Needs Up with Inflation	Partial R	Mean Value (Proportion with That Event)
Male Heads			
Head quit working	−.34%	−.180	.139
Wife quit working	−.19	−.139	.139
Number of years kids left home	+.06	.134	.592
Number of births	−.09	−.115	.296
Female Heads			
Got married	+.23	+.172	.186
Head quit working	−0.19	−.137	.198
Head stayed working	+.16	+.119	.384
Head started working	+.22	+.113	.078
Working Male Heads			
Wife quit working	−.22	−.168	.135
Number of years kids left home	+.06	+.149	.685
Number of births	−.09	−.134	.374
Stayed union	+.11	+.106	.215

been included. But after using that measure to select the variables, what we
want to note is their actual effect—how much a change in that variable alters
the probability of keeping up with inflation or getting ahead.

For all male heads of households, quitting working dominated changes in
economic status, reducing by 34 percent the probability that the family income/
needs would keep up. This event occurred to about one-seventh of the individuals
in this group. Having a working wife who dropped out of the labor force also
reduced the probability of keeping up with inflation, but only by 19 percent.
These changes were followed in importance by a 6 percent increase in the
likelihood of keeping up for each year when a child left home and a 9 percent
decrease for each child born, the latter presumably reducing the wife's earnings
as well as increasing needs.

If we omit from the analysis the male heads who did not work continuously
during the whole period, we automatically eliminate the large "head quit working"
effect, the other three effects remain, and one additional event is powerful

enough to be listed--staying in a labor union increased by 11 percent the likelihood that the family income/needs would keep up with inflation or surpass it.

For female heads, the probability of keeping up was increased 23 percent by getting married. Beyond that, the woman's own own labor force participation dominated the outcome with substantial effects from starting, stopping, or even staying at work, compared with staying out of the labor force.

Combined with our accumulating evidence of little or no effect of individuals' attitudes or behavior on their earnings, these results imply that in at least two historic periods of rather different aggregate economic trends, what control we do have over our own destinies is far more likely to occur through decisions about family composition and our ability and willingness to stay in the labor force than through getting a better job or a promotion. Whether a period of stable prices, high employment, and rapid growth in real income would give a different picture remains to be seen. We hope we shall have a chance to find out.

References

Atkinson, John W., ed. Motives in Fantasy, Action and Society. Princeton, New Jersey: D. Van Nostrand, 1958.

Atkinson, John W., and Feather, Norman T., eds. A Theory of Achievement Motivation. New York: Wiley, 1966.

Atkinson, John W., and Raynor, Joel O., eds. Motivation and Achievement. New York: Wiley, 1974.

Duncan, Greg, and Morgan, James N. "Sense of Efficacy and Subsequent Change in Earnings--A Replication." Forthcoming in Journal of Human Resources, 1981.

Hoffman, Saul D., and Holmes, John W. "Husbands, Wives, and Divorce." In Five Thousand American Families--Patterns of Economic Progress, Vol. IV, edited by Greg J. Duncan and James N. Morgan. Ann Arbor, Michigan: Institute for Social Research, The University of Michigan, 1976.

Juster, F. Thomas. "The Psychology of Inflation. I. Why is Inflation Bad?" Economic Outlook USA, 7 (Winter 1979): 16-17.

Morgan, James. "Voluntary and Involuntary Job Changes: Are there Compensating Differentials?" Proceedings of the Social Statistics Section. American Statistical Association, Houston, Texas, August 1980.

Morgan, James; Dickinson, Katherine; Dickinson, Jonathan; Benus, Jacob; and Duncan, Greg. Five Thousand American Families--Patterns of Economic Progress, Vol. I. Ann Arbor, Michigan: Institute for Social Research, The University of Michigan, 1974.

Rees, Albert. The Economics of Trade Unions, revised edition. Chicago:
    University of Chicago Press, 1977.

Veroff, Joseph; McClelland, Lou; and Marquis, Kent. "Measuring Intelligence and
    Achievement Motivation in Surveys." Final Report to U.S. Dept. of Health,
    Education and Welfare and Office of Economic Opportunity, Survey Research
    Center, Institute for Social Research, The University of Michigan. Ann
    Arbor, Michigan, October 1971.

Appendix to Chapter 1

Table A1.1

EFFECTS OF BACKGROUND VARIABLES ON CHANGES IN ECONOMIC STATUS 1971-1978[a]

(For all male household heads who worked 500 hours or more 1971-1978.)

	Hourly Earnings				Annual Earnings				Total Family Income			Family Income/Needs		Mean Value (Standard Deviation) of Variable
	Annual Growth Rate (%)	1978 Minus 1971 ($)	Beat Inflation?	Insta-bility	Annual Growth Rate (%)	1978 Minus 1971 ($)	Beat Inflation?	Insta-bility	Annual Growth Rate (%)	1978 Minus 1971 ($)	Beat Inflation?	Annual Growth Rate (%)	Beat Inflation?	
Efficacy	.001 (.001)	.140+ (.083)	b	b	.001 (.001)	231 (146)	b	-.011 (.009)	b	b	.009 (.007)	b	.007 (.006)	4.54 (1.77)
Future orientation	b	b	b	.016** (.005)	b	b	b	.021** (.007)	b	b	b	-.001 (.001)	-.008 (.005)	3.09 (1.98)
Risk avoidance	-.003* (.001)	-.192* (.100)	b	-.021** (.008)	-.005** (.001)	-498** (176)	-.013 (.008)	-.028** (.011)	-.003** (.001)	-695** (224)	-.016* (.008)	-.004** (.001)	-.020** (.007)	5.27 (1.57)
Connectedness	-.002+ (.001)	-.124 (.088)	-.018* (.007)	-.015* (.007)	b	b	b	b	b	b	b	-.001 (.001)	-.009 (.006)	6.26 (1.58)
Test score	-.001 (.001)	-.092 (.078)	b	b	b	-205 (138)	b	-.018* (.008)	-.002* (.001)	-260 (175)	b	-.002+ (.001)	-.009 (.006)	10.07 (1.99)
Achievement motivation	b	b	b	.011* (.004)	b	b	b	.011* (.006)	b	b	b	.001 (.001)	b	9.42 (2.62)
Education (in years)	.001 (.001)	.128* (.058)	b	b	.002* (.001)	264** (98)	b	b	.002** (.001)	519** (125)	.009+ (.005)	.001* (.001)	.011** (.004)	12.53 (3.08)
Whether black	b	b	.082+ (.048)	b	b	b	.101* (.047)	b	.007 (.007)	-1358 (1264)	.058 (.046)	b	b	.067 (.250)
Age (in 1972) <30	.022** (.004)	1.10** (.33)	.090** (.028)	.056** (.025)	.040** (.005)	3526** (588)	.194** (.028)	.095** (.035)	.013** (.004)	b	.037 (.027)	-.010* (.004)	-.054* (.024)	.295 (.456)
45-59	-.009* (.004)	-.706* (.340)	-.057* (.029)	-.037 (.026)	-.017** (.005)	-2460** (601)	-.091** (.029)	-.039 (.036)	-.025** (.004)	-5124** (766)	-.189** (.028)	b	.036 (.024)	.278 (.448)
60 or older	-.043** (.011)	-1.42 (.88)	-.261** (.074)	.287** (.066)	-.072** (.013)	-7485** (1548)	-.233** (.074)	.564** (.093)	-.039** (.010)	-5057** (1975)	-.339** (.072)	-.031** (.011)	-.117+ (.063)	.026 (.159)
R^2 (adjusted)	.046	.023	.020	.032	.107	.076	.061	.040	.071	.052	.054	.012	.010	

Number of observations: 1764

+ Significant at .10 level.
* Significant at .05 level.
** Significant at .01 level.
a All dollar amounts in 1978 prices.
b Variable included in regression but t-ratio less than 1.0.

Table A1.2

EFFECTS OF JOB AND RESIDENTIAL MOBILITY VARIABLES ON CHANGES IN ECONOMIC STATUS[a]

(For all male household heads who worked 500 hours or more, 1971-1978.)

	Hourly Earnings				Annual Earnings				Total Family Income			Family Income/Needs		Mean Value (Standard Deviation) of Variable
	Annual Growth Rate (%)	1978 Minus 1971 ($)	Beat Infla-tion?	Insta-bility	Annual Growth Rate (%)	1978 Minus 1971 ($)	Beat Infla-tion?	Insta-bility	Annual Growth Rate (%)	1978 Minus 1971 ($)	Beat Infla-tion?	Annual Growth Rate (%)	Beat Infla-tion?	
Number of residential moves	.004** (.001)	b	b	.018* (.008)	.005** (.002)	346+ (190)	.009 (.009)	.018+ (.011)	.004** (.001)	418+ (238)	.016+ (.009)	.005** (.001)	.011 (.007)	1.43 (1.76)
Number of voluntary job changes	.002 (.002)	b	b	.039** (.011)	.003 (.002)	b	b	.039** (.015)	.005** (.002)	b	.014 (.012)	.005** (.002)	.016 (.010)	0.82 (1.13)
Number of involuntary job changes	-.008** (.003)	-.371+ (.200)	-.056** (.017)	.023 (.014)	-.009** (.003)	-703+ (354)	-.050** (.017)	.075** (.020)	-.007** (.002)	-876+ (443)	-.041* (.016)	-.007** (.002)	-.036** (.014)	0.38 (0.80)
Number of years unemployed more than one month	-.004* (.002)	-.288* (.128)	-.021+ (.011)	.052** (.009)	-.003+ (.002)	-432+ (228)	b	.078** (.013)	b	b	b	b	-.010 (.009)	.655 (1.303)
Change in ln city size	.008** (.001)	.258* (.115)	.019+ (.010)	-.016 (.008)	.008** (.002)	329 (203)	.027** (.010)	-.013 (.012)	.005** (.001)	277 (255)	.015+ (.009)	.006** (.001)	.018* (.008)	-.09 (1.18)
Regional change: Stayed South	b	b	.028 (.027)	.068** (.023)	b	b	b	.093** (.033)	-.005 (.004)	b	b	-.005 (.004)	b	.271 (.445)
Left South	b	b	b	b	b	b	b	b	b	b	b	b	.176* (.083)	.013 (.111)
Went South	b	-1.19 (.93)	-.095 (.078)	.090 (.067)	.026** (.013)	b	b	.118 (.094)	b	-2090 (2054)	b	b	-.092 (.063)	.023 (.150)
Union status change: Stayed union	.012** (.005)	.726+ (.374)	.104** (.032)	-.170** (.027)	.011* (.005)	1095+ (662)	.049 (.032)	-.160** (.038)	.005 (.004)	b	.058+ (.030)	.007 (.004)	.113** (.025)	.215 (.411)
Left union	-.014* (.006)	-.948+ (.502)	-.077+ (.042)	-.077* (.036)	-.012+ (.007)	-1233 (889)	-.095* (.042)	b	-.006 (.006)	-1114 (1113)	-.085* (.040)	b	b	.089 (.285)
Became union	.022** (.007)	b	.117* (.049)	-.061 (.042)	.015+ (.008)	b	b	-.090 (.059)	.008 (.006)	b	b	.009 (.007)	.068 (.039)	.061 (.240)
Disability: Always disabled	b	b	b	.524* (.220)	b	b	b	1.16** (.31)	-.099** (.034)	b	b	-.072* (.035)	b	.002 (.044)
Became disabled	.021+ (.011)	3.17** (.912)	b	.252** (.066)	b	-2896+ (1616)	b	.306** (.093)	b	b	b	b	b	.023 (.149)
R² (adjusted)	.046	.023	.020	.032	.107	.076	.061	.040	.071	.052	.054	.012	.010	

Number of observations: 1764

+ Significant at .10 level. * Significant at .05 level. ** Significant at .01 level.

[a] All dollar amounts in 1978 prices.

b Variable included in regression but t-ratio less than 1.0.

Note: All regression coefficients have been adjusted for the effects of background and family change variables.

Table A1.3

EFFECTS OF FAMILY VARIABLES ON CHANGES IN ECONOMIC STATUS[a]

(For all male household heads who worked 500 hours or more, 1971-1978.)

	Hourly Earnings				Annual Earnings				Total Family Income			Family Income/Needs		Mean Value (Standard Deviation) of Variable
	Annual Growth Rate (%)	1978 Minus 1971 ($)	Beat Inflation?	Insta-bility	Annual Growth Rate (%)	1978 Minus 1971 ($)	Beat Inflation?	Insta-bility	Annual Growth Rate (%)	1978 Minus 1971 ($)	Beat Inflation?	Annual Growth Rate (%)	Beat Inflation?	
Labor Force Status of Wife:														
Wife stayed working	b	b	b	-.047+ (.026)	b	-634 (628)	.041 (.030)	-.065+ (.036)	b	b	b	.004 (.004)	.071** (.024)	.256 (.436)
Wife quit working	b	b	b	.044 (.033)	b	b	.047 (.038)	b	-.028** (.005)	-4684** (1004)	-.221** (.036)	-.023** (.005)	-.219** (.031)	.135 (.342)
Wife started working	-.009+ (.005)	-.673+ (.388)	-.078* (.033)	-.044 (.028)	-.014** (.005)	-1769* (687)	-.077* (.033)	-.045 (.039)	.025** (.004)	3259** (861)	.146** (.031)	.022** (.004)	.070** (.027)	.197 (.398)
Marital Status of Head:														
Head stayed married	.013 (.009)	b	.135* (.060)	.070 (.052)	b	b	b	b	b	b	b	-.018* (.008)	-.105* (.049)	.853 (.354)
Head became unmarried	.016 (.011)	b	.114 (.075)	b	b	b	b	b	-.024* (.010)	-3150 (1965)	-.090 (.071)	b	.071 (.061)	.059 (.236)
Head got married	.014 (.012)	b	.117 (.079)	.097 (.068)	.019 (.013)	b	b	b	.017+ (.010)	2107 (2084)	b	-.016 (.011)	-.239** (.064)	.044 (.204)
Number of births	.005+ (.003)	b	.044* (.020)	-.026 (.017)	-.008* (.003)	650 (417)	.046* (.020)	-.058* (.024)	b	-1073* (522)	-.026 (.019)	-.012** (.003)	-.091** (.016)	.374 (.700)
Number of years kids left home	-.002 (.002)	b	b	b	b	b	b	b	-.002 (.002)	b	b	.017** (.002)	.062** (.010)	.685 (1.070)
Mean value (standard deviation)	.012 (.073)	1.17 (5.72)	.624 (.484)	.543 (.433)	.009 (.085)	2293 (10378)	.596 (.491)	.565 (.610)	.024 (.068)	5015 (13069)	.659 (.474)	.050 (.069)	.789 (.408)	
Number of births (omitting change in wife's labor force status)	.006* (.003)	b	.054* (.019)	b	.009** (.003)	838* (408)	.053** (.019)	-.049* (.023)	-.006* (.003)	-1724** (517)	-.058** (.019)	-.016* (.003)	-.121** (.016)	
R² (adjusted)	.091	.044	.052	.123	.143	.089	.079	.128	.170	.099	.119	.148	.132	

Number of observations: 1764 *Significant at .05 level. **Significant at .01 level.

+Significant at .10 level.

a All dollar amounts in 1978 prices.

b Variable included in regression but t-ratio less than 1.0.

Note: All regression coefficients have been adjusted for the effects of background and job and residential mobility variables.

Chapter 2

DYNAMICS OF WAGE CHANGE

Greg J. Duncan and Saul D. Hoffman

INTRODUCTION

Why some people earn more than others is a question that has long been the subject of both popular speculation and professional inquiry. Many models of income distribution have been developed (see Sahota, 1978, for a recent summary) and each has been judged by the empirical evidence available at the time. Until the past decade, the vast majority of empirical work was done on cross-sectional data, which show, at a single point in time, the earnings and demographic characteristics of some collection of individuals. Data from a representative cross-sectional sample of workers can show a great deal about the nature of the distribution of income: its average, its inequality, how it differs among population subgroups defined by race, sex, education, and so on.

Although restricted to a single point in time, cross-sectional data have been used to test models of the dynamic processes that produce the earnings distribution observed at a point in time. The human capital model of self-investment, for example, predicts that the declining pattern of on-the-job investments will cause an individual's earnings to grow dramatically when young and inexperienced and then increase much less rapidly (if at all) later on. When this hypothesis is tested with cross-sectional data, other characteristics that affect earnings (e.g., education) are statistically controlled, and the future earnings for individuals with a given amount of labor market experience are then predicted from the earnings of otherwise "identical" individuals with more experience. The parabolic experience-earnings profile that shows up in virtually all cross-sectional datasets is taken as confirmation of the human capital investment hypothesis and, often implicitly, as the likely earnings path of most workers as they acquire more labor market experience.[1]

Theories of labor market segmentation are supported by cross-sectional evidence that women and minority workers are consistently overrepresented in low-wage, unstable jobs in "secondary sector" industries, while the high-wage, stable, "primary sector" jobs seem to be reserved for white men. Furthermore, experience-earnings profiles for minorities are flatter and this fact, combined with the pattern of overrepresentation in low-wage jobs that shows up repeatedly in cross-sectional data, is interpreted as evidence of immobility between sectors, with minorities locked into the low-wage jobs.

The availability of large, representative sets of panel data, with repeated observations on the same individuals, greatly enhances our ability to describe and explain labor market processes. We can look behind the stable aggregate income distribution and see whether aggregate stability is caused by individual stability or by a great deal of individual mobility that is cancelled out by aggregation. We can look behind the apparent economic progress of the typical black worker and see whether it is due to real relative improvement in his or her economic status or to the fact that most recent cohorts of black workers are becoming more like their white counterparts. We can also develop much more stringent tests of hypotheses that have been supported by cross-sectional data. For example, is the on-the-job investment behavior implied by the cross-section supported by multiple wage observations on the same individuals? Is the inter-sector immobility implied by segmented labor market theories supported by the direct mobility information afforded by panel data? An added virtue of panel data is that one does not have to rely on statistical controls to identify otherwise identical workers in order to estimate the effects of education or such labor market events as joining a union or experiencing a spell of unemployment. Individuals are, in effect, their own controls, and so the effects of unchanging and elusive concepts like "ambition" and "ability" will no longer interfere with the estimation of the effects of the variables of interest.[2]

---

[1]Strictly speaking, these projected earnings paths are expected to hold only in a "stationary" world with no changes in relative demand, productivity growth, and so on. The expected effects of such changes can be incorporated into the model.

[2]It is possible that the wage effects of unchanging characteristics will change over time. These complications are considered below.

The purpose of this chapter is to provide an overview of methods and results from studies of the dynamics of earnings using panel data. It is organized in three sections. In the first, the advantages of panel data vis-a-vis cross-sectional data are presented, along with a selective summary of the panel data literature. The second and third sections consist of two applications of data from the Panel Study of Income Dynamics to topics of current interest. The second section contains an examination of recent trends in the relative earnings of black and white workers. The apparent increase in the economic status of black workers is shown to be caused primarily by the converging earnings of recent cohorts of black and white workers and the departure of older cohorts with very large race differences in average earnings. An additional contributing factor is the improvement over time of black workers' earnings within a given cohort. The third section examines earnings mobility. Both hourly and annual earnings are found to fluctuate widely from year to year for most workers, a result that contradicts labor market segmentation models which predict immobility for certain worker subgroups. Persistent earnings "affluence" and "poverty" are also described and it is found that the long-term economic position of blacks and women is much less favorable than is indicated by cross-sectional comparisons of "average" or "median" workers.

THE ADVANTAGES OF PANEL DATA

A useful point of departure is Mincer's (1974) widely used human capital earnings equation:

$$(1) \quad \ln Y_i = B_0 + B_1 \, Ed_i + B_2 \, Exp_i + B_3 \, Exp_i^2 + e_i$$

where $\ln Y_i$ is the natural logarithm of the annual or hourly earnings of the ith individual, Ed_i is the ith individual's years of educational attainment, Exp_i is the ith individual's years of labor market experience and e_i is an error term. Theory suggests that the natural logarithm of earnings is the most appropriate form of the dependent variable; coefficients on independent variables are interpreted as the <u>percentage</u> changes in earnings associated with unit changes in the independent variables. The assumption that post-schooling investment in on-the-job training (OJT) declines linearly over the life cycle implies a parabolic, rather than linear, experience-earnings profile; hence, the square of work experience is included in the equation. Mincer estimated his model with cross-sectional data from the 1960 Census. Mincer's equation has served as the basis for hundreds, if not thousands, of articles investigating some aspect of earnings with cross-sectional data, e.g., the wage effects of such institutional factors

as the labor unions and industry, earnings differences between the races and
sexes, wage effects of socioeconomic background, ability, school quality, health,
working conditions, and so on.

There are three fundamental limitations to the inferences that can be made
about these kinds of models from cross-sectional data. First, as pointed out by
Lillard and Willis (1978), cross-sectional models are cast in terms of "typical"
or "representative" workers and lead "to an empirical emphasis on the effects of
independent variables on the mean earnings of an average individual and to a
relative lack of interest in individual differences" (1978, p. 985). Although
the tone of most earnings models seems to imply relatively small year to year
fluctuations in economic position, in fact cross-sectional data cannot measure
individual fluctuations. When the earnings changes of individual workers are
actually calculated with panel data, the extent and diversity of the observed
changes are staggering. For those unfamiliar with these findings, consider the
following question (from Hoffman, 1977): Using eight consecutive annual
observations (1967-1974) on the nominal hourly wage rates of a national sample of
white men who were working each year, we count the number of times wage rates
increased from one year to the next (the maximum possible is seven). What
fraction of workers had seven consecutive wage rate increases? The answer for
these years was 3 percent for all workers. It was only slightly higher than that
for the young and white-collar workers and substantially higher for only one
group--government workers (9 percent). Fewer than one-fifth had six increases,
and these results did not change in going from hourly to annual earnings. It is
tempting to ascribe these fluctuations to errors in measuring earnings, but even
if small (less than 10 percent) decreases in nominal earnings are counted along
with the increases, the proportion of workers with seven consecutive increases
was barely one-quarter.

A more conventional way of summarizing earnings changes is with transition
matrices (see the section on "Earnings Mobility" later in this chapter) or by
simply computing the absolute change in earnings between two points in time.
When the latter calculation was made for deflated annual labor incomes between
1967 and 1974, it was found that the mean change was small, about $400, but the
standard deviation of change was huge--over $5,000. This means that roughly one-

third of male workers each experienced labor income increases or decreases that exceeded $5,000.[3] (See Hill and Hoffman, 1977.)

Year-to-year changes in earnings, then, are frequent, large, and usually come as a shock to the analyst brought up seeing smooth, parabolic wage-earnings profiles of the "typical" worker. The fluctuations are only slightly larger for blacks than whites and vary little by age, union status, or job tenure. Although this evidence does not constitute a formal test, the extent and pattern of the fluctuations cast considerable doubt on segmented labor market models which predict much more earnings mobility for some groups than others and also contradict the spirit of the human capital investment model in which the monotonically declining pattern of investment in on-the-job training ought to produce a pattern of earnings increases that are not thoroughly overwhelmed by exogenous forces or transitory disturbances.[4]

As chaotic as these patterns may seem, it is still possible to estimate wage change equations with sensible results. Many of the wage change analyses are beginning to use the statistical advantages afforded by panel data to overcome the other two limitations of cross-sectional data. These other two limitations deal with the validity of estimates from the models themselves.[5] The usefulness of cross-sectional data is often limited because they do not include crucial time-invariant personality factors such as motivation and ability. It is well known that omitted variables which are correlated with included independent variables may bias the estimated effects of the included variables. Ability is the classic example of such an omitted variable. Since more able people both earn more and complete more schooling, education picks up some of the effects of ability and therefore overstates the true effects of education. So while Mincer estimates that an additional year of education increases earnings by ten percent, we would not expect that sending a typical individual back to school for a year would increase his earnings by the full ten percent. Panel data sets often exclude these crucial time-invariant measures as well but, as will be explained

---

[3]These are 1967 dollars. The mean annual earnings level for this group was about $10,000.

[4]There are, of course, reasons to expect a decline in real earnings rates in some years: depreciation, obsolescence, sudden changes in the prices attached by the market to certain skills, unusually rapid inflation, and so on. Note that the figures on monotonicity cited in the text refer to nominal earnings.

[5]The general arguments are presented here in the text with the econometric detail given in the Appendix.

below, the biases caused by their omission can be reduced or eliminated completely.

The third limitation of cross-sectional data also concerns omitted variables, but in this case they are variables which change over time. These measures fall into two groups: period and cohort variables. Period variables are conditions of the macro-environment at a point in time. By definition, they are constant in any given cross-section. To estimate the effects of period variables on individual economic status, it is necessary to have observations at several points in time, as with panel data or repeated cross-sections pooled together. As an example, Holmes (1977) used Panel Study data to show that incomes of black families are substantially more sensitive to macroeconomic fluctuations than are the incomes of white families.

Cohort variables are conditions which may face persons born in a given year, conditions such as public school quality, discrimination against new labor market entrants in a particularly bad period, and so on. The classic example of problems arising from omitted cohort variables is in the analysis of temporal patterns of black-white earnings ratios. Typically, conclusions about the relative growth rates of the earnings blacks and whites are based on cross-sectional estimates from coefficients on the experience variables in Equation 1. These growth rates are usually much higher for white men than for other subgroups. There are situations in which these cross-sectional estimates would predict future wage growth patterns--in a stationary state in which the underlying earnings-generating function is constant over time--so that each individual's expected earnings (conditional on his/her relevant characteristics) M years in the future is exactly equal to the earnings of an otherwise identical individual today with exactly M additional years of work experience. Among the list of factors that could shift or alter the shape of the earnings-generating function and thereby destroy the cross-section/life-cycle correspondence are changes in a mixture of cohort and period variables: quality of education, both within and especially across races (see Welch, 1973); discrimination; cohort size and composition by education; demand for different educational groups (see Freeman, 1975, on the declining value of college education); female labor force attachment; government policy; technological change; and so on.[6] Most of this

---

[6]Generally speaking, period and cohort variables can cause parallel shifts in experience-earnings profiles or can alter the slope of those profiles. Jonsson and Klevmarken (1980) show how macroeconomic conditions affect the earnings of young and old Swedish workers in different ways--an example of period effects that alter the slope of the profiles.

set of possible earnings-related changes are difficult to measure or, in the use
of period variables, have no variance in a cross-section. As a result, they are
invariably omitted from the cross-sectional equations. Since cohort factors
change over time, omitted cohort variables will necessarily be correlated with
years of work experience, which in turn are highly correlated with the calendar
year in a cross-section. Thus, the relative earnings of black men with 20 years
of work experience may be low because of the discrimination they faced when
entering the labor market. If this discrimination has decreased, then the
relative earnings of these older men will not forecast the relative position that
young blacks will face 20 years from now.

Panel data can be used to help reduce both the unobservable and time-
invariant-variable statistical limitations inherent in cross-sectional data.
There are two basic strategies. The first involves estimating an earnings level
equation similar to Equation 1 and assuming that unobservable permanent
characteristics and dynamic aspects of earnings change are built into the error
term. Lillard and Willis (1978) typified this approach with a model in which
individual earnings levels are a function of measured skills, unmeasured
permanent individual traits, random events with persistent but deteriorating
effects (serial correlation), and purely random effects. A second approach
involves estimating an equation of wage change rather than level. Although both
approaches use panel data to overcome the statistical limitation inherent in
cross-sectional data, the emphasis in this section is on wage change equations.
Wage level equations are better able to characterize the statistical properties
of wage mobility, while wage change equations are more suitable for models of the
labor market processes producing wage growth (quits, layoffs, occupational and
industrial changes, migration, and so on) and also to public policy questions
regarding labor market phenomena. Our summary of the applications of panel data
to wage studies will concentrate on those involving models of wage change.

The statistical problems that arise from time-invariant unobserved variables
can be handled by estimating a change equation with panel data. Let us consider
the problem of estimating the wage effects of labor union membership. With
cross-sectional data, the strategy is to "hold constant" the effects of all other
wage-related characteristics (e.g., education, experience) and then compare the
average earnings of union members to the average for nonunion workers. Any
personal characteristics that are omitted from the equation and are correlated
with both union status and wages will bias the estimated union effect. With
panel data, on the other hand, there are a number of workers who, as time passes,

either join unions or leave them. Wage changes for these job changers can provide a much more reliable estimate of union effects since personal characteristics are, by definition, held constant for the same individuals.[7] Mellow (1979) estimated a wage change model of this type using a two-year panel from the Current Population Survey and found symmetrical union wage effects of about 7 percent.[8]

Panel data also allow the analyst to tackle problems of period and cohort effects that plague cross-sectional data analysis. As with the work by Holmes cited earlier, period effects can be estimated by including direct measures of period variables of interest. This was not possible in a cross-section since they had no variance. Cohort effects can be eliminated with panel data in the same way that time-invariant effects are handled, since repeated observations on a single cohort will be purged of cohort effects. Hoffman (1979) used this procedure and found, contrary to cross-sectional results, that earnings growth rates of black and white workers in their 30s are roughly equal. Growth rates for white workers in their 20s, on the other hand, are roughly twice as large as those of black workers in the same age cohort, although the difference is smaller than estimated from corresponding cross-sectional data.

In fact, wage change analyses using panel data have covered a variety of topics using a variety of methods. A detailed survey of all of them is beyond the scope of this paper. We can, however, summarize a number of the most interesting and important, and in so doing, give the reader a notion of the diversity of topic, method, and result.

------

[7]It is, of course, possible that some personal characteristics may change over time or that the wage effects of measured or unmeasured characteristics may change. Both of these possibilities would interfere with the simple interpretation of the coefficient on the union status change variable as the "true" union effect. In addition, there is the possibility that job changers are themselves an odd group so the wage changes of those joining or leaving unions ought to be compared with wage changes of those who changed job but did not change union status. But these selection biases are easier to treat when the demographic effects are neutralized.

[8]An additional way of using panel data to shed light on the issue of union-nonunion differences in unmeasured worker quality is by estimating adjusted wage differences between workers who were about to become union members and those who remained nonunion. Here the panel data are used only to identify workers who are about to change union status. Mellow finds that black workers who were about to become unionized earned considerably more than those who remained nonunion, implying that some of their apparent union wage benefits reflect higher quality workers.

Wage change models estimated with panel data have been used to test the human capital investment model. There have been two major attempts to do this. Hanushek and Quigley (1980) tested a basic Mincer-type model with data from the Panel Study and found very limited support for it. Lazear (1976) estimated a much more loosely specified wage growth/human capital model with data from the National Longitudinal Study youth sample and obtained estimates for the parameters of interest that are reasonably consistent with the model.[9] Since the Hanushek and Quigley paper is both competent and disturbing in its results, it deserves some further discussion.

Hanushek and Quigley developed the longitudinal analogue to Mincer's cross-sectional human capital equation to test if earnings changes are consistent with the basic post-schooling investment model. In very rough terms, their model can be developed by differencing a cross-sectional model at two points in time. If the two points in time are a year apart then the change model becomes:

(2) $\quad \Delta \ln Y_i = \Delta B_0 + \Delta B_1 \, Ed_{i,t} + B_{1,t+1} \, \Delta Ed + \Delta B_2 \, Exp_{i,t} + B_{2,t+1} + \Delta B_3 \, Exp^2_{i,t} + 2B_3 \, Exp_{i,t} + \Delta e_i$

where t and t+1 denote the two points in time and "Δ" denotes changes from t to t+1.

Note that the initial level of variables such as education belong in a change equation only if there is reason to believe that the cross-sectional effects of education on earnings have changed from one time period to the next. If it is assumed as Hanushek and Quigley have done, that the cross-sectional parameters (the $\tilde{B}$'s) do not change, then Equation 2 becomes:

(3) $\quad \Delta \ln Y_i = B_1 \Delta Ed_i + 2B_3 Exp_i + \Delta e_i$

The coefficient on change in education corresponds to the cross-sectional coefficient on this variable. The same would hold for other variables such as region or city size if they were included in a similar analysis. This coefficient on change in such variables is likely to be a better estimate of the effects of these variables since the biasing effects of the correlation between them and unobserved variables such as ability are eliminated.[10]

_____

[9] Borjas and Mincer (1978) use retrospective earnings data from the Coleman-Rossi Life History Study to estimate and explain the basic parameters from a human capital model. Their empirical work is plagued by measurement error in the earnings data, although their procedures seem promising enough to deserve replication on truly longitudinal earnings data.

[10] In the simplest case, this can be seen by noting that, in a cross-section, observed education and unobserved ability are correlated. In the change equation, unchanging ability drops out and the estimated relationship between change in education and change in earnings is not confounded by a correlation

Different assumptions about the shape of investment profiles will alter the functional form somewhat but the basic point is that the important parameters of the post-schooling investment relationship (e.g., rate of return) can be estimated.

Hanushek and Quigley, however, did not find broad support for the investment model. In their words,

"(f)or males, OJT investments do appear to offer some explanation for wage differences. However, the investment profiles interact with schooling levels (and offer no consistent explanation of wage differences in the lowest schooling group.) Furthermore, the estimates are unstable and generally implausible over time periods of differing length. For females, OJT explanations of wage differences are unsupported, except perhaps for college educated white females" (p. 15).

Not enough time has passed to permit an adequate evaluation of the scope of their findings. But they have raised enough questions to warrant a careful examination of the basic post-schooling investment model with panel data.

Despite the tenuous relationship between wage growth patterns and the on-the-job investment behavior predicted by the human capital model, wage growth is often used as a proxy measure of training. Mincer and Leighton (1980) have examined the effects of minimum wage laws on training by regressing absolute wage growth on a set of human capital variables (measured as initial levels and not changes), plus two state-level variables related to the minimum wage: the ratio of employment covered by the minimum wage law relative to total state employment and the percentage differential between the minimum wage and an adjusted state average wage. Absolute rather than relative wage growth is argued to be a theoretically superior measure of the dollar value of training acquired. Generally, they find significant, negative effects for the state wage variables but not for the coverage measure.

Since panel data allow the analyst to control for unobserved individual differences, they would seem ideal for an investigation of a long-standing hypothesis of tradeoffs between wages and working conditions. The typical result from cross-sectional data is that desirable working conditions have a positive association with wages. This anomalous result is usually attributed to unmeasured skill differences that correlate positively with wage and with

---

with ability. This example assumes, of course, that some individuals acquire more education between times t and t+1. The argument also applies to changes that are frequently observed in panel data, e.g., locational, occupational, and industrial changes. Measurement error may cause estimates from change equations to be worse than those of the level equation.

desirable working conditions. It is somewhat surprising, then, that Brown (1980) has continued to find no support for the compensating wage differential hypothesis when he used panel data from the National Longitudinal Survey of Young Men to perform the test.

Wage growth is an additional employment characteristic that might be expected to produce a (negative) compensating wage differential, regardless of whether or not it reflects past investments in on-the-job training. The trade-off between wage level and growth is the basis for Lazear's (1979) argument that the apparent recent increase in the earnings of blacks has come at the expense of future wage growth; employers, in other words, are responding to affirmative action pressures by offering blacks high initial wages but fewer training opportunities (and lower subsequent wage growth). He tested this hypothesis with panel data from the NLS Young Men sample and the Survey of the High School Class of 1972 and found support for it, although there appears to be little evidence of differential actual growth rates within our Panel Study data in recent years (see the next section of this chapter).

The economic consequences of various kinds of job and residential mobility are a natural topic for longitudinal data analysis since it is crucial to measure economic status both before and after the change. Bartel (1979) used the NLS samples of young and mature men (as well as the cross-sectional Coleman-Rossi Retrospective Life History Study) to distinguish wage effects of quits, layoffs, and migration. Her wage growth model uses the absolute change in earnings as the dependent variable and includes, as controls, a standard set of human capital variables presumably measured at the initial time. She found that the biggest wage gains go to those young and middle-aged men who migrate but remain with the same employer (i.e., transfer). The wage effects of migration after a quit or layoff are much smaller, often insignificant, and depend critically on the sample under investigation.

Certain attitudinal measures have a strong association with earnings in a cross-section but the causality of this relationship is unclear: Did the attitudes lead to higher earnings or does economic success produce positive attitudes? Panel data would appear to be ideal for differentiating between these two explanations, since initial attitudes can be related to subsequent change in economic status. Andrisani (1977) used the Young Men NLS data to support a causal link between an initial feeling of internal control (efficacy) and subsequent change in economic status, although his results do not seem to generalize to other population subgroups (See Duncan and Morgan, forthcoming).

Furthermore, even a strong association between initial attitudes and subsequent change in economic status is not necessarily conclusive proof of the theory. Initial attitudes might reflect the real situation of an individual in a good job, with promise of advancement, and thus be an implicit forecast of the future. In other words, the attitude and subsequent success may both result from some prior unobserved factor rather than the individual's self-confidence.

Duncan (1979) estimated a recursive wage growth model that included a variety of background measures (education, experience, attitudes, location, work habits, etc.) and a number of intervening job-related events (unemployment, quits, changes in union and industry status, etc.). His strategy was to see if there was empirical support for the wage growth processes described in the various theories of earnings determination. For example, did bad working habits inhibit wage growth by keeping workers locked into secondary sector jobs, as segmented labor market theorists allege? Did education lead to higher wage growth by increasing a worker's chances of making voluntary investments in job changes? In general, he found that earnings growth rate functions were quite similar for black and white workers and accounted for a substantial fraction of the variance in individual growth rates. But there appeared to be little empirical support for the labor market processes described in either the human capital or segmented labor market models.

This review of findings on wage change models from panel data has been cursory and incomplete. We have attempted to show the diversity of topics that can be and have been addressed with these kinds of data as well as some of the results. A general comment is in order, however. There is little consensus on the form of wage change equations. Typically, independent variables are entered in a very ad hoc manner--some measuring initial levels, some measuring change-- with little regard for the appropriate functional form. Our prior discussion of the cross-sectional Equation 1 and the change Equations 2 and 3 indicated that a properly specified unchanging cross-sectional equation implies a change equation with no initial level variables on the right-hand side. Some studies estimate wage change relationships with a direct measure of change on the left-hand side of the equation; others put the final wage on the left hand side and initial level on the right hand side; and still others regress change on the initial level. It can be shown that the latter two methods are equivalent but, more important, it has been shown empirically that there are substantial differences in coefficient estimates when the initial wage level is included on the right hand side (Duncan, 1979). As Augustyniak shows in another chapter in this volume, neither measurement error nor regression to the mean provide a justification for including the initial wage on the right hand side of the equation. Clearly, it is time to pay more attention to functional form and to work toward a generally agreed upon wage change equation that can be used as a basis for future wage change analyses in the same way that Mincer's basic cross-sectional equation has been used as the consensus wage level equation.

RECENT TRENDS IN BLACK-WHITE EARNINGS RATIOS

There is little doubt that available aggregate measures have shown steady and substantial improvement in the relative economic status of black workers over the last two decades. Studies Freeman (1973), Welch (1973), and Smith and Welch (1977) are among those that have documented and analyzed the rising relative earnings ratios. The ratio of black-to-white median wages for males rose from 58 percent in 1959 to 67 percent in 1969, 73 percent in 1975, and 76 percent in 1978.[11] The rate of increase in the ratio has apparently risen as well since 1964. In addition to improvement in the aggregate data, there are many other findings of improvement: earnings ratios for the youngest cohorts and for the better educated are considerably higher than the overall averages; occupational distributions also show convergence; and, finally, the general upward trend in the earnings ratio seems to have survived the economic downturn of the early 1970s.

A number of alternative explanations for these findings exist. Freeman (1973) has attributed the improvement to governmental actions—the 1964 passage of the Civil Rights Act and the cumulative impact of Equal Employment Opportunity Commission expenditures—which has altered the relative demands for black and white workers. Smith and Welch (1977) and Welch (1973) have stressed instead "vintage effects"—the fact that in terms of productivity-related characteristics, younger black cohorts are more similar to their white counterparts than are older black cohorts. They argue that earnings ratios converge because, even with discrimination levels constant, average productivity levels have converged for the two races.[12]

---

[11] Note that these trends refer to earned income for individuals. The corresponding trends for family income, which is influenced by the number of earners in a family, show much less improvement.

[12] Butler and Heckman (1978) have argued that the apparent improvement has occurred because of declining labor force participation among those black workers who would otherwise be low earners.

There are, however, a set of less optimistic findings concerning race differences in economic status. Unemployment rate differentials have remained at historical levels for black workers generally and have even widened considerably for teens and 20-24 year olds. Similar differences in participation rates have also developed.[13] More directly relevant to findings of aggregate secular improvement has been evidence of continued within-cohort declines in relative earnings ratios. Using longitudinal data from the Panel Study, Hoffman (1979) examined life-cycle earnings growth for black and white males, aged 20-29 in 1967, over the time period from 1967 to 1974 and found that differences in earnings within cohorts actually _increased_ as the sample members acquired additional years of work experience. Similar results for workers with less than a college degree were presented in Smith-Welch's analysis of CPS data over the same time period.[14]

In this section, we attempt to reconcile the findings of aggregate secular improvement in earnings ratios by race with the less optimistic evidence on within-cohort earnings patterns. We also provide evidence on whether the observed secular earnings convergence reflects structural change in relative earnings functions (due, perhaps, to an easing of discrimination), a change in relative productivity levels (as Smith and Welch have argued), or a change in the composition of a constant-aged sample across comparison years. Our analysis takes advantage of the longitudinal data available in the Panel Study to identify within- and between-cohort effects and to analyze their influence on the secular changes in the black-white earnings ratio.

The analysis which follows is based on 12 years of information (1967-1978) on individual earnings. We begin by presenting simple, descriptive information and then proceed to regression analysis. To highlight within- and between-cohort trends and to examine changes in trends over the 12 years, we treated the 12 years of information as three four-year panels for the time-periods 1967-1970, 1971-1974, and 1975-1978. We followed the same individuals within each four-year period, thus observing within-cohort trends. Comparing the three periods, we observed between-cohort trends as the samples change. In each of the periods, the sample was restricted to males aged 25-54 in the first year of the period

---

[13]See Bowers (1979) for details on this.

[14]Both Hoffman and Smith and Welch found that the within-cohort life-cycle earnings decline was less severe than that predicted from a cross-sectional analysis.

(1967, 1971, and 1975, respectively) who worked at least 500 hours in all years of the period. All earnings figures were inflated to 1978 levels with the CPI. We further focused on two subgroups of interest: workers between ages 25 and 34 and those with at least a high school degree.

Table 2.1 provides information on black-white ratios for four-year average and annual wage rates and annual earnings from 1967 to 1978. Note first the figures in columns 1, 6, and 11 which correspond to the secular improvement figures referred to earlier. For a representative sample of working 25-54 year olds, the ratio of average wage rates rose from about 65 percent in 1967 to almost 70 percent in 1971 and to 76 percent in 1975; average annual earnings showed lower ratios but similar trends. Similarly, for the younger cohort in the sample, the wage rate ratio rose from 72 percent to over 80 percent, and the annual earnings ratio improved from 69 percent to almost 77 percent. This merely confirms the trends indicated in data from the Current Population Survey.

The within-cohort trends shown in columns 2-5, 7-10, and 12-15 show a strikingly different pattern, especially for the 25-34 year old cohort. Rather than approximating the secular trend, within-cohort ratios are generally flat or slightly falling. For example, although aggregate wage ratios for 25-54 year olds rose from 65 percent to 70 percent from 1967 to 1971, the within-cohort trend from 1967 to 1970 showed only a 1 percent increase. Similar trends also occurred in the two subsequent periods: while aggregate ratios continued to rise, the within-cohort ratio actually fell between 1971 and 1974 and rose by only one percentage point between 1975 and 1978. Even for the young cohort, where wage convergence has been most highly publicized, the same conflicting between- and within-cohort trends appeared. Between 1967 and 1970, the within-cohort wage ratio fell 5 percent, while the between-cohort ratio for 25-34 year olds in 1967 and 1971 rose 5 percent. Within-cohort ratios also fell sharply over the 1971-1974 period and were stable over the final four-year period. The general conclusion of Table 2.1 is straightforward: the observed rising secular trend in the black-white earnings ratio appears to be mostly a between-cohort phenomena which masks the quite different underlying within-cohort trends.[15]

---

[15] The Panel Study data can also be used to examine 12 year earnings patterns. When this was done for the 25-54 year old cohort in 1967, it was found that the ratio of average black-white wages showed a very modest upward trend of about 3-4 percent. The ratio of median wages, less influenced by the high-income tail of the white distribution, rose considerably from 1974 through 1977, but fell back in 1978 to just one percent above the 1967 figure. The full 12-year within-cohort trend for the 25-34 year olds showed no improvement whatsoever.

Table 2.1

AVERAGE WAGE AND EARNINGS RATIOS BY RACE

(For three separate cohorts of 25-54 year old male household heads.)

	(1) 1967-70	(2) 1967	(3) 1968	(4) 1969	(5) 1970	(6) 1971-74	(7) 1971	(8) 1972	(9) 1973	(10) 1974	(11) 1975-78	(12) 1975	(13) 1976	(14) 1977	(15) 1978
All															
Wage Rate															
Black men	$5.33					$6.27					$6.67				
White men	8.24					9.02					8.79				
Ratio	.647	.64	.66	.64	.65	.695	.71	.70	.70	.69	.759	.75	.76	.77	.76
Annual Earnings															
Black men	$11,871					$13,519					$14,088				
White men	18,689					20,275					19,431				
Ratio	.635	.62	.65	.64	.64	.667	.68	.67	.67	.65	.725	.72	.72	.75	.71
Age 25-34															
Wage Rate Ratio	.720	.75	.73	.70	.70	.781	.81	.81	.78	.73	.804	.81	.80	.80	.81
Annual Earnings Ratio	.686	.67	.72	.69	.67	.726	.73	.74	.73	.70	.766	.77	.78	.76	.76
Finished High School															
Wage Rate Ratio	.731	.74	.73	.74	.71	.755	.76	.75	.76	.75	.790	.79	.77	.80	.78
Annual Earnings Ratio	.739	.72	.76	.74	.74	.726	.73	.72	.75	.70	.765	.77	.76	.79	.74

Note: All wage rates and earnings have been inflated to 1978 levels with the CPI.

Accounting for Secular Change on Black-White Earnings Ratios

In this section, we present the results of regression analysis of the causes of the rising secular trend in the black-white earnings ratio from 1967-1978, ignoring for the moment the within-cohort trends noted above. In this analysis, we estimated a set of identical four-year earnings regressions for blacks and whites, aged 25-54 in 1967 and 1975. we then adopted a decomposition procedure, previously used in the analysis of cross-sectional differences in average wages,[16] in order to identify the portion of the change in the earnings ratio due to changes in black-white coefficient differences and a second portion due to changes in the average level of productivity differences. The first portion represents the potential structural changes, while the second part summarizes the vintage-related productivity effects. We then further decomposed the observed change into coefficient and productivity effects within a cohort and similar effects between cohorts.

Our basic regression equation in each year has the general form:

$$(4) \quad \ln W_i = \sum_j B_j X_{ij} + \varepsilon_i$$

Using the estimated regression coefficients, we can write

$$(5) \quad \overline{\ln W} = \sum_j \hat{B}_j \bar{X}_j$$

Defining R as the race difference in the mean of the logarithmic four-year average wage and ΔR as the change over time in that difference, we can use (4) and (5) to write

$$(6) \quad \Delta R = (\overline{\ln W}_2^B - \overline{\ln W}_2^W) - (\overline{\ln W}_1^B - \overline{\ln W}_1^W)$$

$$(7) \quad \Delta R = (\sum_j \hat{B}_{j2}^B \bar{X}_{j2}^B - \sum_j B_{j2}^W \bar{X}_{j2}^W) - (\sum_j \hat{B}_{j1}^B \bar{X}_{j1}^B - \sum_j \hat{B}_{j1}^W \bar{X}_{j1}^W)$$

where the superscripts refer to race and the subscripts to year.

Finally, we can decompose ΔR as:

$$(8) \quad \Delta R = [\sum_j (\hat{B}_{j2}^B - \hat{B}_{j1}^B) \bar{X}_{j1}^B - \sum_j (\hat{B}_{j2}^W - \hat{B}_{j1}^W) \bar{X}_{j1}^W]$$

$$+ [\sum_j \hat{B}_{j2}^B (\bar{X}_{j2}^B - \bar{X}_{j1}^B) - \sum_j \hat{B}_{j2}^W (\bar{X}_{j2}^W - \bar{X}_{j1}^W)]$$

The first bracketed term represents the portion of change in the earnings ratio due to differences by race in changes in estimated coefficients, while the second

---

[16] The decomposition technique we adopt was first used by Oaxaca (1973). See Corcoran and Duncan (1979) and Smith and Welch (1978) for recent applications.

term accounts for the portion due to the differences in changes in average worker characteristics.[17]   Note that in this decomposition procedure, greater wage equality can result from falling coefficients and/or average productivity levels for blacks, as long as the decline is greater for whites; similarly, rising figures for blacks do not necessarily cause wage convergence if the increases for whites are even larger.

Our basic regression equation is a conventional one: the dependent variable is the natural logarithm of four-year average hourly earnings and the independent variables include years of work experience, experience squared, a two-variable spline function for years of education,[18] and measures of city size and southern residence.[19]   Our sample was again limited to males, aged 25 to 54 in 1967 and 1975 who worked at least 500 hours in each of the subsequent four years.   The mean values and regression coefficients for the independent variables are presented in Appendix Table A2.1.   The ratio of black-white four-year average wages was 60.7 percent for the 1967 to 1970 period; for the 1975 to 1978 period, it was 74.9 percent, an increase of 14.2 percentage points.[20]   Average real earnings for blacks rose by almost 20 percent, while for whites they rose just under 6 percent.

Table 2.2 shows the detail of the decomposition.   All the figures in the table show the proportion of the total ratio change accounted for by that

---

[17]Note that we have not attempted to decompose the change in the ratio of mean earnings or even the logarithm of that ratio (i.e., $\ln R = \ln \bar{W}^B - \ln \bar{W}^w$), since those terms are not appropriate for a decomposition based on Equation 5. The decomposition in Equation 6 is based on differences in the mean logarithmic wage ($\overline{\ln W}^B - \overline{\ln W}^w$) rather than the logarithm of the mean wage ($\ln \bar{W}^B - \ln \bar{W}^w$). See Smith and Welch (1978), pp. 64-67.

[18]The spline function used allows the return to an additional year of education to differ between the first 12 years and all additional years, but returns to an additional year within the two groups are constrained to equality.

[19]The southern residence variable equals one-fourth of a count of the number of years out of the four that the region of residence was the South.   The city size variable equals one-fourth of a count of the number of years that the largest city in the Primary Sampling Unit was 100,000 or more.   These variables are not strictly dichotomous but do take on values of zero and one for individuals remaining in the same region or city size category all four years. For those remaining for one, two or three years, the variables take on values of one-fourth, one-half and three quarters, respectively.

[20]These ratios are for the geometric mean of 4-year average wages in each time period.   The change in the ratio of the arithmetic means (shown in Table 2.1) is 11.2 percentage points.

variable alone. Columns 1-2 and 4-5 show the coefficient and mean value effects
for blacks and whites separately, if there had been no changes affecting the
other race, while columns 3 and 6 show the net coefficient and mean value effects
(i.e., the across-year change in the differences by race in coefficients or
variable means).[21] The sum of the effects for each independent variable are in
column 7. The bottom row summarizes the general findings: about three-quarters
of the increase in the black-white earnings ratio is due to coefficient changes,
leaving one-quarter explained by changes in the mean values of the independent
variables.

The most dramatic numbers in Table 2.2 are the coefficient effects for years
of work experience and for the constant term of the equation. The two effects
are of roughly equal but opposite magnitudes, each accounting for over
190 percent of the actual change in the earnings ratio; their joint effect,
consequently, is quite small. The constant term in each regression equation
shows the average earnings of an individual with zero values for each of the
independent variables--e.g., zero years of work experience. The large
explanatory power of the constant term in Table 2.2 shows that the projected
relative earnings of blacks just starting out have increased substantially
between these two four-year periods. In fact, this improvement was almost
exclusively due to a substantial change in the black equation from 1967 to 1975.
The experience effect represents both a flatter cross-sectional experience-
earnings profile for blacks in 1975 and a steeper one for whites. Interpretation
of the experience term in a cross-sectional equation is complex, since it
reflects both the accumulation of work experience (and, perhaps, proxies the
acquisition of on-the-job training) and any cohort (or vintage) effects resulting
from school attendance and labor market entry in an earlier time period. We
suspect that cohort effects for blacks are dominant here. The simultaneous
rising constant term and falling cross-sectional returns to additional experience
probably reflect the more advantaged position of younger blacks relative to older
blacks (in ways unaccounted for by the basic regression equation) rather than an
increase in discrimination with respect to accumulated work experience.

That age-earnings profiles for blacks have become flatter is also consistent
with Lazear's (1979) hypothesis that employers are reacting to affirmative action

---

[21]In terms of equation (8), the first and second columns of Table 2.2
correspond to the first two summation terms, expressed as a fraction of ΔR. The
fourth and fifth columns correspond to the third and fourth summation terms, also
expressed as a fraction of ΔR.

Table 2.2

PERCENTAGE CONTRIBUTION TO CHANGE IN BLACK-WHITE EARNINGS RATIO, 1967-75
(For male household heads age 25-54 in 1967 and 1975.)

Variable	Coefficient Effects			Mean Value Effects			Total
	Black (1)	White (2)	Net (3)	Black (4)	White (5)	Net (6)	(7)
Constant	204.0%	12.1%	191.9%	–	–	–	191.9%
Work experience	-104.8	88.7	-193.5	-18.1	-25.2	7.1	-186.4
Southern residence	-4.8	3.4	-8.2	-.4	.3	-.7	-8.9
Large city residence	39.3	-16.0	55.3	6.4	-4.6	11.0	66.3
Low education	-30.9	-38.6	7.7	24.0	8.2	15.8	23.5
High education	4.8	-16.0	20.8	21.9	29.0	-7.1	13.7
	107.6%	33.6%	74.0%	33.8%	7.7%	26.1%	100.1%

Total change in earnings ratio = .142

rules by placing blacks in initially higher paying jobs with lower future growth
rates. A more direct test is to calculate whether four-year individual earnings
growth rates have become less favorable for blacks relative to whites. Using the
slope of the regression of log wage rates on time as a measure of annual growth
rates, the following average growth rates for the black and white workers in our
three samples were obtained:

Subgroup		1967-70	1971-74	1975-78
All:	Black Men	4.3%	0.9%	4.3%
	White Men	3.4	2.8	2.8
Age 25-34:	Black Men	3.3	0.8	5.4
	White Men	4.7	4.1	5.0

Although there appears to have been a deterioration in the wage growth of black
workers between the first two periods, the situation had more than reversed
itself by the third, thus lending little support to Lazear's hypothesis.

From a policy standpoint, the coefficient effects for the two education
variables are interesting and quantitatively important. Changes in race
differences in estimated education coefficients accounted for 28.5 percent of the

total change in the black-white earnings ratio. Almost three-quarters of that
figure was accounted for by the effects of higher education. Returns to an
additional year of education through the 12th grade from 1967 to 1975 fell about
.5 percent for both blacks and whites. But for post-high school years of
education the across-years race effects were quite different. For whites, the
returns fell from 9.4 percent to 7.6 percent, a change consistent with other
reports of the declining value of higher education,[22] while for blacks the
returns actually rose--from 7.6 percent to 9.8 percent per additional year.
Estimated returns to years of higher education were over 2 percent lower for
blacks than for whites in 1967; by 1975, they were 2 percent higher.[23] Again,
there are at least two possible explanations for the shifting pattern of
coefficients: they could be due either to race convergence in (unmeasured)
college quality or to affirmative action effects among highly visible and easily
identified groups. Although the college quality effects could lead to
coefficient equality, it is difficult to see how, in the absence of some external
pressure, the higher black coefficients observed in 1975 could be explained in
that way.

Of the two locational variables--residence in the South or in a large city--
only the latter had a substantial impact. The effects of urban residence were
positive for both blacks and whites in both years, but from near equality in
1967, with about a 27 percent wage advantage for those living in large cities,
the wage effect for whites fell by about 4 percent and rose for blacks by
13 percent. Given the high percentage of blacks living in large cities, the net
effect of these coefficient changes accounted for about 55 percent of the total
eight-year wage ratio change.

Since the city size effects alone accounted for more than half of the
increase in the black-white earnings ratio, it is important to attempt to
discover the cause. One possible explanation is that the city size effect was
really a union effect. When a measure of union status [24] was added to the

---

[22] See Freeman (1975).

[23] In a comparable 1971 regression, the estimated higher education
coefficients for both blacks and whites fell between those for 1967 and 1975.

[24] The union status variable was set equal to one-fourth of a count of the
number of years the individual was a union member during the four year period.
It ranges from zero to one but takes on intermediate values as well.

regression equation, the city size effect all but disappeared. The pattern of coefficients was as follows (standard errors are given in parentheses):

	1967–70				1975–78		
	Black	White		Black	White		
Large city resi- dence	.282** (.056)	.246** (.056)	.265** (.026)	.251** (.026)	.357** (.051)	.204** (.047)	.227** (.024)	.216** (.024)
Union member	– –	.264** (.066)	– –	.215** (.037)	– –	.403** (.039)	– –	.185** (.029)

The addition of the union status variable had little effect on the two city size coefficients for whites--both fell by about .01. For blacks, on the other hand, the large increase in the city size coefficient was actually reversed when union status was added; instead of rising from .28 to .36, it fell from .25 to .20. The union effect for blacks rose substantially between the two periods, from .26 to .40, as did the fraction of blacks unionized (from .34 to .47). Thus the apparent contribution of the increased payoff to living in a large city for blacks appears to be an increase in the wage premium received by unionized blacks.

Equation 8 shows that the effects of changes in the mean values of independent variables, which are shown in columns 4-6 of Table 2.2, are the product of racial differences in mean values and the coefficients used to "value" the mean differences. Thus, the effects of these changes can occur either because blacks or whites have greater changes in the average value of some characteristics, or because--even for equal changes by race over time--the final year's estimated coefficient, used as a multiplicative weighting factor, differs by race.[25] Most of the changes attributed to changes in differences in means are of this second type, since for most of the independent variables, the changes in means by race are quite similar. As a result, we are inclined to give the apparent effects of changing means less weight than if the effects were caused by substantial changes in race differences in means.

---

[25]The same potential problem exists in the decomposition of coefficient effects, since coefficient changes are weighted by the respective means. It turns out the problem is minor in that case, because the means are similar enough that pure coefficient changes dominate.

The fairly substantial wage ratio convergence associated with the low education variable is a combination of both effects. Average education levels for this lower portion of the spline function rose somewhat more for blacks than whites; additionally the black coefficient was substantially larger. The negative effect for higher education represents an increase in mean levels for both blacks and whites, with the large increase for whites outweighing the large coefficient for blacks.[26] Finally, the large city residence effect of 11 percent is due to small but opposite changes in mean levels and to quite substantial differences in the relevant coefficients.

An Extension of the Accounting Procedure

One might conclude from the preceding analyses that the rate of convergence of black-white earnings has been substantial since 1967 and that the primary cause of the upward trend has been relative changes in coefficients, especially those for education and urban residence. Thus, the findings might provide support for a structural change explanation of the improvement. However, this result is difficult to reconcile with the findings noted earlier of little or no change in the within-cohort earnings ratios. In particular, if the coefficient effects represent genuine structural change in relative demand functions, we might expect to find that the benefits were broadly distributed across age groups and that within-cohort earnings ratios would show improvement roughly comparable to the aggregate change.[27]

In order to reconcile and account for the disparate secular and within-cohort trends, it is important to recognize how the secular trends are constructed. Typically, the secular trends are based on time-series data on a representative sample of workers in a given age interval--i.e., all workers ages 14-65 or 25-54, etc.--in some set of comparison years. Obviously, as the time frame for such calculations is extended, the composition of the sample itself changes as some older workers are excluded because they exceed the maximum age limit and some younger ones who reach the minimum are included. For example, in

---

[26]From 1967 to 1975, the average level of education increased by just over a year for blacks and just under a year for whites.

[27]This statement implicitly assumes that the observed stable within-cohort ratios are not caused by the effects of changes in means compensating for coefficient improvement. In fact, there is little opportunity for an effect through changes in means, since most variables are either held constant over time or change equivalently for blacks and whites.

our comparison of 25-54 year olds in 1967 and 1975, workers who were 47-54 in 1967 were no longer part of the 1975 comparison group of 25-54 year olds, while those between 25 and 32 in 1975 were not a part of the 1967-70 group.

Because of these changes in the composition of the sample, it is possible that the observed structural change across years is actually the spurious result of age-related interaction effects which differ by race and year and which are not explicitly considered in the underlying regression format. Suppose, for example, that the oldest black workers—those who were in the 1967 sample but had departed by 1975—were subject to discrimination which was more severe and more extensive than that which confronted younger workers and that this discrimination had lasting wage effects. Alternatively, older black workers might be most severely disadvantaged, compared to white workers, in terms of relevant but unobservable characteristics.[28] For either reason, this group might have received smaller returns than younger black workers for the skills and characteristics they did possess, which suggests that a set of age-interactions would be the appropriate regression specification. But if, as is usually the case, age-interactions are ignored, then the mere departure of these individuals from the sample over time could have generated the appearance of structural change in earnings functions. Precisely the same kind of argument (in reverse) holds if the youngest black workers—those who joined the sample after the first comparison year—received the primary benefits of structural changes or possessed relatively more favorable unmeasured traits.

More formally, this explanation suggests that the regression equations underlying the previous decomposition are actually misspecified because they fail to account for the possible age-related interaction effects outlined above. As in the case of all omitted variables the estimated regression coefficients will be biased, and the stronger the interaction effects the greater the estimation bias. If racial differences in the strength of the interaction effects were greater in the initial four years than in the final four years, precisely because of the entering and departing cohorts, then the resulting changes in the extent of the bias could create the appearance of structural change even if the true change in coefficient differences was zero.

We can examine the possible effects of entering and departing cohorts on changes in black-white earnings ratios by modifying the underlying regressions to allow for age-related interactions and then extending the decomposition procedure

---

[28]Both of these could be considered vintage effects.

to identify the separate contributions of within-cohort changes and changes due
to entering and departing cohorts. To isolate the latter effects, we separated
both the 1967 and 1975 samples into two age groups. We divided our initial
sample of 25-54 year olds into 25-46 and 47-54 year olds. The latter group was
not part of the 1975 sample.[29] The 1975 sample was separated into the 25-32 year
olds, who were not part of the 1967 group, and the 35-54 year olds, who were.
This structure permitted us to examine changes within a continuing cohort (25-46
year olds in 1967 compared with 33-54 year olds in 1975) as well as differences
between the departing cohorts (47-54 in 1967) and entering cohorts (25-32 in
1975).

The total change in the black-white earnings ratio over this time period is
simply the weighted sum of the changes in the earnings ratio for the respective
cohorts. Where n is the fraction of persons in the continuing cohort for both
blacks and whites and the subscripts c, d, and e denote the continuing,
departing, and entering cohorts respectively. We can express the total change in
the earnings ratio as:

$$(9) \quad \Delta R = n[(\overline{\ln W}_c^{75B} - \overline{\ln W}_c^{75W}) - (\overline{\ln W}_c^{67B} - \overline{\ln W}_c^{67W})]$$

$$+ (1-n)[\overline{\ln W}_e^{75B} - \overline{\ln W}_e^{75W}) - (\overline{\ln W}_d^{67B} - \overline{\ln W}_d^{67W})]$$

The first bracketed term is the portion of the earnings ratio change due to
within-cohort ratio changes, while the second term is the portion due to earnings
differences between the entering and departing cohort. Thus, for example, an
increase in the overall black-white earnings could reflect a constant within-
cohort earnings ratio combined with a between-cohort effect in which ratios are
higher for the entering cohort than they were for the departing cohort. Finally,
we can use the decomposition procedure and express Equation 9 as:

$$(10) \quad \Delta R = n[\Sigma(\hat{B}_c^{75B} - \hat{B}_c^{67B})\bar{X}_c^{75B} - \Sigma(\hat{B}_c^{75W} - \hat{B}_c^{67W})\bar{X}_c^{75W}]$$

$$+ n[\Sigma(\bar{X}_c^{75B} - \bar{X}_c^{67B})\hat{B}_c^{75B} - \Sigma(\bar{X}_c^{75W} - \bar{X}_c^{67W})\hat{B}_c^{75W}]$$

$$+ (1-n)[\Sigma(\hat{B}_e^{75B} - \hat{B}_e^{75W})\bar{X}_e^{75B} - \Sigma(\hat{B}_d^{67B} - \hat{B}_d^{67W})\bar{X}_d^{67B}]$$

$$+ (1-n)[\Sigma(\bar{X}_e^{75B} - \bar{X}_e^{75W})\hat{B}_e^{75W} - \Sigma(\bar{X}_d^{67B} - \bar{X}_d^{67W})\hat{B}_e^{67W}].$$

---

[29]Note that not all of the 25-46 year olds in 1967 were members of the 1975
group. Those dropping out of the labor force through death, disability or
discouragement or otherwise failing to meet our filter requirements of 500 work
hours in each of the four years between 1975 and 1978 were excluded.

The first two bracketed terms are the within-cohort coefficient and means effects and are analogous to those used in the previous decomposition. The third and fourth terms summarize the contribution to the earnings ratio change of the change in entering and departing groups. They are derived from a comparison of the within-year decomposition of the difference in average earnings by race for the departing and entering cohorts. The third term in Equation 10 shows the difference between the 1975 entering cohort and the 1967 departing cohort in coefficient differences by race, while the final term represents the corresponding difference between the cohorts in race differences in mean levels of independent variables. Using this decomposition procedure, we can determine not only the portion of the aggregate ratio improvement due to entering and departing cohorts, but also whether that effect operates through a greater similarity in measured traits of young blacks and young whites than had existed for older blacks and older whites or through a greater similarity of estimated coefficients for the younger cohort than for the older one.

The basic regression equation used for these analyses is identical to that used previously, except that the quadratic experience term is not included.[30] The regression results and the means of the independent variables are provided in Appendix Tables A2.2 and A2.3. The separate cohort decompositions are summarized in Tables 2.3 and 2.4.

We found that the changes in the entering and departing cohorts alone accounted for about 60 percent of the improvement in the aggregate black-white earnings ratio from 1967 to 1975, simply because the ratio was so much higher for the entering group (83 percent for the 25-32 year olds) than for the departing group (55 percent for the 47-54 year olds). Even if there had been no improvement for the continuing cohort, the aggregate ratio would have increased about 8.5 points. But additionally, the earnings ratio also increased for the 25-46 year old group from 62.5 percent in 1967 to 71.5 percent for the corresponding 33-54 year olds in 1975.

Here again, we are interested in accounting for these within- and between-cohort ratio increases, in order to determine the relative importance of structural changes and changes in the mean characteristics of the black and white samples. That distinction is especially important in trying to account for the

---

[30]In preliminary regressions, the quadratic term was statistically insignificant.

Table 2.3

PERCENTAGE CONTRIBUTION OF WITHIN COHORT CHANGE IN COEFFICIENTS AND
MEAN VALUES IN ACCOUNTING FOR CHANGE IN BLACK-WHITE
EARNINGS RATIOS, 1967-1975
(For male household heads, age 25-46 in 1967, 33-46 in 1975.)

| Variable | Coefficient Effects | | | Mean Value Effects | | | |
	Black (1)	White (2)	Net (3)	Black (1)	White (2)	Net (3)	Total (7)
Constant	-1.3%	110.5%	-111.8%	–	–	–	-111.8%
Work experience	-6.0%	-32.2	26.2	42.2	25.0	17.2	43.4
Southern residence	1.0	3.2	-2.2	0.1	1.7	-1.6	-3.8
Large city residence	49.6	-5.5	55.1	-7.0	-3.0	-4.0	51.1
Low education	17.1	-43.8	60.9	-2.6	0.6	-3.2	57.7
High education	2.3	-9.3	11.6	4.1	10.6	-6.5	5.1
Total	62.7%	22.9%	39.8%	36.8%	34.9%	1.9%	41.7%

Total change in earnings ratio due to within-cohort difference=.085.
Note: All numbers are expressed as a percentage of the total
difference in the black-white earnings ratio between 1967 and 1975.

very substantial difference in the earnings ratio between the departing and
entering cohorts.

As Table 2.3 shows, the within-cohort improvement was almost entirely due to
coefficient effects; changes in black-white differences in coefficients accounted
for 39.8 percent of the total increase in the earnings ratio and 95 percent
(39.8/41.7) of the within-cohort improvement. The work experience and constant
term effects, which figured so prominently in the previous analysis, were quite
different here. Since our analysis follows the same cohort as it ages over time,
vintage-related effects were not a complicating factor. The constant term for
this cohort of blacks (shown in Table A2.2) was almost unchanged from 1967 to
1975, supporting the contention that the observed increase in the constant term
for the 25-54 year olds was primarily a vintage effect stemming from the higher
relative earnings of the younger cohort. In the white cohort, however, the
constant term rose substantially. The experience coefficients fell for both
groups, since they were now computed for an older age group, for whom experience-
earnings profiles are typically flatter. Because the coefficient drop was
greater for the whites than the blacks, the net effect was to contribute to wage

Table 2.4

PERCENTAGE CONTRIBUTION OF ENTERING AND DEPARTING COHORT CHANGES IN
COEFFICIENTS AND MEAN VALUES IN ACCOUNTING FOR
CHANGE IN BLACK-WHITE EARNINGS RATIO 1967-1975
(For male household heads, age 47-54 in 1967 and age 25-32 in 1975.)

Variable	Coefficient Effects			Mean Value Effects			
	25-32 Year Olds (1)	47-54 Year Olds (2)	Net (3)	25-32 Year Olds (4)	47-54 Year Olds (5)	Net (6)	Total (7)
Constant	77.5%	271.7%	-194.2%	-	-	-	-194.2%
Work experience	-78.5	-338.1	259.6	0.4	-8.0	8.4	268.0
Southern residence	4.1	-16.1	20.2	-5.9	-4.2	-1.7	18.5
Large city residence	-24.9	-62.2	37.3	10.7	3.5	7.2	44.5
Low education	-12.8	83.4	-96.2	-1.9	-8.1	6.2	-90.0
High education	5.8	-13.0	18.8	-11.3	-5.0	-6.3	12.5
Total	-28.8%	-74.3%	45.5%	-8.0%	-21.8%	13.8%	59.3%

Note: All numbers are expressed as a percentage of the total
difference in the black-white earnings ratio between 1967 and 1975.

equality. The most important coefficient effects were those for education and
urban residence, as in the 25-54 year old comparisons. Returns to an additional
year of both low education and high education increased for blacks and fell for
whites. The same pattern of change occurred for the effects of urban location;
for urban blacks in 1975, the estimated wage premium was almost 50 percent. As
with the earlier analysis, we suspect that the city size variable actually shows
a union effect.

The effects of the entering and departing groups are presented in Table 2.4.
Columns 1-2 and 4-5 are drawn from the third and fourth bracketed terms,
respectively, in Equation 10 and show the contribution of racial differences
between the entering and departing cohorts in estimated coefficients and a second
part reflecting the differences in mean levels of characteristics. (The
underlying regression and mean value information is presented in Table A2.3.) As
in Table 2.3, each entry in the table shows the contribution of that factor to
the total difference in the earnings ratio.

The important conclusion from this decomposition is that coefficient effects, rather than convergence in means, are the primary cause of the higher wage ratio of younger workers. Over three-quarters (45.5/59.3) of the difference in the earnings ratios can be accounted for by differences between cohorts in coefficient differences. Coefficient differences for the entering cohort still favor whites, but to a much smaller extent than for the older group; estimated coefficient differences alone would cause a 35 percent wage disadvantage for the older cohort, but only a 14 percent wage differential for the younger group.

In looking at the coefficient effects separately, the constant term and the effects of work experience again stand out. In the regressions for both groups of older workers (shown in Table A2.3), the constant terms are positive and extremely large and the experience coefficients are negative, with the constant term more positive and the experience coefficient more negative for blacks. These results are indications of vintage-related effects—lower wages for workers with more experience and hence of older vintage, more so for blacks than whites. At the mean level of work experience, the net effect of the constant term and experience coefficients is strongly negative. Vintage effects also appear for the younger cohort of blacks in the form of a large constant term and a negative experience effect, but the black-white differences here are milder and, evaluated at the mean level of work experience, there is a negligible effect on earnings differences. As a result, years of work experience and the constant term account for a very large portion of the difference in the earnings ratio.

In addition, there are strong coefficient effects due to urban and southern residence. Southern residence raised the earnings ratio for young workers—it depressed black wages by less than white wages—but it lowered the ratio for older workers. Urban residence for these cohorts increased earnings more for whites than for blacks, but the coefficient difference was smaller for the younger workers. The education effects were also somewhat surprising. In the younger cohort, returns over the low education range were roughly equal for blacks and whites, and, as in all other 1975 regressions, we found that blacks had higher returns to years of higher education. But we also found a very large return to years of lower education for the older blacks—indeed, much higher than that for whites. As a result, differences by cohort in differences in coefficients for high education explained just over 30 percent of the overall difference in earnings ratio, but the differences in low education coefficients operate to the disadvantage of younger blacks.

In contrast to these large coefficient effects, the contribution of differences in mean value on the independent variables were very small for both age cohorts.

EARNINGS MOBILITY

Each year, the Census Bureau issues a report on poverty, showing the proportion of the population living in families with incomes below the official poverty line. Over time, this fraction has fallen somewhat, but it has generally been within one-half of a percentage point of its value the year before. The stability of this poverty fraction seems to have led to the conventional wisdom that stability exists within the poverty population itself, that there is little turnover in the composition of the poor. But there is no necessary relationship between the temporal stability of the fraction poor and in the composition of the poor. Indeed, identical poverty counts in two consecutive years could be consistent with either absolutely no turnover or with complete turnover in the poverty population. Two of the most important findings from past work with the Panel Study are that there is a great deal of turnover in the poverty population and the composition of the persistently poor is strikingly different from those who are poor during any one year. Only about half of those who are poor one year are also poor in the next, and only about one-tenth of the one year poor are poor for seven consecutive years. These facts about family income mobility could not have been inferred from cross-sectional data.

Similar issues arise in the analysis of earnings mobility. A snapshot picture of the earnings distribution in a given year will show the existence of wage inequality among various groups. A more sophisticated analysis could "control" for differences in the characteristics of workers and use the pattern of earnings for workers of different ages to predict the future wage of a typical worker as he or she ages. But beyond such synthetic estimates, cross-sectional data cannot shed much light on the earnings mobility of individual workers. The distribution of earnings may have a very similar structure in two consecutive years and yet there may be complete turnover in the composition of those on the bottom and those on top.

Evidence on earnings mobility helps to answer several crucial questions about economic status. Do labor markets operate to produce immobility, with certain groups locked into low paying, high turnover jobs while others enjoy security and advancement? Or does mobility prevail, made possible by individual or governmental investments in job skills or by "connections" or by chance?

Excessive, unexpected mobility, or instability of earnings is itself a component of economic status to be avoided if possible. Similar questions arise in response to the relative economic position of women and minority workers. Has the apparent convergence of black-white earnings led to the formation of an identifiable black upper middle class, who show up with persistently high earnings? Does the empirical rule that the economic status of women is three-fifths that of men apply to their respective chances of occasional or persistent residence in the top end of the income distribution and does that fraction's inverse apply to their relative chance of being earnings poor?

In the following sections, we use Panel Study data to describe several aspects of earnings mobility. After a brief review of the literature on earnings mobility, an overview of 12 year mobility patterns is presented. Following that, attention is focused on mobility in the top and bottom ends of the earnings distribution.

Review of Prior Studies of Earnings Mobility

The earliest theories of income distribution were based on the role of ability, and were used to reconcile the knowledge that ability was distributed normally in the population with the empirical fact, discovered by Pareto, that incomes were distributed log normally. Many elegant mathematical models of the earnings distribution have been proposed since then (see Sahota, 1978, for a recent summary), but most have addressed questions about the aggregate distribution of income and not about individual mobility. In the words of Schiller: "Perhaps Pareto was leading us down the wrong road when he directed us towards universal mathematical characterizations of the income distribution, the kind of inquiries that have encouraged neglect of individual mobility and welfare" (1978, p. 926).

The human capital theory of individual self-investment has usurped much of the interest in these models because it is much richer and is based on the same utility-maximizing framework as most other current economic theories. Although typically cast in terms of the average worker, the human capital theory does have numerous implications for earnings mobility. Lillard and Willis (1978) developed a sophisticated earnings mobility model which combines features of the statistical theories of income distribution and the human capital theory. In their model, individual earnings are a function of measured skills (education, experience, etc.), unmeasured individual traits, random events with persistent but deteriorating effects (serial correlation) and purely random effects. When

they estimated the effects for black and white men with data from the Panel
Study, Lillard and Willis found that most of the differences in earnings were due
to permanent measured or unmeasured differences in the individuals themselves,
although more than one-fifth of the variation in earnings was due to purely
random fluctuations. Random effects which are correlated over time played a
relatively minor role. When used to predict mobility into and out of the bottom
segment of the earnings distribution, the model does reasonably well, especially
for whites.

Shorrocks (1980) approached the measurement of income mobility as an
extension of the measurement of inequality. He defined an index, R, that
measures the degree to which incomes are equalized as the accounting period is
extended. The value of R is computed as the ratio of multi-year inequality to a
weighted average of short run (e.g., one-year) inequality. R ranges from zero to
one (one indicates identical long and short run inequality) and can be computed
for a variety of inequality measures. He then argued that R can be taken to
indicate the stability or rigidity of the income structure. A plot of the value
of R as the time period is extended shows whether incomes are completely immobile
(R=1 for all time periods), whether lifetime incomes are essentially equal (R
falls monotomically toward zero), or whether fluctuations in income are largely
transitory rather than permanent (R falls rapidly to some asymptotic value). He
illustrated the use of his index with data from the Panel Study of Income
Dynamics, but his empirical work was flawed by the fact that he included the low-
income SEO subsample and did not weight for their different sampling
probabilities.

One of the most recent and ambitious descriptive studies of earnings
mobility was done by Schiller (1977), using data on covered earnings from the
Social Security Administration LEED file. When comparing the relative earnings
positions (measured in ventiles)[31] of male workers between 1957 and 1971,
Schiller found a tremendous amount of annual earnings mobility. Less than one-
third of the workers remained in the same ventile between the two end years; the
average absolute change in ventile position was 4.2. Mobility was markedly
higher for whites than blacks, although it was large enough for blacks to cast
doubt on theories of labor market segmentation which characterize the economic
position of blacks as basically fixed. Interestingly, Schiller found that black

---

[31]Earnings ventiles are formed from demarcation of 20 proportional,
ascending earnings intervals.

workers at the upper end of the earnings distribution had considerably more fluctuation in economic position than did black workers at the bottom end. The earnings affluence of blacks, in other words, was much more transitory than was their earnings poverty. In sum, Schiller found an unexpected amount of earnings mobility which was generally inconsistent with the labor market segmentation model and only a little more supportive of the human capital model.

An Overview of Earnings Mobility

A common method for showing earnings mobility is with a transition table, comparing the earnings position of the same individuals at two points in time. This is done in Tables 2.5 and 2.6 for white and black men, respectively. The time interval is the maximum afforded by the Panel Study data—from 1967 to 1978. The sample was restricted to male household heads between the ages of 25 and 50 in 1968 who worked at least 500 hours in each of the 12 years. This sample was ranked according to wage rate in both 1967 and 1971 and was divided into five equal groups, or quintiles. Table 2.5 shows the distribution of white men according to their wage rate quintile in 1967 and 1978. The first entry in the table shows that 8.3 percent of all white men were in the lowest earnings quintile in both 1967 and 1978. Adding up the four numbers to the right of 8.3 shows that more than half (9.7/17.9) of the white men who began the period in the lowest quintile ended up in one of the higher four quintiles. Analogous information for black men is presented in Table 2.6.

Consistent with the evidence presented by Schiller, Tables 2.5 and 2.6 show a great deal of earnings mobility, especially for whites. Less than 40 percent of white men and 50 percent of black men were in the same wage rate quintile in the two years, and the proportion that moved at least two quintiles was nearly one-quarter for whites and about one-eighth for blacks. Mobility out of the lower end of the earnings distribution was also higher for whites than blacks: nearly one-quarter of the whites who began in the bottom quintile ended up in the top three quintiles; the comparable figure for blacks was about one-eighth. A summary measure of association (Tau-B) between rankings in the two end years was quite similar for the two groups (.439 for whites and .435 for blacks).

The 11-year interval between 1967 and 1978 is a long one and it is of interest to see how rapidly the two racial groups approached the mobility figures shown in Tables 2.5 and 2.6. Four summary mobility measures are shown in Table 2.7 for the intervals between 1967 and the even years between 1967 and 1978. As might be expected, one year mobility (from 1967 to 1968) was much less

Table 2.5

WAGE RATE MOBILITY TABLE, 1967 TO 1978--WHITE MEN
(For all white male household heads, age 25-50 in 1968 with
500 hours worked in each year between 1967 and 1978.)

Wage Rate Quintile in 1967	Wage Rate Quintile in 1978					
	Lowest	Fourth	Third	Second	Highest	All
Lowest	8.3%	5.3%	3.2%	1.0%	0.2%	17.9%
Fourth	4.7	5.5	3.8	3.2	2.1	19.3
Third	1.9	5.0	6.4	5.5	2.1	20.8
Second	1.6	2.5	4.6	7.4	5.3	21.3
Highest	2.2	1.1	2.2	4.1	11.1	20.7
All	18.7%	19.3%	20.1%	21.2%	20.8%	100.0%

Number of observations: 809

Tau B = .439

Table 2.6

WAGE RATE MOBILITY TABLE, 1967 TO 1978--BLACK MEN
(For all black male household heads, age 25-50 in 1968 with
500 hours worked in each year between 1967 and 1978.)

Wage Rate Quintile in 1967	Wage Rate Quintile in 1978					
	Lowest	Fourth	Third	Second	Highest	All
Lowest	25.6%	11.2%	3.2%	2.1%	0.5%	42.6%
Fourth	10.2	12.9	7.1	2.3	0.1	32.6
Third	0.5	4.4	7.8	4.0	0.7	17.4
Second	0.2	2.3	0.6	0.7	0.3	4.1
Highest	0.9	0.0	0.9	0.0	1.6	3.4
All	37.4%	30.8%	19.6%	9.1%	3.2%	100.0%

Number of observations: 233

Tau B = .435

than the mobility over the 11 years from 1967 to 1978. The proportions remaining
in the same wage quintile were considerably higher for one-year than for 11-year
mobility, while the proportion moving at least two quintiles were much lower,
especially for whites. Generally speaking, white mobility increases
monotonically as the time interval was lengthened, while black mobility generally
increased as well, but much less uniformly. The final column of the table shows
that the extent of annual earnings mobility was similar to the amount of hourly
earnings mobility.

Earnings Affluence and Poverty

In this section, we describe recent trends in earnings mobility using the
concepts of earnings "affluence" and earnings "poverty." Affluence and poverty
are defined by the top and bottom quintiles, respectively, of the male earnings
distribution. Obviously, one-fifth of the men will be shown to have been
earnings affluent or earnings poor in any one year. If there was complete
earnings immobility, then one-fifth would also have been affluent or poor in both
of two years, all three of three years, etc. Smaller proportions poor or
affluent in multi-year periods would indicate earnings mobility; complete
turnover would be indicated if none of the workers were found to have occupied
the top or bottom segments of the earnings distribution persistently.

As in the section on trend's in black-white earnings ratio, our analysis of
persistent earnings poverty and affluence treated the 12 years of earnings data
as three separate four-year segments. Samples from each of the segments included
male household heads between the ages of 25 and 54 in the first of each of the
four periods who worked at least 500 hours in each year. An otherwise similar
sample of female household heads and wives was drawn from the 1975-78 period.

The Anatomy of Earnings Affluence

Using the top fifth of the male earnings distribution to denote affluence
and the hourly wage rate to measure earnings, we found that in a given year (1978
in this case) 3.5 percent of black men, 3.6 percent of white women, and virtually
none of black women were wage affluent. (Since white men dominate the male
earnings distribution, it is true by definition that about 20 percent of the
white men are wage affluent in any given year.) Because women are more likely to
work part-time or part year, their chances of being in the top fifth of the
distribution of annual earnings was much less than for hourly earnings: only
one percent of white women were earnings affluent in 1978.

Table 2.7

EARNINGS MOBILITY BETWEEN 1967 AND VARIOUS YEARS, BY RACE
(For all male household heads, age 25-50 in 1968 with
500 hours worked each year between 1967 and 1978.)

| Mobility between 1967 and: | Wage Rate | | | | | | | | | Annual Earnings | |
| | Proportion in Same Quintile | | Proportion Moving At Least Two Quintiles | | Proportion in Bottom Quintile in 1967 and in Top Three Quintiles in End Year | | Tau-B | | | Tau-B | |
	White	Black	White	Black	White	Black	White	Black		White	Black
1968	58.8%	64.9%	7.5%	8.1%	7.8%	7.8%	.724	.664		.763	.691
1970	52.7	53.9	12.4	11.3	11.5	3.2	.644	.640		.693	.619
1972	47.3	51.3	14.1	10.6	14.7	3.7	.586	.532		.598	.452
1974	46.1	56.0	18.2	13.0	22.1	5.3	.555	.543		.576	.504
1976	39.0	38.2	23.0	18.6	27.7	10.5	.441	.485		.440	.609
1978	38.7	48.6	23.0	13.7	24.4	13.7	.439	.435		.474	.401

We examined the extent of earnings mobility at the upper end of the earnings distribution by looking at the fractions of the different groups who were <u>ever</u> in the top fifth of the earnings distribution (occasional affluence) and at the fractions who were <u>always</u> on top (persistent affluence). The closer these fractions were to the one year fractions listed above, the less earnings mobility there was. In fact, the right half of Table 2.8 indicates considerable earnings mobility within each group over the four year period from 1975-78. Occasional earnings affluence was enjoyed by nearly one-third of all white men and by about one-sixth of black men--results which did not change when earnings were measured on an annual basis rather than hourly. For women, the earnings measure made as much of a difference for occasional affluence as it did for one-year affluence. The fraction of white women with earnings in the top fifth of the male earnings distribution in at least one out of four years was nearly 10 percent for hourly earnings and only 2 percent for annual earnings. For black women, the comparable fractions were 2.7 percent and 0.1 percent, respectively.

By comparing the occasionally affluent with the one year affluent, we can see that relative earnings mobility was higher for black men than for any other group. More than three times as many black men were affluent in at least one of the four years between 1975 and 1978 than were affluent in one year alone, indicating a very large turnover among the black men with high earnings. The ratio of occasionally affluent white men to the one year affluent was smaller--a little over 1.5. For white women the ratio was about 2.0, while for black women the ratio depended critically upon the definition of earnings and were based non a very small number of observations.

The gradual improvement in the relative economic status of black men during the past two decades has dramatically increased the likelihood of observing black men who are occasionally affluent. The first six columns of numbers in Table 2.8 show the proportions of black and white men who were occasionally affluent in the first four years of the panel period (1967-70) and in the next four (1971-74). The proportion of white men who were in the top fifth of the earnings distribution in at least one of the four year changed little with the earnings concept or the time period. For black men, the fraction occasionally affluent more than doubled for wage affluence and more than quadrupled for annual earnings affluence.

Table 2.8

ONE-YEAR, OCCASIONAL AND PERSISTENT WAGE AND EARNINGS AFFLUENCE[a] BY RACE AND SEX

	1967-70 (Men)			1971-1974 (Men)			1975-1978 (Men)			1975-1978 (Women)				
	Black Men	White Men	Black Men / White Men	Black Men	White Men	Black Men / White Men	Black Men	White Men	Black Men / White Men	Black Women	White Women	Black Women / White Women	Black Women / White Men	White Women / White Men
One Year Affluence: (Percentage in top fifth of earnings distribution in last year)														
Wage rate	0.2%	21.5%	.009	7.0%	20.9%	.335	3.5%	21.2%	.169	0.1%	3.6%	.028	.005	.170
Annual earnings	0.2	21.3	.009	1.8	21.4	.084	5.1	21.2	.241	0.1	1.2	.083	.005	.057
Occasional Affluence: (Percentage ever in top fifth of earnings distribution)														
Wage rate	6.6	33.9	.195	10.4	32.8	.317	15.5	32.5	.478	2.7	8.6	.314	.080	.254
Annual earnings	3.9	32.0	.122	4.7	31.0	.152	18.6	31.2	.596	0.1	2.0	.050	.003	.063
Persistent Affluence: (Percentage always in top fifth of earnings distribution)														
Wage rate	0.0	11.7	.000	0.3	13.2	.023	1.7	11.4	.149	0.0	1.7	.000	.000	.145
Annual earnings	0.0	13.3	.000	0.0	13.2	.000	1.6	13.0	.123	0.0	0.4	.000	.000	.030

[a]Affluence is defined as falling into the top fifth of male earnings distribution during any year. "Occasional affluence" is defined as affluence in at least one of the four years. "Persistent affluence" is defined as affluence in every one of the four years.

Persistent Affluence

Occasional affluence may be the result of one exceptional year with abundant overtime, a lucrative second job, or favorable business conditions for the self-employed. <u>Persistent</u> affluence, on the other hand, depends much less on chance and much more on a permanent earnings advantage afforded by abundant job skills or by an unusually secure, well-paid job. It is, therefore, a much better indicator of income "class" than is one year or occasional affluence. If, as some have claimed, improvement in the economic status of blacks has led to the formation of a black upper middle class, then that ought to be indicated by a substantial proportion of persistently affluent blacks. Furthermore, it is of interest to compare a black worker's likelihood of persistent wage affluence with that of whites to see if the notion that black economic status is three-quarters that of whites applies to wage affluence as well.

In many respects, persistent affluence is the complement of occasional affluence; both depend upon mobility in the upper end of the income distribution. If there is substantial turnover in the one-year affluent, then the counts of the one-year year affluent will be substantially lower than the counts of occasionally affluent and substantially higher than counts of the persistently affluent. Since the figures on occasional affluence showed considerable mobility, especially for black men, it should come as no surprise that the data on persistent affluence, shown in the bottom two rows of Table 2.8, indicate that persistent affluence is quite rare, especially among minority workers. For white men, nearly half of the one year affluent were also persistently affluent; in each of the three four-year periods, more than one-tenth of all white men were persistently affluent. In contrast, persistent earnings affluence was virtually nonexistent among minority workers. In the first four-year period for black men and the most recent one for black women, <u>not one single black individual in the PSID sample was persistently in the top fifth of the male hourly wage or annual earnings distributions</u>. For white women, and for black men during the more recent time periods, very small fractions were persistently affluent. At most, the fraction of either group that showed up as persistently affluent was 1.7 percent--a number too close to zero to warrant confidence. In sum, there did not appear to be sufficient numbers of minority workers who were persistently in the upper end of the earnings distribution to show up in a national survey sample of this size.

The Anatomy of Earnings Poverty

We have defined earnings poverty as the bottom fifth of the male earnings
distribution. Although it is analogous to earnings affluence, the
characteristics of the earnings poor may not be the converse of the
characteristics of the earnings affluent. For example, we found considerably
more turnover in the earnings affluence of black men than for the other groups--
the likelihood that a black man's one-year affluence was occasional rather than
permanent was quite high. Whether one-year wage poverty is occasional or
persistent also depends upon turnover, but there are reasons to suspect less
turnover for the black one-year poor than for white men. The time-series
evidence on the relative wages of blacks and whites showed that the gains were
strongest for the young and highly educated and for those in high-status
occupations. Thus, the older, less-skilled blacks appeared to have benefited
little from the recent improvements to an overrepresentation of blacks among the
persistently poor. The right half of Table 2.9 shows that this indeed appears to
be the case. During one year (1978 in this case), about one-third of the black
men and about one-fifth of the white workers were earnings poor. The fraction of
workers who were earnings poor in any one of the four years from 1975 through
1978 was half again as large as the one-year fractions; half of all black male
workers were occasionally poor, compared to one-third of all white male workers.
The incidence of persistent earnings poverty was proportionately higher among
black workers than among whites, characterizing one-fifth of all black male
workers and less than one-tenth of all whites. Black men, then, were less than
twice as likely to be one-year earnings poor than white men but were about two
and one-half times as likely to be persistently poor. Although the relative
incidence of earnings poverty among black men may seem disproportionate, the
situation has improved considerably over the past 12 years. One-third of the
blacks were found to be earnings poor in a given year during the most four year
period, while the comparable fraction was close to one-half during the first
four-year period. Similar improvement showed up for persistent earnings poverty,
which included one-fifth of the blacks in the most recent period but considerably
higher fractions for the earlier periods. So while there has indeed been
progress for black men at the lower end of the earnings distribution, the
incidence of wage poverty is still much higher among blacks than whites, and the
disproportionate impact is greatest for persistent wage poverty.

Although the earnings disadvantages faced by black men may seem large, they
are nowhere near as large as those found for women. The last columns of

Table 2.9

ONE YEAR, OCCASIONAL AND PERSISTENT WAGE AND EARNINGS POVERTY,[a] BY RACE AND SEX

	1967-70 (Men)			1971-1974 (Men)			1975-1978 (Men)			1975-1978 (Women)				
	Black Men	White Men	Black Men/White Men	Black Men	White Men	Black Men/White Men	Black Men	White Men	Black Men/White Men	Black Women	White Women	Black Women/White Women	Black Women/White Men	White Women/White Men
One Year Poverty														
(Percentage in bottom fifth of earnings distribution in last year)														
Wage rate	49.5%	18.1	2.74	45.0%	17.5	2.57	29.4%	19.3%	1.52	74.2%	53.6%	1.38	3.85	2.78
Annual earnings	50.3	17.5	2.87	47.0	18.0	2.61	36.4	18.8	1.94	83.6	69.4	1.21	4.45	3.69
Occasional Poverty:														
(Percentage ever in bottom fifth of earnings distribution)														
	66.0	28.9	2.28	56.5	31.4	1.80	45.7	31.6	1.45	81.6	65.1	1.25	2.82	2.25
Annual earnings	68.4	27.6	2.48	57.3	31.1	1.84	50.2	31.5	1.59	92.0	79.2	1.16	3.33	2.87
Persistent Poverty:														
(Percentage always in bottom fifth of earnings distribution)														
Wage rate	28.3	8.9	3.18	25.4	6.4	3.97	19.8	8.0	2.48	54.2	37.0	1.46	6.09	4.16
Annual earnings	33.8	9.0	3.76	32.4	7.4	4.38	21.8	8.6	2.53	71.5	55.9	1.28	7.94	6.21

[a] Poverty is defined as falling into the bottom fifth of the male earnings distribution in one year. "Occasional Poverty" is defined as poverty in at least one of the four years. "Persistent Poverty" is defined as poverty in every one of the four years.

Table 2.9 show that when annual labor income was used as the earnings measure, the vast majority of women of both races experienced at least some earnings poverty and at least half of the women were persistently in the bottom fifth of the male earnings distribution. Shorter work weeks made wage-rate poverty somewhat less wide-spread among women, although persistent wage rate poverty was still a way of life for more than one-half of the black women.

For those accustomed to thinking that the economic status of women is a little over half that of men, the figures on earnings affluence and poverty are striking. In any given year, half of the white women and three-quarters of the black women fell into the bottom fifth of the male wage rate distribution. One-year annual earnings poverty was even more widespread among women. Occasional wage rate poverty reached more than four-fifths of the black women and two-thirds of the white women. If annual labor income is used to define poverty, more than 90 percent of the black women were earnings poor during at least one of the four years.

Persistent wage rate poverty is, of course, less widespread than occasional poverty, but it still characterizes more than half of black women and more than one-third of the white women. Comparable figures for persistent annual earnings poverty are considerably higher.

Summary

Repeated observations on the labor market and demographic characteristics of individuals provides an opportunity for a much richer analysis of labor market phenomena than is afforded by cross-sectional observations. Analysis of longitudinal data is still in its infancy, but holds great promise. In addition to reviewing methods and results from other studies of the dynamics of earnings using panel data, this chapter has presented new evidence on black-white earnings differentials and on earnings mobility.

The facts that black-white earnings ratios have risen dramatically over time and that earnings ratios for a given group of workers have not, are not contradictory. We have shown that most of the increases are due to the changing composition of the cross-section sample used to construct the ratio trends. Earnings ratios of older black and white workers are very low, and the passage of time eliminates many of those older workers from the sample because they retire or pass the maximum age limit that we placed in our sample. Earnings ratios of the very young workers who joined the sample were somewhat higher than average.

Specifically we find that the changes brought about by the entering and departing cohorts accounted for almost three-fifths of the total change.

The black-white improvement in <u>average</u> wage ratios has been accompanied by improvement at the extremes of the earnings distribution as well. Economic mobility out of the bottom of the earnings distribution and into the top seems to have increased for black male workers over the past dozen years. However, the transient nature of their earnings affluence and the permanent nature of their earnings poverty is striking. Relative to white men, black men have one-seventh the chance of persistent earnings affluence and two and a half times the chance of persistent earnings poverty.

For women, the likelihood of persistent earnings affluence is virtually nonexistent. Not a single one of the 405 black women in the Panel Study sample enjoyed hourly or annual earnings in the top fifth of the male earnings distribution in each of the four years between 1975 and 1978. Less than two percent of white women were persistently affluent. Earnings poverty, on the other hand, did indeed characterize these women. The vast majority of black women (over 80 percent) were hourly earnings poor in at least one of the four years between 1975 and 1978. Half of the black women and more than one-third of the white women were persistently earnings poor. Part-time work makes poverty defined by annual earnings much more widespread than for hourly earnings poverty.

References

Andrisani, Paul J. "Internal-External Attitudes, Personal Initiative, and the Labor Market Experiences of Black and White Men." <u>Journal of Human Resources</u> 12 (Summer 1977): 308-28.

Bartel, Ann P. "The Migration Decision: What Role Does Job Mobility Play?" <u>American Economic Review</u> 69 (December 1979): 775-786.

Blau, Francine D., and Kahn, Laurence M. "Race and Sex Differences in the Probability and Consequence of Voluntary Turnover." University of Illinois, 1979. Mimeograph.

Bowers, Norman. "Young and Marginal: An Overview of Youth Employment." <u>Monthly Labor Review</u> (Oct. 1979): 4-10.

Brown, Charles. "Equalizing Differences in the Labor Market." <u>Quarterly Journal of Economics</u> (February 1980): 113-134.

Butler, Richard, and Heckman, James. "Government's Impact on the Labor Market Status of Black Americans: A Critical Review." University of Chicago, 1977. Mimeograph.

Corcoran, Mary, and Duncan, Greg J. "Work History, Labor Force Attachment, and Earnings Differences Between Races and Sexes." Journal of Human Resources (Winter 1979): 3-20.

Chamberlain, G. "On the Use of Panel Data." Harvard University, 1978. Mimeograph.

Duncan, Greg J. "An Empirical Model of Wage Growth." In Five Thousand American Families--Patterns of Economic Progress, Vol. VII, edited by Greg J. Duncan and James N. Morgan. Ann Arbor: Institute for Social Research, 1979.

Duncan, Greg J., and Morgan, James N. "Sense of Efficacy and Changes in Economic Status--A Comment on Andrisani." Journal of Human Resources, forthcoming.

Freeman, Richard B. "Overinvestment in College Training?" Journal of Human Resources (Summer 1975): 287-311.

Freeman, Richard B. "The Changing Labor Market for Black Americans." Brookings Papers on Economic Activity, 1973.

Freeman, Richard B. "Black Economic Progress After 1964: Who Has Gained and Why?" NBER Conference on Low-Income Labor Markets, 1978.

Hanushek, Eric A., and Quigley, John M. "Life-Cycle Earnings Capacity and the OJT Investment Model." Discussion Paper 7904, University of Rochester Public Policy Analysis Program, 1978.

Hill, Daniel H., and Hoffman, Saul D. "Husbands and Wives." In Five Thousand American Families--Patterns of Economic Progress, Vol. V, edited by Greg J. Duncan and James N. Morgan. Ann Arbor: Institute for Social Research, 1977.

Hoffman, Saul D. "Black-White Life-Cycle Earnings Differences and the Vintage Hypothesis: A Longitudinal Analysis:" American Economic Review (Dec. 1979): 855-867.

Hoffman, Saul D. "Patterns of Change in Individual Earnings." In Five Thousand American Families--Patterns of Economic Progress, Vol. V, edited by Greg J. Duncan and James N. Morgan. Ann Arbor: Institute for Social Research, 1977.

Holmes, John W. "Economic Growth and Family Well-being." In Five Thousand American Families--Patterns of Economic Progress, Vol. V, edited by Greg J. Duncan and James N. Morgan. Ann Arbor: Institute for Social Research, 1977.

Jonsson, Anita, and Klevmarken, Anders. "Disequilibrium and Non-Neutral Effects on Age-Earnings Profiles." University of Gothenburg, 1980. Mimeograph.

Lazear, Edward. "Age, Experience and Wage Growth." American Economic Review 66 (September 1976): 548-58.

Lazear, Edward. "The Narrowing of Black-White Wage Differentials is Illusory." American Economic Review 69 (Sept. 1979): 553-64.

Lillard, Lee A., and Willis, Robert J. "Dynamic Aspects of Earnings Mobility." Econometrica 46 (Sept. 1978): 985-1012.

Mellow, Wesley. "Unionism and Wages: A Longitudinal Analysis." Bureau of Labor Statistics, 1979. Mimeograph.

Mincer, Jacob. Schooling, Experience and Earnings. New York: National Bureau of Economic Research, 1974.

Mincer, Jacob, and Leighton Linda. "Effects of Minimum Wages on Human Capital Formation." NBER Working Paper 441, 1980. Mimeograph.

Oaxaca, Ronald. "Male-Female Wage Differentials in Urban Labor Markets." International Economic Review (Oct. 1973).

Sahota, Gian Singh. "Theories of Personal Income Distribution: A Survey." Journal of Economic Literature 16 (March 1978): 1-55.

Shorrocks, Anthony F. "Income Stability in the United States." In Statics and Dynamics of Income, edited by Klevmarken and Lybech. TIETO, forthcoming.

Schiller, Bradley R. "Relative Earnings Mobility in the United States." American Economic Review 67 (December 1977): 926-941.

Smith, James, and Welch, Finis. "Black-White Male Wage Ratios: 1960-1970." American Economic Review (June 1977): 323-38.

Smith, James P., and Welch, Finis. "Race Differences in Earnings: A Survey and New Evidence." Rand Corporation, R-2295-NSF. Santa Monica, 1978.

Welch, Finis. "Black-White Differences in Returns to Schooling." American Economic Review (Dec. 1973): 893-907.

Appendix to Chapter 2

Table A2.1

BLACK-WHITE MEAN VALUE AND WAGE REGRESSION COEFFICIENTS
(For male household heads aged 25-54 years in 1967 and 1975.)

Variable	Mean Value				Regression Coefficients			
	1967-70		1978-79		1967-70		1975-78	
	Black	White	Black	White	Black	White	Black	White
Work experience	20.94	20.54	18.97	18.79	.043** (.012)	.035*** (.006)	.014 (.009)	.039** (.006)
Work experience squared	519.2	499.4	456.2	449.3	-.00094*** (.00027)	-.00075** (.00015)	-.00005 (.00027)	-.00068** (.00014)
Southern residence	.502	.236	.516	.233	-.030 (.048)	-.138** (.029)	-.043 (.042)	-.118** (.027)
Large city residence	.731	.583	.756	.555	.282** (.056)	.265** (.026)	.357** (.051)	.227** (.024)
Low education	9.97	10.94	10.69	11.39	.050** (.009)	.030** (.007)	.046** (.010)	.025** (.009)
High education	0.33	1.23	0.64	1.77	.078** (.021)	.094** (.008)	.098** (.017)	.076** (.006)
Constant					.484	1.097	.768	1.114
R^2					.305	.345	.371	.239
ln Average wage	1.622	2.015	1.821	2.072				
Number of observations	293	961	340	1220				

**Significant at .01 level.

Table A2.2

BLACK-WHITE MEAN VALUE AND WAGE REGRESSION COEFFICIENTS FOR CONTINUING COHORT
(For male household heads, age 25-46 in 1967 and age 33-54 in 1975.)

Variable	Mean Value				Regression Coefficients			
	1967-70		1978-79		1967-70		1975-78	
	Black	White	Black	White	Black	White	Black	White
Work experience	17.39	17.22	25.61	24.46	.011** (.004)	.011** (.002)	.010** (.004)	.007** (.002)
Southern residence	.519	.238	.510	.208	-.031 (.047)	-.140** (.032)	-.028 (.053)	-.113** (.040)
Large city residence	.753	.577	.724	.551	.353** (.059)	.253** (.029)	.486** (.062)	.234** (.033)
Low education	10.21	11.10	10.08	11.15	.038** (.011)	.033** (.008)	.041** (.010)	.025* (.010)
High education	.295	1.322	.384	1.578	-.077** (.027)	-.099** (.008)	-.093** (.023)	-.084** (.009)
Constant	-	-	-	-	.800	1.227	.798	1.450
R^2					.283	.336	.487	.239
ln Average wage	1.650	2.025	1.852	2.141				
Number of observations	233	753	193	699				

* Significant at .05 level.
** Significant at .01 level.

Table A2.3

BLACK-WHITE MEAN VALUES AND WAGE REGRESSION COEFFICIENTS FOR ENTERING AND DEPARTING COHORTS
(For male household heads, age 47-54 in 1967 and age 25-32 in 1975.)

| | Mean Value | | | | Regression Coefficients | | | |
| | 1967-70 | | 1978-79 | | 1967-70 | | 1975-78 | |
Variable	Black	White	Black	White	Black	White	Black	White
Work experience	33.39	31.93	8.60	8.51	-.074* (.030)	-.026* (.012)	-.021+ (.013)	.022** (.007)
Southern residence	.441	.227	.525	.278	-.265 (.184)	-.093 (.072)	-.079 (.063)	-.114** (.037)
Large city residence	.655	.603	.806	.562	-.130 (.184)	-.319** (.062)	.061 (.084)	.207** (.034)
Low education	9.128	10.413	11.654	11.839	.073** (.018)	.030* (.014)	.044+ (.026)	.050+ (.027)
High Education	.463	.930	1.045	2.110	-.083 (.065)	.050* (.023)	.077** (.024)	.050** (.011)
Constant	-	-	-	-	3.559	2.274	1.350	.983
R^2	-	-	-	-	.441	.364	.263	.126
ln Average wage	1.526	1.979	1.773	1.947				
Number of observations	70	208	147	521				

+ Significant at .10 level.
* Significant at .05 level.
**Significant at .01 level.

Chapter 3

SOME DYNAMIC ASPECTS OF POVERTY

Martha S. Hill

INTRODUCTION

At the onset of the War on Poverty in the mid-1960s, approximately one
individual out of five was counted as poor--living in a family with income
inadequate to meet their minimal needs, as defined by the Census Bureau. This
proportion dropped steadily during the 1960s, but by 1970 it had ceased its
monotonic decline. Since then the proportion officially poor each year has been
about one out of eight individuals, with only small year-to-year increases and
decreases.

Stability in the annual poverty rate does not necessarily mean, however,
that most poor individuals remain in poverty year after year. Individuals poor
in any given year may be quite heterogeneous in terms of their long-run poverty
status; for some it may be an off-year not to be repeated again, for others
poverty may be occasional, and for others poverty may persist year after year.
The importance of the long-run poverty patterns underlying annual cross-sectional
observations of the poverty population should be recognized by poverty
researchers and policy-makers alike. An especially important policy issue is the
proper allocation of federal funds to the poverty population. The present
allocation system, based on single-year income figures, encourages identical
treatment of individuals poor in that year without regard to their differing
long-run economic situations and ignores possible needs of individuals atypically
non-poor that year. Policies should be properly matched to the long-run economic
outlook for the individual, with income transfers directed more toward those
experiencing a single off-year and support programs to alter the long-run
economic possibilities directed toward those tending to remain in poverty from
one year to the next.

This chapter concentrates on long-run poverty patterns. It starts with a
review of the literature on poverty and then turns to empirical analysis. Panel
Study data are used to track the poverty status patterns of individuals over the

past decade, varying the time horizon and the poverty definition. Incidence and duration of poverty are examined first, then the chapter focuses on the effect of present poverty status on the subsequent likelihood of being poor. The primary concern here is to isolate the components of state dependence and heterogeneity. The effect of state dependence, independent of a form of heterogeneity, is measured, then characteristics are examined which differentiate individuals temporarily poor from those persistently poor.

REVIEW OF POVERTY LITERATURE

Measurement issues relating to poverty have attracted substantial attention in the literature.[1] One issue often discussed is whether a definition of poverty based solely on economic well-being is sufficient, or if noneconomic circumstances should also be used in identifying the poor. Choosing and measuring appropriate noneconomic factors presents problems which have been solved by depending on an economic definition both for policy purposes and for empirical analysis. While economic circumstances lend themselves to more easy quantification, there are problems associated with economic definitions of poverty as well. Another measurement issue is the choice of an absolute or relative measure. The absolute measure involves establishing an income level high enough to satisfy minimal physical needs. The relative measure involves setting a cut-off point in the income distribution, with individuals below the cut-off point considered to be poor. An additional measurement issue attracting substantial attention is how to treat welfare money payments—whether pre-transfer or post-transfer money income is most appropriate for defining poverty.[2] A related issue is whether in-kind welfare transfers, such as food stamp bonus value, should be included along with money welfare transfers in the definition of post-transfer poverty.[3]

Discussion of these measurement issues often leads to pointing out deficiencies in the official government definition—an economic, absolute, post-

---

[1]See, for example, Lazear and Michael, 1980; Kakwani, 1980; Schiller, 1980; Garfinkel and Haveman, 1977; Goedhart, Halberstadt, Kapteyn, and van Praag, 1977; Smeeding, 1977; Sen, 1976; Perlman, 1976; Plotnick and Skidmore, 1975; Rein, 1967; Watts, 1967.

[2]Plotnick and Skidmore (1975) perform empirical analyses based on absolute and relative measures and pre- and post-transfer measures in addition to presenting a general discussion of the measurement issues.

[3]See Smeeding (1977) and Plotnick and Skidmore (1975).

money-transfer measure. As defined by the government, a family is considered poor if its total money income during the year is less than the amount of money deemed necessary to meet minimal physical needs for a family of that particular composition. Despite the criticisms of this poverty definition, it is the one most frequently used in poverty analysis, no doubt, because it facilitates both comparisons with government figures and the drawing of policy implications from research findings.

The official statistics and much of the research on poverty have tended to disregard another important measurement issue related to understanding poverty and its causes--the time horizon over which poverty is measured. Ignoring this issue has tended to lead to the concept that the poverty population is a relatively constant group of individuals. Most of the research on poverty has been based on single year cross-sectional measures. Over the long run there can be substantial turnover in the poverty population that comparisons of cross-sectional data could understate if subgroup incidences of poverty remained fairly stable. Over the 1965-1972 period Plotnick and Skidmore's (1975) cross-sectional comparisons did, however, show changes in the poverty incidence of subgroups; but little was made of this finding as an indication of long-run mobility in the poverty population. The reasons for this may well have been that longitudinal data are needed to really ascertain the extent of turnover and what differentiates individuals moving in or out of poverty from those remaining poor. It was not until recently that longitudinal data well suited to analyzing this topic have become available, and the works addressing this issue of time horizon have mostly been done in about the last five years using the Panel Study of Income Dynamics data.

This work, including that of Levy (1975), Coe (1978a, 1978b), and Rainwater (1980), found that the proportion of the population poor in a single year is substantially larger than the proportion consistently poor over the long run. However, these works differ in their measurement of poverty and in their approach to comparing the extent of it over the short and long run. In so doing, they found differing magnitudes of persistent as opposed to temporary poverty. Both Coe and Levy used the official poverty definition but Coe defined persistent poverty as being in poverty every year over the long run, whereas Levy defined it as being poor in at least two-thirds of the years. Rainwater, on the other hand, examined a relative measure of poverty--setting the poverty line at one-half of median family income relative to needs.

Coe's approach showed that during 1967 through 1975, while one-quarter of the population was poor in at least one year only 1 percent were poor all nine years; these persistently poor amounted to about 10 percent of the 1975 poor. Allowing for a less stringent definition of persistent poverty and looking at the 1968 to 1973 period, Levy found that about 40 percent of the 1967 poor were persistently poor. Half of the remaining 1967 poor were poor at most one other year in the six year period. Rainwater's relative measure also yielded estimates of the persistent poverty population higher than Coe's measure. Over the period 1967 through 1976 Rainwater found that about 40 percent of the population was poor in at least one year with 5 percent poor all ten years. Averaging economic welfare over the full ten-year span he found that 14 percent of the population was relatively poor. All of these results, though, showed substantial transience in poverty.

Much of the empirical work on poverty has concentrated on identifying the demographic and socioeconomic characteristics of the poor. This work has shown that in the cross-section, poverty incidence has been higher for blacks, the aged, the disabled, female-headed families, the poorly educated, residents of rural areas, and residents of the South (Schiller, 1980; Garfinkel and Haveman, 1977; Plotnick and Skidmore, 1975; Perlman, 1976). Most of this work involved bivariate analyses, but some multivariate analyses have been done. This work includes that of Plotnick and Skidmore (1975) and Garfinkel and Haveman (1977). Using early 1970s cross-sections, both sets of authors found positive independent effects of the family head being black, being female, having low education, living in a rural area, and living in the South. These effects appeared for the standard post-transfer absolute poverty measure, for Plotnick and Skidmore's relative measure of poverty, and for Garfinkel and Haveman's absolute poverty measure based on earnings capacity rather than actual annual income. A variety of effects of age were found in these analyses, the effect varying with the poverty definition and regression specification.[4]

_____

[4]Garfinkel and Haveman found differing effects of age for the standard poverty definition and their earnings capacity one. Whereas the likelihood of being poor declined monotonically with age using the standard poverty definition, the relationship was more J-shaped using their earnings capacity poverty definition. Plotnick and Skidmore, allowing for some interactive effects, found evidence of an age/sex interaction, both with the standard poverty definition and with their relative definition. Whereas among female-headed families the odds of being poor declined monotonically with age, among male-headed families the likelihood of poverty was higher in both the young and old age brackets.

Coe (1978a, 1978b) examined the bivariate relationship between many of these same characteristics and long-run as well as short-run poverty. Comparing the 1976 poverty population with the population of individuals who were poor in every year from 1967 through 1976, he found that demographic subgroups with higher probabilities of poverty in the short-run tended to have even higher probabilities of poverty continuing throughout the long run. This was especially true for individuals living in families with household heads who were black, female, or unmarried with children in the household. Whereas such individuals comprised 30 to 40 percent of the 1975 poor, they comprised almost twice that percentage of those poor in every year 1967 through 1975.

Detailed discussions of the causes of poverty (Schiller, Perlman) have focused on aspects of the labor market (low wages, restricted labor supply, restricted labor demand) and family composition (marital instability and high fertility). The relationships between these factors and poverty have been looked at separately rather than being integrated into a unified model of poverty causation. Emphasis is usually placed on the labor market factors. Schiller, for example, examined cross-sectional relations between poverty and several labor market factors. He found that while about half of the 1977 poor participated in the labor force sometime during the year, they were more likely to be part-time than were non-poor workers. The work time of poor workers tended to be further reduced by their greater susceptibility to unemployment. In the cross-section the poor were also more likely to be in lower paying occupations. Garfinkel and Haveman's multivariate analysis of labor market as well as demographic characteristics associated with poverty confirmed independent effects of annual hours worked, full-time versus part-time work, and being in a low-paying occupation.

Analyses by both Coe and Rainwater emphasize the important role of earnings in persistent poverty. With their differing definitions of poverty, they both found that among all of the potential sources of family income the earnings component was the one keeping the largest percentages of people out of persistent poverty. In fact, Coe found that income received from labor and assets kept a larger percentage of the population out of persistent poverty than out of single-year poverty. Levy investigated the effects of earnings in a different manner, finding an estimate of permanent earnings to be a good predictor of poverty status.

Analysis of restricted labor demand in the form of unemployment suggests a relationship in the long run but not one strong enough to cause most poverty.

The poor are more susceptible to unemployment (Gramlich, 1974; Corcoran and Hill, 1980b) but over a recent nine-year period only half of the poor were ever in a family with an unemployed head and only 10 percent of the poor would have been moved out of poverty entirely if household heads had never been unemployed during the nine years.

While there are various theories associated with wage, labor supply, and family composition determination and their interrelationships, there is no theory linking these factors to poverty status determination in a precisely-formulated model. What has developed instead are concepts about the most important forces underlying the poorer labor market positions, more unstable family conditions, and larger family sizes observed for the poor in cross-sections. One concept which Schiller refers to as "flawed character" views poverty as the result of a lack of sufficient initiative and diligence on the part of individuals experiencing it. The same opportunities are thought to be available to the poor as to the non-poor, and the poor simply fail to take advantage of them. This concept tends to suggest that elimination of poverty is of little public importance.

A very different concept of poverty is what Schiller terms "restricted opportunity"--that access to economic opportunity is restricted for the poor and that regardless of their initiative and diligence they cannot gain access to it. This concept places emphasis on improving the access of the poor to economic opportunities. The access barrier most frequently cited (Schiller; Perlman; Thurow, 1969) is discrimination, especially in the provision of quality education and in access to stable, good-paying jobs.

Another major concept about the forces underlying poverty has been termed the "culture of poverty." This concept hypothesizes that poor attitudes developed and perpetuated by the social conditions of the poor underlie their poverty. Such attitudes result in deviant behavior and serve as barriers to taking advantage of the economic opportunities available to the rest of society. This approach to what generates poverty implies a relatively immobile poverty population, with poverty passed on via cultural conditions from one generation to the next, and to be alleviated only by changing those cultural conditions. Proponents tend to vary in their ideas about the degree to which the poverty population is part of the culture of poverty. Harrington (1962) implied that most of the poor are in this situation, whereas Lewis (1969) stated that he thought that about 20 percent of the poor were part of the culture of poverty. That the culture of poverty concept is the most useful one for understanding poverty is certainly dubious given the Coe, Levy, and Rainwater findings concerning long-run turnover in the poverty population. Further doubt about its applicability to most poverty situations is cast by Levy's investigation of the degree to which poverty status is automatically passed from one generation to the next. While subject to some statistical problems, his analysis showed that after forming their own households most of the children from poor families moved out of poverty.

DATA AND EMPIRICAL ANALYSIS

The empirical analysis of poverty dynamics presented in this chapter concentrates on the ten-year period from 1969 through 1978. Analysis pertaining to the decade as a whole is based on observations of all Panel Study individuals present throughout that period. To try to detect any structural differences over the decade, the two component five-year periods 1969-1973 and 1974-1978 have been examined separately, with the samples shifting to individuals present throughout the respective five-year periods. The definition of poverty used for the core of this analysis corresponds to the official Census definition--having total family money income during the year less than that needed to meet the Census Bureau's minimal annual needs level for a family of that composition.[5] To test whether the results were sensitive to the definition of poverty, several variants of the official poverty definition have been examined. The official definition has been criticized for across-time comparisons of the size of the poverty population because it ignores non-cash transfers, predominately Food Stamps, which in recent years have increasingly substituted for cash transfers. Consequently, one variant examined here adds the Food Stamp bonus value to family income. Other variants either delete welfare money income from total money income or raise the poverty line to include as poor all individuals with family money income less than 1.25 times their official needs levels. These latter variants allow us to see the effects of broadening the poverty population to include individuals who were poor prior to receipt of welfare income or who were hovering near poverty even with welfare income.

---

[5]Although poverty status is based on family income and needs, the individual is the unit of analysis. Since families can dissolve or be created over time, a "family" is not a stable unit for long-run analysis.

Poverty Incidence and Duration

Over the period of observation, poverty incidence about doubled in size as the horizon widened from one year to five years, and about tripled as the time horizon expanded from a single year to a full decade. The duration of poverty for those who were poor during the specified period underwent quite similar changes as the length of the period expanded. In any single year during the period 1969–1978, 6.6 to 8.9 percent of the individuals were poor; but during either one of the two component five-year periods, 16.6 to 17.5 percent of the individuals were poor at some time, and over the entire ten years 24.4 percent of the individuals were poor at some time. The short-run versus long-run patterns of poverty incidence and duration differed little for the two five-year periods comprising the decade, and we found that they changed little when we substituted different poverty definitions in the analysis.

For the years in poverty of the individuals who were ever poor, we found highly skewed distributions. By far the largest percentages of those who were ever poor were only temporarily poor. For either of the five-year periods, about 40 percent of the individuals poor at some time were poor only one year, whereas only 11 or 12 percent were poor each of the five years. When the period was extended to a full decade, the percentage poor in only one year remained at 40 while the proportion poor each year dropped to 3 percent.

The reader is referred to the appendix for the detailed tables pertaining to poverty incidence and duration and for a more comprehensive discussion of these results.

Effects of Past Poverty on Present Likelihood of Being Poor

Despite substantial transience in the poverty population over the long run, there remain important associations between poverty in one year and poverty in subsequent years. With the Panel data it is possible to see whether an individual was poor the previous year, the year before that, and so on back to the initial year of observation. Tracking poverty status in this way showed that prior years of poverty are powerful predictors of the subsequent likelihood of being poor. Dividing Panel Study individuals into those initially poor and those initially non-poor, we found that five years later 41.1 percent of those who were initially poor were again poor, whereas only 3.4 percent of those initially non-poor were in poverty in that later date. Extending the time horizon to a ten-year period, the first percentage dropped only to 32.1 and the latter rose to only 4.4. Thus even ten years after a given year of poverty, those individuals poor in that year were as much as seven times more likely to be poor again.

Does this strong association between past poverty and present poverty alone tell us much about the poverty process and what generates it? It may or it may not, because this association could either reflect a strong causal link between the poverty itself and subsequent poverty or it could merely reflect a persistent and strong correlation between poverty and other factors that vary across people and that are the true sources of poverty. More succinctly, the observed effect of a year of poverty on subsequent chances of being poor can incorporate two quite different components, one being what is known as state dependence, the other being what is termed heterogeneity. State dependence is that part of the effect due to an actual causal link between being poor at one time and the likelihood of being poor later, and it is invariant across people. With state dependence, regardless of who is poor at a specific time and what their other circumstances are, the poverty at that time causes a given increase in their subsequent likelihood of being poor. If, for example, poverty causes deterioration of health, then past poverty could cause subsequent poverty by eliminating economic opportunities requiring sound health. This effect of past poverty on subsequent likelihood of being poor would be a state dependence effect. Heterogeneity, on the other hand, is that portion of the effect of past poverty on the present likelihood of being poor that is generated by individual differences in the likelihood of becoming poor. These individual differences may involve either characteristics of the individuals themselves or characteristics of their environments that make them more susceptible to poverty. Returning to the health example, a positive association between past poverty and the likelihood of subsequently being poor could be generated by ill-health, caused by something other than poverty, occurring, persisting, and leading to continuing poverty. Such a causal link would reflect heterogeneity effects rather than state dependence association between past and present poverty.

To derive any estimate of the effect of prior poverty status on current poverty status requires information for the same people for two different times. With a time series of this type of information we can tell what proportions of individuals remained poor from one year to the next and what proportions became poor. This type of information is presented in Tables 3.1 and 3.2, first for the entire decade 1969-1978 and then for the component five-year intervals.

As Table 3.1 shows over the decade an average of about 60 percent of the individuals poor in one year remained poor the next year, whereas only about

Table 3.1

YEAR-TO-YEAR POVERTY TRANSITION PROBABILITIES OVER THE TEN-YEAR PERIOD, 1969-1978
(For sample individuals present in all years of specified ten-year period.)

Percentage Poor

Year	Counting All Money Income			Counting All Nonwelfare Income			Counting All Money Income with Poverty Line at 1.25		
	All	Prior Year Poor	Prior Year Nonpoor	All	Prior Year Poor	Prior Year Nonpoor	All	Prior Year Poor	Prior Year Nonpoor
1969	8.6			9.8			14.3		
1970	8.8	64.0	3.6	10.7	72.4	4.0	13.9	71.3	4.3
1971	8.9	58.0	4.2	11.0	70.1	4.0	13.3	68.3	4.4
1972	7.4	55.1	2.7	9.3	63.6	2.6	11.5	62.4	3.7
1973	6.6	54.1	2.7	8.5	61.3	3.1	10.5	63.5	3.6
1974	7.1	57.6	3.4	9.2	68.2	3.7	11.9	65.7	5.6
1975	8.4	64.8	4.1	10.3	72.8	4.0	13.0	69.7	5.4
1976	7.4	54.8	3.1	9.3	66.0	2.8	11.4	59.2	4.3
1977	7.2	60.8	2.9	8.8	65.6	3.0	11.3	66.7	4.1
1978	6.8	58.3	2.8	8.3	65.9	2.7	11.0	65.5	4.1
Average	7.7	59.0	3.3	9.6	67.0	3.3	12.1	65.9	4.3
Sample Size		12,474			12,474			12,474	

Table 3.2

YEAR-TO-YEAR POVERTY TRANSITION PROBABILITIES OVER TWO FIVE-YEAR PERIODS
(For sample individuals present in all years of specified five-year period.)

Percentage Poor

	1969-1973 Counting All Money Income			1974-1978 Counting All Money Income			Counting All Money Income Plus Food Stamp Bonus Value			Counting All Nonwelfare Money Income			Counting All Money Income with Poverty Line at 1.25		
	All	Prior Year Poor	Prior Year Nonpoor	All	Prior Year Poor	Prior Year Nonpoor	All	Prior Year Poor	Prior Year Nonpoor	All	Prior Year Poor	Prior Year Nonpoor	All	Prior Year Poor	Prior Year Nonpoor
Year 1	8.6			7.2			5.9			9.7			12.0		
Year 2	8.8	64.0	3.6	8.6	65.3	4.2	7.5	59.3	4.1	10.8	73.2	4.1	13.4	70.8	5.0
Year 3	8.9	59.1	4.2	7.6	55.8	3.1	6.6	52.0	2.9	9.7	65.7	2.9	11.7	59.0	3.8
Year 4	7.4	55.1	2.7	7.5	60.5	3.0	6.5	54.5	3.1	9.2	66.0	3.1	11.7	67.5	3.8
Year 5	6.6	54.1	2.8	7.1	58.7	2.9	6.4	56.9	2.9	8.7	67.4	2.9	11.3	65.8	3.6
Average	8.1	58.3	3.4	7.7	59.7	3.4	6.7	55.7	3.3	9.6	68.1	3.3	12.1	65.8	4.7
Sample size		12,474			14,073			14,073			14,073			14,073	

3 percent of the individuals not poor in a given year became poor the subsequent year. These percentages varied only somewhat across the years: the percentage of the preceding-year poor remaining poor ranged from 54.1 percent (in 1972-1973) to 64.8 percent (in 1974-1975), and the percentage of the preceding-year non-poor becoming poor ranged from 2.7 percent (in 1971-1972 and 1972-1973) to 4.2 percent (in 1970-1971). Both the average and the range for these percentages differed very little between the component five-year periods (Table 3.2). In addition, changes in the definition of poverty showed relatively small effects. Deleting welfare income somewhat increased the mean percentage of poor remaining poor, while adding Food Stamp bonus value worked in the opposite direction; neither of these changes, though, altered the mean percentage of non-poor becoming poor each year. Raising the poverty line affected both the percentage of poor remaining poor from one year to the next and the percentage of non-poor becoming poor, but the increases in both of these percentage were rather small.

These percentage figures can be used to estimate the total effect of the preceding year's poverty status on the present year's poverty status. They represent conditional probabilities, with the overall probability of being poor increasing from about .03 to .60 if the individual was poor the preceding year. This information tells us the size of the total "effect" of prior year's poverty status on the current year's likelihood of being poor: on average, an individual was about 20 times more likely to be poor a given year if his or her status was "in-poverty" rather than "out-of-poverty" the preceding year.

Another way of looking at the relation between prior status and current status is to translate the probabilities into odds. As Table 3.3 shows (column 1), the odds that an individual was poor in a given year increased by a factor of 40 if that individual was poor the preceding year. This factor remained at about the same level whether or not Food Stamp bonus value was included in family income and whether the poverty line was set at 1.0 or at 1.25. It was somewhat higher, however, under the non-welfare income variation of the poverty definition.

The previous finding of pervasive transient poverty and isolated persistent poverty suggests that any effect of the prior poverty state itself that is uniform across people is a relatively small component of the total effect of prior poverty state on the odds of being poor. The overall effect shown in Table 3.3 sets the upper limit of this effect at a factor of about 40 (65 with only non-welfare income), but part or even all of this effect could actually be heterogeneity rather than state dependence.

Table 3.3

EFFECTS OF PRECEDING YEAR´S POVERTY STATUS
ON THE ODDS OF BEING POOR IN A GIVEN YEAR
(For all sample individuals present throughout specified five-year period.)

	Factor by Which Odds Increase if Preceding Year´s Poverty Status is Poor rather than Non-poor	
	With No Controls for Effects of Heterogeneity	With Controls for the Effects of Stationary Heterogeneity
POVERTY LINE AT 1.0		
Counting all money income:		
1969-1973	$39.7 = e^{3.71}$	$e^{1.15} = 3.2$
1974-1978	$42.1 = e^{3.77}$	$e^{1.29} = 3.6$
Counting all money income plus food stamp bonus value:		
1974-1978	$36.8 = e^{3.69}$	$e^{1.38} = 4.0$
Counting only non-welfare income:		
1974-1978	$64.6 = e^{4.13}$	$e^{1.43} = 4.2$
POVERTY LINE AT 1.25		
Counting all money income:		
1974-1978	$39.0 = e^{3.69}$	$e^{1.10} = 3.0$

Investigating the Issue of Heterogeneity Versus State Dependence

There are several different ways to analyze the state dependence versus heterogeneity issue using panel data. The technique referred to here is computationally simple, requiring only information about the frequencies of alternative year-to-year patterns of either being in the given state--in this case poverty--or not being in the state. Developed by Chamberlain (1978, 1979) and Anderson (1970), this technique is applicable to analysis of other topics as well that involve movement in and out of a particular state over time (such as female labor force participation [Chamberlain, 1978] and unemployment [Corcoran and Hill, 1980a]). This technique is informative about what general classes of variables should be most important in understanding the causes of poverty, but it is also limited to the extent that effects of specific individual variables are not being measured. Techniques for investigating the specific effects of individual variables in the context of a state dependence/heterogeneity decomposition have been developed by Chamberlain as well as by James Heckman. They are considerably more complex than the technique used in this paper. The simplicity of the technique used here makes it a useful tool for illustrating the way that such decompositions can be done. Even though it is not informative about the specific role of factors associated with poverty, it can direct us to classes of factors that play important roles in the poverty process.

To better isolate the effect of state dependence, the present technique allows estimation of the degree of association between past and present poverty, independent of the effects of one form of heterogeneity—stationary heterogeneity. This type of heterogeneity refers to differences in poverty propensities that remain constant over time but vary from individual to individual. The resulting estimate of the effect of past poverty on present poverty still incorporates any effects of serially correlated exogenous factors which affect propensities for poverty but change over time (i.e., high aggregate unemployment rates that persist from one year to the next). Despite this incomplete decomposition, though, removing the influence of stationary heterogeneity can still be informative about which type of factors to concentrate efforts on to further understand the causes of poverty. If the effect of prior poverty status drops substantially when controls for stationary heterogeneity are imposed then research should concentrate on identifying characteristics that vary across people and affect individual-specific poverty propensities. If, on the other hand, the effect of the history of poverty status remains at the same level after controls for stationary heterogeneity are introduced, then research on the sources of poverty should concentrate less on identifying these varying characteristics of individuals or environments which affect poverty propensities and more on what it is about poverty itself that causes recurrence in a uniform fashion across all sorts of people.

Here we briefly describe the basis for this technique and discuss the results of using it to investigate the long-run poverty process. More comprehensive information on the derivation of the technique and other uses for it are presented by Chamberlain (1978) and by Corcoran and Hill (1980a).

The technique is based on the following autoregressive logistic specification for an individual's probability of being poor in year t, conditional on poverty status in the previous year, t-1:

$$(1) \quad \mathrm{Prob}(y_{it}=1 \mid y_{i,t-1}) = \frac{\exp(\alpha_i + \gamma y_{i,t-1})}{1 + \exp(\alpha_i + \gamma y_{i,t-1})}$$

where y_{it} = 1 if poor in year t, otherwise 0,

α_i = the effect of personal characteristics that influence the ith individual's probability of being poor,

γ = the degree to which being poor last year affects the probability of being poor this year.

This equation states that the conditional probability that an individual is poor in year t, given his/her poverty status in the previous year--Prob $(y_{it}=1 \mid y_{i,t-1})$--depends upon (1) the effect on the likelihood of being poor, α_i, which reflects the influence of personal characteristics and remains constant for the individual over the observation period, and (2) whether the individual was poor in the previous year, $(y_{i,t-1})$. If the influence of these personal characteristics completely explains poverty persistence, then γ will be equal to zero. This can be tested by constructing a confidence interval for γ.

Chamberlain has shown that from this specification an estimate of γ, as well as a confidence interval for it, can be obtained if at least four years of panel data are available. Probabilities of across-time sequences of being in or out of a state--in this case the state is poverty--are used to make these calculations. From the above specification of an individual's probability of being poor in a given year, certain conditonal probabilities for patterns of being either in or out of poverty from year to year over the observation period will contain a γ term but no α_i term. The α_i term drops out of the specification of the probability of any particular sequence when that probability is conditional on a fixed beginning and end state (either of which can be being in poverty or being out of poverty) and on a fixed total number of years of being in poverty over the observation period.

At least four years of panel data are required to estimate the γ term and its confidence interval from these conditional probabilities because no such conditional probabilities of sequences will retain a γ term if fewer than four years are represented in the sequence. The following is the specification for the conditional probabilities:

$$(2) \quad \text{Prob} \left((y_{it} \cdots y_{iT}) \mid y_{i1}, \, y_{iT}, \, \sum_{t=1}^{T} y_{it} \right) = \frac{\exp{(\gamma)}^{\sum_{t=1}^{T} y_{it} \, y_{i,t-1}}}{\sum_{d \varepsilon B_i} \exp{(\gamma)}^{\sum_{t=1}^{T} d_t \, d_{t-1}}}$$

where $B_i = \{ \underset{\sim}{d} = (d_1 \cdots d_T) \mid d_t = 0 \text{ or } 1, \, d_1 = y_{i1}, \, d_T = y_{iT}, \, \sum_{t=1}^{T} d_t = \sum_{t=1}^{T} y_{it} \}$

and $\quad T$ = the final year of the observation period.

This derived specification, in essence, means that within a set of sequences that cover the same time frame, of those that contain the same number of years in which poverty occurs and which have the same beginning state and the same end state, the sequences containing more consecutive years of poverty are more likely if there is, in fact, state dependence. If there is state dependence, with a constant effect, γ, of prior year's occupancy of the state of poverty on present year's chances of being poor, then those sequences in the conditional set with more consecutive years of poverty are more likely, and they are more likely by a factor of e^γ for each additional set of consecutive years of poverty over and above that of other sequences in that conditional set.

The sets of sequences $y_{1t} \cdots y_{it}$ which retain γ terms in their corresponding conditional probabilities vary with the number of years in the observation period. The ones that do so with five years of data are listed in Table 3.4, along with the observed percentage of the sample with each such sequence pattern. For each sequence, "1" designates being in poverty in a given year and "0" designates being out of poverty. The frequencies listed for the sequences are ones observed for the years 1969-1973 and 1974-1978 using the official poverty definition, and ones for the years 1974-1978 varying the poverty definition in ways discussed earlier. These variants allow us to see if the heterogeneity/ state dependence decomposition differs across the two halves of the 1969-1978 decade and if it is sensitive to the way poverty is defined. The lower half of this table presents the resulting estimates of γ and its variance based on these observed frequencies. Across all of these variants, $\hat{\gamma}$ was significantly different from zero at conventional levels and did not differ much in size.

Table 3.4

FREQUENCY DISTRIBUTIONS OF VARIOUS POVERTY STATUS PATTERNS PRODUCING AN ESTIMATE OF γ USING FIVE YEARS OF PANEL DATA AND RESULTING ESTIMATE OF γ

Poverty Pattern:[a]	Counting All Money Income		Adding Food Stamp Bonus Value	Counting Only Non-welfare Money Income	Moving Poverty Line from 1.0 up to 1.25
	1969–1973	1974–1978	1974–1978	1974–1978	1974–1978
	PERCENTAGE OF SAMPLE WITH SPECIFIED PATTERN				
11000	1.0	0.9	0.4	0.9	1.4
10100	0.5	0.2	0.2	0.2	0.3
10010	0.1	0.2	0.2	0.2	0.1
	1.6	1.3	0.8	1.3	1.8
00011	0.3	0.9	0.7	0.6	0.8
00101	0.2	0.2	0.1	0.1	0.3
01001	0.1	0.1	0.1	0.1	0.2
	0.6	1.2	0.9	0.8	1.3
11100	0.7	0.4	0.4	0.7	0.6
11010	0.2	0.1	0.2	0.3	0.4
10110	0.3	0.1	0.0	0.0	0.1
	1.2	0.6	0.6	1.0	1.1
00111	0.4	0.5	0.6	0.5	0.7
01101	0.1	0.2	0.1	0.2	0.2
01011	0.1	0.1	0.1	0.1	0.1
	0.6	0.8	0.8	0.8	1.0
01100	0.6	0.4	0.6	0.4	0.5
00110	0.6	0.3	0.3	0.3	0.5
01010	0.1	0.2	0.1	0.2	0.3
	1.3	0.9	1.0	0.9	1.3
11001	0.3	0.3	0.3	0.3	0.4
10011	0.2	0.1	0.1	0.2	0.3
10101	0.1	0.1	0.1	0.0	0.1
	0.6	0.5	0.5	0.5	0.8
	RESULTING ESTIMATES				
$\hat{\gamma}$	1.15	1.29	1.38	1.43	1.10
$\mathrm{Var}(\hat{\gamma})$	.009	.009	.012	.010	.007

[a]Each "1" represents a year in poverty and each "0" represents a year out of poverty.

The effect, γ, of prior-year poverty status (apart from heterogeneity) on the probability of being poor in a given year raises the odds of being poor by a factor of e^γ. Table 3.3 lists these values of $e^{\hat{\gamma}}$ along with the observed effect of prior-year poverty states before dropping out the effect of stationary heterogeneity. As can be seen from Table 3.3, the effect of dropping out the influence of stationary heterogeneity was quite substantial. The factor by which the odds of being poor this year were increased by being poor last year fell from a magnitude of about 40 to a magnitude closer to 3 or 4. Expressing the effect in odds terms accentuated the effect on probabilities, but there clearly was a drop in the effect of prior poverty status on present status when stationary heterogeneity was controlled for. The effect of prior poverty status remained significant, and we still do not know to what extent this effect represents a causal link rather than an influence of serially correlated exogenous factors which change over time. But we do have a very good indication that differences across people or their circumstances are an important source of variation in the likelihood of being poor.

Some Important Characteristics of the Different Long-Run Poverty Groups

If state dependence had accounted for most of the total effect of prior-year poverty status on the current likelihood of being poor, there would be little need to investigate characteristics associated with varying extents of long-run poverty. All individuals poor in a given year could simply be given money transfers sufficient to move them above the poverty line that year (i.e., to the non-poor state). This one-year transfer would eliminate not only all of the poverty that year but most poverty the next year as well. Continuing to give cash transfers to each year's smaller and smaller group of poor would quickly result in poverty becoming a very rare occurrence. However, the results concerning the state dependence/heterogeneity investigation suggest the need for a more complex approach to poverty reduction.

Examining the composition of the various long-run poverty groups—the temporarily poor, the occasionally poor, and the persistently poor[6]—according to characteristics found to be strongly related to poverty in the cross-section can provide some idea of the complexity of the problem. As Table 3.5 indicates,

---

[6]Here temporarily poor refers to individuals poor 1 or 2 years 1969–1978, occasionally poor refers to those poor 3 to 7 years 1969–1978 and persistently poor refers to those poor 8 to 10 years 1969–1978.

the composition of the three poverty groups was quite different. As the extent of long-run poverty increased, the poverty population shifted away from individuals with household heads who were full-time workers toward ones with household heads working fewer than 500 hours per year. Whereas 63 percent of the temporarily poor were in full-time worker households, 70 percent of the persistently poor were in households with the head working fewer than 500 hours per year. Two other characteristics dominated the persistently poor group and were far from dominating the temporarily poor group. Whereas 20 percent of the temporarily poor were black, the majority (60 percent) of the persistently poor were black. Similarly, about 30 percent of the temporarily poor were in female-headed households as compared to the majority (60 percent) of the persistently poor. As poverty became more persistent, there were also substantial shifts toward larger proportions with disabled heads, female heads age 65 or older, and unmarried female heads with children.

These results suggest that in developing and applying programs for reducing permanent poverty, particular attention should be paid to the causes of the poverty of household heads who are black, female, or working few hours in the labor market. Programs designed for females should take into consideration whether they are aged and whether or not they are unmarried with children. Programs for reducing temporary poverty, on the other hand, apparently should be directed mostly toward full-time workers. Considerably further investigation into the identifying characteristics of the various long-run poverty groups is needed, along with better understanding of the causes underlying the variations in susceptibility to persistent long-run poverty.

SUMMARY AND CONCLUSIONS

Tracking changes in the poverty status of Panel Study individuals, this chapter examines long-run poverty patterns over the past decade. Like other work on long-run poverty, a substantial degree of transience is found in the poverty population. Despite the predominance of temporary poverty, however, there is clear evidence that being poor in one year increases the likelihood of being poor the subsequent year. Part, or even all, of this year-to-year association might reflect a causal link between poverty status at one time and future likelihood of being poor. A causal relationship of this sort has been termed "state dependence." But the strong positive relationship of poverty status from one year to the next could also be due to another factor--one known as "heterogeneity." This factor refers to individual-specific differences in the

Table 3.5

COMPOSITION OF VARIOUS POVERTY POPULATIONS ACCORDING TO THE HOUSEHOLD HEAD'S CHARACTERISTICS
(For sample individuals present in all years of specified observation period.)

Observation Period	Percentage of Population	Percentage of Specified Population in a Household in 1978 Whose Head was....										
		Black Population	Female	Disabled	Male Age 65 or Older	Female Age 65 or Older	Unmarried Male with Children	Unmarried Female with Children	Employed at Least 1500 Hours	Employed Less than 500 Hours	In City of Less than 10,000	In City of 500,000 or More
Population of Individuals Poor One or Two Years During Observation Period												
1969-1978	13.6	18.5	28.1	16.5	6.6	7.0	0.8	12.1	62.9	24.9	18.9	32.5
Population of Individuals Poor Three to Seven Years During Observation Period												
1969-1978	8.1	37.7	40.8	24.8	7.0	9.7	1.2	21.8	44.3	40.3	26.5	27.5
Population of Individuals Poor Eight to Ten Years During Observation Period												
1969-1978	2.6	61.8	60.9	38.5	14.9	17.5	3.0	34.2	16.0	69.8	32.6	20.5
Entire Population of Individuals Present During Observation Period												
1978	100.0	12.2	19.0	9.9	8.4	4.5	1.0	8.9	71.7	19.4	15.1	31.7
1969-1978	100.0	11.6	19.2	10.8	9.7	5.2	1.0	7.5	70.3	20.7	14.9	32.5
Population of Individuals Poor at Least One Year During Observation Period												
1978	7.2	42.1	58.8	30.8	9.4	12.6	1.8	36.5	15.4	66.4	21.4	26.2
1969-1978	24.4	29.5	35.8	21.6	7.6	9.0	1.2	17.7	51.7	34.8	22.9	29.6
Population of Individuals Poor Exactly One Year During Observation Period												
1969-1978	9.5	16.7	26.0	15.4	7.7	6.8	0.4	10.9	65.4	24.7	19.5	30.1
Population of Individuals Poor Every Year During Observation Period												
1969-1978	0.7	60.8	81.1	32.3	4.2	22.2	0.2	48.4	9.2	75.4	16.8	26.5

propensity to be poor. Characteristics of the individual and the environment can influence the individual-specific poverty propensities. Using a technique to test the importance of the state dependence effect controlling for heterogeneity, a significant state dependence effect is found. But this effect is quite small relative to the overall effect of last year's poverty status on this year's likelihood of being poor. This suggests that the more important source of the tendency toward recurrence of prior poverty status is differences in individuals' propensities for being poor.

These results imply that persistent, occasional and temporary poverty call for different poverty policies. If state dependence were a large component of the likelihood of recurrence of prior poverty status, then provision of income transfers sufficient to move all poor individuals out of poverty in one year would keep most people out of poverty in all subsequent years. Since the state dependence effect, while significant, appears to be relatively small, elimination of poverty seems to require more complex solutions.

A look at some aspects of the composition of the temporarily, occasionally, and persistently poor suggests some important characteristics to consider. Individuals in households with full-time workers form the majority of the temporarily poor, whereas individuals in households with heads working fewer than 500 hours annually form the majority of the persistently poor. The persistently poor are also predominantly female as well as predominantly black. Relative to the other long-run poverty groups, the predominantly poor are also disproportionately in households with a head who is disabled, an aged female, or an unmarried female head with children. This analysis primarily, though, points to the need for further investigation of factors affecting individuals' poverty propensities. Without such understanding there will continue to be impediments to proper development and allocation of poverty programs for effectively eliminating poverty.

References

Andersen, E. B. "Asymptotic Properties of Conditional Maximum Likelihood Estimators." Journal of the Royal Statistical Society, Series B, 32 (1970): 283-301.

Chamberlain, Gary. "On the use of Panel Data." Unpublished manuscript, Harvard University, 1978.

_____. "Heterogeneity, Omitted Variable Bias, and Duration Dependence." Unpublished manuscript, Harvard University, 1979.

Coe, Richard D. "Dependency and Poverty in the Short Run and Long Run." In _Five Thousand American Families--Patterns of Economic Progress, Vol. VI_, edited by Greg J. Duncan and James N. Morgan. Ann Arbor: Institute for Social Research, University of Michigan, 1978.

_____. "The Poverty Line: Its Function and Limitations." _Public Welfare_ (Winter 1978): 32-36.

Corcoran, Mary, and Hill, Martha S. "Persistence in Unemployment Among Adult Men." In _Five Thousand American Families--Patterns of Economic Progress, Vol. VIII_, edited by Greg J. Duncan and James N. Morgan. Ann Arbor: Institute for Social Research, University of Michigan, 1980.

_____. "Unemployment and Poverty." _Social Science Review_ (September 1980): 407-13.

Garfinkel, Irwin, and Haveman, Robert. "Earnings Capacity, Economic Status, and Poverty." _Journal of Human Resources_ (Winter 1977): 49-70.

Goedhart, Theo; Halberstadt, Victor; Kapteyn, Arie; and van Praag, Bernard. "The Poverty Line: Concept and Measurement." _Journal of Human Resources_ (Fall 1977): 503-20.

Gramlich, Edward M. "The Distributional Effects of Higher Unemployment." Brookings Paper on Economic Activity, No. 3. Washington, D.C.: The Brookings Institution, September 1974.

Harrington, Michael. _The Other America: Poverty in the United States_. New York: Macmillan, 1962.

Kakwani, Nanak. "On a Class of Poverty Measures." _Econometrica_ (March 1980): 437-46.

Lampman, Robert J. _Ends and Means of Reducing Income Poverty_. Chicago: Markham Publishing Co., 1971.

Lazear, Edward P., and Michael, Robert T. "Family Size and the Distribution of Real Per Capita Income." _The American Economic Review_ (March 1980): 91-107.

Lewis, Oscar. "The Culture of Poverty." In _On Understanding Poverty_, edited by Daniel P. Moynihan. New York: Basic Books, 1969.

Levy, Frank. "How Big is the American Underclass?" Working Paper No. 0090-1, The Urban Institute, September 1977.

Perlman, Richard. _The Economics of Poverty_. New York: McGraw-Hill, 1976.

Plotnick, Robert D., and Skidmore, Felicity. _Progress Against Poverty: A Review of the 1964-1974 Decade_. New York: Academic Press, 1975.

Rainwater, Lee. "Persistent and Transitory Poverty: A New Look." working paper, Joint Center for Urban Studies of MIT and Harvard University, October 1980.

Rein, Martin. "Problems in the Definition and Measurement of Poverty." In
    Poverty in America, edited by Louis A. Ferman, Joyce L. Kornbluh, and
    Alan Haber. Ann Arbor: The University of Michigan Press, 1972.

Schiller, Bradley R. The Economics of Poverty and Discrimination. Englewood
    Cliffs, New Jersey: Prentice-Hall, Inc., 1980.

Sen, Amartya. "Poverty: An Ordinal Approach to Measurement." Econometrica
    (March 1976): 219-31.

Smeeding, Timothy M. "The Antipoverty Effects of In-Kind Transfers." Journal of
    Human Resources (Summer 1977): 360-78.

Thurow, Lester C. Poverty and Discrimination. Washington, D.C.: The Brookings
    Institution, 1969.

Watts, Harold W. "The Measurement of Poverty--An Exploratory Exercise."
    American Statistical Association Proceedings of the Social Sciences Section,
    1967.

Appendix to Chapter 3

LONG-RUN POVERTY INCIDENCE AND DURATION

The figures in Table A3.1 show how poverty patterns changed as the time horizon widened. Looking first at the patterns for the official poverty definition, we see that poverty incidence about doubled as the horizon widened from one year to five years, and about tripled as the time horizon expanded from a single year to a full decade. The duration of poverty for those ever poor during the specified period underwent quite similar changes as the length of the period expanded. In any single year during the period 1969-1978, 6.6 to 8.9 percent of the individuals were poor; but during the component five-year periods, 16.6 to 17.5 percent of the individuals were poor at some time and, over the entire ten years, 24.4 percent of the individuals were poor at some time. The duration of this poverty for those who were ever poor during the corresponding time frames increased from one year (by definition) for single-year periods, to 2.3 years for a five-year period, to 3.2 years for the full ten-year period.

These short-run versus long-run patterns of poverty incidence and duration differed little for the two five-year periods comprising the decade and were fairly insensitive to the poverty definition. Relative incidence and duration ratios, short-run to long-run, remained at about the same level when either the transfer components of income were changed or the poverty line was raised. The absolute levels for incidence and duration did vary in the long run in the same manner as in the short run. Long-run as well as short-run incidence and duration were somewhat higher when welfare transfers were deleted from income and slightly lower when Food Stamp bonus value was added to income. More substantial absolute changes occurred when the poverty line was raised from 1.0 to 1.25, with incidence most strongly affected. With this change in the poverty definition came substantial increases in poverty incidence in all of the time spans, with long-run incidence rising from one-quarter to one-third of the sample who were poor at some time during the decade. By either definition, it is clear that, over the long-run, poverty affects a very substantial portion of the population.

Examining in more detail the years in poverty of the individuals who were ever poor during the five or ten-year intervals (Tables A3.2 and A3.3), we found highly skewed distributions. By far the largest percentages of those who were ever poor were temporarily poor. In either five-year interval, 40 percent of those individuals were poor in one year only; an additional 20 percent were poor

Table A3.1

INCIDENCE AND DURATION OF POVERTY
(For sample individuals present in all years of specified period.)

	Percentage of Sample Poor		Average Number of Years Poor	
	A Given Year During Observation Period	At Sometime During Observation Period	Individuals Poor at Sometime During Observation Period	Entire Sample
POVERTY LINE AT FAMILY MONEY INCOME/NEEDS=1				
Counting all family money income:				
1969-1978	6.6-8.9	24.4	3.16	0.77
1969-1973	6.6-8.9	17.5	2.34	0.41
1974-1978	7.1-8.6	16.6	2.29	0.38
Counting all family money income plus food stamp bonus value:				
1974-1978	5.9-7.5	15.3	2.16	0.33
Counting all non-welfare money income:				
1969-1978	8.3-11.0	25.8	3.69	0.95
1969-1973	8.5-11.0	19.0	2.59	0.49
1974-1978	8.7-10.8	18.5	2.59	0.48
POVERTY LINE AT 1.25				
Counting all family money income:				
1969-1978	10.5-14.3	32.5	3.47	1.23
1969-1973	10.6-14.3	24.0	2.65	0.64
1974-1978	11.3-13.4	24.0	2.51	0.60

in two of the five years, bringing the percentage of those who were poor less than half the time during that interval up to 60 percent. Only about 11 or 12 percent of the individuals poor at some time during the five-year interval were poor in every one of the five years. Again, the figures were quite similar for the two five-year periods but were somewhat sensitive to alterations in the poverty definition, shifting mostly between the two extremes of one year in poverty and all years in poverty. The largest shifts occurred when either welfare income was deleted or the poverty line was raised. In both cases, the percentage of those who were poor in only one year dropped to about 37 percent, whereas the percentage poor every year rose to about 20 percent.

The distribution of those who were poor at some time according to the number of years in poverty continued to be quite skewed when the period was extended to a decade. While there was a slight reduction in the percentage poor in one year only, the percentage poor in less than half of the years covered by the period rose from about 60 percent up to almost 80 percent. At the other extreme, the percentage poor in every year of the interval dropped from 11-12 percent down to only 3 percent. As with the five-year intervals, excluding welfare income or raising the poverty line shifted the distribution toward the upper end of the scale, but the shift was small in magnitude. Regardless of the definition of poverty, over the long run, poverty is a transient state, by and large. Quite sizeable portions of the population experience poverty at some point, but the persistently poor comprise only a small subgroup of these individuals.

Table A3.2

PERCENTAGE OF INDIVIDUALS POOR AT SOMETIME IN
FIVE-YEAR PERIOD BY NUMBER OF YEARS BELOW
POVERTY LINE, 1968-1973 AND 1974-1978
(For sample individuals present in all years of specified five year period.)

	1	2	3	4	5
POVERTY LINE AT 1.0					
Counting all money income:					
1969-1973	42.3	20.6	14.3	11.4	12.0
1974-1978	42.8	21.1	13.3	12.0	10.8
Counting all money income plus food stamp bonus value:					
1974-1978	47.1	19.6	14.4	10.5	8.5
Counting all non-welfare income:					
1969-1973	37.4	17.4	12.1	12.6	20.0
1974-1978	37.3	17.3	14.1	12.1	19.5
POVERTY LINE AT 1.25					
Counting all money income:					
1969-1973	35.0	16.7	15.0	13.3	19.6
1974-1978	38.3	18.8	13.3	12.5	17.1

Table A3.3

PERCENTAGE OF INDIVIDUALS POOR AT SOMETIME IN THE TEN-YEAR
PERIOD 1969-1978 BY NUMBER OF YEARS BELOW POVERTY LINE
(For sample individuals present in all years of specified ten-year period.)

	Number of Years Below Poverty Line									
	1	2	3	4	5	6	7	8	9	10
Counting all money income	38.9	16.8	11.9	6.1	5.7	5.7	3.7	4.1	3.7	2.9
Counting all nonwelfare income	35.7	17.1	8.5	6.2	6.2	5.4	4.3	4.3	6.2	6.6
Counting all money income, with Poverty Line at 1.25 instead of 1.0	33.8	13.8	10.5	8.3	5.8	7.4	4.9	4.0	5.2	6.5

Chapter 4

A PRELIMINARY EMPIRICAL EXAMINATION OF THE DYNAMICS OF WELFARE USE

Richard D. Coe

INTRODUCTION

Since 1965 the number of persons receiving public assistance has grown tremendously, with an attendant jump in costs.[1] The "welfare explosion," as it has come to be called, has been the source of a great deal of political controversy, and naturally has attracted the attention of a number of researchers. The purpose of this chapter is to provide some idea of what has been learned over the last decade about the use of welfare in our society and examine what the PSID data contribute to this knowledge. In particular, we wish to focus our attention on the issue of the dynamics of welfare use: What is the long-run experience of households with the welfare system?

The welfare explosion of the late 1960s occurred in a period of relatively vigorous economic activity, with unemployment rates at low levels. The question became "Why the explosion?" The generally accepted answer, to quote Lyon (1976, p. 25), was that "increased knowledge about the welfare system combined with a legitimatizing of dependency, both fostered by the welfare rights movement, resulted in an outpouring of applications by female-headed families." Rising benefit levels were also considered to have had an impact on increasing welfare use, but they were of secondary importance. Although these arguments seem reasonable and consistent with numerous observations, it is fair to say that

---

[1]According to the 1979 Statistical Abstract (Table No. 566), between 1965 and 1970 the number of recipients of assistance more than doubled in the case of AFDC (going from 4.4 million to 9.7 million) and increased ten-fold in the case of food stamps (going from 0.4 million to 4.3 million). Associated costs rose in a similar fashion, increasing from $1.8 billion to $4.9 billion for AFDC and from $60 million to $577 million for food stamps. By the year 1975, food stamp recipients outnumbered AFDC recipients (19.1 million compared to 11.0 million), and Supplemental Security Income (which one year earlier had consolidated Old-Age Assistance, Aid to the Blind, and Aid to the Disabled into one program) was being received by 4.3 million persons, up 1.6 million from the number of recipients of the combined programs of a decade earlier.

121

there has been little systematic documentation to suggest that knowledge or attitudes toward welfare use changed dramatically during the 1960s. This is undoubtedly due in part to the inherent difficulty of measuring such subjective concepts.

The growth of the number of welfare recipients raised the fear that our nation was seeing the formation of a "welfare class"--a segment of society which made extensive and extended use of welfare. The predictable cry of malingering was raised. The only data available--cross-sectional data, which covered the welfare population at one point in time--provided some inferential support to fuel these fears. In the last ten years, however, the availability of new data sets has enabled researchers to examine directly some of the major questions involving welfare use. In particular, these data have allowed direct inquiry into the issue of the long-run experience of households with the welfare system.

In this chapter we examine welfare participation patterns and factors associated with welfare use. We begin with an overview of past work on the topic, looking first at welfare use patterns and then at theoretical as well as empirical models of the welfare decision. This review, as well as the analysis following it, focuses predominantly on the AFDC and food stamp programs. In the analysis section of the chapter, we focus on the welfare experience of a representative national sample over an extended period of time. The sample is all sample individuals who were in the Panel Study of Income Dynamics throughout the ten-year period from 1969 through 1978.

Analysis of this data includes both a descriptive overview of welfare use and an investigation of the determinants of welfare use. We first focus on how many people and what subgroups of the population received welfare for differing lengths of time. Evidence is also presented on the dynamic nature of welfare use: Are individuals on welfare for an extended, unbroken time spell, or do they cycle on and off the welfare rolls? In investigating the determinants of welfare use, we also look at it from both a static and a dynamic perspective.

LITERATURE REVIEW

Most of the studies reviewed here are concerned with the AFDC program. As a result they deal largely with the experience of women, who comprise the vast majority of AFDC recipients. The justification for this focus on AFDC is that historically it has been the largest and most expensive of the social welfare programs (with the exception of the OASDHI[2] program, if one wishes to categorize that as a social welfare program). While this was true in the late sixties and early seventies, the food stamp program now rivals AFDC in size and expense. We will review the few studies that have looked at the long-run utilization of food stamps. The most recent of the federal public assistance programs—the SSI program, which in 1974 consolidated the various federal assistance programs for the aged, blind, and disabled—has had no research done on its dynamic aspects.

Descriptive Analysis of the Dynamics of Welfare Use

Rydell's study in 1974 was the first to document the tremendous turnover in the welfare population, using case records of the major assistance programs in New York City. From 1967 to 1972 New York City had almost one million separate welfare cases—90 percent more than in any single month during that period and 55 percent more than in any single year. Over the five-year period, 19.2 percent of the population of New York City had received some assistance, and by the end of the period there were almost as many former cases as there were current welfare cases. On average, each case was on welfare less than 40 percent of the time during this period.

Looking at one point in time, Rydell found that indeed it was easy to get the impression that there was a permanent "welfare class." In a given month, 63 percent of the cases were continuous long-term (over three years) cases, while an additional 19 percent were multiple-time long-term cases. Consequently, it appeared that at a given point in time, over 80 percent of welfare cases were long-term cases. Only 4 percent of the cases were short-term cases (received welfare for less than a year). However, because long-term cases cumulate on the welfare records, this figure overstates the time on welfare of the typical recipient. Of an opening cohort of cases (individuals who began receiving welfare at the same time), 26 percent received welfare for less than a year, 21 percent received it for a period of one-to-three years, and 53 percent were long-term cases. Finally, looking at all welfare cases over the five-year period, Rydell found that fully one-half were short-term cases, 23 percent were intermediate-term, and only 5.7 percent were long-term continuous cases. (An Additional 21 percent were multiple-time cases which were not broken down by length of time on welfare.)

---

[2] Old Age, Survivors, Disability, and Health Insurance.

Rydell also calculated the "half-life" of various types of welfare cases--
the length of time it took for one-half of the cases in an opening cohort to go
off the welfare rolls. He found that AFDC cases in which two or more children
were involved had the longest half-life (2.5 years), while AFDC-UP cases had the
shortest half-life (0.7 years). In addition to the large amount of aggregate
turnover in welfare cases, Rydell also found a substantial amount of cycling of
individual cases, that is, cases which went off welfare only to return at some
later date.[3]

Like Rydell, Boskin, and Nold (1975) discovered little long-term utilization
of welfare. Employing a monthly time frame and examining the experience from
1967 to 1972 of female-headed households who came on the California AFDC case
records in 1967 (N=440), they found that 73 percent of the cases received welfare
for one continuous period (accounting for 37 percent of the five-year period, on
average), 20 percent received welfare for two or more spells for 47 percent of
the period), and 7 percent of the cases had three or more spells of receiving
welfare (for 50 percent of the period). Their results imply somewhat less
cycling than Rydell's findings for New York City.[4]

One major problem with the Rydell and Boskin and Nold studies is that they
were quite limited geographically, applying only to New York City and the state
of California. One could justifiably argue that these areas are not
representative of the country as a whole. Using data from the Panel Study of
Income Dynamics, Rein and Rainwater (1978) examined the pattern of welfare[5] use
from 1967 to 1973 of a nationally representative sample of 3,086 women aged 18 to
54 in 1968. During any one year of this seven-year period, an average of

---

[3]Almost 40 percent of an opening cohort of cases were multiple-time
recipients of welfare, with about half of these being long-term cases. Rydell
estimated that approximately one-half of closed cases eventually reopen, and that
one-half of each month's case openings had previously received welfare. However,
these figures overstate the "true" turnover in welfare cases, for they include
spurious closings--closings due to administrative error or temporarily lost
contact. Spurious closings, most of which reopen in the same or first succeeding
month, accounted for approximately 11 percent of average monthly closings.

[4]Of an opening cohort of cases, Rydell found that 38 percent had multiple
spells on welfare, compared to the 27 percent found by Boskin and Nold. However,
the latter study did not report how spurious closings were handled, which may
account for the lower estimate of cycling.

[5]"Welfare" is defined as AFDC, AFDC-UP, and General Assistance Payments,
Old Age Assistance, Aid to the Blind, and miscellaneous public cash transfer
systems.

5.5 percent of these women were in a household which received $100 or more in welfare benefits. Over the entire seven-year period, 11.9 percent (weighted) of the women received welfare during at least one year (25 percent on an unweighted basis). Of these women, 16 percent received welfare for the entire seven years, while 33.0 percent were recipients for only one year. Rein and Rainwater found that if a woman wasn't on welfare in a given year, she had a 1.5 percent likelihood of receiving welfare in the next year. If a woman went on welfare, she had a 60 percent likelihood of staying on the next year, a 70 percent likelihood of staying on for a third year, and so on up to an 80 percent steady-state likelihood after four continuous years of receiving welfare. On the other hand, if a woman was off welfare one year, she had a 25 percent likelihood of returning the next year. If she was off two years, the probability dropped to 20 percent. After four years off, the probability of returning dropped to 7 percent. (These are all unweighted probabilities.)

Rein and Rainwater concluded that "Overall, ... the welfare class is a definite minority among recipients. It represents less than 10 percent of those who ever go on welfare, and only a little over a fifth of those already on it at any one time" (p. 524).

The above studies focused almost solely on AFDC, and analyzed primarily the experience of women. As was mentioned above, AFDC has historically been the largest and most expensive of the social welfare programs, but the food stamp program now rivals AFDC in size and expense. Food stamp usage has been analyzed by Coe (1979) using data from the Panel Study of Income Dynamics. In the four-year period encompassing 1973 through 1976, the percentage of households which received food stamps in any one year varied between 7.1 and 8.5 percent. However, only 2.8 percent of the households used food stamps in every one of the four years, while 14.8 percent used food stamps in at least one of the four years. In addition, Coe found that of the 835 panel households which were using food stamps in 1973, one-half were not using food stamps in 1976, even though the aggregate percentage of households using food stamps in a given year had increased.

This variance could have been partially in response to aggregate economic conditions. In 1973 and 1976, two relatively strong economic years, the rate of food stamp use was 7.1 and 7.8 percent, respectively. In 1974 and 1975, two years of relatively recessed economic conditions, the rate was 8.1 and 8.5 percent, respectively.

A series of analyses aimed at determining the responsiveness of welfare program caseloads to the cyclical behavior of the economy were conducted by the Office of Income Security Policy of HEW. Changes in the AFDC caseload were found to be not greatly affected by changes in aggregate macroeconomic variables. The rapid growth in the caseloads from 1952 to 1972 was attributed primarily (80 percent) to increased benefit levels and decreased job availability. However, other public assistance caseloads were found to be sensitive to changes in aggregate economic conditions. Changes in AFDC-UP caseloads were significantly related to changes in the manufacturing layoff rate and to the aggregate unemployment rate. These cyclical fluctuations exhibit substantial regional variation, with the North and West most affected and the South least affected.

The recent rapid growth in the aggregate food stamp caseloads was attributed primarily to noncyclical forces, most notably the extended geographical coverage of the program which occurred in 1974. (Puerto Rico was the major addition to the program.) However, it was estimated that a one percentage point increase in the national unemployment rate resulted in a one million person increase in the number of food stamp recipients. Because the SSI program was so recently initiated, no analysis was done on it.

The point has been made, most explicitly by Rein and Rainwater, that the receipt of welfare income per se presents an incomplete picture of the real importance of welfare to a household. In order to learn about dependency on welfare, one must know how important welfare income is in the total income package of a household. We do not attempt here to review the findings of Rein and Rainwater on this issue. However, an example of the type of results they discover may be informative. In regard to long-term dependency on welfare, they found, of the households which received welfare for four or more years in the seven-year period studied, two-thirds received less than 50 percent of their total seven-year income from welfare.

SUMMARY OF PREVIOUS FINDINGS

The evidence reviewed above enables us to draw some conclusions on the patterns of welfare use over time. At any single point in time, it would appear that the percentage of welfare recipients who are long-term welfare users is quite high. Rydell estimated that almost 80 percent of welfare cases in a given month receive welfare for more than three years during a five-year period. Rein and Rainwater found that of the women who received welfare in 1967, 63 percent received welfare in four or more years of the seven-year period they studied. Coe discovered that, on average, 33 percent of the food stamp users in a given year received food stamps in each of the four years he examined.

However, because the long-term cases tend to cumulate on the welfare rolls over time, these figures overstate the proportion of all welfare recipients who are long-term users. Of all persons who received welfare at some time over a multi-year period, the percentage who were long-term recipients was considerably smaller. Rein and Rainwater found this figure to equal 38 percent; Rydell estimated the maximum number to be 27 percent. Coe found that only 19 percent of food stamp users over a four-year period were recipients in every year. On the other hand, the percentage of ever welfare recipients on welfare for a year or less is substantial. With respect to the AFDC program, Rein and Rainwater discovered that 33 percent of all recipients received welfare for only one year; Rydell found that half of the cases for New York City were on the rolls for a year or less. With respect to the food stamp program, Coe found that of all users over a four-year period, 41 percent used food stamps for only one year.

Another way to describe the long-run pattern of welfare use is to follow an opening cohort of cases over time. Rydell estimated that 26 percent of an opening cohort stayed on welfare for less than a year, while 53 percent stayed on for over three years. Rein and Rainwater found that, of a cohort, 18 percent received welfare for just one year, while 49 percent received it for more than three years (and 16 percent received it in each of the seven years they examined). Coe found that, of all food stamp recipients in 1973, 50 percent had stopped receiving the stamps four years later.

This evidence demonstrates that there is considerable aggregate turnover in the population of welfare recipients. These studies have also discovered that a substantial number of individual welfare recipients cycle on and off the welfare rolls. Boskin and Nold found that 27 percent of AFDC mothers had at least two distinct spells of welfare use. Rydell found that between 21 and 38 percent (depending on the base) of welfare recipients were multiple-spell users. (Rydell´s 38 percent estimate is technically equivalent to Boskin and Nold´s 27 percent figure.) Rein and Rainwater (who defined a "spell" as a year rather than a month, as Rydell and Boskin and Nold did) found that 18 percent of welfare recipients had more than one spell of welfare receipt. Coe found that, out of all food stamp users over a four-year period, 6.8 percent had multiple spells of use.

Explaining the Dynamics of Welfare Use

Whichever way one chooses to view the issue, it seems clear that there is a considerable flow of people into and out of the various assistance programs. In addition to the volume of these flows the factors which account for this welfare dynamism have also received some attention from researchers. Economists are the main proponents of the models reviewed here which have been put forth to explain why people receive welfare benefits. The theoretical models and the relevant empirical evidence vary somewhat according to the assistance program being examined. Virtually all of the theoretical models involve a static analysis of the decision to participate. No theoretical model, with the possible exception of Coe´s (1979), has directly analyzed the dynamic issue of change in welfare status although several hypotheses can be inferred from the static models. Most of the empirical studies have utilized cross-sectional data, often across years. Some recent empirical work, mainly by the authors discussed above, has addressed specifically the issue of the determinants of change in welfare use.

Most of the theoretical work reviewed below focuses on what has been labelled the demand side of the market for welfare, that is, on the individual´s decision to receive welfare income. This is not to say that researchers are unaware of the importance of supply side factors. Administrative practices are universally recognized as crucial in the determination of who receives welfare. However, analysts have found it difficult to make any general statements on the effect of administrative practices because of the tremendous diversity across localities and programs.

Two more points are worth mentioning at this time. Available data have dictated that most of the empirical work use the number of recipients as the dependent variable. In other words, the analysis is directed at explaining differences in caseloads, or the number of recipients, across time and/or across geographical areas--usually states. A second approach has been to determine which factors distinguish eligible persons who decide to receive welfare from eligible persons who do not participate. This type of analysis uses the individual (or the household) as the unit of analysis, with the dependent variable being a dichotomous zero/one, based on whether the individual received any welfare income.

The second point to note is that in the empirical work, demographic characteristics of individuals often turn out to be statistically important to welfare status. The problem is that demographics per se never enter a theoretical model. The demographic characteristics are thought to proxy for one or more of the theoretical concepts, but the results are more suggestive than conclusive.

The Welfare Decision

An early attempt at modelling the welfare decision was made by Brehm and Saving (1964), who were interested in explaining why households choose to receive General Assistance payments. The essence of their model was the labor/leisure tradeoff, with the additional twist of incorporating an individual's "taste" for welfare into the decision. As might be expected, the benefit level available from welfare plays a primary role in a straight labor/leisure model. Indeed, Brehm and Saving found that differences in state benefit levels were the most powerful factor in explaining differences in the percentage of a state's population which received General Assistance payments in the period 1951-1959. Other significant variables were the state unemployment rate and the degree of urbanization in the state, which the authors interpreted as measuring the ease of getting on the General Assistance rolls. Brehm and Saving concluded that their results "... indicate that the G.A.P. recipients are like the remainder of consumers in that they react to economic incentives" (p. 1018). What they mean by this, apparently, is that "the demand for G.A.P. can be treated as a special case of the traditional theoretical treatment of the demand for leisure" (p. 1017).

This work was sharply criticized by Stein and Albin (1967), who characterized the conclusions as having "in effect revived the view that high benefits encourage sloth" (p. 576). They argued that Brehm and Saving erred in their selection of their dependent variable, which focused on number of cases rather than number of recipients. Using cases ignored interstate differences in average case size, which resulted in measured benefit levels not being equivalent across states. Correcting for this, Stein and Albin found no significant relationship (in fact, the coefficient was generally negative) between number of recipients in a state and the average benefit per recipient. They concluded from their findings that "... the 'demand for leisure' approach and its theoretical underpinnings must be questioned... (it) seeks to describe voluntary behavior in a situation in which restricted behavior is the general rule" (p. 584). In a later article, Albin and Stein (1968) formally introduced a work requirement restraint into the labor/leisure choice model and demonstrated that the individual's decision changed dramatically from the free choice situation. They concluded from their model that "conditions imposed by the supply side may dominate the relief transaction" (p. 310), but they presented no empirical evidence to support their claim.

The Brehm-Saving and Stein-Albin exchange left unsolved the empirical question of whether benefit levels or unemployment rates were the most important variable in explaining interstate differences in General Assistance caseloads. Kasper (1968) further refined the estimation equations of the aforementioned authors and found mixed support for both. In a linear specification with number of GA cases (and/or recipients) as the dependent variable, he found the average level of benefit payments to be insignificant and a more precisely defined unemployment rate (which related closely to the job market of low-income people) to be significant. In a _log_ linear specification, however, the average benefit level was significant. Kasper concluded from this that benefit level may be significant at low levels but insignificant at higher levels in predicting GA caseloads Bryant (1972) found the unemployment rate to be significant in predicting food stamp caseloads, as did Seagrave (1975). However, neither one of these authors included benefit levels in their work. Walker and Tweeten (1973) attempted to explain interstate differences in AFDC recipients for selected years between 1950 and 1967. Like Stein and Albin, they found benefit levels to be _negatively_ related to case levels. The most important factor in explaining interstate differences was differences in illegitimate births, indicating that eligibility criteria are crucial. Other factors which were significant were the percentage of the population which was rural and certain administrative regulations of the program, such as mandatory school attendance and the suitable home requirement (both of which tended to restrict participation). Garfinkel and Orr (1974) examined AFDC recipients' decisions to work, using state data for 1967, and found that the decisions were quite responsive to the economic parameters, such as the guarantee level and the marginal tax rate, of the various state programs. Their results supported the Brehm-Saving argument that welfare recipients respond rationally to economic incentives in their labor/leisure choice. Evidence from the Negative Income Tax experiments (not reviewed here) further supported this view.

In sum, then, the basic model of the decision to receive welfare has centered around the labor/leisure tradeoff, with several extensions to incorporate various other factors, such as personal attitudes, which have been thought to be important. (See Durbin, 1973, for perhaps the most extensive elaboration.) The empirical evidence has been mixed at best. One reviewer summed up the evidence as follows:

> (The pre-1975 research) found that indeed indigent families were quite rational in making their decision between work and welfare, but that their movement on and off the rolls was affected as much by personal attitudes toward welfare and changing administrative policies as it was by the level of benefits and the benefit-loss rate built into the programs. The basic decision to choose or not to choose welfare was quite rational within the rules of the game, but as it turned out, the rules were frequently changed. (Lyon, 1976, p. 13.)

The pre-1975 research was motivated largely by the tremendous growth in the number of welfare recipients which occurred in the late sixties and early seventies. The underlying assumption of this research and of the labor/leisure tradeoff approach was that by voluntary action (not working) individuals would make themselves eligible for welfare benefits. In the mid-seventies, however, it became clear that, despite the rapid growth in caseload levels, a substantial number of eligible households were not participating in the various assistance programs. Several studies (Bicket and MacDonald, 1975; Bureau of Census, 1976; Coe, 1977; MacDonald, 1977; Coe, 1979) estimated that the participation rate among eligible households in the food stamp program was approximately 40 percent. The participation rate in the SSI-Elderly program has been placed at around 55 percent (Warlick, 1979). The issue became not one of whether people voluntarily make themselves eligible for welfare, but rather: If eligible, why don't they participate?

As might be expected from economists, benefit levels again played a major role in attempts to explain the difference between eligible participants and eligible nonparticipants. If benefit levels were too low, then, for some eligible persons, welfare might not be worth the time and inconvenience involved in dealing with the welfare bureaucracy in order to apply for it. MacDonald (1977) found benefit levels to be significant in predicting participation in the food stamp program, while Warlick found the same with respect to the SSI program for the aged. On the other hand, Clarkson (1976) found nominal benefit levels to be insignificant in predicting participation in the food stamp program. Rather, the cash equivalent value[6] of the food stamp bonus, as estimated by Clarkson, was significant.

---

[6]The advent of many in-kind public assistance programs, such as food stamps, Medicaid, and the housing allowance programs, resulted in some theoretical developments on the issue of what the real benefit of these programs were to the participants. This generally involved introducing the household's preferences for that particular good. The debate continues whether the benefits from these programs should be valued at their cost to the government (Browning, 1979) or their cash equivalent value, as evaluated by the recipient (Smeeding, 1979).

Even those who believed benefit levels were important in predicting participation recognized that other factors might indeed be crucial. Researchers began to suspect that large numbers of eligible households simply did not have sufficient knowledge of the program. As stated by MacDonald, "...(it) is difficult to believe that eligible nonparticipants qualifying for sizeable bonuses were well informed" (p. 106). This suspicion was soon confirmed. Based on responses given by Panel Study households, Coe (1979) found that fully 60 percent of eligible nonparticipants did not think or did not know that they were eligible to receive food stamps. No other reason, such as low bonus value or administrative hassle, accounted for as much as 10 percent of the eligible nonusers´ responses. (Benefit levels were an insignificant predictor of participation, although that result was sensitive to which other variables were entered into the analysis.) Poor information was particularly important in explaining the low participation rates of the elderly, the employed, the childless, the people who were not receiving other welfare, and people residing in the West. While Coe found that other barriers to participation affected specific subgroups of eligible households, he concluded that "if the government wishes to increase participation in the food stamp program among eligible households, it must devote its energies to informing such households that they are eligible for food stamps...(Other) reforms cannot hope to have much impact on participation until eligible households realize that they do indeed qualify for food stamps."

Coe´s results bring us back to square one--how useful is it to model the welfare decision as a voluntary, individual free choice situation? The Negative Income Tax results have shown that welfare recipients respond in quite rational ways to economic incentives when they are fully informed of the choices available and are not subject to arbitrary decisions of welfare officials. However, the findings of Coe and others indicate that rational free choice might be the exception in a world of misinformation, illegitimacy, unemployment, and regulatory confusion.

Empirical Examination of Welfare Use in the Long Run

The empirical evidence discussed above concerned primarily cross-sectional data--a one-year look at who was (or was not) receiving welfare. Some studies combined this cross-sectional data over a number of years, but it was always at the aggregate level. None of the above studies was able to follow the same households over time in order to examine the reasons why households enter and

leave the welfare system, or why a substantial number of households cycle onto
and off the welfare rolls. While reasonable inferences could be made from the
cross-sectional studies, it wasn't until the availability of the longitudinal
data sets discussed in the first section of this paper that researchers were able
to study directly the <u>reasons</u> for the tremendous dynamism in welfare use. In
this section we review the empirical work in this area.[7]

Rydell (1974), although not particularly concerned with the behavioral
reasons for changing caseloads, did attempt to determine some of the correlates
of case openings, closings, and case length for New York City. He found that,
for all types of welfare cases, change in household composition accounted for
30 percent of case openings. This factor was particularly important for the AFDC
cases, of which 45 percent opened for this reason. Medical reasons accounted for
26.3 percent of all case openings, including 17.5 percent for AFDC and
13.6 percent for Old-Age Assistance. Unemployment accounted for 13.4 percent of
AFDC case openings, while administrative reasons accounted for an additional
13 percent. In modeling caseload openings, Rydell's basic predictor was average
openings over the last 12 months, not an important behavioral variable. He also
found that the number of births in the last 12 months was also important in
predicting changes in the AFDC caseload. The benefit level was significant only
in predicting Old-Age Assistance and AFDC-UP openings, while the unemployment
rate was significant only for the AFDC-UP program.

Looking at the reasons for case closings, Rydell found that the overwhelming
identifiable reason was administrative, which accounted for 62 percent of all
closings. (Another 15 percent was attributed to "Other Reasons.") Change in
household composition accounted for 8.5 percent of AFDC closings, while finding
employment accounted for 11.4 percent. (Death accounted for 44 percent of the
closings of Old-Age Assistance cases.)

But Rydell's most important findings concerned case length. First of all,
he found that AFDC cases with two or more children had significantly longer case
lengths (2.5 years) than any other type of assistance, including AFDC cases with
only one child. He also found that as the length of time on welfare increased,
the chances of getting off it decreased--a finding also supported by Rein and
Rainwater's analysis of data from the Panel Study. This provides some empirical

---

[7]It might be noted that little theoretical work has been directed
explicitly at the change in welfare use. Coe (1979b) presented a path analytic
framework for examining the change in food stamp use, but that was more
descriptive than behavioral in focus.

support for the "settling-in" hypotheses—the argument that households can become accustomed to dependency on welfare over time. He also found that the larger the amount of non-welfare income, the shorter the stay on welfare; and the older the welfare recipient, the longer the case length. A surprising finding was that the receipt of employment income actually led to a longer time on welfare, indicating that employment is not necessarily a stepping stone to self-sufficiency. Rydell attributed this to the persons whose productivity was so low that employment would not lead to high enough incomes to disqualify them from welfare. (Rein and Rainwater found that, of long-term welfare users, two-thirds received less than 50 percent of their total income from welfare. Lyon reported that long-term cases tend to have lower per-capita benefits.)

Despite these findings, Rydell concluded that, "at the current state of knowledge about welfare dependency, chance events play a large part in determining whether a welfare case is a short-term or long-term one" (p. 8). By "chance events," he means factors other than those measured in his study. Omitted factors that he suggests might be important include health, job skills, ambition, and personality of welfare recipients.

Boskin and Nold (1975) examined the probabilities of going off welfare versus staying on for their opening cohort of 440 AFDC recipients in California. They found that recipients who had an expected wage less than the minimum wage were less likely to go off welfare.[8] They also found that the briefer a person's expected duration of unemployment, the shorter his or her stay on welfare. However, both of these variables were constructed "from a not very rich data source," and thus they "may be picking up the influence of other characteristics." Boskin and Nold also found that blacks were less likely to leave welfare than whites. Perhaps of equal importance are the factors they found not to be significant in predicting the probability of leaving welfare. Such factors were age less than 23, unskilled occupation, adverse health affecting employability, and presence of preschool children. The latter finding seems particularly odd, given the findings of Rydell.

Perhaps the most extensive analysis of the welfare use over the long run was done by Harrison (1977). His sample was 2,688 women from the Panel Study, aged 24 to 54 in 1968 (Note: His lower age cutoff of 24 years could be crucial, given that in 1973 half of mothers on AFDC were less than age 30.) He looked at their

---

[8]They attributed this finding to the minimum wage precluding such people from employment. This explanation is somewhat questionable, given the finding that work and welfare often go together, especially in long-term welfare cases.

experience over the five-year period from 1967 through 1971. Two questions which he looked at are of particular concern to us: Over the five-year period, how many households were there that ever received welfare (AFDC, AFDC-UP, GA, etc.)? Of these, how many had multiple spells of receiving it? He attempted to explain these experiences with four types of variables: class inheritance, human capital, eligibility status, and labor market structure.

Harrison found that the class inheritance variables[9] and all the human capital variables[10] except age were insignificant predictors of whether the household was ever on welfare during the five-year period. Age was positively related to the likelihood of ever being on welfare, but at a decreasing rate. The eligibility variables (age of youngest child, number of dependent children) were highly significant. Three of the six labor market variables were also significant. If the unemployment rate in the county of residence was greater than 6 percent, the probability of going on welfare increased. If the household head had ever belonged to a labor union, the probability of ever being on welfare was decreased by 5.5 percent. Finally, if the household head worked in a job (defined as a specific industry-occupation combination) which had a high national wage rate, the probability of going on welfare was reduced. Labor market variables such as whether the county had a surplus of unskilled labor or a typical unskilled wage rate of less than $2.50, or whether the household lived within 30 miles of the nearest SMSA, were insignificant.

Turning to multiple spells (a "spell," incidentally, was not precisely defined—this writer believes he means more than one year), Harrison again found the class inheritance variables to be insignificant. He did find that veteran status reduced the probability of repeated welfare use by 11 percent. A similar reduced effect was found for whether the household head had grown up in the South. Other human capital variables were either insignificant or had very small effects. Each additional dependent child increased the probability of repeated welfare use by 5 percent. Two of the labor market variables exerted strong effects. If the family resided in a city with an unemployment rate greater than

---

[9] These variables were: whether their parents were poor and whether the father had a blue-collar job.

[10] These variables were: high school graduate, whether a veteran, whether the household head had completed a formal training program, opportunity wage, whether the household head had grown up in the South or in a rural area, and other family income.

6 percent, the probability of multiple welfare spells <u>increased</u> by 19 percent;
and union membership decreased the probability of multiple spells by 24 percent.

Summarizing his remarks, Harrison concluded that the variables which
systematically were most powerful were those over which the individual had little
control. Human capital variables, often thought to be the most important, were
generally insignificant.

Neither Boskin nor Nold and Harrison attempted explicitly to link <u>change</u>
variables to <u>change</u> in welfare status; in other words, they did not examine the
actual dynamics of the welfare use. One of the few attempts to do this was by
Coe (1979b), who looked at the determinants of change in food stamp use between
1973 and 1976. Using an elaborate path model, he found that the act of going on
or off food stamps was closely linked to the AFDC status of the household. Those
households which had become AFDC recipients during the four-year period were
50 percent more likely to become food stamp recipients also. Households
receiving AFDC in 1976 were 30 to 40 percent less likely to stop using food
stamps by 1976. Coe found that the number of children in the household and
whether the household head was female were significant in predicting changing
food stamp patterns, primarily through their effect on AFDC status. One puzzling
aspect of these results, however, was that the steady state variables were often
as powerful as the change variables in predicting change. For example, in
predicting which households joined the food stamp program between 1973 and 1976
joining the AFDC program during that period had a strong effect, but remaining on
AFDC had an equally strong effect. Thus, it seems clear that Coe's analysis of
change failed to capture some of the dynamic aspects of changing welfare use.

One additional point of potential importance should be mentioned here. Lyon
(1976) reported that a Rand study had found short-term and multiple-time AFDC
cases had much higher levels of Medicaid-paid health care than did long-term
continuous cases. The authors of that study concluded that "a good deal of the
movement onto the rolls is caused by a demand for health care not covered by
private insurance plans, and ...welfare may mask a large number of families in
need of health insurance more than income maintenance" (p. 18).

The end result of the research on the welfare decision is that we appear to
know very little about the dynamics of welfare use. Much effort has been
directed toward the General Assistance and AFDC programs, some to the food stamp
program, and virtually none toward the more recent SSI program. The numerous
cross-sectional studies have yielded ambiguous results on the major question of
the benefit level/participation relationship. In any event, by its very nature,

cross-sectional data cannot allow the researcher to address explicitly the dynamic nature of welfare use. The longitudinal data bases have been less extensively examined, and few of those examinations have attempted to link change in causal conditions to change in welfare use. We do know that there is a tremendous amount of dynamism in welfare use, and it appears that factors such as family composition change, health, and the presence of children are important in the process. However, much needs to be learned, and the following additional analysis is intended to shed some further light on the topic.

EMPIRICAL ANALYSIS

We now have 12 years of Panel Study data, which is useful in analyzing both the patterns of welfare use and its determinants. The data on welfare income, unfortunately, are somewhat inconsistent across the years, particularly the early years. Consequently, the present empirical analysis is confined to the more recent years, spanning the decade from 1969 through 1978.

A Descriptive Look at Welfare Use Over a Ten-Year Period

We began by looking at all sample individuals in 1970 (broken down into selected subgroups) and examining the incidence and length of welfare receipt[11] between 1969 and 1978 (Table A4.1). (Appendix Table A4.1 provides more comprehensive information on number of years of welfare receipt by different types of welfare income.) Of the 12,562 sample individuals in 1970, one-quarter (weighted percentage) received welfare during at least one year. Of all household heads and wives in 1970, 20 percent received welfare during at least one year. This percentage remained virtually unchanged both when female heads and wives alone were considered, and when elderly heads and wives were the group of interest. Children under the age of ten in 1970 were especially likely to have experienced welfare over the following ten years—over 30 percent were in households which received welfare during at least one year.

Black households were far more likely to receive welfare. Over 60 percent of all black individuals were in households which at some time between 1969 and 1978 received welfare. Of all black household heads and wives, slightly more than 50 percent received welfare. Sixty percent of the black wives and female heads and the elderly black household heads and wives were welfare recipients

---

[11]Welfare income includes receipt of AFDC, SSI, General Assistance payments, Old Age Assistance, Aid to the Disabled, and food stamps.

during at least one year. Black children were particularly prone to be in households which received welfare, with over 70 percent living in a household which received welfare during at least one year.

Welfare receipt, however, was not necessarily synonymous with welfare dependency--which is defined as meaning that at least one-half of the household head's and wife's combined income was welfare.[12] While over 25 percent of all sample individuals were on welfare in at least one year, somewhat less than 10 percent were in households which were dependent on welfare income for at least one year. This percentage did not vary much across the different subgroups of individuals. Blacks, however, were more likely than whites to be dependent on welfare income. One-third of all black individuals lived in households which were dependent on welfare income during at least one year out of the ten, and almost one-half of the black children were in welfare dependent households for at least one year. We found that a larger percentage of individuals were likely to receive food stamps than cash assistance. It is also interesting to note that children in general, and black children in particular, were especially likely to be in households where food stamps were used. Appendix Table A4.2 breaks down the pattern of receipt (for a different sample over a slightly different time period) by the various individual welfare programs.

That long-term welfare receipt is the exception rather than the rule among welfare recipients can be seen from Table 4.2 (based on the results shown in Table 4.1). Of all sample individuals who were in households receiving welfare during at least one year, one-quarter (25.8 percent) received it for more than five years. Almost one-third (31.3 percent) received it for just one year. (Given the problem of overlapping years this is a lower bound estimate on short-term welfare use.) Young children were more likely than other groups to be long-term users. One-third of them who were in households which received welfare at some time received it for six years or more. Black welfare recipients were clearly more likely to be long-term recipients. Almost one-half (46.1 percent) of black welfare recipients received it for more than five years during the ten-year period. Black children were particularly prone to long-run welfare receipt, with almost 60 percent of such recipients receiving it for more than five years.

---

[12]Food stamps were evaluated at the cash value of the bonus value.

Table 4.1

DISTRIBUTION OF WELFARE USE PATTERNS, 1969-1978

Source of Welfare	All Sample Individuals		Heads and Wives[a]							
			All		Female[b]		Elderly[c]		Children[d]	
	All	Black	All	Black	All	Black	All	Black	All	Black
Percentage Receiving Welfare in At Least One Year										
All welfare programs	25.2	61.8	19.5	52.5	22.6	60.3	19.4	58.9	32.8	73.3
Cash welfare programs	16.1	49.0	12.0	38.6	14.1	45.9	15.8	49.9	20.8	59.2
Food stamp program[a]	21.7	56.4	16.0	46.4	19.5	56.2	12.8	45.7	30.6	70.7
Percentage for Whom Welfare Amounted to at Least Half of Income in at Least One Year										
All welfare programs	8.7	33.9	5.8	23.7	8.0	31.9	6.7	25.0	13.3	45.8
Cash welfare programs	8.7	33.9	5.4	22.2	7.7	30.6	6.4	22.9	12.6	42.8
Food stamp program[e]	1.3	6.2	0.7	3.3	1.3	5.2	0.4	1.4	1.9	9.3
Sample size	12,562	5,013	5,573	1,676	2,700	996	1,008	196	3,150	1,501

[a] Head or wife in 1970.
[b] Age 55 or less in 1970.
[c] Age 56 or more in 1970.
[d] Age less than 10 in 1970.
[e] For food stamps the ten year period covers 1968-1971 and 1972-1978. No data were available for food stamp use in 1972. Food stamp income was defined as equal to the bonus value of the stamps.

Table 4.2

DISTRIBUTION OF WELFARE RECIPIENTS BY LENGTH OF
WELFARE RECEIPT FOR SELECTED SUBGROUPS, 1969-1978

Number of Years of Welfare Receipt	All Sample Individuals		Heads and Wives[a]							
			All		Female[b]		Elderly[c]		Children[d]	
	All	Black	All	Black	All	Black	All	Black	All	Black
1	31.3	14.9	35.4	21.0	33.6	19.6	27.3	13.4	26.5	10.0
2-5	42.9	39.0	41.5	38.5	39.8	34.5	38.1	44.1	39.6	30.4
6-9	17.9	30.9	15.4	27.0	17.3	29.4	19.1	30.2	22.0	37.7
10	7.9	15.2	7.7	13.5	8.8	16.7	10.8	12.4	11.9	22.1

[a]Head or wife in 1970.
[b]Age 55 or less in 1970.
[c]Age 56 or more in 1970.
[d]Age less than 10 in 1970.

The Composition of the Welfare Population

Table 4.3 shows the composition of the welfare population, broken down according to the number of years of welfare receipt. (Table 4.4 presents similar results for the welfare dependent population.) Reading across row 2 of Table 4.3, we see that black individuals accounted for 13.7 percent of all individuals who received welfare for one year only. Individuals who were either household heads or wives in 1970 accounted for 46.2 percent of all one-year welfare recipients. Black household heads and wives comprised 6.6 percent of all one-year recipients, and non-black household heads and wives accounted for 39.6 percent of this group.

Table 4.3

COMPOSITION OF WELFARE RECIPIENT POPULATION, BY
NUMBER OF YEARS OF ANY WELFARE RECEIPT, 1969–1978

Number of Years of Welfare Receipt	All Black Individuals	Percentage of Individuals with Specified Number of Years of Welfare Receipt							
		Heads and Wives[a]		Female Heads and Wives[b]		Elderly Heads and Wives[c]		Children[d]	
		All	Black	All	Black	All	Black	All	Black
0	6.0	56.7	3.0	23.4	1.3	13.3	0.5	17.8	1.0
1	13.7	46.2	6.6	21.7	3.6	8.3	1.0	21.9	2.6
2–5	26.3	39.6	8.9	18.9	4.7	9.7	2.4	24.0	5.9
6–9	49.6	35.3	14.9	20.0	9.4	10.0	3.9	31.6	17.4
10	54.8	38.1	16.8	22.3	12.2	12.7	3.6	38.6	23.1
All	11.7	52.7	4.7	22.6	2.4	12.4	1.0	19.8	2.9

[a]Head or wife in 1970.
[b]Female head or wife under age 56 in 1970.
[c]Head or wife age 56 or more in 1970.
[d]Age less than 10 in 1970.

The point of interest in Table 4.3 is the comparison of these percentages as the number of years of welfare receipt increased. Such a comparison shows that black individuals--in particular black female heads of households, black wives and black children--accounted for a substantially larger percentage of the long-term than the short-term welfare population. For example, while black individuals comprised 13.7 percent of all one-year welfare recipients, they accounted for over one-half (54.8 percent) of the ten-year welfare recipients. This finding can be seen most dramatically in the results for young black children. they were 2.6 percent of the one-year welfare population but 23.1 percent of the ten-year welfare population (almost ten times their proportion of the sample of individuals). Black female heads of households and black wives also showed a substantial increase in the larger time frame, from 3.6 percent of the one-year population to 12.2 percent of the ten-year population. The black female heads and wive, it might be concluded, have the major responsibility for caring for the young black children.

Table 4.4

COMPOSITION OF WELFARE-DEPENDENT[a] POPULATION,
BY NUMBER OF YEARS OF DEPENDENCY, 1969-1978

Number of Years of Welfare Dependency	All Black Individuals	Heads and Wives[b]		Female Heads and Wives[c]		Elderely Heads and Wives[d]		Children[e]	
		All	Black	All	Black	All	Black	All	Black
0	8.5	54.4	4.0	22.8	1.8	12.6	0.8	18.8	1.7
1	40.6	39.2	9.4	19.5	4.9	13.1	2.7	25.6	10.7
2-5	41.4	35.8	13.2	21.0	8.7	9.9	3.0	29.0	12.6
6-9	56.9	29.5	14.6	19.5	10.8	7.3	3.5	32.7	20.4
10	55.3	34.2	16.3	28.2	15.6	3.9	0.5	44.5	27.0
All	11.7	52.7	4.7	22.6	2.4	12.4	1.0	19.8	2.9

Percentage of Individuals with Specified
Number of Years of Welfare Dependency

[a] Dependency is defined as at least half of head and wives' total income coming from welfare.
[b] Head or wife in 1970.
[c] Female head or wife under age 56 in 1970.
[d] Head or wife age 56 or more in 1970.
[e] Age less than 10 in 1970.

A comparison of Tables 4.3 and 4.4 shows how the composition of the welfare-recipient population differed from the welfare-dependent population. The major difference of note was that elderly household heads and wives comprised a substantially smaller proportion of the ten-year dependent population (3.9 percent) than they did of the ten-year recipient population (12.7 percent).

This may reflect the fact that elderly persons had alternative sources to draw on over the more extended period, such as help from relatives or social security.

The Dynamic Nature of Welfare Use

In addition to looking at differences in the length of time individuals spent on welfare, it is also interesting to see whether welfare was received in one continuous spell or intermittantly. Tables 4.5 and 4.6 address this aspect of welfare use. Table 4.5 shows the percentage of all household heads and wives in 1970 who received welfare in each of the individual years, along with the percentage who received it in one year and in the following year. Corresponding figures are provided for elderly household heads and wives, female heads of households and wives, and black female heads of households and wives. Some points of note from this table:

1. From 1970 to 1978, the aggregate percentage of the group of individuals who received some welfare in a given year did not change much. In 1970, 7.4 percent of all household heads and wives received welfare, 7.6 percent received it in 1978. This implies that the increase in the number of welfare recipients which the country has experienced in the last decade is a result of younger people forming their own households and receiving welfare, and not from the fact that a given group of household heads and wives have become more likely over the ten-year period to receive welfare. An exception to this is the group of elderly household heads and wives (over age 55). In 1970, 7.1 percent received welfare, but by 1978 that percentage had increased to 11.4 percent. The big increase occurred in 1974, the year the Supplemental Security Income program was initiated.

2. By the end of the observation period food stamp receipt equalled or exceeded cash welfare receipt, for all welfare recipients except elderly persons.

3. In general, between 70 and 75 percent of the welfare recipients in any one year received some welfare in the following year. This figure was somewhat lower for food stamp recipients and was higher for elderly household heads and wives and for black female heads and wives.

Perhaps more to the point on the welfare cycling issue are the results presented in Table 4.6, which show the percentage of welfare recipients with multiple spells of welfare receipt. Because the individuals with just one year of welfare receipt and those who received welfare for the entire ten years did not cycle on and off welfare, our attention now focuses on those individuals who received welfare for an intermediate length of time. Of those individuals who

Table 4.5
YEAR-BY-YEAR TRANSITION PROBABILITIES OF
WELFARE USE BY TYPE OF WELFARE, 1969-1978
(Heads and wives in 1970.)

Year	All		Female[a]		Black Female[a]		Elderly[b]	
	All	Prior Year Recipients	All	Prior Year Recipients	All	Prior Year Recipients	All	Prior Year Recipients

Percentage Receiving Welfare/All Welfare Programs

Year	All	Prior Year Recipients	All	Prior Year Recipients	All	Prior Year Recipients	All	Prior Year Recipients
1969	4.3		5.7		23.0		5.0	
1970	7.4	83.9	9.2	85.0	30.0	90.2	7.1	89.7
1971	7.4	71.0	9.8	75.1	32.9	87.1	6.9	77.7
1972	4.1[c]	47.8[c]	6.1[c]	54.4[c]	25.5[c]	67.2[c]	4.2[c]	52.9[c]
1973	6.6	78.1	8.4	79.0	33.3	86.3	7.4	83.5
1974	8.0	73.9	9.2	72.4	36.6	84.0	10.2	84.6
1975	8.9	73.6	10.1	74.7	38.3	82.2	11.4	81.5
1976	7.9	66.4	9.5	68.8	32.8	72.1	9.4	71.5
1977	7.4	70.9	8.9	72.5	34.1	83.3	10.0	80.5
1978	7.6	74.5	8.6	73.0	32.3	76.9	11.4	88.0

Cash Welfare Programs

Year	All	Prior Year Recipients	All	Prior Year Recipients	All	Prior Year Recipients	All	Prior Year Recipients
1969	3.6		5.0		19.0		4.0	
1970	4.5	83.9	6.1	84.9	22.3	92.5	4.9	88.1
1971	4.4	69.6	6.4	75.2	25.1	86.9	4.5	69.6
1972	4.1	70.8	6.1	75.5	25.5	83.3	4.2	72.5
1973	4.1	67.2	6.0	70.8	25.7	79.3	4.0	69.0
1974	4.8	76.3	6.0	73.8	26.6	84.8	7.2	88.3
1975	5.6	76.5	6.1	75.7	25.1	77.1	9.7	80.5
1976	5.2	72.5	6.2	75.5	24.2	79.8	8.1	72.9
1977	5.1	75.0	5.9	76.4	24.6	78.3	8.4	77.5
1978	5.4	76.7	6.0	74.7	22.1	73.1	9.1	82.4

Food Stamp Program

Year	All	Prior Year Recipients	All	Prior Year Recipients	All	Prior Year Recipients	All	Prior Year Recipients
1969	2.1		2.6		10.9		2.8	
1970	5.5	82.9	6.8	79.9	23.4	78.2	5.1	91.4
1971	5.4	67.3	7.2	71.3	25.1	84.0	5.0	78.7
1972	--	--	--	--	--	--	--	--
1973	5.5	--	6.8	--	27.4	--	6.1	--
1974	6.5	73.0	8.1	75.5	30.5	80.4	6.4	73.5
1975	6.6	67.9	8.6	71.1	31.9	76.2	5.6	72.6
1976	5.9	61.3	7.8	63.5	26.3	65.8	4.7	65.7
1977	5.3	63.3	7.0	63.3	24.8	71.7	4.9	81.8
1978	5.4	67.7	6.8	69.2	26.9	75.4	6.3	85.3
Sample size		5,573		2,700		996		1,008

[a] Age 55 or less in 1970.
[b] Age 56 or more in 1970.
c Does not include food stamp recipients in 1972.

145

Table 4.6

PERCENTAGE WITH MORE THAN ONE SPELL[e] OF WELFARE USE, 1969-1978

(Heads and wives in 1970.)

Number of Years Received Welfare	All Welfare Programs				Cash Welfare Programs				Food Stamp Program[a]			
	All	Female[b]	Black Female[b]	Elderly[c]	All	Female[b]	Black Female[b]	Elderly[c]	All	Female[b]	Black Female[b]	Elderly[c]
Zero	--	--	--	--	--	--	--	--	--	--	--	--
One	--	--	--	--	--	--	--	--	--	--	--	--
Two	32.8	34.4	51.6	20.6	36.0	36.5	32.8	34.6	27.4	32.1	52.4	15.7
Three	55.4	48.5	50.1	64.7	39.0	35.3	39.4	52.3	50.7	50.9	57.1	35.5
Four	56.7	63.7	54.2	44.9	43.4	52.3	32.1	29.2	45.9	45.8	58.5	56.4
Five	63.8	60.1	54.3	57.9	49.2	40.1	41.8	51.7	60.7	63.1	67.0	48.2
Six	67.4	64.3	83.6	72.0[d]	61.6	51.6	54.0	93.6[d]	45.0	39.0	35.0	63.6[d]
Seven	74.6	86.3	89.9	72.9[d]	69.7	67.0	57.8	80.1[d]	50.7	54.7	54.6	43.2[d]
Eight	57.4	47.8	61.0	61.3[d]	59.4	50.6	68.4	65.0[d]	15.4	9.5	16.5	21.0[d]
Nine	61.0	53.3	49.5	79.5	71.0	63.3	57.7	96.3[d]	47.6	55.2	37.3	31.0[d]
Ten	--	--	--	--	--	--	--	--	--	--	--	--

[a] For food stamps the ten year period covers 1968-1971 and 1973-1978. No data were available on food stamps use in 1972.
[b] Age 55 or less in 1970.
[c] Age 56 or more in 1970.
[d] Fewer than 20 observations.
[e] "Spell" is defined as consecutive years of welfare receipt.

received welfare from three to eight years, over one-half had multiple spells of welfare use (a spell is defined as consecutive years of welfare receipt). This is a clear indication that there is considerable cycling on and off welfare by welfare recipients. This result is reinforced by the results shown in Appendix Table A4.3, which gives the distribution of the number of starts and quits of welfare use from one year to the next (for a slightly different time period). These figures demonstrate that once people are on welfare they are not inescapably locked into the welfare system, nor once off of it are they necessarily freed from it for life. Instead, a substantial number of welfare recipients cycle on and off the welfare rolls. The reasons for such cycling will be examined in the next section.

THE DETERMINANTS OF WELFARE USE

We have seen in the previous section that a large percentage of the population receives welfare in at least one year over a ten-year period, that the percentage varies across subgroups of the population; that among the population of welfare recipients the length of time of welfare receipt varies considerably, and that there appears to be considerable cycling on and off welfare use. In this section we examine the factors which determine who receives welfare (and who is dependent on welfare income), the length of time that they receive welfare, and the dynamic nature of welfare use.

Caveats are in order. The analytical results presented here are not based on a precisely defined theory of welfare use and have not been subjected to the full battery of econometric tests. Consequently they should be viewed primarily as illustrative of the type of findings which can be revealed by long-term panel data.

Welfare Use and Dependency in a Given Year

The results of a pooled (over ten years) cross-sectional regression on welfare use and dependency are presented in Table 4.7. Because of possible simultaneity problems between welfare use and dependency and the work hours of the individual, two sets of results (one including work hours and one omitting them) are presented.[13]

Table 4.7 indicates that the primary determinants of welfare receipt in a given year were the composition of the household and the labor market experience of the head of the household. Being unmarried increased the probability of receiving welfare in a particular year by 2.3 percent (as shown in column one). If the unmarried head of household was female, the probability increased by an additional 6.5 percent. The effect of being unmarried was greatest on those persons who had at least one child under the age of seven in the household. While married persons with a young child in the household actually had a decreased probability of receiving welfare, being unmarried with a young child increased the probability by 20.2 percent. The result is perhaps not too surprising, given that one of the larger welfare programs, AFDC, requires a dependent child in the household and an absent or incapacited (and, in some states, unemployed) parent as a condition for eligibility.

The other crucial factor in explaining the receipt of welfare is the labor market experience of the head of the household. For every increase of 1000 hours of unemployment for the household head, the probability of receiving welfare increased 9.3 percent. This implies that if the head of the household went from working full-time to not working, he was 18.6 percent more likely to receive welfare. Furthermore, if the head of household lost his job as a result of an involuntary job change (the closing of the business, being fired, or laid off), the probability of welfare receipt increased an additional 5.4 percent. It is also of interest to note that the local unemployment rate also showed a positive effect on the probability of receiving welfare, even when the unemployment hours

---

[13]Omitting work hours of the individual from the equation predicting welfare receipt had two effects of note--the sign of the coefficient for both whether female and over the age of 55 switched from negative to positive. Both of these groups are more likely to have zero work hours, and when this factor is controlled for, their probability of welfare receipt is negative. That is, if an elderly person or a female is working, he/she is less likely to receive welfare. If work hours are not controlled for and we look at the probability of welfare receipt of a female or elderly person regardless of work hours, (but controlling for other factors listed in Table 4.7), the coefficient is positive, indicating that females and the elderly are more likely to receive welfare.

What these results indicate, then, is that women and the elderly are more likely to receive welfare, but a primary reason for this is their low work hours. The issue then becomes what are the determinants of their work hours. If the availability of welfare is a reason for their low work hours, then a simultaneity problem exists. If so, then a more properly specified model than estimated here is called for.

Table 4.7 (page 1 of 2)
POOLED REGRESSIONS ON ONE-YEAR WELFARE USE AND ONE-YEAR WELFARE DEPENDENCY, 1969-1978
(Heads and wives 1970, N=10,070.)

Independent Variables	Whether Received Any Welfare in Given Year (Mean=.088)				Whether Welfare Income Accounted for at Least One-Half of Income of Head and Wife (Mean=.046)			
	(1)	(2)	(3)	(4)	(1)	(2)	(3)	(4)
Constant	.077	-.075	.021	-.034	.078	-.029	.040	-.004
Personal Characteristics								
Whether female	-.032** (.009)	.017** (.008)	-.015* (.007)	.003 (.006)	-.032** (.007)	.003 (.006)	-.021** (.006)	-.006 (.005)
Whether black	.104** (.009)	.106** (.009)	.027** (.007)	.027** (.007)	.039** (.007)	.041** (.007)	-.011+ (.006)	-.0111* (.006)
Education in 1970	-.003** (.001)	-.004** (.001)	-.001 (.001)	-.0010+ (.0005)	-.0012* (.0006)	-.0020** (.0006)	.000 (.000)	-.000 (.000)
Expected wage	-.0035** (.0005)	-.0045** (.0005)	-.0010* (.0004)	-.0014** (.0004)	-.0022** (.0004)	-.0029** (.0004)	-.0006+ (.0003)	-.0008* (.0003)
Under age 35 in 1970	.001 (.007)	-.001 (.007)	-.002 (.006)	-.003 (.006)	-.014* (.006)	-.016** (.006)	-.017** (.005)	-.017** (.005)
Age 35-55 in 1970	--	--	--	--	--	--	--	--
Over Age 55 in 1970	-.027** (.007)	.022** (.007)	-.004 (.006)	.014* (.005)	-.040** (.006)	-.006 (.005)	-.026** (.005)	-.011 (.005)
Family Characteristics								
Whether unmarried	.023* (.010)	.041** (.010)	.066 (.008)	.012 (.008)	.018* (.008)	.031** (.008)	.007 (.007)	.012+ (.007)
Whether unmarried and whether female	.097** (.015)	.045** (.015)	.038** (.012)	.018 (.012)	.064** (.012)	.028* (.012)	.027** (.010)	.011 (.010)
Number of children under age 18	.049** (.002)	.049** (.002)	.015** (.002)	.015** (.002)	.028** (.002)	.028** (.002)	.006** (.001)	.006** (.001)
Whether at least one child age 6 or less	-.039** (.008)	-.034** (.008)	-.002 (.006)	.000 (.006)	-.028** (.006)	-.025** (.006)	-.004 (.005)	-.002 (.005)
Whether child age 6 or less x whether unmarried	.218** (.017)	.230** (.018)	.100** (.013)	.102** (.013)	.241** (.013)	.249** (.013)	.164** (.011)	.166** (.011)
Non-labor, non-welfare income of head and wife ($1,000)	-.0017** (.0003)	-.0010** (.0003)	-.0007** (.0002)	-.0004+ (.0002)	-.0012** (.0002)	-.0008** (.0002)	-.0006** (.0002)	-.0004+ (.0002)

Table 4.7 (page 2 of 2)

Independent Variables	Whether Received Any Welfare in Given Year (Mean=.088)				Whether Welfare Income Accounted for at Least One-Half of Income of Head and Wife (Mean=.046)			
	(1)	(2)	(3)	(4)	(1)	(2)	(3)	(4)
Area Characteristics								
City size (hundred thousands)	-.0004 (.0007)	-.0001 (.0007)	-.0001 (.0005)	-.0000 (.0005)	.0014** (.0005)	.0016** (.0005)	.0016** (.0005)	.0017** (.0005)
Northeast	.040** (.007)	.045** (.007)	.009 (.006)	.010+ (.006)	.025** (.006)	.028** (.006)	.004 (.005)	.005 (.005)
(North Central)	—	—	—	—	—	—	—	—
South	.018** (.007)	.019** (.007)	.007 (.005)	.007 (.005)	.010+ (.005)	.010* (.005)	.002 (.004)	.002 (.004)
West	.019* (.008)	.020* (.008)	.003 (.006)	.003 (.006)	.006 (.006)	.006 (.006)	-.005 (.005)	-.005 (.005)
Whether public transportation	.012* (.006)	.012* (.006)	.004 (.004)	.004 (.004)	.009* (.004)	.009* (.004)	.003 (.004)	.003 (.004)
Economic Environment								
County unemployment rate	.008** (.001)	.008** (.001)	.0043** (.0010)	.0044** (.0010)	.002+ (.001)	.002+ (.001)	-.0004 (.0008)	-.0004 (.0008)
National unemployment rate	.001 (.002)	.009** (.002)	-.003* (.001)	-.000 (.001)	-.001 (.002)	.005** (.002)	-.003** (.001)	-.001 (.001)
National inflation rate	.002+ (.001)	-.000 (.001)	.003** (.001)	.003** (.001)	.002* (.001)	.001 (.001)	.003** (.001)	.003** (.001)
Whether bad unskilled local labor market	.009 (.007)	.008 (.007)	-.001 (.005)	-.002 (.005)	.010+ (.005)	.009+ (.005)	.003 (.004)	.003 (.004)
Individual Labor Market Experience								
Work Hours, Individual (thousands)	-.061** (.003)	—	-.022** (.003)	—	-.043** (.002)	—	-.018** (.002)	—
Unemployment hours of head (thousands)	.093** (.013)	.117** (.013)	.058** (.010)	.065** (.010)	.017+ (.010)	.034** (.010)	-.006 (.008)	-.0001 (.0085)
Whether involuntary job change	.054** (.014)	.052** (.015)	-.022* (.011)	.021+ (.011)	-.004 (.011)	-.006 (.001)	-.024* (.009)	-.024** (.009)
Previous Welfare Experience								
Whether received any welfare in previous year	—	—	.488** (.010)	.496** (.0100)	—	—	.283** (.008)	.289** (.008)
Whether received any welfare two years earlier	—	—	.220** (.010)	.226** (.010)	—	—	.179** (.008)	.184** (.008)
R^2 (adjusted)	.234	.208	.544	.541	.180	.157	.414	.410

Significance Levels:
**.01 *.05 +.10

of the household head were controlled. Local welfare officials may become more inclined to certify welfare applicants as eligible under these conditions, or perhaps individuals apply for welfare earlier when conditions in the local economy begin to deteriorate.

When the results were compared to those for welfare dependency in a particular year, the family composition variables again were quite important, but the labor market experience variables either lost significance or, if still significant, the size of the effect was considerably smaller. This suggests that while a bad labor market experience may force a person to seek welfare assistance, such assistance is more in the nature of supplemental aid (until another job is found) rather than the sole means of existence of the individual. Those persons caught in an unfortunate family situation, however, appeared to have little recourse other than welfare income.

The same equations were estimated with the inclusion of two variables which measured the previous welfare experience of the individual. These variables were quite powerful, so much so that they took away the explanatory significance of several of the variables discussed above. It is clear that previous contact with the welfare system is positively related to future contact, but why this is so is not clear from these results.

Distinguishing between Short and Long-Term Welfare Receipt

In Table 4.8 attention is focused on only those individuals who received welfare in at least one of the ten years between 1969 and 1978 (inclusive). The four columns on the left show the effect of a selected set of variables on whether or not the individual received welfare in just one year out of the ten (short-run receipt); the four columns on the right deal with whether or not the individual received welfare in at least six of the ten years (long-run receipt). A comparison of the two sets of estimates yields some idea of what factors distinguish short-term welfare recipients from long-term welfare recipients. (The omitted category is intermediate-term, or two to five year, welfare recipients.)

The relationship between sex and marital status stands out clearly from these results. A married female welfare recipient was more likely to be a short-term recipient and was considerably less likely to be a long-term recipient. The opposite held true for unmarried women, as evidenced by the interaction term of number of years unmarried times whether female. (But note that male welfare recipients who were unmarried were also more likely to be long-term recipients.)

Table 4.8 (page 1 of 2)
REGRESSIONS ON SHORT AND LONG TERM WELFARE RECEIPT, 1969-1978
(Heads and wives in 1970 who received welfare
in at least one year; N=1,763.)

Independent Variables	Whether 1 Year of Welfare Receipt[a]		Whether 6 Years or More of Welfare Receipt[b]	
	(1)	(2)	(1)	(2)
Constant	.065	.066	.690	.711
Personal Charcteristics				
Whether female	.093** (.034)	.094** (.034)	-.223** (.028)	-.225** (.028)
Whether black	-.093** (.025)	-.110* (.046)	.105** (.021)	.046 (.028)
Education in 1970	.019** (.003)	.019** (.003)	-.011** (.002)	-.011** (.003)
Expected wage	.0008 (.0032)	.0007 (.0032)	-.006* (.003)	-.006* (.003)
Under age 35 in 1970	.086** (.030)	.085** (.030)	.003 (.025)	.004 (.025)
(Age 35-55 in 1970)	--	--	--	--
Over age 55 in 1970	-.089** (.033)	-.086* (.032)	-.039 (.028)	-.042 (.028)
Family Characteristics				
Number of years unmarried	-.011+ (.006)	-.012+ (.006)	.013* (.005)	.013* (.005)
Number of years unmarried x whether female	-.026** (.007)	-.026** (.007)	.031** (.005)	.031** (.006)
Average number of children under age 18	-.028** (.008)	-.028** (.009)	.048** (.007)	.046** (.007)
Number of years with at least one child age 6 or less	-.019** (.005)	-.019** (.005)	-.002 (.004)	-.005 (.004)
Average non-labor, non-welfare income of head and wife ($1,000)	.028** (.006)	.028** (.006)	-.042** (.005)	-.042** (.005)

Table 4.8 (page 2 of 2)

Independent Variables	Whether 1 Year of Welfare Receipt[a]		Whether 6 Years or More of Welfare Receipt[b]	
	(1)	(2)	(1)	(2)
Economic Environment				
Average county unemployment rate	.011+ (.006)	.011+ (.006)	.011* (.005)	.012* (.005)
Individual Labor Market Experience				
Average work hours, individual (thousands)	.143** (.021)	.143** (.021)	-.244** (.017)	-.245** (.017)
Average unemployment hours, head (thousands)	-.360** (.091)	-.358** (.091)	.113 (.076)	.106 (.076)
Number of involuntary job changes	-.048** (.012)	-.049** (.012)	-.029** (.010)	-.027** (.010)
Black Interactions				
Number of years unmarried x whether black	--	.004 (.006)	--	.002 (.005)
Number of years with at least one child age 6 or less x whether black	--	-.000 (.007)	--	.016** (.006)
R^2 (adjusted)	.028	.207	.294	.297

[a] Mean for whether 1 year of welfare receipt is .355.
[b] Mean for whether 6 years or more of welfare receipt is .230.
Significance levels:
**.01 *.05 +.10

Other demographic factors operated for the most part in the expected way. The more educated a person was the more likely he or she was to be only a short-term welfare recipient. Younger people were also more likely to be only short-term recipients, while elderly people were more likely to be intermediate term welfare recipients. The more children in the household, the more likely the household head or wife was to be a long-term welfare recipient.

One of the more powerful variables in distinguishing between short and long-term welfare receipt was race. Blacks were much more likely to be long-term rather than short-term welfare recipients. Two interaction terms were entered into the estimation equation to investigate the reasons for the difference. The interaction terms showed no effect in predicting short-term receipt. In predicting long-term use, however, the interaction between race and the presence of a young child was highly significant. (The race variable per se became insignificant.) Thus, it would seem that a primary reason why blacks are more likely to be long-term welfare recipients is that they often have young children at home, resulting in reduced opportunities to find alternative means of support.

(Appendix Table A4.4 shows the results of a regression for number of years of welfare receipt for all sample individuals and includes the same set of independent variables; the results were similar to those shown in Table 4.8.)

Predicting the Dynamics of Welfare Use

Table 4.7 shows the results of a traditional, static cross-sectional examination of welfare use. That analysis related current year welfare receipt to current state variables. The results allow us to make certain inferences concerning the effects of a change in a particular state on the change in welfare use, although no estimate was made which related changes directly to each other. With cross-sectional data, we must rely on inferences about the effect of change on change. With panel data, however, such propositions can be tested directly. If the two sets of results agree, we can be confident that we have identified the actual determinants of welfare receipt. If the static and the dynamic results differ greatly, then further testing is necessary in order to acquire a complete picture of the determinants of welfare use.

We attempted to capture the dynamic aspects of welfare use in Tables 4.9 and 4.10. In Table 4.9 we looked at individuals who did not receive welfare in a given year to see what changes (or initial conditions) distinguished those who received welfare in the following year from those who did not. In other words, we examined the act of going on welfare from one year to the next.

Some initial unchanging conditions were significant in predicting going on welfare, in particular whether the person was female and whether he or she was black. The effect of being black was similar to that found in the cross-sectional analysis, with the coefficient being relatively large and highly significant. A comparison of the effect of being female was complicated by the fact that initial marital status was not completely controlled for in the dynamic analysis. Still, the effect on women of becoming separated stood out--it increased the probability of going on welfare by 9 percent, the effect for men was insignificant. (This compares to a 9.7 percent increased probability of an unmarried female being on welfare in a given year, as shown in Table 4.7.)

The effect of having children in the household also stood out. The probability of going on welfare increased by 2.5 percentage points for each child

Table 4.9 (page 1 of 2)
POOLED REGRESSION ON WHETHER STARTED RECEIVING WELFARE IN YEAR t, 1969-1978[a]
(Heads and wives in year t-1 who did not receive any welfare; N=8,831.)

Independent Variables	Mean	Regression Coefficient
Constant		.004
Personal Characteristics		
Whether female	.411	.020** (.005)
Whether black	.116	.061** (.008)
Education in 1970	9.7	-.006** (.001)
Expected wage	7.67	-.0013* (.0006)
Under age 35 in 1970	.258	-.006 (.007)
(Age 35-55 in 1970)	--	--
Over age 55 in 1970	.372	-.002 (.006)
Change in Family Characteristics		
Became separated in year t	.031	.007 (.026)
Became separated x whether female	--	.090** (.031)
Change in number of kids under age 18	-.048	.025** (.006)
(Did not have child age 6 or less in year t or year t-1)	--	--
Had child age 6 or less in year t and year t-1	.230	.056** (.007)
Had child age 6 or less in year t-1, did not in year t	.039	.041** (.013)
Had child age 6 or less in year t did not in year t-1	.020	.209** (.040)
Gained child age 6 or less x whether married in year t	--	-.183** (.044)
Change in non-labor, non-welfare income of head and wife ($1,000)	.147	-.0007 (.0007)

Table 4.9 (page 2 of 2)

Independent Variables	Mean	Regression Coefficient
Change in Area Characteristics		
Change in city size (hundred thousands)	-.036	.0026 (.0016)
Change in county unemployment rate	.131	-.001 (.001)
Change in national unemployment rate	.298	-.004 (.002)
Inflation rate	6.63	.010** (.001)
(Local unskilled labor market remained good)	--	--
Local unskilled labor market improved	.123	-.005 (.008)
Local unskilled labor market worsened	.131	.019* (.008)
Local unskilled labor market remained bad	.140	.036** (.007)
Individual Labor Market Experience		
Change work hours, individual (thousands)	-.3154	-.003 (.002)
Change unemployment hours, head (thousands)	.0015	.051** (.010)
Whether involuntary job change	.040	.058** (.013)
Previous Welfare Experience		
Whether received any welfare in year t-2	.106	.069** (.008)
Whether received any welfare in year t-3	.022	.064** (.008)
R^2(adjusted)		.069

[a]Mean for whether started receiving welfare in year t is .059.
Significance levels:
**.01   *.05   +.10

Table 4.10 (page 1 of 2)
POOLED REGRESSIONS ON WHETHER STOPPED RECEIVING WELFARE IN YEAR t, 1969-1978[a]
(Heads and wives in year t-1 who received any welfare; N=2,814.)

Independent Variables	Mean	Regression Coefficient
Constant		.603
Personal Characteristics		
Whether female	.675	-.120** (.018)
Whether black	.400	-.078** (.017)
Education in 1970	8.11	.010** (.002)
Expected wage	6.22	.016** (.003)
Under age 35 in 1970	.221	.039+ (.023)
(Age 35-55 in 1970)	--	--
Over age 55 in 1970	.382	-.008 (.019)
Change in Family Characteristics		
Became married	.024	.084+ (.051)
Change in number of children age 18	-.096	.030* (.013)
(Did not have child age 6 or less in year t or year t-1)	--	--
Had child age 6 or less in year t and year t-1	.266	-.051* (.022)
Had child age 6 or less in year t-2, did not in year t	.056	.113** (.037)
Had child age 6 or less in year t, did not in year t-1	.030	.093+ (.049)
Change in non-labor, non-welfare income of head and wife ($1,000)	.019	.0016 (.0046)

Table 4.10 (page 2 of 2)

Independent Variables	Mean	Regression Coefficient
Change in city size (hundred thousands)	-.040	-.0081 (.0051)
Change in Economic Environment		
Change in county unemployment rate	-.113	.003 (.003)
Change in national unemployment rate	.285	-.001 (.008)
Inflation rate	6.64	-.029** (.004)
(Local unskilled labor market remained good)	--	--
Local unskilled labor market improved	.176	-.047* (.022)
Local unskilled labor market worsened	.135	-.074** (.025)
Local unskilled labor market remained bad	.234	-.019 (.020)
Individual Labor Market Experience Change work hours, individual (thousands)	-.390	.027** (.005)
Change unemployment hours, head (thousands)	-.051	-.100** (.019)
Previous Welfare Experience Whether received any welfare in year t-2	.694	-.125** (.019)
Whether received any welfare in year t-3	.539	-.132** (.018)
R^2(adjusted)		.203

[a]Mean for whether stopped receiving welfare in year t is .292.

Significance levels:
**.01 *.05 +.10

under the age of 18 that was added to the household. If that added child was age six or less, the household's probability of going on welfare increased an additional 20.9 percentage points--unless the household head was married, in which case there was only a 2.6 percentage point increase in the probability. This addition of children to the unmarried household was by far the single greatest contributor to the probability of starting welfare. Furthermore, if a young child was present in the household during the previous year, the probability of going on welfare also increased, even though the presence of the child in the previous year did not result in welfare receipt. In sum, as was found in the cross-sectional results, the presence of children in general and in the household of an unmarried person in particular, was a primary determinant of the change from non-welfare use to welfare use.

Again, however, the foregoing statement should not be read to mean that labor market variables are unimportant. As the results in Table 4.9 indicate, the condition of the local labor market and the individual´s personal experience with it were significant in predicting whether a non-welfare recipient went on welfare or not. If the local labor market for unskilled workers worsened between years or remained bad, the probability of becoming a welfare recipient increased.[14] In addition to this environmental effect, the labor market experience of the head of the household could further increase the probability of going on welfare. If the head of the household went from fully employed in a given year to completely unemployed the following year, the probability of the household going on welfare in that second year increased by 10.2 percent. Moreover, if the job loss occurred because of an involuntary job change, the probability increased by an additional 5.8 percentage points.

Finally, we see that previous experience with the welfare system increased the probability of a nonrecipient going on welfare. Although, again, we cannot tell if this reflects a causal link (such as learning how to apply for welfare), two points are worth noting from the results shown in Table 4.9. First, whatever the operating force behind the significance of previous welfare experience, it did not appear to decrease (or increase) over time, at least over a three year span. The size of the effect of being on welfare three years ago on the current likelihood of going on welfare (6.4 percent increased likelihood) is similar to the size of the effect of being on welfare two years ago. (If the person received welfare in both of these previous years, then the combined effect was considerably larger.) Or, put another way, the effect of previous welfare experience on the probability of going back on welfare, other factors controlled for, was the same whether the previous experience occurred two or three years before. The other point of note is that the effect of previous welfare

---

[14]"Bad" is defined as "many more people looking for jobs than there are jobs available," as reported by county employment officials.

experience appears to be considerably smaller than the effect found from the cross-sectional results presented in Table 4.7. If we wished to predict the third-year welfare status of an individual who had a previous two-year history of welfare receipt/no welfare receipt, the cross-sectional results would imply that the initial year of welfare receipt would increase the probability of receiving welfare in the third year by 22 percent. The dynamic results of Table 4.9 would suggest an increased probability of only 6.9 percent.

Welfare Quits

To round out the story, an attempt was made to ascertain the factors which distinguished welfare recipients in a given year and who did not receive welfare in the succeeding year from those who did receive it in the following year; to determine, in other words, what factors determine welfare quits. The effort was only moderately successful, as some of the results were consistent with earlier findings while others were not (Table 4.10). Blacks and women were less likely to stop receiving welfare. However, contrary to expectations, an interaction term between sex and becoming married was insignificant. The children variables produced some puzzling results. An increase in the number of children in the household increased the probability of quitting, a difficult result to explain. On the other hand, if the household lost a child under the age of seven (either through aging or a change in the composition of the household members), the probability of quitting increased. This was as expected, except that in Table 4.9 we saw that such an event also increased the probability of going on welfare. The lack of interaction terms with marital status may be partially responsible for the conflicting results.

Previous welfare experience was quite significant in distinguishing between welfare recipients who went off welfare and those who did not. Again, the effect did not appear to change over time and it was considerably smaller than was found in the cross-sectional results.

CONCLUSION

The major findings of this research can be summarized as follows:

1. When viewed over a ten-year perspective, welfare receipt is considerably more prevalent than one-year figures would suggest. Approximately one-quarter of all sample individuals lived in households which received welfare at some time during the ten-year period from 1969 to 1978 (inclusive). In any given year during this ten-year period, no more than 8.9 percent of all household heads and

wives received welfare; however, 20 percent received welfare at some time during the ten-years. Blacks were especially liable to get welfare, especially young black children; over 70 percent of the black children in our sample were in a household which received welfare during at least one of the ten years.

2. Although welfare receipt is more prevalent than is perhaps generally recognized, the number of persons who are dependent on welfare income in a given year is considerably smaller. Less than 10 percent of our sample individuals were in households in which the head and wife received at least half of their annual income from welfare. However, young black children were especially likely to be dependent on welfare; almost one-half of them were in households where 50 percent or more of their parent's income came from welfare during at least one of the ten years.

3. Long-term welfare receipt is the exception rather than the rule. Of all welfare recipients in this ten-year period, one-third received welfare during only one year (undoubtedly the upper-bound estimate of welfare receipt for a year or less), while approximately 25 percent received welfare in six or more of the ten years. Again, young black children were considerably more likely to need welfare on a long-term basis; fully 60 percent of them who were in households which ever received welfare received it for at least six of the ten years.

4. The receipt of welfare over an extended period of time is a dynamic occurrence exhibiting considerable cycling. Approximately one-half of the household heads and wives who received welfare for a total of three to eight years received it intermittently.

Preliminary attempts to ascertain the factors which determine who receives welfare, how long they receive it, and what causes them to go on and off of welfare from one year to the next suggest that two distinct factors are at work. One involves the family situation of the individual. The presence of young children in the households headed by unmarried persons, particularly females and blacks, has a considerable impact on both the incidence and length of time of welfare receipt. The other crucial factor in determining the incidence of welfare receipt is adverse labor market experience. A higher county unemployment rate, more unemployment hours of the head of the household, and involuntary loss of the household head's job all increase the probability of welfare receipt. The results suggest, though, that these adverse job market situations are less important than the family situation in explaining long-term welfare receipt. As mentioned earlier, however, these results should not be taken as conclusive but only suggestive of the type of findings which can be revealed by analysis of long-term panel data.

References

Bickel, Gary, and MacDonald, Maurice. "Participation Rates in the Food Stamp Program: Estimated Levels, by State." Discussion Paper 253-75. Institute for Research on Poverty, Madison, Wisconsin, 1975.

Boskin, M., and Nold, F. "A Markov Model of Turnover in Aid to Families With Dependent Children." Journal of Human Resources 10 (1975): 507-81.

Brehm, C., and Saving, T.R. "The Demand for General Assistance Payments." The American Economic Review (December 1964):

Brehm, C. T., and Saving, T.R. "The Demand for General Assistance Payments: Reply." American Economic Review 57 (June 1967): 585-88.

Browning, Edgar. "Reply." Southern Economic Journal (January 1979):

Bryant, Keith. "Theory of the Firm in a Non-Market Environment." The American Journal of Agricultural Economics (1972).

Bureau of Census. Characteristics of Households Purchasing Food Stamps. Current Population Reports, Washington, D.C.: U.S. Department of Commerce, 1976. Series P-23, No. 61, p. 23.

Clarkson, Kenneth. "Welfare Benefits of the Food Stamp Program." Southern Economic Journal (July 1976):

Coe, Richard. "Participation in the Food Stamp Program Among the Poverty Population." In Five Thousand American Families--Patterns of Economic Progress, Vol. V., edited by Greg J. Duncan and James N. Morgan. Ann Arbor: Institute for Social Research, The University of Michigan, 1977.

Coe, Richard. "An Examination of the Dynamics of Food Stamp Use." In Five Thousand American Families--Patterns of Economic Progress, V. VII. edited by Greg J. Duncan and James N. Morgan. Ann Arbor: Institute for Social Research, The University of Michigan, 1979.

Coe, Richard. Participation in the Food Stamp Program. Unpublished doctoral dissertation, University of Michigan, 1979.

Durbin, Elizabeth. "Work and Welfare: The Case of Aid to Families with Dependent Children." The Journal of Human Resources. 8 (Supplement, 1973): 103-25.

Garfinkel, Irwin, and Orr, Larry. "Welfare Policy and the Employment Rate of AFDC Mothers," National Tax Journal (June 1974): 175-85.

Harrison, Bennett. "Labor Market Structure and the Relationship Between Work and Welfare." Department of Urban Studies and Planning, M.I.T., 1977. Mimeograph.

Kasper, Hirschel. "Welfare Payments and Work Incentive: Some Determinants of the Rates of General Assistance Payments." Journal of Human Resources 3 (Winter 1968): 86-110.

Levitan, Sar; Marwick, David; and Rein, Martin. Work and Welfare Go Together. Baltimore: The Johns Hopkins Press, 1972.

Lyon, David W. "The Dynamics of Welfare Dependency: A Survey." The Rand Paper Series, Santa Monica, California, 1976. Mimeograph.

MacDonald, Maurice. Food, Stamps, and Income Maintenance. New York: Academic Press, 1977.

Rein, Martin, and Rainwater, Lee. "Patterns of Welfare Use." Social Service Review (December 1978): 511-34.

Rydell, C. Peter, et al. Welfare Caseload Dynamics in New York City. New York: The Rand Corporation, 1974.

Sanger, Mary Bryna. Welfare of the Poor. New York: The Academic Press, 1979.

Seagrave, Charles. "Food Stamps." The Cyclical Behavior of Transfer Income Programs: A Case Study of the Current Recession. Washington, D.C.: U.S. Department of Health, Education, and Welfare, 1975.

Smeeding, Timothy. "Comment." Southern Economic Journal, (January 1979).

Stein, Bruno, and Albin, Peter. "The Demand for General Assistance Payments: Comment." American Economic Review 57 (June 1967): 575-85.

Walker, Neal, and Tweeten, Luther. "Determination of Participation Rates in Major Federally Subsidized Public Assistance Programs." Rocky Mountain Social Science Journal (1973).

Warlick, Jennifer. An Empirical Analysis of Participation in the Supplemental Security Income Program Among Aged Eligible Persons. Unpublished doctoral dissertation, University of Wisconsin-Madison, 1979.

Appendix to Chapter 4

Table A4.1 (page 1 of 2)

DISTRIBUTION OF WELFARE USE PATTERNS BY NUMBER OF YEARS OF WELFARE RECEIPT, 1969–1978

Source of Welfare	Number of Years	All Sample Individuals		Heads and Wives[a]							
				All		Female[b]		Elderly[c]		Children[d]	
		All	Black	All	Black	All	Black	All	Black	All	Black
		Percentage Receiving Welfare									
All Welfare Programs	0	74.8	38.2	80.5	47.5	77.4	39.7	80.6	41.1	67.2	26.7
	1	7.9	9.2	6.9	11.0	7.6	11.8	5.3	7.9	8.7	7.3
	2–5	10.8	24.1	8.1	20.2	9.0	20.8	7.4	26.0	13.0	22.3
	6–9	4.5	19.1	3.0	14.2	3.9	17.7	3.7	17.8	7.2	27.6
	10	2.0	9.4	1.5	7.1	2.0	10.1	2.1	7.3	3.9	16.2
Cash Welfare Programs	0	83.9	51.0	88.0	61.4	85.9	54.1	84.2	50.1	79.2	40.8
	1	4.9	7.9	4.1	7.1	4.2	7.7	4.5	12.3	4.6	5.9
	2–5	6.6	20.8	4.9	16.9	5.5	18.1	7.4	26.7	8.3	21.4
	6–9	3.2	14.2	2.2	9.9	3.1	13.0	2.4	12.0	5.0	21.1
	10	1.4	6.2	1.0	4.6	1.4	7.1	1.4	4.2	2.7	10.7
Food Stamp Program[e]	0	78.3	43.4	84.0	53.6	80.5	43.8	87.2	54.3	69.4	29.3
	1	7.2	11.1	5.7	12.0	6.5	12.8	3.3	11.6	8.4	7.8
	2–5	10.1	25.1	7.4	21.7	8.9	24.9	6.6	22.0	13.8	28.0
	6–9	3.8	17.1	2.3	11.1	3.4	16.0	2.0	8.4	6.7	28.3
	10	0.7	3.2	0.6	2.4	0.6	2.5	3.7	3.7	1.6	6.6

Table A4.1 (Page 2 of 2)

Source of Welfare / Number of Years	Heads and Wives[a]									
	All Sample Individuals		All		Female[b]		Elderly[c]		Children[d]	
	All	Black	All	Black	All	Black	All	Black	All	Black
Percentage with Welfare Amounting to at Least Half of Income										
All Welfare Programs										
0	91.3	66.1	94.2	76.3	92.0	68.1	93.3	75.0	86.7	54.2
1	1.9	6.6	1.4	3.8	1.6	3.9	2.0	5.2	2.5	7.1
2-5	4.1	14.3	2.8	11.3	3.7	14.7	3.2	12.3	5.9	17.9
6-9	2.1	9.8	1.1	6.2	1.7	9.1	1.2	7.2	3.4	10.0
10	0.7	3.2	0.4	2.3	0.8	4.3	0.2	0.3	1.5	6.3
Cash Welfare Program										
0	91.3	66.1	94.6	77.8	92.3	69.4	93.6	77.1	87.4	57.2
1	1.9	6.6	1.4	3.5	1.7	4.0	2.3	4.2	2.4	6.3
2-5	4.1	14.3	2.8	13.5	3.7	15.5	3.3	16.6	6.2	19.5
6-9	2.0	9.8	0.9	4.1	1.4	7.1	0.5	1.7	2.7	11.3
10	0.7	3.2	0.4	2.1	0.8	3.9	0.2	0.3	1.4	5.6
Food Stamp Program[e]										
0	98.7	93.8	99.3	96.7	98.7	94.8	99.6	98.6	98.1	90.7
1	1.0	4.1	0.6	2.5	1.1	4.1	0.3	0.6	1.3	5.5
2-5	0.3	1.9	0.1	0.7	0.2	1.0	0.0	0.7	0.4	3.5
6-9	0.0	0.1	0.0	--	0.0	0.0	--	--	0.0	0.2
10	--	--	--	--	--	--	--	--	--	--
Sample size	12,562	5,013	5,573	1,676	2,700	996	1,008	196	3,150	1,501

[a] Head or wife in 1970.
[b] Age 55 or less in 1970.
[c] Age 56 or more in 1970.
[d] Age less than 10 in 1970.
[e] Excludes the year 1972. Includes years 1968-1971, 1973-1978.

Table A4.2

DISTRIBUTION OF WELFARE USE PATTERNS BY TYPE OF PROGRAM, 1968-1977

(All household heads and wives in 1969; N=5,335.)

Number of Years Received Income	All Welfare Programs		AFDC		Other Welfare Income		Food Stamps		AFDC + Other Welfare		SSI + Other Welfare	
	Number of Observations	Percentage of Sample[a]	Number of Observations	Percentage of Sample[a]	Number of Observations	Percentage of Sample[a]	Number of Observations	Percentage of Sample[a]	Number of Observations	Percentage of Sample[a]	Number of Observations	Percentage of Sample[a]
Zero	3,709	81.8	4,680	94.4	4,608	92.8	3,671	80.3	4,283	88.9	4,457	90.7
One	427	7.0	178	1.7	283	3.2	632	10.6	318	4.6	300	3.7
Two	235	2.7	112	1.0	149	1.3	265	2.9	147	1.6	171	1.5
Three	179	2.0	62	0.6	83	0.7	188	1.8	105	0.9	103	1.1
Four	154	1.4	78	0.8	74	0.7	167	1.4	85	0.8	88	0.9
Five	87	0.7	40	0.2	53	0.5	102	1.0	70	0.6	44	0.5
Six	74	0.9	42	0.3	53	0.5	99	0.8	94	1.1	44	0.4
Seven	90	0.8	44	0.4	17	0.2	69	0.3	52	0.4	43	0.4
Eight	88	0.6	30	0.2	9	0.1	80	0.5	52	0.4	32	0.2
Nine	98	0.8	25	0.2	5	0.0	61	0.5	101	0.6	29	0.2
Ten	194	1.3	44	0.2	1	0.0	1	0.0	28	0.2	24	0.3

[a]Weighted percentage.

Table A4.3

DISTRIBUTION OF PATTERNS OF TOTAL WELFARE USE, 1968-1977
(All heads and wives in 1969; N=5,335.)

Number of Years Received	Number of Individuals	Percent of All Individuals	Distribution of Changes in Welfare Use Between Years																
			Number of Times Went Off Welfare					Number of Times Went on Welfare					Number of Times on Welfare for Two Consecutive Years				
			0	1	2	3	4	0	1	2	3	4	0	1	2	3	4 or More
Zero	3,709	81.8	100.0	-	-	-	-	100.0	-	-	-	-	100.0	-	-	-	-
One	427	7.0	6.2	93.8	-	-	-	5.2	94.8	-	-	-	100.0	-	-	-	-
Two	235	2.7	8.5	66.4	25.0	-	-	1.5	78.2	20.3	-	-	26.8	73.2	-	-	-
Three	179	2.0	17.4	41.5	39.6	1.5	-	2.3	55.9	39.3	2.5	-	3.2	45.1	51.7	-	-
Four	154	1.4	25.7	26.1	37.6	10.4	0.1	4.8	45.9	41.3	7.9	-	0.4	12.7	43.4	43.5	-
Five	87	0.7	17.1	33.9	45.7	3.3	-	9.1	44.7	43.7	0.9	1.6	-	1.6	2.0	61.4	34.9
Six	74	0.9	5.8	43.2	40.9	9.9	0.2	12.5	50.0	36.2	1.3	-	-	-	0.8	9.5	89.7
Seven	90	0.8	21.1	59.4	16.8	2.6	-	13.9	51.7	31.3	3.2	-	-	-	-	-	100.0
Eight	88	0.6	13.8	58.9	27.3	-	-	3.9	54.8	41.3	-	-	-	-	-	-	100.0
Nine	98	0.8	16.0	84.0	-	-	-	30.2	69.8	-	-	-	-	-	-	-	100.0
Ten	194	1.3	100.0	-	-	-	-	100.0	-	-	-	-	-	-	-	-	100.0

Table A4.4 (page 1 of 2)
REGRESSION OF NUMBER OF YEARS OF WELFARE RECEIPT, 1969-1978[a]
(Heads and wives in 1970; N=2,870.)

Independent Variable	Mean	Regression Coefficient	
Constant		2.11	2.13
Personal Characteristics			
Whether female	.563	-.856** (.098)	-.818** (.097)
Whether black	.089	1.23** (.11)	.274 (.169)
Education in 1970	10.95	-.075** (.010)	-.077** (.010)
Expected wage	8.73	-.024** (.007)	-.024** (.007)
Under age 35 in 1970	.343	-.067 (.092)	-.038 (.092)
(Age 35-55 in 1970)	--	--	--
Over age 55 in 1970	.240	-.108 (.013)	-.040 (.102)
Family Characteristics			
Number of years unmarried	2.03	.058** (.019)	.030** (.020)
Number of years unmarried x whether female	--	.157** (.023)	.151** (.022)
Average number of children under age 18	1.24	.360** (.030)	.350** (.030)
Number of years with at least one child age 6	2.51	.028+ (.015)	.013 (.015)
Average non-labor, non-welfare income of head and wife ($1,000)	3.384	-.025** (.006)	-.027** (.006)

Table A4.4 (page 2 of 2)

Independent Variable	Mean	Regression Coefficient	
Economic Environment			
Average county unemployment rate	6.05	.092** (.018)	.092** (.018)
Individual Labor Market Experience			
Average work hours, individual (thousands)	1.82	-.754** (.060)	-.718** (.060)
Average unemployment hours, head (thousands)	.044	2.89** (.138)	2.88** (.138)
Number of involuntary job changes	.319	-.006 (.052)	-.015 (.051)
Black Interactions			
Number of years unmarried and whether black	--	--	.199** (.027)
Number of years with at least one child age 6 or less x whether black	--	--	.128** (.033)
R^2 (adjusted)		.324	.339

[a] Mean for number of years of welfare receipt, 1969–1978 is .753.
Significance levels:
**.01 *.05 +.10

Chapter 5

INTERGENERATIONAL STATUS TRANSMISSION
AND THE PROCESS OF INDIVIDUAL ATTAINMENT

Mary Corcoran and Linda P. Datcher

INTRODUCTION

Most Americans, if asked, would say that they support equal opportunity.
Yet there is wide popular disagreement over the extent to which equality of
opportunity has been achieved--both because of conceptual and philosophical
disagreements and because of empirical uncertainties. Social scientists have
made extensive investigations of the degree to which a man´s origin determines
his destination and how this process operates. Investigations of this sort can
be divided into two groups according to the type of data used: studies utilizing
data on unrelated individuals and studies using sibling data.

In the first group of studies, some measures of economic success are
estimated as a function of measured aspects of family background. This procedure
gives an estimate of the total impact of measured background on economic
attainment. Next, the coefficients of background measures from these reduced-
form equations are compared to the coefficients obtained when intervening
variables such as education and test scores are added. This reduction in the
size of background coefficients from adding these controls serves as a measure of
the extent to which background characteristics affect status attainment via these
intervening variables.

In the second set of studies, status attainment resemblance among siblings
is used to measure the effect of being born into and reared in the same family.
Researchers divide this resemblance into direct and indirect effects by
estimating the extent to which sibling resemblance across intervening variables
such as education or ability accounts for sibling resemblance on status
attainment. These sibling studies have also been used to indicate the extent to
which demographic background effects capture full "family" effects. These models
typically require some fairly strong assumptions about the ways in which families
operate.

The first part of this chapter reviews empirical literature on the process by which background influences economic success and is limited to two issues: (1) estimates of the size of the overall impact of background on economic attainment (usually defined as the proportion of variance in an attainment measure that can be accounted for by background measures), and (2) estimates of the extent to which background influences attainment indirectly via intervening variables such as aspirations, test scores, and education. In the second part of the chapter, we estimate models of status attainment using a sample of 207 brothers from the Panel Study of Income Dynamics.

LITERATURE REVIEW

Studies of Unrelated Men

We begin by examining models of socioeconomic attainment which regress measures of economic status on measured aspects of family background. A landmark piece of work in this vein was done by Blau and Duncan (1967). Concentrated on the determinants of occupational status, their work was based principally on a sample of 25 to 64 year-old white men with nonfarm backgrounds; their sample was drawn from the March 1962 Current Population Survey Occupational Changes in a Generation Supplement (OCG). Duncan, Featherman, and Duncan (1972) extended this work to examine income as the measure of attainment and, using other data sets, synthesized a measure of cognitive test scores as a predictor variable. They found that father's education, father's occupation, and respondent's number of siblings accounted for about one-quarter of the variance in respondent's education, for less than one-fifth of the variance in occupational status, and for less than one-tenth of the variance in income in reduced-form regressions run on ten-year age cohorts from the OCG sample. When the respondent's education was added to the occupational status regressions, the effects of father's schooling and number of siblings dropped sharply, but the coefficient for father's occupational status remained significant. When the respondent's own education and occupational status were added to the earnings regressions, the coefficients of the included background variables were cut by at least 50 percent and, for the oldest cohorts, dropped to insignificance. With these findings Duncan, Featherman and Duncan concluded that, although background factors influenced later occupational status and earnings, most of the effect was indirect through earlier achievement indicators such as education.

When they modified their model by including a measure of respondent's intelligence at about age 12,[1] their basic findings did not change. However, they indicated that the addition of an intelligence measure lowered the effect of the background variables on education, occupational status, and earnings. The total impact of the background factors on education and earnings as measured by the sizes of the standardized coefficients in reduced form regressions was roughly equal to the direct effect of ability (controlling background).

Jencks et al (1972) took a second look at the questions posed by Blau and Duncan and by Duncan, Featherman, and Duncan. As was the case with the Duncan et al. studies, many of Jencks' analyses of occupational status and income determination were based on the 1962 OCG data. In addition, Jencks et al. analyzed Project Talent and the Coleman data. Their conclusions about the effects of socioeconomic background on status attainment were basically the same as those of earlier studies. They concluded that family background among white men from nonfarm backgrounds had quite small effects on men's occupational status once test scores and schooling were controlled and had very small effects on men's income once these factors plus occupational status were controlled.

Hauser and Featherman (1978) and Featherman and Hauser (1977) used both the OCG sample and the 1973 replication (OCG-II) to investigate whether the process of stratification had changed between 1962 and 1972. For both samples, they regressed attainment measures on six background variables (father's education, father's occupation, number of siblings, race, farm origin, whether raised in a broken family) for men aged 25 to 64. The R^2's for the 1962 education, occupational status, and earning regressions were .332, .249, and .127, respectively. These compared to R^2s of .323, .206, and .077 in the 1972 regressions. Thus, the explanatory power of this class of background variables had declined over the period 1962 to 1972. They also found that over this period, the coefficients of race and farm origin dropped. On the basis of this and other evidence, they suggested that "socioeconomic background and social ascription weigh less heavily in the socioeconomic careers of working men in the early 1970s than was the case in the OCG benchmark of 1962" (Hauser and Featherman, 1978, p. 234).

Sewell and Hauser (1975) used a sample that was more restricted geographically but richer in information for their calculations of background

---

[1]Data sets in addition to the 1962 Occupational Changes in a Generation Supplement were used here.

effects. Relying on data from male graduates of Wisconsin high schools in 1957, they regressed son's education, the Duncan score of son's 1964 occupation, and a canonically weighted average of son's 1965-1967 earnings on an initial set of background variables. Preliminary results showed that father's occupation and education, mother's education, and parents' income had strong, positive effects both on son's education and on son's occupation. Adding a measure of ability reduced the coefficients on the parents' education variables by one-third in the education regression. The coefficients on father's occupation and parents' income fell by a lesser amount. When respondent's education and ability were added to the occupational status regression, the coefficients on the parental education and family income measures dropped by more than two-thirds and became insignificant. When education was added to the earnings regression, the coefficient on family income fell by only a small amount. This is consistent with the later finding of Jencks et al. (1979) that much of the impact of family income on son's income in the OCG-II was independent of schooling.

Sewell and Hauser moved beyond their initial model of the effects of background to try to identify the channels through which background operated. They found that high school rank in class, social support for attending college,[2] and educational and occupational aspirations showed large, significant impacts on educational attainment independent of ability and background. In fact, the coefficients on almost all of the family background and ability measures fell by well over 50 percent with the inclusion of these additional variables.[3] Effects of family income and mother's education dropped to insignificance. This implies that most of the effect of the background and ability variables on years of education were channelled through these intervening mechanisms. Adding the socio-psychological measures of background and ability to the occupation regression produced a similar pattern of results. The effects of parental education and family income on occupational status were mediated by the expectations and aspirations of significant others. The one exception was father's occupation; 16 percent of the overall effect of father's occupation on respondent's occupation was unmediated by ability, by the socio-psychological measures, or by schooling. In contrast, only educational and occupational

---

[2] Social support for attending college was measured by dummy variables for whether teachers and/or parents encouraged going to college, and for whether most of the respondent's friends were planning to go to college.

[3] The only exception was father's education which fell by only 38 percent.

aspirations were significant in the earnings regression specification that included family background, high school rank, social support, and aspirations. Furthermore, there was little change in the coefficient on family income, the only background variable remaining significant with the addition of the socio-psychological measures.

Sewell and Hauser did some additional analysis to determine whether the effect of family income on earnings was due to the type of college attended. Although there were wide variations in the earnings of college graduates depending on the kind of college they attended, neither family income nor educational/occupational aspirations seemed to account for the differences.

There are several other studies (e.g., Freeman, 1978; Griliches, 1972; Hauser and Daymont, 1977; Jencks et al., 1979; Morgenstern, 1973) which analyzed the effect of background on earnings and occupational status. These and the ones discussed so far are in general agreement on several conclusions. First, education is a principal determinant of occupational status and earnings, independent of family background and ability measures. Second, differences in family background and ability are associated with moderate differences in occupational status and with modest differences in earnings in later life. Third, with the exception of family income and, to a lesser extent, father's occupation and ability, family background measures operate almost exclusively through their effect on educational attainment. Fourth, the effect of family background on years of education largely occurs because of changes in high school rank, social support for attending college, and educational and occupational aspirations. Fifth, the total effect of measured background on education, occupational status, and earnings is about the same as the total effect of ability.

Empirical Criticisms of the Blau-Duncan Approach

The validity of these conclusions rests on the belief that the estimated equations do not seriously violate the assumptions required for consistent estimation using ordinary least squares regression (OLS). However, Bowles (1972), Griliches (1977 and 1978), and others have pointed out that, contrary to the necessary assumptions the included explanatory variables may be correlated with the error terms in the background regressions, thereby yielding biased and inconsistent coefficients. This may occur for three reasons. First, there may be errors in measuring amounts of education and family background characteristics such as permanent income. Second, variables such as ambition and unmeasured dimensions of family background may be correlated with the included variables but left out of the estimated equations. By failing to include all relevant background traits, the extent to which background determines economic status may be underestimated and may thus bias estimates of the influence of included background measures and schooling. Third, schooling is, in part, the result of individual maximizing behavior based on an expected earnings function. If the errors in the actual and expected earnings function are correlated, then schooling will be similarly correlated with the error term in the actual earnings regression. Failure to correct for these problems may severely bias estimates of the impact of background on education and earnings.

Measurement Error

Regarding measurement error, it has been argued that retrospective reports of parental status traits may be more subject to error than would be contemporaneous reports of men's status characteristics. It has been further pointed out that failing to correct for measurement error in background variables could lead to underestimates of the extent to which economic outcomes depend on social origins, or to overestimates of the influence of education on economic outcomes (Bowles, 1972; Bowles and Nelson, 1974; Mason et al., 1976).

Until recently attempts to investigate measurement error in retrospective background reports have been constrained by inadequate data and/or models. Bielby, Hauser, and Featherman (1977) have conducted perhaps the most extensive published investigation so far of measurement error using the remeasurement subsample of the OCG-II (N=926: 578 whites and 348 blacks). This subsample was a nationally representative sample of U.S. men who were 20 to 64 years of age in 1973. For each sample member, measures of family background traits, education, first occupation, and current occupation were obtained on two separate occasions. In addition, a third measure of schooling had been obtained prior to the 1973 OCG-II survey. Bielby et al. tested for two kinds of correlated measurement error: first to see whether errors in reports of different characteristics at a point in time were correlated (within-occasion error) and, second, to see if errors in reports of the same characteristic obtained at different times were correlated (within-variable error). To identify within-variable error correlations, the study assumed that the correlations between errors in reports of characteristics obtained at different times were equal for all pairs of

characteristics.[4] They concluded that retrospective reports of parental
background by nonblack men were subject only to random measurement error, and
that retrospective reports of parental status were as reliable as were
contemporaneous reports of men's current status.

Bielby et al. next adjusted the structural equations models of status
attainment from the full OCG-II sample for measurement error by applying
measurement error estimates based on the remeasurement sample. On the basis of
this, they concluded that failing to control for measurement error neither
substantially inflated estimates of the economic returns to schooling nor
substantially underestimated effects of particular background variables on
individual achievement. They also found that failing to correct for measurement
errors resulted in considerable underestimates of the proportion of variance in
occupational status explained by background, but that this underestimate was as
much due to errors in the measurement of the respondent's current occupation as
to errors in his reports of parental characteristics.

Corcoran (1979, 1980) examined measurement error in men's retrospective
reports of parental traits using a nationally representative sample of 217 young
white male heads of households aged 23 to 30 in 1976 who were living with both
parents in 1968. This sample from the the Panel Study of Income Dynamics,
provided reports by the father and son of the father's occupation and education
and reports by the father, son, and mother of the mother's education. Corcoran
found that men's reports of their parents' status had lower reliabilities than
did parents' reports of their own status, but these differences were only
significant for mother's education. She further found that adjustments for
measurement error did not affect the conclusions about the relative importance of
particular background traits in predicting sons' status attainment. Corcoran
(1979) did find that adjustments for measurement error substantially increased
the overall explanatory power in her reduced-form occupational status and
earnings equations, but this conclusion must be qualified since her reliability

---

[4]It is by no means clear why this assumption should hold. In fact, one can
make a case against this assumption. If men consistently misreport a given
variable over time because they are mistaken about its true value, then errors in
reports of that variable will be correlated over time. It seems likely that men
may be misinformed about the characteristics of their parents at some past date
and so retrospective reports of these traits may be subject to nonrandom error.
But, we suspect men are less likely to be misinformed about their own current
characteristics and so one might expect there to be less nonrandom error in men's
reports of their own characteristics than in their reports of their parents'
characteristics.

estimates were based on a small sample and had large standard errors. Given this, the range of possible change in explanatory power is likely to be quite large.[5]

Omitted Background Traits: Including New Measures

Researchers have dealt with the problems of omitted background variables in two ways: by including new measures of parental background in their analyses, and by the use of sibling data. As discussed above, the original three background measures used by Blau and Duncan--father's education and occupation and number of siblings--were augmented in later studies. For example, Jencks et al. (1979) expanded this list to include mother's education, family income, father's birthplace, race, region of birth, whether raised on a farm, and whether raised in an intact home. They reported that with the exception of race, family income, and father's occupation, none of these measures had sizeable significant effects on men's occupational status or earnings once education, experience, and community of residence were controlled. A second example is Greeley's (1977) analysis of the effects of ethnicity and religion on men's status attainment. He reports that most Catholic ethnic groups and Jews have 10 to 20 percent higher family incomes than would be expected on the basis of their background, education, occupational status, and place of residence. Greeley's analysis was not strictly comparable with that of Jencks et al. since he looked at family income rather than men's earnings.

Sibling Studies

Researchers have used sibling data sets for five purposes: (1) to estimate the effects on occupational status and earnings of having and being raised by one set of parents rather than by another; (2) to estimate whether sibling resemblance on economic outcomes can be attributed to similar SES background; (3) to decompose sibling resemblance into direct (independent of schooling and test scores) and indirect components; (4) to estimate the extent to which genetic differences account for inequality in status attainment; and (5) to reduce the bias on the coefficients of test scores and schooling that results from

---

[5]A second problem is that in the 1979 study the coding rules for sons' reports of parental education were somewhat different than those used for parents' reports. In the 1980 study responses were recoded using the same rules for both sons' and parents' reports. A preliminary analysis using these recoded variables still showed that adjustments for measurement error substantially increased overall explanatory power.

unmeasured variables. Sibling data are of two sorts: from studies of brothers and of twins. In general, brothers samples have been used for purposes 1, 2, 3, and 5 and twin samples for purposes 4 and 5.

Estimating the Total and Direct Effects of Background Using Brothers Data

Blau and Duncan were the first to use sibling resemblance as a measure of the potential effect of background. They reported that the correlation between brothers' schooling was higher than the R^2 which obtained in a multiple classification analysis of schooling as a function of father's occupation, father's education, ethnic group, region and number of siblings. They emphasized strongly that in order to use sibling resemblance as a measure of background effects on schooling it must be assumed that one brother's schooling has no effect on that of the other. Duncan, Featherman, and Duncan further explored how one might interpret sibling resemblance on education.

In recent years a number of scholars have extended the work of Blau and Duncan (Taubman, 1976a, b; Corcoran, Jencks, and Olneck, 1976; Brittain, 1977; Jencks et al., 1979) using brothers data. Since Jencks et al. (1979) summarized and compared results from all the data sets used in these analyses, we will focus on their work.

Jencks et al. (1979) defined the effects of family background on men's expected economic success as "all the potentially predictable consequences of having one set of parents rather than another." They measured the magnitude of these effects by estimating the degree of economic resemblance between brothers. This meant that their definition of background subsumed effects not only of parents themselves, but effects of shared heredity, of being raised in the same community, and of being sent to the same schools, along with many other influences. Their measure would not pick up effects of background factors which differ for brothers--which vary within families. However, their measure would pick up any resemblance in brothers' statuses that is due to reciprocal influence and will reallocate it to "common background."

Jencks et al. argued that unless the characteristics of one brother influence those of the other brother, the intraclass correlation between the economic status of two brothers would be equal to the percentage of variance explained by regressing their economic status on all the genetic and environmental factors that brothers had in common. They estimated these intraclass correlations by computing product-moment correlations for all brother pairs twice, with the order reversed.

Jencks et al. examined five samples of brothers. In every sample the sibling correlations on occupational status and ln earnings were about twice as large as the R^2s in the regressions of occupational status[6] and ln earnings on measured demographic background. They then adjusted the sibling correlations to allow for differences between men with brothers and all men and also corrected for random measurement error. After these adjustments, they concluded that family background as a whole accounted for 48 percent of the variance in occupational status and "anywhere between" 15 to 35 percent of the variance in earnings among men aged 25 to 64 years. Their best guess was that demographic background accounted for about two-thirds of this resemblance.

Next they estimated whether the background traits that explain brothers' resemblance on occupation and earnings operated independently of schooling and test scores. They reported that at least half of the impact of shared background on brothers' occupational status but only one-quarter of its impact on brothers' earnings was mediated by test scores and schooling.

There are four things to be kept in mind about the Jencks et al. results. First, as noted above, their definition of shared background will pick up more than men's socioeconomic origins. Until we know what the unmeasured background variables are that cause brothers' attainments to be more alike than would have been predicted by their common demographic background, we cannot argue on the basis of the results obtained by Jencks et al. that the Blau-Duncan approach underestimates the effects of class origins on men's economic destinations. Second, the samples of brothers used by Jencks et al. were either small or drawn from special populations or both. Third, although Jencks et al. investigated the effects of 12 demographic measures in their analyses of unrelated men, none of their samples of brothers contained more than seven of these measures. Fourth, they relied at least in part on using one brother to locate the other in four of their five samples. If brothers who kept in touch were more alike in economic attainments than those who did not, this may have biased sibling correlations upwards. Finally Jencks et al. assumed that the attainments of one brother did not affect those of the other. While they reported checks which lent some support to this assumption, these checks were quite weak--as they readily

---

[6]The one exception is occupational status in the Brittain sample of 151 Cleveland brothers. Brittain did not measure occupational status by the Duncan score.

admitted. As Blau and Duncan stressed, this assumption is very strong, and without it one cannot use sibling resemblance as a measure of the effects of family background.

Use of Twin Data to Estimate Genetic Effects

Some researchers have argued that twin data allow one to estimate the extent to which genetic inheritance influences economic status. For example, Behrman, Taubman, and Wales (1977) compared monozygotic (MZ) and dizygotic (DZ) twins drawn from a sample of white males who served in the Armed Forces during World War II. Their approach was based on the premise that MZ twins are more similar than DZ twins with respect to observed variables and genotype but not to latent environmental variables. From this premise they concluded that the difference between the observed resemblance of MZ twins and the observed resemblance of DZ twins was an estimate of the role of heredity as part of family background effects. Using this approach, one of their principal models concluded that 45 percent of the variance in the 1973 earnings of their sample was due to genetics. This finding was robust regardless of various assumptions about the correlation between genetic and environmental factors.

Goldberger (1977) sharply criticized this application of twin studies. The source of his criticism stemmed from the assumption that MZ twins were no more similar than DZ twins with respect to latent environmental effects. In a simple univariate model, he showed that the excess observed correlation among the MZs over DZs (Δc) is a weighted average of the excess genotypic correlation (Δg) and their excess environmental correlation ($\Delta \rho$), where the weights are the degree of heritability and environmentability, h^2 and $(1-h^2)$ respectively. That is:

$$\Delta c = \Delta g \cdot h^2 + \Delta \rho \cdot (1-h^2)$$

Solving for h^2 yields $h^2 = (\Delta c - \Delta \rho)/(\Delta g - \Delta \rho)$. While Behrman, Taubman, and Wales (1977) assume that $\Delta \rho = 0$, Goldberger showed that estimates of h^2 are extremely sensitive to assumptions about differential environmental correlations. He concluded that, although twin studies show that MZs are more highly correlated than DZs, there is no basis for allocating these differences between genetic and environmental factors.

Use of Sibling Data to Reduce Bias in Estimates
of Returns to Schooling and Test Scores

Finally, it has been argued that sibling data provide a means of reducing the bias that is due to excluded background measures. The basic reasoning is as follows. Siblings share heredity, access to financial resources, and exposure to parental and community influences. In a model such as

$$Y = \alpha + \beta E + \delta A + U$$

where Y is ln earnings, E is education, and A is an unmeasured excluded variable, simply using OLS to estimate β produces a bias equal to b_{AE}, where b_{AE} is the coefficient of regressing A on E. If A is purely a family variable, (i.e., if siblings have exactly the same levels of A), then estimating β using within family data would eliminate the bias so that $E(\hat{\beta}) = \beta$.

Within the last few years several studies (Chamberlain and Griliches, 1975, 1977; Olneck, 1977; Brittain, 1977; Jencks et al. 1979; Behrman and Taubman, 1976) have investigated the problems of the bias in schooling coefficients due to omitted background measures by estimating within-pair regressions on samples of brothers. Results of this research are not consistent. Chamberlain and Griliches reported that ignoring unmeasured background (shared by brothers) did not result in large overestimates of the economic returns to schooling. Brittain, Olneck, and Behrman and Taubman reported the reverse. Goldberger (1977), on the other hand, has noted the advantages of twin studies over ordinary sibling data in obtaining good estimates of the parameters in an earnings regression. This view is based on the observation that, if unmeasured variables are more highly correlated for MZs than DZs, then the within-MZ regressions may be a more effective control for the correlation between unmeasured background variables and the included individual characteristics than the within-DZ regressions.

The principal problems with the procedure used in this work are (1) A probably includes variables that vary within families (e.g., ability and neighborhood influences), and (2) the procedure ignores the other problems with the earnings function such as measurement error and endogeneity of schooling. Griliches (1977) has argued that, because of these two factors, within family estimation is not necessarily less biased than OLS.

Chamberlain and Griliches (1977) indicated that Goldberger's criticism of the ability of twin studies to separate genetic and environmental effects also applies to whether twin data can identify more general models than sibling data. This problem can be illustrated with the following model[7]

(1) $Y_k = X\delta + \beta Y_s + \gamma a + \upsilon_k$

(2) $Y_s = X\alpha + \rho a + w$

(3) $a_{ij} = f_i + g_{ij}$

where Y_k is some measure of later achievement such as income or occupation, Y_s is years of schooling, X represents the independent variables which may vary between equations, and a_{ij} is an unobserved variable for person i in family j which affects both Y_s and Y_k. If $\gamma \neq 0$, then using OLS to estimate Equation 1 yields inconsistent estimates. If there were enough exogenous variables in Equation 2 which did not appear in Equation 1, then this problem could be solved using an instrumental variables procedure. In general there are not enough such variables, so that estimating the parameters can only be done by relying on restrictions the model imposes on the variance-covariance matrix of the residuals of the reduced-form equations. Restrictions imposed by the cross-sibling covariance matrix generated by f_i and the total covariance matrix generated by $f_i + g_{ij}$ produce one fewer equation than parameters to be estimated. Therefore, the sibling model is not identified without further restrictions. In the twin models, there are restrictions imposed by the cross-sibling covariance matrix for DZ twins, the cross-sibling covariance matrix for MZ twins, and the total covariance matrix. Thus, it would appear that the additional restrictions would provide enough equations to estimate the parameters. However, unless one assumes that the correlation on the unmeasured variable, a, between MZ twins is one, the additional restrictions are accompanied by an equal number of additional parameters to be estimated, so that the twin model is just as underidentified as the sibling model. The correlation on the unmeasured variable, a, between MZ twins equals one only if that variable is a genetic or common family background characteristic. Differences in environmental effects between MZ twins would rule out such a correlation.

Summary of Sibling Data Research

To summarize, researchers have concluded the following on the basis of analyses of brothers' data. First, analyses which define background using

---

[7] See Chamberlain and Griliches (1975, 1977) for more details.

standard demographic measures will result in considerable underestimates of the extent to which families affect sons' chances of economic success. Second, the unmeasured background traits that influence men's earnings, unlike measured demographic background, exert a considerable impact on earnings that is independent of test scores and schooling. Third, there is inconsistent evidence from within-family regressions about whether estimates of economic returns to schooling are inflated when only demographic background is controlled. In addition, Taubman and Wales (1977) have argued, that comparisons of identical and fraternal twins, suggest that a considerable amount of economic inequality is due to genetics. Both Goldberger (1977) and Chamberlain and Griliches (1977) have criticized twin studies of this sort, arguing that twin data do not provide enough information to separate out environmental from genetic effects.

ESTIMATING YOUNG MEN'S STATUS ATTAINMENT

The Sample and Variables

The Panel Study of Income Dynamics is uniquely well suited to the study of the early status attainment process. It has followed families' economic fortunes annually since 1967 and has taken separate interviews with children who leave home. This has provided direct measures of an individual's family origin as reported by his parents in 1968 and his own reports of his economic status as of 1979. This sample has three advantages relative to most sibling data sets. First, since background measures were reported in 1968 by parents, this should considerably reduce potential bias due to measurement error. In addition, since this sample contained measures of parental status by two observers, estimates can be corrected for measurement error using the procedures followed by Bielby et al. (1977), Mason et al. (1976) and Corcoran (1979, 1980). Second, the Panel Study has more measures of background traits than other sibling data sets, plus background measures such as family income or father's cognitive test scores which are hard to obtain retrospectively. Third, the Panel Study did not need to rely on one brother to help trace the other since the study followed all children who left home. Jencks et al. (1979) reported that four of the five sibling data sets they examined relied at least in part on one brother to trace another. If brothers in similar economic circumstances are more likely to keep in touch then this may have biased the siblings correlations upwards in their analyses. This problem is minimized with Panel Study data.

As of 1979, there were 915 male household heads aged 23-33 in the Panel Study who were employed at least 250 hours in 1978, who lived with at least one parent in 1968, and who reported their schooling, occupation, and earnings. Among these men, 413 had one or more brothers who like themselves had left home by 1979. Thus, there were 206.5 independent brother pairs. Most of our analyses are run on these 413 men or 206.5 brother pairs.[8]

For each of these 413 men, we have a measure of annual labor income, hourly wage, occupation (a one-digit Census code), and education as of 1978, and measures of the following twelve demographic characteristics:

1) race (nonblack/black)

2) father's years of schooling (coded into eight categories)

3) Duncan score of father's main occupation in 1968 (based on one-digit Census codes)

4) whether lived in female-headed household in 1968

5) mother's education (coded into eight categories)

6) size of nearest city in 1968

7) whether lived outside of the South in 1968

8) whether father was native born

9) whether raised on a farm

10) number of siblings

11) family income in 1967

12) religion (Catholic/Jewish/Other)

None of the sibling studies reported in Jencks et al. included more than seven of these measures;[9] only one brothers study measured family income and this was a retrospective measure; and only one brothers study included a measure of religion.

Measures of the background variables 1 through 7, and 11 were obtained from the 1967 parents' interviews. There were no missing data on race, female head, region, and family income in our sample. Measures of the other background variables were reported by sons in the year the sons left home. Sons also

---

[8]Some of these men are from 1968 households in which more than two sons subsequently left home. Thus there are more than 206.5 unique pairs. The sample was weighted so that no individual appears in more than one unique pair. Thus for two brothers, there are two pairs with brothers in reverse order--each pair having a weight of 1/2. For three brothers there are six pairs of all possible combinations--each with a weight of 1/4. We also tried an alternative weighting scheme, where we weighted pairs by the number of unique families. Since this did not alter the results, we report results only for the first weighting scheme.

[9]Kalamazoo and Taubman actually had more than seven, but had only seven measures where the variance was not severely limited due to sample restrictions.

reported on variables 2, 3, 5, and 7. Whenever there was missing data from parents on variables 2, 3, 5, or 7, we assigned the sons' reports. Whenever there was missing data on one son's interview for variables 8, 9, 10 or 12, we assigned his brother's response for that variable. In the very few remaining cases of missing data, we assigned the sample mean.

Using these background measures, we performed parallel analyses of status attainment models and a study of measurement error using the full sample of 915 employed male household heads aged 23 to 33 years in 1979 who worked at least 250 hours in 1978 and who lived with at least one parent in 1968.

It should be noted that our splitoff sample had some problems of representativeness. First, some men aged 23-25 years might still be in school, so our sample may omit men in this age range with high amounts of schooling. Second, men aged 30-33 years in 1979 would have been 19-23 years old in 1968. Some men in this age range, particularly those with less schooling, would have already left home and would not be children in a sample family. Thus, this sample of splitoffs likely underrepresents the well-educated in the 23-25 year old range and underrepresents the less well-educated in the 30-33 year old range. This problem would be exacerbated in the sibling subset.

We also examined the effects of two other demographic factors and two neighborhood characteristics. We looked at the effects of father's supervisory authority in his main job in 1975[10] and father's cognitive test scores[11] on young men's status attainment for a sample of 702 male household heads aged 23 to 33 in 1979 who lived with their fathers in 1968 and whose fathers were still in the sample in 1979. We looked at the effects of race composition (percentage white) and mean income in the zip code area for 1968 address for a sample of 470 male household heads aged 23 to 32 in 1978 who lived in an SMSA in 1968. This sample and the variables used in its analysis are described in more detail by Datcher (1979).

Extent to Which Brothers' Resemblance Can Be
Predicted by Their Measured Demographic Background

If we assume that the characteristics of one brother do not directly affect those of the other, then the intraclass correlations between brothers' economic

---

[10]This factor was represented by a categorical variable--supervises and has say over others' pay or promotion/supervises but does not have such say/does not supervise.

[11]This was based on a 13-item sentence completion test given in 1972.

outcomes measure the impact of shared background on those outcomes. Recall that this measure will not pick up effects of background which differ for brothers and that this is a much broader definition of background than is typically used in stratification studies. Brothers share more than common class origins. Defining background by brotherly resemblance will pick up the effects of having the same peers, attending the same schools, being raised in the same neighborhood, and so on.

If measured background variables capture the full influence of background on men's education and economic status and if the characteristics of one brother have not affected those of the other, then the intraclass correlations should equal the R^2s obtained when education, Duncan scores, and ln earnings are regressed on measured background variables. To see this look at Figure 5.1. Imagine regressing an outcome measure (Y) on a set of background measures that include all relevant interactions and non-linearities (F_Y); "a" is the correlation between F_Y and Y. If the characteristics of one brother have no effect on those of the other (i.e., if the path from Y_1 to Y_2 is zero) and if, on average, this set of characteristics has the same effect in each brother, then in this model $a^2 = r_{Y1,Y2}$. The assumption that the characteristics of one brother do not affect those of the other brother is crucial here. If brothers do influence one another, then the model pictured in Figure 5.1 would probably overestimate the impact of family background. Jencks et al. (1979) performed several rather weak tests of this assumption and could neither rule out nor confirm it.

Table 5.1 presents our results. In row 1, we present the effects of all ten background measures other than family income and religion for those interested in comparisons with Jencks et al. (1979). There was considerably more resemblance between brothers' schooling and economic outcomes than would have been predicted on the basis of the twelve demographic measures included in our brothers sample. When we regressed our three outcome measures on the twelve demographic background measures, the R^2s were .419 for schooling, .265 for occupational status, and .147 for ln hourly earnings (Table 5.1, row 4). These compare to sibling intraclass correlations of .640, .434, and .288 (Table 5.1, row 13). In every case the sibling correlation exceeded the R^2 by at least .14.

Family Income and Religion

Since only one of the sibling data sets reported by Jencks et al. (1979) measured family income and only one measured religious affiliation, we will discuss the effects of family income and religious affiliation separately.

Figure 5.1

THE TOTAL EFFECT OF SHARED BACKGROUND ON ATTAINMENT OUTCOMES

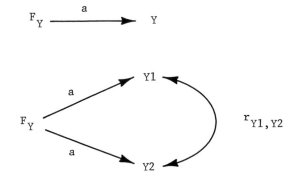

F_Y = Weighted average of all background factors that influence outcome Y

Y = Outcome measure

Yi = Economic outcome for the ith brother in a pair

$r_{Y1,Y2} = a^2$

Table 5.1 (page 1 of 2)

ESTIMATES OF THE IMPACT OF MEASURED BACKGROUND
AND SHARED BACKGROUND ON MEN'S EDUCATION AND ECONOMIC OUTCOMES
(For varying subgroups of 915 employed male household heads, aged 23–33 in
1979 who lived with at least one parent in 1968.)

Demographic Variables	Education	Occupation	Ln Hourly Earnings	Ln Annual Earnings
Incremental R^2 in Regressions Using the Subgroup of 413 Brothers				
1. Race, father's education, father's occupational status, whether lived in female-headed household in 1968, mother's education, size of nearest city in 1968, region where resided in 1968, whether father native born, whether raised on a farm, number of siblings[a]	.400	.221	.101	.104
2. Family income[a]	.002	.006	.019	.022
3. Religion[a]	.017	.039	.027	.036
4. Total effects of measured demographic background	.419	.265	.147	.163
Incremental R^2 in Regressions Using the Subgroups of 702 in Male-Headed 1968 Families				
5. Father's supervisory authority on main job in 1975[b]	.015	.014	(.003)	.010
6. Father's cognitive test score[b]	(.001)	(.000)	(.003)	(.003)
Incremental R^2 in Regressions Using the Subgroups of 470 in an SMSA in 1968				
7. Mean income and racial composition of community where resided in 1968[c]	.015	(.000)	(.005)	–[h]
Incremental R^2 Pooling Results for Various Subgroups				
8. Total measured background[d] (sum of lines 4 and significant contributions in lines 5, 6, and 7)	.449	.279	.147	.173

Table 5.1 (page 2 of 2)

Demographic Variables	Education	Occupation	Ln Hourly Earnings	Ln Annual Earnings
Incremental R^2 Adjusting for Measurement Error Using the Full Sample				
9. Errors in measuring demographic background[e]	.072	.042	.013	–
10. Errors in measuring outcome variables[f]	.045	.052	.012–.026	.013–.028
11. Errors in measuring outcome variables[f]	.055	.071	.022–.047	.020–.042
12. Estimated true R^{2f}	.566	.373	.172–.186	.186–.201
Correlations Between Brothers´ Outcomes Using the Full Sample				
13. Observed correlation	.640	.434	.288	.260
14. Estimated true correlation[f]	.695	.505	.310–.335	.280–.302

[a] In all regressions, age of head in 1968 is controlled.

[b] These increments to R^2 are derived by examining the extent to which adding measures of father´s position in the work hierarchy (obtained in the 1975 Panel Study interview) and of father´s cognitive test score (obtained from a 13-item sentence completion test in the 1972 Panel interview) increase R^2s in the regression of the sons´ status attainment measures on all the background measures listed above. Numbers are in parentheses when the added variable was insignificant.

[c] These increments to R^2 were obtained by comparing regressions of family background on status attainment with and without race composition of local community and community income measures. Numbers are in parentheses when added variables were insignificant. The sample and the measures are described in detail in Datcher (1979).

[d] This is calculated as the sum of line 4 plus significant contributions from lines 5, 6 and 7.

[e] We calculated these adjustments based on estimates of the extent to which corrections for measurement error in fathers´ 1968 reports of their own schooling and occupation and of their wives´ schooling improved the explanatory power in regressions of these variables on sons´ 1978 education, occupational status, and earnings.

[f] We estimated these corrections using the reliabilities for contemporaneous reports of men´s occupation and ln earnings used by Jencks et al. (1979) in their sibling analyses and using Bartlett´s reliability estimate for Panel study men´s reports of schooling from the Panel Study (in Jencks et al., 1979).

Rows 2 and 3 of Table 5.1 give us the increments in R^2 obtained when we added family income and religion measures to our other ten demographic characteristics.[12]   Table 5.2 reports the nonstandardized coefficients of these measures when we ran our regressions on the full sample of 915 young men.

Family income was significantly related to schooling and to earnings; a man's expected schooling was .05 years higher and expected hourly wage was 1.6 percent higher for each $1,000 of 1967 family income. These earnings advantages dropped only slightly (to 1.4 percent) when schooling was controlled.

Religious affiliation consistently and significantly affected all three outcome measures. On average, Catholic young men earned 13.0 percent more per hour and had 5.2 points higher Duncan scores for their current occupation than did Protestants with similar background characteristics. Jewish young men had, on average, 1.31 more years of schooling coupled with occupational status that was 12.5 points higher than those of their Protestant counterparts. All these differences were significant. The occupational status and earnings advantages of Catholics were unaffected when schooling was controlled. The occupational status advantage of Jews was halved and became only marginally significant when schooling was controlled.

Father's Supervisory Authority

Next we attempted to adjust the R^2s in our regressions of economic outcomes for three potentially important omitted background factors: father's position in the work hierarchy, father's cognitive test scores, and community characteristics. First, regarding the work hierarchy, Gintis (1971) and Bowles and Gintis (1976) have argued that parents socialize children differently depending upon the parents' position in the work hierarchy. In particular, they have argued that parents tend to foster noncognitive traits which would be appropriate in the parents' jobs and that this might lead to differences in later economic outcomes for the children. With samples of U.S. and Italian parents Kohn (1969) found that paternal opportunities for occupational self-direction were significantly related to expressed child-rearing values, independently of social class. Of course, it is a large jump to move from paternal values to child-rearing practices to children's later attainment.

---

[12]These ten characteristics are comparable with those available in the five samples of brothers analyzed by Jencks et al. Here the R^2 based on these factors (Table 5.1, row 1) is perhaps the most appropriate one to use for comparisons with their result.

Table 5.2

REGRESSIONS OF EDUCATION, OCCUPATIONAL STATUS, AND LN EARNINGS ON BACKGROUND MEASURES[a]

(For 915 employed male household heads aged 23 to 33 years in 1979 who lived with at least one parent in 1968.)

Characteristic[b]	Education	Occupational Status			Ln Hourly Wage			Ln Annual Earnings		
	No Controls	No Controls	Education Controlled	Education Experience, Region and City Size Controlled	No Controls	Education Controlled	Education Experience, Region and City Size Controlled	No Controls	Education Controlled	Education Experience, Region and City Size Controlled
Size of nearest city	(.046)	(.069)	(-.146)	(-.421)	(.008)	(.006)	(-.015)	(.002)	(.002)	(-.002)
Female household head	(-.287)	(-.480)	(.877)	(.590)	(.029)	.046	(.017)	(.013)	(.033)	(-.015)
Non-farm origins	(-.082)	(2.105)	2.491	2.401	(.058)	.062	(.061)	(-.016)	(-.010)	(.000)
Native father	(-.444)	(-1.076)	(1.020)	(1.635)	(.139)	.164	.214	(.047)	(.078)	(.151)
Father's occupation	.010	.115	.066+	.071+	(.001)	(-.000)	(-.000)	(.000)	(.000)	(.000)
Father's education	.140	1.099	.436	.413+	(.002)	(-.005)	(-.006)	(.001)	(-.009)	(-.008)
Mother's education	.132	.724	(.101)	(.098)	(.002)	(-.003)	(-.004)	(-.001)	(-.010)	(-.006)
Non-south	(-.189)	-3.128	-2.235+	-3.368	.071+	.082	(.068)	(.023)	(.037)	(.041)
White	(.140)	(.811)	(.152)	(.384)	(.026)	(.018)	(.031)	.123	.113+	.117
Number of siblings	-.122	-.650	(-.076)	(-.085)	(-.012)	(-.005)	(-.003)	-.018+	(-.010)	(-.006)
Family annual income in 1967 (1000's of dollars)	.046	(-.225)	(.009)	(-.006)	.016	.014	.012	.022	.019	.016
Catholic	(-.058)	5.433	5.161	5.345	.130	.133	.114	.168	.172	.140
Jewish	1.305	12.480	6.319+	6.424+	(-.115)	-.188+	(-.164)	(-.046)	(-.138)	(-.096)

[a]Coefficients in parentheses were not significant at the .10 level. Coefficients with a "+" superscript were significant of .10 level. All other coefficients were significant at .05 levels.

[b]Characteristic is measured as of 1968 unless noted otherwise.

In 1975 the Panel Study asked household heads about supervisory authority on their jobs. Thus, we have measures (albeit fallible ones) of father's supervisory level for 702 men who were sons in male-headed households in 1968. (These measures also may have picked up permanent income.) Wright (1977) used these questions to explore whether racial differences in economic returns to schooling were due to racial differences in class categories. Table 5.1, row 5, shows the change in R^2 when measures of supervisory authority were added to the regressions of our outcome measures on the 12 demographic measures. Adding measures of father's supervisory authority increased the R^2s in the education and occupational status regressions by about one and one-half percentage points and increased the R^2 in the ln annual earnings regression by one percentage point but had negligible effects on the R^2 for ln hourly earnings. Sons whose fathers had say over others' pay or promotion acquired .91 more years of schooling, had a 7.6 point advantage in Duncan scores, and had a 15.5 percent annual earnings advantage over men with an otherwise similar measured demographic background. All these differences were significant, and controlling for schooling did not appreciably reduce the occupational status or annual earnings advantages.

Effect of Fathers' Test Scores on Son's Achievements

Another possibility was that our brothers' correlations picked up genetic similarities between brothers. Hernnstein (1973), for instance, has raised the possibility that the correlation between parents and sons' socioeconomic attainments may be due in large part to the genetic transmission of IQ. If this were true, then we would expect the coefficients of parental status measures to drop when measures of parental test scores were added to early attainment regressions. One would also predict that parental IQ should affect sons' attainments. We tested to see whether the father's cognitive test scores were associated with the son's economic achievements, using the Panel Study's 13-item sentence completion test administered to respondents in 1972.[13] The coefficients of this measure of father's test score were always insignificant when we added it to the education and to the reduced form occupational status and earnings regressions (see Table 5.1, row 6.) Furthermore, coefficients on other background measures were unchanged by this addition. These results are contradictory to the idea that the impact of demographic background on early

---

[13] Analyses show that the relationships between this test score measure and men's status and earnings were quite similar to those observed in other data with more reliable measures of cognitive test scores (Jencks et al., 1979, Chapter 4).

attainment is due to genetic transmission of IQ. Of course, our measure of paternal test scores was taken in adulthood and is not very reliable. If included demographic background measures such as father's education were a better proxy for the phenotypic component of paternal IQ than was our measure of adult paternal IQ, then these results might simply be due to the fact that we have employed a poor instrument.[14]

Nonetheless, these data provided no support for the argument that the disparities between sibling correlations and R^2s were due to genetic similarities on ability as measured by cognitive test scores. This finding is consistent with the findings of Jencks et al. (1979) that brothers' resemblance on economic outcomes was not predicted by their similarity on test scores. Since we have only examined test scores, we have no evidence that would allow us to say anything about whether genetic similarity or other kinds of talent explains sibling correlations.

Neighborhood Characteristics

We also attempted to examine the impact of the income level and racial composition of childhood community on the status of young men. We measured these childhood community factors by using the average income and the percentage white in the zip code area for the 1968 address. These two community measures had small and insignificant effects on all our outcome measures with one exception. (See Table 5.1, row 7.) Average community income was significantly and positively related to years of schooling. Each increment of $1000 in average community income raised a man's expected education by .09 years. Adding both community measures to our education regressions increased the R^2 by about 1.5 percentage points but had trivial effects in the other regressions. These results provided little evidence of a strong community effect, but our community measures were not very detailed and were unavailable for a large number of young men.

Corrections for Measurement Error in
Reports of Family Background

Our best estimate is that the 12 background characteristics measured in our brothers sample together with father's position in the work hierarchy, father's cognitive test score, and mean income and racial composition of the 1968

---

[14]We are grateful to Paul Taubman for pointing out this possibility.

neighborhood, accounted for 44.9 percent of the variance in sons´ schooling, 27.9
percent of the variance in their occupational status, and 14.7 percent of the
variance in their hourly earnings (Table 5.1, row 8). These figures still were
lower than the sibling intraclass correlations of .640, .434, and .288. We did
not have reports by both father and son for all the demographic variables
included in these analyses, and we had only one report for the son´s attainment
characteristics. Given this, we feel that the uncorrected estimates reported
above (and in Table 5.1, lines 7 and 8) give the best measure of the extent to
which demographic characteristics fail to predict resemblance between brothers.

We have, however, adjusted these estimates for measurement error as follows.
In our full sample of 915 employed men aged 23 to 33 years, we have reports by
parents and by sons of father´s schooling and occupation and of mother´s
schooling. We used pairwise correlations based on this sample to estimate the
following model:

$$(1) \quad ED_{s-s} = \alpha_1 + \beta_1 \, ED_{f-t} + \beta_2 \, OCC_{f-t} + \beta_3 ED_{m-t} + \nu_1$$

$$(2) \quad OCC_{s-s} = \alpha_2 + \beta_4 \, ED_{f-t} + \beta_5 \, OCC_{f-t} + \beta_6 ED_{m-t} + \nu_2$$

$$(3) \quad LN\ WAGE = \alpha_3 + \beta_7 \, ED_{f-t} + \beta_8 \, OCC_{f-t} + \beta_9 ED_{m-t} + \nu_3$$

$$(4) \quad ED_{f-f} = ED_{f-t} + \varepsilon_{1f}$$

$$(5) \quad ED_{f-s} = \lambda_{1s} \, ED_{f-t} + \varepsilon_{1s}$$

$$(6) \quad OCC_{f-f} = OCC_{f-t} + \varepsilon_{2f}$$

$$(7) \quad OCC_{f-s} = \lambda_{2s} \, OCC_{f-t} + \varepsilon_{2s}$$

$$(8) \quad ED_{m-f} = ED_{m-t} + \varepsilon_{3f}$$

$$(9) \quad ED_{m-s} = \lambda_{3s} ED_{m-t} + \varepsilon_{3s}$$

where
ED_{i-j} = the jth person´s report of the ith person´s education
OCC_{i-j} = the Duncan score of the jth person´s report of the ith person´s
            occupation
LN WAGE = ln (hourly wage) of son in 1978
i, j = f for father
        s for son
        t for true

In this model we allowed the stochastic disturbance terms of the endogenous
variables to covary freely. Based on results from previous analyses of
measurement error using father-son pairs from the Panel Study (Corcoran, 1979;
1980) we allowed errors in fathers´ reports of their own schooling and of their
wives´ schooling to covary and errors in sons´ reports of mothers´ and fathers´
schooling to covary; all other error covariances were fixed at zero.

Table 5.3 reports structural equations of the attainment process with and
without adjustments for measurement error. We compared equations estimated under

the assumption that fathers´ reports were without error (assumption 1) to equations estimated under the assumption that measurement error existed and had the structure specified above (assumption 2).

Table 5.3

MODELS OF EARLY STATUS ATTAINMENT UNDER DIFFERENT
ASSUMPTIONS OF MEASUREMENT ERROR
(For 915 employed male household heads aged 23 to 33 in 1979,
who lived with at least one parent in 1968.)

Assumptions About Measurement Error[a]	
1	$ED_{s-s} = .189\ ED_{f-f} + .014\ OCC_{f-f} + .116\ ED_{m-f} \qquad R^2 = .237$
2	$ED_{s-s} = .216\ ED_{f-t} + .011\ OCC_{f-t} + .164\ ED_{m-t} \qquad R^2 = .275$
1	$OCC_{s-s} = 1.270\ ED_{f-f} + .178\ OCC_{f-f} + .418\ ED_{m-f} \quad R^2 = .162$
2	$OCC_{s-s} = 1.486\ ED_{f-t} + .197\ OCC_{f-t} + .449\ ED_{m-t} \quad R^2 = .187$
1	$LNWAGE = .013\ ED_{f-f} + .004\ OCC_{f-f} + .003\ ED_{m-f} \quad R^2 = .033$
2	$LNWAGE = .008\ ED_{f-t} + .005\ OCC_{f-t} + .007\ ED_{m-t} \quad R^2 = .036$

[a]Assumption 1=   Father´s reports assumed true
Assumption 2=   Regressions are corrected for measurement error using model in Equations 1-9, allowing errors in fathers´ reports of their own and of their wives´ schooling to covary and allowing errors in men´s reports of their fathers´ and mothers´ schooling to covary.

In every case, models which assumed no measurement error in fathers´ reports of background traits modestly underestimated the overall effect of background on achievement. The R^2 in the regressions of son´s education on background rose by 16 percent from .237 to .275; the R^2 in the reduced-form equation of occupational status rose by 15 percent from .162 to .187; and the R^2 in the reduced-form equation of ln hourly wage on background rose by 9 percent from .033 to .036.

Table 5.1, row 9, shows the results when we applied these proportional increases to our regressions of all attainment measures on demographic background. We suspect that the increases in R^2s would be proportionately smaller if we had estimates for measurement error in all our background measures. Reports on variables like race, number of siblings, region of birth, whether female-headed household in 1968 and religion probably contained less error than the variables in our measurement models. Reports on family income, father native born and whether raised on a farm probably contained somewhat more error.

Corrections for Measurement Error in
Men's Reports of Their Own Status Traits

We know of no study which has calculated reliabilities for young men's reports of their own schooling, occupational status, or hourly earnings. Therefore, we used the reliability estimates derived by Jencks et al. (1979) in their analysis of sibling data (.86 for occupational status and .86 to .93 for ln earnings), and we used Bartlett's estimate of .92 for the reliability of Panel Study men's reports of their own schooling (Jencks et al., 1979, p. 330). Table 5.1, in lines 10, 11, 12, and 14, show the results of these adjustments. In all cases, there was still a considerable gap between the R^2s and the sibling intraclass correlations.

How Background Influences Economic Status

Most studies which estimated occupational status and earnings as a function of measured demographic background reported that the occupational status and/or earnings advantages associated with demographic characteristics (with the exception of race and family income) either disappeared altogether or dropped sharply once schooling and/or test scores were controlled. If the unmeasured characteristics that produced resemblance between brothers' occupational status and earnings were similar in character to the measured characteristics that produced such resemblance, we would expect these unmeasured traits to exert their influence indirectly via schooling.

We next estimated the extent to which shared background affects brothers' occupational status and earnings via their schooling as follows. In Figure 5.1, "a," the zero-order correlation of F_Y with Y_1, measures the overall impact of shared background on outcome Y. Figure 5.2, on the other hand, shows a model with two hypothetical variables: one (F_{ED}) which accounts for brothers' resemblance on schooling and another (H_Y) which accounts for brothers' resemblance on economic outcome Y over and above what would be expected on the basis of similar educational attainments. H_Y can be defined as the weighted sum of all family traits that influence outcome Y with education controlled; "b" is the standardized coefficient of H_Y when predicting outcome Y. The model in Figure 5.2 is exactly identified and can be estimated with sibling data if we

Figure 5.2

FAMILY EFFECTS ON ECONOMIC OUTCOMES
INDEPENDENT OF SCHOOLING

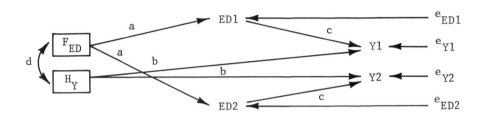

$$r_{ED1,ED2} = a^2$$

$$r_{ED1,Y1} = r_{ED2,Y2} = c + abd$$

$$r_{ED1,Y2} = r_{ED2,Y1} = cr_{ED1,ED2} + abd$$

$$r_{Y1,Y2} = cr_{ED2,Y1}$$

EDi = years of schooling for the ith brother

Yi = the ith brother's score on economic outcome Y

F_{ED} = all family traits that make brothers alike on schooling

H_Y = all family traits that influence economic outcome Y, net of schooling

assume family effects are symmetric and that brothers are not directly affected
by one another's characteristics. The difference between the zero-order
coefficient between Y and F_Y ("a" in Figure 5.1) and "b" in Figure 5.2 measures
how much of shared background operates via schooling.

We constructed a comparable estimate of the extent to which measured
background characteristics influenced occupational status and earnings indirectly
via schooling using the following technique (see Jencks et al., 1979, p. 71). We
calculated the occupational status and earnings advantages of a man who was one
standard deviation above the mean on the 12 demographic variables measured in our
brothers sample with and without controlling for schooling.[15] Table 5.4 shows
the results of these analyses for our sample of brothers and for the full sample.
Table 5.5, gives the sibling correlations used to estimate the models in
Figures 5.1 and 5.2. Table 5.2 reports how controlling schooling affects the
nonstandardized coefficients for particular background measures in the full
sample.

Education explained 70 percent of the impact of demographic background on
occupational status and 42 percent of its effect on hourly wages in our sample of
brothers (Table 5.4, row 4). The comparable figures were 65 and 64 percent in
the full sample (Table 5.4, row 2). Thus, we found that much of the influence of
measured background on men's occupational status and earnings is mediated by
schooling. These large decreases in explanatory power are consistent with
results from similar analyses of effects of demographic background.

Turning to our brothers models, we found that schooling explained 54 percent
of the impact of shared background on brothers' occupational status but only 14
percent of its impact on brothers' earnings (Table 5.4, row 5.) The difference
in the reduction in explanatory power using shared background rather than
demographic background was modest for occupational status (70 versus 54 percent),
but was quite dramatic for hourly earnings (42 versus 14 percent). Jencks
et al. (1979) reported a similar pattern for their sibling data sets.

Table 5.2 shows how particular background measures were affected by adding
controls for schooling. In general most coefficients became insignificant or
dropped substantially when education controls were added. This was not as true

---

[15]Note that we cannot compare these numbers to "a" and "b" in Figures 5.1
and 5.2. A man who is one standard deviation above the mean on all 12
demographic measures will be much more advantaged than a man who is one standard
deviation above the mean on a composite index of these 12 demographic
characteristics.

Table 5.4

PERCENTAGE OF BACKGROUND'S EFFECT ON OCCUPATIONAL STATUS
AND LN EARNINGS THAT IS DUE TO BACKGROUND'S EFFECT ON EDUCATION
(For varying subgroups of 915 employed male household heads age 23 to 33 in 1979
who lived with at least one parent in 1968.)

| | Occupational Status | | | Ln Hourly Earnings | | | Ln Annual Earnings | | |
	1 Coefficients Controlling Nothing	2 Coefficients Controlling Education	3 Percentage Reduction in Coefficients When Education is Controlled	4 Coefficients Controlling Nothing	5 Coefficients Controlling Education	6 Percentage Reduction in Coefficients When Education is Controlled	7 Coefficients Controlling Nothing	8 Coefficients Controlling Education	9 Percentage Reduction in Coefficients When Education is Controlled
Summed Coefficients on Demographic Background Variables Using Full Sample									
Omitting family income and religion[a]	.559	.204	64%	.741	.261	65%	.313	.139	66%
Including family income and religion[a]	.819	.362	65%	.979	.451	64%	.608	.383	37%
Summed Coefficients on Demographic Background Variables Using Subgroup of 413 Brothers (206.5 Brother Pairs)									
Omitting family income and religion[a]	.613	.069	89%	.346	.122	65%	.308	.141	54%
Including family income and religion[a]	.991	.291	70%	.673	.391	42%	.681	.467	31%
Summed Coefficients on Shared Background Variables Using Subgroup of 413 Brothers (206.5 Brother Pairs)									
	.658[b]	.290[c]	54%	.537[b]	.467[c]	14%	.510[b]	.466[c]	9%

[a] This is the sum of standardized coefficients of background measures when these measures (and education) are regressed on economic outcomes.
[b] This is estimated as "a" in Figure 5.1.
[c] This is estimated as "b" in Figure 5.2.

Table 5.5

CORRELATIONS[a] BETWEEN BROTHERS´ CHARACTERISTICS
(For 413 employed male household heads aged 23-33 in 1979 with
brothers, who lived with at least one parent in 1968.)[b]

	U_1	X_1	Y_1	Z_1	U_2	X_2	Y_2	Z_2
U_1	1.000							
X_1	.690	1.000						
Y_1	.264	.317	1.000					
Z_1	.312	.347	.841	1.000				
U_2	.640	.512	.229	.235	1.000			
X_2	.512	.434	.158	.189	.690	1.000		
Y_2	.229	.158	.260	.261	.264	.317	1.000	
Z_2	.238	.189	.261	.288	.311	.347	.841	1.000

U_i = Highest grade completed by the ith brother
X_i = Duncan score of current occupation of the ith brother
Y_i = Ln annual earnings of the ith brother
Z_i = Ln hourly earnings of the ith brother
i = 1,2

[a] All correlations were computed from files in which every pair of
brothers appears twice, with the order reversed. This makes
product-moment correlations equal to intraclass correlations.
[b] There were 206.5 brother pairs in this sample.

for the effects of religion or family income as for other background measures.
For the most part, the status and earnings advantages associated with being
Catholic remained about the same when schooling was controlled. And the hourly
earnings advantage associated with coming from a family with a high family income
dropped only 25 percent once schooling and characteristics of current residence
were controlled.

Does Controlling Family Background
Reduce Returns to Schooling?

It has been argued that failure to adequately specify and measure background
may upwardly bias estimates of economic returns to schooling (Bowles, 1972). By
analyzing the effects of educational differences among brothers on differences in
occupational status and income, we can eliminate biases in the education
coefficient due to the effects of common family background (Olneck, 1977).
Comparing this within-family regression coefficient to the coefficient obtained

with a model regressing men's occupational status and earnings measures on
schooling and measured background traits should allow us to estimate the extent
of bias in the education coefficient when demographic background alone is
controlled. However, this technique will not eliminate bias due to unmeasured
background traits that vary within families. Further, any such estimate is at
best tentative, given the small size of our brothers sample. This means that our
confidence intervals are likely be so large that we cannot draw firm conclusions.

In our sample of brothers, an extra year of schooling was associated with a
6.13 point increase in expected Duncan scores, with a 6.4 percent increase in
expected hourly earnings and with a 6.1 percent increase in expected annual
earnings (Table 5.6, row 1). Controlling measured background had almost no
effect on the Duncan score advantage associated with more schooling, and it
reduced the earnings advantages associated with additional schooling by a
moderate 15 to 25 percent (Table 5.6, rows 2 and 4).

The estimates from within-brother pair occupational status regressions
suggest that failure to control brothers' shared background may impart a modest
upward bias to the education coefficient. The schooling coefficient with our 12
background measures controlled is only 6.4 percent lower than the coefficient
with nothing controlled, but the within-pair schooling coefficient (4.40) is
28 percent lower.

Next we investigated whether or not the extent of potential bias in status
returns to schooling differed by level of schooling. Table 5.7 shows the results
when occupational status was regressed on three measures of schooling (years of
education, years of higher education, and college graduation or BA). The
coefficient on years of education was the average Duncan score advantage
associated with an additional year of elementary or secondary school. The effect
of a year of post-high school education can be obtained by summing the
coefficient on years of higher education with the years of education coefficient.
The BA variable measured the effect of college graduation.

The results (Table 5.7) indicated that effects of a year of elementary and
secondary schooling dropped by about 16 percent when measured background was
controlled but by more than half and became trivial to boot when common
background was controlled. The effects of higher education were more robust.
The estimated effects of four years of college over four years of high school
dropped by only 15 percent when shared background was controlled. This pattern
of effects was similar to that reported in Olneck's (1979, p. 87) analysis of
education effects.

Table 5.6

THE EFFECTS OF SCHOOLING ON OCCUPATIONAL STATUS
AND EARNINGS WITH AND WITHOUT BACKGROUND CONTROLS
(For 413 employed male household heads aged 23 to 33 in 1979
with brothers, who lived with at least one parent in 1968.)

Controlled Independent Variables	Occupational Status	Ln Hourly Earnings	Ln Annual Earnings
Coefficient (Standard Error) on Schooling			
No controls[a]	6.13 (.32)	.064 (.010)	.061 (.011)
Measured background controlled[b]	5.74 (.41)	.054 (.012)	.046 (.014)
Shared background controlled[c]	4.40 (.72)	.023 (.023)	.043 (.020)
Proportionate Reduction in Schooling Coefficient			
Measured background controlled[b]	6.4%	16%	25%
Shared background controlled[c]	28%	64%	29%

[a]These figures were obtained by regressing outcomes on men's years of schooling.

[b]These results were obtained by adding our 12 demographic variables to the regression described in footnote a.

[c]These results were obtained by regressing the differences in brothers' economic outcomes on the differences in their schooling.

Turning to earnings, we obtained a somewhat mixed picture. The analysis on annual earnings suggested that controlling measured background was sufficient to eliminate bias in the schooling coefficient due to unmeasured background factors, while the analysis of hourly earnings suggested the opposite. The annual earnings advantage associated with an extra year of schooling was approximately the same whether one controlled for measured background or for shared background. But the hourly earnings advantage associated with schooling dropped 64 percent

Table 5.7

EFFECTS OF SCHOOLING ON OCCUPATIONAL STATUS
BY LEVEL OF SCHOOLING
(For 413 employed male household heads age 23 to 33 in 1979
with brothers, who lived with at least one parent in 1968.)

Other Variables Controlled	Effects of A Year of Education	Effects of A Year of Higher Education	Effects of A BA	Estimated Effect of 4 Years College
None	2.68[a]	2.31[a]	10.32[a]	30.3[c]
Measured background	2.25[a]	2.32[a]	10.58[a]	28.9[c]
Shared family background	1.20[b]	1.93[b]	13.30[b]	25.8[c]

[a] These coefficients were estimated from the regressions of schooling measures and background measures on occupational status for the 413 brothers' sample.

[b] These coefficients were estimated from within-pair regression on the 206.5 brother pairs.

[c] This figure is equal to the effects of a BA plus 4 times the sum of effects of a year of education and of higher education.

when shared background was controlled. This last result is inconsistent with the pattern of results reported by Olneck (1979). Given this and given the large standard error of the within-pair schooling coefficient (in the ln hourly earnings regression), we suspect that this reduction may be caused by random sampling error.

SUMMARY OF EMPIRICAL RESULTS AND IMPLICATIONS

The results of our empirical analysis of demographic background were consistent with those reported by other researchers. Measured demographic background accounted for a large proportion of the variance in young men's schooling, for a more moderate amount of the variance in their early occupational status, and for a modest amount of the variance in their earnings. In general the occupational status and/or earnings advantages associated with particular demographic background characteristics either became insignificant or very small once men's schooling was controlled. There were three exceptions to this. Most of the occupational status and wage benefits associated with being Catholic, being raised by parents with a large income, and having a father who had supervisory authority at work remained even when schooling was controlled.

The results of our sibling analyses were also consistent with past research. We found both that sibling resemblance could not be predicted by the similarity between siblings' demographic background and that less than one-fifth of shared background's effects on earnings were mediated by schooling. These results provided very strong confirmation of the 1979 work of Jencks and his associates and also the work of others. Our data set, unlike most of those that Jencks examined, did not rely on one brother to locate the other. This should eliminate possible biases due to systematic differences between brothers who stay in touch and those who are out of touch. Second, our sibling data included a much more extensive list of background measures than were available in any sibling data sets analyzed by others (Olneck, 1976; Taubman, 1977; Jencks et al., 1979). In particular, our data included measures of family income and religion. Problems due to measurement error in reports of demographic background were minimized in our data since parents reported on their own characteristics. In addition, since we had reports by two observers for several of our demographic background variables, we were able to gauge the extent to which measurement error affected our estimates of the explanatory power of measured background. Finally, we were able to explore, albeit crudely, several theoretically important background characteristics such as father's position in the work hierarchy, father's test score, and neighborhood characteristics.

These results have confirmed the findings of Jencks et al. that the families into which men are born have a considerable impact upon their chances of economic success. But, the sibling research raises more questions than it answers, and in particular it tells us very little about the following three questions:

1) To what extent do social class origins affect men's life chances?

2) How much of a reality (for men) is equal opportunity?

3) What is the process by which parents enhance a son's chances of economic success?

Obviously, if we knew the answer to this last question, we could answer the first two better. Sibling research of the sort reported here subsumes all the things that result in similarities between brothers' attainments. One could think of processes such as parents encouraging a work ethic or the genetic transmission of talent which need not imply either class rigidities or a denial of equal opportunity. On the other hand, one might argue that our omitted background factors include effects of social class attributes or ascriptive

characteristics which are not fully captured by the included demographic
background measures.

Results from sibling data do allow us to reject certain alternatives.
Jencks and his associates showed that three-quarters of the effects of shared
background on occupational status and earnings remained when men's cognitive test
scores were controlled. Thus, whatever these unmeasured background traits are,
they do not depend on cognitive test scores to influence economic success. And
we have shown that a measure of father's test score was unrelated to measures of
son's success. Both these results fail to confirm the notion of an IQ-
meritocracy. Furthermore, both Jencks' results and ours suggest that much of the
impact of shared backgrounds on men's earnings operates independently of
education.

Our most important finding is that men's backgrounds have a large impact on
their socioeconomic attainments. The challenge is to find out how this influence
works. Two approaches should prove fruitful. The first is to track a sample of
young men over time as they complete school and enter the labor market (e.g.,
Sewell and Hauser, 1975). The second is to move away from supply-side analyses
and to investigate how men are sorted and evaluated within institutions such as
schools, personnel offices, and firms. (See Baron and Bielby, 1980, for an
elegant essay about the potential of such investigations.)

References

Berhman, Jere, and Taubman, Paul. "Intergenerational Transmission of Income and
    Wealth." American Economic Review 66 (May 1976): 436-40.

Behrman, Jere; Taubman, Paul; and Wales, Terence. "Controlling for and Measuring
    the Effects of Genetics and Family Environment in Equations for Schooling
    and Labor Market Success." In Kinometrics: The Determinants of Socio-
    economic Success within and between Families, edited by Paul Taubman.
    New York: North-Holland, 1977.

Bielby, William I.; Hauser, Robert M.; and Featherman, David L. "Response Errors
    of Black and Nonblack Males in Models of the Intergenerational Transmission
    of Socio-economic Status." American Journal of Sociology 84 (May 1977):
    1242-88.

Blau, Peter, and Duncan, Otis Dudley. The American Occupational Structure.
    New York: John Wiley and Sons, 1967.

Bowles, Samuel. "Schooling and Inequality from Generation to Generation."
    Journal of Political Economy 80 (May/June 1972): S219-51.

Bowles, Samuel, and Gintis, Herbert. Schooling in Capitalist America: Educational Reform and the Contradictions of Economic Life. New York: Basic Books, 1976.

Bowles, Samuel, and Nelson, Valerie. "The ´Inheritance of IQ´ and the Intergenerational Reproduction of Economic Inequality." Review of Economics and Statistics 56 (1974): 39-51.

Brittain, John A. The Inheritance of Economic Status. Washington, D.C.: Brookings Institution, 1977.

Chamberlain, Gary. "Are Brothers as Good as Twins?" In Kinometrics: The Determinants of Socio-economic Success with and between Families, edited by Paul Taubman. Amsterdam: North-Holland, 1977.

Chamberlain, Gary, and Griliches, Zvi. "Unobservables with a Variance-Components Structure: Ability, Schooling, and the Economic Success of Brothers." International Economic Review 16 (June 1975): 422-49.

_____. "More on Brothers." In Kinometrics: Determinants of Socioeconomic Success within and between Families, edited by Paul Taubman. New York: North-Holland, 1977.

Corcoran, Mary. "Sex Differences in Measurement Err in Status Attainment Models," Sociological Methods and Research (November 1980): 199-217.

Corcoran, Mary. "Measurement Error in Status Attainment Models." In Five Thousand American Families, Vol. VII, edited by Greg J. Duncan and James N. Morgan. Ann Arbor, Michigan.: Institute for Social Research, University of Michigan, 1979.

Corcoran, Mary; Jencks, Christopher; and Olneck, Michael. "The Effects of Family Background on Earnings." American Economic Review 66 (May 1976): 430-35.

Duncan, Otis Dudley; Featherman, David; and Duncan, Beverly. Socioeconomic Background and Achievement. New York: Seminar Press, 1972.

Featherman, David, and Hauser, Robert M. Opportunity and Change. New York: Academic Press, 1978.

Gintis, Herbert. "Education, Technology, and the Characteristics of Worker Productivity." American Economic Review 61 (1971): 266-79.

Goldberger, Arthur S. "Twin Methods: A Skeptical View." In Kinometrics: The Determinants of Socio-economic Success with and between Families," edited by Paul Taubman. New York: North-Holland, 1977.

Greeley, Andrew. The American Catholic: A Social Portrait. New York: Basic Books, 1977.

Griliches, Zvi. "Sibling Models and Date in Economics: Beginning of a Survey." Journal of Political Economy 87 (1979): S37-S63.

_____. "Estimating the Returns to Schooling: Some Econometric Problems." Econometrica 45 (January 1977): 1-22.

Griliches, Zvi; Hall, B.; and Hausman, J. "Missing Data and Self-Selection in Large Panels." Annales de L´INSEE 30-31 (1978): 137-76.

Hauser, Robert M., and Featherman, David L. The Process of Stratification: Trends and Analyses. New York: Academic Press, 1977.

Hauser, Robert M., and Daymont, Thomas N. "Schooling Ability and Earnings: Cross-sectional Findings 8 to 14 Years after High School Graduation." Sociology of Education 50 (July 1977): 182-206.

Hernstein, Richard T. IQ and the Meritocracy. Boston: Little, Brown, 1973.

Jencks, Christopher; Smith, Marshall; Acland, Henry; Bane, Mary Jo; Cohen, David; Gintis, Herbert; Heyns, Barbara; and Michelson, Stephan. Inequality: A Reassessment of the Effect of Family and Schooling in America. New York: Basic Books, 1972.

Jencks, Christopher; Bartlett, Susan; Corcoran, Mary; Gouse, James; Eaglesfield, David; Jackson, Gregory; McClelland, Kent; Meuser, Peter; Olneck, Michael; Schwartz, Joseph; Ward, Sherry; and Williams, Jill. Who Gets Ahead: The Determinants of Economic Success in America. New York: Basic Books, 1979.

Kohn, Melvin. Class and Conformity. Homewood, Illinois.: The Dorsey Press, 1969.

Morgenstern, Richard. "Direct and Indirect Effects on Earnings of Schooling and Socioeconomic Background." Review of Economics and Statistics 55 (May, 1973): 225-33.

Olneck, Michael. "On the Use of Sibling Data to Estimate the Effects of Family Background, Cognitive Skills, and Schooling: Results from the Kalamazoo Brothers Study." In Kinometrics: The Determinants of Economic Success within and between Families, edited by Paul Taubman, Amsterdam: Horth-Holland, 1977.

_____. "On the Use of Sibling Data to Estimate the Effects of Family Background, Cognitive Skills, and Schooling: Results from the Kalamazoo Brothers Study." In Kinometrics: The Determinants of Socio-economic Success within and between Families, edited by Paul Taubman. Amsterdam: North-Holland, 1977.

Sewell, William H., and Hauser, Robert M. Education, Occupation and Earnings. New York: Academic Press, 1975.

Taubman, Paul. "The Determinants of Earnings: Genetics, Family, and Other Environments: A Study of White Male Twins." American Economic Review 66 (December 1976a): 858-70.

_____. "Earnings, Education, Genetics, and Environment." Journal of Human Resources 11 (Fall 1976b): 447-61.

Taubman, Paul, and Wales, T. "Mental Ability and Higher Educational Attainment in the 20th Century." National Bureau of Economic Research, Occasional Paper 118. Berkeley, California., 1972.

Chapter 6

ANTECEDENTS AND CONSEQUENCES OF RETIREMENT

James N. Morgan

BACKGROUND

Concern for the economic aspects of aging and retirement has a long history, even though the amount of quantitative research beyond simple description has been relatively small and some of it has been ignored in discussions of policy. When it became obvious in the fifties and sixties that the years of postwar prosperity had not eliminated poverty in the United States, the plight of the aged was one of the problems in the forefront when the poor were discussed (Bond, 1954; Steiner and Dorfman, 1957; Strumpel, 1972; U.S. Department of Commerce, Bureau of the Census, 1978; U.S. Department of Health Education and Welfare, 1953; U.S. House of Representatives, 1979).

It was relatively easy to produce cross-sectional data showing the low incomes of the aged, and the usual technical issues arose about adjustment for their smaller family sizes and larger nonmoney income resulting from imputed rent. Even distributional issues arose as in the public discussions over medical care when some analysts pointed out that people over 65 had higher average assets or net worth than people under 65, and more careful analysts pointed out that inequality of both income and assets increases with age, so that the largest proportion of people with no assets is found among the aged (Morgan, 1962, 1965; Blue Cross, 1962).

During the last few decades there has been a substantial amount of writing on non-economic aspects of aging, including the affective effects of retirement, attempts to show gradual "disengagement" from society, and beliefs that retirement was bad for one's health (Atchley, 1976; Berghorn, 1978; Binstock, 1977; Butler, 1975; Eisdorfer, 1972; Filenbaum, 1971; Friedman and Havighurst, 1954; Glamser, 1976; Havighurst et al, 1969; Jaslow, 1976; Kimmel et al., 1978; Larson, 1978; Pollak, 1957; Pollam, 1975; Price et al., 1979; Riley, 1968, 1969, 1972; Shanas, 1958, 1972; Thompson, 1973). Of course some studies showed retirement to be desired and enjoyed.

In the sixties and seventies improved data were provided by a number of large quantitative studies: the HEW surveys of the aged in 1963 and 1968 (Bixby, 1970; Epstein and Murray, 1967), a 1973-1974 two-wave survey of the low-income aged and the disabled (Tissue, 1979), a Survey of Newly Entitled Beneficiaries, (Lauriat, 1970b Kolodrubetz, 1971, 1973 Reno, 1971 U.S. HEW, 1975). However, most of the data were from cross sections, not panels or reinterviews, and age comparisons are beset with well-known difficulties of separating age, cohort, and period-of-history effects. For example, in spite of popular beliefs, older people generally report few dissatisfactions, even though they have lower incomes, and frequently poorer health, though health does affect individual satisfactions (U.S. House of Representatives Select Committee on Aging, 1979).

Interestingly enough, the first major study with interviews of people before and after retirement has largely been ignored (Streib and Schneider 1971). This study's findings flew in the face of conventional wisdom but have been replicated since then. People reported some fears of retirement beforehand, but after retirement their reports of general satisfaction and of their own health generally improved. It is gradually becoming clear that retirement is a desirable goal, much sought after and enjoyed so long as health and adequate income persist. Confirmation exists in HEW's Longitudinal Retirement History (LRH) Study, a panel started at preretirement ages and followed biennially for six waves (Irelan 1968, 1976; Motley 1978; Murray 1978; Schwab 1974, 1977; Sherman 1973; Thompson 1978a, 1978b, 1979;). That panel also documented the fact, unwelcome to some, that only a fragment (about one-tenth) of the retired was able and eager to work (Motley, 1978). Similar findings appeared in the National Longitudinal Study's panel of older men (Parnes, 1979). And while it focused more on affective than economic aspects, the Duke Longitudinal study of the aged also showed no loss of satisfaction (George and Maddox, 1977).

The aggregate statistics bore out the pervasive desire to retire. As soon as the Social Security system allowed women and then men to retire at 62, even though at actuarially reduced benefits, the vast majority of both started doing so. And they continue to do so, in spite of inflation, although a substantial minority reported in the 1979 wave of the Panel Study that inflation had caused them to change their ideas about retirement (see below).

In spite of growing current unemployment, this surge of early retirement, combined with demographic factors of the expected future growth of the aged population and shrinkage of the working-age population, aroused concern about future labor shortages and even about difficulties for the nation in producing enough to support a larger dependent population. Much of this discussion ignored the simultaneous diminution of the dependent population under 18 resulting from the baby bust and the increment in women working outside the home, further facilitated by lower fertility. The encouragement of people to retire later or getting the aged back to work was long supported by normative beliefs that work was good for their mental health and life satisfaction. This concern was further stimulated by the effects of population changes and inflation on a Social Security system based on the assumption of a stable rate of population growth (at the real rate of interest) and no inflation.

We shall not review that literature here except to point out that it mixes up three problems in a misleading and politically disruptive way: First, there are the basic economic-productive problems of a society with a current period of a high ratio of potential workers to the total population but an expectation that that ratio will fall. (This requires large investments now that will increase output per person-hour in the future.) The second issue concerns the funding arrangements of the Social Security system and their impact on the national economy (e.g., on saving and investment). It is quite clear that the golden rule algebra, by which the misnamed "pay-as-you-go" worked with stable prices and a stable rate of population growth, no longer works. Actuarially sound interpretations of the system will have to replace insistence that the contributions of about 40 working age cohorts or generations should balance the benefits of some 15 retired generations if we are to avoid continual politicized interference with the system. Third, we must consider intergenerational equity and the question whether each generation in some aggregate sense pays its own way. Analysis of this issue must deal with the relation between expected benefits and expected lifetime contributions plus interest (at market interest rates, which reflect inflation). To illustrate where this leads, we can think of an imaginary trust fund into which a generation pays its contributions and which accrues interest at standard market interest rates (3 percent plus the rate of inflation). Then the indexing of benefits reflects nothing more nor less than higher interest rates occasioned by the current inflation, and those increased benefits become a legitimate right of the retired and a legitimate part of the interest burden on the government debt--a debt that, unlike government bonds, happens to pay proper interest rates.

More relevant to our discussion of research rather than policy is that this concern led to studies of the retirement decision in general, to studies of the effects of Social Security on retirement, and finally to studies of more complex models of lifetime planning where Social Security affects desired retirement age which in turn induces extra saving to facilitate that retirement. Strangely enough, in spite of all the discussion about Social Security, there have been no official data collected on people's retirement plans or expectations, and only very recently have there been data on pension coverage (U.S. Department of Health Education and Welfare, 1972; Rogers, 1980). Understanding of the large changes in actual retirement age is hampered by lack of data on changes in pension coverage, savings, and expected retirement among age cohorts. The President's Commission on Pension Policy is doing a two-wave survey (September 1979 and September 1980) of asset accumulations and pension coverage. Econometric studies of the effect of Social Security on saving have disagreed, and the confusion was increased by the discovery that several studies which showed that Social Security reduced saving no longer did so when a computer error was corrected.[1]

There have been several other recent studies of the possible effects of the Social Security system on individual saving (Kotlikoff, 1979; Pellechio, 1979; Feldstein, 1980; Feldstein and Pellechio, 1979). These studies appear to produce findings quite sensitive to the model used, and perhaps more dependent on precise data than the available data would allow. The latest, not summarized by Morgan (1980), is Martin Feldstein's 1980 working paper which used the Retirement History Survey file to estimate the effects of Social Security wealth on total asset accumulation. His estimate, close to -1, indicates that Social Security discourages or replaces other saving. Martin David is doing a similar analysis with Wisconsin estate data.

The Institute for Social Research (ISR) conducted a set of studies in the 1960s on small national samples and on a sample of United Auto Workers members, 58 to 61 years old who were affected by the union-negotiated Supplemental Early Retirement Benefits (Barfield and Morgan, 1969). These studies indicated that both plans for early retirement and satisfaction with retirement were dominated by health and an adequate retirement income. There were some added effects of being free of mortgage payments and obligations to children, and a small effect from a combination of having little or no control over one's work pace and having difficulty keeping up. A follow-up of the UAW workers to see whether their euphoria continued even after they reached 62 when the UAW supplement stopped indicated that they mostly continued to be well satisfied (Barfield, 1979).

---

[1]The original, much cited article, which was wrong, was Feldstein (1974).

An earlier ISR study which focused on poverty and its intergenerational transmission permitted some supplemental analyses of the economic status of the aged (Morgan and David, 1962; Morgan, 1965). Some funds from the Ford Foundation made it possible to repeat the questions on expected or actual retirement in 1977 (Barfield and Morgan, 1978). The national confusion at that time about whether private pension plans would pay off, plus some controversy over Social Security, increased people´s uncertainty about what they could expect and even about when they would retire. In general the data seemed to show that the previous negative correlation between current age and planning to retire early was neither a pure age effect of people getting more realistic as they get older nor a time trend brought about by succeeding generations who were less imbued with the work ethic. Rather, it represented different historic experiences of cohorts, so the age-curve now had a kink in it. Some people who had spent their whole working lives in prosperous times, and were now close to retirement were nearly as likely to plan early retirement as some younger people who came into the labor market after unemployment started rising and without the seniority enjoyed by their elders (Morgan, 1980; Barfield and Morgan, 1978).

There were also studies in Denmark (Skade, 1957; and Svane, 1973) and in England (Great Britain, 1966). The British have been experimenting since 1977 with a scheme to induce people to retire a year earlier (Makeham and Morgan, 1980). The Swedish also have a new partial retirement plan (Crona, 1980).

The importance of health and financial ability to retire had already been noted in analyses of the Survey of Newly Entitled Beneficiaries (Reno, 1971), although those who retired at 65 in that study often gave a compulsory retirement age as an the additional reason. The same basic findings appeared also in analysis of the Longitudinal Retirement History Study (Quinn 1977, 1979) and the National Longitudinal Study (Parnes, 1979), and in our analysis of the retirement questions included in the eleventh wave of the Panel Study of Income Dynamics (Morgan, 1980).

However, the concern over the state of Social Security and the possible need for a later retirement age in the future has led to much attention being given, not to the income effect (retiring because one can afford it) but to substitution effects where the Social Security earnings tax is seen as an inducement to retire (Boskin, 1977; Burkhauser, 1979; Quinn, 1977; Pellechio, 1977).

On the other hand, Kotlikoff (1979) who adjusted for selection bias, found no "Social Security effect." We noted in Volume VIII of this series that all these studies of Social Security effects have been forced to use models which make multiple use of recent earnings. We can illustrate with a study which was overlooked in that discussion (Boskin, 1977).

Michael Boskin used the first five years of the Panel Study to investigate retirement, defined as dropping below quarter time, with an analysis focused on the effect of estimated Social Security benefits (Boskin, 1977). The statistics were sophisticated, but the estimation of Social Security benefits was ambiguous and potentially subject to a severe selection-bias effect. For those not likely to be eligible for the maximum, Boskin estimated Social Security benefits by estimating the primary insurance amount, which was in turn estimated from average monthly earnings. These were "imputed either from a regression of earnings on education, occupation and other personal characteristics, or from actual benefits received and information on age, earnings, etc." (p. 9). If those with better than average actual earnings records, and hence potentially higher Social Security benefits, were more likely to retire, then using that higher actual benefit in comparison with a lower estimated benefit for those who did not retire would produce the appearance of a substantial Social Security effect.

Sophisticated econometrics appeared to prove that Social Security discouraged working, when in fact none of the studies really modelled the full set of provisions of the system. A recent study which looked at the implications of Social Security for a real sample--the Longitudinal Retirement History Study-- pointed out that, properly understood, the system affected people quite differently depending on their circumstances and earning history, and for most it even provided a net incentive to work between ages 62 and 65 (Blinder, Gordon and Wise, 1978, 1981). The reason is the combination of the actuarial adjustment between 62 and 65 which was estimated for a typical 62-year old to be fair at a real discount rate of 4 percent (higher than the recent real interest rates), and the recalculation of benefits whenever there were some higher earnings that could be averaged in, dropping out a year of lower earnings. For many typical cases from the LRH study, the authors estimated that this recalculation was equivalent to a 50-percent wage subsidy, or was until the 1977 law started indexing covered earnings of early years upward to allow for inflation since then. But that same law also tripled the increase in benefits from 1 to 3 percent for each extra year of work after age 65, so that after 65 an adjustment of benefits reduced the tax rate implicit in the earnings test to 25-35 percent instead of the apparent 50 percent, not counting the recalculation of benefits from dropping low-earning years. The authors concluded:

...it seems likely that the social security law--if understood by the public--would provide work disincentives for only a small minority of individuals. For the vast majority, it seems that social security should either be irrelevant to labor supply decisions or induce them to work harder.

It is possible, therefore, that social security is discouraging labor supply only because its provisions are poorly understood.

The same study modelled the retirement decisions as a function of increasing reservation wage (taste for leisure) and decreasing (actual or potential) market wage, as age increases. It also estimated a wealth accumulation model including a desire to make bequests and found that both Social Security wealth and private pension wealth resulted in reductions in other private saving. However, the authors noted that with private pensions there was a parallel saving in the pension fund, whereas there was none with Social Security. The policy implications are not clear, since few would want the government to create a huge Social Security trust fund which would have to be invested in private industry.

So far as we know, there have been no recent studies in the United States of people's awareness of the provisions of the Social Security system, but it is instructive that a recent national study in England revealed a substantial amount of ignorance of the crucial provisions relative to retirement decisions (Parker, 1980). In that survey of men aged 55 to 72 and women aged 50 to 72, nearly half the men under pension age and two-thirds of the women said they were not aware that working after the pension age would increase their pension benefits later on. Of those working past pension age, one-fourth had not heard of a rule that earning too much might reduce their pensions, and more than half did not know at what earnings level the reduction started. When even more direct questions were asked, a third of working pensioners said they were keeping down the amount they earned because they knew their pension would be cut if they earned too much, but a third of these were not actually subject to the rule. And of the 30 percent who said they would try to increase their earnings if they could do so without having their pension cut, a quarter were not even subject to the earnings rule (p. 46). For those who do not trust what people say and look for preferences revealed by behavior, "There was no evidence to suggest that pensioners' earnings were concentrated in the band immediately below the earnings limit of Ł35" (Parker, 1980, p. 45).

Analyses of two of the National Longitudinal Study panels by Hall and Johnson (1980) are strikingly similar to our analysis in Volume VIII. They used logit rather than ordinary regression; but, given the substantial sample sizes and the non-extreme proportions, that would make little difference. They had a better subjective health measure, which worked, and a days-in-hospital report which did not (perhaps because it did not also encompass days lost at home through illness or accident).

They found, as we did, that private or non-Social Security government pensions were more likely to encourage very early retirement than was Social Security, and their data had expected amounts where we only had coverage. They did not make use of mortgage timing or previous unemployment or illness (they found days in hospital had no effect); we found rather, that people with continuing mortgage payments were less likely to plan to retire and that a history of illness encouraged plans for early retirement, but unemployment (insignificantly) discouraged retirement plans. They found that spouse's Social Security encouraged retirement; we found that it did not, but that a wife's expectation of a private pension did encourage retirement.

But both Hall and Johnson's analysis and ours found essentially that people retire if and when they can afford it, and/or when their health demands it. Compulsory retirement apparently affects only a few.

Hall and Johnson used logit analysis, but they took the group planning never to retire as the comparison for each of the expected retirement ages. We, on the other hand, treated the decision as a conditional one, the very early retirement (before 62) being compared with anything later, the early retirement (before 65) being compared with all later possibilities. Our method provides a stabler base for comparisons and appears closer to the logic of retirement planning. Recently, with more working wives approaching retirement, attention has focused on the jointness of the retirement decision (Fox, 1977; Clark et al, 1980). As the first step in a simulation study, Anderson, Clark and Johnson have produced logit regression analyses of labor force participation of husbands and wives in the Longitudinal Retirement History Study as a function of both of their ages, imputed wages, and the other's labor force participation (Anderson, Clark and Johnson, 1980). The wife's wage, age and eligibility for pension affect both their participations, but the husband's affect neither. And each's participation affects the other's. There is clearly a related and possibly simultaneous decision about retirement.

In addition to the studies of the financial resources available to retirees discussed above, there have been many studies of housing of the aged and some attention to the possibility of converting their housing equity into annuities (Newman, 1976; Struyk, 1977; Neubig, 1980).

Another way to look at aging is to list the data bases which have been and will continue to be used in studying the retirement process, and the condition of the aging:

Census data

Current Population Survey

1951 Survey of Beneficiaries (HEW)

1968 Survey of Aged (Bixby)

1968-70 Survey of Newly Entitled Beneficiaries (HEW 1976)

Longitudinal Retirement History Study (Social Security Administration, HEW, 1968-1978)

Duke Longitudinal Study (George and Maddox, 1977)

National Longitudinal Studies--Panel of Middle Aged Men (1967-, Parnes, et al., 1979)

Studies in England and Denmark (Great Britain, Danish National Institute for Social Research); longitudinal one planned in France

Panel Study of Income Dynamics (Duncan and Morgan, 1972, ff)

All except the last are samples of cohorts embedded in a particular period of history. The Panel Study of Income Dynamics, if it continues, will allow analysis (in a very small but representative sample) of changing patterns of retirement, with extensive prehistory and later data on consequences.

As a first step toward that long-range possibility, we present some analysis of the antecedents and consequences of retirement for those in the panel who retired during the period from 1971 through 1974. And as a control group we include along a sample of people of similar ages some of whom had retired before 1971, and some of whom had still not retired by 1975.

ANALYSIS

Before and After Retirement

There are too few people retiring in any one year to allow much annual analysis with the Panel Study data. But by taking all those who retired in 1971-1974, we have for analysis four years before their year of retirement and four years after that year. We simply shift time scales so that everything is dated relative to the year of retirement. These preliminary findings could easily be expanded by allowing only three years before and three years after and considering all those who retired in 1970-1975.

But time trends may be occurring that cannot be corrected for by putting dollar amounts into 1978 dollars, and it is useful to have a control group. For this purpose, we show in some tables all those who did not retire in 1971-1974 but were 67-73 years old in 1979 (59-65 in 1971). We divided them into three groups: those who had retired before 1971, those who had retired after 1974, and those who were not yet retired in 1979 (see Appendix Tables A6.1 and A6.2).

Table 6.1 gives the averages "pre" and "post" for the combined subsample, those who retired in 1971-1974 and the similar aged control group. Table 6.2 shows results for persons who retired in 1971-74 both those who retired before they were 65 and those who retired at age 65 or later. The similarities were many, and reassuring. Retirement was real: work hours dropped from close to full time to trivial amounts and earnings dropped also. Transfer incomes rose to make up two-fifths of the decrease in the family heads' annual earnings for those who retired early, while transfers made up less than one-fourth of the drop in income for those who retired on time at age 65 or later. Reinforcing that difference was a larger decline in food expenditures for the later retirees and a decline in an index of personal efficacy compared with an increase for the early retirees, although this latter difference was at the borderline of significance.[2] The trends, averages of time-fitted individual regressions, all seem appropriate, when we remember that with inflation adjustment a constant dollar amount can show up as a declining trend in 1978 dollars.

The standard deviations are measures of temporal instability, based on the four years for each individual. Table A6.2 in the appendix gives the interpersonal variability for the 152 1971-1974 retirees and for all the 351 cases.

When we follow the same people over time, and assume that comparing situations before and after an event reveals something about the causes and consequence of the event, we must remember that historic time is also changing, affecting not only price levels but real earnings and unemployment. And individuals are getting older so that some changes may merely be the result of aging. Comparisons with our three "control groups" are useful, particularly for seeing whether people in the same age group who did not retire during the period were experiencing some of the same changes. Of course, the measures that involve earnings, hours of work, or transfers are distorted for the other groups by containing some years called "preretirement" that were really postretirement (for

---

[2]The efficacy index is the number of positive answers to three questions on sense of control over one's own life. It was measured in 1970 and 1975 and not shifted according to year of retirement.

Table 6.1

SOME "PRERETIREMENT" AND "POSTRETIREMENT" AVERAGES
(For 351 unchanged-heads who retired in 1971-1974 <u>or</u>
who were 67-73 years old in 1979
"control group.")

	Four Years Before Retirement or Control Period[a]	Four Years After Retirement or Control Period[a]
Four-Year Averages		
Work hours	1,683	500
Annual earnings in 1967 Dollars)	$9,664	2,954
Income/needs	3.8	2.9
Transfer income	$2,365	4,718
Food expenditures	$2,723	3,038
Food needs	$1,329	1,236
Trends (Real per Year)		
Work hours	-107	-102
Annual earnings	$-1,897	-750
Income/needs	-0.04	-0.14
Transfer income	$-551[c]	315
Food expenditure	$39	-251
Change in house equity	$2,939	$9,084[d]

[a]Immediately preceding year of retirement, or for those aged 59-65 in 1971 and already retired, we use 1967-1970; and for those aged 62-68 in 1974 and not yet retired, we use 1971-1974.

[b]For those aged 59-65 in 1971 and already retired, we use 1972-1975; and for those aged 62-68 in 1974 and not yet retired, we use 1975-1978.

[c]Highly variable, standard deviation=1,982.

[d]Differential inflation.

those who retired before 1971) and some called "postretirement" that were still preretirement for the other two groups.

For someone aged 67-73 in 1979 who retired before 1971, we ended up comparing 1967-1970 with 1972-1975, the first period including one or more years after retirement and the second period being not immediately after retirement but

Table 6.2

FOUR YEARS BEFORE RETIREMENT AND FOUR YEARS AFTER
(For those who retired in 1971-1974.)

	Retired Before Age 65			Retired at Age 65 or Later		
	Pre	Post	Change	Pre	Post	Change
Hours						
Level	1,963	237	-1,726	1,559	181	-1,378
Trend	-69	-20		-133	-8	
Standard deviation[a]	287	97		278	88	
Annual Earnings						
Level	11,692	1,097	-10,595	9,112	823	-8,289
Trend	-1,925	-36		-1,180	-110	
Standard deviation[a]	4,775	361		2,594	505	
Transfer Income						
Level	1,320	5,647	+4,327	2,887	4,812	+1,925
Trend	-179	-41		-571	15	
Standard deviation[a]	1,199	3,348		2,189	2,551	
Income/Needs						
Level	3.93	2.75	-1.18	3.49	2.45	-1.04
Trend	0.32	-0.35		0.01	-0.40	
Standard deviation	0.53	0.21		0.50	0.18	
Food Expenditures						
Level	3,070	3,059	-11	3,099	2,533	-566
Trend	-165	-140		-279	-87	
Efficacy[b]	2.09	2.34	+.25	2.20	2.05	-.15
Change in house equity (unadjusted for price level)	2,743	9,611		2,749	8,037	
Number of Cases	97	97	97	55	55	55

[a]Standard deviation of four years, averaged across individuals, not interpersonal variation. Interpersonal standard deviations are mostly proportionate to mean levels except for trends where means can be zero.
[b]Pre=1970, post=1975.

somewhat later. For someone who retired in 1975-1978, we compared 1971-1974 with 1975-1978, so some of the "post" years were really the year of retirement or before. Perhaps the group not yet retired in 1979 was the cleanest because both four-year periods were preretirement for it. As Table 6.3 shows an increase in food expenditures for this group, perhaps reflecting inflation, and a small decline in income/needs in 1978 dollars. This group also had a small insignificant increase in "efficacy" with which we can compare the increase for early retirees and the small decrease for late retirees.

Table 6.3

SOME COMPARISONS WITH "CONTROL GROUPS"

| | Retired in 1971-1974 | | Did Not Retire in 1971-1974 (Aged 59-65 in 1971) | | |
	Before Age 65	At Age 65 or Older	Retired Before 1971	Retired After 1974	Not Yet Retired in 1977
Efficacy in 1970	2.09	2.20	1.93	2.24	2.00
Efficacy in 1975	2.34	2.05	2.09	2.33	2.07
Change	+.25	-.15	+.16	+.09	+.07
Change in annual food expenditure (1978 dollars)	-$1,1	-$566	-$670	+$1133	+$988
Change in income/needs	-.31	-.32	-.39	+.17	-.18

We are also able to make some pre/post comparisons for all those who were retired by 1978, since we asked a sequence of questions about whether their retirement was planned/unexpected or willing/unwilling (remember that the timing of the pre and postmeasures was not precise when we included the pre-1971 retirees and the 1975-1978 retirees). Table 6.4 indicates that, interestingly enough, the planned and the willing retirees had a smaller drop in income/needs and little difference in efficacy change (although their levels were higher on both), but their food expenditures showed less of a reduction.

Some Effects of Inflation on Retirement Plans and Attitudes

In 1979, we asked both retired and nonretired people whether inflation had caused them to change their attitudes toward retirement. The actual question came after a sequence on inflation which asked:

"Prices and costs have been rising generally--are there some particular increases that have hit you especially hard?"

"What are they?"

"Have you been able to do anything about it?"

"What have you done?"

TABLE 6.4

EFFECTS OF THE CIRCUMSTANCES OF RETIREMENT

	Reported in 1978 That:			
	Had Retired as Planned	Had Retired Unexpectedly	Was Willing or Glad to Retire	Had Retired Only Because Had to
Efficacy 1970	2.16	2.01	2.30	1.88
Efficacy 1975	2.31	1.97	2.30	2.04
Change in efficacy	+.15	−.04	0	+.16
Change in food expenditure	+79	−223	+8	−15
Pre income/needs	4.17	3.37	4.41	2.95
Post income/needs	3.03	2.41	3.14	2.24
Change in income/needs	−1.14	−0.96	−1.27	−0.71
Number of cases	119	108	131	104

"Has inflation caused you to change your ideas about retirement?"

"How have they changed?"

Two responses to the last question were coded, but very few gave a second response. Answer codes were designed to handle both the nonretired and retired:

Now planning to retire later

Now planning not to retire

Now not sure when will/can retire

Planning to retire earlier

Planning to retire from one job and get another

Went back to work

Might go back to work

Regrets retiring

No change in plans, but only about ideas about retirement

Save more for retirement

The startling finding from the responses was the small effect of inflation. We present the data separately for the retired respondents, since it has a different meaning. Table 6.5 containing the main replies given by retired people according to the age at which they retired, shows that even the few who said inflation had affected their retirement ideas were indicating that it affected their feelings rather than their actions or plans.

Table 6.5

EFFECT OF INFLATION ON IDEAS ABOUT RETIREMENT
(For 574 retired by 1979.)

Respondent Reaction to Inflation	Retired by 1978 and Retired at Age:				
	45-61	62-64	65	66-97	All Retired
Went back to work	2	1	2	0	1.0
Might go back	1	1	0	1	0.6
Regrets retiring	3	3	3	3	3.2
No change but feels different	7	4	11	3	5.3
Should save more for retirement	1	1	1	1	0.9
Other	2	4	5	4	4.2
No effect	84	86	78	88	84.8
	100	100	100	100	100.0
Number of cases	192	181	62	139	574

A somewhat larger (but still small) proportion of the 1,046 respondents 45-64 years old and not retired in 1978, reported some change in retirement plans (Table 6.6). About one in seven said he or she would retire later than originally planned, 3.8 percent said that due to inflation they would not retire at all, and another 3.9 percent said that they now didn't know when they would retire. Combining those groups would mean that for about one-fifth of the sample, their expected retirement age had at least been pushed back. Like most quantitative measures, the truth is more moderate than the conjectures, but in the same direction.

In 1978, those aged 45-64 and not retired were also asked:

> Taking everything into account, if you retired at 65 would you expect to have a retirement income that was not enough, just enough, more than enough or what?

Table 6.6

EFFECT OF INFLATION ON RETIREMENT PLANS
(For 1,046 who were aged 45-64 and not retired in 1978 or 1979.)

Respondent's Reaction:	In 1979, Planned to Retire:				All
	Before 62	62-64	At 65	66-	
Will retire later	21	7	14	19	13.6
Will not retire	3	3	4	7	3.8
Not sure when	3	6	3	3	3.9
Will retire and get another job	1	1	1	0	0.6
No change in plans but in attitude	5	6	6	3	5.9
Other or NA	9	5	5	7	6.4
No effect	58	72	67	61	65.8
	100	100	100	100	100.0
Number of cases	190	306	449	101	

Table 6.7 shows that those who thought in 1978 that they would not have enough or only just enough retirement income to retire at 65 were more likely in 1979 to say that they had changed their retirement plans, though again the differences were small.

Is there any difference in how inflation affects people who are and who are not retired? Table 6.8 shows the responses to a question about which price increases hit them especially hard. The responses are shown according to whether they retired early or late, compared with the whole sample of 5,819 unchanged household heads between 1978 and 1979. There was a remarkable similarity across all groups as to which price increases they felt most. Transportation remained important even after retirement, and utility bills appear to be no more important than before even though most older people were relatively overhoused, particularly in relation to their cash income. Perhaps the various homeowner relief programs for older people have already had their effect. Table 6.9 shows that, for those 45-64 years old and not retired in 1978, differential perceptions of where inflation hit hardest were not associated with retirement plans.

In general then, inflation has had a real, though small and rather undifferentiated effect on people's attitudes and retirement plans. The 1979 interviews were taken between March and August of 1979, before the serious inflation had persisted very long. We repeated the question in the 1980 questionnaire and will soon know whether people's responses will have changed as they have realized just how serious continuing inflation can be. We plan to repeat the question about expected retirement age in the 1981 interviews.

SUMMARY

It is apparent that we are in a state of confusion and changing views about retirement and Social Security. Neither Social Security's effect on saving nor its effect on retirement is clear. There is, however, accumulating evidence that most people want to retire, like retirement if their health and income are adequate, and even benefit from it. Even inflation, at least in its early stages, has not had much apparent effect on people's retirement plans or driven them back to work. Our analysis of a small group who retired during the period from 1971 through 1974 shows the expected substantial drop in income but little or no change in such indicators as food expenditures or sense of personal efficacy.

Table 6.7

EFFECT OF INFLATION ON RETIREMENT PLANS
BY WHETHER PLANNED TO RETIRE EARLY AND WHETHER
EXPECTED TO HAVE ENOUGH RETIREMENT INCOME

Attitudinal Change	All Aged 45-64 Who Planned to Retire Early				All Aged 45-64 Who Planned to Retire			
	Expect to Have:				Expect to Have:			
	Not Enough	Just Enough	More than Enough	All[a]	Not Enough	Just Enough	More than Enough	All[a]
Will retire later	9	14	10	13	12	15	10	14
Now won't retire	9	2	1	3	7	3	1	4
Not sure when	9	3	1	5	5	3	2	4
Will retire and get another job	0	1	1	1	0	1	2	1
	27	20	13		24	25	15	
No change in plans, only attitude	10	5	5	6	8	6	4	6
Other changes	7	7	8	4	8	6	6	5
No change	56	67	73	68	60	66	75	66
Number of cases	107	269	75	496	287	525	122	1,046

[a]Includes some uncertain expectations.

Table 6.8

RETIRED PEOPLE'S ASSESSMENTS OF WHERE
INFLATION HIT THEM HARDEST

(For persons who retired during or before 1978, by age.)

What Price Increases Have Hit Especially Hard?	45-62		62-64		65		66-97		All 5,819 Retired or Not	
	First Mention	Second Mention	First Mention	Second Mention	First Mention	Second Mention	First Mention	Second Mention	First Mention	Second Mention
Food	57	10	54	0	47	0	42	9	51	0
Housing	4	0	3	5	0	19	6	1	3	3
Utilities	9	15	16	7	19	16	13	11	13	11
Transport	8	23	8	25	6	19	10	15	12	26
Med	2	5	2	3	2	0	1	4	1	2
Taxes	1	2	1	2	2	4	0	3	1	2
Taxes	1	2	1	2	2	4	6	3	1	2
Appliances and repair	1	0	0	0	0	1	0	0	0	0
Clothing	1	2	0	5	0	1	0	3	0	4
Other	1	3	1	3	2	2	1	3	1	2
Number of cases	192		181		62		139			

Table 6.9

WHICH PRICE INCREASE HIT ESPECIALLY HARD?
(For persons aged 45 or older in 1978
who planned to retire sometime.)

| What Hit Especially Hard | Before 62 | | 62-64 | | 65 | | 65 or Later | |
	First Mention	Second Mention	First Mention	Second Mention	First Mention	Second Mention	First Mention	Second Mention
Food	52	0	45	0	52	0	51	0
Housing	1	2	1	1	3	3	0	2
Utilities	19	13	16	13	12	13	10	18
Transport	10	34	15	25	14	28	17	18
Med	1	1	1	1	0	1	0	2
Taxes	0	3	1	1	1	4	1	4
Appliance repair	0	0	0	0	0	0	0	0
Clothing	0	4	0	3	0	4	0	3
Other	1	1	1	3	1	1	3	7
Number of cases	190		306		449		101	

References

Anderson, Kathryn; Clark, Robert L.; and Johnson, Thomas. "Retirement in Dual-Career Families." In retirement Policy in an Aging Society, edited by Robert L. Clark. Durham, North Carolina: Duke University Press, 1980.

Atchley, Robert C. The Sociology of Retirement. Cambridge, Massachusetts: Schenkman Publishing Co., 1976.

_____. "Adjustment to Loss of Job at Retirement." International Journal of Aging and Human Development 6 (1975): 17-17.

Back, K.W. "Transition to Aging and the Self Image." In Normal Aging II, edited by E. Palmore. Reports from the Duke Longitudinal Studies (1970-73), Durham, North Carolina, Duke University Press, 1974.

Barfield, Richard E. The Automobile Worker and Retirement: A Second Look. Ann Arbor, Michigan: Institute for Social Research, The University of Michigan, 1970.

Barfield, Richard, and Morgan, James. Early Retirement, The Decision and the Experience. Ann Arbor, Michigan: Institute for Social Research, The University of Michigan, 1969.

_____. "Trends in Planned Early Retirement." The Gerontologist 18 (1978): 13-18.

_____. "Trends in Satisfaction with Retirement." The Gerontologist 18 (1978): 19-23.

Barker, David T., and Clark, Robert L. "Mandatory Retirement and Labor-Force Participation of Respondents in the Retirement History Study" Social Security Bulletin 43 (November 1980): 20-29.

Berghorn, Forrest J.; Schafer, Donna E.; Steere, Geoffrey H.; and Wiseman, Robert F. The Urban Elderly, A Study of Life Satisfaction. New York: Universe Books, 1978.

Binstock, R.H., and Shanas, E., eds Handbook of Aging and the Social Sciences. New York: Van Nostrand Reinhold Co., 1977.

Bixby, Lenore E. "Income of People Aged 65 and Older: Overview from 1968 Survey of the Aged." Social Security Bulletin 33 (April 1970): 3-34.

_____. "Retirement Patterns in the United States: Research and Policy Interaction." Social Security Bulletin 39 (August 1976): 3-19.

Bixby, Lenore E.; Finegar, Wayne W.; Grad, Susan; Kolodrubetz, Walter W.; Lauriat, Patience; and Murray, Janet. Demographic and Economic Characteristics of the Aged, 1968 Social Security Survey U.S. Dept. of Health , Education and Welfare, Social Security Administration, Office of Research and Statistics, Research Report No. 45, DHEW Pub. No. (SSA) 75-11802. Washington, D.C.: United States Government Printing Office, 1975.

Bixby, Lenore, and Reno, Virginia. "Second Pensions among Newly Entitled Workers: Survey of New Beneficiaries." Social Security Bulletin 34 (November 1971): 3-7.

Bixby, Lenore, and Rings, E. Eleanor. "Work Experience of Men Claiming Retirement Benefits." Social Security Bulletin 32 (August 1969): 3-14.

Blinder, A.S.; Gordon, R.H.; and Wise, D. An Empirical Study of the Effects of Pensions and the Saving and Labor Supply Decisions of Older Men. Report to U.S. Department of Labor, Washington, D.C., 1978.

_____. "Reconsidering the Work Disincentive Effects of Social Security." Forthcoming in National Tax Journal.

Bond, Floyd, and others. Our Needy Aged a California, study of a national problem. New York: Henry Hoit and Co., 1954.

Bond, Kathleen. "Retirement History Study's First Four Years: Work, Health, and Living Arrangements." Social Security Bulletin 41 (December 1978): 1-13.

Boskin, Michael. "Social Security and Retirement Decisions." Economic Inquiry 15 (January 1977): 1-25.

Boskin, Michael, and Hurd, Michael. "The Effect of Social Security on Early Retirement. " Journal of Public Economics 10 (December 1978): 361-77.

Bould, Sally. "Unemployment as a Factor in Early Retirement Decisions." American Journal of Economics and Sociology 39 (April 1980): 123-136.

Brennan, Michael, Taft, Philip, and Schupack, Mark. Economics of Age, New York, W.W. Morton, 1967.

Burkhauser, Richard V. "The Pension Acceptance Decision of Older Workers." Journal of Human Resources, 14 (Winter 1979): 63-75.

Burkhauser, Richard V., and Tolley, G.S. "Older Americans and Market Work." The Gerontologist 18 (1978): 449-53.

Burkhauser, Richard, and Turner, John. "A Time Series Analysis of Social Security and its Effect on the Market Work of Men at Younger Ages." Journal of Political Economy 86 (August 1978): 701-15.

Burns, Robert K. "Economic Aspects of Aging and Retirement." American Journal of Sociology 59 (January 1954): 384-90.

Butler, Robert N. Why Survive? Being Old in America. New York: Harper and Row, 1975.

Campbell, C.D. and Campbell, R.G. "Conflicting Views on the Effect of Old-Age and Survivors Insurance on Retirement." Economic Inquiry 14 (September 1976): 369-88.

Clague, Ewan; Polli, Balraj; and Cramer, Leo. The Aging Worker and the Union. New York: Pragger, 1971.

Clark, Robert L.; Johnson, Thomas; and Archibald-McDermed, Ann. "Allocation of Time and Resources by Married Couples Approaching Retirement." Social Security Bulletin 43 (April 1980): 3-16.

Clark, Robert; Kreps, Juanita; and Spengler, Joseph. "The Economics of Aging: A Survey." Journal of Economic Literature 16 (September 1978): 919-62.

Crona, Goran. "Partial Retirement in Sweden=Development and Experiences." Sartryckur Aging and Work 1 (198): 113-120.

Cutler, Stephen J. "Aging and Voluntary Association Participation." Journal of Gerontology 32 (July 1977): 470-79.

Droffil, E.J. "Life-Cycles with Terminal Retirement ." International Economic Review 21 (February 1980): 45-62.

Duncan, Greg, and Morgan, James, eds. Five Thousand American Families--Patterns of Economic Progress, Volumes I through VIII. Ann Arbor, Michigan: Institute for Social Research, The University of Michigan, 1972-1980.

Eisdorfer, C. "Adaptation to Loss of Work." In Retirement, edited by F.M. Carp, New York: Behavioral Publications, 1972.

Ekerdt, David J.; Bosse, Raymond; and Mogey, John M. "Concurrent Change in Planned and Preferred Age for Retirement." Journal of Gerontology 35 (March 1980): 232-40

Ekerdt, David J.; Rose, C.L.; Bosse, Raymond; and Custa, P.T. "Longitudinal Change in Preferred Age of Retirement." Journal of Occupational Psychology 49 (1976) 161-169.

Epstein, Lenore A. "Early Retirement and Work Life Experience." Social Security Bulletin 29 (March 1966): 3-10.

Epstein, Lenore A., and Murray, Janet H. The Aged Population of the United States, the 1963 Social Security Survey of the Aged, Research Report No. 19 Office of Research and Statistics, Social Security Administration, U.S. Dept. of Health, Education and Welfare. Washington, D.C.: United States Government Printing Office, 1967.

_____. "Employment and Retirement." In Middle Age and Aging, edited by B. Neugarten. Chicago: University of Chicago Press, 1968.

Feldstein, Martin. "Social Security Benefits and the Accumulation of Preretirement Wealth." Working Paper 477, National Bureau of Economic Research. Cambridge, Massachusetts, May 1980.

_____. "Social Security, Induced Retirement, and Aggregate Capital Formation." Journal of Political Economy 82 (Sept./Oct. 1974): 905-26.

Feldstein, Martin, and Pellechio, Anthony J. "Social Security and Household Wealth Accumulation: New Microeconomic Evidence." Review of Economics and Statistics 61 (1979): 361-68.

Filenbaum, G.G. "On the Relation between Attitude to Work and Attitude to Retirement." Journal of Gerontology 26 (1971): 244-48.

Foner, Anne, and Kertzer, David I. "Transitions over the Life Course: Lessons from Age-Set Societies." American Journal of Sociology 83 (March 1978): 1081-1104.

Fox, Alan. "Earnings Replacement Rates of Retired Couples: Findings from the Retirement History Study." Social Security Bulletin 42 (January 1979): 17-39.

_____. "Work and Retirement Patterns of Married Couples." Proceedings from the Gerontological Society Meetings San Francisco, November, 1977.

_____. "Work Status and Income Change, 1968-72: Retirement History Study Preview." Social Security Bulletin 39 (December 1976): 14-30.

Fox, J.H. "Effects of Retirement and Former Work Life on Women´s Adaptation in Old Age." Journal of Gerontology 32 (1977): 196-202.

Friedmann, E.A., and Havighurst, R.J., eds. The Meaning of Work and Retirement, Chicago: University of Chicago Press, 1954.

Friis, H., and Manniche, E. Old People in a Low Income Area in Copenhagen, Copenhagen: Danish National Institute of Social Research, 1961..

George, Linda K, and Maddox, George L. "Subjective Adaptation to Loss of the Work Role: A Longitudinal Study." Journal of Gerontology 32 (July 1977): 456-62.

Glamser, Francis D. "Determinants of a Positive Attitude Toward Retirement" Journal of Gerontology 31 (January 1976): 104-07.

Gordon, Roger, and Blinder, Alan. "Market Wages, Reservation Wages and Retirement." Working Paper No. 513, National Bureau of Economic Research, Cambridge, Massachusetts, July 1980.

Goudy, Willis J.; Powers, Edward A.; Keith, Patricia; and Reger, Richard A. "Changes in Attitudes Toward Retirement: Evidence from A Panel Study of Older Males." Journal of Gerontology 35 (November 1980): 942-948.

Great Britain Office of Population and Census and Surveys, St. Catherine House, Kingsway, London WC2. Forthcoming report on a survey in 1977 on why people retire when they do, of 3,500 people within a few years of minimum pension age. (See Parker.)

Great Britain Ministry of Pensions and National Insurance, Financial and Other Circumstances of Retirement Pensioners, London: Her Majesty´s Stationery Office, 1966.

Great Britain, U.K. Ministry of Pensions and National Insurance. National Insurance Retirement Pensions: Reasons Given for Retiring or Continuing at Work. London: Her Majesty´s Stationery Office, 1954.

Great Britain. Report of the Committee for the Economic and Financial Problems of the Provision for Old Age (Phillips Committee), CMD9333. London: Her Majesty's Stationery Office 1954.

Hall, Arden, and Johnson, T.R. "The Determinants of Planned Retirement Age." Industrial and Labor Relations Review 33 (January 1980): 241-54.

Havighurst, Robert J., and Albrecht, Ruth. Older People. New York: Longmans Green and Co., 1953.

Havighurst, R.J.; Munnichs, J.M.A.; Neugarten, B.; and Thomas, H. Adjustment to Retirement: A Cross National Study. Netherlands: Royal Van Gorcum, 1969.

Health and Welfare Canada. Retirement in Canada: Summary Report, Vol. 2. Ottawa: Canada, Social and Economic Concerns, March 1977.

_____. Retirement in Canada, Volume 2. Ottawa, Canada: Social and Economic Concerns, May 1977.

Honig, Marjorie, and Hanoch, Giora. "A General Model of Labor-Market Behavior of Older Persons." Social Security Bulletin 43 (April 1980): 29-39.

_____. "The Labor Market Behavior of Older People: A Framework for Analysis." Paper for Workshop on Elderly of the Future, Committee on Aging, National Research Council, Annapolis, Maryland, 1979.

Irelan, Lola M., and Bell, D. Bruce. "Understanding Subjectively Defined Retirement: A Pilot Analysis." The Gerontologist 12 (Winter 1972): 354-56.

Irelan, Lola M., et al. Almost 65: Baseline Data from the Retirement History Study Social Security Administration Office of Research and Statistics, Research Report No. 49, HEW Publishing, 1976.

Irelan, Lola M. and Steinberg, Joseph. "A Retirement History Survey." Proceedings of the Social Statistics Section American Statistical Association, 1968.

Jaslow, P. "Employment, Retirement and Morale among Older Women." Journal of Gerontology 31 (1976): 212-18.

Katona, George. Private Pensions and Individual Saving. Ann Arbor, Michigan: Institute for Social Research, The University of Michigan, 1965.

Katona, George, and Morgan, James. "Retirement in Prospect and Retrospect." Symposium on Old Age Income Assurance, Joint Economic Committee, U.S. Congress. Washington, D.C.: United States Government Printing Office, 1968. Also reprinted in Retirement and the Individual, Hearings before the Subcommittee on Retirement and the Individual of the Special Committee on Aging, U.S. Senate, 90th Congress, 1st, Part 2, Washington D.C.: United States Government Printing Office, July 1967.

Kimmell, Douglas C.; Price, Karl F.; and Walker, James W. "Retirement Choice and Retirement Satisfaction." Journal of Gerontology 33 (July 1978): U.S. Government Printing Office, 575-85.

Kingson, Eric R. Men Who Leave Work Before Age 62: A Study of Advantaged and Disadvantaged Very Early Labor Force Withdrawal. Report for the Employment and Training Administration, U.S. Dept. of Labor under Grant 91-25-78-48 Washington, D.C.: U.S. Government Printing Office, May 1979.

Kitchings-Johnson, Carolyn, and Price-Bonham, Sharon. "Women and Retirement: A Study and Implications." Family Relations 29 (July 1980): 380-85.

Kolodrubetz, Walter W. "Characteristics of Workers with Pension Coverage on longest Job: New Beneficiaries." Social Security Bulletin 34 (November 1971): 8-28.

_____. "Private and Public Retirement Pensions: Findings from the 1968 Survey of the Aged." Social Security Bulletin 33 (September 1970): 3-22.

_____. "Private Retirement Benefits and Relationship to Earnings: Survey of New Beneficiaries." Social Security Bulletin 36 (May 1973): 6-37.

Kolodrubetz, Walter W., and Landay, Donald M. "Coverage and Vesting of Full-Time Employees Under Private Retirement Plans." Social Security Bulletin 36 (November 1973): 20-36.

Kotlikoff, Laurence J. "Testing the Theory of Social Security and Life Cycle Accumulation" American Economic Review, 69 (June 1979): 396-410.

Kutner, Bernard. Five Hundred Over Sixty. New York: Russell Sage Foundation, 1956.

Laing, Jersey, and Fairchild, Thomas J. "Relative Deprivation and Perception of Financial Adequacy Among the Aged." Journal of Gerontology 34 (September 1979): 746-59.

Larson, Reed. "Thirty Years of Research on Subjective Well-Being of Older Americans." Journal of Gerontology 33 (1978): 109-25.

Lauriat, Patience. "Benefit Levels and Socio-Economic Characteristics: Findings from the 1968 Survey of the Aged." Social Security Bulletin 33 (August 1970): 3-20.

Lauriat, Patience, and Rabin, William. "Men who Claim Benefits before Age 65: Findings from the Survey of New Beneficiaries." Social Security Bulletin 33 (November 1970): 3-29.

Lawton, M. Powell. "Employment and the Well-Being of Elderly Inner-City Residents." Environment and Behavior 6 (June 1976): 199-211.

Liang, Jersey; Kahana, Eva; and Doherty, Edmund. "Financial Well Being Among the Aged: A Further Elaboration." Journal of Gerontology 35 (1980): 409-20.

Lininger, Charles A. "Some Aspects of the Economic Situation of the Aged: Recent Survey Findings." In Aging and the Economy, edited by Harold L. Orbach and Clark Tibbitts. Ann Arbor: University of Michigan Press, 1963.

Makeham, Peter, and Morgan, Philip. "Evaluation of the Job Release Scheme," Research Paper 13, Department of Employment, Great Britain, 1980 (summarized in Employment Gazette (July 1980): 720-26.

Morgan, James N. "The Anatomy of Income Distribution." Review of Economics and Statistics 44 (August 1962): 270-83.

_____. "Behavioral and Social Science Research and the Future Elderly." In Aging: Social Change edited by Sara Kiesler, James Morgan, and Valerie Oppenheimer. New York: Academic Press, 1981.

_____. "Measuring the Economic Status of the Aged." International Economic Review 6 (January 1965): 1-17. (Also in Age with a Future, Copenhagen: Munksgaard, 1964.)

_____. "Retirement in Prospect and Retrospect." In Five Thousand American Families:--Patterns of Economic Progress, Vol. 8, edited by Greg J. Duncan and James N. Morgan. Ann Arbor, Michigan: Institute for Social Research, The University of Michigan, 1980.

_____. "What with Inflation and Unemployment, Who can Afford to Retire?" In Aging from Birth to Death Interdisciplinary Perspectives, edited by Matilda White Riley. Boulder, Colorado: AAAS Selected Symposium, Westview Press. 1979.

Morgan, James, and David, Martin. "The Aged: Their Ability to Meet Medical Expenses." In Financing Health Care of the Aged, Part 1. Blue Cross Association, American Hospital Association, Chicago, Illinois, 1962.

Motley, Dena K. "Availability of Retired Persons for Work: Findings from the Retirement History Study" Social Security Bulletin, 41 (April 1978): 18-39.

_____. "Paying for Health Care in the Years Before Retirement." Social Security Bulletin 38 (April 1975): 3-22.

_____. "Health in the Years before Retirement." Social Security Bulletin 35 (December 1972): 18-36.

Mulanaphy, James M. "1972-73 Survey of Retired TIAA-CREF Annuitants Statistical Report." Educational Research Division, TIAA and CREF, New York, 1974.

Murray, Janet. "Subjective Retirement," Social Security Bulletin 42 (November 1979): 1-7.

_____. "Changes in Food Expenditures, 1969-1973: Findings from the Retirement History Study." Social Security Bulletin, 4 (July 1978): 3-11.

_____. "Food Expenditures," Paper presented at the Gerontological Society meetings, San Francisco, 1977.

_____. "Activities and Expenditures of Preretirees." Social Security Bulletin 38 (August 1975): 5-21.

_____. "Living Arrangements of People Aged 65 and Older: Findings from 1968 Survey of the Aged." Social Security Bulletin 34 (September 1971): 3-14.

Myers, Robert J. Indexation of Pensions and Other Benefits Homewood, Illinois: Richard D. Irwin, 1978.

Neubig, Thomas. "Reverse Annuity Mortgages: A Dissaving Mechanism for Older Home Owners." In Five Thousand American Families:--Patterns of Economic Progress, Vol. 8, edited by Greg J. Duncan and James N. Morgan. Ann Arbor, Michigan: Institute for Social Research, The University of Michigan, 1980.

Newman, Sandra J. "Housing Adjustments of the Disabled Elderly." The Gerontologist 16 (August 1976): 312-17.

Olsen, Henning, and Hansen, Gert. Retirement from Work (in Danish with English summary). Copenhagen, Denmark: Danish National Institute for Social Research, 1977.

Oregon University College of Business Administration. Preretirement Counselling, Retirement Adjustment and the Older Employee. Eugene, Oregon: Oregon University Press, 1969.

Palmore, Erdman B. ed. Normal Aging II: Reports from the Duke Longitudinal Study. Durham, North Carolina: Duke University Press, 1974.

Palmore, Erdman B. "Why do People Retire?" Aging and Human Development 1 (1971): 169-83.

Palmore, Erdman, ed. Normal Aging I: Reports from the Duke Longitudinal Study 1955-1969. Durham, North Carolina: Duke University Press, 1970.

Palmore, Erdman B. "Differences in the Retirement Patterns of Men and Women." The Gerontologist 5 (1965): 4-8.

Parker, Stanley. Older Workers and Retirement, an enquiry carried out on behalf of the Department of Employment and the Department of Health and Social Security London, Office of Population Census and Surveys, Social Survey Division, Her Majesty's Stationery Office, 1980.

Parnes, Herbert S., and Nestel, Gilbert. "Early Retirement." In The Preretirement Years: Five Years in the Lives of Middle-Aged Men Vol. 4, by H.S. Parnes, et. al. Center for Human Resource Research. Athens, Ohio: Ohio University, December 1974. (And Washington, D.C.: United States Government Printing Office, 1975).

Parnes, Herbert S. From the Middle to the Later Years: Longitudinal Studies of the Pre and Post-Retirement Experiences of Men. Conference on Demographic and Health Information for Aging Research, National Institute on Aging, Bethesda, Maryland, June 1979.

Parnes, Herbert S., and Nestel, Gilbert. Retirement Expectations of Middle-Aged Men. Columbus, Ohio: Center for Human Research, Ohio State University, September 1971.

Parnes, Herbert S.; Nestel, Gilbert; Chirikos, Thomas L.; Daymont, Thomas N.; Mott, Frank L.; Parsons, Donald O.; and associates. From the Middle to the Later Years: Longitudinal Studies of the Preretirement and Postretirement Experiences of men. In The Retirement Experience (Vol. Five in the Series The Preretirement Years). Columbus, Ohio: Center for Human Resource Research, Ohio State University, 1979.

Patton, Carl Vernon. "Early Retirement in Academia." The Gerontologist 17 (August 1977): 345-54.

Pellechio, Anthony J. The Effect of Social Security on Retirement. Discussion paper, National Bureau of Economic Research, April 1979.

_____. "Social Security Financing and Retirement Behavior." American Economic Review 69 (May 1979): 284-87.

Poitrenaud, Jean; Vallery-Masson, Janine; Valleron, Alain J.; Demeestere, Michelle, and Lion, Marie R. "Factors Related to Attitude Towards Retirement Among French Preretired Managers and Top Executives," Journal of Gerontology 34 (September 1979): 723-27.

Pollak, Otto. Positive Experience in Retirement: A Field Study (Pension Research Council Monograph Series). Homewood, Illinois: Richard D. Irwin Inc., 1957.

Pollam, A.W. "Early Retirement; Relationships to Variation in Life Satisfaction." The Gerontologist 11 (1975): 43-47.

Price, Karl F.; Walker, James W.; and Kimmel, Douglas C. "Retirement Timing and Retirement Satisfaction," Aging and Work 2 (Fall 1979): 235-45.

Quinn, Joseph F. "Labor-Force Participation Patterns of Older Self-Employed Workers." Social Security Bulletin 43 (April 1980): 17-28,

_____. "Retirement Patterns of Self-Employed Workers." In Retirement Policy in an Aging Society, edited by Robert L. Clark. Durham, North Carolina: Duke University Press, 1980.

_____. "Microeconomic Determinants of Early Retirement: A Cross Sectional View of White Married Men." Journal of Human Resources 12 (Summer 1977): 329-46.

_____. The Microeconomics of Early Retirement: A Cross Sectional View. Unpublished report prepared for the Social Security Administration, 1975.

_____. "Wage Determination and Discrimination Among Older Workers." Journal of Gerontology 34 (September 1979): 728-35.

Reno, Virginia. "Why Men Stop Working at or Before age 65." Social Security Bulletin 34 (June 1971): 3-17.

_____. "Why Men Stop Working at or before Age 65." Survey of New Beneficiaries Report 3, U.S. Department of Health, Education and Welfare. Washington, D.C.: United States Government Printing Office, 1971.

236

_____. "Why Men Stop Working before Age 65." In Reaching Retirement Age, Research Report No.47, Office of Research and Statistics, Social Security Administration U.S. Department of Health, Education and Welfare, Washington, D.C.: United States Government Printing Office, 1976.

_____. "Retirement Patterns of Men at OASDHI Entitlement." SNEB Report No. 2, Office of Research and Statistics, Social Security Administration, March 1971.

_____. "Retired Women Workers." In Reaching Retirement Age, Research Report No. 47 Office of Research and Statistics, Social Security Administration, U.S. Department of Health, Education and Welfare, Washington, D.C.: United States Government Printing Office 1976.

Riley, Matilda White, et. al. Aging and Society (3 Vols.). New York: Russell Sage; 1968, 1969, and 1972.

Schiller, Bradley R., and Weiss, Randall D. "The Impact of Private Pensions on Firm Attachment." Review of Economics and Statistics 61 (August 1979): 369-80.

Schultz, James H. The Economic Status of the Retired Aged in 1980 (simulation projections). Research Report No. 24, Office of Research and Statistics, Social Security Administration U.S. Department of Health, Education and Welfare, Washington, D.C., 1968.

_____. "Income Distribution and the Aging." In Handbook of Aging and the Social Sciences, edited by Robert H. Binstock and Ethel Shanas. New York: Van Nostrand Reinhold, 1976.

_____. "Some Economics of Aged Home Ownership." The Gerontologist, 7 (1967): 73-74 80.

_____. "The Future Economic Circumstances of the Aged: A Simulation Projection: 1980." Yale Economic Essays 7 (Spring 1967).

Schwab, Karen. "Early Labor-Force Withdrawal of Men: Participants and Nonparticipants Ages 58-63." Social Security Bulletin 37 (August 1974): 24-38.

_____. "Gradual Retirement and Adjustment in Retirement." Paper presented at the Gerontological Society meetings, San Francisco, November 1977.

Scitovsky, Anne A., and Snyder, Nelda M. Medical Care Use by a Group of Full Insured Aged, U.S. Department of HEW, Public Health Service, Health Resources Administration, National Center for Health Services Research, DHEW Pub. No. (HRA)75-3129, 1975.

Shanas, Ethel. "The Family as a Social Support System in Old Age." The Gerontologist 19 (April 1979): 160-74.

_____. "Adjustment to Retirement." In Retirement, edited by F.M. Carp. New York: Behavioral Publications, 1972.

_____. "Facts versus Stereotypes: The Cornell Study of Occupational Retirement." The Journal of Social Issues 14 (1958).

_____. Financial Resources of the Aging. Washington D.C.: Health Information Foundation Research Series 10, U.S. Department of Health, Education, and Welfare, Social Security Administration, Research and Statistics Note No. 34, 1959.

Shanas, Ethel. "Work and Retirement." In Final Report—National Survey of the Aged (HEW, OMB 90-A-389).

Shanas, Ethel, et al. Old People in Three Industrial Societies. London: Rutledge and Paul Kegan, 1968.

Shanas, Ethel, and Streib, Gordon, eds., Symposium on the Family: Intergenerational Relationships and Social Structure. Englewood Cliffs, New Jersey: Prentice Hall, 1965.

Sheldon, Henry D. The Older Population of the United States. Census Monograph Series for the Social Science Research Council in cooperation with the U.S. Department of Commerce, Bureau of the Census, U.S. Department of Health, Education, and Welfare. New York: Wiley, 1958.

Sheppard, Harold L. Employment-Related Problems of Older Workers: A Research Strategy, R and D Monograph 73, Employment and Training Administration, U.S. Department of Labor. Washington, D.C.: United States Government Printing Office, 1979.

_____. "New Perspectives of Older Workers." Upjohn Institute for Employment Research, Kalamazoo and Washington, 1971.

Sheppard, Harold L., and Rix, Sara E. The Graying of Working America: The Coming Crises of Retirement-Age Policy. New York: The Free Press, 1977.

Sheppard, Harold L. "Work and Retirement." In Handbook of Aging and the Social Sciences, edited by R.H. Binstock and E. Thanas. New York: Van Nostrand and Reinhold, 1976.

Sherman, Sally R. "Assets on the Threshold of Retirement." Social Security Bulletin 36 (August 1973): 3-17.

Sherman, Susan R. "Mutual Assistance and Support in Retirement Housing." Journal of Gerontology 30 (July 1975): 579-83.

Silk, Leonard S. "The Housing Circumstances of the Aged in the United States 1950." Journal of Gerontology 7 (1952): 87-91.

Skade, Rigmor. "Living Conditions" (A Survey of Old Age Pensioners in Denmark; (Danish Statistical Department) in Cross-National Surveys of Old Age, Report of a Conference at Copenhagen, October 19-23, 1956, International Association of Gerontology, Social Science Research Commission. Published by Division of Gerontology, University of Michigan, Ann Arbor 1957.

Sobol, Marion G. "Factors influencing Private Capital Accumulation on the Eve of Retirement." Review of Economics and Statistics 61 (November 1979): 585-93.

238

Steiner, P.O., and Dorfman, R. The Economic Status of the Aged. Berkeley, California, University of California Press, 1957.

Stirner, Fritz W. "The Transportation Needs of the Elderly in a Large Urban Environment." The Gerontologist 18 (April 1978): 207-11.

Streib, Gordon F. and Schneider, Clement J. Retirement in American Society: Impact and Process: Ithaca, New York: Cornell University Press, 1971.

Streib, Gordon F.; Thompson, Wayne E.; and Suchman, Edward A. "The Cornell Study of Occupational Retirement." The Journal of Social Issues 14 (1958): 3-17.

Strumpel, Burkhard. "The Aged in an Affluent Economy." In Report on the Task Force on Aging, edited by P. Lawton and C. Eisdorfer> Washington, D.C.: American Psychological Association, 1972.

Struyk, Raymond J. "The Housing Expense Burden of Households Headed by the Elderly." The Gerontologist 17 (1977): 1447-52.

_____. "Housing Adjustments of Relocating Elderly Households." The Gerontologist 20 (February 1980): 45.

Svane, Ole. Assessment of Needs of Care for the Elderly. Copenhagen: Danish National Institute of Social Research, 1973.

Taves, Marvin J., and Hansen, Gary D. "Seventeen Hundred Elderly Citizens." In Aging in Minnesota, edited by Arnold M. Rose. Minneapolis: University of Minnesota Press, 1963.

Thomae, H., et al. Einstellung und Verhaltensweisen Aelderer Fussgaenger in de Grossstadt (Attitudes and Behavior of Elderly Pedestrians in a Large City). Bonn, West Germany: Psychologisches Institut den Universitaet Bonn, 1976.

Thomas, Geoffrey, and Osborne, Barbara. Older People and Their Employment, Part I: The Older Worker and His Attitudes to Employment: Part II: The Policy of Employers. An inquiry made by the Social Survey in April 1950 for the Ministry of Labour and National Service (Reports Nos. London, 150/1 and 150/2), The Social Survey, 1951.

Thompson, Gayle B. "Black-White Differences in Private Pensions: Findings from the Retirement History Study." Social Security Bulletin 42 (February 1979): 15-22.

_____. "Impact of Inflation on Private Pension Findings from the Retirement History Study." Social Security Bulletin 41 (November 1978): 1-10.

_____. "Pension Coverage and Benefits, 1972: Findings from the Retirement History Study." Social Security Bulletin 41 (February 1978): 3-17.

_____. "Work vs. Leisure: An Investigation of Morale among Employed and Retired Men." Journal of Gerontology 15 (1973): 165-69.

_____. "Work Experience and Income of the Population Aged 60 and Older, 1971." Social Security Bulletin 37 (1974): 3-20.

Thompson, Wayne E., and Streib, Gordon F. "Situational Determinants: Health and Economic Deprivation in Retirement." The Journal of Social Issues 14 (1958): 18-34.

Thompson, Wayne E. "Pre-Retirement Anticipation and Adjustment in Retirement." The Journal of Social Issues 14 (1958): 35-45.

Thompson Rogers, Gayle. "Pension Coverage and Vesting Among Private Wage and Salary Workers, 1979: Preliminary Estimates from the 1979 Survey of Pension Plan Coverage." Working Paper No. 16, Division of Retirement and Survivor Studies, Office of Research and Statistics, Social Security Administration, U.S. Department of Health, Education and Welfare, June 1980.

Tissue, Thomas. "Low-Income Widows and Other Aged Singles." Social Security Bulletin 42 (December 1979): 3-10.

Toseland, Ron, and Rasch, John. "Factors Contributing to Older Persons' Satisfaction with their Communities." The Gerontologist 18 (August 1978): 395-402.

Townsend, Peter. The Family Life of Old People: An Inquiry in London. London: Routledge and Kegan Paul, 1957.

Tracy, Martin. "Retirement Age Practices in Ten Industrial Societies, 1960-1976." Studies and Research No. 14, International Social Security Association, Geneva 1980.

Tuckman, Jacob, and Lorge, Irving. "Retirement and the Industrial Worker." Teachers College, Columbia University, 1953.

U.S. Department of Commerce, Bureau of the Census. Social and Economic Characteristics of the Older Population. 1978, Current Population Reports P-23 No. 85, August, 1979. Washington, D.C.: United States Government Printing Office, 1979.

U.S. Department of Health, Education and Welfare, U.S. Department of Labor, and U.S. Department of the Treasury. Coverage and Vesting of Full-Time Employees under Private Retirement Plans, Findings from the April 1972 Survey, September 1973 (DHEW Pub. No. SSA 74-11908; BLS Report No. 423).

U.S. Department of Health, Education and Welfare. "Selected Findings of the National Survey of Old-Age and Survivors Insurance Beneficiaries, 1951." Washington, June 1953. (Also reported in Social Security Bulletins of Aug. 1952, June 1952, and Aug. 1953, and in Public Welfare, April 1953).

U.S. Department of Health, Education and Welfare, Social Security Administration, Office of Research and Statistics. Reaching Retirement Age. Findings from A Survey of Early Entitled Beneficiaries 1968-70, Research Report No. 47, Washington, D.C.: United States Government Printing Office, 1976.

U.S. Department of Health, Education and Welfare, Office of Income Security Policy, Office of the Assistant Secretary for Planning and Evaluation, Work, Income, and Retirement of the Aged: Report of a Workshop. Technical Analysis Paper No. 18 (edited by Thomas A. Gustafson). Washington, D.C., 1979.

U.S. Department of Labor, Bureau of Labor Statistics. _Retired Couples´ Budget for a Moderate Living Standard_, Bulletin #1570-4. Washington, D.C.; United States Government Printing Office, 1970.

U.S. House of Representatives, Select Committee on Aging American Attitudes toward Pensions and Retirement, Hearings, February 17, 1979, Appendix. _1970 Study of American Attitudes Toward Pensions and Retirement_ (a nationwide survey of employees, retirees, and business leaders, commissioned by Johnson and Higgins and conducted by Louis Harris and Associates, Inc.). Washington, D.C., 1979.

Waters, William R. "The Effect of Pension Plan Membership on the Level of Household Non-Pension Wealth." San Francisco Econometric meetings, December 1966.

Wedderburn, Dorothy. "Prospects for the Reorganization of Work." _Gerontologist_ 15 (June 1975): 236-41.

Wentworth, Edna C., and Motley, Dena K. _Resources after Retirement_ (A Study of Income, Assets and Living Arrangements of Social Security Beneficiaries, 1941 through 1962), Research Report No. 34, Office of Research and Statistics, Social Security Administration, Department of Health, Education and Welfare. Washington, D.C.: United States Government Printing Office, 1970.

Appendix to Chapter 6

Table A6.1 (page 1 of 2)

WORK HOURS AND INCOME FOUR YEARS BEFORE AND FOUR
YEARS AFTER RETIREMENT FOR A COMPARISON YEAR

| | | Retired 1971–1974 | | | |
	Retired Before 1971	Before 65	65 or Older	Retired After 1974	Not Retired Even by 1979
Levels					
Pre work hours	1,263	1,963	1,559	2,055	1,439
Post work hours	271	237	181	732	1,159
Pre earnings	7,747	11,692	9,112	10,562	8,385
Post earnings	435	1,997	823	4,13	8,365
Pre income/needs	2.92	3.93	3.47	4.99	3.59
Post income/needs	2.15	2.75	2.45	3.73	3.16
Pre transfer income	5928	1320	2887	529	2040
Post transfer income	5124	5647	4812	5231	2591
Pre food	2882	3070	3094	2741	2449
Post food	2212	3059	2533	3874	3437
Trends					
Pre work hours	−331	−69	−133	−31	−21
Post work hours	−26	−20	−8	−454	−42
Pre earnings	−2,526	−1,925	−1,180	−2,521	−1,604
Post earnings	−84	−36	−110	−3,174	−642
Pre income/needs	−.264	.032	.005	−.164	.067
Post income/needs	060	−.035	−.040	−.500	−.009
Pre transfers	−2,701	−179	−571	124	68
Post transfers	50	−41	15	1,606	110
Pre food expenditures	~ 108	−1651	−279	5	612
Post food expenditures	−36	$ −140	$ −87	$ −486	$−526

Table A6.1 (page 2 of 2)

| | Retired 1971-1974 | | | |
	Retired Before 71	Before 65	65 or Older	Retired After 1974	Not Retired Even in 1979
Standard Deviations					
Pre work hours	540	287	278	310	249
Post work hours	138	97	88	649	228
Pre earnings	3,938	4,775	2,594	6,914	5,267
Post earnings	562	361	505	4,483	1,685
Pre income/needs	.577	.526	.503	.867	.575
Post income/needs	-183	.213	.180	1.032	-393
Pre transfers	5,331	1199	2,189	257	902
Post transfers	2,993	3,348	2,551	3,735	1,579
Pre efficacy (1970)	1.93	2.09	2.20	2.24	2.07
Post efficacy (1975)	2.09	2.34	2.05	2.33	2.04
Change in house equity 1969-1972	1,905	2,743	2,749	4,215	3,033
Change in house equity 1976-1979	8,112	9,611	8,037	8,335	10,620
Total change in change in house equity	7,938	13,854	9,287	10,674	11,006
Change in average income/needs	-.785	-1.157	-1.079	-1.287	-.638
Number of cases	59	97	55	55	85

Table A6.2 (page 1 of 2)

FOUR YEARS BEFORE AND FOUR YEARS AFTER RETIREMENT

	All 351 (Retired in 1971–1974) or Age 59–65 in 1971		152 Who Retired in 1971–1974	
	Mean	Standard Deviation	Mean	Standard Deviation
Levels				
Pre work hours	1,683	825	1,779	710
Post work hours	500	712	211	341
Pre earnings	9,681	8,734	10,518	758
Post earnings	2,954	6,769	972	1,826
Pre income/needs	3.81	3.22	3.73	2.23
Post income/needs	2.95	2.59	2.61	1.61
Pre transfer income	2,365	3,089	2,033	2,439
Post transfer income	4,718	3,205	5,267	3,039
Pre food expenditures	2,866	1,269	3,083	1,298
Post food expenditures	3,038	1,253	2,820	1,260
Pre food needs	1,329	722	X	X
Post food needs	1,315	668	X	X
Trends				
Pre work hours	−107	273	−98	237
Post work hours	−102	235	−15	68
Pre earnings	−1,906	3,374	−1,586	2,342
Post earnings	−750	2,075	−70	490
Pre income/needs	−.05	.64	.020	.500
Post income/needs	−.11	.58	.037	.190
Pre transfers	−551	1,983	−357	2,143
Post transfers	31,5	1379	−16	509
Pre food expenditures	−67	471	−217	472
Post food expenditures	$ −200	403	−116	313

244

	All 351 (Retired in 1971–1974) or Age 59–65 in 1971		152 Who Retired in 1971–1974	
	Mean	Standard Deviation	Mean	Standard Deviation
Standard Deviation				
Pre work hours	336	394	284	254
Post work hours	228	325	93	194
Pre earnings	465	565	3,783	4,053
Post earnings	$143	276	427	1,013
Pre income/needs	.601	1.049	.515	.719
Post income/needs	.356	.829	.198	.473
Pre transfers	1,822	2,918	1,650	2,795
Post transfers	$2,850	2,241	2,085	2,027
Pre efficacy (1970)	2.11	.95	2.21	.86
Post efficacy (1975)	2.17	.92	2.14	.87
Change in house equity 1969–1972	2,939	7,208	2,746	7,071
Change in house equity 1976–1979	9,084	17,578	8,95	15,103
Change in house equity pre to post[a]	10,829	10,561	11,275	14,453
Change in average income/needs	−.89	1.51	−1.12	1.41

[a]Equity (1976+1979)/2 − (1969+1972)/2

Chapter 7

EXPECTED WAGES AND MEN'S LABOR SUPPLY

Mary Corcoran and Abigail MacKenzie

INTRODUCTION

Unemployment has been a serious national problem for at least a decade. Since 1970, unemployment rates have consistently exceeded the traditionally accepted levels for frictional unemployment that are compatible with a full-employment economy.[1] These high unemployment rates suggest that the likelihood of individual workers experiencing unemployment are quite high, and there is some evidence to support this. Among prime-age male household heads with a ten-year history of labor force attachment (a group with relatively low unemployment rates), four out of ten reported at least one spell of unemployment between 1967 and 1977 (Hill and Corcoran, 1979). Since, at any point in time, young workers and women have higher unemployment rates than prime age men, one suspects that the ten-year unemployment incidence would have been even higher among these two groups.

Given the current high incidence of unemployment, it is interesting to ask how unemployed workers get jobs. This paper focuses on the answers suggested by job search theory. Job search theorists argue that the length of unemployment depends on workers' reservation wages (lowest wage for taking a job). This implies that workers who are willing to work at jobs which pay less than their previous jobs (i.e., who are willing to take a pay cut) ought to be re-employed more quickly than otherwise similar workers who are unwilling to take a reduction in pay (Kasper, 1967).

Despite the importance of reservation wages in search theory, there have been few direct empirical analyses of either the relationship between reservation wages and unemployment duration or of those factors which influence workers' reservation wages. This chapter examines the job search behavior of unemployed male household heads and attempts to answer some major questions: Are workers'

---

[1]The generally accepted level of frictional unemployment is 3 to 4 percent. Since 1970 the annual unemployment has ranged from 4.9 percent to 8.5 percent.

expectations about future wages realistic? How do these expectations affect their chances of finding employment? Do workers who expect a pay cut find jobs more quickly?

The first section of this chapter presents search theory and the model to be estimated. The second describes the sample and the variables. This is followed by a presentation of empirical results of the analysis. And, finally, the implications of these results are discussed.

A SEARCH THEORY OF UNEMPLOYMENT

Much recent theoretical work in unemployment is derived from search theory, which emphasizes the voluntary aspect of unemployment. Search theory argues that unemployed workers face a distribution of wage offers and assumes that workers know the shape of this distribution. Workers do not know what wages will be offered to them by a specific firm, but they are assumed to set a reservation wage for themselves based on their expectations about job offers. This search process may be conceptualized as a random sampling of job offers one at a time, where workers must decide whether to accept or reject a particular offer as it is sampled. A worker searches for a job until he receives a wage offer which is as large as or exceeds his reservation wage. In theory, the individual would determine his reservation wage so that the marginal cost of additional search equals (or is larger than) the marginal benefit, keeping in mind that costs of additional search include foregone earnings while searching as well as direct search costs. Benefits to additional search are the expected increase in lifetime earnings which would result from a better offer.

Thus, search theory's basic premise is that a worker's probability of accepting a job should increase as the gap between his reservation wage and potential wage decreases. Anything that increases wage offers or lowers the reservation wage should increase the probability of employment. This expectation is captured in the following set of equations:

(1)　potential wage offers = $k(X_1, X_2)$

(2)　reservation wage = $f(X_1, X_2, X_3)$

(3)　probability of employment = h(reservation wage, potential wage offers) = $h(X_1, X_2, X_4)$

where:

X_1 = measures of worker quality such as education or work experience

X_2 = measures of local demand conditions

X_3 =   anything which reduces the cost of being unemployed such as UI, assets, wife's earnings, etc.

X_4 =   reservation wage

Wage offers would depend both on labor market conditions and on worker quality. The reservation wage depends on these and on a worker's available resources. The probability that a worker takes a job is a function of the gap between wage offers and reservation wages.

To summarize, search theory argues that a worker would remain unemployed so long as his reservation wage exceeds the wage rates of currently available job offers. To test search theory adequately, it would be useful to have data on workers' reservation wages and on the wages of jobs offered to them. Although the Panel Study of Income Dynamics does not provide such data, it does provide a measure of expected wages and information on a variety of worker qualification and local demand measures, including a worker's wage on his last job. This last wage measure and the worker qualification and local demand measures are used here as proxies for possible wage offers. With controls for worker quality and local demand, the expected wage measure should pick up workers' willingness to accept jobs at the low-paying end of their wage offers distribution. Thus, using the Panel Study data, we can estimate the following revised version of Equation 3.

(3a)   probability of employment = $k(X_1, X_2, X_4')$ where X_4' = expected wage.

Empirical Tests of Reservation Wages and Re-employment Probabilities

Much of the empirical work based on search theory models has tested whether reservation wages decline with unemployment duration (Kasper, 1967; Stephenson, 1976; Kiefer and Neumann, 1979) or has explored the determinants of unemployment duration (Ehrenberg and Oaxaca, 1976; Rosenfeld, 1977; Solon, 1978; Welch, 1976). In general, such analyses have been based on samples of special populations and have not directly measured workers' reservation wages. There are a few exceptions to this general rule. Kasper (1967) used a measure of both past wage and asking wage for a 1961 sample of 3,000 long-term unemployed persons in Minnesota. He reported that these persons were willing to take an average pay cut of 3.5 percent, but he was unable to ascertain whether willingness to take a reduction in pay increased the probability of employment and whether unemployed persons actually received a pay cut. Stephenson (1976) used a two-stage least squares procedure to estimate the relationship between unemployment duration and reservation wages for a 1971 sample of 300 unemployed male youths in

Indianapolis. He found that workers were more willing to take a pay cut as their unemployment time increased but that reservation wages showed no significant effect on unemployment duration. Barron and Mellow (1980) estimated a relative reservation wage measure for a sample of 1,090 persons who were unemployed in May of 1976. This measure was the ratio of the reported reservation wage to an estimate of the worker's expected wage offer based on his or her occupation, region, and other demographic characteristics. The wage equation was estimated using a national sample of employed individuals. Barron and Mellow reported that workers' probabilities of being employed in June 1980 decreased significantly as their relative reservation wage increased.

SAMPLE

The sample used in the analysis reported here consisted of 470 male heads of households who were unemployed at the time of the 1974, 1975, 1976, or 1977 interview date, who had completed school at least two years prior to the interview date when they were unemployed,[2] and who were still heads of households in the year subsequent to their unemployment. Men on temporary layoff were omitted from analysis. Analysis was restricted to men who had left school at least two years prior to their unemployment to avoid picking up effects of "unemployment" between periods of schooling. This also meant that most of these men (91 percent) were able to report a wage for the year prior to their unemployment. A previous wage measure was helpful in attempting to find out whether willingness to take a pay cut increased employment probabilities.

On the interview date these men reported (1) their work hours and wages in the previous year, (2) the occupation and wages they expected to obtain, and (3) their job search behavior. The Panel Study also provided data on whether these men were employed at the following interview date and, for those who were employed, the length of time they had been in their current job.

Table 7.1 lists the wage expectations and job search questions. It might be argued that since respondents were not asked about the lowest wage they would take, the wage expectations question did not measure workers' reservation wages but was instead a measure of worker quality. The author tested this theory by regressing ln expected wages on measures of worker quality, local demand, and financial resources. If ln expected wages dropped as financial resources

---

[2] This was done indirectly by excluding any men for whom the age minus schooling was less than 8.

dropped, this would suggest that responses about wage expectations picked up whether or not a worker planned to accept a job at the low-paying end of his wage offers distribution. This is a weak test, however, since there are other interpretations of a relationship between resources and expected wages. Other available income, for example, would include wife's earnings and asset income, both of which might be positively related to worker quality.[3] At the very least, the expected wage question should allow us to test whether unrealistically high wage expectations had delayed employment. This question was quite similar to that analyzed by Kasper (1967).

In addition, men interviewed in 1974, 1975, and 1977 were asked a series of four questions about their willingness to move to get a job and about the nature of available jobs. (See Table 7.1, questions E8-E11.) These questions provided additional information about the flexibility of job seekers and about the quality of available job opportunities.

The Panel Study also provided a number of measures of worker quality (X_1), local demand conditions (X_2), and available resources during unemployment (X_3). Table 7.2 describes these measures. The Panel Study did not measure job offers received between two interview dates, but it did provide an hourly wage measure for the previous year. In the analysis reported in this chapter, this measure was used as a proxy for the mean of a worker's wage offer distribution. Additional proxies for wage offers included the other worker qualification and the labor market demand measures listed in Table 7.2.

The sample studied in this analysis has several advantages over the samples used in other research on the topic. It is a nationally representative sample of unemployed male household heads. Thus unlike many studies of unemployment behavior, the data can safely be used to generalize to a national population. The data include a measure of workers' expected wages and of their previous wages and, thus, can be used to investigate explicitly the effects of expected wages and/or expectations of pay cuts on workers' employment probabilities. Restricting the analysis to male heads of households who had been out of school for two or more years and eliminating men on layoff reduced the problems of including in the analysis groups of men for whom a search model would be inappropriate. Finally, since the Panel Study follows individual panel members over time, it is possible to investigate whether the wages on the jobs which workers actually took were consistent with their expressed expectations.

---

[3] We would like to thank Charles Brown for pointing out this possibility.

Table 7.1

QUESTIONS ASKED OF UNEMPLOYED WORKERS

EXPECTATIONS

E1.   What kind of job are you looking for?

_____

E2.   How much would you expect to earn? $_____ PER _____

E3.   Will you have to get any training to qualify? _____

JOB SEARCH QUESTIONS

E5.   How many places have you been to in the last four weeks to find out
       about a job?

       0. NONE   1. ONE   2. TWO   3. THREE   4. FOUR   5. FIVE OR MORE

JOB OPPORTUNITIES AND WILLINGNESS TO MOVE

E8.   Are there jobs available around here that just aren't worth taking?

       1. YES   5. NO   (GO TO E10)

       E9. How much do they pay? $_____ PER _____

E10.   Would you be willing to move to another community if you could get a
       good job there?

       1. YES, MAYBE, OR DEPENDS   5. NO

E11.   How much would a job have to pay for you to be willing to move?
       $_____ PER _____

Table 7.2 (page 1 of 2)

VARIABLES USED IN ANALYSES OF UNEMPLOYED WORKERS' WAGE EXPECTATIONS

Variable	Code
Measure of Employment Transition	
Whether employed at next interview date	= 1 if yes 0 if otherwise
Proportion of time employed in current job	= number of months in job held at next interview divided by number of months? between interviews = 0 if not employed at next interview
Worker Quality Measures (X_1)	
Education	= highest grade completed
Experience	= age-education-6
Ln previous wage	= ln of average hourly wage in year prior to interview (workers with no hourly wage were assigned the mean)
Not employed last year[a]	= 0 if worked in year prior to interview 1 otherwise
Hours/week worked last year	= hours/week worked when working in year prior to interview
Weeks unemployed last year	= weeks unemployed in previous year
Local Labor Market Condition Measures (X_2)	
Region dummies	= South, Northeast, North Central (West was the excluded category)
County unemployment rate	= unemployment rate in county of residence at time of interview
City size	= population size of nearest city (1000's)
Interview year dummies	= 1975, 1976, 1977 (1974 was the excluded category)
Other Controls	
White	= 1 if nonblack 0 otherwise
Married	= 1 if currently married 0 otherwise
Number of places looked	= number of places looked for a job in four weeks prior to interview

Table 7.2 (page 2 of 2)

Dependent Variable	Code
Resource Measures (X_3)	
Other available income (in 1000s of dollars)	= total family income-household head's labor income-households head's unemployment compensation in year prior to interview
Family size	= number of individuals in the family at time of interview
Received UI	= 1 if received unemployment compensation in year prior to interview 0 otherwise
Attitudinal Measures (X_1) [b]	
Whether jobs not worth taking [c]	= 1 yes to question E8, Table 7.1 0 otherwise
Ln (pay for poorly paid jobs)	= ln (wages for poorly paid jobs) if yes to question E8, otherwise assigned the value ln (.50)
Would move for a job [d]	= 1 yes to question E10, Table 7.1 0 otherwise
Ln (pay to move)	= ln (hourly wage for which respondent would move) if yes to question E10, otherwise assigned a value of ln(.50)

[a]This measure was included to pick up effects of assigning a past wage for those who were unemployed in the previous year.

[b]These measures were not collected in 1976.

[c]This variable will also pick up the effects of assigning a $.50 wage for respondents who said no.

[d]This variable will also pick up effects of assigning a $.50 wage for respondents who said no.

There are some problems with these data, however. The expected wage question did not ask about the minimum acceptable wage. There was no direct measure of exactly when a man's unemployment spell ended. While there was data on employment status at the next interview date and on tenure in the job held as of that date, we do not know whether or not a man who was unemployed at the next date had been unemployed continuously between the two interviews. Nor do we know whether employed men worked at more than one job between interviews.

There are also two conceptual issues to be considered. First, the expected wage question is being used as a proxy for the reservation wage, but it did not ask about minimum acceptable wage. If, however, reservation wages and expected wages are positively correlated when worker quality and wages are controlled, this should reduce the conceptual problem.[4]

The second issue arises in any attempt to measure reservation wages. A worker may report a high expected wage or reservation wage because he has already been offered a job or expects to be offered a particular job sometime in the future. This should attenuate the relationship between responses to expected wage questions (or to acceptable minimum wage questions) and the concept of reservation wage.[5]

ANALYSIS

The analysis which follows is in two parts. We begin by describing the characteristics of unemployed men and addressing the important questions of whether unemployed men were willing to take pay cuts, whether they actually took pay cuts, and whether those who were willing to take pay cuts were more likely to become employed. In the second phase of the analysis, an attempt was made to model the transition from unemployment to employment using Equation 3a.

After adjusting for inflation, we found that men's average expected wages exceeded their past wages, but the average wages on jobs the men actually accepted were lower than their past wages. Contrary to theoretical expectations, men who expected to take pay cuts were slightly _less_ likely to be employed by the time of the next interview than were men who expected pay raises. Holding constant past wages, other worker qualifications characteristics and local labor

---

[4]We have actually added a reservation wage question to the 13th wave of the Panel Study in order to test this assumption.

[5]We are thankful to Thomas Daymont for bringing this point to our attention.

market conditions, we found no evidence that workers with lower expected wages were more likely to get and retain jobs.

Past Work Experience and Job
Search Behavior of Unemployed Men

A large percentage of the unemployed household heads in our sample had a past history of work, and when they worked they worked quite a lot. Most of these men (91 percent) had been employed during the previous year (see Table 7.3). These men earned, on average, $5.26 per hour (in 1978 dollars) when they last worked[6]; they worked an average of 34 weeks during the previous year; and they worked 44.8 hours per week when working.

The majority of these men reported having engaged in some job search activity within the previous month; four-fifths of these men had looked for a job in at least one place during the past four weeks. And about half had searched in five or more places.

Willingness to Move and Job Opportunities

During three of the four years, unemployed men were asked whether there were any jobs that were not worth taking in their area, what these jobs paid, whether they would move to get a job, and how much a job would have to pay to get them to move. The answers to these questions gave us some idea about the types of job opportunities unemployed men were passing up and about their geographic flexibility in taking a job.

Responses suggested that men did not generally pass up job opportunities for which wages fell somewhat below their expectations. Almost half (45 percent) of the men, when asked whether there were jobs available that were not worth taking, said there were no such jobs (Table 7.4). Men who did report that they knew of available jobs which were not worth taking said that these jobs paid considerably less than their most recent job. On average, jobs not worth taking paid $2.83 per hour (in 1978 dollars)[7]; this compares to a 1978 minimum wage of $2.65 per hour. The $2.83 hourly wage averaged about 60 percent of these workers' past hourly wages and about half of their expected hourly wages.

There was some evidence of geographic flexibility in job search. The majority (69 percent) of the unemployed workers reported that they would move for

---

[6]Here, $5.26 = e^{1.66}$.

[7]Here, $2.83 = e^{1.04}$.

Table 7.3

PAST WORK BEHAVIOR and EXPECTED WAGES, AND ACCEPTED WAGE[a]
(For male heads of households unemployed at the interview and
who had completed school at least two years prior to the interview date.)

	All Men	Men Employed Last Year	Men Employed and Reporting Wage at Next Interview	Men Employed Last Year and Employed and Reporting a Wage at Next Interview
Expected Wages, Past Wages and Accepted Wages				
Mean of ln expected wage[b]	1.74	1.75	1.74	1.74
Mean of ln past wage	–	1.66	–	1.66
Mean of ln accepted wage[c]	–	–	1.57	1.58
Mean of ln expected/past wage[c]	–	.07	–	–
Mean of ln accepted/past wage[c]	–	–	–	-.03
Mean of ln accepted/expected wage[b,c]	–	–	-.13	-.14
Percentage who said job sought required training	14.44	14.09	15.75	14.75
Work Behavior in Year Prior to Interview				
Percentage employed last year	91.0	100%	95.0	100%
Mean weeks employed	31.1	34.1	32.9	34.6
Mean weeks unemployed	14.6	14.8	14.3	15.0
Hours/week worked when employed	40.8	44.8	42.1	44.3
Search Activity in Last Four Weeks				
Percentage who looked in at least one place	82.8	83.4	86.4	87.8
Percentage who looked in				
1 place	7.7	7.8	7.8	8.2
2 places	8.6	8.2	9.3	9.8
3 places	10.1	10.7	12.6	13.1
4 places	10.0	9.6	9.7	8.8
5 or more places	46.4	47.0	47.1	47.8
Median number of places looked	4.0	4.0	4.0	4.0
N	470	415	244	226

[a]This is a pooled sample of unemployed men from the 1974, 1975, 1976, and 1977 interviews.

[b]Of the 470 respondents, 438 reported an expected wage. The others were omitted from these estimates.

[c]Note: men who did not report an accepted wage were excluded from these estimates.

Table 7.4

AVAILABLE JOB OPPORTUNITIES AND WILLINGNESS TO MOVE[a]
(For male heads of households who were unemployed at the interview date
and who had completed school at least two years prior to the interview date.)[b]

All Workers	
Percentage who said there were jobs not worth taking	55.0%
Percentage who would move for a job	69.0%
N	341
Workers Who Said There Were Jobs Not Worth Taking	
Mean ln (wage in these jobs)	1.04
Mean ln (wage in these jobs/past wage)[c]	−.68
Mean ln (wage in these jobs/expected wage)[d]	−.73
N	174
Workers Who Said They Would Move for a Job	
Mean ln (wage to move)	1.84
Mean ln (wage to move/past wage)[e]	.15
Mean ln (wage to move/expected wage)[f]	.08
N	248

[a]All wages were inflation adjusted to 1978 dollars.

[b]This is a pooled sample of unemployed male household heads from the 1974, 1975, and 1977 interviews. In 1976, household heads were not asked about available jobs or willingness to move.

[c]Workers with no past wage were excluded, giving an N of 163.

[d]Workers who did not report expected wages were excluded, giving an N of 165.

[e]Workers with no past wage were excluded, giving an N of 224.

[f]Workers who did not report expected wages were excluded, giving an N of 227.

a job. But, while workers were flexible, they wanted a pay premium for this flexibility of an average of 15 percent over their past wages and 8 percent over their expected wages.

Expectations

Since part of the analysis was a test of whether or not men who were willing to take pay cuts became employed more quickly, it was useful first to examine

men's wage expectations. Looking at men who worked in the previous year, we
found that they typically did not aspire to higher status occupations. About
two-thirds of the men with past jobs expected to again be employed in the same
occupation and only 15 percent expected to be employed in a higher status
occupation (Table 7.5).[8] These figures were consistent with the training
questions as well; only 14.4 percent of the men reported that they would require
training for their expected occupations (Table 7.3).

Table 7.5

OCCUPATIONAL STATUS OF JOB SOUGHT RELATIVE TO PAST JOB
(For male heads of households who were unemployed at the interview date,
who have been employed in the previous year, and who had completed
school at least two years prior to the interview date.)[a]

| | Percentage Seeking: | | | |
	Lower Status Occupation	Same Status Occupation	Higher Status Occupation	Total
White men (N=197)	14.5	67.6	18.1	100
Black men (N=169)	18.1	58.6	23.3	100
All men (N=366)	15.1	66.2	18.7	100

[a]This is a pooled sample of unemployed male household heads from the 1974,
1975, 1976, and 1977 interviews. Sample members who did not report either
their past occupation or the occupation they were seeking were eliminated
from this table.

Although men's occupational aspirations were consistent with their past
occupations, they did expect to be paid more, an average of 7 percent adjusted
for inflation, than they had received in their previous jobs (Table 7.3). This
figure was higher for those who had voluntarily left their jobs than for those
whose unemployment was involuntary (19 vs. 4 percent).

Further investigation showed that a large proportion of men expected to take
pay cuts. Table 7.6 categorizes unemployed men who were employed the previous
year into two groups: men who expected to take a pay cut and men who expected a
pay raise. About half of the unemployed men (51.5 percent) expected a pay raise

[8]Here occupation is coded at the 1-digit level and then recoded using the
Duncan Socioeconomic Index.

(i.e., their expected wage exceeded their past wage) and half expected a pay cut
(their expected wage was less than their past wage).[9]

Table 7.6

PROBABILITY OF EMPLOYMENT AT NEXT INTERVIEW BY
EXPECTATIONS ABOUT A PAY CUT
(For male heads of households who were employed at the interview date,
who had been unemployed in the previous year, and who had completed
school at least two years prior to the interview date.)[a]

Expected Wage Relative to Past Wage	Percentage of Sample	Percentage Who Were Employed at Next Interview
Expected a pay cut[b]	48.5	68.3
Same or expected a pay increase[c]	51.5	74.4

[a]This is a pooled sample of unemployed male household heads from the 1974, 1975,
1976 and 1977 interviews. Sample members who did not report expected wage were
excluded from the analysis.

[b]Expected wage less than past wage.

[c]Expected wage the same or greater than past wage.

But there was no evidence that men who were willing to take a pay cut were
more likely to become employed by the next interview. Indeed, those who expected
a pay raise were slightly more likely to be employed at the next interview than
were those who were willing to take a pay cut (74 vs. 68 percent).

It should be noted, however, that the expected wage measure may pick up
three quite different factors: (1) reservation wages, (2) worker quality, or
(3) local demand conditions. That is, a high expected wage could have meant
either that a worker was holding out for a job in the high paying end of his wage
offers distribution, or that he had a great deal of human capital, or that there
was a tight labor market. These interpretations have quite different
implications for employability. High quality workers, all else being equal,
should be more likely to get job offers and so become employed. Similarly, in a

---

[9]In fact, no one in this sample reported an expected wage which equalled
their past wage.

tight labor market it should be easier to find jobs. On the other hand, high
reservation wages should reduce employment probabilities. A related problem is
that workers with relatively low expected wages may have been unemployed for a
longer period of time than other workers. This would be consistent with the
search theory prediction that workers´ reservation wages decline over time. If
the group of workers who expected pay cuts was dominated by the long-term
unemployed--who may have differed systematically from other unemployed men (i.e.,
had fewer qualifications, less motivation, or a "taste" for leisure)--then we
would expect to observe more unemployment persistence among the men who expected
pay cuts. This is again a case of quality differences. We used multivariate
analyses in order to isolate these different effects by including specific
measures of worker qualifications and local labor market conditions, as well as
controls for search activity and extent of past unemployment.

How do Accepted Jobs Compare to
Past Jobs and to Job Expectations?

One way to test whether expectations about the level of future wages were
realistic is to examine the wages for the jobs accepted by workers. We have
already seen that workers´ expected wages averaged 8 percent higher than their
past wages. But Table 7.3 shows that, on average, the real wages in jobs
actually taken by workers were considerably lower than either their expected
wages (by 15.3 percent) or their past wages (by 8.3 percent). Thus, some workers
must have taken a drop in their real earnings.

Indeed, as Table 7.7 shows, only 35 percent of those workers who were
employed by the time of the next interview had obtained jobs in which the pay was
equal to or greater than the wage level they expected to receive. Not
surprisingly, people who expected a pay increase were less likely to find jobs
where the pay level at least equalled the expectations they had expressed in the
previous year; only 27 percent of them managed to do so.

Table 7.8 looks at pay expectations in a slightly different way--by asking
whether expectations about getting pay cuts or raises were actually met. About
89 percent of those who expected a drop in pay actually received a cut in real
wages and about 63 percent of those who expected a raise in pay actually received
an increase in wages. Thus, peoples´ expectations about the direction of their
wage change in a future job relative to pay in their last job were likely to be
met.

Table 7.7

EMPLOYMENT AND WAGE STATUS RELATIVE TO EXPECTED WAGES
BY EXPECTATIONS ABOUT A PAY CUT [a]

(Male heads of households unemployed at the interview data,
who had completed school at least two years prior to the interview date,
employed in the previous year, and who reported a wage at the
next interview date; N=212.) [b]

Accepted Wage Relative to Expected Wage	Expected Wage Relative to Past Wage		
	Proportion of the Sample	Expected Pay Cut [c] [a]	Same or Expected Pay Increase [a] [d]
Accepted wage was less than expected wage	64.9	56.6	73.2
Accepted wage was equal to or greater than expected wage	35.1	43.4	26.8

[a] All wage figures are in 1978 dollars.

[b] This is a pooled sample of unemployed male heads from the 1974, 1975, 1976 and 1977 interviews; cases not reporting an expected wage were excluded.

[c] Expected wage less than past wage.

[d] Expected wage the same or greater than past wage.

Table 7.8

EMPLOYMENT AND WAGE STATUS RELATIVE TO PAST WAGES BY
EXPECTATIONS ABOUT A PAY CUT[a]

(For male heads of households unemployed at the interview date,
who had completed school at least two years prior to the interview date,
who had been employed in the previous year, and who reported a wage at the
next interview date; N=212.)[b]

Accepted Wage Relative to Past Wage	Expected Wage Relative to Past Wage		
	Proportion of the Sample	Expected Pay Cut[c]	Same or Expected Pay Increase[d]
Accepted wage was less than past wage	62.3	89.1	36.7
Accepted wage was equal to or greater than past wage	37.7	10.9	63.3

[a]All wage figures are in 1978 dollars.

[b]This is a pooled sample of unemployed male household heads from the 1974, 1975, 1976 and 1977 interviews. Cases where respondents did not report an expected wage were excluded.

[c]Expected wage less than past wage.

[d]Expected wage the same or greater than past wage.

To summarize, most workers who found jobs were working in jobs which paid less than they had expected to earn. This was particularly the case for workers who expected to earn more than their past job paid. On the other hand, workers' expectations about whether they would receive a pay cut or a pay raise were likely to be realized, suggesting that these expectations about the direction of their wage change were quite realistic.

Multivariate Analyses

As we have already noted, search theory predicts that employment probabilities increase as the gap between workers' wage opportunities and reservation wages drops. This suggests that workers who are willing to take a pay cut (i.e., with relatively low reservation wages) should find jobs more quickly. But a preliminary analysis of the data indicated that workers who expected pay raises were <u>more</u> likely to be employed a year later than were workers who expected a pay cut. On the other hand, workers who expected a pay raise were less likely to obtain a job where the level of pay met or exceeded their expectations than were other workers.

A number of factors might obscure the true relationship between expected wage and employment probabilities. Expected wages may pick up aspects of workers' quality which were not captured by their past wages or may pick differences in local labor markets. Since both the length of time a worker was unemployed and the extent of his search activity could not be controlled for, their effects may also be obscuring the true relationship.

Table 7.9 reports the results when Equation 3a was estimated with the Panel Study data. Employment was measured in two ways: (1) by whether the respondent had a job at the next interview date (column 1 in Table 7.9), and (2) by the proportion of time the worker was employed between the two interview dates in the job he held by the time of his next interview (column 2, Table 7.9). The predictor variables included: ln hourly wage on the last job; other measures of worker quality (hours worked per week on last job, education, work experience, whether worked last year, weeks unemployed last year); measures of labor market conditions (region, year interviewed, area unemployment rate, city size); and controls for race, marital status, and extent of search activity. The equation predicting employment status at the next interview was estimated as a logit function; the equation predicting the proportion of time employed was estimated using ordinary least squares techniques.

Even when controlling for previous wage, worker qualifications, labor market conditions, and search activity, high expected wages were shown to be associated with a significantly higher probability of employment. A one-standard deviation increase in ln expected wages[10] was associated with an increase of 5.7 percent in

---

[10]Those who did not report an expected wage were assigned a 50¢ wage.

Table 7.9 (page 1 of 2)

MULTIVARIATE ANALYSIS OF RE-EMPLOYMENT
(For male heads of households who were unemployed at the interview date
and who had completed school two years prior to the interview date.)

Predictor Variable (Excluded Category)	Dependent Variable		
	Whether Employed at Next Interview[a]	Proportion of Time Employed in Job at Next Interview[b]	Ln Expected Wage
ln expected wage	.7909* (.3547)	.0821 (.0537)	–
Worker Quality Measures (X_1)			
ln previous wage	-.1957 (.2401)	-.0258 (.0369)	.2780** (.0307)
Education	.1517* (.0546)	.0192* (.0080)	.0171* (.074)
Experience	.0216 (.0341)	.0105* (.0050)	.6186** (.005)
Experienced Squared	-.0010 (.0007)	-.0002[+] (.0001)	-.0003** (.0001)
Not employed last year	.3387 (.6757)	-.2293* (.1032)	.0678 (.0940)
Hours/week worked last year	.0241* (.0131)	.0008 (.0019)	.0058** (.0016)
Weeks unemployed last year	.0029 (.0077)	-.0013 (.0012)	-.0002 (.0011)
Local Labor Market Condition Measures (X_2)			
South	.6937* (.3611)	.0693 (.0545)	-.1176* (.0491)
Northeast	.5517[+] (.3432)	.2185** (.0522)	-.6241 (.0466)
North central	1.105** (.3656)	.1341* (.0536)	-.1105* (.0462)
(West)			
Area unemployment rate	-.0619 (.0571)	.0074 (.0084)	.0022 (.0078)
City size	-.0016** (.0004)	-.0003** (.0001)	.0001 (.0001)
Interviewed in 1975	.6938[+] (.3994)	.0948 (.0648)	-.2000** (.0559)

Table 7.9 (page 2 of 2)

Predictor Variable (Excluded Category)	Dependent Variable		
	Whether Employed at Next Interview[a]	Proportion of Time Employed in Job at Next Interview[b]	Ln Expected Wage
Interviewed in 1976	.6567 (.4054)	.1479* (.0669)	−.2497** (.9562)
Interviewed in 1977	1.2125** (.3973)	.2570** (.0644)	−.1587** (.0541)
(Interviewed in 1974)			
Other Controls			
White	1.2498** (.3317)	.0355 (.0542)	.0871+ (.0480)
Married	.2172 (.2712)	.0362 (.0405)	.1312** (.0462)
Number of places looked	−.0455 (.0495)	−.0064 (.0075)	−
Resource Measures			
Other available income	−	−	.0118** (.0034)
Family size	−	−	−.0433** (.0126)
Received UI	−	−	.0104 (.0230)
Sample size	470	459[c]	450[d]
$\bar{R}^2$		.154	.411

[a]This was estimated using logit.

[b]This was estimated using OLS.

[c]Eleven employed respondents did not report their job tenure and were excluded from the analysis.

[d]This was run only for people who reported an expected wage.

**significant at .01 level.

*significant at .05 level.

+significant at .10 level.

the probability of being employed by the next interview (Table 7.9, column 1).[11]
Expected wages had a positive but insignificant effect on the proportion of time
the worker had been employed in his job by the time of the next interview. Thus,
these results provided no support for the hypothesis that men with relatively low
expected wages were more likely to become employed.

There were a number of interesting other findings. Unemployed men
interviewed in 1975, 1976, or 1977--rather than in 1974--were considerably more
likely to be employed by the next interview and had a larger proportion of time
employed between interviews. (However, 1977 was the only year significant for
both dependent variables). This finding is consistent with national statistics
which showed unusually high unemployment rates in 1974. Men who lived in the
South, Northeast, and North Central regions had higher employment probabilities
and had been employed for a larger proportion of time than were men from other
parts of the country. City size was negatively related to employment probability
and to time employed.

As expected, employment probabilities and time employed increased with
worker qualifications. Education was positively related to both the likelihood
of getting a job and to the proportion of time in subsequent employment.
Experience was positively related to the proportion of time employed. Men who
did not work at all in the previous year spent a smaller proportion of time
working between interviews. Hours worked per week in the previous year were
positively related to the probability of getting a job the following year.

---

[11]In a logit equation the probability that the ith person works at the next
interview, p_i can be estimated by

$$P_i = \frac{1}{1+e^{-\sum_{j=1}^{m} \beta_j X_{ij}}}$$

X_{ij} = The ith person's values on the predictor variables
$j=1...M$

β_j = The coefficient in the logit equation for the jth
predictor variable

To calculate the effect of one standard deviation increase in ln expected
wages on the probability of working when all X's are at the mean, one first
calculates the value of p_i, when all X_{ij} are assigned their mean values; this
gives p_o. Next one calculates the value of p_i when all X_i's (other than ln
expected wages) are assigned their mean values, and ln expected wages is assigned
a value of one standard deviation above the mean, this gives p_1. The difference
$p_1 - p_o$ is equal to 5.7 percent.

Surprisingly, past wages did not predict either employment status at the next interview or the proportion of time employed between interviews. This finding did not change if an instrumented past wage measure was substituted in the employment equations. Nor was there any evidence that increased search activity (measured as the number of places a worker looked for a job in last four weeks), increased the likelihood of employment.

One might argue that wage expectations do not measure reservation wages. Table 7.9, column 3, shows the results when measures of worker quality, local demand, and available resources at the time of unemployment were regressed on ln expected wages. Men's expected wages increased with other available income and decreased with family size. That is, men with fewer resources expected lower wages. This is what one would predict if expected wages were picking up effects of being willing to accept jobs at the low end of one's wage offer distribution.[12] In order to reduce measurement error, we estimated an instrumented expected wage measure from the expected wage equation and reestimated the equations for probability of employment and for proportion of time worked (Griliches and Mason, 1976). This had no effect on the pattern of results. The attitudinal measures in Table 7.2 provide some measure of workers' motivations. Adding these to the equations reported in columns 1 and 2 in Table 12.9 had no effect on the reservation wage coefficient.

One can always argue that this expected wage measure still may be picking up unmeasured aspects of worker qualifications or worker motivations or of labor market opportunities. However, these analyses do include a number of qualification and labor market measures.

IMPLICATIONS

This chapter has described an investigation of the relationship between unemployed workers' expectations about wages and their employment probabilities. We began by asking whether workers' pay expectations were realistic and found that those expectations appeared to be unrealistically high. Among those unemployed workers who had obtained jobs before the following year's interview, only 35 percent had obtained jobs which met their pay expectations. On average, unemployed workers expected a pay raise of 7 percent, in real terms, in their

---

[12]The positive coefficient on other available income might also be interpreted as an effect of worker quality.

next job. But a year later, the average unemployed worker who had taken a job reported a wage that was 15 percent lower, in real terms, than his expected wage.

Although unemployed workers´ expectations about their level of pay were high, their expectations about whether or not they would receive a pay cut or pay raise seemed more realistic. Among workers who found jobs, 89 percent of those who expected a pay cut received one and 63 percent of those who expected a raise in pay received one.

Next we investigated whether unemployed workers who expected pay cuts were more likely to have obtained a job a year later. This was not the case. Indeed, the reverse was true; men who expected an increase in wages were more likely to be employed a year later. A test was made to see whether this occurred because men with relatively high pay expectations had more qualifications or were in areas with more favorable labor market conditions. But an increase in expected wages significantly increased the probability of employment at the next interview, even when we controlled for past wages, worker qualifications, labor market demand, search activity, and past unemployment. There was some evidence that workers´ expected wages dropped with available financial resources and demands, suggesting that expected wages included a component of being willing to take jobs at the low end of one´s wage offers distribution.

These results clearly show that controlling for past wages, workers with high pay expectations were no more likely to become employed than were workers with similar qualifications but with low pay expectations. The crucial question is whether this finding can be extended to rebut the argument that men continue in unemployment as a consequence of their unwillingness to accept pay cuts. This raises the question of the relationship between expected wages and reservation wages. The analysis reported here suggested that expected wages varied with financial resources. This supports a reservation wage interpretation but is also consistent with unmeasured ability differences.

Further, even if expected wages were a good proxy for reservation wages, it may still be possible that high or low reservation wages, relative to opportunities and endowments, can affect employment. If so, that effect is being swamped by more powerful forces, including, probably, unmeasured differences in ability and training and differences in whether the prior wage was unusually high or low.

268

References

Barron, John M., and Mellow, Wesley. "Search Effort in the Labor Market." The
    Journal of Human Resources (Summer 1979): 389-404.

Ehrenberg, Ronald G., and Oaxaca, Ronald L. "Unemployment Insurance, Duration of
    Unemployment, and Subsequent Wage Gain." American Economic Review 66
    (December 1976): 756-66.

Feldstein, Martin S. "Temporary Layoffs in the Theory of Unemployment." Journal
    of Political Economy 84 (October 1976): 937-57.

Hill, Martha S., and Corcoran, Mary. "Unemployment Among Family Men: a 10-Year
    Longitudinal Study." Monthly Labor Review (November 1979): 19-23.

Kasper, Hirschel. "The Asking Price of Labor and the Duration of Unemployment
    Review of Economics and Statistics 49 (May 1967): 165-72.

Kiefer, Nicholas M., and Neumann, George. "Estimation of Wage Offer
    Distributions and Reservation Wages." In Studies in the Economics of
    Search, edited by S. Lippman and J. McCall. Amsterdam: North-Holland,
    1979.

Lippman, Steven A., and McCall, John J. "Job Search in a Dynamic Economy."
    Journal of Economic Theory 12 (June 1976): 665-90.

_____. "The Economics of Job Search: A Survey." Economic Inquiry 14
    (Pt. I, June 1976): 155-89; (Pt. II, September 1976): 347-68.

Rosenfeld, C. "Job Search of the Unemployed, May 1976." Monthly Labor Review
    100 (November 1977): 39-43.

Stephenson, Stanley P., Jr. "The Economics of Youth Job Search Behavior." Review
    of Economics and Statistics 58 (February 1976): 104-11.

Stigler, George. "The Economics of Information." Journal of Political Economy
    69 (June 1961): 213-25.

_____. "Information in the Labor Market." Journal of Political Economy 70
    (October 1962 Supp.): 94-104.

Welch, Finis. "What Have We Learned from Empirical Studies of Unemployment
    Insurance?" Industrial and Labor Relations Review 30 (July 1977): 451-61.

Chapter 8

THE GASOLINE PRICE RESPONSIVENESS
OF PERSONAL TRANSPORTATION DEMAND

Daniel H. Hill

Over the past ten years, understanding and quantifying the response of American households and enterprises to increased petroleum prices has become a research topic of major policy importance. The overall extent of the welfare transfer from oil consuming to oil producing nations and sectors resulting from the recent formation of cartels in the oil industry is crucially affected by the degree of price responsiveness among the oil consumers. If consumers are willing and able to substitute other commodities for petroleum when its price increases then relatively little is to be gained by monopolistic producers who arbitrarily increase prices. Indeed, if the negative response of consumers to such price increases is sufficiently strong, arbitrary price increases will lead to a reduction in producer revenues. Economics predicts and history verifies that under these conditions it is very difficulty to maintain pricing discipline among members of a cartel and these organizations are generally short lived.

A policy relevant aspect of this high responsiveness of demand (elastic demand) is that the governments of consuming nations could recapture much of the welfare (consumer surplus) lost due to exogenous monopolistic pricing by imposing taxes on petroleum. Redistributing the resulting revenue could mitigate many of the adverse effects of the increased petroleum prices and at the same time reduce the petroleum demands of consumers.

Conversely, of course, the inability or unwillingness of consumers to alter their demands for a commodity when its price is arbitrarily increased provides producers with a very strong incentive to organize and raise prices collectively. The total amount of revenue to be captured by such a policy is large. Pricing discipline is much easier to maintain when the profits of cartel members are high and any unilateral or secret action by one member to sell larger quantities at lower prices becomes readily apparent to all the other members as they see their sales drop. Such a situation deprives the governments of consuming nations of much hope in reducing demand and recapturing consumer surplus via taxation.

Under conditions of inelastic demand, consuming governments are more severely restricted in their response to exogenous monopoly pricing.

The speed with which consuming nations and sectors respond to price changes also affects the amount of welfare transfer which monopolistic pricing policies can induce. Even if the long-run price responsiveness of consumers is large, a very slow adjustment to rising prices will allow large potential welfare transfers due to monopolistic pricing as well as conditions favorable to the maintenance of pricing discipline among cartel members. The fact that long-run demand is sensitive to price suggests that the taxing policies of consuming governments can substantially reduce the amount of consumer surplus extracted from their citizens. That consumers are slow to respond, however, argues for phased in taxes such as those proposed by the Carter Administration in 1977.

Finally, even if demand is only moderately responsive in the long-run, if consumers respond very rapidly to current changes in price, then on immediate imposition of taxes by consuming governments when exogenous price increases are announced may succeed in destabilizing foreign cartels while retaining most of the welfare which would otherwise be transferred abroad.

In this chapter we attempt to use data from the Panel Study of Income Dynamics (PSID) to estimate the temporal pattern of household response to changes in gasoline prices. Because we obtained information only on the total amount of driving done in panel households' automobiles, our investigation is limited to one component of the overall response of households to price changes. As we shall see in the literature review, other studies have suggested that the response of annual miles driven to price changes comprises roughly one-half the total response of gasoline demand to price. Examination of the Panel Study data is justified despite this limitation because it is the only data set which allows one to examine the dynamics of response at the individual household level.

REVIEW OF THE LITERATURE

Prior to 1978 virtually all modern empirical investigations of the responsiveness of American consumers to the price of gasoline were based on state or even national aggregate gasoline consumption or aggregate automotive transportation data and aggregate price measures. While there have been many such studies, the essence of their methods and findings can be gleaned from examining three of them--Houthakker, Verliger, and Sheehan (1974), Dahl (1978) and Kwast (1980).

The analysis of Houthakker, Verliger, and Sheehan is typical of modern gasoline demand analyses not only with respect to the type of data, but also with respect to the behavioral model and technique of statistical estimation. The model assumes that each individual j living in state i in time period t has a desired demand for gasoline q^*_{jit}. This demand is representable as a log-linear function of the local current gasoline prices (P_{jit}) he faces and his income (Y_{ijt}). That is

$$q^*_{jit} = f(P_{jit}, Y_{jit}) \ .$$

The individual's full response to changes in gasoline prices or income will take time, partly because old habits take time to change, but primarily because actual gasoline consumption is constrained by the technical characteristics of the individual's automobile. Houthakker, Verliger, and Sheehan assumed a dynamic adjustment process in which the observed percentage change in demand resulting from a price change in any two consecutive periods is a constant fraction of the desired percent change. That is:

$$q_{it}/q_{it-1} = (q^*_{it}/q_{it-1})^\theta \ .$$

Thus, $\ln q^*_{it} = \ln q_{it} - (1 - \theta) \ln q_{it-1}$

Taking logarithms of the first equation, substituting for q* from this last equation, and rearranging terms yields the following Koyck equation which allows the estimation of the parameters of the unobserved desired demand equation in terms of observed variables:

$$\ln q_{it} = \theta + \theta \gamma \ln P_{it} + \theta \beta \ln Y_{it} + (1 - \theta) \ln q_{it-1} \ .$$

From a theoretical perspective there are several problems with this approach. First, but probably least important as a practical matter, is that log-linear demand models are "theoretically implausible." By this we mean that there is no well behaved representation of preferences consistent with utility maximization which yields log-linear demand equations. A far more serious problem hindering our attempt to understand the dynamics of change is that the Koyck estimation technique is appropriate only if the true adjustment paths are characterized by large initial impacts which decay exponentially. The authors recognized this problem, but they neither offered nor investigated alternative dynamic adjustment processes. An empirical problem not addressed was that the model was motivated as reasonable for individuals but was estimated with aggregates.

The data set used by Houthakker, Verliger, and Sheehan is a quarterly time series of 40 state level cross sections derived from the American Petroleum Institute's weekly estimates. This data source is perhaps the one most widely used data set in aggregate analysis of its kind primarily because of its wide and timely availability. While quarterly data on wholesale sales of gasoline are probably fairly representative of actual retail sales, the same cannot be said for the gasoline price data which are based on weekly, city-wide, "typical" prices for major brand regular gasoline. The authors noted that because major brand retailers generally are able to sell at higher prices, than independents the price data may be biased upwards. The problem is actually more serious than this, however, not only because the portion of gasoline sold by independent dealers varies greatly across states but also because during their sample period, 1963-1972, there was a substantial rise in the proportion of cars requiring high octane premium fuel. This, of course, results in serially correlated measurement errors in an independent variable.

Houthakker, Verliger, and Sheehan used the Belestra-Nerlov error components technique in estimating the parameters of Equation 3, because use of OLS would result in biased estimates when lagged dependent variables are employed. This procedure yielded short-run or impact elasticities of $-.075$ for price and $.303$ for income. The estimated speed of adjustment is $.304$, which implies a long-run price elasticity of $-.247$ and a long-run income elasticity of $.997$. The authors concluded that:

> "...the arguments made for energy rationing by many politicians and some economists are unfounded. The market mechanism by itself appears to be capable of bringing about the necessary adjustments in demand. Consequently there are also limits to the price increases that a producer cartel can exact."

Kwast (1980) used a model which differed from that of Houthakker, Verliger, and Sheehan only in so far as he included regional dummies and a dummy indicating the OPEC embargo years. His data extended from 1963 through 1977, rather than 1963 through 1972 as in the earlier work, and it was annual rather than quarterly. While the coefficient on price estimated by Kwast was virtually identical to that found in the earlier analysis, his estimated speed of adjustment was only one seventh as large. Kwast stated:

> "This value of [θ] implies a long-run price elasticity of demand of −1.59, which seems implausibly large...A possible explanation for our result is that it merely indicates the dynamic structure of the partial adjustment model is over simplified."

While Kwast was probably justified in saying the partial adjustment model represents an over simplification, he based his statement regarding the implausibility of his estimated long-run elasticity at least partly on the results of the Houthakker, Verliger, and Sheehan analysis of quarterly data. The use of quarterly observations of gasoline demand in a lagged dependent variable model may overstate the speed of adjustment due to the strong seasonal component of gasoline demand. Monthly gasoline demand data, however, clearly indicates that within year variance of demand is far greater than across year variance. Thus, the correlation of gasoline demand during one quarter with the previous quarter's measure will be much lower than its annual counterpart for reasons entirely apart from any dynamic adjustment process. Indeed, if quarterly change were driven by a partial adjustment process we would expect annual correlations to be _lower_ than quarterly ones.[1] Thus, Kwast was probably unjustified in rejecting his long-run estimate. While a gasoline demand price elasticity of −1.59 does seem extremely large, one must note that in Kwast's case, because of the very slow speed of adjustment, the "long-run" represents a time period which is best measured in decades while in the earlier piece the full long-run adjustment is accomplished in a few years.

Given these arguments it is unfortunate that Kwast ignored the dynamic nature of the response when evaluating the impact of a federal gasoline excise tax and concluded that "an increase in the federal excise tax on gasoline equivalent to a 29 percent jump in the real price of gasoline would result in only modest short-run reductions in quantity demanded."

One further aspect of the Kwast analysis warrants discussion here − his tests of structural stability of the demand relation before and after the oil embargo of 1973 through 1974. Two tests were preformed. The first was a simple

---

[1] The fact that Houthakker, Verliger, and Sheehan ignored the seasonality problem while Kwast (perhaps unwittingly) finesses it would imply that the variance of the estimated coefficient on lagged consumption should be higher in the earlier work. An examination of the separated standard errors indicates that once one adjusts for differences in sample size, the variance of the earlier estimate is 2.7 times greater than the latter.

Chow test of structural stability for the subsample periods 1963 through 1972 and 1975 through 1977. The calculated F statistic obtained was not sufficiently large to reject the null hypothesis of stability. The second test employed all possible combinations of a dummy variable taking the value of one for the years 1975, 1976, and 1977 and zero for all other years with the independent variables. Significant coefficients on these interaction terms indicated structural instability. While this test is asymptotically equivalent to the Chow test, it is more powerful for small samples. Because only 10 of the 80 possible interaction coefficients in the 32 models estimated were significant, Kwast concluded that:

> "In summation, virtually no evidence is found of structural change in either the slope coefficients or intercepts term of the gasoline demand equations."

That this conclusion is misleading is clear when one examines the findings in greater detail. Kwast based his conclusion on a time series of only three post embargo cross-sections. All ten of the significant interaction coefficients appeared in the models with less than three interaction variables. Thus, 40 percent of the interactions in the smaller models were significant. While only one model yielded a significant post embargo price interaction which indicates price responsiveness decreased after the embargo, three of the five smaller models containing an interaction term for lagged consumption were significant and negative. Thus, Kwasts´ results do provide evidence of a structural shift toward less long-run price responsiveness combined with a more rapid adjustment process.

The Dahl (1979) analysis is the last example of work done using time series of highly aggregated data and representative of studies which do not employ partial adjustment models. A major objective of these models is to purge estimates of simultaneity bias resulting from the endogeneity of gasoline prices. As in the above analyses, Dahl assumed household demand for gasoline is a log-linear function of gasoline prices and income. Because her data spanned a much longer period of history (1947-1972) during which automobile ownership increased dramatically, she also included a measure of the stock of automobiles per capita in the demand function. Because the price of gasoline affects both its supply and household demand for automobiles, it is necessary to identify these functions

and estimate them simultaneously with the gasoline demand function.[2] This
procedure yielded an estimated short-run gasoline price elasticity of -.442 and
an income elasticity of .322.

Dahl next performed separate estimations for annual miles traveled (AMT) and
automobile efficiency (MPG). Since total gasoline consumption is equivalent to
miles driven divided by miles per gallon it follows that

$$\ln(QD) = \ln(AMT) - \ln(MPG) \text{ and } \frac{\partial \ln QD}{\partial \ln P} = \frac{\partial \ln(AMT)}{\partial \ln P} - \frac{\partial \ln MPG}{\partial \ln P} .$$

While Dahl was unable with any degree of precision to estimate the gasoline
price responsiveness of miles drive, she was able to obtain a significant
coefficient of .212 on price in the efficiency equation. This implies that
roughly half of the short-run response to changes in gasoline prices is due to
reductions in miles driven and the remainder due to changes in driving habits and
automobile maintenance which improves efficiency of the existing stock of
automobiles. The magnitude of this latter response seems implausibly high, but
is not far out of line with estimates from vintage capital models which examine
car purchases and decisions to scrap old models to provide dynamic estimates of
efficient responses. Dahl quoted an Office of Energy Systems study estimating a
one-year efficiency price elasticity of .097 and a long efficiency price
elasticity of .686. The reduction in miles driven induced by an increase in the
price of gasoline can be expected to decline as the efficiency of the vehicle
fleet increases. Combining her own estimate with those of the OES study, Dahl
concluded by stating:

> "...The short-run estimated elasticity of demand is -.442 of which half
> comes from changes in miles per gallon. In the long-run, demand is more
> elastic than -.778, of which nine-tenths come from changes in miles per
> gallon."

Dahl also concluded that a 25¢ per gallon tax on gasoline results in "a
23 percent reduction in gasoline [demand which] means an 11 percent reduction in
crude oil consumption, which in turn means a 27 percent reduction in crude oil
imports."

While there are numerous problems with all gasoline demand analyses based on
historical aggregate data, the Dahl study suggests some interesting behavioral

---

[2]The identifying variables for the gasoline supply equation are the
wholesale prices of kerosene distillate fuel oils (diesel) and residual fuel oil
all relative to wholesale gasoline price, and for the auto stock equation the
price of new automobiles.

underpinnings for the dynamic adjustment process as well as some testable
hypotheses.

One major criticism of all the models based on historical aggregate data is
that the period of history to which they pertain is one characterized by
secularly increasing gasoline consumption and declining real prices, commuter
flight to the suburbs, the extension of the interstate highway system, and the
practices of automotive manufacturers which resulted in secularly increasing
vehicle weight and in an even more rapid increase in engine horsepower. Each of
these factors tend to increase demand. Futhermore, while one might argue that
none of these factors would have been possible if gasoline prices were higher, it
stretches credibility to argue that urban flight and completion of an interstate
highway system were direct consequences of declining gasoline prices.

Another problem with gasoline demand analyses based on aggregate data is
that they often seek to infer individual or household behavior from the behavior
of measures from large geographic areas. These measures do not separate
commercial, industrial, and government demands for gasoline from private demand.
The former demands are tied to the demand for final products much more strongly
than the latter and, therefore, a properly specified model should at least
include measures of business output at the same level of observation.
Alternatively, demand functions for each sector should be developed and estimated
separately. Prior to 1975 there was very little household level data available
for analysis. To date published analysis of household demand for gasoline has
been confined to two data sets.--Panel Study of Income Dynamics and the 1972-73
Consumer Expenditure Survey[3]--and only two analyses (Archibald and Gillingham,
1978; and Hill, 1980 summarize the state of the art in this area.

Archibald and Gillingham employed a Lancasterian home production model in
which gasoline demand is viewed as a derived demand for transportation services.
This model aids empirical estimation only in so far as it suggests which measures
belong in the estimating equation. In this instance, these measures are prices
of gasoline and other goods, household income (or total expenditures), and
numerous household and vehicle characteristics. The authors employed a modified
log linear estimating equation to estimate a gasoline demand function for a
subset of the consumer expenditure survey sample. Individuals in the subset
owned and operated an automobile, resided in one of the 23 large metropolitan

---

[3]Several other data sets are becoming available at this writing; these
include the National Personal Transportation Survey conducted by the Census
Bureau for DOE and DOT, The Household Energy Consumption Survey.

areas for which the Department of Labor estimated commodity specific price data, completed all five interviewed and did not use their automobiles for business purposes. Archibald and Gillingham modified the traditional log-linear estimating equation by including square terms for the log of gasoline prices and income in one model and a measure of recent rate of change in gasoline price in another. Both specifications were estimated separately for one car and multi-car families. The specification, including recent price change and the logarithm of price, provided a superior fit using interview information and was not worse than the alternative specification using information from the diary portion of the survey. The price coefficients obtained were negatively significant and generally in the neighborhood of -.6. Contrary to general practice, Archibald and Gillingham interpreted these cross-sectional level coefficients as short-run elasticities. They concluded:

> "Thus, our results indicate a short-run response to changes in the relative price of gasoline roughly comparable to the long-run response previously estimated by others."

In their first analysis, based on interview information, the authors found significantly less price responsiveness in households with more than one car (-.387) than in one automobile household (-.651). They rationalize this seemingly perverse finding by arguing that multi-automobile households are more heavily reliant on automotive transportation than are one-car households.

Other findings include the fact that households with more, or more powerful, automobiles consumed more gasoline; while households headed by older persons, whites, the college-educated, or women consumed less. Archibald and Gillingham concluded from their analysis that "...price increase, however engineered, should be effective in reducing gasoline consumption."

The final study to be discussed as part of this literature review is this author's earlier analysis of data from the Panel Study of Income Dynamics for 1973 through 1977 (Hill, 1980). The author began his analysis by using data on annual miles driven to estimate gasoline expenditures. These expenditures increased both absolutely and relative to income as income increased in the cross-section. This pattern indicates that, even in the absence of price responsiveness, a tax on gasoline would be highly progressive.[4] The author then used 1973 cross-sectional data and change data from 1973 through 1977 to estimate

---

[4]The author did note that some small number of poor households with commuting commitments would be severely burdened by such a tax, but this situation could easily be remedied by means of various rebate schemes.

long-run and intermediate (five-year) gasoline price elasticities of miles driven
using both a simple log linear model and more sophisticated structural log-linear
equations model. Because of precision problems in the computer algorithm, the
elasticities reported by the author at that time are seriously biased, especially
the long-run estimates from the simple model, this latter elasticity was reported
to be -2.084. Once the precision problems are eliminated, the correct figure is
-1.236 a figure significant at the 99 percent level of confidence. Even this
revised figure is considerably larger than that found by others, especially when
it is recalled that this is but one component of the total gasoline demand price
elasticity. As we can see from the corrected estimates in Appendix Tables A8.1
and A8.2, this long-run estimate drops to -.708 when statistical controls are
made for family characteristics, numbers, of cars and location measures. Because
members of older households drive fewer miles, and because the major retirement
centers are in the South and southwest where gasoline prices were low in 1973,
much of the apparent impact of gasoline prices on miles driven is due to a
spurious correlation of prices and age.

There are a number of other potential biases associated with using cross-
sectional data to estimate household reaction to gasoline price changes. A major
portion of the cross-sectional variance in gasoline prices, for instance, is
variance in state taxes. If citizens of states where settlement is sparse and
travel distances are long refuse to allow themselves to be taxed as highly as
those in more densely populated areas, then there may be a negative association
between prices and miles driven where the causation is opposite to the one
posited by theory.

Such a situation can be represented as:

$$\ln(AMT_{it}) = \alpha + \beta_1 \ln P_{it} + \beta_2 \ln Inc_{it} + e_i' + e_{it}$$

Where $E(P_{it}, e_i) > 0$.

Because the offending component of the error e_i' does not vary with time,
differencing observations at two points in time and estimating the resulting
change equation can alleviate the bias. That is, one can estimate:

$$\ln\Delta AMT_{it} = \alpha + \beta_1 \ln\Delta P_{it} + \beta_2 \ln\Delta Inc_{it} + \Delta e_{it}.$$

The βs in this case are, however, interpretable as short or intermediate run
elasticities depending on the length of time between the observation periods. In
his 1980 analysis, the author used a modification of this procedure to estimate

five-year change elasticities for stable Panel households. His major finding was
that miles driven showed substantial price responsiveness, but only among those
households that had changed residential locations over the five-year period.
These households had intermediate run price elasticities in excess of -2, while
households who had not moved had insignificantly positive elasticities. Overall,
the intermediate run elasticity of miles driven was -.34.

There are two major problems with the author's 1980 analysis, above and
beyond the precision errors encountered in computation. The first is a
conceptual problem in the recursive model he employed. While miles driven and
number of cars probably are determined by prices and income, it is not clear that
gasoline prices affect income or weeks worked. This means that the "total
effect" coefficients he presents should be taken with a grain of salt. The
direct effects are not affected by the causal ordering in this path analysis.
The second problem with that analysis is its failure to check alternative time
periods for the change equation; as we shall see below, the results are sensitive
to the exact specification of beginning and end periods.

The Model

In the present analysis, we assume that the demand for personal automotive
transportation as measured by household Annual Miles Traveled(AMT) is a composite
derived demand of all utility yielding home production activities or "home
commodities" for which transportation is an input. That is, households are
assumed to maximize a utility function of the form:

$$(1) \quad U = U(A_1(Q_{1j}M_{1j1}), \; \dots \; A_n(Q_n, M_{nn})^5$$

subject to the budget constraint:

$$(1a) \quad P_j Q_j + P_{Mj} M_j = Y$$

Following Archibald and Gillingham, we assume the necessary aggregation and
regularity conditions are met so that the annual demand for personal
transportation can be represented by the following indirect utility function:

---

[5]Time is also an input to most activities and utility maximization is
constrained by the limitedness of life. We suppress it in this analysis because
we are dealing with annual data and not with time allocation decisions.

$$(2) \quad AMT = M(P, P_m^*, Y, Z);$$

where Z is a vector of all household characteristics which affect either the marginal utility of a home produced commodity which has travel as an input or the marginal product of travel in producing that commodity. The marginal cost of driving P_m^* is both a function of the price of gasoline, oil, and other variable costs of driving, and a function of the fuel efficiency and other characteristics of the household's vehicle fleet.

While it is well known that addilog demand equations do not satisfy the adding-up constraint of utility theory and, hence, are theoretically implausible in the strictest sense, we assume here that the function M above is additive in logs. Our reasons for doing so are twofold: first, because constant elasticity systems in general provide a better fit to a wider range of data than alternative systems (see, for example, Houthakker, 1961) and, second, because we wish to compare our empirical estimates with those of Houthakker, Verliger, and Sheehan (1975), Kwast (1978), Hill (1980), and Archibald and Gillingham (1980). Thus:

$$(2') \quad \ln AMT_i = \alpha + \beta_1 \ln P_{mi}^* + \beta_2 \ln Y_i + \sum_{j=3}^{n} \beta_3 \ln Z_{ij} + \epsilon_i$$

Partly because households are reluctant to make rapid changes in consumption in response to prices and income changes (habit persistence), but also because their response is constrained by the characteristics of major household capital goods such as the automobile and the house and its proximity to work and to markets (partial adjustment), it takes households quite some time to respond to changes in prices and/or incomes. Thus, the effects of changes in the parameters will be likely to be distributed over several time periods. That is:

$$(3) \quad \ln AMT_{it} = \alpha + \sum_{\ell=0} \beta_{1j} \ln P_{m,t-\ell}^* + \sum_{\ell=0} \beta_{2t-\ell} \ln Y_{t-\ell}$$
$$+ \sum_{j=3} \beta_j \ln Z_j + \epsilon_{it} .$$

If the dominant reason for delayed response is that it takes households time to adjust their capital stock to be compatible with price-induced changes in demand, then Equation 3 can be simplified considerably. This is the situation assumed by Houthakker, Verliger, and Sheehan, Kwast and many others. The model reduces to:

$$(3') \quad \ln AMT_{it} = \alpha + \beta X_{it} + (1-\gamma) \ln AMT_{it-1} + \epsilon_{it}$$

where X_{it} is the vector $(P^*_{it}:Y_{it}:Z_{ij})$ and β is $(\beta_1:\beta_2:\beta_3)$

This model implies large initial responses which decline geometrically with time. Since psychological factors may also delay response to changes in prices and/or incomes, however, theory provides very little a priori information on the pattern of response. In the case of gasoline price changes in the 1970s, there is good reason to believe that households had doubts about the permanence of the radical increases in gasoline prices during and after the 1973-1974 oil embargo. It is well known in psychological economics that uncertainty tends to inhibit changes in behavior. This being the case, the imposition of simple dynamic structures, such as those implied by the partial capital adjustment model, represent a serious misspecification of the empirical model; thus, one should estimate the full model represented in Equation 3. In practice there are several problems in estimating such a model. First, the total length of the lag is not known and the investigator must decide before estimation how far back to go. In the present instance, however, this problem is not terribly severe since gasoline prices were quite stable up to and through much of 1973, and we can assume that 1973 represents an equilibrium base year. Thus, we need go no further back than 1973. A second problem, arising when estimating unconstrained distributed lag models, is particularly troublesome given that we must use state average gasoline prices whose year to year changes are highly correlated. This is a problem of multicolinearity and there is no satisfactory solution beyond being aware of its existence and its effect on estimates. A final problem in estimating models such as that presented in Equation 3 is that OLS estimates will be biased, inefficient, and inconsistent if there is any correlation of error terms from one period to the next. Such auto-correlation is likely to be a problem with annual household level transportation demand equations, so the estimating procedure must deal with it.

The literature on distributed lag models provides numerous suggestions for compromise between estimation of models such as Equation 3 in which no restrictions are placed on the pattern of responses and estimation of the simple partial adjustment or adaptation models which impose severe restrictions (see Almond, Griliches, Front...). As Griliches (1967) points out, all of these techniques involve a certain degree of "ad-hocery," especially with respect to deciding on the length of the lag. Here we employed the modified Koyck adaptive expectations model mentioned by Griliches (1967). By adding additional lagged independent variables to the Koyck model, one can let the model retain much of its elegance while allowing for household behaviors as diverse as delayed initial reaction to initial over reaction followed by geometrically declining readjustments to desired levels of demand. With these modifications the Koyck model generalizes to

$$(4) \quad \ln AMT_{ht} = \gamma_k a + \beta_1 \sum_{i=1}^{k} (\gamma_{i+1} - \gamma_i) + \sum_{j=1}^{i} (-1)^j \gamma_i \sum_{\ell=i+1}^{k} \gamma_\ell \ln X_{ht-i}$$

$$+ \gamma_k \beta_2 Z_{ht} + (1-\gamma_k) \ln AMT_{ht-1} + \mu_{ht}$$

where $\gamma_j = 0$ whenever $0 \geq j > k + 1$.

While this modified Koyck model is an "infinite" lag model, the researcher must specify the number of periods required for the dynamic responses to settle into their geometrically declining pattern—a drawback similar to that of finite distributed lag models such as the Almond model. Nevertheless, it is more flexible and no more difficult to estimate than the Koyck.

In order to obtain unbiased estimates of parameters of the modified Koyck model, we utilized a maximum likelihood algorithm (LISREL) to simultaneously estimate the dynamic adjustment coefficient and the error variance covariance matrix ψ. Basically this approach required us to create an instrument for the lagged dependent variable. This means we had two equations to estimate jointly, Equation 4 and 4´:

$$(4´) \quad \ln AMT_{t-1} = a´ + \sum_{i=1}^{k-1} \beta_i´ X_{ht-1} + \beta_2´´ Z_{ht-1}´´ + \mu_{ht-1}$$

Because equation 4´ is not intended to provide behaviorally interpretable coefficients, we included in the $Z_{ht-1}´$ vector variables which would result in "over-control" if included in the structural Equation 4. The variance-covariance matrix implied by the model is:

$$(5) \quad \Sigma = \begin{bmatrix} \emptyset^{-1} \beta \phi \beta´\theta´^{-1} + \theta^{-1} \psi \theta´^{-1} & \vdots & \theta^{-1}\beta\phi \\ \cdots \cdots \cdots \cdots \cdots \cdots \cdots \cdots & \vdots & \cdots \cdots \\ \emptyset\beta´\theta´^{-1} & \vdots & \phi \end{bmatrix}$$

where $\emptyset$ is the variance-covariance matrix of all the independent variables; β is the (2 X R) matrix of effects of these independent variables on the dependent variables; θ is a 2 X 2 matrix containing ones on the diagonal and the dynamic adjustment coefficient in the upper right corner; and, finally, ψ is the (2 X 2 symmetric) variance covariance matrix of residuals. The LISREL algorithm estimates the model by iteratively adjusting the elements of the $\hat{\Sigma}$ matrix so as to minimize:

$$F = \log|\hat{\Sigma}| + tr\ (S\hat{\Sigma}) - \log\ |S| - (p+q)$$

where S is the variance covariance matrix of the data. With the X and y variables distributed multi-normally, the fitting function is the concentrated (un)likelihood function and the resulting estimates are full information maximum likelihood estimates.

The Data Sample and Results

Each year since the 1974 interviewing year the Panel Study of Income Dynamics has included toward the beginning of the interview the following sequence of questions.

How many cars and trucks do you (and family living here) own?____

During the last year how many miles did you (and your family) drive in (your car/all of your cars)? _____

Responses to the latter question in the 1979 interviewing year formed the basis of our analysis. So as to remove the effects of time invariant household specific components of the error term, we scaled this variable (and all other variables) by expressing it as the deviation from the household's 1973 values. This scaling was done to make the estimated effects much more easily interpreted as the changes induced in the dependent variable resulting from changes in independent variables—the interpretation desired of coefficients of any econometric model. This gain in interpretability, however, comes at price of limiting our sample to households which were relatively "stable" (having no changes in head or wife) over the 1973-1978 period.

Because the Panel Study has not obtained information on gasoline prices, we obtained this information from other sources on the basis of residential location (state). Gasoline prices for regular major brand gasoline in 57 major U.S. cities are reported weekly in the American Petroleum Institute's Weekly Petroleum Report. A random sample of ten weeks for each year from 1973 through 1978 was taken to obtain average annual prices for each of the 57 cities. These data were then used in conjunction with gasoline tax data to assign average annual gasoline prices by state. States with more than one reporting city (e.g., Texas) were assigned the average (across cities) of average prices, while states with no reporting cities (Idaho) were assigned the average price of surrounding states, adjusted for differences in state taxes. While the resulting data are superior to the data used, for instance by, Houthakker, Verliger, and Sheehan, or by Kwast, they remain rather crude estimates of what individual households actually paid for gasoline in any given year. Sources of error include, among other things, price differences between branded and unbranded dealers and between various grades of gasoline. Of lesser importance, the assignment procedure ignored the large seasonal aspects of travel demand by assigning equal weight to each week's observation in computing annual averages.

For income, the other primary economic variable in the model, we used total family money income, taken directly as edited. As mentioned above, each variable was expressed as its natural logarithm scaled by the natural logarithm of its 1973 value, and it is interpretable as the percentage change from 1973. The two economic variables, price and income, were deflated by the national average consumer price index for each year to allow change to be interpreted as a percentage change in real terms.

There were two categories of non economic controls employed in the model. The first included variables viewed as having an impact on personal transportation demand and which may be spuriously correlated with prices and income: measures of family size (both total family size and number of household members of driving age); weeks of employment of head and wife; age of head; and dummy variables for whether the household had moved in the particular year and whether they were homeowners. The non-economic variables of the second category were included only to improve the instrument of the previous year's demand. Because they would have resulted in over-control if included in the current-year demand equation, these variables only appeared in the equation which created an instrument for the prior year's travel demand. They included: changes in miles to work, ...and dummy variable for whether there was public transportation within walking distance of the residence which was good enough to use to get to work.

Because prior work with 1978 data indicated that only families that had moved exhibited any price responsiveness (Hill, 1980), we limited our sample of to otherwise stable families who either moved or changed jobs sometime between 1973 and 1979. This reduced our sample to 906. Table 8.1 presents maximum likelihood regression coefficient estimates for the economic variables of five nested models of dynamic personal transportation demand. The first column of coefficients corresponds to the Koyck transformation employed by Houthakker, Verliger, and Sheehan, Kwast, and Dahl. This is the most restrictive of the five models in that coefficients on all lagged _independent_ variables were constrained to zero. In other words, only current values of prices, incomes (as well as the non-economic variables) and lagged Annual Miles Traveled (the dependent variable) were allowed to affect the dependent variable. The zero constraints on coefficients of lagged independent variables were relaxed sequentially to obtain the coefficients presented in columns two through five in Table 8.1. In addition to the parameters estimate of the models and the estimated error covariance terms, each column contains the value of the concentrated (un)likelihood function at its minimum, as well as the number of parameters estimated, including the variances and covariances of the independent variables. This information can be used in testing the hypothesis that the generalization of the model obtained by relaxing zero constraints on the lagged independent variables represents a significant improvement in fit. Specifically, if F_j is the minimum value of F for the specification with independent variables lagged j times, then under the hypothesis that there should be only $j-1$ lags:

$$\frac{N}{2} (F_{j-1} - F_j) \sim \chi^2 \quad d.f.= K_j - K_{j-1}.$$

The pairwise calculations of this statistic from the least restrictive to the most restrictive model in Table 8.1 are presented in Table 8.2.
It would not be unusual to observe the results presented in column 5 of Table 8.1 even if the true model contained only three lags (nor those in column 4 if the true model contained two lags). However, it is highly unlikely that the improvement obtained in the estimates presented in column three (resulting from adding a second lag term) are due solely to chance. Thus, the simple dynamic adjustment process upon which the Koyck transformation is based is clearly

Table 8.1

MAXIMUM LIKELIHOOD COEFFICIENTS OF ECONOMIC VARIABLES
FOR FIVE DYNAMIC TRANSPORTATION DEMAND MODELS
(All stable households who moved during 1973-1978.)

	k=0	k=1	k=2	k=3	k=4
ln Gas Price$_{78}$	-2.49+ (1.41)	-2.07 (1.92)	-2.49 (1.91)	-2.44 (1.92)	-2.46 (1.92)
ln Gas Price$_{77}$	- (-)	-1.17 (2.05)	-1.86 (2.69)	-2.03 (2.77)	-2.18 (2.77)
ln Gas Price$_{76}$	- (-)	- (-)	1.76 (2.61)	1.87 (2.95)	1.88 (2.94)
ln Gas Price$_{75}$	- (-)	- (-)	- (-)	-.063 (2.71)	-1.06 (3.12)
ln Gas Price$_{74}$	- (-)	- (-)	- (-)	- (-)	2.08 (3.51)
ln Income$_{78}$	.176* (.080)	.085 (.089)	.037 (.089)	.058 (.089)	.066 (.089)
ln Income$_{77}$	- (-)	.258* (.115)	-.083 (.126)	.007 (.132)	.006 (.132)
ln Income$_{76}$	- (-)	- (-)	.532** (.127)	.608** (.138)	.608** (.138)
ln Income$_{75}$	- (-)	- (-)	- (-)	-.299* (.131)	-.246 (.166)
ln Income$_{74}$	- (-)	- (-)	- (-)	- (-)	-.083 (.142)
ln AMT$_{77}$	.637* (.284)	.283 (.329)	.236 (.334)	.202 (.340)	.194 (.345)
$E(\mu_{78}\mu_{78})$	2.05** (.096)	2.21** (.278)	2.19** (.294)	2.20** (.312)	2.21** (.322)
$E(\mu_{77}\mu_{78})$	.086 (.246)	.391 (.284)	.411 (.287)	.433 (.290)	.441 (.292)
F	.1331	.1215	.0635	.0469	.0349
d.f.	29	31	35	39	43
N	906	906	906	906	906

Table 8.2

CHI-SQUARE TEST STATISTIC FOR GOODNESS OF FIT
OF FIVE TESTED DYNAMIC DEMAND MODELS
(All stable households who moved during 1973-1978.)

j	$N/2(F_{j-1}-F_j)$	d.f.	$P=\text{Prob}(F_j|H_{j-1})$
4	5.436	4	.5 > P > .1
3	7.520	4	.5 > P > .1
2	26.274	4	.01 > P > .0001
1	5.255	2	.05 > P > .02

rejected in favor of a process where it took at least two years for responses to settle into a geometrically declining pattern.

The simple Koyck adaptive expectations/partial adjustment model is also inferior to the model which allows two periods of reaction in terms of the reasonableness of the empirical results. Table 8.3 presents the full results from which the coefficients in columns one through three of Table 8.1 were abstracted. The first and third columns of coefficients pertain to the creation of the instrumental variable for the lagged dependent variable in the actual demand equations whose coefficients are given in the second and fourth columns. The coefficients on price, income, and lagged dependent variables in the Koyck model (Column 2) are of the proper sign and significant at at least the 90 percent level of confidence. The rather large coefficients on the lagged dependent variable of .637 implies a rather slow adjustment process and long-run elasticities roughly two and three-quarters times the initial year impact elasticities.

The price elasticity is very imprecisely measured for all specifications. Although highly negative in the Koyck model, it is barely significantly different from zero even at the 90 percent level of confidence. The point estimate of the long-run gasoline price elasticity from the Koyck model is a truly incredible -6.86. The size of the coefficients of other variables when divided by the speed of adjustment (1-.637) is also incredible in the Koyck specification. For instance these coefficients, homeowners increased their miles driven by over 100 percent more than otherwise similar renters, and moving resulted in a 60 percent increase in AMT. Each one-percent increase in the age of the household head was accompanied by a one percent decrease in miles driven, even controlling for

Table 8.3 (1 of 2)

MAXIMUM LIKELIHOOD COEFFICIENTS FOR THE FULL KOYCK AND TWICE LAGGED KOYCK MODELS
(All stable households who moved during 1973-1978.)

	k = 0		k = 2	
	j = 77 $\ln AMT_j$	j = 78 $\ln AMT_j$	j = 77 $\ln AMT_j$	j = 78 $\ln AMT_j$
ln Gasoline Price$_{78}$	– (–)	–2.49+ (1.40)	– (–)	–2.49 (1.91)
ln Gasoline Price$_{77}$	–1.43 (.91)	– (–)	–1.40 (1.43)	–1.86 (2.69)
ln Gasoline Price$_{76}$	– (–)	– (–)	.135 (1.62)	1.76 (2.61)
ln Income$_{78}$	– (–)	.176* (.079)	– (–)	.037 (0.89)
ln Income$_{77}$	.128* (.059)	– (–)	.003 (.075)	–.083 (.125)
ln Income$_{76}$	– (–)	– (–)	.193** (.067)	.532** (.127)
ln Number Adults	.335* (.148)	–.089 (.239)	.301* (.145)	–.013 (.244)
ln Retirement Expenditures$_j$	.037** (.012)	.014 (.021)	.037** (.012)	.016 (.021)
ln Family Size$_j$	.010 (.020)	–.002 (.035)	.003 (.020)	–.010 (.032)
ln Weeks Worked Head$_j$	–.003 (.021)	.005 (.026)	–.004 (.017)	–.003 (.026)
ln Weeks Worked Wife$_j$	–.312** (.106)	.266 (.173)	–.289** (.104)	.204 (.177)

Table 8.3 (2 of 2)

| | k = 0 | | k = 2 | |
	j = 77 ln AMT$_j$	j = 78 ln AMT$_j$	j = 77 ln AMT$_j$	j = 78 ln AMT$_j$
ln Age$_j$	-.245* (.066)	-.289+ (1.78)	-.236* (.098)	-.387* (.185)
ln Whether Own$_j$	-.041 (.065)	.431** (.102)	-.053 (.063)	.387** (.104)
ln Whether Moved$_j$	.153* (.065)	.238* (.106)	.166** (.062)	.227* (.105)
ln Public Transportation$_j$	-.118+ (.064)	- (-)	-.094 (.061)	- (-)
ln Miles to Work$_j$	.032 (.023)	- (-)	.026 (.022)	- (-)
ln Number of Cars$_j$	.182** (.067)	- (-)	.178* (.064)	- (-)
ln AMT$_{77}$	- (-)	.637* (.284)	- (-)	.236 (.335)

differences in commuting distance (i.e., even in the coefficient of the first column which control for both weeks work, public transit, and miles to work).

The estimates from the second model presented in table 8.3 were uniformly more reasonable than those from the first and yielded a much better fit in terms of the likelihood function. The point estimate of the speed of adjustment was much higher, but there was a two-year delay in the reaction of households to changes in income. Once the reaction did take place, it was quite dramatic, with a third year impact income elasticity of .532. The long-run income elasticity was only moderately larger at .631 ([.037 - .087 + .532]/[1-.236]). One possible explanation of this delayed reaction is that much of the response of transportation demand operates through changes in the residential location, and, because of the transaction costs (partly time costs) of moving, households were slow to move. Alternatively, because of the general economic validity of the 1970s, households were initially skeptical of the permanence of changes in income and did not respond until the income change demonstrated some permanence.

While the point estimate of the long-run gasoline price elasticity in the delayed response model is a somewhat more reasonable -3.5, it is even less precisely estimated than the elasticity in the Koyck model. The reason is, of course, the high correlation between gasoline prices and price changes in consecutive years. The pattern of response nevertheless suggests rapid initial over-response to increased gasoline prices.

Up to this point we have been dealing with a sample of otherwise stable households who had changed residential location or jobs at some time during the 1973-1978 period. Such households have been found by this author (1980) to exhibit the greatest price responsiveness. Such households, however, accounted for only one-third of the total sample of stable households. In the following section we shall examine the transportation demand of the larger group of households. Before going on to the analysis of households who did not move or change jobs between 1973-1978, there are two points which should be made about the results already presented. The first point is that in none of the five models examined were the covariance of residuals of the dependent variable and its lagged counterpart large enough to attain statistical significance. Thus, the strategy of removing time invariant individual components of the error term by scaling observations as deviations from the household's 1973 values seems to have been successful. The second point is that only in the case of the Koyck model did the estimated speed of adjustment $(1-\gamma_k)$ differ substantially and significantly from unity. This, combined with the goodness of fit measure, indicates that after three years most of the response to changes in gasoline prices or incomes has been realized, at least for movers. One year, however, is too short a period for responses to be made.

Table 8.4 presents the maximum likelihood regression coefficients for the Koyck model and four of its generalizations for households that did not move or change jobs over the 1973-1978 period. The differences in the goodness of fit among these five models for stayers are not sufficiently large to indicate that any one specification is superior to any other--they all fit the data equally well (or poorly). One must use criteria other than goodness of fit in deciding which specification is superior. With the exception of the Koyck model, which yields small insignificant price and income elasticities of the right sign, the pattern of response seems quite robust with respect to the number of lags of economic variables included. In each case with one to four lagged values of price and income, initial responses to income changes were positive and significant, followed by small negative readjustment. This pattern implies long-run elasticities smaller than impact elasticities. Furthermore, initial price responses were insignificantly positive but became negative in the second year.

In the specifications with three and four lagged values the negative second year response was sufficiently large to attain significance at the 90 percent level of confidence. In each of the three specifications containing more than one period's lag of independent variables, the negative second year price response was followed by positive readjustments. While we must be careful in interpreting these highly imprecise estimates, the pattern of point estimates of price response is consistent with behavior characterized by initial skepticism regarding price changes followed by a period of strong negative reaction to the increases which decays and becomes positive, presumably as a result of the household's models. Surveys of consumer attitudes in the 1973-1974 period provide ample evidence of households uncertainty and hence, skepticism regarding gasoline price levels and expected changes (see, for example, Hill and Hill 1978). This lends some credence to the apparent finding of delayed response to price changes, while Dahl's analysis supports the hypothesis that the (delayed) impact price elasticity of miles driven will be greater than the long-run elasticity because households will gradually replace existing automobiles with more fuel efficient models.

Table 8.4

MAXIMUM LIKELIHOOD COEFFICIENTS OF ECONOMIC VARIABLES
FOR FIVE DYNAMIC TRANSPORTATION DEMAND MODELS
(All stable households who did not move during 1973-1978.)

	k=0	k=1	k=2	k=3	k=4
ln Gas Price$_{78}$	-.066 (.911)	1.05 (1.19)	1.17 (1.21)	1.65 (1.26)	1.61 (1.26)
ln Gas Price$_{77}$	- (-)	-1.72 (1.21)	-3.22 (2.21)	-3.83* (2.26)	-3.99+ (2.36)
ln Gas Price$_{76}$	- (-)	- (-)	1.66 (2.09)	.69 (2.24)	.86 (2.29)
ln Gas Price$_{75}$	- (-)	- (-)	- (-)	2.03 (1.62)	1.83 (1.77)
ln Gas Price$_{74}$	- (-)	- (-)	- (-)	- (-)	.34 (1.94)
ln Income$_{78}$	.080 (.045)	.103* (.049)	.120* (.050)	.123* (.051)	.130* (.051)
ln Income$_{77}$	- (-)	-.072 (.063)	-.038 (.067)	-.039 (.067)	-.034 (.068)
ln Income$_{76}$	- (-)	- (-)	-.077 (.050)	-.076 (.074)	-.078 (.075)
ln Income$_{75}$	- (-)	- (-)	- (-)	-.003 (.072)	.005 (.072)
ln Income$_{74}$	- (-)	- (-)	- (-)	- (-)	-.053 (.045)
ln AMT$_{77}$	.628** (.158)	.729** (.178)	.747** (.178)	.761** (.178)	.754** (.179)
$E(\mu_{78}\mu_{78})$	.876** (.032)	.876** (.030)	.871** (.030)	.871** (.031)	.870** (.032)
$E(\mu_{77}\mu_{78})$	.040 (.087)	-.015 (.098)	-.026 (.098)	-.033 (.098)	-.029 (.098)
F	.0524	.0487	.0438	.0392	.0368
d.f.	27	29	33	37	41
N	1807	1807	1807	1807	1807

Summary and Conclusions

While individual estimates of household response to changes in prices and incomes are very imprecise several things can be concluded from our analysis. First, households do react to increased gasoline prices by reducing miles driven. Second, increases in real incomes lead to increases in miles driven. Finally, the dynamic pattern of response is quite complicated. Increases in income are translated into increases in miles driven only after a one or two year delay. Price increases have a more immediate impact on miles driven which eventually is counteracted presumably as a result of increased fuel efficiency of the vehicle fleet.

All dynamic gasoline and transportation demand models in the literature employ the Koyck transformation in estimating partial adjustment or adaptive expectations models. Longitudinal data from the Panel Study of Income Dynamics were used to estimate a nested set of dynamic transportation demand models of which true Koyck is the most restrictive special case. In the case of households that had moved or changed jobs sometime during the 1973-1978 period, the pattern of response assumed in the Koyck transformation is significantly restrictive. Response in annual miles driven to changes in income took two full years before materializing for these households, presumably because the major response of travel demand to income changes operates through or in conjunction with residential location decision.

Unfortunately, estimates of gasoline price elasticities of miles traveled derived from state average gasoline prices merged with the panel data, while in every model negative are estimated very imprecisely. We cannot at present, therefore, make firm statements regarding the degree of responsiveness of households to increased prices. In general, both the short and long-run point price elasticity estimates were too large to be believed for households who moved during the post embargo years. This may reflect inadequate control for local transportation characteristics. The regions of the country which enjoyed net immigration during the 1970s are regions characterized by generally lower gasoline prices and longer typical urban suburban circuities. Households moving into such areas from more compactly settled, high gasoline price areas would have experienced increases in gasoline prices much smaller than average and may be driving more not so much as a result of the lower gasoline prices directly but rather as a result of established transportation patterns in their new locations. Future analysis of travel demand for mobile households may benefit from more detailed consideration of these factors as well as from paying more attention to the determinant of interstate household mobility.

In terms of goodness of fit, the simple Koyck dynamic demand model is neither better nor worse than more general forms for households that remained in the same residence and job over the post-embargo period. Point estimates from the more general specifications, however, are suggestive of a more complicated dynamic structure than those imposed by the assumptions of the Koyck transformation. The gasoline price responses, while still imprecisely estimated for nonmovers suggest delayed response during the, first year after a change in price, followed by a strong negative response which is later mostly reversed, presumably as households gradually replace their automobiles with more efficient models. Response to changes in income seem to be more immediate than to changes in price, but they also seem to be transitory. IN either case, the long-run elasticities are smaller in absolute value than are the immediate impact elasticities.

References

Archibald, Robert, and Gillingham, Robert. "An Analysis of Consumer Demand for Gasoline Using Household Survey Data." Bureau of Labor Statistics, Washington, D.C., October 1978. Mimeograph.

Dahl, Carol A. "Consumer Adjustment to a Gasoline Tax." The Review of Economics and Statistics (November 1979): 427-432.

Griliches, Zvi. "Distributed Lags: A Survey." Econometrica 36, (January 1967): 16-49.

Hill, Daniel H. "The Relative Burden of Higher Gasoline Prices." In Five Thousand American Families--Patterns of Economic Progress--Vol. VIII, edited by Greg J. Duncan and James N. Morgan. Duncan. Ann Arbor: Institute for Social Research, The University of Michigan, 1980.

Houthakker, Hendrik S.; Verliger, Phillip K.; and Sheehan, Dennis P. "Dynamic Demand Analysis for Gasoline and Residential Electricity." American Journal of Agricultural Economics 56 (May 1974): 412-418.

Kwast, Myron L. "A Note on the Structural Stability of Gasoline Demand and the Welfare Economics of Gasoline Taxation," Southern Economics Review (April 1980): 1212-1220.

Appendix to Chapter 8

Table A8.1
DIRECT AND TOTAL EFFECTS OF FACTORS INFLUENCING MILES DRIVEN 1973
[Dependent Variable: ln(Miles Driven 1973)]

Variable Name	Direct	Total
Market orientation	.0132* (.0055)	.0132* (.0055)
ln(Number of cars owned)	.2967** (.0493)	.2967** (.0493)
ln(Income)	.2933** (.0294)	.3529** (.0274)
Whether public transit	-.1844** (.0311)	-.1877** (.0319)
ln(Miles to work)	.0623 (.0121)	.0872** (.0124)
ln(City size)	-.0172 (.0087)	.0005 (.0088)
ln(Weeks worked)	.0353** (.0111)	.0805** (.0109)
ln(Weeks worked, spouse)	.0121 (.0080)	.0332** (.0080)
ln(Miles to city)	-.0351* (.0163)	-.0468** (.0168)
ln(Number of adults)	.1126** (.0435)	.3415** (.0406)
ln(Number of children)	.0091 (.0238)	.0102 (.0243)
ln(Age of head)	-.0093** (.0010)	-.0134** (.0009)
ln(Gasoline price)	-.7080* (.3556)	-.0780 (.3791)
N	3232	3232
R^2	.229	INAP

Table A8.2

DIRECT AND TOTAL EFFECTS OF FACTORS INFLUENCING CHANGE IN MILES DRIVEN
[Dependent Variable: ln(Miles77)-ln(Miles 73)]

	Direct Effects of		Total Effects of	
	Change in Variable	Change in Coefficient	Change in Variable	Change in Coefficient
Market orientation	.0229** (.0090)	.0308** (.0092)	.0289*** (.0090)	.0308** (.0092)
ln(Number of cars owned)	.2357** (.0654)	.0936 (.0760)	.2357** (.0654)	.0936 (.0760)
ln(Income)	.1639** (.0457)	.0166 (.0408)	.2206** (.0443)	.0861* (.0362)
Whether public transit	.0295 (.0438)	.0937 (.0463)	.0266 (.0440)	.0899 (.0463)
ln(Miles to work)	.0200 (.0167)	-.0080 (.0180)	.0332* (.0167)	-.0024 (.0179)
ln(City size)	-.0144 (.0165)	.0077 (.0119)	-.0089 (.0166)	.0108 (.0119)
ln(Weeks worked)	.0118 (.0112)	.0103 (.0714)	.0208 (.0112)	.0280 (.0162)
ln(Weeks worked, spouse)	.0183 (.0151)	.0019 (.0115)	.0360* (.0147)	.0057 (.0114)
ln(Miles to city)	-.0091 (.0141)	.0507* (.0209)	-.0060 (.0142)	.0492* (.0210)
ln(Number of adults)	.2281** (.0657)	.1329* (.0631)	.3769** (.0598)	.1697** (.0575)
ln(Number of children)	-.0568 (.0468)	.0457 (.0359)	-.0640 (.0470)	-.0349 (.0356)
Age	-0- (-0-)	-.0011 (.0017)	-0- (-0-)	-.0022 (.0016)
ln(Gasoline price)	1.3328 (.9130)	.2448 (.4715)	1.0876 (.9161)	.0342 (.4710)
Whether moved	1.8119** (.5938)	-0- (-0-)	1.7141** (.5962)	-0- (-0-)
Moved price interaction	-3.7691** (1.1991)	-0- (-0-)	-3.5818** (1.2044)	-0- (-0-)

N = 3232

R^2 = .0498

Chapter 9

INTERTEMPORAL VARIABILITY IN INCOME AND THE
INTERPERSONAL DISTRIBUTION OF ECONOMIC WELFARE

Scott Grosse and James N. Morgan

INTRODUCTION

Intertemporal variation in individual earnings is an important dimension of
economic welfare which has been largely overlooked in studies of income
distribution (for a critique see Chapter 2 in this volume by Duncan and Hoffman).
Because during any single period many households have atypically high or
atypically low incomes, static measures of income distribution show a greater
degree of economic inequality than is true over time. Richard Coe (1978) has
shown with Panel Study data that there is a very high turnover in the poverty
population. But this implies that a large proportion of households classified as
non-poor are highly vulnerable to sinking below the poverty line and hence are
not really as well off as their average income would seem to indicate. Two other
studies using Panel Study data (Benus, 1974; Benus and Morgan, 1975) have already
examined the relationship between income instability and certain individual
characteristics; the present study extends the previous work by introducing a
longer time frame, more independent variables, and alternative measures of
income.

Taking intertemporal variability in income into account may not only change
the relative ranking of individuals´ economic status (Benus and Morgan, 1975), it
may also reveal the extent to which certain groups are more vulnerable to
economic instability. In particular, it may be of interest to know whether more
privileged or more disadvantaged groups experience greater instability in
earnings. The theory of compensating differentials first proposed by Adam Smith
suggests that one might expect to find a positive relation between income level
and instability because higher incomes presumably contain risk premiums
compensating the recipients for facing greater economic instability. While such
a risk premium may be found across job types for individuals of the same level of
human capital, for the labor force as a whole one might expect an inverse

297

relationship between income level and variability if greater variability is a "bad," because individuals with greater earning power would presumably seek lower variability as part of a compensation package. Alternatively, one could account for such an inverse relationship by reference to a segmented labor market with "good jobs" and "bad jobs" (see Kalleberg and Sorenson, 1979; Brown, 1980).

A few studies have supported the existence of compensating differentials to ´risk´, but none of these results appear to be directly applicable to intertemporal variability in annual earnings. Using evidence that across professions cross-sectional variability in income is positively associated with mean incomes (Friedman and Kuznetz, 1945), Milton Friedman (1953) has argued that a significant fraction of income inequality is attributable to individuals being compensated for being exposed to different degrees of income variability. King (1974) presents similar evidence with the same interpretation. However, Adam Smith to the contrary, it is not clear that cross-sectional variance is equivalent to risk or individual uncertainty. For example, simply because the occupation "medical practitioners" includes both lowly-paid staff members of free clinics and highly-paid neurosurgeons does not by itself make the practice of medicine a risky business. John Leigh (1979) pooled Panel Study data by time series and cross sections for industry groups and found that industries with greater income variability have higher average earnings, but this is essentially the same result as those found by Friedman and King. John Abowd and Orley Ashenfelter (1980) provide evidence that wages are somewhat greater in industries with higher unemployment probabilities, but they did not test the proposition of Adam Smith that wages can be expected not only to adjust for differences in the number of days of work available so as to equalize total earnings but also to include a pure wage premium so as to compensate workers for greater uncertainty. On the other hand, Morgan (1980) related change in income level to change in unemployment for voluntary and for involuntary job changers and found no evidence of a tradeoff between income level and stability.

THE DISTRIBUTION OF INCOME INSTABILITY

This section explores the distribution of instability in income among different groups in the labor force using an analytical framework derived in part from Benus (1974). The dependent variable in Benus´s analysis was "that portion of an individual´s income variation not explained by either his cohort income movements or his consistent deviations from the cohort income pattern." Benus chose to limit himself to exploring income variability among the full-time labor force and consequently screened out all those who worked less than 1,500 hours in any of the consecutive five years (including hours missed due to involuntary unemployment and sickness). The independent variables considered by Benus were the average income level for an individual during 1967–1971, the occupation and educational attainment as reported in 1972, age, race, sex, and county unemployment rate. Using Multiple Classification Analysis, his most significant finding was that instability is high at both ends of the income scale even after other variables were taken into account. Regarding occupation, Benus found blue-collar workers to have higher instability than white collar workers, but most notably, he found that farmers and the self-employed had very high income instability. The other variables were found to be of much lesser importance. The net effects of race and sex were insignificant, the net relationship with educational level displayed an erratic pattern, and age and county unemployment rates distinguished only at the very small extreme categories (the youngest age group and the counties with very high unemployment). Overall, according to Benus, about 19 percent of the variance was explained by seven variables for a sample of 2275.

Our analysis differs from that of Benus with regard to both the specification of the dependent variable and the sample filter, and it employs an expanded set of predictor variables as well. It seems reasonable to expect that most people would regard a constant percentage increase in real income each year as perfect stability and predictability. Consequently, we took the standard error of the regression of annual earnings in logarithms deflated by the Consumer Price Index on time (i.e. the square root of the sum of squared deviations around the trend) as the measure of individual income instability. (Benus used a similar measure in his unpublished dissertation.) In contrast to Benus, we believe that irregular labor force activity of even a voluntary nature is an important component of instability and, consequently, we established a less restrictive filter, screening out only those household heads who had earnings of less than $100 in any year from 1967 to 1977 in 1967 dollars. Income trend and industry were the two most important variables we added to the set of explanatory variables. Since increases or decreases in wage or salaries tend to occur in discrete "steps," a substantial trend in either direction will almost invariably be associated with relatively high measured instability. We decided to include both occupation and industry in our analysis (as reported at the time of the 1978 interview), because, for example, an operative in construction might expect higher instability than an operative in manufacturing. We excluded county unemployment rate because of its lack of significance in the Benus study. We decided to experiment by using variables reflecting geographic mobility and physical disability, both expected to be associated with higher instability, and by using change in marital status, which, in cases of divorce, might also have been associated with somewhat higher instability.

The unadjusted means shown in Table 9.1, which represent zero-order relationships with instability, resemble in many respects the patterns found by Benus. There is a pronounced J-curve relationship between level and instability. Instability was highest for those with the lowest income level, and declined with income up to $10,000 in 1967 dollars (over $20,000 in current dollars). Only above $15,000 (over $30,000 in current dollars) did instability start increasing somewhat. Farmers and self-employed managers had very high levels of instability, while service workers and medical and legal professionals also had levels of instability well above the average for the sample. The remaining occupational differentials were all much smaller than those found by Benus, and the large gap between blue-collar and white-collar workers observed by Benus did not appear. The pattern of unadjusted means by age was as expected, with both the young (under age 35 in 1968) and the small numbers of old people in the sample experiencing much higher levels of instability than the rest. The unadjusted differentials by sex and race, while substantial, were much smaller than those found by Benus. For education we did not find the monotonically inverse relation we expected. Instead, there was a tipping point such that those with at least a high school degree had substantially less instability than those with less education.

The variables added in this analysis also yielded unadjusted means largely in accord with expectations. Those workers with either a large wage increase or decrease over the period had proportionally higher instability around their time trend. Workers in agriculture, construction, and nonprofessional services all experienced atypically high instability, while instability was relatively low for workers in manufacturing, utilities, and the government sector. The marital status, mobility, and disability variables had the expected effects: those who stayed married for the whole period had much less income instability than those who remained single or changed status; those who moved across county lines more than once had significantly higher instability; and those who reported being disabled also experienced more instability.

Not being satisfied that the unadjusted means satisfactorily describe the distribution of instability among subgroups in the labor force, we developed two

Table 9.1 (page 1 of 3)

INSTABILITY IN THE LABOR EARNINGS OF THE HOUSEHOLD HEAD, 1967-1977

Predictor	Percentage	Unadjusted Means	Medians	Percentage in Top Decile	Adjusted Means
Average Income (In 1967 Dollars)					
Less than $2500	4.2	1.37	1.37	43.2	1.36
$2500-4500	11.3	1.10	1.00	28.5	1.01
$4500-6500	19.5	.83	.74	13.5	.78
$6500-8000	15.7	.62	.46	6.7	.62
$8000-10,000	18.1	.52	.41	2.3	.56
$10,000-12,000	12.4	.45	.32	1.6	.53
$12,000-15,000	9.2	.45	.32	2.2	.52
$15,000-20,000	6.1	.52	.39	5.1	.59
Over $20,000	3.4	.66	.60	4.4	.53
Income Trend					
Less than -5%	10.1	1.35	1.25	35.7	1.19
-5 to -1%	18.4	.73	.60	10.6	.71
-1 to 0%	7.8	.49	.36	1.7	.52
0 to 1%	9.9	.51	.34	6.5	.59
1 to 3%	21.9	.45	.34	2.7	.53
3 to 6%	18.7	.56	.42	4.7	.60
6 to 10%	7.5	.81	.69	11.5	.73
Over 10%	5.7	1.18	1.02	23.3	1.01
Occupation (1978)					
Medical and legal professionals	2.1	.92	.80	14.2	1.04
Other professionals	15.3	.60	.37	9.4	.70
Salaried managers	17.2	.55	.36	4.1	.69
Self-employed managers	4.2	1.08	1.03	21.1	.86
Clerical workers	6.9	.62	.42	9.9	.58
Sales workers	5.2	.68	.62	4.1	.74
Craftsmen and kindred	22.7	.65	.46	8.2	.67
Operatives	13.2	.66	.50	9.4	.65
Laborers	3.9	.76	.60	10.3	.58
Service workers	5.4	.89	.80	14.6	.55
Farmers	2.9	1.31	1.30	40.2	1.04
Misc. not in labor force	0.9	1.00	.87	33.5	.46

Table 9.1 (page 2 of 3)

Predictor	Percentage	Unadjusted Means	Medians	Percentage in Top Decile	Adjusted Means
Industry (1978)					
Agriculture	4.6	1.14	1.01	32.2	.73
Durables manufacturer	21.4	.58	.40	7.5	.71
Nondurables manu.	8.4	.49	.36	3.3	.60
Construction	8.4	.92	.82	16.2	.84
Transp., comm., util.	7.9	.56	.38	7.6	.69
Retail trade	10.3	.73	.60	7.9	.57
Wholesale trade	2.9	.64	.44	8.4	.68
Finance, insur. realestate	3.9	.70	.56	4.6	.71
Misc. services	7.9	.84	.66	14.8	.73
Professional service	15.9	.67	.49	8.9	.66
Government (non-prof.)	7.2	.58	.51	6.4	.66
Not in labor force, Misc.	1.2	1.13	1.00	30.9	.92
Age (1968)					
25-35	11.6	.93			.78
35-45	27.2	.67			.71
45-55	35.3	.62			.68
55-65	21.5	.63			.64
65-75	4.0	1.01			.68
Over 75	0.4	1.08			.54
Race					
White	88.5	.67			.68
Black	7.8	.79			.73
Other	3.7	.84			.87
Sex					
Male	90.2	.67			.71
Female	9.8	.83			.52

Table 9.1 (page 3 of 3)

Predictor	Percentage	Unadjusted Means	Adjusted Means
Education			
Functionally illiterate	1.5	.79	.54
0-5 years of school	1.9	.94	.70
6-8 years	10.8	.75	.68
9-11 years	16.0	.81	.79
High school graduate	16.8	.64	.66
High school plus advanced training	16.3	.58	.67
Some college	14.3	.69	.70
Bachelor's degree	13.6	.68	.67
Advanced degree	8.8	.62	.65
Marital Status			
Remained single	12.1	.86	.76
Remained married:			
wife works	44.5	.65	.68
wife doesn't work	32.6	.64	.67
Changed status:			
wife works	3.5	.94	.78
wife doesn't work	7.3	.75	.67
Mobility			
One or no moves	78.8	.66	.67
Two moves	13.6	.75	.74
Three or more moves	7.7	.91	.77
Disability			
Never disabled	76.3	.66	.67
Disabled 1 year	10.7	.78	.75
Disabled 2 years	4.7	.78	.70
Disabled 3 or more years	8.2	.83	.74

alternative statistics for instability. The first of these was the median level
of instability, which reflects the level of instability experienced by the
average member of the group. The second alternative measure is the percentage of
the group in question whose level of income instability would have placed them in
the top decile of the whole sample. This variable was intended to indicate for
each subgroup the probability of experiencing extraordinarily high instability.
The median indicates the midpoint of the distribution, and the percentage in the
top sample decile reflects the existence of more very high incomes than normal,
i.e. a distribution skewed to the right. If two different distributions are
differentially skewed, then a comparison of the means will not necessarily
reflect similarities or differences adequately. Thus one should ideally look at
all three measures in conjunction with one another.

Turning again to Table 9.1, we can see that the three different measures of
(unadjusted) instability yielded almost precisely the same ranking of income
groups but with very different proportional differences. That is, the medians
and percentages in the top decile were proportionally lower than the means for
the more stable groups. This was because these groups had relatively skewed
distributions so that the mean was further to the right of the median. Yet, few
members of the more stable income groups actually found themselves in the top
decile.

A comparison of the medians and means for each of the occupational
categories allowed us to distinguish four occupations among which instability was
fairly evenly distributed: farmers, self-employed managers, sales workers, and
service workers. While sales workers typically had fairly high instability, very
few experienced it at a really high level. Perhaps sales workers have greater
flexibility in altering work effort so as to avoid extreme fluctuations in
earnings. The remaining variable for which the two alternative classifications
of instability were constructed was industry of respondent. While workers in
government experienced the same mean level of instability as workers in durables
manufacturing, the median instability was much lower for those in nondurables
manufacturing. Further, while workers in transportation, communication, and
utilities had higher mean instability than workers in nondurables manufacturing,
their median instability was almost the same.

Regression-Adjusted Effects

The last column in Table 9.1 presents the adjusted means produced by the MCA algorithm simultaneously adjusting for the effects of other variables.[1] The differentials were much smaller for the majority of the sample. Thus, there was no pattern for income categories above $6,500 (1967 dollars) or for income trend between -1 percent and +6 percent. For occupation and industry, many differentials were not only attenuated but even reversed reflecting high intercorrelations. Service workers, laborers, and clerical workers all had adjusted means significantly below the average for the whole sample. Only self-employed groups had instability actually higher net of income level and other variables. For industry, only construction appeared particularly high and nondurables manufacturing and retail trade appeared particularly low.

With one exception, gender, the net effects of the remaining variables were sharply reduced to or below the borderline of significance. However, the finding that female heads of households in this particular sample had lower instability after other variables were taken into account is not applicable to women workers as a whole. Curiously, while the black/white differential was rendered insignificantly small by the other variables, the white/"other" differential widened.[2]

Finally, a word should be said about education. It appears that not only did high school dropouts have significantly higher instability than those with either more or less education, but that this phenomenon became even more pronounced after all the other variables, including income, were taken into account. This is in agreement with much other evidence that finishing some level of education is more important than starting one. This may reflect the operation of credentials to some extent, but probably more important are the psychological differences between those who quit and those who either finish or do not start a particular level.

In order to investigate changes over time in the patterns described above, we ran MCAs separately for the first and the last five-year periods of the decade 1967-77 for the same sample used in the larger analysis. Only education, age,

---

[1] It is equivalent to a regression using 52 dichtomous variables for the various characteristics but transforming the coefficients so that their weighted sum for each set of characteristics equals the grand mean.

[2] There were enough Hispanics in our sample and others who were neither black nor white, and they are sufficiently different, so that they could not be combined with either major group.

race, and sex necessarily had the same value for individuals for both subperiods. Summary results indicating the explanatory power of each variable are shown in Table 9.2. Note that the R^2 for both subperiods was substantially below the R^2 for the entire eleven-year period, indicating that the shorter the time frame the more important random noise becomes. The mean level of instability increased by about 10 percent for the sample as a whole between 1967-71 and 1973-77. Interestingly, the highest ranking socio-economic categories by income (over $15,000 in 1967 dollars) and education (at least a bachelor's degree) experienced a slight decrease in instability while every other income and educational category suffered higher instability during the latter subperiod. The youngest age category, had a decrease in instability, reflecting a more settled employment pattern for the group aged 25-34 in 1968 and 35-44 in 1978.

The occupational codes for 1972 were not strictly comparable to those for 1978, but a comparison of the results for industry groups is illuminating. Workers in agriculture and in the construction industry experienced substantially higher income instability during the 1973-77 period, when farm prices fluctuated wildly and the home construction industry had an unusually severe recession. While workers in these two industries experience high instability in the best of times, four industrial categories with the lowest unadjusted mean levels of instability for the 1967-71 Vietnam War-era boom period also had fairly large increases in average instability. These were durables and nondurables manufacturing, wholesale trade, and transportation, communication, and utilities. On the other hand, workers in government, the professional services (e.g., health, law, education), and the single category of finance, real estate, and insurance managed to insulate themselves from the recession and stagflation of 1973-77 with reduced levels of instability, but the professional service workers were the only group to have a decrease in the adjusted mean as well.

Not too surprisingly, those sectors which suffered least from the increase in instability were those which were least involved in the handling of commodities, since physical output is most cyclically unstable. Moreover, workers in service sectors were more likely to have high education and high incomes. The MCA results suggest that primarily the college-educated, upper-income individuals within the three service industries listed above best managed to avoid increased unemployment as well as increased fluctuations in real income caused by erratic changes in wages. There was a sharp increase in the "explanatory" power of four variables—income level, occupation, industry, and education—because of the widened differentials described above. Yet,

Table 9.2

GROSS AND NET EFFECTS OF EXPLANATORY VARIABLES
ON INCOME INSTABILITY

	Household Head's Labor Earnings 1967-1977		1967-1971		1973-1977	
	Eta^2	$Beta^2$	Eta^2	$Beta^2$	Eta^2	$Beta^2$
Income	.207	.143	.209	.147	.172	.175
Income trend	.265	.138	.192	.093	.144	.064
Occupation	.089	.035	.045	.018	.087	.067
Industry	.085	.017	.041	.015	.066	.035
Age	.047	.006	.051	.010	.010	.005
Race	.006	.005	.002	.000	.013	.006
Sex	.007	.011	.006	.002	.003	.007
Education	.023	.003	.015	.002	.028	.006
Marital status	.025	.003	.020	.002	.010	.003
Mobility	.016	.004	.011	.000	.003	.001
Disability	.012	.002	.023	.005	.006	.000
R^2		.446		.365		.339
R^2 Adjusted		.423		.339		.311

	Head-Wife Taxable Income Only (1967-1977)		With Transfers (1968-1977)	
	Eta^2	$Beta^2$	Eta^2	$Beta^2$
Income	.206	.123	.123	.066
Income trend	.194	.081	.135	.059
Occupation	.161	.051	.176	.100
Industry	.135	.031	.132	.033
Age	.054	.007	.019	.007
Race	.004	.003	.004	.002
Sex	.021	.017	.006	.017
Education	.020	.002	.026	.006
Marital status	.049	.011	.036	.022
Mobility	.016	.007	.010	.005
Disability	.040	.004	.017	.002
R^2		.428		.375
R^2 Adjusted		.405		.351

interestingly, the fit of the set of variables as a whole diminished between the two periods, 1967-71 and 1973-77, as variability of a random sort presumably became more important.

Thus far we have considered only the instability of the household head's annual labor earnings, but other components of family income may have important influences on overall instability in available resources. Consequently, we considered instability in two other measures of income, total head-wife taxable income including non-labor income and the wife's labor earnings and total head-wife income including transfer payments as well. Non-labor income may be either stabilizing or destabilizing depending upon whether it is largely fixed or highly variable. Wives' earnings may be either stabilizing or destabilizing depending upon whether the "added worker" or the "discouraged worker" effect predominates. That is, instability may be reduced if a decline in their husbands' earnings induces women to increase work effort, whereas if women react to their husbands' inability to obtain employment by giving up job search through discouragement, (of if the husband and wife work in the same plant) then instability may be accentuated. The fact that both cross-sectionally and over time aggregate female labor force participation rates are negatively related to male unemployment rates appears to offer support for the discouraged worker effect (Finegan, 1975; Niemi, 1975). Contrarily, dynamic studies with individual data reveal that while women do not respond to husbands' current unemployment, over time the wives of husbands with histories of unemployment or irregular labor force attachment are more likely to be in the labor force (Spencer, 1973), thus stabilizing household income. Transfers are assumed to be stabilizing for all groups, but much more so for some groups than for others.

Using head-wife taxable income in place of the household head's earnings did not substantially affect either the mean level of instability or the explanatory power of the model. The relative levels of instability experienced by different groups, though, changed fairly dramatically. The reader may compare the unadjusted means for head-wife taxable income in column A of Table 9.3 with those for the head's labor earnings found in the second column of Table 9.1 (the patterns of adjusted means are roughly similar for the two income measures). The figures for the income trend variables appear to indicate that where the household head had a pronounced decline in income, having a wife in the labor force cushioned the blow, while for those household heads with low instability this had a slightly destabilizing effect. With regard to occupational categories with very high instability in labor earnings, we found that the combined head-

wife taxable incomes of farmers and self-employed managers was _less_ stable than
the household head´s labor earnings, while for medical and legal professionals
joint incomes were _more_ stable. For the two entrepreneurial categories, the most
unstable component of total income was presumably profits, but a contributing
factor may have been the greater participation of wives in family enterprises
during busy times. On the other hand, doctors, dentists, and lawyers were likely
to have had wives who either did not work or had salaried jobs, while non-labor
income consisted largely of relatively invariable interest and dividend receipts.

The last two columns of Table 9.3 allow us to look at the impact of transfer
payments on instability. Since a question on transfers was first asked in 1969,
we had only ten years of data available, which modestly reduced the instability
means (by well under one-tenth). The income and income trend variables were
coded on the basis of taxable income only, to allow direct comparability.
Turning to the last column of Table 9.3, we see that transfers do not appear to
have raised instability for any group, and they reduced it substantially among
the poor and among those with large gains or losses in income. The latter result
suggests that the extreme income trend categories contained disproportionate
numbers of people who either started or stopped receiving public assistance,
Social Security support, or unemployment insurance coverage during the eleven-
year period. Not surprisingly, farmers and self-employed managers benefited less
than did any other occupations from direct transfer payments. Workers in
government seemed to succeed more than did those in any other industrial sector
in reducing instability through the receipt of transfers although this might
reflect a greater likelihood of transfer recipients to work for government units.
With the young, the old, females, and the non-white non-black group who were in
the labor force continuously for at least a decade, income transfers succeeded in
reducing income instability substantially.

Good Jobs-Bad Jobs or Compensating Differentials

The results described in the previous section suggest that income level and
stability are positively associated for most of the population. A direct test of
the hypothesis of compensating income differentials (compensating for risk and
uncertainty), though, entails controlling for human capital and comparing
instability and level of income across industries for those who remained in the
same industry. The argument is that if people have a choice, between high paying
jobs and stable jobs, it is likely to involve finding a job requiring about the
same background and skills, but in a different industry. People cannot change

Table 9.3 (page 1 of 2)

INSTABILITY IN HEAD—WIFE TAXABLE INCOME (1967-1977)
AND HEAD—WIFE TOTAL INCOME (1968-1977)

Predictor	Percentage	Taxable Only	With Transfers	Ratio B/A
Average Income (In 1967 Dollars)				
Less than $2500	4.6	1.45	.98	.68
$2500-4500	7.7	1.14	.83	.73
$4500-6500	11.1	.86	.68	.80
$6500-8000	11.5	.74	.59	.79
$8000-10,000	17.5	.63	.53	.84
$10,000-12,000	15.5	.55	.47	.86
$12,000-15,000	14.6	.48	.42	.88
$15,000-20,000	10.7	.50	.46	.91
Over $20,000	6.7	.67	.60	.90
Income Trend				
Less than -5%	9.9	1.19	.87	.73
-5 to -1%	14.5	.75	.63	.83
-1 to 0%	7.4	.52	.43	.83
0% to 1%	10.2	.59	.51	.86
1 to 3%	22.0	.49	.43	.86
3 to 6%	18.9	.57	.49	.86
6 to 10%	10.8	.77	.64	.84
Over 10%	6.3	1.20	.86	.72
Occupation (1978)				
Medical and legal prof.	2.1	.70	.59	.84
Other professionals	15.0	.57	.45	.79
Salaried managers	16.4	.57	.49	.86
Self-employed managers	4.4	1.07	.98	.91
Clerical workers	6.8	.66	.49	.74
Sales workers	5.0	.64	.53	.83
Craftsmen and kindred	21.9	.60	.50	.83
Operatives	12.8	.65	.54	.83
Laborers	3.7	.77	.67	.87
Service workers	5.3	.91	.73	.80
Farmers	2.9	1.43	1.27	.89
Misc. not in labor force	3.8	1.31	.74	.56

Table 9.3 (page 2 of 2)

| Predictor | Percentage | Unadjusted Means | | Ratio B/A |
		Taxable Only	With Transfers	
Industry(1978)				
Agriculture	4.6	1.21	1.09	.90
Durable manufact.	20.8	.59	.48	.81
Nondurable manufact.	8.0	.55	.45	.82
Construction	8.2	.84	.71	.84
Transp. comm., util.	7.7	.58	.49	.84
Retail trade	9.8	.70	.59	.84
Wholesale trade	2.7	.66	.52	.79
Finance, insur.				
realestate	3.9	.63	.54	.86
Misc. services	7.7	.82	.69	.84
Prof. services	15.6	.64	.51	.80
Government	7.0	.56	.42	.75
Misc. not in				
labor force	4.0	1.33	.78	.59
Age (1968)				
25-35	11.2	.88	.93	.78
35-45	26.1	.68	.58	.86
45-55	35.3	.63	.53	.84
55-65	21.4	.63	.53	.84
65-75	4.7	1.04	.70	.67
Over 75	1.4	1.21	.74	.61
Race				
White	88.7	.69	.56	.82
Black	7.6	.77	.65	.84
Other	3.7	.84	.62	.75
Sex				
Male	88.9	.67	.56	.83
Female	11.1	.92	.66	.72

their age, race, sex, nor very easily their education or main occupation, but they can change industry. Hence the best test of the theory is to compare very similar groups of individuals across different industry groups. In order to do this we stratified the sample by race and sex and further subdivided the most numerous subsample--white males--on the basis of age and education. A substantial majority of the men in the sample did not remain in the same industry between 1973 and 1977, including almost all of those under the age of 35, and most of those who had either college degrees or had not finished high school were concentrated in two different clusters of industries. Consequently, we only had two useable subsamples: white men with only high school degrees between 35 and 44 years of age and those over age 45. We are using correlations of group means (ecological correlations) which have very few "cases" (degrees of freedom) but can be expected to produce high correlations because much of the extraneous variation is averaged out. There were ten industry groups (data points) for the 35-44 year old white male and non-college group and for the other men with at least 10 cases per group.

For the two subsamples we regressed average instability in annual earnings against the average levels of both hourly and annual earnings. A positive association with hourly earnings would support the finding of Abowd and Ashenfelter (1980) that industries with relatively high wage levels are subject to greater economic instability. A positive association with the level of annual earnings if found would be the first evidence of a pure income differential compensating workers for risk. For industry groups with at least ten cases, the correlation between instability and hourly earnings was +0.32 for the 35-44 age group and -.07 for the older group of men. The correlations with average annual earnings were -0.13 and +0.02, respectively. Thus, only for white male high school graduates aged 35-44, was there evidence of compensating differentials. The other three correlations provide no support at all for the existence of compensating differentials. As workers over age 45 are relatively immobile, it is not surprising that compensating differentials fail to appear among them. With regard to intertemporal variability in annual earnings, these results provide no support for either the theory of compensating differentials or theories of segmented labor markets (at least for relatively homogeneous classes of labor). In other words, for similar individuals income level and instability are independently assorted across industry groups.

CONCLUSION

We first investigated the relationship of economic and demographic variables to various measures of income instability. Except among the young, high school dropouts, and the self-employed, income instability appeared to vary in a consistent manner only with income and income trend. That is, low income and large change in income over time were associated with greater instability in income. The second result is partly mechanistic, a product of our specification of instability. The connection with income level, though, is substantively interesting, for it is consistent with the segmented labor market paradigm which maintains that individuals in the primary or "good" job market have high and stable incomes, while those in the secondary or "bad" job market have low and unstable incomes. On the other hand, the data provide no support for the existence of separate, bounded labor markets; rather, the relationship between income level and instability appears continuous and not kinked (see Freiman, 1976, and Chapter 2 by Duncan and Hoffman in this volume for analogous conclusions). It is true that a discrete shift downwards in the level of instability is associated with the attainment of a high school degree, but this cannot be taken as evidence that those who do not finish high school are necessarily relegated to inferior jobs.

The opposing hypothesis of compensating wage differentials receives only modest support from the analysis presented in the third section. This is in accord with other research which supports the existence of compensating differentials for certain kinds of unfavorable job attributes, most notably risk of death, but not for other characteristics such as stress and repetitiveness (Brown, 1980). While we did find a positive association between hourly earnings and instability for at least some workers, there was no evidence of a positive association between annual earnings and instability for any single group, and differences among groups with different demographic attributes and stocks of human capital led to a strongly negative relation between instability and earnings in the whole sample.

The remaining findings are new and significant. Income transfers appeared to cushion the incomes of those employed persons whose labor market earnings were subject to the most instability. Having a secondary earner in the labor market and/or income-earnings assets may be either stabilizing or destabilizing for individual households, but overall these things make little difference. Not surprisingly, income instability grew significantly during the mid-1970s as deep recession and double-digit inflation hit the U.S. economy, but it is interesting

to note that those in the highest income groups and the highest status
occupations managed to avoid the increased vulnerability the rest of the labor
force was exposed to during recent years.

References

Abowd, John, and Ashenfelter, Orley. "Unemployment and Compensating Wage
Differentials." Working paper No. 120, Industrial Relations Section,
Princeton University, March 1979.

_____. "Anticipated Unemployment, Temporary Layoffs and Compensating Wage
Differentials." Working Paper No. 137, Industrial Relations Section,
Princeton University, June 1980.

Benus, Jacob. "Income Instability." In Five Thousand American Families--
Patterns of Economic Progress, Vol. 1. Ann Arbor, Michigan: Institute for
Social Research, The University of Michigan, 1974.

Benus, Jacob, and Morgan, James. "Time Period, Unit of Analysis and Income
Concept in the Analysis of Income Distribution." In The Personal
Distribution of Income and Wealth, edited by James D. Smith. Columbia
University Press, New York: 1975.

Brown, Charles. "Equalizing Differences in the Labor Market." Quarterly Journal
of Economics (February 1980): 114-134.

Coe, Richard D. "Dependency and Poverty in the Short and Long Run." In Five
Thousand American Families--Patterns of Economic Progress, Vol. VI edited by
Greg J. Duncan and James N. Morgan. Ann Arbor, Michigan: Institute
University of Michigan, 1978.

Finegan, T. Aldrich. "Participation of Married Women in the Labor Force." In
Sex, Discrimination, and the Division of Labor, edited by C.B. Lloyd. New
York: Columbia University Press, 1975.

Freiman, Marc P. Empirical Tests of Dual Labor Market Theory and Hedonic
Measures of Occupational Attainment. Unpublished doctoral dissertation,
University of Wisconsin, Madison, 1976.

Friedman, Milton. "Choice, Chance, and the Personal Distribution of Income."
Journal of Political Economy (April 1953): 277-290.

Friedman, Milton, and Kuznets, Simon. Income from the Independent Professional
Practice. New York: National Bureau of Economic Research, 1975.

Kalleberg, Arne L., and Sorensen, Aage B.. "Sociology of Labor Markets." Annual
Review of Sociology 5 (1979): 351-379.

Leigh, John Paul. Earnings, Risk and the Wage Structure of Industry.
Unpublished doctoral dissertation, University of Wisconsin, Madison,
Wisconsin, 1979.

Lillard, Lee A., and Weiss, Yoram. "Components of Variation in Panel Earnings Data: American Scientists, 1960-70." Econometrica 47 (March 1979): 437-454.

Morgan, James N. "Voluntary and Involuntary Job Changes: Are There Compensating Differentials?" Proceedings of the Social Statistical Association. Houston, Texas: American Statistical Association, 1980.

Niemi, Beth. "Geographic Immobility and Labor Force Mobility: A Study of Female Unemployment." In Sex, Discrimination, and the Division of Labor, edited by C.B. Lloyd. New York: Columbia University Press, 1975.

Spencer, B.G. "Determinants of the Labour Force Participation of Married Women: A Micro-Study of Toronto Households." Canadian Journal of Economics 6 (May 1973): 227-238.

Chapter 10

TRENDS IN NON-MONEY INCOME THROUGH
DO-IT-YOURSELF ACTIVITIES, 1971 TO 1978

James N. Morgan

A complete measure of the economic status of a family should include non-money as well as money income. The most obvious example of non-money income is the imputed net rental return on a homeowner´s equity in his or her house. However, non-money income is also derived from various do-it-yourself activities such as fixing one´s own car or growing and preserving one´s own food. It is an income even though it entails costs, in materials, in hours of work. (A full measure of well-being should take leisure into account.) There are problems both in separating the recreational aspects of do-it-yourself projects from the production aspects and in distinguishing the surplus of benefits over the money outlays for equipment and supplies. A compromise can be reached by asking people how many hours of work they put into each activity and how much money they think they saved by doing it themselves. The assumption is that a person growing flowers for fun would be less likely to think of it as saving money than someone growing potatoes. But it is likely that the reports on hours spent are more uniformly reliable than estimates of the amount of money saved.

Unpaid productive activity ranges from housework (which someone does for almost every household), through child care (which is demanded of parents), to a variety of optional and open-ended possibilities. Any unpaid productive activity can be thought of as having diminishing marginal productivity and increasing disutility of the work itself as more hours are devoted to it. Even if we believed that we could measure the marginal possibilities for earning money by work and that home production is extended to that same margin, we could not measure the total contribution of home production to family well-being by valuing the hours at that rate, because there is a kind of producer´s surplus inside the margin. In addition, most do-it-yourself activities also involve some money outlays for materials, tools, rentals, and so on.

The most important thing to measure, it seems, is the total net contribution of the do-it-yourself activity. For each of the three activities we measured in

the 12th wave of the Panel Study of Income Dynamics—repairs and renovation to
the house, car repairs, and growing or preserving food, we asked respondents how
much they thought that they saved by doing the work themselves. The implication
was that they could have bought the food and paid for the work done on their cars
and houses. This way of stating the question was also intended to discourage the
inclusion of recreational activities, though an argument could be made that
growing flowers for pleasure adds to a family's total well-being.

One might think that the totals saved by these activities would have been
greater when alternative opportunities were smaller or the time pressures less—
that is, when money wage rates were lower or when paid work hours were fewer. In
fact, however, the very families with the most counter-pressures and the least
need for more real income did the most unpaid work. This does not mean that
people do not make rational marginal choices, but that there are vast differences
in the pressures to perform such unpaid productive activities and in the
opportunities to do so.

Using data from the 1973 wave of the Panel Study, Gronau (1980) estimated
the value of housework, by assuming that the marginal contribution of housework
equals the alternative earning opportunity for each married woman and that the
housework productivity function must have a particular form. Since middle-aged
couples generally have children, larger houses, and higher earning opportunities
than average, and also higher family incomes, adding the value of housework to
income might be expected to increase measured inequality.

We were concerned here not with housework but with three other main
components of unpaid work—work on the house, on the car, and in growing and
preserving food. Our analysis showed that such work was dominated by differences
in opportunities and capacities—age, homeownership, sex, and marital status.
When we took account of these basic factors, neither income nor wage rate nor the
number of hours worked for pay had much association with unpaid work hours.

Difficult though they are to value, regular housework and child care are a
much larger component of real income than the three do-it-yourself activities we
analyzed here. But, because market alternatives are more readily available for
working on the house or car or obtaining food, there is much more freedom of
choice about undertaking these optional activities than in doing regular
housework. If the tax advantages of do-it-yourself affected people, it should be
these optional activities that would be affected.

Trends

    A penny saved is worth more than a penny earned because it is tax-free, and the popular press is full of stories about how people are coping with inflation by doing more work around the house themselves.

    "More and more Americans are pushing themselves away from the TV set and doing their own home improvements. Do it yourselvers this year are expected to spend nearly $28 billion, about three times as much as just seven years ago. He (or increasingly she) is doing complicated electrical and plumbing jobs that used to be considered hands-off for amateurs" (Time, July 18, 1980).

    These comments seem to fly in the face of our data. It is true that Time compared 1980 with 1973 while we compared 1978 with 1971, that there were small changes in our questions, and that we asked about amounts saved rather than amounts spent. But Table 10.1 (with the 1971 dollar amounts increased 61 percent for price inflation), shows modest increases in the proportions of people who reported that they worked on their cars or on growing and preserving food and in dollars saved in all three kinds of unpaid work. However, there was a decline in the proportion who said they worked on their houses and no offsetting increase in the hours of work on the house reported by those who did work on their houses. Thus, the average hours per household spent working on the house decreased. This result might have been due to a minor change in question wording in 1979 that could have eliminated the mention of some trivial repairs.[1]

---

[1]The questions were:

    1972: Did you (or your family) do any work yourself (yourselves) on this (house/apartment) during 1971?

    1979: Did you (or your family) do any work (yourself/yourselves) on your (house/apartment) during 1978? I mean repairs or remodelling.

The details asked about were as follows:

    1972: What did you do?
    Who in the family did this work?
    About how much do you think you saved doing it yourself—was it about $25, $50, $100, $200 or what?
    About how much time did it take altogether?

    1979: We would like a rough idea of how much time you spent and how much money you saved. What did you do?
    About how much time did that take?
    About how much do you think you saved by doing it yourself?

Table 10.1

TRENDS IN DO-IT-YOURSELF WORK

	1971[a]	1978
Percentage who		
Worked on car	35%	42%
Worked on house	43	36
Grew or preserved food	29	32
Amount Saved per Household[b]		
On car	$ 69	$118
On house	252	327
On food	47	62
Spent 100 Hours or More		
On car	1.8%	2.8%
On house	10.3%	8.6%
Hours Spent[c]		
On car	8	14
On house	41	32
Implied Amount Saved per Hour[b]		
On car	$8.54	$8.49
On house	6.19	10.09
Number of cases	5,060	6,373

[a]Based on the 1972 sample, not the 1979 panel which would contain duplicate 1972 families because of splitoffs or divorce. Dollar amounts increased 61 percent for inflation (i.e., they are shown in 1978 prices).

[b]In 1978 dollars.

[c]Includes zeros for those who did none.

Table 10.2 summarizes the trends on the eight basic items, comparing 1971 and 1978 for the four subgroups which differed the most from one another. Among married couples, homeownership made the most difference. Among the unmarried, do-it-yourself work differed according to sex, particularly work on cars. Beyond that, age had the most effect on the propensity to engage in do-it-yourself activities, and differentially across the three activities, as we shall see later. The age patterns did not change much over time. Among all four groups in Table 10.2 (married homeowners, married non homeowners, unmarried men, and unmarried women) there was an increase in the proportion who worked on their cars and an increase in the hours spent and the dollars reported saved. Among all four groups there was also a decrease over the years in the proportion who reported working on their houses and in the hours spent in such work; except among single men, however, there was an increase in the money saved on that work. The cost of having work done around the house has increased greatly, so that it is quite possible that the savings per hour did indeed go up as our respondents' reports would indicate. Finally, all but the single men were more likely to report growing or preserving food, but the changes in proportions and in the dollars saved were small.

It is not unreasonable to expect, given the increased number of young two-earner families with relatively new houses, that doing one's own repairs or remodelling would decline: they presumably have more money to pay to have someone else do the work and perhaps less time to do it themselves. The decline in hours worked on the home was largest among those under age 55, particularly for married homeowners.

In an earlier study covering the year 1964, questions were asked about housework, major housecleaning and painting, sewing and mending, growing food, canning or freezing food, and other activities "that saved money," and about hours spent in these activities, but not about any estimate of money saved (Morgan, Sirageldin and Baerwaldt, 1966). That analysis focused on the whole set of home-production activities and found that they were most often performed by married couples with large families who lived in single family structures, who were well educated, lived in rural areas, and had no child under age two

---

(If don't know) Was it more than $100?
If yes, Was it more than $200?
If yes, About how much do you think you saved?
If yes, Was it more than $50?
If no, Was it more than $25?

Table 10.2

WORK ON CAR, HOUSE, OR FOOD, BY MARITAL STATUS,
HOMEOWNERSHIP, AND SEX—1971 AND 1978

(Averages include zeroes so they can be added and divided.)

| | Married | | | | Unmarried | | | | All | |
| | Home Owner | | Non-Home Owner | | Men | | Women | | | |
	1971	1978	1971	1978	1971	1978	1971	1978	1971	1978
Whether Worked on										
Car	.47	.56	.45	.57	.29	.47	.08	.11	.35	.43
House	.59	.53	.36	.30	.26	.25	.23	.18	.43	.36
Food	.39	.49	.23	.24	.15	.13	.18	.27	.29	.35
Hours Spent on										
Car	10	16	12	23	9	20	6	3	8	14
House	62	53	32	13	22	12	9	17	41	32
$ Saved[a] Working On										
Car	$88	145	97	205	73	141	11	18	69	118
House	414	599	127	136	161	127	56	63	252	326
Food	72	99	39	34	17	18	16	35	47	62
Total	574	844	263	376	251	285	83	117	368	506
$ Saved/Hr.[a] On Car and House (Ratio of Means)	$7	11	5	9	6	8	7	4	7	10

[a] In 1978 dollars.

(requiring lots of extra time). Since the question wording varied, estimates of changes over time in the amount of work on the house are treacherous, but about half of the 1964 sample reported doing some work on the house, compared with 43 percent in 1971 and 36 percent in 1978. So there may really be a declining trend over the 14 years in work on the house, despite the popular stereotypes. Changes in the questions make comparison difficult, to be sure, but the fact that mostly the same individuals were in the 1971 and 1978 samples makes comparisons more precise. Our analyses generally revealed meaningful correlations between background or environmental factors and whether people engaged in such activities, but not with the amounts of time they reported spending or the amounts of money they reported saving.

Trends among Families with Unchanged Heads

A better test for behavioral trends, as distinct from aggregates, is to compare panel families who did not experience any change in household head between 1972 and 1979, even though there may be some important changes in aggregates resulting from difference between newly formed families and families which disappeared. For the 3,323 households with no change in head in the 1971–1979 period, the proportion reporting any home repair or remodelling dropped from 46.8 percent to 37.9 percent. In fact, 40 percent reported no such work either time, 25 percent did something both times, 13 percent went from none to some, and 22 percent went from some to none. The proportions spending 200 hours or more went down from 5.2 percent to 4.3 percent, but the proportion reporting savings of $200 or more went up from 26.1 percent to 28.6 percent, in constant dollars adjusted for inflation. (See Appendix Tables A10.2 and A10.5) Finally, a two-way table based on the complexity of the work and the skill level involved shows the proportion who said they did some house fixing which took much skill or very extensive work (e.g., electrical and/or complex plumbing) only increased from 9.2 percent to 10.4 percent, even though the question in 1979 seemed to focus on the more extensive repairs and remodelling rather than painting and fixing up little things (Table 10.3).

This cohort, however, can reflect only aging or historic trend effects, not the differences between generations, and perhaps it was the newer cohorts (younger generations) who were doing more work. An aggregate can increase because new families differ from those they replace in the population. The average dollar amounts reportedly saved by the two representative samples were:

	1971[a]	1978
Car repairs	$ 69	$118
House repairs	252	326
Growing and processing food	47	62

[a]Multiplied by 1.61 to reflect general price increases by using "1978 dollars."

This would seem to reflect modest increases in activity, adjusted for price levels, but surely not the tripling Time estimated for house repairs, unless the ratio of amounts spent to amounts saved has changed radically. They report on amounts spent, we report on amounts saved.

Turnover or Persistence

It is interesting to look at the extent to which there is turnover or persistence in those who engage in home production. Focusing on the unchanged panel families, Table 10.4 summarizes the turnover in families spending any time on each of the three activities and compares the net change among these same families with the change estimated from the two representative samples. There was substantial persistence of behavior, compared with a model of independence where the proportion expected to do something both years would be the product of the proportion in each of the years. Thus, the expected proportion working on the car in each of the two years, if a random 37.7 percent did so in 1971 and 40.7 percent in 1978, would have been the product of those probabilities, or 15.3 percent, but 27.7 percent of the families actually worked on the car in each of the two years. Appendix Tables A10.1-A10.3 give the turnover relations for amounts saved working on the car or house or growing food; Tables A10.4-A10.5 show hours spent working on the car or house; and Table A10.6 shows the complexity of skill level for car repairs in 1971 compared with 1978. The rank correlations are all highly significant: some people did these activities regularly, some did not. The correlations might have been even higher if we had pooled the three activities.

Comparison of Two Samples with Heavy Overlap

In view of the possible "selection bias" resulting from looking only at families with unchanged heads over an eight-year period, we compared the age

Table 10.3

COMPLEXITY AND SKILL REQUIREMENT OF WORK DONE ON HOMES IN 1971 AND 1978
(For 3,323 households with the same head.)

1971	1978						
	No Work Done	Simple Repairs	Some Skills	Fair Amount of Skill	Much Skill Required	Extensive and Complex	All
No work done	40.1	2.7	2.0	5.2	2.4	0.8	53.2
Simple repairs	6.7	2.0	0.8	1.4	0.9	0.3	12.2
Some skill	2.5	0.4	1.0	0.9	0.5	0.3	5.6
Fair amount of skill	9.3	1.8	1.6	4.1	1.8	1.1	19.7
Much skill required	2.3	0.4	0.5	1.5	0.7	0.6	6.1
Extensive and complex	1.0	0.2	0.3	0.6	0.7	0.4	3.1
All	62.0	7.5	6.2	13.7	7.0	3.4	100.0

Rank correlation: Tau-B = .22
Transition Proportions

More complex	8.6
Less complex	8.0
None to some	13.1
Some to none	21.9
None to none	40.1
Same complexity	8.2
	99.9

Table 10.4

TURNOVER AND PERSISTENCE OF DO-IT-YOURSELF ACTIVITIES
(For 3,323 households with the same head.)

1971	1978			Net Change	Change In 2 Full Samples
	Yes	No	All		
Worked on Car					
Yes	27.7	10.0	37.7	13.0-10.0=	42-35=+7
No	13.0	49.3	62.3	+3%	
All	40.7	59.3	100.0		
Worked on House					
Yes	24.9	21.9	46.8	13.1-21.9=	35-43=-8
No	13.1	40.1	53.2	-8.8%	
All	38.0	62.0	100.0		
Grew Food or Preserved it					
Yes	22.1	9.7	31.8	18.7-9.7=	32-29=+3
No	18.7	49.5	68.2	+9%	
All	40.8	59.2	100.0		

cohorts within the representative sample of families in the panel in 1972 with that of 1979. These analyses are superior to those of two totally independent samples because of the large proportion of identical families in both years. Table 10.5 shows both the rank correlation coefficients when amounts of time spent or dollars saved were bracketed and the correlations ratios when the actual amounts were used where we determine what fraction of the variance could be explained. The two results are similar, since the loss of the information from grouping a dependent variable is very small, and the rank correlations allow non-linear effects. The rank correlations also preserve the sign (direction) of the effect.

Marital status and type of housing also affected these activities, as we have seen, and much of the apparent effect of income disappeared in a multivariate analysis. But we focused here on age because we wanted to look at cohort versus age effects, and we focused on income or earnings level because we were interested in comparing the opportunity cost implied by money earnings with the implied wage--the amount saved per hour--in home production activities.

Age, Cohort, and Period of History Effects

We looked first at proportions who did any of the three types of do-it-yourself activities, first comparing 1971 with 1978 for those of the same current age, and then comparing those of the same birth-cohort (age in 1972). (See Table 10.6.) The results were most dramatic for work on cars where the young have always done more of that type of work. It is apparent, particularly if one plots the changes for the same cohorts (shown in Figure 10.1), that the young not only did the most do-it-yourself work but also showed the greatest increase in the proportions working on cars, while the decline in reported work on the house was pervasive except among the younger age groups who traditionally do the least, partly because they are least likely to own a home. Appendix Tables A10.7 and A10.8 give similar age-cohort data for hours spent and amounts saved. The patterns are similar, because the amounts did not vary much, by any characteristic including age; only the presence or absence of the activity varied systematically.

There was, then, increasing activity in car repairs, particularly among the young, while work on the house decreased among older people but increased among the young. A small increase was reported at all age levels in growing or preserving food and in dollar amounts saved. Given these different patterns, analysis of total do-it-yourself activity is likely to be misleading.

Table 10.5 (page 1 of 2)
IMPORTANCE OF FACTORS AFFECTING DO-IT-YOURSELF WORK

	1971			1978		
	Dollars Saved			Dollars Saved		
	$ Car	$ House	$ Food	$ Car	$ House	$ Food
Rank Correlation (Tau-B)						
Income decile	.18	.26	-.01	.23	.24	.06
Income/needs decile	.08	.15	-.05	.14	.24	.06
Age in 1979	-.22	-.07	.11	-.25	-.10	.12
Age in 1972	-	-	-	-.26	-.10	.12
Hourly earnings	.18	.23	-.05	.22	.21	-.00
After-tax hourly earnings	-	-	-	.22	.20	.00

	Hours Spent On		Hours Spent On	
	Car	House	Car	House
Income decile	.19	.27	.24	.22
Income/needs decile	.09	.15	.15	.16
Age in 1979	-.23	-.18	-.26	-.11
Age in 1972	-	-	-.27	-.11
Hourly earnings	.19	.25	.24	.20
After-tax hourly earnings	-	-	.23	.19

Table 10.5 (page 2 of 2)

	$ Saved			$ Saved		
	Car	House	Food	Car	House	Food
			Eta^2			
Income decile	.023	.036	.002	.024	.033	.004
Income/needs decile	.013	.017	.003	.013	.022	.002
Age in 1979	.042	.019	.011	.031	.019	.009
Age in 1972	.042	.019	.011	.032	.018	.012
Hourly earnings	.025	.034	.006	.015	.024	.001
After-tax hourly earnings	-	-	-	.014	.020	.002

	Hours Spent On		Hours Spent On	
	Car	House	Car	House
Income decile	.012	.025	.009	.012
Income/needs decile	.008	.012	.005	.010
Age in 1979	.021	.015	.013	.000
Age in 1972	-	-	.013	.006
Hourly earnings	.012	.022	.006	.009
After-tax hourly earnings	-	-	.006	.008

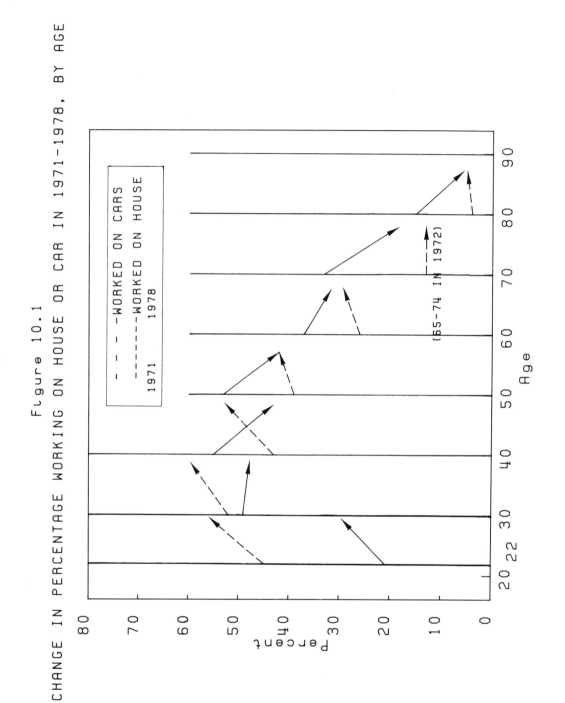

Figure 10.1

CHANGE IN PERCENTAGE WORKING ON HOUSE OR CAR IN 1971-1978, BY AGE

Table 10.6

PERCENTAGE WHO SAVED ANY MONEY WORKING ON CAR OR HOUSE, BY AGE AND AGE COHORTS

Age	Car 1971 1972 Age	Car 1978 1979 Age	Car 1978 1972 Age	House 1971 1972 Age	House 1978 1979 Age	House 1978 1972 Age	Food 1971 1972 Age	Food 1978 1979 Age	Food 1978 1972 Age
18-24	45	51	55	21	25	29	11	16	19
25-34	50	58	57	49	44	48	27	25	28
35-44	43	54	51	55	46	45	31	35	34
45-54	30	45	42	53	45	42	31	38	39
55-64	26	33	29	37	34	32	32	41	43
65-74	13	18	13	33	23	20	38	40	37
75+ / All ages	$\frac{4}{35}$	$\frac{6}{42}$	$\frac{5}{42}$	$\frac{15}{43}$	$\frac{9}{35}$	$\frac{6}{35}$	$\frac{32}{29}$	$\frac{32}{32}$	$\frac{32}{32}$
Eta^2 (Adj.)	.22	.25	.26	.07	.10	.10	.11	.12	.12

Implied Earnings of Do-It-Yourself Work

We asked how many hours were spent working on the car or house and how much money was saved by doing the work. It is interesting to see whether people with alternatives for higher money earning or with more outside pressures on their time restricted themselves to those unpaid activities with higher payoffs in saving per hour. The ratio of the mean savings to the mean hours spent is a good approximation to the average savings per hour; these figures are given in Table 10.7 according to the level of the head's after-tax hourly earnings. Of course, the head's marginal wage may have differed from his hourly wage after tax if he had overtime at a higher wage, or if he could only earn more by working at a second job at a lower wage. Wives were also involved in some of these activities and their opportunity costs in both money and foregone family activities might have been different.

Do people value their time according to their wage and expand their home production until it pays off at that rate? We cannot be sure, because we were looking at the average not at the marginal amount saved. If there had been a different pattern of falling marginal productivity in do-it-yourself activities among low and high wage people, the latter might still have been saying no to added activities at a higher marginal payoff. It is difficult to believe that such a pattern existed. If substantial "rationality" was being exhibited, it was largely masked by differential constraints and urgent pressures.

Perhaps the opportunity cost is more closely related to the total time demands on people than on their market wage rates, particularly since many people do not have choices about the amount of market work they do anyway. Hence, we looked at age patterns, assuming that middle aged people, in mid-career and often with children, would have had the most pressures to spend time either earning money or caring for children.

Table 10.8 does indicate a tendency for middle aged people to have reported higher dollar savings per hour both for car work and for work on the house. Since the middle aged also were more likely to do work on the house, where average savings per hour were higher, than on the car or on growing food, their average return per hour on all their do-it-yourself work could have been expected to be still higher relatively to people younger or older than themselves. (We did not ask about hours spent growing or preserving food, and so we do not have an estimate of savings per hour for that activity.)

Appendix Tables A10.9-A10.11 show the effect of hourly earnings and age on do-it-yourself activities in 1971 and 1978. Earnings are not net of taxes

Table 10.7

IMPLIED HOURLY EARNINGS WORKING ON CAR OR HOME,
BY HOURLY PAID EARNINGS OF HEAD (NET OF MARGINAL TAX RATE), 1978

Hourly Earnings Net of Marginal Tax Rate[a]	Cars			House			Number of Cases
	$	Hours	$/Hour	$	Hours	$/Hour	
$2.50	69	8.6	8.02	130	20.4	6.37	2086
2.50-3.49	110	13.8	7.97	23.9	22.8	10.48	1021
3.50-4.49	253	18.4	8.32	351	30.8	11.30	912
4.50-5.49	142	16.0	8.87	397	29.7	13.37	777
5.50-6.49	150	17.5	8.57	466	4.82	9.67	622
6.50-7.49	254	27.5	8.80	558	65.5	8.52	415
7.50-8.49	129	14.2	9.08	611	44.6	13.70	235
8.50-9.49	230	25.9	8.88	693	50.8	13.64	123
9.50-10.49	83	7.0	11.86	429	61.5	6.98	50
10.50 or more	128	15.6	8.21	629	42.2	14.91	132
All	118	13.9	8.40	327	32.4	10.09	6373

[a]Hourly earnings X (1-Marginal Tax Rate). Marginal tax rate is estimated on the basis of taxable income, without exemptions, assuming standard deduction at low incomes, average itemized deductions of 16% above that.

Table 10.8

1978 IMPLIED HOURLY EARNINGS FROM
DO-IT-YOURSELF SAVINGS, BY AGE

Age in 1979	Cars			House			Number of Cases
	$	Hours	$/Hour	$	Hours	$/Hour	
18–24	163	21.8	7.48	194	27.8	6.98	947
25–34	176	18.1	9.72	502	41.9	11.98	1,995
35–44	138	14.5	9.52	531	42.1	12.61	928
45–54	142	19.2	7.40	349	31.6	9.54	923
55–64	73	8.5	8.59	252	37.6	6.70	770
65–74	27	5.3	5.09	112	11.9	9.41	539
75 or more	5	1.0	5.00	43	7.8	5.51	271
All ages	118	13.9	8.49	327	32.4	10.09	6,373

because we did not code the marginal tax rate in 1971. Interestingly enough, the average saving reported per hour worked on cars remained stable ($8.54 in 1971 and $8.49 in 1978), while the reported saving per hour working on the house rose (from $6.19 to $10.09). This implies that the small change in the question might have led to the omission of a lot of small or simple repairs, exaggerating the reduction in do-it-yourself activities around the house. On the other hand, the increase between 1971 and 1978 in the proportion of wives who worked may well have led to a reduction in do-it-yourself hours and an increased willingness to hire others. There have also been many new products which cut the time but increase the money cost of and perhaps the payoff for do-it-yourself activities.

Overall, then, we found differential changes in reported hours spent but a general increase in amounts saved per household on each of the three do-it-yourself activities: 70 percent on cars, and 30 percent both on houses and on food.

FACTORS ASSOCIATED WITH DO-IT-YOURSELF ACTIVITIES

In general we can say that young people fix their own cars, the middle aged fix their houses, and older people grow or preserve food, although the age differences are most substantial in the case of cars.

Figures 10.2 and 10.3, for 1971 and 1978, show the dramatically different age patterns for the three types of activity. Together they reveal that the proportions who reported some such activity increased in all age groups for work on car repairs and growing food and decreased for reports of work on the home, despite the increase in the proportion owning a home. The differences in age pattern were even more striking when we restricted the sample to married homeowners, who tended to own a car as well (Figures 10.4 and 10.5).

Looking now at the four groups--married homeowners, married non-homeowners, all unmarried men, and all unmarried women--the most dramatic differences were in whether they reported doing any work on their cars. Figures 10.6 and 10.7 show the static differences and indicate a dramatic increase in reports by unmarried women under age 45 of doing some work on their own cars.

We do not present the age patterns among the four demographic groups for work on the house, since we have already shown the pattern for married homeowners in discussing time trends, and the non-homeowners were much less likely to do such work and did not differ by age, sex, or marital status.

Figure 10.8 shows the percentages growing or preserving food in 1978. Here, the married non-homeowners reversed the age pattern, doing less and less after age 45, while all the other groups were more likely to report growing or preserving food until they were 65. Many of the unmarried women in the older age groups were homeowners, of course, and there were not many unmarried men in the older age groups.

Figure 10.9 shows the estimated total amounts saved in 1978 by all three types of do-it-yourself activity combined, illustrating once again the dramatic differences between married homeowners, married non-homeowners, unmarried men and unmarried women.

Given these effects of homeownership, marital status, sex, and age on do-it-yourself activities--and given the fact that many of the other usual explanatory factors like income, education, and children present were highly correlated with one or more of these factors--any investigation of these other effects requires a multivariate analysis. When we tried such analyses using as dependent variables whether work was done on the house, or on the house plus car, or hours spent on the house, these other "explanatory" variables mostly dropped to insignificance. Appendix Tables A10.12 and A10.14 give the estimated gross and net explanatory power of a set of categorical predictors, illustrating that once allowance was made for homeownership, sex, and age, little else mattered.

336

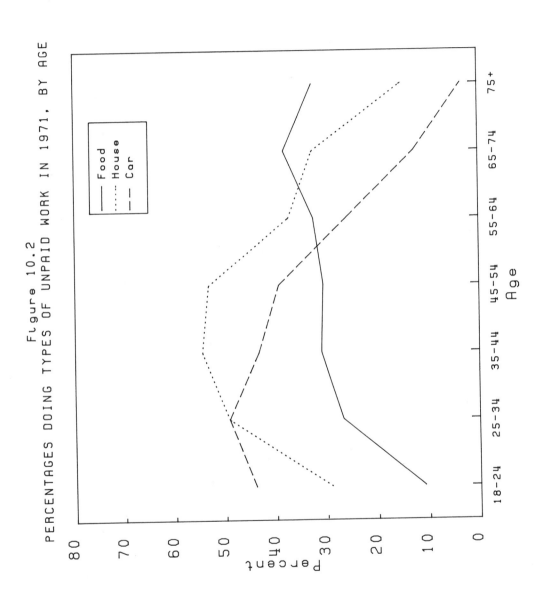

Figure 10.2

PERCENTAGES DOING TYPES OF UNPAID WORK IN 1971, BY AGE

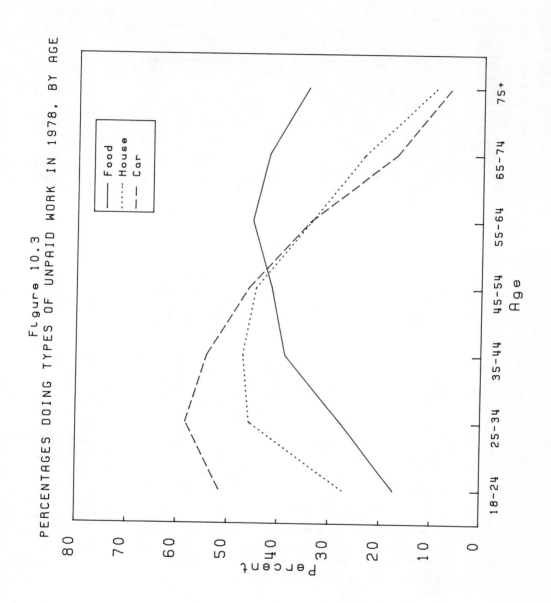

Figure 10.3

PERCENTAGES DOING TYPES OF UNPAID WORK IN 1978, BY AGE

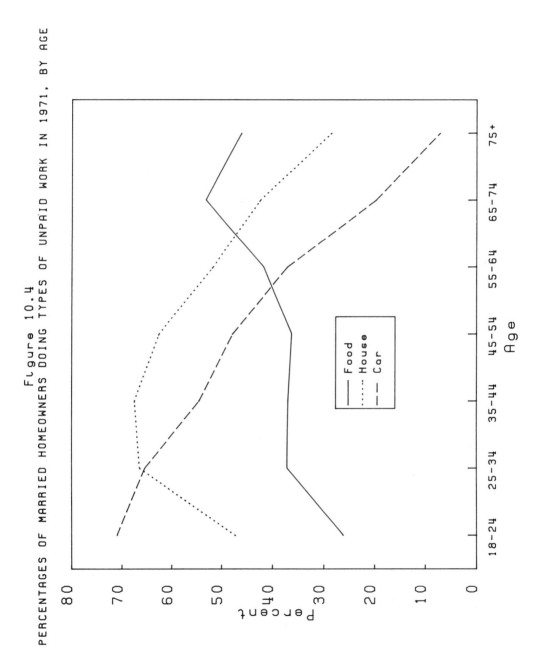

Figure 10.4
PERCENTAGES OF MARRIED HOMEOWNERS DOING TYPES OF UNPAID WORK IN 1971, BY AGE

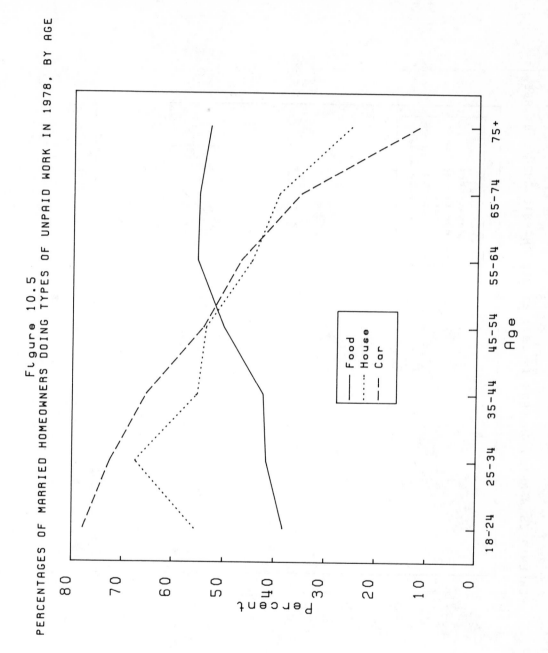

PERCENTAGES OF MARRIED HOMEOWNERS DOING TYPES OF UNPAID WORK IN 1978, BY AGE

Figure 10.5

340

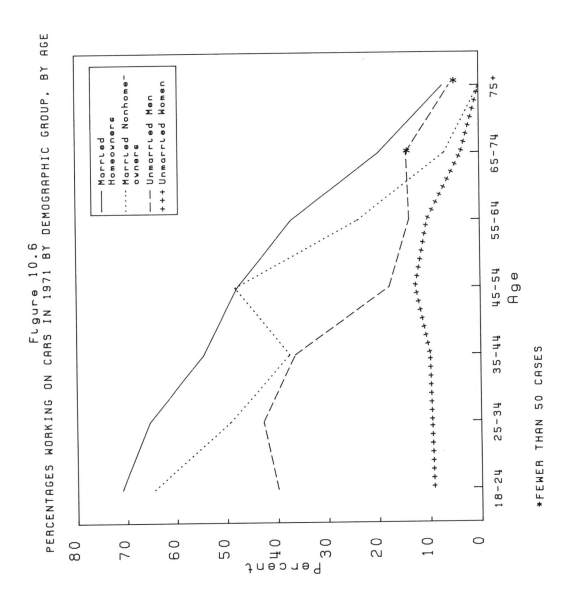

Figure 10.6
PERCENTAGES WORKING ON CARS IN 1971 BY DEMOGRAPHIC GROUP, BY AGE

*FEWER THAN 50 CASES

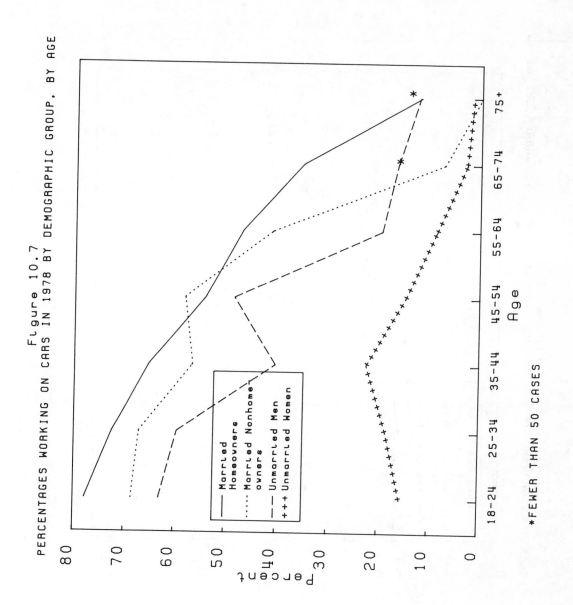

Figure 10.7

PERCENTAGES WORKING ON CARS IN 1978 BY DEMOGRAPHIC GROUP, BY AGE

*FEWER THAN 50 CASES

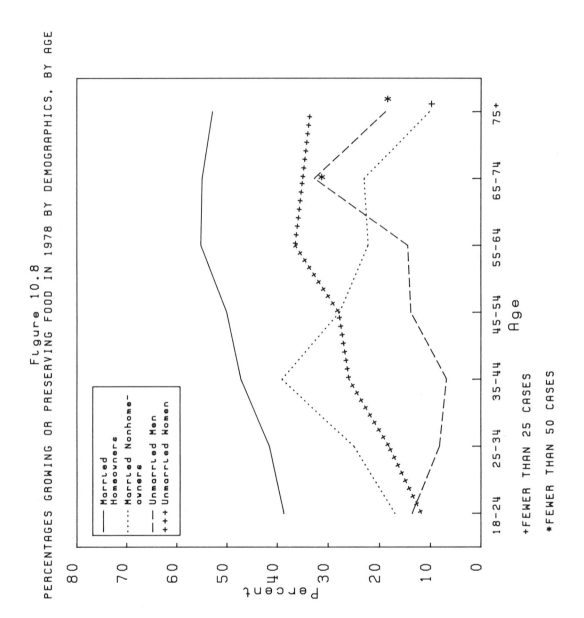

Figure 10.8

PERCENTAGES GROWING OR PRESERVING FOOD IN 1978 BY DEMOGRAPHICS, BY AGE

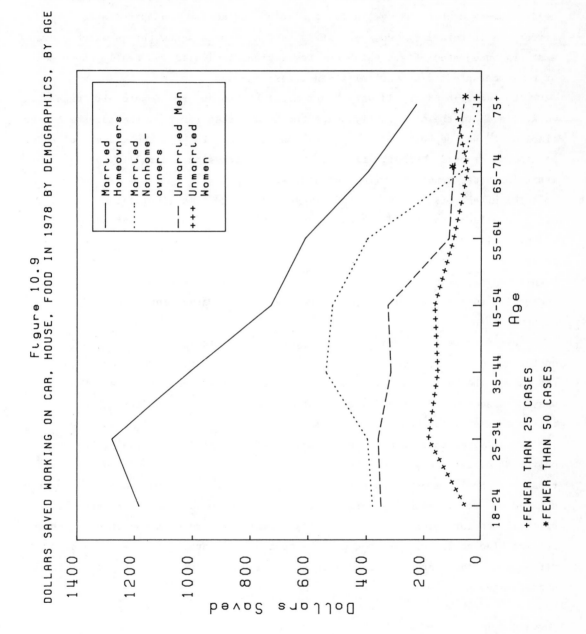

DOLLARS SAVED WORKING ON CAR, HOUSE, FOOD IN 1978 BY DEMOGRAPHICS, BY AGE

Figure 10.9

+FEWER THAN 25 CASES

*FEWER THAN 50 CASES

Whether we looked at the probability of working on the house, or the house and car, or the total amount saved working on house-car-food, once we took account of marital status, whether the wife worked, the sex of single household heads, homeownership and age, nothing else accounted for any appreciable difference in behavior. However, it is useful to note a few things which showed a strong unadjusted effect which our regressions indicated was really the effect of homeownership and/or marital status, sex, and age.

The family head's paid work hours might be thought to compete with unpaid work. In fact, the more family hours the head worked for pay, the more he or she also worked on the house or car or on growing food. But all the effects of paid work hours dropped to insignificance when the regression controlled for age, sex, marital status, a working wife, and homeownership.

The effect of the family head's wage rate, net of marginal income taxes, might have been considered ambiguous, reflecting both a money opportunity cost and an indicator of a higher tax incentive to work at unpaid and hence untaxed activities. We found, in fact, that--up to about $7.50 an hour--people with higher wages did more unpaid work. This "effect" again disappeared when the regression took account of age, sex, marital status, a working wife, and homeownership.

Having extra people in the family might have left less time for unpaid work on the house or car unless they were old enough to do some of the work. In fact, the larger the household (at least up to five persons) the more likely the family was to do some work on the house and/or car; but, again, this "effect" withered in the multivariate analysis.

Finally, occupation appeared to account for something by itself, but the only real difference was between those not in the labor force and the rest, with those not earning money also doing less unpaid work. There was some tendency for skilled and semi-skilled workers to be more likely to work on their cars, for clerical and for sales workers to be less likely to work on house or car, and for skilled blue-collar workers to save the most on all three activities. And these differences, too, largely appeared to be spurious effects reflecting other things such as age.

SUMMARY

Do-it-yourself activity was important to many of our sample families, but we found no evidence that it has increased dramatically over time. Work on cars was done largely by young people; work on houses was mainly done by the middle-aged;

and work growing food was done mostly by older people. The trends were consistent with our expectations, with apparent increases in do-it-yourself activities except in the proportions working on their homes.

There was an appreciable increase in the proportion of young female household heads who reported working on their own cars. And there were increases in the reported amounts saved per hour, even though those amounts were not correlated with hourly dollar earnings or with the marginal tax rate. The decline in the proportions of people working on their homes appears to fit a declining trend since 1964 and may reflect a relatively young or recently renovated stock of houses, people's ability to pay to have the work done, or a scarcity of enough free time to accomplish this kind of work.

References

Gronau, Reuben. "Home Production--a Forgotten Industry." Review of Economics and Statistics 62 (August 1980): 408-16.

Morgan, James; Sirageldin, Ismail; and Baerwaldt, Nancy. Productive Americans, A Study of How Individuals Contribute to Economic Progress. Ann Arbor, Michigan: Institute for Social Research, 1966.

Appendix to Chapter 10

Table A10.1

AMOUNTS SAVED BY FIXING CAR IN 1971 AND 1978
(For 3,323 Households with the same head 1971-1979.)

Dollars Saved In 1971[a]	Dollars Saved in 1978						
	None	1-99	100-199	200-499	500+		All
None	48.7	5.3	2.9	3.3	1.4		61.3
1-99	7.0	4.4	3.0	2.5	1.1		19.9
100-199	2.3	1.8	1.9	2.9	1.0		9.9
200-499	1.7	1.2	1.2	2.9	1.6		8.5
500+	0.2	0.3	0.3	1.0	0.6		2.4
All	59.9	13.0	9.2	12.6	5.3		100.0

Tau-B = .48

[a]At 1978 prices, i.e., increased 61%.

Table A10.2

AMOUNTS SAVED BY WORKING ON HOUSE IN 1971 AND 1978
(For 3,323 households with the same head 1971-1979.)

Dollars Saved In 1971[a]	Dollars Saved in 1978					All
	None	1-99	100-199	200-499	500+	
0	40.4	1.6	2.0	4.1	5.0	53.2
1-99	7.3	0.8	0.7	1.7	1.7	12.2
100-199	4.2	0.6	0.6	1.7	1.4	8.5
200-499	6.4	0.3	0.8	2.9	3.4	13.8
500+	4.4	0.7	0.6	2.2	4.5	12.3
All	62.7	4.0	4.7	12.7	15.9	100.0

Tau-B = .29

[a] At 1978 prices, i.e., increased 61%.

Table A10.3

AMOUNTS SAVED BY GROWING OWN FOOD IN 1971 AND 1978
(For 3,323 households with the same head 1971-1979.)

Dollars Saved In 1971[a]	Dollars Saved In 1978						
	None	1-99	100-199	200-499	500+		All
0	52.4	10.4	2.4	2.0	0.9		68.2
1-99	8.4	5.4	2.7	2.3	0.5		19.3
100-199	1.2	0.9	1.0	1.2	0.7		4.9
200-499	1.1	0.8	0.5	2.0	0.9		5.4
500+	0.1	0.2	0.3	0.4	1.2		2.2
All	63.3	17.7	6.9	7.9	4.2		100.0

Tau-B = .44

[a] In 1978 prices, i.e., increased 61%.

Table A10.4

HOURS SPENT FIXING CAR IN 1971 AND 1978
(For 3,323 households with the same head 1971-1979.)

Hours spent In 1971			Hours Spent in 1978				
	None	1-99	100-199	200-499	500+		All
None	48.5	12.2	0.4	0.1	0.1		61.3
1-99	11.5	24.0	1.0	0.3	0.0		36.8
100-199	0.1	1.1	0.1	0.1	0.0		1.5
200-499	0.1	0.2	0.0	0.1	0.0		0.4
500+	0.0	0.1	0.0	0.0	0.0		0.1
All	60.2	37.5	1.5	0.5	0.2		100.0

Tau-B = .48

Table A10.5

HOURS SPENT FIXING HOUSE IN 1971 AND 1978
(For 3,323 households with the same head 1971-1979.)

Hours Spent In 1971			Hours Spent in 1978				
	0	1-99	100-199	200-499	500+		All
0	32.7	5.1	1.1	0.3	0.1		39.5
1-99	26.5	16.5	3.1	1.9	0.8		48.8
100-199	2.0	3.0	0.8	0.5	0.2		6.5
200-499	1.7	1.3	0.4	0.3	0.0		3.7
500+	0.6	0.7	0.1	0.1	0.0		1.5
All	63.6	26.7	5.4	3.1	1.2		100.0

Tau-B =.32

Table A10.6

STABILITY AND CHANGE IN COMPLEXITY OF
CAR REPAIR--1971 VERSUS 1978
(For 3,323 households with the same head 1971-1979.)

1971	1978						
	None	Little or No Skill	Some Skill	Some Amount	Much Skill	Complex Repairs	All
None	48.5	3.0	5.7	2.9	1.2	0.2	61.4
Little or no skill	1.7	0.9	0.9	0.4	0.1	0.0	4.1
Some skill	5.3	1.7	5.4	3.1	1.0	0.2	16.7
Fair amount	2.7	1.3	3.3	2.8	0.9	0.2	11.1
Much skill	1.2	0.3	1.5	1.5	0.8	0.2	5.5
Complex repairs	0.2	0.1	0.1	0.2	0.2	0.1	1.0
All	59.6	7.4	16.9	11.0	4.2	0.9	100.0

Tau-B = .39

Transition Proportions

None to none	48.5
Same complexity	10.0
More complex	7.1
Less complex	10.2
None to some	13.1
Some to none	11.1
	100.0

Table A10.7

HOURS SPENT IN DO-IT-YOURSELF CAR AND
HOUSE REPAIR, BY AGE GROUPS AND AGE COHORTS

Age	Hours on Car			Hours on House		
		1978			1978	
	1971	1979 Age	1972 Age	1971	1979 Age	1972 Age
18–24	12	22	22	35	28	29
25–34	11	18	15	58	42	47
35–44	9	14	16	56	42	37
45–54	10	19	17	45	37	40
55–64	5	9	7	29	38	29
65–74	2	5	4	20	12	13
75+	0	1	1	7	8	2
All ages	8	14	14	41	32	32
Eta^2 (Adj.)	.021	.013	.013	.015	.006	.006

Table A10.8

DOLLARS SAVED WITH DO-IT-YOURSELF WORK, BY AGE GROUP AND AGE COHORTS

(For 5,080 families in 1972, 6,373 families in 1979.)

Age	$ Car 1971ᵃ 1972 Age	$ Car 1978 1979 Age	$ Car 1972 1972 Age	$ House 1971ᵃ 1972 Age	$ House 1978 1979 Age	$ House 1972 1972 Age	$ Food 1971ᵃ 1972 Age	$ Food 1978 1979 Age	$ Food 1972 1972 Age
18-24	$104	$163	$185	$127	$194	$297	$15	$22	$25
25-34	96	176	154	352	502	535	34	45	58
35-44	88	137	151	390	531	478	61	77	91
45-54	79	141	113	304	349	348	58	80	63
55-64	42	73	60	162	252	182	62	89	102
65-74	14	27	15	143	112	99	50	59	52
75+	3	5	3	36	43	11	34	69	69
All ages	69	118	118	252	327	327	47	62	62
Eta² (Adj.)	.042	.031	.032	.019	.019	.018	.011	.009	.011

ᵃIn 1978 dollars.

Table A10.9

1971 IMPLIED HOURLY EARNINGS BY PAID
HOURLY EARNINGS, FOR DO-IT-YOURSELF WORK

Hourly Earnings (in 1978$)	Cars			House		
	$ Saved	Hours Spent	Implied Earnings	$ Saved	Hours Spent	Implied Earnings
<2.50	29	3.7	$7.84	113	20.6	$5.49
2.50-3.49	69	8.5	8.12	123	22.2	5.54
3.50-4.49	87	10.2	8.53	177	34.2	50.03
4.50-5.49	91	10.2	9102	14.6	32.0	4.56
5.50-6.49	86	10.8	7.96	210	40.5	5.19
6.50-7.49	94	9.8	9.59	296	49.2	6.02
7.50-8.49	84	10.1	8.32	449	76.0	5.91
8.50-9.49	97	10.5	9.24	459	69.3	6.62
9.50-10.49	85	12.6	6.75	483	58.6	8.24
10.50+	74	7.6	9.74	503	642	7.83
All	69	8.1	8.54	252	40.7	6.19

Table A10.10

1978 IMPLIED HOURLY EARNINGS BY PAID HOURLY
EARNINGS FOR DO-IT-YOURSELF WORK

Hourly Earnings	Cars			House		
	$ Saved	Hours	$/Hour	$ Saved	Hours	$/Hour
<$2.50	58	7.4	$7.84	114	15.1	$7.55
2.50-3.49	114	13.5	8.44	153	35.3	4.33
3.50-4.49	119	15.4	7.72	236	25.8	9.15
4.50-5.49	135	16.2	8.33	392	30.4	12.89
5.50-6.49	174	20.6	8.45	425	31.3	13.58
6.50-7.49	161	16.1	10.00	362	30.8	11.75
7.50-8.49	156	17.9	8.72	431	56.6	7.61
8.50-9.49	146	17.8	8.20	588	48.0	12.25
9.50-10.49	125	17.9	6.98	474	40.1	11.82
10.50+	152	15.9	9.56	629	56.1	11.21
All	118	13.9	8.49	327	32.4	10.09

Table A10.11

IMPLIED HOURLY EARNINGS
FOR DO-IT-YOURSELF WORK IN 1971 BY AGE
(In 1978 dollars.)

Age in 1972	Car			House			N
	$	Hours	$/Hour	$	Hours	$/Hour	
18-24	104	12.5	8.32	127	34.6	3.67	780
25-34	96	11.1	8.65	352	58.4	6.02	1,101
35-44	88	9.3	9.46	390	55.6	7.01	957
45-54	79	9.6	8.23	305	44.7	6.82	928
55-64	42	5.3	7.92	162	29.2	5.54	707
65-74	14	2.0	7.00	143	20.5	6.98	384
75+	341	0.3	9.75	36	6.7	5.37	202
All ages	69	8.1	8.54	252	40.7	6.19	6,373

Table A10.12

GROSS AND NET EXPLANATORY POWER OF SETS
OF CATEGORICAL PREDICTORS FOR WORK ON HOUSE

	Number of Cate-gories	Whether Worked on Home		Hours, If Worked[a]	
		Gross (Eta^2)	Net $(Beta^2)$	Gross (Eta^2)	Net $(Beta^2)$
Sex, married, wife employed[b]	4	.075	.017	.010	.008
Own home	3	.060	.048	.017	.017
Age	7	.058	.031	.008	.018
Education	10	.024	.005	.004	.002
Wage rate net of marginal tax	8	.051	.003	.008	.003
Distance to city	5	.003	.003	.007	.006
Number in family	5	.052	.003	.002	.005
Occupation	7	.048	.002	.003	.005
Head's paid work hours	5	.047	.001	.002	.001
Number of cases		6,373		135	
Y		35%		89 hours	
R^2 (Adj.)		.150		.209	

[a] Hours truncated at 2000.
[b] Single men, single women, married, with wife employed, wife not employed.

Table A10.13

GROSS AND NET EXPLANATORY POWER OF SETS OF
CATEGORICAL PREDICTORS FOR WORK ON HOUSE OR CAR

	Number of Cate-gories	Whether Worked on House or Car		Hours, If Worked[a]	
		Gross (Eta^2)	Net $(Beta^2)$	Gross (Eta^2)	Net $(Beta^2)$
Sex, married, wife employed[b]	4	.169	.073	.003	.3
Own home	3	.028	.018	.006	.008
Age	7	.133	.067	.002	.008
Education	10	.042	.005	.003	.003
Wage rate net of marginal tax	8	.094	.002	.004	.003
Distance to city	5	.011	.001	.002	.001
Number in family	5	.075	.002	.002	.002
Occupation	7	.128	.008	.002	.002
Head's paid work hours	5	.118	.001	.001	.001
Number of cases		6,373		3,426	
Mean		55%		84 hours	
R^2 (Adj.)		.269		.009	

[a] Hours truncated at 2000.
[b] Single men, single women, married with employed wife, wife not employed.

Table A10.14

GROSS AND NET EXPLANATORY POWER OF SETS OF CATEGORICAL PREDICTORS
FOR TOTAL DOLLARS REPORTED SAVED WORKING ON HOUSE, CAR, OR FOOD

| | Number of Categories | Total Saved Working on House, Car, Food[a] | |
		Gross (Eta^2)	Net ($Beta^2$)
Sex, married, wife employed[b]	4	.058	.014
Own home	3	.039	.028
Age	7	.033	.024
Education	10	.009	.003
Wage rate Marginal tax	8	.032	.002
Distance to city	5	.010	.003
Number in family	5	.036	.002
Occupation	7	.040	.004
Head's paid work hours	5	.033	.013
Number of cases		6373	
Mean		$489	
R^2 (Adj.)		.108	

[a] Amount truncated at $10,000
[b] Single men, single women, married with employed wife, wife not employed.

Chapter 11

RACE/SEX DIFFERENCES IN THE EFFECTS
OF BACKGROUND ON ACHIEVEMENT

Linda P. Datcher

INTRODUCTION

Many individuals interested in eliminating the effects of discrimination on different groups in the society argue that equal opportunity policies should be the sole instruments used. Their challenges to affirmative action programs rest on the premise that, in trying to redress past violations of the rights of particular groups in the society, these programs operate by subverting the rights of others. Given that the violation of individual rights is generally regarded as illegitimate in this society, it is incumbent on the advocates of affirmative action to present arguments in support of partially abrogating the rights of majority individuals to compensate for past injustices.

One such argument is that, because the current economic status of individuals depends in part on the past status of their parents and their community, equal opportunity alone is not enough to generate equal outcomes within a reasonable time period. As a result, the achievement of equal opportunity in itself would be a hollow victory since the deleterious consequences of past discrimination would not have been eliminated and might persist long into the future. This argument is strengthened by the observation that not only do particular minority groups face disadvantages in the levels of background characteristics, but they also have lower prospects than majority individuals for benefiting from gains made by previous generations.

This latter contention has been questioned in recent work on racial differences in the impact of family background by Featherman and Hauser (1976b and 1976c), Freeman (1978), and others. The prevailing notions developed from this work are that the impact of family background on older blacks is small and substantially lower than that for older whites and that, over time, the effect on blacks has become so much closer to that of whites that background influences on young blacks are roughly equal in size to those of young whites. These notions suggest a number of conclusions. First, while in the past black families in more favorable socioeconomic circumstances were much less able than white families to pass that advantage on to their children, the mechanisms by which families affect their children's later status now function as well for blacks as for whites. Second, while in the past much progress toward eliminating racial income differentials could be made by identifying the sources of the lower effectiveness of black families, such efforts would be much less fruitful in the current environment. Third, the future for black Americans is now much brighter because progress made by one generation will significantly aid the advancement of the next.

This chapter presents evidence that challenges the prevailing notions about racial differences in the effect of family background. Analysis of the effects of background for both men and women is based on re-examination of the findings of past studies of men combined with new data from the Panel Study of Income Dynamics. The findings show that the case for racial convergence in male background effects has been largely overstated and, furthermore, that important distinctions between the sources of earnings inequality by race and by sex arise from considering the role of family background.

This chapter first describes a theoretical analysis of differential family background effects on education and earnings, then tests the resulting hypotheses, and finally compares these results to those of similar studies.

Theoretical Framework

Economic theory explaining the effects of background on achievement examines the decisions made by parents as well as those made by their offspring. Parents choose alternative levels of the family's consumption now and investment in raising their children's income as adults in order to maximize the family's utility subject to the budget constraint. If investment in children is a normal good, then the theory of consumer behavior implies that lower prices, higher income, and higher preferences for investment raise the amount parents make in their children.

Children, at maturity, decide on the total amount of investment in various activities, such as schooling, they will obtain. Assuming that children act to maximize their earnings power, the optimal choice occurs at the level where the marginal benefit equals the marginal cost. The marginal benefit is measured by the rate of return on each additional dollar of investment, while marginal costs consist of all financing expenses.

In Figure 11.1, the optimal choice of investment for an individual with marginal cost curve MC_1 and marginal rate of return curve MR_1 is S_1. More favorable family backgrounds are represented in this diagram by downward shifts in the marginal cost curve from MC_1 to MC_2 and MC_3. The greater the slopes of the demand and supply curves, the smaller is the effect of a given shift in marginal cost on the level of investment. Similarly, the smaller the shift in marginal cost with a given change in the background, the smaller is the effect of background on investment. This implies that race, sex, and age differences in the effects of family background on later achievement can be determined by examining differences in the slopes of supply and demand curves for human capital and in the sensitivity of marginal cost to background changes.

For simplicity, the analysis has been divided into three steps. The first examines the implications on the model for investment in schooling, assuming that the slope of the marginal rate of return curve is the same for all individuals. The second specifies the modifications required given variations in the marginal rate of return curve slopes. The third discusses the relevance of the model in examining the effects of background on earnings.

If the slope of the marginal rate of return curve for schooling were the same for all individuals, the following implications could be drawn. First, we might expect to find greater effects of family background on schooling among white families than among black families. Because of discrimination against blacks in such areas as housing, education, credit, and job opportunities, the amount of resources for investment available to black families with a given set of characteristics are smaller than those available to identical white families. This handicap would show up not only as smaller monetary sums that could be used for investment, but also as higher prices to be paid for a given acquisition, say, attending high schools of a particular caliber. Discrimination against blacks could be represented by a steeper marginal cost curve and by a smaller downward shift in marginal cost with a given improvement in family background compared to white families. Figure 11.1, which assumes no racial difference in the slope of the marginal cost curves, shows that if the father's education increased by one year, the downward shift in marginal costs for blacks would be from MC_1 to MC_2 while for whites it would be from MC_1 to MC_3. As a result, the change in family background would generate smaller additional investment in education for blacks than for whites. This difference would be further accentuated by the added factor of racial differences in the slopes of the marginal cost curves.

362

Figure 11.1

INVESTMENT IN MARKET-VALUED CHARACTERISTICS WITH
DIFFERENT MARGINAL COSTS AND IDENTICAL RATES OF RETURN

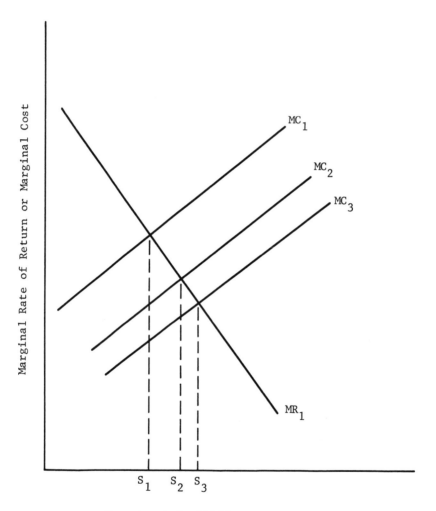

Investment in Children

A second implication of the model is that the effect of background for women should be smaller than the effect for men. Sex-based differences in parents' preferences for investing in their children would have the same effect on women that racial discrimination has on blacks. A third prediction of the model results from the amelioration of discriminatory practices over time and changing societal norms about the roles of women. Given these advancements, we should expect to find that race and sex differences in the effect of background would decline between young and old age cohorts. While black parental preferences for investing in their daughters may reflect the traditionally higher labor force activity of black women, white parental preferences may be undergoing more dramatic change in recent years as white women close the gap between their own and black women's level of labor market attachment. This implies the fourth prediction of the model, that the male/female gap should be smaller for blacks than whites and should decline faster for whites.

These four hypotheses were derived assuming that the slope of the marginal rate of return curve was the same for all individuals. As indicated above, taking into account differences in marginal return across these groups requires some modifications. A major source of differences in the marginal rate of return curves is the existence of compulsory attendance laws for schooling below the college level. By 1918, all states and territories except Alaska had enacted compulsory school attendance laws. By 1935 the maximum compulsory age in almost all states was 16 years. Thus, in the absence of exemptions and nonenforcement of the law, the marginal rate of return curve would be completely inelastic over the range 0-10 years of schooling. There is evidence, however, that, because of exemptions and nonenforcement, the elasticity of the marginal rate of return curve has varied considerably across race groups over time.

Table 11.1 shows the fraction of individuals in different race, sex, and age groups who attended school at various times during the period from 1920 through 1960. For younger individuals the marginal rate of return curve appears to be highly inelastic, given that almost all individuals aged 7-15 attended school in 1950 and 1960. For older individuals, however, liberal granting of work permits to those under 16 and nonenforcement of the attendance laws appear to have generated much more elasticity in the marginal return curves for blacks than for whites. This suggests that the black marginal rates of return curves were initially relatively elastic and became more inelastic compared to whites over time. They were almost completely inelastic over the 9-10 years of schooling range for individuals educated after 1960.

Table 11.1

SCHOOL ATTENDANCE BY YEARS OF AGE, RACE, AND SEX 1920-1960

Race and Age	Males					Females				
	1920	1930	1940	1950	1960	1920	1930	1940	1950	1960
Black 7-13 years	75.5	86.4	90.5	93.7	95.9	77.6	88.2	91.8	94.3	96.2
White 7-13 years	92.4	96.5	95.4	95.8	97.7	92.6	97.7	95.7	96.1	97.9
Difference	16.9	10.1	4.9	2.1	1.8	15.0	9.5	3.9	1.8	1.7
Black 14-15 years	65.0	75.3	80.1	88.5	90.1	72.3	80.7	84.3	89.6	90.1
White 14-15 years	81.4	90.8	90.9	93.7	94.8	81.6	90.1	91.1	93.6	94.5
Difference	16.4	15.5	10.8	5.2	4.7	9.3	9.4	6.8	4.0	4.4
Black 16-17 years	34.1	42.7	51.5	63.8	73.9	43.8	49.7	56.6	65.2	73.3
White 16-17 years	41.0	58.4	70.3	75.7	82.4	45.7	59.3	70.9	76.2	81.1
Difference	6.9	15.7	19.2	11.9	8.5	1.9	9.6	14.3	11.0	8.1

Source: U.S. Bureau of the Census, Fifteenth Census of the U.S., 1930, Population, Vol. II, General Report, Statistics by Subjects, p. 1096; U.S. Bureau of the Census, U.S. Census of Population, 1960, Vol. I. Characteristics of the Population, part I, U.S. Summary 1-372; U.S. Bureau of the Census, U.S. Census of Population, 1950, Vol. II, Characteristics of the Population, Part 1, U.S. Summary, 1-206.

Figure 11.2 presents an example of how these considerations may affect expectations about the effects of background on years of pre-college schooling. The curve for marginal rate of return for older and young whites and for younger blacks is represented by MR_1 which is almost vertical, while the marginal rate of return curve for older blacks, MR_2, is substantially more elastic. Even though a given change in background (e.g., one more year of father's education) shifts the marginal cost curve further to the right for whites than for blacks (MC_1 to MC_3 and MC_1 to MC_2, respectively), the effect of the change in background is greater for older blacks than for whites. Furthermore, the effects for young blacks and young whites are much closer than those for the older cohort.

Although this is a simple example, it shows that, if relative slopes of the marginal rate of return curves are more important determinants of the effects of family background on years of pre-college education than differential shifts in marginal costs, then the effects of background by race for years of pre-college schooling may differ from the effects for years of college education. Because of relatively more elastic marginal rates of return curves, the effects of background may be larger for older blacks than for older whites. Because the marginal rates of return have become more inelastic over time, the effects of background among persons with no college education may be smaller for young persons than for older persons. Given that school enrollment figures are virtually identical by sex within racial groups, the first of these conclusions apply only to the comparisons between blacks and whites. However, the second should hold for all groups.

The final step in this analysis is to examine the relevance of the supply/demand model for looking at race/sex/age differences in the effects of background on earnings. Explicit hypotheses are much more difficult to formulate than the education hypotheses presented above. There is little agreement on the relative roles of differential marginal returns and costs for acquiring other market-valued characteristics such as on-the-job training, information about job opportunities, or particular attitudes or behavioral norms. Therefore, developing a theory about the net effect of family background on earnings through a combination of these other avenues is beyond the scope of this study.

In addition, the lack of measures of the various aspects of ability would complicate estimation problems. For example, holding constant levels of market-valued characteristics, the omission of ability would bias the effect of background on earnings downwards for all race/sex groups, with the largest impact occurring for white males. In Figure 11.3 it is assumed that all high ability

366

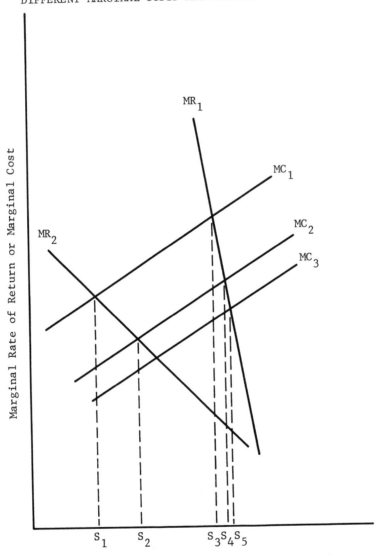

Figure 11.2

INVESTMENT IN MARKET-VALUED CHARACTERISTICS WITH
DIFFERENT MARGINAL COSTS AND DIFFERENT RATES OF RETURN

Marginal Rate of Return or Marginal Cost

MR_1

MC_1

MC_2

MR_2

MC_3

S_1 S_2 $S_3S_4S_5$

Investment in Schooling

individuals have marginal return curve MR_{HA} and marginal cost curve MC_{HA}, so that they invest I*. A given improvement in family background shifts the marginal cost for white men to MC_{WM}. The same improvement in family background shifts the marginal cost for blacks and women a lesser amount to MC_{BW} because of discrimination and sex-based parental preferences, as mentioned earlier. Only white men with lower abilities (i.e., those corresponding to MR_{LA}^1) would invest I* with marginal cost MC_{WM}. Similarly, only lower ability blacks and women (i.e., those corresponding to MR_{LA}^2) would invest I*. This means that, holding market-valued characteristics constant, ability and background are negatively correlated and generate a downward bias in background effects. Because the shift in the marginal cost was greater for white men than for the other groups, the resulting downward bias and negative correlation between background and ability are also larger for them.

Holding family background constant, the omission of measures of ability would also produce an overestimate of the effects of education on earnings and, thus, of the indirect effect of background on earnings through education. The size of the upward bias would be higher for blacks and women than for white men. To illustrate this result, assume that the marginal return for all low ability individuals is MR_{LA} in Figure 11.4 and that there is no variation in background characteristics within race/sex groups. The resulting marginal cost curve for white men is ABC, while the corresponding curve for blacks and women is ABD. The slope of ABD is greater than that of ABC at levels of investment larger than I_1 because of the discrimination and sex-based differences in parental preferences mentioned earlier. Holding background constant, an increase in investment to I_2 for white men occurs only if there is a corresponding increase in ability to that level represented by the MR_{HA}^W. The same increase in investment for blacks and women occurs only if there is a larger jump in ability, i.e., to that represented by the MR_{HA}^B. This implies a positive correlation between education and ability, holding background constant, that will lead to an overestimate of the rate of return on an additional unit of investment independent of ability. Furthermore, because the slope of the marginal cost curve is higher for blacks and women, the size of that bias will be greater for these groups.

The final remaining problem that arises in trying to make explicit hypotheses about the differences in the effects of family background on earnings for different race/sex/age groups occurs because these effects may vary according to the individual's position in the life cycle. In such instances, a cross-section comparison of younger and older age cohorts may not accurately reflect

368

Figure 11.3

MARGINAL RATES OF RETURN AND MARGINAL COSTS CORRESPONDING TO
THE SAME LEVEL OF INVESTMENT IN MARKET-VALUED CHARACTERISTICS

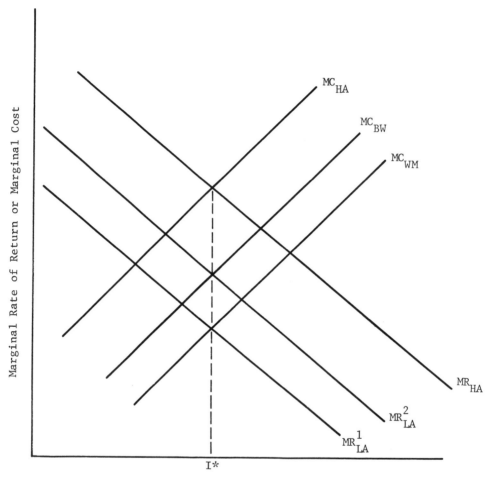

Investment in Market-Valued Characteristics

Figure 11.4

MARGINAL RATES OF RETURN AND MARGINAL COSTS CORRESPONDING TO THE
SAME CHANGE IN LEVEL OF INVESTMENT IN MARKET-VALUED CHARACTERISTICS

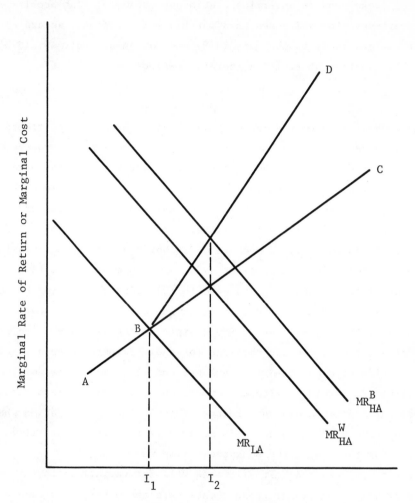

Investment in Market-Valued Characteristics

time-series changes in the impact of background on earnings. One example of such
life-cycle effects arises because of on-the-job training. If individuals with
favorable backgrounds invest more in on-the-job training, holding education
constant, and if training is costly in terms of earnings foregone, then the
effects of background on current earnings of the younger cohort will understate
the importance of background in determining earnings capacity. The problem is
likely to be more severe for white men than for black men because, according to
the findings of various analysts (Lazear, 1979, and Duncan and Hoffman, 1978),
blacks acquire less on-the-job training, ceteris paribus.

DATA

The Panel Study of Income Dynamics data was used to examine the effects of
family background by race, sex, and age. Regressions on college attendance,
years of pre-college education for those with 12 or fewer years of education,
total years of education, and ln hourly earnings were run for a sample of black
and white men and women ages 25-64 in 1978. The family background factors
included in the regressions were years of father's education, years of mother's
education, number of siblings, and a measure of father's occupation. This latter
variable was constructed using the Panel Study's eight-category occupation code
for father's occupation. Values were assigned to individuals according to Census
figures for the logarithm of median male earnings in their fathers' race/
occupational category in various years. For example, blacks 25-34 years old were
assigned 1970 values of black median earnings for their fathers' occupational
group, 35-44 year olds were assigned 1960 values, and 45-64 year olds were
assigned 1950 values. Therefore, with the exception of men 55-64 years old, the
assigned figures correspond to median earnings of the father's occupation when
the son was 17-26 years old. Although this measure is far from ideal, it does
control partially for the age of the son at the time when his father's
occupational status was measured. It allows as well for variations in the
economic status of one occupational group relative to the others over time and by
race. In addition to the family background variables, indicators of rural or
southern origin were also included in the regressions.

Mean values of the background variables, nominal years of education, and
hourly earnings for different race/sex/age groups are given in Table 11.2. This
table shows that there were only small sex differences in background within age/
race groups. It also shows that differences between blacks and whites in
earnings and years of schooling narrowed between the older cohort and the younger

cohort for both men and women. However, it does not appear that blacks' gains in background characteristics were as dramatic or as uniform as those of whites. Even though there was a substantial drop in the racial disparity in father's education from the older male cohort to the younger male cohort and a narrowing of differences in type of place of origin for both women and men, the other background characteristics for blacks showed little or no improvement relative to whites. In fact, in some cases, the relative status of blacks deteriorated.

EMPIRICAL RESULTS

In this section we first discuss the outcome of the education analysis and then describe the estimated effects of background on earnings. A sampling of the results for education are presented in Tables 11.3-11.5. To indicate how background effects on education have changed over time by race, these tables report results of a logit analysis of college attendance, regressions on years of pre-college schooling, and regressions on total years of education, separately for black and white women and men ages 25-34 and 45-64 in 1978. The logit coefficients were estimated by a maximum likelihood procedure in which the dependent variable, the probability of college attendance (p) is affected by the explanatory variables (X_i) according to the following equation $p=1/(1-\exp\Sigma\beta_i X_i)$.

In general, the coefficients in Tables 11.3-11.5 have the expected signs and are significant at the 5-percent level. Since the parental education variables serve as proxies for parents' preferences for investing time and effort in their children (see Hill and Stafford, 1978) and as indicators of parents' economic status, they should have the observed positive coefficients. The larger coefficients on mother's education for daughters compared to sons reflects the greater role it plays in daughters' achievements. Father's occupational status and number of siblings are correlated with the level of resources available to invest in any given child so that, as was generally found, the former should be positive and the latter negative. Finally, regional and community differences in tastes for and knowledge of available opportunities (Sewell, Haller, and Strauss, 1957; Sewell, 1964) might be expected to produce the observed negative coefficients for rural or southern origin.

Although comparing the sizes of the coefficients across the various groups would provide some indication of relative family background effects, the fact that the explanatory variables are expressed in different units makes such simple comparisons between variables rather limited in value. A more useful approach is taken in Tables 11.3-11.5. The line of numbers below the standard errors of each

Table 11.2

MEAN VALUES OF EDUCATION, EARNINGS, AND BACKGROUND
VARIABLES BY AGE, RACE, AND SEX

| | Blacks | | | | Whites | | | | Black/White Differences | | | |
| | Men | | Women | | Men | | Women | | Men | | Women | |
	25-34	45-64	25-34	45-64	25-34	45-64	25-34	45-64	25-34	45-64	25-34	45-64
Father's education	9.22	6.51	8.11	7.33	10.16	8.11	10.80	8.02	-0.94	-1.60	-2.69	-0.69
Mother's education	9.94	7.35	9.50	7.41	11.09	8.59	11.46	8.63	-1.15	-1.24	-1.96	-1.22
Father's occupation	8.33	7.49	8.38	7.47	8.90	8.27	8.91	8.17	-0.57	-0.78	-0.53	-0.70
Number of siblings	4.31	4.94	4.33	5.01	3.09	3.75	2.92	3.67	1.22	1.19	1.41	1.34
Rural origin	0.26	0.45	0.17	0.44	0.21	0.31	0.16	0.27	0.05	0.14	0.01	0.17
Southern origin	0.65	0.86	0.68	0.71	0.27	0.23	0.24	0.23	0.38	0.63	0.44	0.48
Years of education	12.55	9.11	12.52	10.87	13.77	12.29	13.32	12.21	-1.22	-3.18	-0.91	-1.34
1967 hourly earnings		2.37		1.42		3.69		2.04		-1.32		-0.62
1977 hourly earnings	5.00	5.92	3.95	3.30	5.93	7.39	4.21	4.12	-.93	-1.47	-0.26	-0.82

Table 11.3

EFFECTS OF BACKGROUND FACTORS ON COLLEGE ATTENDANCE

Race, Sex, and Age in 1978	Total	Effects of Family Background Factors				Effects of Type of Place of Origin	
		Father's Education	Mother's Education	Father's Occupation	Number of Siblings	Rural origin	Southern Origin
Black men 25-34 (N=181)	1.5050	.2846* (.0756) .9996	-.0550 (.0714)	1.0233* (.5157) .5054	.0163 (.0844)	.9838 (.5923)	.1717 (.4261)
Black women 25-34 (N=244)	1.1986	.0104 (.0548)	-.2246* (.0700) .7843	-.3270 (.4683)	-.1723* (.0599) .4143	-.1143O+ (.6533)	-1.1208* (.3273)
White men 25-34 (N=494)	2.0791	.1228* (.0371) .4313	.1712* (.0434) .5978	1.6347* (.4579) .8074	-.1009* (.0490) .2426	-.0738 (.2893)	-.3166* (.2389)
White women 25-34 (N=544)	1.8545	.1790* (.0377) .6287	.1834* (.0443) .6404	1.1853* (.4713) .5854	-.0621 (.0507)	-.2205 (.3094)	-.2595 (.2496)
Black men 45-65 (N=151)	1.0329	.1709 (.1092) .6003	-.0594 (.1294)	.8758 (.8481) .4326	.7971* (.2596)	1.2860 (.8518)	-.2293 (1.1568)
Black women 45-64 (N=263)	.9196	.1553* (.0658) .5455	.0502 (.0693)	.7206 (.5840)	-.1556+ (.0846) .3741	1.5450* (.6243)	-1.6198* (.4460)
White men 45-64 (N=574)	2.0869	.1924* (.0374) .6758	.0833* (.0347) .2909	1.0716* (.3887) .5293	-.2458* (.0482) .5909	.0640 (.3047)	-.0218 (.2612)
White women 45-64 (N=575)	1.4116	.1329* (.0367) .4668	.1452* (.0386) .5070	.1442 (.1930)	.1821* (.0528) .4378	-.3089 (.3844)	-.3282 (.2850)

The symbols * and + indicate that the coefficient is significant at the 5 percent and 10 percent levels, respectively. Numbers in the parentheses are standard errors. Numbers below the standard error indicate the effect on college attendance if each explanatory variable were changed by one standard deviation in the direction of raising years of education.

[1] The coefficient of number of siblings for older black men was significant with the wrong sign. The other coefficient estimates for older black men are not very precise because only 7 out of the sample of 151 attended college. Estimates of the effect of a one standard deviation change in father's education and occupation were included even though these were insignificant to provide an estimate of the likely effect if more data had been available.

Table 11.4

EFFECTS OF BACKGROUND FACTORS ON YEARS OF PRE-COLLEGE EDUCATION FOR INDIVIDUALS WHO DID NOT ATTEND COLLEGE

Race, Sex, and Age in 1978	Total	Effects of Family Background Factors				Effects of Type of Place of Origin	
		Father's Education	Mother's Education	Father's occupation	Number of Siblings	Rural Origin	Southern Origin
Black men 25-34 (N=140, R²=.21)	.2255	.0642+ (.0363) .2255	.0482 (.0425)	.2658 (.2590)	-.0384 (.0371)	-.4973+ (.2887)	.2509 (.2245)
Black women 25-34 (N=197, R²=.16)	.5846	.0290 (.0339)	.1674* (.0400) .5846	.0678 (.2256)	-.0491 (.0351)	.1719 (.2414)	-.4192+ (.2270)
White men 25-34 (N=223, R²=.14)	.3305	.0941* (.0312) .3305	.0246 (.0318)	.1254 (.3708)	-.0444 (.0342)	-.0441 (.1994)	0.3951* (.1798)
White women 25-34 (N=326, R²=.18)	.5579	.0406* (.0205) .1426	.0540* (.0208) .1886	.1171 (.2488)	-.0943* (.0253) .2267	.0883 (.1494)	-.4584* (.1236)
Black men 45-64 (N=144, R²=.35)	2.1862	.2026* (.0882) .7116	.2775* (.0750) .9690	1.0238+ (.5299) .5056	-.0670 (.1046)	-.4253 (.5487)	-2.6692* (.7914)
Black women 45-64 (N=230, R²=.31)	.7871	-.0069 (.0408)	.2254* (.0374) .7871	-.0832 (.3020)	-.0203 (.0497)	-.9242* (.3258)	-.9190* (.3113)
White men 45-64 (N=381, R²=.22)	1.3953	.0707 (.0446)	.1370* (.0367) .4784	1.0078* (.3901) .4978	-.1743* (.0437) .4191	.1166 (.2797)	-.8808* (.2481)
White women 45-64 (N=445, R²=.12)	.7210	.0573+ (.0323) .2013	.1169* (.0288) .4082	.2257+ (.1230) .1115	-.0531 (.0339)	-.2307 (.1924)	-.3340+ (.1913)

For explanation of symbols and numbers, see Table 11.3.

Table 11.5

EFFECTS OF BACKGROUND FACTORS ON TOTAL YEARS OF SCHOOLING

Race, Sex, and Age in 1978	Total	Effects of Family Background Factors				Effects of Type of Place of Origin	
		Father's Education	Mother's Education	Father's Occupation	Number of Siblings	Rural origin	Southern Origin
Black men 25-34 (N=181, R^2=.24)	1.0858	.2104* (.0478) .7390	.0084 (.0529)	.7021* (.3549) .3468	-.0216 (.0586)	.6023 (.3768)	.0097 (.3144)
Black women 25-34 (N=244, R^2=.30)	1.4226	.0377 (.0432)	.3240* (.0512) 1.1314	.0533 (.3277)	-.1211* (.0447) .2912	-.1502 (.3698)	.4580+ (.2686)
White men 25-34 (N=494, R^2=.24)	2.3174	.1673* (.0366) .5876	.1238* (.0411) .4323	1.9369* (.4539) .9566	-.1418* (.0484) .3409	.1235 (.2901)	-.3255 (.2351)
White women 25-34 (N=544, R^2=.29)	1.7783	.1583* (.0315) .5560	.1878* (.0346) .6561	.6724+ (.4048) .3321	-.0932* (.0426) .2241	-.0859 (.2607)	-.5088 (.2101)
Black men 45-64 (N=151, R^2=.40)	2.4253	.3207* (.0858) 1.1264	.1946* (.0848) .6795	1.2540* (.6115) .6194	.1194 (.1112)	-.7311 (.6229)	-2.8032* (.8297)
Black women 45-64 (N=263, R^2=.32)	1.2065	.1396* (.0478) .4903	.2051* (.0457) .7162	.1030 (.3827)	-.0451 (.0584)	-.4138 (.3916)	-1.7810* (.3230)
White men 45-64 (N=574, R^2=.31)	2.9898	.1791* (.0435) .6291	.1844* (.0415) .6439	1.8365* (.4518) .9070	-.3368* (.0522) .8098	.3904 (.3473)	-.6311* (.2984)
White women 45-64 (N=575, R^2=.53)	1.4977	.1299* (.0352) .4563	.1990* (.0338) .6949	.2319 (.1500)	-.1441* (.0415) .3465	-.0130 (.2341)	-.4951* (.2325)

For explanation of symbols and numbers, see Table 11.3.

variable shows the effect on years of education if each statistically significant[1] family background variable were changed by one standard deviation in the direction of raising years of education.[2] These numbers were then used to compare background effects across the different demographic groups.

The sizes of the effects of family background in the logit analysis of college attendance shown in Table 11.3 generally conform to the college education predictions of the theoretical model presented earlier. In most cases, these effects were higher for men than for women and higher for whites than for blacks. Furthermore, although background effects were significantly higher for white men than for black men in both age cohorts, the large differences between older black and white men were substantially eroded over time, indicating rising efficacy of black backgrounds. Differences by sex in the impact of black family background were not statistically different from zero for either the younger or older cohorts. However, the increasing importance of family background for white women substantially narrowed the gap between them and white men.

These findings support the view that the initially large differential shifts in the marginal cost curve with a given change in family background between black and white men and between white women and white men lessened over time due to the amelioration of discriminatory practices and changing perceptions of sex-roles. It is important to note, however, that, although the convergence between white women and white men makes the difference within the younger cohort not statistically different from zero, convergence between black and white men still leaves a significant gap in the impact of family background. As predicted, the male/female gap was smaller among older blacks than among older whites, and the difference declined faster for whites. However, contrary to the expectations of the model, there was no substantial change in the total effect of family background between the older cohort of black women and the younger one.

As mentioned earlier, if expectations about the impact of family background on elementary and secondary school education rest more on differences in the elasticities of the marginal rate of return curves across race/sex/age groups than on differential shifts in marginal costs, then these expectations about the impact of family background should differ considerably from those for college

---

[1] At the 10 percent level.

[2] Common standard deviation levels were used across each race/age/sex group. These levels were calculated using a sample of all men ages 25-64 with earnings in 1977.

attendance. Table 11.4 presents the results of regressing years of pre-college schooling on background characteristics for individuals who did not attend college.[3] For men, these results show that the effect of family background was initially highest for older black men and that there was a sharp decline between the younger and older cohorts of both races. The effect for white men dropped by 1.07 years from 1.40 to 0.33. The effect for blacks started at 2.19 and fell much farther, 1.96 years to 0.23. Although the effect was significantly higher for older black men than for older white men, differences between the younger cohort were small. The findings for the older men and the changes over time to the younger cohort were consistent with evidence presented earlier showing highly inelastic marginal return curves for individuals educated after 1960, moderately more elastic curves for older whites, and substantially more elastic curves for older blacks. The results for women supported this story less strongly. Although the effects of family background for younger women were small and virtually equal for both races, there was no evidence of noticeably larger effects for older black women.

Table 11.5 combines the effects of family background on college attendance and years of pre-college schooling in looking at the impact on total years of education. It shows that, as in the case of college attendance, family background effects within age cohorts were generally higher for men than for women and for whites than for blacks. However, unlike the analysis for college attendance, the effects of family background fell over time for men but rose for women. Although the drop was largest for black men, the changes for black and white women were identical. As a result, the gap in background effects between white men and white women fell from 1.49 to 0.54 years, while the racial difference between males rose from 0.56 years of schooling for the older cohort to 1.23 years for the younger one. The effects of mother's education, father's occupation, and number of siblings were significantly greater for young white men than for young black men, while only the coefficient on number of sibling was significantly greater for older whites compared to older blacks. It appears, therefore, that changes in the impact of family background on total years of schooling over time are dominated by the changes in years of pre-college education rather than by the changes in college attendance.

---

[3]The selectivity bias created by censoring the sample will be corrected later using the Heckman (1978) technique.

Before turning to the earnings regressions, it should be noted that the education findings do not control for the effects of offspring's ability on levels of schooling. Assuming that parents' ability is correlated with children's ability and that, because of discrimination, high ability black parents are less able to achieve improved socioeconomic status than high ability white parents, then the correlation between offspring ability and family background would be lower for blacks than whites. It would also be lower if current ability is influenced by environment in earlier periods and if black parents with a given set of characteristics are less able than white parents with the same characteristics to provide a high quality environment. In these cases, the upward bias in family background would be higher for whites than for blacks. The size of the bias for both groups is likely to be small, however, given the indirect nature of the linkage between family background and the offspring's ability.

Table 11.6 presents the results from the earnings regressions. The dependent variable for the younger cohort was ln 1977 hourly earnings, while the dependent variable for the older cohort was ln 1967 hourly earnings. These two earnings variables were used to reduce the extent to which life-cycle changes were confounded with time-series shifts in background effects. In addition to the background characteristics, the dependent variables were regressed on years of schooling, years post schooling, experience and its squared term, whether married, whether had children under 18, whether union member, average county wage of low-skilled workers and the county unemployment rate. These last variables were included, in part, to control for differences in local economic conditions in 1967 and 1977. As in the case of the education regressions, the numbers below the standard errors indicate the effects of a one standard deviation change in the significant background variables.[4]

The sizes of the standard deviation changes suggest that the effects of family background on earnings, independent of education, have declined over time for all groups except black women. While such changes would raise hourly earnings of older white women and men by 9 and 16 percent, respectively, there were no significant background effects for either young white men or women. The one standard deviation change would raise earnings of older black men by 31 percent. However, the effects for young black men were relatively small.

---

[4]See footnotes 1 and 2.

Table 11.6

EFFECTS OF BACKGROUND FACTORS ON LN HOURLY EARNINGS

Race, Sex and Age in 1978	Total	Effects of Family Background Factors				Effects of Type of Place of Origin		Own Education
		Father's Education	Mother's Education	Father's Occupation	Number of Siblings	Rural Origin	Southern Origin	
Black men 25–34 (N=170, R²=.41)	.0625	-.0031 (.0138) .0903	.0171 (.0148)	.0067 (.0930)	-.0260+ (.0151) .0625	.0383 (.1028)	-.0181 (.1061)	.0797* (.0283)
Black women 25–34 (N=188, R²=.28)	.0903	.0257+ (.0137) .0903	.0097 (.0172)	-.0373 (.1091)	-.0078 (.0124)	-.0616 (.1168)	.0221 (.0773)	.1178* (.0253)
White men 25–34 (N=478, R²=.18)	0	.0052 (.0079)	-.0027 (.0086)	.1284 (.0966)	-.0054 (.0102)	-.0741 (.0621)	.0481 (.0517)	.0631* (.0120)
White women 25–34 (N=373, R²=.23)	0	.0042 (.0114)	-.0164 (.0125)	.1093 (.1440)	-.0008 (.0150)	-.0484 (.0882)	.0958 (.0755)	.0972* (.0187)
Black men 45–64 (N=172, R²=.54)	.3126	.0334* (.0123) .1173	.0235* (.0114) .0821	-.1063 (.0794)	-.0471* (.0152) .1132	.0013 (.0831)	-.1300 (.1115)	.0001 (.0154)
Black women 45–64 (N=16, R²=-.38)	0	-.0078 (.0147)	-.0014 (.0145)	-.1337 (.1210)	.0388+ (.0160)	-.2526* (.1117)	-.0283 (.1032)	.1059* (.0213)
White men 45–64 (N=611, R²=.34)	.1556	.0183* (.0068) .0643	-.0015 (.0063)	.1138+ (.0673) .0562	-.0146+ (.0082) .0351	-.1559* (.0520)	.0039 (.0451)	.0629* (.0078)
White women 45–64 (N=291, R²=.26)	.0899	.0256+ (.0129) .0899	-.0155 (.0132)	.0139 (.0474)	-.0001 (.0159)	-.2962* (.0860)	-.0377 (.0871)	.0880* (.0177)

For explanation of symbols and numbers, see Table 11.3.

Within age cohorts, background effects were generally greater for blacks then for whites, but there was no distinct pattern of sex differences.

The coefficient estimates of the effects of years of schooling indicate that, except among older men, there were no significant differences in the rates of return to schooling within sex groups. Black and white women exhibited rates that varied from .09 to .12. Young men and older white men had much lower rates, in the .06 to .08 range. A frequent explanation for the tiny schooling coefficients found for older black men is the lower quality of education received per year of attendance. The findings of substantially higher rates of return for older black women who presumably attended the same schools suggest that this interpretation should be re-examined. However, a full discussion of such issues would require another paper. As mentioned earlier, the earnings results should be qualified by noting the potential biases that may arise. The omission of measures of ability biases downward estimates of background effects, especially for white men. It also biases upwards estimates of the returns to schooling, particularly in the case of women and blacks.

The discussion so far has largely centered around comparing the effects of a one standard deviation change in family background measures across groups to uncover differences in the efficacy of background. In looking at race/sex differences in background effects, it would also be useful to examine the role of differences in the level of family background on achievement. Here, the first important point to note is that, as Table 11.2 demonstrated earlier, there are no sex differences in the mean levels of background characteristics within race groups in the same age cohort. This means that, although blacks may be disadvantaged relative to white men in terms of parental resources, no such disparity exists between white men and white women.

In order to indicate the extent to which the poorer backgrounds of blacks contribute to lower average levels of schooling, Table 11.7 presents estimates of the nominal and percentage changes in the gap between schooling level of blacks in the various sex and age groups and that of white males in the same cohort. It assumes that blacks retained the estimated black coefficients for total years of schooling shown in Table 11.5 but acquired mean levels of the background characteristics of white males in their age cohort. Table 11.7 shows that for young blacks and older black men, differences in the levels of family background between black and whites accounted for approximately 50 percent of the difference in years of schooling. For older black women, an even greater gap remained after equating their backgrounds to those of older white men.

Table 11.7

ESTIMATES OF THE CONTRIBUTION OF DIFFERENCES IN BACKGROUND CHARACTERISTICS
TO DIFFERENCES IN YEARS OF SCHOOLING COMPLETED BY BLACKS AND WHITES

	Total Difference	Hypothetical Effects of Changing Black Means to White Means				
		Total	Father's Education	Mother's Education	Father's Occupation	Number of Siblings
Men						
25–34	1.22 (100%)	.60 (49%)	.20 (16%)		.40 (33%)	
45–64	3.18 (100%)	1.73 (54%)	.51 (16%)	.24 (8%)	.98 (31%)	
Women						
25–34	1.25 (100%)	.67 (54%)		.52 (42%)		.15 (12%)
45–64	1.42 (100%)	.35 (25%)	.11 (8%)	.24 (17%)		

Table 11.8 presents figures showing the total impact on average ln hourly earnings of blacks relative to white males in the same age cohort of changing mean black family backgrounds to mean white backgrounds. The direct impact is computed by multiplying the significant background coefficients in the black earnings regressions by the difference in backgrounds between blacks in a given sex/age group and white males in the same age group. The indirect impact through education is determined by multiplying the returns to schooling by the effect on total years of schooling of the mean background differences for the significant variables in the total years of education regressions of Table 11.5. Table 11.8 shows that the importance of differences in the level of family background between blacks and whites in contributing to earnings disparity has risen over time. While only 4 percent and 31 percent, of the gaps between older white men and older black women and men respectively, were due to background differences, the figures for young black women and men were 35 percent and 46 percent respectively. Much of this change is due to rising background influences operating indirectly through educational attainment. Although differences in background characteristics can account for much of the greater earnings of white men, large gaps between blacks and whites still remain to be explained by other phenomena.

Table 11.8

ESTIMATES OF THE CONTRIBUTION OF DIFFERENCES IN BACKGROUND CHARACTERISTICS
TO DIFFERENCES IN AVERAGE LN HOURLY EARNINGS OF BLACKS AND WHITES

Hypothetical Effects of Changing Black Means to
White Male Means in Same Age Cohort

	Total Differ- ence	Total Effects	Direct Effects					Indirect Effects				
			Total	Father's Educa- tion	Mother's Educa- tion	Father's Occupa- tion	Number of Siblings	Total	Father's Educa- tion	Mother's Educa- tion	Father's Occupa- tion	Number of Siblings
Black men												
25–34	.172 (100%)	.080 (46%)	.032 (18%)				.032	.048 (28%)	.061		.032	
45–64	.446 (100%)	.138 (31%)	.138 (31%)	.053	.029		.056	0				
Black women												
25–34	.407 (100%)	.144 (35%)	.053 (13%)	.053				.091 (22%)		.061		
45–64	.956 (100%)	.038 (4%)	0					.038 (4%)	.012	.026		.030

Summarizing the education and earning findings from this analysis reveals a number of important points. In the case of the effects of background on schooling, the evidence has shown that the outcomes varied depending on the level of schooling considered. Within both age cohorts, the effects of background on college attendance were highest for white men. Although there was little change in background effects over time for black women compared to white men, there was considerable convergence between white men and black men and between white men and white women due to rising background effects for black men and white women. In fact, no significant differences remained between white men and women in the younger cohort. Our examination of years of pre-college schooling, on the other hand, showed that within both age cohorts the effects of background were highest for black men. Instead of increasing over time, background effects fell for all groups and were uniformly small for the younger cohort. The largest declines occurred for black men.

The findings for total years of schooling reflected a combination of these results. Although background effects within each age cohort were highest for white men, they fell over time for men and rose for women. These changes resulted in convergence in background effects between white men and women and divergence between white men and black men. Differences in mean levels of background characteristics accounted for up to 50 percent of the difference in educational attainment between blacks and whites.

The combination of (1) divergence in background effects on total years of schooling between black men and white men versus convergence between white women and white men, (2) elimination of significant differences in background effects on college attendance between white men and white women versus a large remaining gap between white men and black men, and (3) the large contribution of mean background differences to the disparity between average black educational attainment and average white male achievement compared with no mean background differences between white men and white women all suggest that important distinctions should be made between the sources of inequality by sex and by race. At least in the case of years of schooling, white women have access to as much parental resources as do white men, while blacks both have fewer resource units available and benefit less from each unit.

The earnings results shows that the effects of family background independent of schooling and the other measured market-valued characteristics were, in general, highest for blacks but declined over time for all groups except black women. These effects were uniformly small for all individuals in the younger cohort. The contribution of differences in levels of background characteristics to the earnings disparities between blacks and whites has risen substantially over time. However, it still accounts for at most 50 percent of the earnings differentials.

COMPARISONS WITH OTHER STUDIES

In order to judge the generality of these results, it would be useful to compare them to some of the other studies of race/sex differences in the effects of background over time. Table 11.9 shows the results of calculating the effects of a one-standard deviation change in family background characteristics on total years of schooling using the Panel Study data as well as samples of individuals examined by other analysts. The results are shown by years of birth, sex, race, and data source. Ignoring the figures for black men in the 1907-1916 and 1907-1921 cohorts reveals a number of findings that are consistent across studies. First, background effects for men have declined over time, while those for women have remained relatively stable. Second, the decline in background effects has been larger for black men than for white men. Third, the net effect of the differential changes in background influences over time is convergence between women and white men and divergence between white men and black men.

The findings of convergence between women and white men are supported by other studies which report the estimated standardized coefficients of background variables in various educational attainment analyses. Using a sample from a 1970 followup study to a 1955 survey conducted by the Educational Testing Service, Alexander and Eckland (1974) showed that a canonically weighted measure of family background variables has a greater effect on years of schooling for women than for men. Similarly, Sewell and Shah (1968) demonstrated that, in their samples from a 1965 followup study on 1957 high school seniors in Wisconsin schools, family background is as important for college attendance and graduation for women as for men.

As Table 11.9 shows, one of the main differences across studies is that, compared to the Panel Study findings, the NLS data show the background effects for young black men to be much closer to those of young white men. Some of this discrepancy may be explained by the omission of number of siblings from the NLS regression analysis. Number of siblings is an important variable affecting the resources available for each child within a family. However, this information was not collected by the NLS survey, and Table 11.5 suggests that its omission would lower the effect of family background for young whites relative to young

Table 11.9

COMPARISON OF BACKGROUND EFFECTS ON TOTAL YEARS OF SCHOOLING ACROSS STUDIES

Years of Birth, Date Education Observed	Panel Study of Income Dynamics[1]				CPS Occupational Changes in a Generation Survey (OCG)[2]				National Longitudinal Studies (NLS)[3]			
	Black Men	White Men	Black Women	White Women	Black Men	White Men	All Men	All Women	Black Men	White Men	Black Women	White Women
1914-1933(1978)	2.43[4]	2.99	1.21	1.50								
1944-1953(1978)	1.09	2.32	1.42	1.78								
1907-1916(1973)					0.81	2.49						
1917-1926(1973)					2.04	2.16						
1927-1936(1973)					1.74	2.17						
1937-1946(1973)					1.53	2.04						
1898-1942(1962)							1.91	1.37				
1909-1953(1973)							1.71	1.37				
1907-1921(1969)									1.01	1.86		
1923-1937(1967)											1.46	1.56
1942-1952(1969)									1.35	1.63		

[1] These figures are taken from column 1 of Table 11.5.
[2] These figures for black men and white men are based on the analysis of Hauser and Featherman (1976a). The figures for all men and all women are based on the analysis of Hauser and Featherman (1976b).
[3] The numbers for black men and white men are derived from Freeman (1978). The numbers for black women and white women are derived from Treiman and Terrell (1975).
[4] Common standard deviation units were used for all calculations within a given study.

blacks and therefore overstate the extent of the similarity between young men. In addition, since many young men in the sample had not completed their schooling as of the survey date, the NLS analysis used expected years of education as the dependent variable for those still in school. If, as seems likely, expected schooling is less correlated with background than actual schooling when completed and if 17-27 year old whites are less likely to have finished their education than 17-27 year old blacks, then the effects of background would be biased downwards for whites relative to blacks.

A second discrepancy across studies is the relative size of background effects for the oldest black men compared to the oldest white men. In the two examples that include black men born before World War I, their background effects are extremely small compared to whites. For those born afterwards, the patterns of initially roughly comparable effects and divergence over time mentioned earlier appear to hold. This seemingly abrupt change may be related to widening opportunities for blacks brought about by World War I and the subsequent migrations to urban areas and to the North.

Table 11.10 shows the results across studies of calculating the effects of a one-standard deviation change in family background characteristics on earnings, holding education and market-valued characteristics constant.[5] Here there is much less consistency than there was in the case of the education analyses. With the exception of older women, background effects within a given age/sex cohort are greater for blacks than for whites according to the Panel Study data, but the opposite was true with the OCG data. Furthermore, differences between men and women are generally smaller with the Panel Study sample. Since background effects for older white women operate exclusively through father's education according to the latter study, the omission of this variable in the OCG analysis may account for some of this discrepancy. Similarly, the omission of mother's education may explain part of the differential sizes of background effects for black and white men.

---

[5]Although Freeman (1978) also analyzed differences between blacks and whites in the effects of background on earnings, he did not report the coefficients and standard errors of the background variables holding education constant. Consequently, the Freeman results could not be used for comparison purposes in Table 11.10.

Table 11.10

COMPARISON OF BACKGROUND EFFECTS ON EARNINGS ACROSS STUDIES

	Panel Study of Income Dynamics[1]				CPS Occupational Changes in a Generation Surveys (OCG)[2]			
	Black Men	White Men	Black Women	White Women	Black Men	White Men	All Men	All Women
1914-1933(1967)	.312	.155	0	0				
1944-1953(1977)	.063	0	.090	0				
1898-1942(1961)					0	.064	845	137
1909-1953(1972)					0	.018	878	0

[1]These figures are taken from column 1 of Table 11.6.
[2]The figures for black and white men are based on regressions on log annual earnings from Hauser and Featherman (1978). The figures for all men and women are based on regressions on annual earnings from Hauser and Featherman (1976). The estimates for white men born 1909-1953 include only the effects of significant variables with the correct sign. The regression coefficient for father's education was significant and negative, while the coefficient of number of siblings was significant and positive.

SUMMARY AND POLICY IMPLICATIONS

The prevailing notions about racial differences in the impact of family background on achievement stress findings of convergence over time. The analysis in this paper suggests that these prevailing notions about convergence are overstated and somewhat simplistic. In the case of acquisition of schooling, the theoretical and empirical models support the view that the effects of family background vary by level of education. Background effects for college attendance were greater for men than for women and greater for whites than for blacks. However, there has been substantial convergence across race and sex groups due to rising effects over time for black men and white women. Although the gap between young black men and young white men was still statistically greater than zero, the difference between young white women and young white men was insignificant. In the case of pre-college schooling, background effects were highest for older black men and second highest for older white men. Male background effects, which have fallen considerably over time, were small and roughly equal for young blacks and whites. Finally, the findings for schooling show that background effects were highest for white men and that over time they have been converging between women and white men but diverging between black men and white men. The effects of background on earnings operate principally through influencing years of schooling. Direct impacts independent of education and other market-valued characteristics have declined over time and now appear to be relatively small for all groups.

These findings suggest that a complete understanding of the causes of racial earnings differentials requires more than an explanation of disparities in returns to the market-valued characteristics emphasized by Becker's "taste for discrimination" approach. This implies that important sources of the difference are accessible only by considering a more historical, dynamic view of the acquisition of market-valued characteristics through intergenerational links. This theory assumes that blacks suffer not only because of poorer background, but also because they are less effective at translating parental economic gains into offspring achievement. This finding points to an important distinction between sources of earnings differentials by race and by sex. Although both blacks and white women are subject to labor market discrimination, white women do not carry the additional burdens imposed by poorer family backgrounds and, in the case of total years of education achieved, by lower background effectiveness. This suggests that educational policies that provide equal opportunity alone are much more likely to be sufficient for white women than for blacks.[6]

References

Alexander, Karl, and Eckland, Bruce. "Sex Differences in the Educational Attainment Process." American Sociological Review (1974): 668-682.

Becker, Gary. Human Capital. New York: Columbia University Press, 1975.

Becker, Gary, and Tomes, Nigel. "An Equilibrium Theory of the Distribution of Income and Intergenerational Mobility." Journal of Political Economy (1979): 1153-89.

Ben-Porath, Yoram. "The Production of Human Capital and Life-Cycle Earnings." Journal of Political Economy (1967): 352-65.

Duncan, Greg, and Hoffman, Saul. "Training and Earnings." In Five Thousand American Families--Patterns of Economic Progress, Vol. VI, edited by Greg J. Duncan and James N. Morgan. Ann Arbor, Michigan: Institute for Social Research, The University of Michigan, 1978.

Featherman, David L., and Hauser, Robert M. "Sexual Inequalities and Socioeconomic Achievement in the U.S., 1962-1973." American Sociological Review (1976a): 462-483.

Featherman, David L., and Hauser, Robert M. "Changes in the Socioeconomic Stratification of the Races, 1962-1973." American Journal of Sociology (1976b): 621-51.

Featherman, David L., and Hauser, Robert M. "Equality of Schooling: Trends and Prospects." Sociology of Education (1976c): 99-120.

Featherman, David L., and Hauser, Robert. Opportunity and Change. New York: Academic Press, 1978.

Freeman, Richard. "Changes in the Labor Market for Black Americans, 1948- 972." Brookings Papers on Economic Activity 1 (1973): 67-131.

Freeman, Richard. "Black Economic Progress After 1964: Who Has Gained and Why?" Paper presented at National Bureau of Economic Research Conference on Low-Income Labor Markets, June 9-10, 1978.

Heckman, James. "Sample Selection Bias As A Specification Error." Econometrica (1979): 30-55

Hill, C. Russell, and Stafford, Frank. "Allocation of Time to Preschool Children and Educational Opportunity." The Journal of Human Resources (1978): 323-41.

---

[6]This analysis does not address questions of differences in type and quality of education between white men and women. Affirmative action programs may be required to equalize women and men along these dimensions.

Lazear, Edward. "The Narrowing of Black-White Wage Differentials is Illusory." *American Economic Review* (1979): 553-64.

Loury, Glenn. "Essays in the Theory of the Distribution of Income." Ph.D. Dissertation, Massachusetts Institute of Technology, 1976.

Sewell, William. "Community of Residence and College Plans." *American Sociological Review* (1964): 24-38.

Sewell, William; Haller, A.O.; and Strauss, M.A. "Social Status and Educational and Occupational Aspirations." *American Sociological Review* (1957): 67-73.

Sewell, William H. and Shah, Vimal. "Parents' Education and Children's Educational Aspirations and Achievements." *American Sociological Review* (1968): 191-209.

Smith, James P., and Welch, Finis R. "Black-White Male Wage Ratios: 1960-1970." *American Economic Review* (1977): 323-38.

Treiman, Donald, and Terrell, Kermit. "Sex and the Process of Status Attainment: A Comparison of Working Women and Men." *American Sociological Review* (1975): 174-200.

Chapter 12

TRENDS IN RESIDENTIAL PROPERTY TAXES

James N. Morgan, Michael Ponza, and Renata Imbruglia

The apparent widespread popular resistance to property taxes and claims that they have increased to excessive amounts have led us to look at actual increases in property taxes in relation to increases in income or in house values. Inflation can cause increased assessments and taxes without any required popular vote, but that same inflation means the house is worth more, and it often means that the family income has also risen. Increases in tax rates, which usually require voter approval, raise taxes relative to house values. People accustomed to having control over their property taxes through millage votes may resent seeing inflation-caused reassessments raise their taxes without their permission.

There are several ways to examine empirically the distribution of residential property tax burdens. Assuming that the tax is borne by the homeowner in the case of owner-occupied residential property and by the tenant in rental residential property, the distribution of burdens depends on (1) which measure of family economic welfare or ability to pay is chosen;[1] (2) whether

---

[1]There are several possible measures of economic well-being. Annual family money income is one measure typically used. This measure doesn't fully represent a family's true relative economic position since it neglects differences in family size and composition. A second measure of economic well-being, the ratio of annual family money income to family needs, takes into account family characteristics such as size, composition, and family income in determining ability to pay. Annual measures of economic welfare may often present a distorted view of a family's economic position due to transitory income changes. Permanent income (or permanent income/needs) is used to control for this phenomenon, where permanent family income is family income averaged over a number of years. For each of the economic welfare measures, the family income component may either be the typically used family money income figure, or family money income plus imputed rent from owner-occupied housing net of income taxes.

property tax payments are defined "gross" or "net"[2] of tax; and (3) whether the analysis considers only homeowners or includes both homeowners and renters.[3] In an earlier volume of this series, using both family money income and family money income/needs as single-year measurements of economic well-being, Coe and Hill (1978) found that residential property tax payments as a percentage of income are regressive. This regressivity was accentuated when the federal income tax offset was included.[4] When a nine year average of family money income was used to approximate permanent or normal income, the regressivity of the property tax was sharply reduced, becoming proportional throughout much of the income range. Again, including the federal income tax offset reintroduced regressivity, but of a substantially smaller magnitude than with the single year estimates.

We present here two sets of estimates of property tax/income ratios for the years 1976 and 1978. We examined the traditional ratio of gross property taxes to family money income and also the ratio of net property taxes to family income net of taxes, but including imputed rental income from owner-occupied housing.[5] We examined these ratios as they varied across families, first according to family money income deciles and then by deciles of family money income relative to a needs standard controlled for family size and composition.

---

[2]Homeowners who itemize their federal income tax deductions can deduct property tax payments in arriving at their federal income tax liability. This has the effect of shifting some of the property tax burden onto the federal government and therefore represents a reduction in property tax payments to the individual homeowner. The reduction in property tax payments depends on the individual's marginal tax rate, i.e., it equals the marginal tax rate times the gross property tax payment. This reduction in effective property tax payments is referred to as the federal income tax offset.

[3]There is a selection bias from omitting renters and those who receive their housing without payment. See Morgan, David, Cohen and Brazer (1962) for a detailed description of a procedure which assigns property tax payments to non-homeowners.

[4]Inclusion of the federal tax offset has this effect since the value of the property tax reduction depends on the taxpayer's marginal tax rate: the higher that rate, the greater the reduction in effective property tax payments. The tax reduction varies from negligible amounts for low income families to substantial amounts for high income households, having the effect of significantly lessening property tax burdens in the upper income levels.

[5]Imputed rental income from owner-occupied housing is valued at 6 percent of net equity in the house.

Table 12.1 shows the property tax burden measures according to the two measures of family economic well-being for 1976 and 1978.[6] Except among the lowest deciles, which typically contain some families whose incomes are only temporarily low, property tax payments for homeowners were just slightly regressive, and the degree of regressivity was substantially smaller for the more sophisticated property-tax-to-income ratio. Since the federal income tax offset to property taxes and the effects on disposable income occur predominantly at the upper income levels, the pattern of property tax burden by income level was most altered by the inclusion of imputed rent of owner-occupied housing. If we had included non-homeowner families and made specific assumptions concerning the assignment of property tax payments to their dwellings, and if we had substituted permanent income for annual income (or permanent income/needs for annual income/ needs), the remaining regressivity could have been eliminated.[7]

Table 12.1 indicates also that there was very little trend in the distribution of residential property tax burdens. If anything, property tax to income ratios fell slightly from 1976 to 1978, indicating that incomes were rising faster than property taxes.[8] An exception was the startling increase between 1976 and 1978 in the property tax to income ratio for the lowest decile families. This increase presumably reflected some older, fixed-income families with escalating house values and property taxes, or even recently retired family heads with large homes (hence high property taxes) who experienced a substantial drop in income. But it may also have reflected more temporarily low incomes since, apart from the very slight increase in tax burden for those families headed by persons between 55 and 65 years of age, there was no concentration of increases in property tax burden for any particular age subgroup (see Table 12.1).

---

[6]Appendix Table A12.1 gives the decile breakpoints for the two ability to pay measures for the years 1976 and 1978.

[7]See Morgan, et al. (1962) and Coe and Hill (1978).

[8]These data contain some families who moved in order to adjust their housing stock to conform to changed income, family size, and/or family composition conditions. Changes in property taxes therefore arose both from rising property taxes on the same house and from different taxes on different houses for those who moved. Restricting the analysis to non-movers would have created selection-bias problems but would have permitted a better focus on changes in property taxes relative to both income and house value trends. We do this below.

Table 12.1 (page 1 of 2)

ALTERNATE ESTIMATES OF PROPERTY TAXES AS A PERCENTAGE OF FAMILY INCOME BY FAMILY MONEY
INCOME DECILES, FAMILY MONEY INCOME/NEEDS DECILES, AND AGE OF HEAD FOR 1976 AND 1978

	1976		1978		1976		1978	
	Weighted Percentage of Observations	Gross Taxes as Percentage of Family Money Income[a]	Weighted Percentage of Observations	Gross Taxes as Percentage of Family Money Income[a]	Weighted Percentage of Observations	Net Taxes as Percentage of Disposable Money Income[b]	Weighted Percentage of Observations	Net Taxes as Percentage of Disposable Income[b]
Income Decile								
1	5.0	8.7	5.0	13.6	5.0	5.0	5.0	5.6
2	6.8	5.8	6.1	5.8	6.8	4.5	6.1	6.0
3	6.5	6.0	6.9	5.0	6.5	4.8	6.9	3.8
4	7.9	3.8	7.6	3.6	7.9	3.4	7.6	2.8
5	8.0	3.3	8.9	3.5	8.0	3.1	8.9	2.9
6	10.9	3.4	10.3	2.9	10.9	3.2	10.3	2.6
7	11.3	3.2	12.7	3.0	11.3	3.1	12.7	2.4
8	12.4	2.6	13.0	2.6	12.4	2.3	13.0	2.8
9	15.2	2.9	14.7	2.5	15.2	2.3	14.7	1.8
10	16.0	2.6	14.8	2.4	16.0	1.8	14.8	1.9
Total	100.0	3.7	100.0	3.7	100.0	3.0	100.0	2.9
Income/ Needs Decile								
1	2.4	7.7	2.9	17.8	2.4	4.3	2.9	13.9
2	6.4	4.3	4.6	3.5	6.4	3.4	4.6	2.7
3	7.3	4.6	7.5	4.3	7.3	3.6	7.5	3.6
4	9.3	4.8	9.3	4.0	9.3	4.1	9.3	3.1
5	11.3	3.9	12.7	3.9	11.3	3.4	12.7	3.0
6	13.4	3.7	13.1	3.7	13.4	3.1	13.1	2.6
7	11.6	3.4	13.7	3.2	11.6	3.0	13.7	2.5
8	13.2	2.9	13.2	2.6	13.2	2.5	13.2	2.1
9	13.4	3.1	13.2	2.8	13.4	2.5	13.2	2.1
10	11.7	2.8	9.8	2.5	11.7	2.0	9.8	1.7
Total	100.0	3.7	100.0	3.7	100.0	3.0	100.0	2.9

Table 12.1 (page 2 of 2)

Age of Head	1976			1978		
	Weighted Percentage of Observations	Gross Taxes as Percentage of Family Money Income[a]	Net Taxes as Percentage of Disposable Money Income[b]	Weighted Percentage of Observations	Gross Taxes as Percentage of Family Money Income[a]	Net Taxes as Percentage of Disposable Income[b]
Less than 25	2.2	2.6	2.6	2.6	2.4	1.9
25-34	18.9	2.8	2.6	20.5	2.8	2.3
35-44	18.1	3.6	2.6	17.0	2.7	2.0
45-54	22.1	3.3	2.8	20.6	3.0	2.8
55-64	17.5	3.9	3.2	17.1	5.5	3.0
65-74	13.3	4.7	3.8	14.1	4.4	3.5
75 and older	7.9	5.2	4.0	7.1	5.1	5.1
Total	100.0	3.7	3.0	100.0	3.7	2.9

[a]Property taxes used here are the gross reported amounts. Income is annual family money income.
[b]Property taxes used here are gross reported property taxes less federal income tax offset (i.e., marginal tax rate multiplied by gross property tax). Income used here is annual family money plus imputed rental income from net equity in house (i.e., 6 percent net equity in home) plus tax credits less taxes paid.

A more detailed look at property tax trends and how they specifically compared with movements in incomes and house values required us to restrict the analysis to those families who did not move between 1976 and 1978. We restricted the sample to non-moving homeowners in which the original husband or wife or single head or both husband and wife remained.[9] The sample was thus reduced from 2,697 homeowners in 1976 and 2,853 homeowners in 1978 to 1,667 cases.

Table 12.2 presents means and mean ratios for each of the three years from 1976 to 1978 for the four principal regions of residence, as well as for the entire country. For this three-year period, average house values increased dramatically by 43 percent, incomes rose by 27 percent, and property taxes increased by 19 percent. The mean property tax/income ratio remained virtually unchanged at 3.7 percent, and the mean property tax/house value ratio fell from 1.64 percent in 1976 to 1.45 percent in 1978. Given these relationships among property taxes, house values, and family incomes, one wonders why there exists such great fervor regarding property taxes. Presumably, capital gains in the form of appreciating house values were not available to pay for higher property taxes or for increased living costs in general. The fact is not generally appreciated that the average property tax/income ratio was stable and the average property tax/house value was falling somewhat, particularly in the western United States. People accustomed to having control over their property taxes through millage votes apparently resent seeing inflation-caused reassessments raise their taxes without their permission.

To assess property tax trends for the aged, identical age-subsamples for the three years were examined. Table 12.2 shows the mean values and mean ratios obtained for all families with heads aged 45 to 64 and aged 65 or older, and among each age group, presents these same statistics for those in the lowest two deciles of family money income. Average house values, incomes, and property taxes each increased during the three year observation period for all heads aged 45 to 64, resulting in a smaller average property tax to house value ratio and a slightly larger property tax to income ratio. For family heads 65 or older, average house values and property taxes both increased while average incomes fell; this produced a modest increase in the ratio of their mean property tax/ house value and a 20 percent increase in the property tax/income ratio. More

---

[9]Specifically, the sample consisted of non-moving homeowners satisfying any one of the following family composition changes: no family composition change; change in members other than head or wife; head same but wife left/died and/or head has new wife, previous wife now head, or previous female head got married.

Table 12.2

AVERAGE HOUSE VALUES, PROPERTY TAXES, FAMILY MONEY INCOME, PROPERTY TAX/INCOME RATIO, AND PROPERTY TAX/HOUSE
VALUE RATIO BY REGION OF RESIDENCE, AGE OF FAMILY HEAD, AND LOWEST INCOME-AGE DECILE FOR YEARS 1976-1978

	Average House Value[a]			Average Property Tax			Average Family Income[b]			Average Property Tax to House Value Ratio			Average Property Tax to Family Income Ratio		
	1976	1977	1978	1976	1977	1978	1976	1977	1978	1976	1977	1978	1976	1977	1978
Region of Residence															
Northeast	$38.6	$42.1	$51.6	$970	$1040	$1130	$21.1	$23.2	$26.3	.0262	.0240	.0221	.0572	.0566	.0618
North Central	32.4	35.2	45.2	520	550	650	18.8	20.6	23.8	.0169	.0168	.0165	.0378	.0351	.0370
South	30.1	33.1	38.9	230	310	330	15.1	16.7	19.5	.0084	.0102	.0092	.0201	.0223	.0196
West	36.6	43.6	65.2	540	600	520	18.9	21.1	24.4	.0152	.0142	.0089	.0373	.0390	.0295
All regions	33.9	37.7	48.4	550	610	650	18.4	20.3	23.4	.0164	.0162	.0145	.0374	.0370	.0368
Age of Head															
45-64	36.5	40.9	52.6	640	730	770	22.2	23.9	28.1	.0172	.0179	.0159	.0354	.0361	.0360
65 or older	13.3	13.4	17.6	170	180	190	34.2	35.1	29.8	.0128	.0144	.0135	.0533	.0550	.0622
Low Income and age 45-64[c]	25.2	23.0	31.4	394	287	313	8.6	7.4	3.9	.0148	.0124	.0130	.0657	.0576	.1355
Low income and age 65 or older[d]	18.0	18.2	23.9	248	254	265	4.6	4.8	4.2	.0151	.0156	.0138	.0595	.0568	.0617

[a] House values measured in thousands of dollars.
[b] Incomes measured in thousands of dollars.
[c] Refers to non-moving homeowners with incomes in the lowest two deciles for that particular year and who are age 45-64.
[d] Refers to non-moving homeowners with incomes in the lowest two deciles for that year who are age 65 or older.

important, Table 12.2 documents that low-income, middle-aged homeowners were the only subgroup to experience a substantial increase in the mean property tax to family income ratio. Although their property tax/house value ratio was stable (1.3 percent in 1978), the average property tax/income ratio for low-income, middle-aged homeowners doubled, rising from 6.6 percent in 1976 to 13.5 percent in 1978.[10] Close inspection of this group's average values reveals the source of this two-fold increase. Average house values appreciated by 25 percent, and average property taxes actually declined by 21 percent, but average family income also fell by 55 percent during the three years studied.[11] Presumably, some of these family heads were retiring during the period, producing a selection bias by forming an age bracket around retirement age.

The above results were based on average values or averages of ratios. If the distribution of increased property taxes was the problem, with certain individuals facing substantial increases in property taxes and no concurrent increase in family income, then inferences based on average values or ratios could have been misleading. To control for this potential bias we considered, for individual homeowners, changes in property taxes against changes in house value or in family money income, with all change variables measured in dollars (See Tables 12.3 and 12.4). We found that, despite the attention given to sky-rocketing property taxes, the overall national picture appeared to be one of modest increases. Most of these accrued to families with substantial increases in house value or in family money income. An examination of the upper righthand corners of the tables, which represent those families whose property taxes rose substantially but whose house values or incomes did not, documents that this occurs for only a small fraction of the population.

In summary, the apparent sharp regressivity of the residential property tax when annual family money income was used to characterize family economic welfare was substantially reduced when the empirical analysis took the federal tax offset, imputed rental income from owner-occupied housing, and family size and composition into account when quantifying a family's ability-to-pay, even though the federal tax offset worked in the opposite direction. Including non-homeowners and using a more "permanent" income concept would erradicate the

_____

[10]The reader is warned to treat these results with caution. They are based on a sample size of 56 cases.

[11]These are current dollars not adjusted for changes in the general price level.

Table 12.3

CHANGE IN PROPERTY TAX BY CHANGE IN HOUSE VALUE AND FAMILY MONEY INCOME 1976-1978

(Percentage distribution of non-moving homeowners.)[a]

	Change in Property Taxes 1976-1978								
	Less than -$150	-$149 to -$50	-$49 to $50	$51 to $150	$151 to $250	$251 to $550	$551 to $1050	$1051 or More	Total
Change in House Value									
Less than -$1,500	9.1%	8.4%	38.3%	19.2%	12.3%	10.4%	2.2%	0.1%	100%
-$1,499 to -$500	0.0	13.4	44.5	22.9	7.2	12.0	0.0	0.0	100%
-$499 to $500	4.1	5.9	36.9	24.0	16.7	8.0	4.4	0.0	100%
$501 to $1,499	5.6	9.4	46.1	19.5	10.2	3.8	0.0	5.4	100%
$1500 to $2,499	4.0	14.2	48.4	9.1	16.0	5.9	2.5	0.0	100%
$2,500 to $5,499	7.0	2.8	36.7	27.1	12.6	10.5	2.3	1.1	100%
$5,500 to $10,499	4.1	6.8	35.2	22.0	13.8	13.6	2.6	1.9	100%
$10,500 or more	10.9	5.1	24.2	24.6	13.8	14.8	5.5	1.1	100%
Change in Family Money Income									
Less than -$1,500	8.3	7.3	27.7	24.2	15.3	10.0	6.1	1.0	100%
-$1,499 to -$500	5.6	7.8	41.2	17.8	13.1	7.7	3.8	3.0	100%
-$499 to $500	8.3	6.3	53.0	18.6	6.2	5.7	1.7	0.0	100%
$501 to $1,499	6.0	4.1	46.5	22.5	12.0	6.0	2.7	0.0	100%
$1,500 to $2,499	10.1	4.1	24.6	33.2	11.3	11.9	3.6	1.2	100%
$2,500 to $5,499	10.0	6.1	32.1	21.7	13.1	15.1	0.6	1.2	100%
$5,500 to $10,499	6.8	7.1	26.2	23.9	14.9	17.2	3.1	0.7	100%
$10,500 or more	8.2	3.9	23.2	24.1	15.3	15.2	7.7	2.4	100%
All Non-moving Homeowners	8.1	5.8	30.9	23.5	13.6	12.8	4.0	1.2	100%

[a]Sample consists of non-moving homeowners between 1976 and 1978 who satisfied any one of the family composition changes listed in footnote 9 of the text. Unweighted case count is 1,667.

Table 12.4

CHANGE IN PROPERTY TAX BY 1978 INCOME DECILES FOR ALL NON-MOVING HOMEOWNERS AND FOR THOSE 65 YEARS OLD OR OLDER

	Change in Property Taxes 1976-1978								
	Less than -$150	-$149 to -$50	-$49 to $50	$51 to $150	$151 to $250	$251 to $550	$551 to $1,050	$1,051 or More	Total
1978 Family Money Income Decile									
1	2.9%	7.7%	68.4%	10.1%	7.8%	1.5%	1.6%	0.0%	100%
2	8.6	11.2	40.6	16.8	16.6	3.6	2.6	0.0	100%
3	11.0	8.9	36.4	23.4	8.1	6.7	2.6	2.9	100%
4	7.1	1.4	45.1	30.9	3.0	11.3	1.2	0.0	100%
5	5.9	3.8	38.9	25.8	9.1	12.2	3.2	1.1	100%
6	6.7	5.1	25.9	32.1	16.5	10.6	3.1	0.1	100%
7	7.0	7.2	30.2	22.5	15.2	14.7	3.1	0.0	100%
8	7.2	9.2	24.8	25.6	11.9	14.8	4.6	1.9	100%
9	8.8	4.0	19.8	26.0	19.6	17.2	2.6	1.9	100%
10	11.7	3.0	18.8	18.8	17.2	18.7	9.5	2.3	100%
1978 Family Money Income Deciles for the 65 or Older Subsample									
1	2.1	9.2	65.0	11.9	7.6	1.9	2.2	0.0	100%
2	8.9	13.5	39.2	19.7	12.3	3.0	3.4	0.0	100%
3	8.2	9.6	36.0	20.8	10.4	9.0	4.2	1.8	100%
4	9.5	2.2	42.1	26.8	1.6	15.5	2.3	0.0	100%
5	4.3	0.0	38.5	27.3	8.5	17.4	0.0	4.0	100%
6	0.0	4.2	29.3	38.0	22.0	6.5	0.0	0.0	100%
7	15.0	6.0	30.7	34.5	5.2	8.5	0.0	0.0	100%
8	9.1	15.7	22.7	22.8	14.0	0.0	7.8	7.8	100%
9	11.9	7.0	33.6	14.4	13.3	19.8	0.0	0.0	100%
10	0.0	0.0	20.9	29.8	10.7	33.9	4.8	0.0	100%

remaining regressivity, leaving the tax proportionate in incidence. Little trend in the distribution of property tax burdens was found to exist between 1976 and 1978. While our analysis suggested that some individuals did experience sharp increases in property taxes with no concomitant increases in family income or house value, these represented only a small percentage of the entire population. In view of these data, the popular pressure for property tax reductions must stem largely from popular perceptions which fail to link increases in property taxes to increases in house value, much less to increases in family money income, and perhaps which focus on property taxes as one of the few areas concerning government finance commonly voted on directly rather than by electing representatives to make informed decisions.

References

Coe, Richard D., and Hill, Martha S. "An Empirical Note on the Residential Property Tax." In Five Thousand American Families--Patterns of Economic Progress, Vol. VI, edited by Greg J. Duncan and James N. Morgan. Ann Arbor: Institute for Social Research, The University of Michigan, 1978.

Morgan, James N.; David, Martin; Cohen, Wilbur; and Brazer, Harvey. Income and Welfare in the United States. New York: McGraw-Hill, 1962.

Appendix to Chapter 12

Table A12.1

DECILE BREAKPOINTS FOR FAMILY MONEY INCOME AND FAMILY MONEY INCOME/NEEDS RATIO FOR 1976 AND 1978

Decile	1976				1978			
	Unweighted Cases	Range for Money Income	Unweighted Cases	Range for Money Income/Needs	Unweighted Cases	Range for Money Income	Unweighted Cases	Range for Money Income/Needs
1	141	$ 0- 3,714	125	0.00-1.50	134	$ 0- 4,154	109	0.00- 1.80
2	186	3,715- 5,959	245	1.51-2.23	151	4,155- 6,719	183	1.81- 2.60
3	187	5,960- 7,999	254	2.24-2.89	194	6,720- 9,299	275	2.61- 3.40
4	247	8,000-10,512	277	2.90-3.52	224	9,300-12,103	289	3.41- 4.20
5	241	10,513-12,999	320	3.53-4.21	261	12,104-15,328	376	4.21- 5.10
6	329	13,000-15,999	350	4.22-5.08	330	15,329-18,849	369	5.11- 6.00
7	311	16,000-19,199	294	5.09-5.96	387	18,850-22,650	370	6.01- 7.10
8	338	19,200-23,499	303	5.97-7.24	384	22,651-27,473	331	7.11- 8.50
9	375	23,500-30,999	291	7.25-9.20	401	27,474-36,293	319	8.51-11.00
10	342	31,000 or more	238	9.21 or more	367	36,294 or more	212	11.01 or more
Total	2697		2697		2833		2833	

Table A12.2

CHANGE IN HOUSE VALUE AND FAMILY MONEY INCOME BY CHANGE IN PROPERTY TAX 1976-1978
(Percentage distribution of non-moving homeowners)[a]

Change in Property Taxes	Less than -$1,500	-$1,499 to -$500	-$499 to $500	$501 to $1,499	$1,500 to $2,499	$2,500 to $5,499	$5,500 to $10,499	$10,500 or More	Total
			Change in House Value 1976-1978						
Less than -$150	6.1%	0.0%	2.8%	1.7%	1.3%	11.4%	9.7%	67.0%	100%
-$149 to -$50	7.8	3.0	5.6	4.0	6.7	6.4	22.6	43.8	100%
-$49 to $49	6.7	1.9	6.6	3.7	4.3	15.9	21.9	39.0	100%
-$50 to $149	4.4	1.3	5.6	2.1	1.1	15.4	18.0	52.1	100%
$150 to $249	4.9	0.7	6.8	1.9	3.2	12.4	19.6	50.6	100%
$250 to $549	4.4	1.2	3.4	0.7	1.3	10.9	20.4	57.6	100%
$550 to $1,049	3.0	0.0	6.0	0.0	1.7	7.8	12.7	68.8	100%
$1,050 or more	0.3	0.0	0.0	10.9	0.0	12.0	30.2	46.6	100%
All non-moving homeowners	5.4	1.3	5.5	2.5	2.7	13.4	19.3	49.9	100%
			Change in Family Money Income 1976-1978						
Less than -$150	15.8	3.1	5.7	6.8	8.6	23.7	16.0	20.2	100%
-$149 to -$50	19.5	6.0	6.1	6.5	4.9	20.2	23.3	13.5	100%
-$49 to $49	13.8	6.0	9.6	13.8	5.5	20.0	16.3	15.0	100%
$50 to $149	15.8	3.4	4.4	8.8	9.8	17.7	19.5	20.5	100%
$150 to $249	27.3	4.3	2.6	8.1	5.8	18.5	21.0	22.4	100%
$250 to $549	12.1	2.7	2.5	4.3	6.4	22.7	25.7	23.7	100%
$550 to $1,049	23.8	4.3	2.5	6.3	6.3	3.1	15.1	38.7	100%
$1,050 or more	12.2	10.9	0.0	0.0	19.2	19.2	11.7	39.2	100%
All non-moving homeowners	15.4	4.5	5.6	9.2	7.0	19.2	19.2	20.0	100%

[a] Sample consists of non-moving homeowners between 1976 and 1978 who satisfied any one of the family composition changes listed in footnote 9 of the text. Unweighted case count is 1,667.

Chapter 13

SOME ECONOMETRIC ADVANTAGES OF PANEL DATA

Sue Augustyniak

The availability of panel data has been a fairly recent phenomena, enabling a closer scrutiny of many economic theories which could not be estimated or tested using other kinds of data. Time series data are typically aggregated to an extent which precludes analysis at the household level. The effect of a variable such as age on investment or retirement is lost as is the effect of family composition on demand. Cross-section data provide information about individual variables but do not provide enough information to estimate relationships which occur with a time lag. Any given cross-section of data will include responses from households which have had a chance to adjust to their present position and from those that have recently been, for instance, unemployed or have experienced a rise in income and haven't yet had a chance to modify their behavior.

Panel data allow more flexibility; they make it possible to use the household as the unit of analysis and to follow the household over time to observe directly how it reacts to changes in its environment. This procedure has proven very useful in testing a wide range of economic theories. Among these are the use of individual characteristics to determine wage levels, model the timing and assess the consequences of retirement decision, examine the incidence and persistence of poverty and the use of welfare programs. The individual reactions to changing variables that are available in panel data are also vital for determining consumer demand for goods such as gasoline, food, and utilities.

Panel data has been used extensively to analyze the determinants of an individuals wage and the change in that wage. Chapter 2 provides an example of this analysis as well as a discussion of other work in the area. This note corresponds to the structure set up in Chapter 2 and uses some of the existing analysis in the literature on income determination as a framework. A simple model of income determination is used to illustrate the merits of longitudinal or panel data vis-a-vis cross-sectional data in estimating income determination

405

models. We begin with a basic cross-sectional model, supplemented by unobservable individual measures and period and cohort variables:[1]

$$(1) \quad \ln Y_{it} = \beta_0 + \beta_1 Ed_i + \beta_2 Exp_{it} + \eta_1 Ind_i + \eta_2 Macro_t + \eta_3 Qual_c + \varepsilon_{it}$$

where:

$\ln Y_{it}$ is the natural logarithm of earnings of the ith individual in year t.

Ed_i represents observable variables which vary over individuals but remain constant over time (education, for example). This variable also represents other background variables.

Exp_{it} represents variables that vary with time and across individuals (the most familiar is work experience). We are allowing for a more general measure of work experience than total time spent in the labor force or the number of hours on the current job.[2]

Ind_i represents unobservable, time invariant individual effects (such as achievement motivation or ability). I.Q. may be one of these variables if it was not measured in the sample but many other facets of an individual are included in this variable.

$Macro_t$ represents effects that vary with time but are constant across individuals; these are sometimes called period effects (an example is the aggregate unemployment rate in a given year).

$Qual_c$ represents measures that vary over time but are constant for individuals born in a given year (c); these are sometimes called cohort effects.[3]

ε_{it} is a random serially uncorrelated disturbance term, distributed independently of the explanatory variables in Equation 1, with $E(\varepsilon_{it}^2) = \sigma^2$.

---

[1] The explanatory variables are typically assumed to be non-stochastic, but the analysis would be unchanged if they were considered random variables and their expectations were taken conditional on their observed values.

[2] If Mincers variable j = Age − Ed − 5 were used as a proxy for one of the experience variables there would be a linear relationship between the Exp variable j, one of the Macro variables representing current year, an individual measure representing years of school, and the cohort measure. Current year minus j minus years of school is equal to the individuals year of birth plus 5. This makes estimation of this model impossible and emphasizes the number of problems not solved by the use of panel data.

[3] Some cohort effects (e.g., implications of cohort size on labor market supply and demand, or the effect of growing up during the depression) are constant across all individuals born in a given year. Others, such as school quality, may vary within a cohort by race, region, city size, etc. For simplicity, we will assume that cohort effects are of the first type and we will use the "c" subscript to denote cohort.

CROSS-SECTIONAL DATA

Single Cross-Section

When we attempt to estimate a wage equation using a single cross-section of data, the unobserved variables are lumped together with the disturbance term and the effect of the time invariant variables can not be distinguished from the constant term. As a result we are in fact estimating:

$$(2) \quad \ln Y_{it} = \beta_0^* + \beta_1 Ed_i + \beta_2 Exp_{it} + \varepsilon_{it}^*$$

where:

$$\varepsilon_{it}^* = \varepsilon_{it} + \eta_1 Ind_i + \eta_3 Qual_c$$

$$\beta_0^* = \beta_0 + \eta_2 Macro_t$$

To the extent that the explanatory variables Ed_i and Exp_{it} are correlated with ε_{it}^* through the omitted variables Ind_i and $Qual_c$, ordinary least squares (OLS) estimates of the parameters of Equation 2 will yield biased estimates of the effects of Ed and Exp and biased estimates of their standard errors as well.[4] Since the correlation between the excluded variables and the included variables is not expected to diminish as the sample size increases, the estimates of the parameters will be inconsistent and the standard tests of significance will be inappropriate.

Consistent estimates for the effect of Ed and Exp might be obtained through the use of instrumental variables which are correlated with Ed and Exp but not correlated with the disturbance term ε_{it}^*. In practice, this solution may not be feasible because such instrumental variables are virtually impossible to find.

Repeated Cross-Sections

The use of successive cross-sections represents an improvement over the use of a single cross-section because it allows for some variation in the period effects. By obtaining more than one observation on these variables, we can explicitly control for their effect on earnings. The model to be estimated is now:

$$(3) \quad \ln Y_{it} = \beta_0 + \beta_1 Ed_i + \beta_2 Exp_{it} + \eta_2 Macro_t + \varepsilon_{it}^*$$

---

[4] The individual characteristics are assumed to be correlated with the amount of Ed and Exp attained, while the cohort effects are correlated with the Exp variables because the older cohorts have been in the labor force longer and have accumulated more experience.

where: $$\varepsilon_{it}^* = \varepsilon_{it} + \eta_1 \, \text{Ind}_i + \eta_3 \, \text{Qual}_c$$

The OLS estimates of β_1 and β_2 will be biased and inconsistent if there is any correlation between the explanatory variables and ε_{it}^*, but an unbiased estimate of the effect of Macro_t can be obtained. The inclusion of more cross sections of data also means the inclusion of more independent observations increasing the degrees of freedom for the estimates.[5]

PANEL DATA

Repeated observations on the same individuals provide the analyst with several ways of improving upon single or repeated cross-sections. Panel data can be used to gain efficiency in the estimation of a wage level equation or to estimate a change equation directly. Each of these uses is discussed in turn.

Models of Wage Levels

The most common use of panel data in improving estimates of a wage level equation has been its use in estimating the components of the disturbance term. To illustrate this methodology we return to the disturbance term (ε_{it}^*) in Equation 2 and introduce the following specification for it:

(4) $$\varepsilon_{it}^* = \varepsilon_{it} + \eta_1 \text{Ind}_i + \eta_3 \, \text{Qual}_c$$

$$\varepsilon_{it}^* = \varepsilon_{it} + \delta_i$$

where: $\varepsilon_{it} = \rho\varepsilon_{i,t-1} + u_{it}$, and δ_i represents the time invariant component of the disturbance.

This disturbance term has a random component represented by ε_{it} and an individual component introduced by Ind_i and Qual_c. It is often assumed that the exclusion of variables specifying local labor market conditions or other factors which

---

[5]That this model produces biased estimates of both the parameters and their standard errors when estimated with pooled cross-section data does not in itself make the estimates worthless. For some cases, particularly for use as policy indicators, minimum mean square error is the relevant criteria. The mean square error of an estimator is the sum of its variance and its squared bias. For a given bias we can obtain estimates displaying a smaller distribution around the true parameter if we can reduce the variance of the disturbance. We can reduce the variance by increasing the dispersion in the data matrix or by increasing the number of observations. By pooling together several cross-sections we increase the number of observations.

fluctuate with the business cycle result in the random components of the disturbance being serially correlated. An alternative but less flexible method would be to specify a time varying component to the disturbance and assume that the random portion of the disturbance is serially uncorrelated.

The unmeasured variables are represented by components of the disturbance in Equation 4. Although the individual effects of the unmeasured variables can not be estimated, their total effect can be determined by estimating the parameters of the disturbance. The variance of δ_i and u_{it} and the parameter ρ of Equation 4 can be estimated by using a maximum likelihood estimation on the residuals from a consistent estimation of Equation 2. This assumes that a consistent estimation of Equation 2 is possible which will only be the case if there are variables which can be used as instruments for the explanatory variables found to be correlated with the disturbance. If a consistent estimation is possible then by estimating the variance of δ and u and the parameter of serial correlation ρ , we can break down the total unexplained variance in wages into (1) a portion representing permanent differences--usually taken to represent permanent differences in individuals, (2) a portion which is purely stochastic, and (3) a portion which reflects the correlation of wages over time. Assuming that we accept the individual and serially correlated component of the disturbance as measuring the effect of excluded variables, this gives a consistent estimate of the unexplained variance in earnings, $var(u_{it})$.

Lillard and Willis (1978) used panel data to identify the permanent portion of the disturbance. They included dummy variables representing the year to account for the effect of the measured and unmeasured time varying variables, thereby eliminating the serial correlation. Their model assumes that the disturbance term is uncorrelated with the explanatory variables. This means that individual variables such as ability are uncorrelated with explanatory variables such as education and experience. This is a much stronger assumption than we made in Equation 1 and is indeed a stronger assumption about independence than most studies are willing to make. If this assumption is not valid, their estimates for the effects of the explanatory variables, as well as their estimate of the individual component of the variance, will be biased. Using their model, it would be impossible to separate the respective effects of the unobserved and the observed time invariant variables if they are correlated, but one can look at the joint effect that the time invariant variables have upon earnings and this is what they set out to do.

Other studies using panel data have sought to explain the relative quantities of state dependence and heterogeneity responsible for the correlation between past and present values of the dependent variable and its effect on the variance of earnings across individuals and over time using a wage level equation. The analysis of state dependence requires the separation of the effect that past earnings have upon present earnings from the effects that unmeasured individual variables which are correlated with past earning levels have upon present earnings. The past earnings of the individual may have influenced his investment in skills which in turn affect his current earnings. It is typically assumed that periods of unemployment from an individuals desired or primary occupation are characterized by low earnings and the deterioration of skills necessary for employment in the higher wage occupation in the future. In the case of state dependence, the hypothesis is that past earnings affect behavior in a way which directly affects current earnings, so that a lagged earnings structure should be included in an explanation of current earnings. With heterogeneity, it is characteristics of the individual which affect both past and present earnings; the inclusion of past earnings is not justified since it has no direct effect. As we discuss below, lagged dependent variables are not valid proxies for either the unmeasured variables or the lagged independent variables and, if the correlation between past and present values of the dependent variables is due to serial correlation of the disturbances, it should be dealt with directly through the use of GLS. In all the above cases the inclusion of the lagged dependent variable would increase the R^2 since it picks up some of the effect of the excluded variable. This is sometimes mistakenly used as a justification for the inclusion of the lagged dependent variable regardless of the causal relationship specified in the model. Under the assumption of state dependence, our model would become

$$(5) \quad \ln Y_{it} = \beta_0 + \beta_1 Ed_i + \beta_2 Exp_{it} + \eta_1 \hat{Ind}_i$$

$$+ \eta_2 Macro_t + \eta_3 Qual_c + \eta_4 \ln Y_{i,t-1} + \varepsilon_{it}$$

where $\hat{Ind}_i$ is an instrumental variable for Ind_i.

The coefficient of the lagged dependent variable gives the degree of state dependence. If we believe that the disturbances are serially correlated and that we have state dependence, we must use an instrumental variable for the lagged dependent variable as well. Chamberlain (1978) suggested that the coefficient of the lagged independent variables be used to distinguish between serial correlation and state dependence. Chamberlain developed a model with serial correlation where $\varepsilon_{it} = \rho\varepsilon_{it-1} + \xi_{it}$. A differencing operation would then produce:

$$(6) \quad \ln Y_{it} = \beta_0(1-\rho) + \beta_1(1-\rho) \, Ed_i + \beta_2(Exp_{it} - \rho \, Exp_{i,t-1})$$

$$+ \quad \eta_1(1-\rho) \, \hat{Ind}_i + \eta_2 (Macro_t - \rho \, Macro_{t-1})$$

$$+ \quad \eta_3(1-\rho) \, Qual_c + \rho \ln Y_{i,t-1} + \xi_{it}$$

If the coefficient of the lagged time-varying variables are close to the product of their unlagged counterparts with $-\rho$ (an estimate of ρ is given by the parameter of the lagged dependent variable), then there is evidence of serial correlation rather than state dependence. However, if we hypothesize that in the absence of state dependence there is at least one variable whose lagged values would not be included as an explanatory variable, and if we estimate a significant coefficient for that variable which differs from the coefficient that variable would have if there were serial correlation, then the implication is that there is state dependence.

The use of state dependence models provides a justification for the inclusion of the lagged dependent variable as an explanatory variable. If the state dependence hypothesis is justified, then the inclusion of the lagged values of earnings reduces the portion of unexplained variance in earnings between groups, although it does not explain why different groups have different past values of earnings. If we believe there is state dependence we are still left with the question of what it is about the past state that affects the current one.

Models of Wage Change

The previous models attempted to estimate the expected value of an individual's earnings, given certain levels of the explanatory variables. An equation of wage change would have a slightly different emphasis in that we would be trying to estimate the expected change in the level of wages given a change in the level of the explanatory variables. The two problems are closely related because a theory that explains the determinants of the wage level must also explain a change in this level.

If we were to use our wage model (Equation 1), solve for the change in variables between two consecutive time periods, and allow all the parameters to vary uniformly over individuals between the two points in time, we would have:

$$(7) \quad \Delta \ln Y_{i,t+1} = \Delta \beta^*_{0,t+1} + \Delta \beta_{1,t+1} \, Ed_i + \beta_{2,t+1} \, \Delta Exp_{i,t+1}$$

$$+ \Delta \beta_{2,t+1} \, Exp_{it} + \Delta \eta_{2,t+1} \, Macro_t + \varepsilon^*_{it}$$

where:

$$\varepsilon^*_{it} = \varepsilon_{i,t+1} - \varepsilon_{it} + \Delta \eta_{1,t+1} \, Ind_i + \Delta \eta_{3,t+1} \, Qual_c \quad \text{and}$$

$$\beta^*_{0,t+1} = \beta_{0,t+1} - \beta_{0t} + \eta_{2,t+1} \Delta Macro_t.$$

Some of the biasing effects of the unobserved Ind_i and $Qual_c$ remain in this change equation if their parameters have been changing over time. As in the case of a cross-sectional model, the effects of Ind_i and $Qual_c$ are lumped together with the disturbance term because we are unable to measure them and control for their effects.[6] Their presence as part of the disturbance in Equation 7 together with our assumption that they are correlated with other explanatory variables in the model, results in biased estimates of the coefficients. The smaller the change in the coefficients η_1 and η_3, the smaller will be the bias that is introduced by excluding $\Delta \eta_{1,t+1} \, Ind_i$ and $\Delta \eta_{3,t+1} \, Qual_c$ as explanatory variables in Equation 7. In most cases, if we believe that the parameters vary little over time, if at all, a change equation represents a substantial improvement over the cross-sectional equation with regard to the biasing effects of omitted individual and cohort measures.

The assumption that the parameters do not change over time is often used. This seems reasonable, particularly if the time period is short and relatively consistent; it results in the following change equation.[7]

$$(8) \quad \Delta \ln Y_{i,t+1} = \beta^*_0 + \beta_2 \, \Delta Exp_{i,t+1} + \Delta \varepsilon_{i,t+1}$$

---

[6]Since we are dealing with the change in the explanatory variables between two points in time, we have only one observation for the aggregate macro variables, and the value of these variables will be the same for all individuals in the sample. With only one observation on a variable we cannot control for its effect and so we cannot estimate the effect that $Macro_t$ has upon wages.

[7]The Exp notation stands for all observable variables that vary with time and across individuals. If years of labor force experience were the only Exp variable, then $\Delta Exp_{i,t+1} = 1$ for all individuals with jobs and the term would drop out of the regression. Any variables for which $\Delta Exp_{i,t+1}$ equals a constant will be added to the constant term. We have left $\Delta Exp_{i,t+1}$ in Equation 8 to allow for other variables of this type.

where
$$\beta_0^* = \eta_2 \, \Delta Macro_{t+1}$$

Mellow (1979), however, allowed the parameters of some of the observable variables to vary but did not discuss the problems caused if the parameters of the unobservable variables vary as well. Presumably he was assuming that the parameters of the unobservable variables do not vary, in which case our change equation would become:

$$(9) \quad \Delta lnY_{i,t+1} = \Delta\beta_0^* + \beta_{2,t+1} \, \Delta Exp_{i,t+1} + \Delta\beta_{2,t+1} \, Exp_{it}$$

$$+ \Delta\eta_{2,t+1} \, Macro_t + \Delta\varepsilon_{it}$$

There are two further aspects to note about these change equations. If we believe that the model as stated in Equation 1 is true, then we introduce some complications by estimating a change equation. First, it is impossible to estimate the influence that the time invariant variables (e.g., education) have upon wages since they drop out of the change in wages equation. Second, our disturbance term is no longer independent; we have introduced serial correlation into the model. The serial correlation takes the form of a negative correlation between adjacent terms which arises because the disturbances for the change equation are the differences between two initially uncorrelated disturbances;

$$E(\Delta\varepsilon_t \, \Delta\varepsilon_{t-1}) = E(\varepsilon_t - \varepsilon_{t-1}) \, (\varepsilon_{t-1} - \varepsilon_{t-2})$$

$$= E(\varepsilon_t \varepsilon_{t-1}) - E(\varepsilon_{t-1}^2) - E(\varepsilon_t \varepsilon_{t-2}) + E(\varepsilon_{t-1} \varepsilon_{t-2}) \quad .$$

The first, third, and fourth terms drop out when we take expectations under the assumption that the ε's are uncorrelated, leaving $E(\Delta\varepsilon_t \, \Delta\varepsilon_{t-1}) = -\sigma^2$. [8]

The introduction of serial correlation is not too serious because it still permits unbiased and consistent estimation of the parameters of the model. The use of OLS will result in the loss of efficiency and give biased estimates of the standard errors, but since the form of this covariance matrix is known Atkin's estimation can be used and the estimates will have all the desirable properties.

---

[8] As an example, consider a person whose wage is moving exactly on the expected growth path. At time t there is a random disturbance which moves him off this path and at time t+1 he moves back onto the path. There will be a negative correlation between the change in his wage at time t and at time t+1; if the disturbance was positive, he will have a larger than average wage change at time t and a smaller than average wage change in period t+1.

We wish to emphasize that the simple answer for this problem is a result of the strong assumptions made regarding the disturbance term when we set up the model. In the case where the covariance matrix is not scaler, and its form is not known up to a multiplicative constant, the feasable Atkin estimation procedure must be used in place of Atkin estimation. This procedure will result in asymptotically unbiased, asymptotically efficient, and consistent estimates of the parameters as well as asymptotically unbiased estimates of the standard errors, providing a large sample justification for the application of the usual tests.

Some models seeking to explain wage changes include the initial wage level as an explanatory variable, often as a proxy for an unobserved variable such as ability. Although ability can be assumed to remain relatively constant over time, it may still affect the pattern in which wages change over time and should therefore be included as an explanatory variable in the wage change equation. For example, it might be that people with more drive (Ind_i) not only get more education, which affects their initial wage, but also acquire more on-the-job training. If this is the case, a cross-sectional model should include interaction terms between Ind_i and Exp_{it} to allow for the fact that the effect of an additional year of experience on wages increases with the level of Ind_i. Once we take the change between time periods, making the usual assumption of invariant parameters, the change equation becomes:

$$(10) \quad \Delta \ln Y_{it} = \beta_0^* + \beta_2 \Delta Exp_{i,t+1} + \Delta \varepsilon_{it}^*$$

$$\Delta \varepsilon_{it}^* = \Delta \varepsilon_{i,t+1} + \beta_4 \, Ind_i \times Exp_{i,t+1}$$

$$\beta_0^* = \eta_2 \Delta Macro_t$$

Once again we have a situation where the inclusion of the individual characteristics as explanatory variables would save us from inconsistent estimates. However, the inclusion of initial wage will not do this, and in any case it would be a poor proxy for ability.

Another problem in adding the initial wage to the right-hand side of the equation is that it complicates the interpretation of the coefficients. Suppose we add $\eta_4 \ln Y_{it}$ to the right hand side of Equation 8. Then our change equation would become:

$$(11) \quad \ln Y_{i,t+1} - (1+\eta_4) \ln Y_{it} = \beta_0^* + \beta_2 \Delta Exp_{i,t+1} + \Delta \varepsilon_{i,t+1}$$

The dependent variable in this equation is no longer the simple difference in the natural log of wages and causes problems of interpretation for the remaining coefficients.

A second justification for the inclusion of initial wage as an explanatory variable was advanced by Blau and Kahn (1979). They stated that the inclusion of the initial wage level "controls for possible regression to the mean" (p.19). Regression toward the mean refers to the negative correlation between the initial level and the change in this level for a given variable. It can be caused by behavioral responses due, say, to risk aversion, with individuals of different wage levels, or by systematic decisions by firms to equalize differences in wages. If regression to the mean is caused by a behavioral mechanism, then this mechanism should be included in the model. Regression toward the mean will also occur in a well specified model simply as a result of the differencing operation. The reason for this phenomenon can easily be seen by recalling the assumptions about the error term in change Equation 8:

$$\Delta\varepsilon_{i,t+1} = \varepsilon_{i,t+1} - \varepsilon_{it} \text{ and } E(\Delta\varepsilon_{i,t+1}\varepsilon_{it}) = E(\varepsilon_{i,t+1} - \varepsilon_{it})\varepsilon_{it} = -\sigma^2$$

With the assumption of random disturbances in the initial equation, we have introduced a negative correlation between the change in wage variable and the initial level of wages. At first glance this problem appears to be rather serious because regression toward the mean will arise whenever the correlation between wage observations over time is less than perfect. The resulting negative correlation between the change in wages and the initial level would seem to cause problems for any of the explanatory variables present in the wage change equation that are also correlated with the initial level of wages. In ordinary circumstances the exclusion of a variable which is correlated with the dependent variable and other explanatory variables would lead to biased estimates of the parameters of the explanatory variables. This seems to argue for the inclusion of initial wage as an explanatory variable in the wage change equation to allow the unbiased estimation of the parameters of interest.

That this is not, in fact, a problem can be seen by postulating a wage change equation that includes the initial level of Ed_i. The only way that the correlation between Ed_i and lnY_{it} could bias the estimated effect of Ed_i on ΔlnY_{it} would be if Ed_i were correlated with the disturbance term in the wage change equation. But if Equation 1 is properly specified then Ed_i is uncorrelated with the disturbance term ε_{it} for all t. Therefore Ed_i is uncorrelated with $\Delta\varepsilon_{it}$. If there is a correlation between Ed_i and ε_{it}, then the problems we have are not unique to the change equation and cause problems in estimating the level of wages as well. This misspecification problem is not caused by regression to the mean but rather by correlation between regressors and disturbances, and it can be solved by using instrumental variables if appropriate instruments can be found.

It is possible that one of the <u>change</u> variables in our equation is correlated with the disturbance. As an example, assume that $\Delta Exp_{i,t+1}$ is causing the problem, then:

$$(12) \quad E(\Delta Exp_{i,t+1} \; \Delta\varepsilon_{i,t+1}) \neq 0 \text{ or}$$

$$E(Exp_{i,t+1} \; \varepsilon_{i,t+1} + Exp_{i,t+1} \; \varepsilon_{it} + Exp_{it} \; \varepsilon_{i,t+1} + Exp_{it} \; \varepsilon_{it}) \neq 0$$

When we take expectations through Equation 12, recalling our assumption that the disturbances are serially uncorrelated (which implies that a disturbance is not correlated with a prior value of an explanatory variable) and that disturbances are contemporaneously uncorrelated with explanatory variables, we have:

$$(13) \quad E(Exp_{i,t+1} \; \varepsilon_{it}) \neq 0.$$

If this is the case we have a relationship which allows unbiased estimation of the level of wages but which cannot be estimated in the change in wages equation. This situation is certainly not improved by the inclusion of initial wage in the change equation. If we were to use this technique we would find that $\Delta Exp_{i,t+1}$ is still correlated with $\Delta\varepsilon_{i,t+1}$ and we will have introduced other problems as well.

The use of initial wage as an explanatory variable in a wage change equation may be warranted for other reasons specific to the models being estimated, as in the case of state dependence; but its inclusion as a proxy for unobserved variables or to control for the initial levels of some variables is not justified.

The use of two years of panel observations eliminates the need to include the unobserved time invariant variables in the estimated equation by controlling for these variables through its disturbance term. This represents a large improvement over the use of cross-sectional data because it eliminates the bias portion of the error, allowing inferences about the relative effects of the explanatory variables to be made for the population as a whole.

A potentially serious problem in the use of panel data to estimate change equations should be noted. Change equations, particularly single changes between two points in time are more sensitive than a level equation to self-selection bias in the data. Self-selection bias occurs when the group observed to be changing differs in some unmeasured way from the nonchangers. Job changers, for example, may have more motivation or may be leaving unusually low-paying jobs. In addition, change equations require that the sample be restricted to those in the labor force at both points in time, therefore intermittent labor force participation causes proportionately larger losses in a change equation than in the estimation of a cross-sectional levels equation. Other problems often noted with a change equation are the decrease in the number of degrees of freedom and the elimination of a substantial amount of the variation among both the dependent and independent variables.

Multiple Years of Panel Data

By generalizing the change in earnings function to cover more than one change in aggregate macroeconomic conditions, we can include these variables in our equation. The most straight-forward generalization of the wage change equation would be to use several years of panel data and observe the change between successive years in a given individual's earnings. The presence of more than one observed change for each individual allows some fluctuation in the Macro_t variables so that we can control for them in our regression equation. The model to be estimated is now

$$(14) \qquad \Delta \ln Y_{i,t+1} = \beta_2 \; \Delta \text{Exp}_{i,t+1} + \eta_2 \; \Delta \text{Macro}_{t+1} + \Delta \varepsilon_{i,t+1}$$

$$E(\Delta \varepsilon_{i,t+1})^2 = E(\varepsilon_{i,t+1} - \varepsilon_{it})(\varepsilon_{i,t+1} - \varepsilon_{it})$$

$$= E(\varepsilon_{i,t+1}^2 - 2\varepsilon_{it}\varepsilon_{i,t+1} + \varepsilon_{it}^2) = 2\sigma^2$$

$$E(\Delta \varepsilon_{i,t+1} \Delta \varepsilon_{it}) = E(\varepsilon_{i,t+1} - \varepsilon_{it})(\varepsilon_{it} - \varepsilon_{i,t-1})$$

$$= E(\varepsilon_{i,t+1}\varepsilon_{it} - \varepsilon_{i,t+1}\varepsilon_{i,t-1} - \varepsilon_{it}^2$$

$$+ \varepsilon_{it}\varepsilon_{i,t-1}) = -\sigma^2$$

This model exhausts all the information and leaves only the truly random component in the disturbance term. Although the Macro_t variables are now controlled for, their variation between any two years is likely to be small, making it difficult to estimate their effects precisely. The small range of values observed for these variables introduces imprecision into the estimate of their effect, which results in relatively large estimated standard errors and makes it difficult to single out individual effects of the explanatory variables. The greater the variation in the observations of the explanatory variables, the more precise our estimates of their effects will be. If there was no serial correlation in the disturbances before there will be a negative correlation between adjacent time periods in the present model.

A second method of utilizing the information in several years of panel data was used by Hanushek and Quigley (1978). For their change variables, they looked at the change in each year from the first year rather than looking at the change between adjacent years. This transformation has the benefit of controlling for the time invariant variables, and it has the additional advantage of allowing more variation among the explanatory variables.[9] This model would be specified as:

$$(15) \quad \ln Y_{i,t+s} - \ln Y_{it} = \beta_2 \, (Exp_{i,t+s} - Exp_{it})$$

$$+ \eta_2 \, (Macro_{t+s} - Macro_t) + \varepsilon_{i,t+s} - \varepsilon_{it}$$

$$E(\varepsilon_{i,t+s} - \varepsilon_{it})^2 = E(\varepsilon_{i,t+s}^2 - 2\,\varepsilon_{i,t+s}\,\varepsilon_{it} + \varepsilon_{it}^2) = 2\sigma^2$$

$$E(\varepsilon_{i,t+s} - \varepsilon_{it})\,(\varepsilon_{i,t+r} - \varepsilon_{it}) = E(\varepsilon_{i,t+s}\,\varepsilon_{i,t+r}$$

$$- \varepsilon_{i,t+s}\,\varepsilon_{it} - \varepsilon_{i,t+r}\,\varepsilon_{it}$$

$$+ \varepsilon_{it}^2) = \sigma^2$$

where t is the first year of panel data and t+s represents subsequent years. If there are s years of panel data there will be s-1 observations. This specification introduces an additional complication over the specification in Equation 14 because all the equations are serially correlated through their relation to the initial disturbance term ε_{it}. Due to the assumption that there was no serial correlation among the original disturbances the form of the serial correlation will be known and not to troublesome. In conjunction with other assumptions about the disturbance term the effect of this transformation on the

---

[9] OLS estimates of either change equation will not be efficient or asymptotically efficient under the assumptions of the model due to the serial correlation of the disturbance terms.

variance-covariance matrix may increase the difficulty of estimation. Another potentially serious problem with using this model is the choice of the base year. For some analysis the base year chosen will have important consequences on the resulting conclusions. This will be particularly true if there are period effects taking place, or if the nature of the problem has been changing somewhat with time. In either case the problems arise because our model is misspecified but nevertheless it is disconcerting that deviation from an arbitrarily chosen year may provide different results then the same analysis using a different base year.

To circumvent this problem we could take the deviation for each variable from its mean value over time. This could be done for each individual and then we could restructure the data matrix to consist of the individuals deviation from the mean value of the variable at each point in time. The equation covering T time periods is:

$$(16) \quad \ln Y_{it} - \ln \bar{Y}_i = \beta_2(\text{Exp}_{it} - \overline{\text{Exp}}_i) + \eta_2(\text{Macro}_t - \overline{\text{Macro}}) + \varepsilon_{it} - \bar{\varepsilon}_i$$

$$E(\varepsilon_{it} - \bar{\varepsilon}_i)^2 = E(\varepsilon_{it}^2 - 2\varepsilon_{it}\bar{\varepsilon}_i + \bar{\varepsilon}_i^2) = \sigma^2 - \sigma^2/T$$

$$E(\varepsilon_{it} - \bar{\varepsilon}_i)(\varepsilon_{is} - \bar{\varepsilon}_i) = E(\varepsilon_{it}\varepsilon_{is} - \varepsilon_{it}\bar{\varepsilon}_i - \varepsilon_{is}\bar{\varepsilon}_i + \bar{\varepsilon}_i^2) = -\sigma^2/T$$

where the bar is used to denote the mean value of the variable for that individual over the T time periods.

This method includes one more observation than the procedures described in Equations 14 and 15 since one of the observations is not dropped. The problem with this procedure is that for variables which do not change much over time our new data matrix will be composed of variables that are very small in magnitude. Even for variables which do vary extensively over time this method will result in less variation in the data matrix then there would be with the procedure described in Equation 15. The decrease in variance increases the imprecision of the estimates we obtain. A slight advantage which will at least partially offset this increased imprecision caused by the decreased variance of the data is that this method results in a smaller variance and covariance among the disturbance terms. The longer the period under consideration the greater the gain in precision this will lead to.

Strong assumptions concerning the error structure were made in this note to simplify the discussion and comparison of models. Attempts to use the procedures discussed in the context of analyses may involve further complications if the error structure and model specified are not the simple ones on which most of this note is based. This does not invalidate the resulting advantages to be obtained from panel data, it only complicates the procedure used. The assumptions we made were the typical ones used in comparisons of procedures, and the advantages they imply generalize to more complex models. The basic result is that there are large advantages to be obtained from the repeated observations of the same individuals, particularly when there are individual specific effects to be accounted for. The purpose of this note is to make people aware of the potential benefits since the advantageous aspect of panel data is often not exploited to the analysts advantage. The primary advantage of panel data is the potential it provides for holding constant individual specific effects. This is accomplished through the use of a change equation such as those described by Equations 14 – 16. The nature of a panel in providing information over several time periods also yields advantages in controlling for macro economic or time specific effects.

References

Blau, Francine D., and Kahn, Laurence M. "Race and Sex Differences in the Probability and Consequence of Voluntary Turnover." University of Illinois, 1979. Mimeograph.

Chamberlain, G. "On the Use of Panel Data." Harvard University, 1978. Mimeograph.

Hanushek, Eric A., and Quigley, John M. "Life-Cycle Earnings Capacity and the OJT Investment Model." Discussion Paper 7904, University of Rochester Public Policy Analysis Program, 1978.

Lillard, Lee A., and Willis, Robert J. "Dynamic Aspects of Earnings Mobility." Econometrica 46 (September 1978): 985–1012.

Mellow, Wesley. "Unionism and Wages: A Longitudinal Analysis." Bureau of Labor Statistics, 1979. Mimeograph.

Chapter 14

SOME TESTS OF WAGE TRADE-OFF HYPOTHESES

James N. Morgan

Theories involving unmeasured concepts sometimes have implications for variables we <u>have</u> measured. In such cases we can at least see whether the data are consistent with the theoretical hypothesis, even though alternative explanations are still possible. One example is the on-the-job training hypothesis which says that an individual may face a choice of jobs which offer trade-offs between level of initial wage and chances for subsequent increases, the alternative being 1) a higher initial salary with smaller likelihood of increases and 2) a lower initial salary but more on-the-job training which will lead to a more rapid increase in salary in the future. If market forces have made the discounted present value of the two alternatives roughly equivalent for the individual (or for all those with roughly the same initial human capital) then the time paths of earnings in the two jobs should cross at some "overtaking" point. The point would occur where the investment in training has resulted in the accumulation of sufficient additional "human capital" to offset any continuing costs of the on-the-job training.[1] That is, after a few years, the earnings of individuals in the jobs with training overtake the initially higher earnings of individuals in the jobs that go nowhere and after that earnings on the "good jobs" are not only higher but they increase more rapidly.

If individuals within a group are sufficiently similar in their initial endowments (of human capital), then the original job alternatives that were open to them should be apparent by comparing their later earnings experiences, and it would not be necessary to find out precisely what alternatives each person

---

[1]For recent discussions, see Brown (1980) and Hause (1980). For the main presentation, see Mincer (1974).

faced.[2] Our operational hypothesis is that, for any group with reasonably
similar "endowments," there should be a negative correlation between the level
and time-trend of earnings in their early years, and a positive correlation
later--after the "overtaking" point. A realistic categorization of endowments,
for this purpose, would include not just formal education but also race and sex,
which represent differences based on historical discrimination. In the present
analysis the necessity for separating by age restricted the fineness of our
classifications. Hence, we created five groups of unchanged (1974 through 1979)
household heads. The groups consisted of (1) all the nonwhites, (2) the white
women, and (3) the remaining group of white men, which was divided into three
subgroups according to their education.

For each group, including only those with more than $100 in earnings (in
1967 dollars) in each of the five years and still in the labor force in 1979, we
fitted a time regression on the logarithm of their deflated annual earnings. The
regression coefficient was thus an annual percentage increase in real earnings.
The standard error around that time trend for each individual was a measure of
instability or uncertainty of earnings. If people expect their own earnings to
change at a constant rate (percent) this measure would indicate unexpected
departures.

We could then ask whether early in life there was a negative correlation
between the level and the time-trend of earnings, and later in life a positive
correlation. We used the five-year average level to avoid the semi-automatic
negative correlation between initial level and trend arising from measurement
errors, transitory incomes, or real regression to some norm. Since we averaged
logs, the level is really a geometric mean.

Tables 14.1 and 14.2 show that there was indeed a tendency for the level and
trend of earnings to be negatively correlated among the younger age groups of
each subgroup. And there was a positive correlation later on. However, for

---

[2]This is a leap of faith, of course, because the appearance of trade-offs
across persons and jobs does not prove that individuals really have alternatives
to choose among. One could have jobs allotted by sheer chance, which happened to
have similar present expected values but different time paths of earnings.
Furthermore, we are implicitly assuming that a single job choice affects the
whole future even if there are subsequent job changes, perhaps by narrowing the
range of alternatives for the future. We also assume that those in the same
education-race-sex group have a narrower range of total-job qualities available,
as measured by their discounted present value of earnings, so that the negative
correlations between level and trend across competing jobs would not be swamped
by positive correlations across a wide range of generally good to generally bad
jobs.

nonwhites and the educated white men a small negative correlation reappeared at later ages. These groups had a flat or even falling income trend in real dollars, however, so a negative correlation meant that those older workers at a lower level were more likely to be keeping up with inflation.

Table 14.1

RELATION OF LEVEL TO TREND OF EARNINGS FOR VARIOUS SUBGROUPS[a]

Subgroup	N	Trend (%/Yr.)	Intercept (a)	Effect of Level (b)	Average Level	Correlation (R)
All	3038	.0104	.0722	-.0070	$6904	-.03
Nonwhite						
18-34	43	.1652	1.236	-.1360	2644	-.22
35+	983	.0090	-.0414	.0059	5219	.03
White Women						
18-34	54	.1352	1.47	-.1633	3533	-.62
35+	154	-.0079	-.186	.0215	3984	.14
White Men						
0-11 grades						
18-34	106	.017	-.034	.0060	4915	.02
35-44	87	-.011	-.138	.0146	6248	.08
45+	223	-.034	-.862	.0946	6310	.36
12 + no college degree						
18-34	400	.034	.318	-.0323	6438	-.11
35-44	193	-.012	-.212	.0220	8604	.10
45+	295	-.020	.091	-.0121	9045	-.07
College graduate						
18-34	207	.107	1.11	-.1126	7259	-.28
35-44	99	.0057	-.024	.0032	12457	.03
45+	134	-.0064	.194	-.0210	14045	-.20

[a]Trend = a + b (level); level = average of ln (deflated annual earnings).

Thus, the data did corroborate the notion that there may be some jobs with lower initial earnings but more chances for advancement. The fact that the differences by age were stronger within the more homogeneous groups in Table 14.2 than for the whole sample reinforces the notion that the tradeoffs are possible for those with similar initial endowments. We used annual earnings rather than hourly earnings, even though the latter might seem closer to a productivity measure affected by investment in human capital, because much of the variation in

Table 14.2

"EFFECT" OF LEVEL ON TREND IN ANNUAL EARNINGS
BY AGE FOR SOME POPULATION GROUPS
(Regression coefficients of deflated ln-earnings.)

Age Subgroup	All	Nonwhites	White Women Heads	White Men 0-11 Years of College	White Men 12+ but No College Degree	White Men College Graduate
18-24	-.134	-.136	-.134[a]	-.111	-.127	-1.07[a]
25-34	-.060	-.028	-.177	.069	-.022	-.107
35-44	.005	.007	-.027	.015	.220	.003
45-54	.018	.062	-.006	.125	-.014	-.011
55-64	.002	-.012	.016	.084	-.032	-.044
All ages	-.007	-.007	-.021	.061	-.012	-.031

[a]Fewer than 25 cases.

work hours could have been involuntary, a second indicator of the quality of a job. A substantial number of workers said they wanted more work than they had. If, as seems true, lower wage jobs also have more unemployment, our measure takes account of both.

There is a second hypothesis about workers´ job choices which says that they might trade off lower wages for more job stability. We have shown elsewhere that this was not borne out in our data (Grosse and Morgan, Chapter 9 in this volume; Morgan, 1980), but we thought that it might be useful to test the compensating differential hypothesis again with the subsample and time period we have used here. We correlated instability with level of earnings for all of our subgroups (Table 14.3) and again found a persistent negative correlation, the reverse of what the hypothesis would have predicted.[3] Indeed, we searched each of the groups in Table 14.3 further to see whether there was a positive correlation between level and instability of earnings for any subgroup (defined by a number of characteristics including occupation and industry). We found only an

---

[3]Instability is the standard error of deflated ln (earnings) around the regression-fitted trend line, hence is a relative measure. It seems reasonable that a zero-instability base-line would be a predictable constant percentage increase in earnings.

occasional small group with a positive correlation; the negative correlations
were pervasive. If there are individuals who face a choice between a stable low-
paying job and an unstable high-paying one, that choice is overwhelmed by strong
positive correlations among job qualities. There is a positive correlation
between growth trend and instability but it could be an artifact of measurement,
if promotions do not come every year.

Table 14.3

REGRESSION OF INSTABILITY ON LEVEL OF EARNINGS[a]

Subgroup	N	Instability (Standard Error)[b]	Intercept (a)	Effect of Level (b)	Average Level	Correlation (r)
All	3038	.37	2.67	-.260	$6905	-.43
Nonwhite	1026	.48	2.98	-.292	5115	-.43
18-34	411	.59	5.00	-.466	4447	-.61
35+	615	.43	2.16	-.200	5486	-.32
White Women	208	.41	2.39	-.240	3866	-.48
In or near city	156	.42	3.18	-.331	4188	-.57
30+ miles from nearest city of 5000	52	.37	1.23	-.108	3041	-.30
White Men						
0-11 grades						
18-34	106	.56	5.15	-.541	4915	-.56
35-44	87	.42	3.21	-.319	6248	-.48
45+	223	.37	3.05	-.305	6311	-.49
12+ grades, no college degree						
18-34	460	.37	3.69	-.379	6438	-.48
35-44	193	.34	2.45	-.233	8604	-.29
45+	295	.27	2.06	-.196	9045	-.35
College graduate or more						
18-34	207	.41	4.09	-.414	7259	-.54
35-44	99	.26	1.23	-.103	12057	-.26
45+	134	.23	1.92	-.177	14045	-.48

[a] Instabiilty = a + b(level).
[b] Standard deviation of residuals of log earnings around a regression on time.

426

Conclusion

In contrast to the lack of confirmation of the level/stability tradeoff hypothesis, the hypothesis that there is a tradeoff between level and trend in earnings, perhaps reflecting differences in on-the-job training, does appear to be borne out in dynamic panel data. Further analysis should use tenure on the job rather than age, dividing groups at the ten year "overtaking" point Mincer suggested. We should also provide better controls for interpersonal differences in initial endowments. Convincing evidence that individuals face such tradeoffs, however, might require information on the job alternatives actually perceived as available by individuals. Also a more in-depth examination of mechanisms by which individuals learn on the job should prove fruitful.

References

Brown, Charles. "Equalizing Differences in the Labor Market." Quarterly Journal of Economics 94 (February 1980): 113-134.

Brown. Charles. "The Overtaking Point Revisited." Review of Economics and Statistics 62 (May 1980): 309-313.

Grosse, Scott, and Morgan, James N. "Level and Instability of Earnings: Good Jobs-Bad Jobs or Compensating Differentials?" Chapter 9, this volume.

Hause, John C. "The Fine Structure of Earnings and On-the-Job Training Hypothesis." Econometrica 48 (May 1980): 1013-1030.

Mincer, Jacob. Schooling, Experience and Earnings. New York: National Bureau of Economic Research, 1974.

Morgan, James N. "Voluntary and Involuntary Job Changes--Are There Compensating Differentials?" Proceedings of the Social Statistics Section, American Statistical Association, Houston, Tx., August 1980.

Chapter 15

CONSISTENCY OF REPORTS OF HOURLY EARNINGS

James N. Morgan

For the last nine years of the Panel Study of Income Dynamics we have asked
enough questions to allow us to estimate in two different ways the average hourly
earnings of family heads. Thus, we are able to see whether the two estimates
agree, and, if they do not, whether there is any systematic pattern in the
differences between them. Since we do not know whether the differences between
the measures result from systematic biases in one or the other or both or random
errors in one or the other or both, there is no formal model to test. When
either measure is used as a dependent variable, systematic measurement biases can
cause errors in estimates, but random errors in measuring earnings do no harm
beyond some reduction in levels of significance. When either measure is used as
an explanatory variable, either systematic biases or random errors can distort
estimated relationships. New statistical programs allow multiple measures to be
used simultaneously to estimate the true earnings, its variance, and a less
biased set of relationships with other variables. But a useful preliminary is to
examine the two measures and their differences.

We shall look first at individual correlations for unchanged household heads
across nine years, then at across-individuals correlations between estimates
based on the eleventh wave report of 1978 wage rates and the twelfth wave reports
of 1978 earnings for unchanged household heads between those two years.[1]

One measure of hourly earnings termed "calculated wage" was derived by
asking people for their annual earnings from work (wages and salaries), including
overtime, bonuses, commissions, extra jobs, and income from professional practice
or trade. The total number of hours worked during the year was calculated by
asking how many weeks a person worked the previous year minus time missed due to
his or her own sickness (or that of some other member of the family) and also

---

[1]The wage rate is as of the time of interview, but the annual hours and
earnings for that year are asked in the subsequent interview. Wage rates, of
course, can vary during a year.

subtracting time spent on vacation, on strike, or unemployed. Next, we asked people approximately how many hours a week they worked--making sure that hours spent on overtime or second jobs were included. We then estimated hourly earnings by dividing total earnings by the total number of hours worked.

A second estimate of average hourly earnings, termed "stated wage," was derived from a series of questions about salary rates that we started asking nine years ago of those employed by others. A filter question is: Are you salaried, paid by the hour, or what?

The three resulting groups are asked:

Salaried: How much is your salary: $ per ____.

If you were to work more hours than usual during some week, would you get paid for those extra hours of work?

If yes, about how much would you make per hour for that overtime?

Hourly: What is your hourly wage rate for your regular work time?

What is your hourly wage rate for overtime?

Other: If you worked an extra hour, how much would you earn for that hour?

Those who reported extra jobs or other ways of making money were also asked: "How much did you make per hour at this?" We assumed that the overtime rate on extra work on the main job or the second job rate applied to any hours beyond the first 2000 per year, and we created a weighted average earnings measure.

For the nine years for which we can make the stated-wage estimate, we can calculate for each individual the correlation between the two earnings estimates. Even if there were systematic exaggerations of work hours, there might still be a perfect correlation between the two estimates, but with a regression line slope coefficient which differs from unity.

The overall correlation for the 519 cases that met our specifications was .565. These cases included individuals who were household heads for the whole 12 years, with some hourly earnings and non-zero work hours for each of the last 9 years, and with no reported wage rate over $9.98 for the years when only three digits were allowed in the code (usually a small fraction exceeded the limit). Table 15.1 shows the results of an analysis of factors affecting reliability of reports of earnings--various factors accounting for more than a third of the variability in the correlation between the two earnings reports. (In the table, the individual correlations are treated as the dependent variable in a regression.)

Situational factors such as having years of only part-time work or being self-employed clearly led to the greatest discrepancies in the reports of wage

Table 15.1

REGRESSION ANALYSIS OF THE CORRELATION BETWEEN HOURLY
EARNINGS BASED ON CALCULATED WAGE[a] AND HOURLY EARNINGS BASED ON STATED WAGE[b]
(For 519 individuals who were household heads 1968-1979
and employed in the nine years 1971-1979.)

| Independent Variable | Number of Classes | Explanatory power | | Direction of Effect |
		Gross (Eta Squared)	Net (Beta Squared)	
# Years worked less than 1000 hours	5	.275	.215	-
Number of years self-employed	4	.071	.057	-
Years of job tenure	6	.097	.019	+
Years in white-collar job	5	.045	.016	-
Education	8	.016	.015	?
Age	5	.133	.010	-
Race (black)	3	.002	.005	-
Marital status	5	.018	.004	?
Sex	2	.019	.001	?

Average Correlation (Mean of Dependent Variable) = .565

R^2 (Adj.) = .354

[a] Calculated wage is derived by dividing annual earnings by annual work hours.
[b] Stated wage is the wage reported as hourly, weekly, or monthly earnings.
This stated wage was adjusted for overtime and second jobs by assuming such
work time applied to any hours beyond 2000 per year.

rates (Table 15.2). The usual demographic variables made little difference, except for education, which was not monotonic. The people with some high school education but no college appeared to be the most consistent; the college graduates were the least so. The people with part-time work may have had low correlations if our adjustment for second jobs or overtime was incorrect, but the overall reliability of the commonly used hourly earnings measure was clearly lower for those working part time.

The various restrictions necessary to have nine years of information for each included case not only kept our number of cases small (519) but also allowed a possible selection bias by eliminating younger and older respondents, individuals becoming household heads, and those with higher wage rates. It did allow a measure of agreement between the two earning rate reports for each individual (across the nine years). But we are also able to use group correlations for a single year, 1978, and to search for what subgroups of respondents seemed most consistent. We took the 3,541 family heads in the sample who did not change between 1978 and 1979, who were currently working in 1978 so that they reported wage rates, who reported 1978 earnings in 1979 that came to $0.50 an hour or more, and who answered all the wage questions. For this entire group and for its subgroups, we looked at the correlation of the two measures between (a) hourly earnings derived by dividing 1978 annual earnings by 1978 annual hours as reported in 1979 (calculated wage), and (b) average wage derived from 1978 reports on the regular or current wage (stated wage), adjusted for a different overtime rate if any (for all hours over 2,000) and for a different second-job rate if any (for all hours on the second job). Overall, the correlation was .719, higher than the average individual cross-year correlation of .565. If we assume that the errors are most likely in the reports on hours per week and weeks worked, and next most likely in annual earnings, we should treat the hourly earnings figure derived from those replies--the calculated wage--as the dependent variable (with the errors) and the stated hourly wage as the truer estimates. This would give:

(Calculated Wage) = 2.55 + .696(Stated Wage)

	Average	Standard Deviation
Calculated Wage	$7.83	$4.31
Standard Wage	$4.31	$4.46

(Note that the correlation is equal to the regression slope times the ratio of the standard deviations .695(4.46/4.31) = .719.) Since the standard deviations of the two estimates are usually similar, the regression slope is a good proxy

Table 15.2

EFFECTS OF SHORT HOURS OR SELF-EMPLOYMENT ON CORRELATION
BETWEEN CALCULATED WAGE[a] AND STATED WAGE[b]
(For 519 individuals who were household heads 1968-1979
and employed in the nine years 1971-1979.)

Independent Variable	N	Unadjusted Correlation	Correlation Adjusted by Regression for Other Factors
Number of years (out of 9) worked less than 1000 hours			
0	394	68	67
1	55	46	42
2	29	14	20
3-4	25	10	22
5 or more	16	6	9
Eta Squared		.28	
Beta Squared			.22
Number of years self-employed			
0	431	61	59
1	36	53	60
2	26	37	54
3 or more	26	23	21
Beta Squared		.07	
Eta Squared			.06

[a] Calculated wage is derived by dividing annual earnings by annual work hours.
[b] Stated wage is the wage reported as hourly, weekly, or monthly earnings. This stated wage was adjusted for overtime and second jobs by assuming such work time applied to any hours beyond 2000 per year.

for the similarity of the two estimates (though not of the bias, as we shall see). Table 15.3 gives the correlations between the two estimates for a number of subgroups, showing again that the most discrepancies occur among the part-time workers. When we searched in a non-hierarchical way for subgroups with widely differing relationships between the two measures, we obtained the results given in Figure 15.1, where the R-squareds varied from .058 to .864; the former were for young women heads of families in the lower six deciles of family income/needs, and the latter were for men with some college in the top income/needs decile working full time (2,000 hours or more). However, a group of men in the lowest income/needs decile and with very low earnings also had a very high correlation (R^2 = .860).

Given that most researchers use the calculated wage measure of hourly earnings and assuming that the stated wage measure might be more accurate, what can we say about possible biases from this choice? Random errors in a dependent variable cause no biases in estimated relations, but biased (non-random) errors in that variable can do so.

The average difference between the calculated wage and the stated wage (for 3541 heads working in 1979, unchanged since 1978 and able to give wage rate figures) was $0.24, with a standard deviation of $3.29. (The higher estimate was for the calculated wage.) The major differences in this "bias," aside from some automatic relations with the level of each of the two earnings estimates, appeared to depend on the number of hours worked in 1978:

Hours Worked	N	Average Difference Between Calculated Wage and Stated Wage	Standard Deviation of Difference
Fewer than 500	64	$1.29	$4.74
500-999	111	.45	4.72
1000-1499	277	.31	3.07
1500-1999	1064	.99	2.61
2000-2499	1407	.37	2.61
2500 or more	618	-1.24	4.36
All	3541	.24	3.29

Aside from this, which mostly affects those with substantial overtime or second jobs, little systematic bias appeared. Table 15.4 shows the mean differences by age, education, race, and income/needs decile for all those sampled and for those who worked 2,500 hours or more. The standard deviation of the differences also varied very little from one subgroup to another.

Table 15.3 (page 1 of 3)

REGRESSION OF CALCULATED WAGE[a] ON STATED WAGE [b,c]
(For 3541 individuals who were household heads
and employed in both 1978 and 1979.)

Subgroup	N	R^2	Regression Coefficient
Education			
Cannot read or write	57	.24	.41
0-5 grades	69	.67	.77
6-8	296	.50	.69
9-11	642	.37	.57
12 (high school)	769	.34	.52
12+ non-academic	585	.43	.67
Some college	549	.44	.73
College degree	394	.75	.82
Advanced or professional degree	180	.69	.78
Income/Needs Decile			
1 (Lowest)	193	.85	1.01
2nd	277	.36	.55
3rd	358	.53	.71
4th	401	.31	.69
5th	454	.32	.61
6th	394	.31	.55
7th	425	.38	.53
8th	370	.27	.47
9th	374	.38	.50
10 (Highest)	295	.74	.86

Table 15.3 (page 2 of 3)

Subgroup	N	R^2	Regression Coefficient
Age			
18-24	409	.36	.61
25	1407	.36	.57
35	652	.42	.70
45-54	619	.63	.77
55-64	395	.66	.77
65-74	54	.47	.62
75	5	.99	1.03
Hours Worked			
1-499	64	.25	.69
500-949	111	.18	.37
950-1499	277	.50	.67
1500-1999	1064	.62	.93
2000-	2025	.52	.64
Hourly Earnings			
.50-2.99	378	.61	.86
3.00-4.99	875	.50	.65
5.00-6.99	802	.25	.31
7.00-8.99	645	.25	.03
9.00-10.99	418	.28	.42
11.00-12.99	189	.47	.56
13.00 or more	234	.71	.97

Table 15.3 (page 3 of 3)

Subgroup	N	R^2	Regression Coefficient
Marital Status			
Married	2479	.52	.69
Single	403	.38	.62
Widowed	138	.79	.90
Divorced	370	.52	.73
Separated	151	.66	.64
Race			
White	2233	.50	.68
Black	1181	.60	.76
Hispanic	98	.35	.84
Other	29	.95	1.07
Sex			
Male	2880	.50	.68
Female (heads)	661	.63	.78

[a] Calculated wage is derived by dividing annual earnings by annual work hours.

[b] Stated wage is the wage reported as hourly, weekly, or monthly earnings. This stated wage was adjusted for overtime and second jobs by assuming such work time applied to any hours beyond 2000 per year.

[c] The regression specification was Calculated Wage = a+b (Stated Wage). Overall, Calculated Wage = 2.55 + .695 (Stated Wage).

436

Figure 15.1

RESULTS OF A SEARCH FOR DIFFERENT RELATIONS BETWEEN TWO ESTIMATES OF EARNINGS RATES
(Hourly Earnings) = a+b (Wage Rate)

(For 3,541 individuals who were household heads
and employed in both 1978 and 1979.)

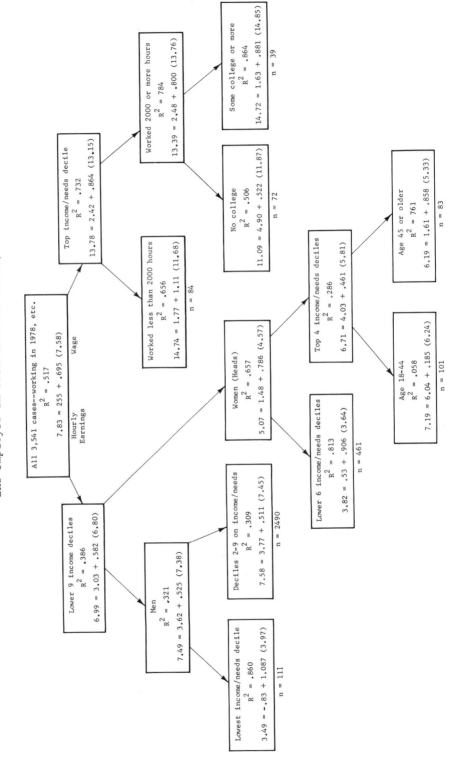

Table 15.4 (page 1 of 2)

MEAN DIFFERENCE BETWEEN CALCULATED WAGE[a] AND STATED WAGE[b]
(For 3541 individuals who were household heads
and employed in both 1978 and 1979.)

Characteristic	All	Worked Less than 2500 Hours	Worked 2500 Hours or More
Age			
18-24	$ .12	$.33	$ -1.03
25-34	.28	.61	-1.03
35-44	.25	.59	-.79
45-54	.23	.83	-1.90
55-64	.34	.57	-1.08
65-74	-.13	.72	-3.67
Education			
Cannot read or write	-1.14	-.95	-1.76[c]
0-5 grades	.41	.44	.34[c]
8	.29	.55	-1.26
9-11	.24	.39	-.48
12 (high school)	.07	.50	-1.78
12+ non-acad.	.41	.81	-1.50
Some college	.66	.83	-.04
College degree	-.08	.63	-1.66
Advanced degree	-.20	.69	-2.16
Race			
White	.23	.65	-1.43
Black	.37	.50	-.29
Spanish American	.19	-.14	1.44[c]
Other	.47	.58[c]	.03[c]

Table 15.4 (page 2 of 2)

	All	Worked Less than 2500 Hours	Worked 2500 Hours or More
Income/Needs Decile			
1 (Lowest)	-.10	-.07	-1.92^c
2nd	-1.12	-.99	-2.10
3rd	-.19	-.02	-1.17
4th	.10	.46	-1.57
5th	.44	.66	-.58
6th	.41	.63	-.59
7th	.40	.68	-.77
8th	.47	1.00	-1.26
9th	.07	.63	-2.28
10 (Highest)	.63	1.61	-1.31
All	.024	.062	-1.64

[a] Calculated wage is derived by dividing annual earnings by annual work hours.
[b] Stated wage is the wage reported as hourly, weekly, or monthly earnings. This stated wage was adjusted for overtime and second jobs by assuming such work time applied to any hours beyond 2000 per year.
[c] Fewer than 25 cases.

SUMMARY

The use of an average hourly earnings estimate based on dividing annual earnings by annual hours (the "calculated wage") will produce some small downward bias in estimates of the effects and of the strength of effects of hourly earnings on other variables, if we assume stated wage rates are more accurate. However, we found no substantial variations in the size of the measurement error that could bias comparisons among subgroups, except for those working only part time and those working much more than full time. The simplest explanation for the discrepancies for those who reported either very low or very high annual work hours is that there were errors in the reports of those hours. Therefore, in analyzing earnings it would seem appropriate to eliminate from the analyses those workers with extremely high or low work hours, or to truncate their hourly earnings figures by compressing work hours to a range of 500 to 2500 before dividing annual earnings by annual work hours.

In using earnings as an explanatory variable one might want to treat the two measures as separate but flawed indicators of a true earnings rate, using some maximum likelihood computer program such as LISREL to determine simultaneously their weights and the rest of the relationships. But one might also prefer to deal separately with the different rates for overtime or second jobs, since they may show that the overall average earning rate is not fixed but depends on the total hours worked.

Chapter 16

CHILD CARE WHEN PARENTS ARE EMPLOYED

James N. Morgan

INTRODUCTION

The massive increases both in the proportion of mothers employed and in the number of single-parent families with children have left many families with the difficult problem of coordinating market work with caring for children. There have been demands for more day care facilities and for subsidies in addition to those created by recent changes in the Federal Income tax law allowing deductions for some of the costs of child care. There have also been concerns that child care problems are keeping some women from paid employment, or making their attendance at work less dependable.

PRIOR DATA AND ANALYSIS

Questions were included during five different years[1] of the Panel Study asking about child-care arrangements of households where there were children under 12 and where both parents or the single parent worked. The 1973 data were analyzed in two chapters in the third volume of Five Thousand American Families (Dickinson, 1975, and Duncan and Hill, 1975). These chapters reported that the informal and family sources of child care predominated, that nearly half the families paid nothing for child care, and that breakdowns in child care arrangements causing loss of time from work were quite rare. Regression analysis on whether the family relied on its own members for child care, whether a sitter was employed, and whether day care centers were used, revealed that the first two options were largely affected by the number of children and by the mother's wage, but the third appeared to be more a matter of supply, dependent on region, religion, the age of the youngest child, city size, and whether the family had moved recently.

---

[1]1973, 1974, 1976 (Wife's Interview), 1977, and 1979.

A later analysis by Duncan and Hill (1977) used the interviews from 1974 instead of 1973 and restricted the sample to two-parent families with both parents working and a child six years of age or younger. They focused on the use of formal day care arrangements and used logit regression. They found that formal methods were much more common in the larger urban areas, and in the South.

The overall proportions using the various modes of child care have changed little over the years since 1973, with no discernible trend. Comparisons are complicated by the fact that employed single parents were asked about child care only in 1973, 1974, and 1979. However, the only substantial difference between the single and the married parents was that a single parent could not rely on juggling work hours or splitting shifts so one parent could always be at home. In 1979 we attempted to reduce the complexity of the questions by asking only how the youngest child was cared for.

The only other recent national data on mode of child care appears to be a supplement to the June 1977 Current Population Survey of the U.S. Census Bureau. Some of its findings were recently reported by Presser and Baldwin (1980). The CPS survey questioned 15 to 44 year old mothers with children under five years of age. There were 8,331 such women 18-44 years old--of whom 2,996 were employed-- out of a sample of 53,500 households. Out of this group, 30 percent reported that nuclear family members provided the child care--a parent or siblings. Another 28 percent said it was provided by other relatives (10 percent in the home, 18 percent elsewhere). Individuals other than relatives accounted for another 30 percent, with 7 percent of them providing child care in the child's own home. Only 12 percent used institutional care like day care centers. More than half of the relatives who cared for children were paid, as of course were almost all of the non-relatives. That same study also asked non-working mothers whether they would work if satisfactory child care were available at a reasonable cost, and 17.4 percent said yes. Working mothers were asked if they would work more if more care were available at reasonable cost, and 16.2 percent of them said yes. This seems to indicate that there is a small but significant demand for more organized child care. The fact that such care has not developed during a period of increased work and wages for women would seem to reveal a reluctance to pay for such care, or lack of entrepreneurial talents in setting up commercial day-care facilities, or high costs resulting from regulation of child-care facilities. Another analysis of the same data set indicated that the use of day-care facilities was associated with expecting fewer additional children (Powers and Salvo, 1980). A summary analysis (Hofferth, 1979) refers to another study we have not seen (ABT, 1978).

Two earlier studies (Low and Spindler and Westinghouse) are summarized in a chapter in Setting National Priorities: the 1973 Budget (Schultze, Rivlin and Teeters). The data are not directly comparable, because each child was counted separately, and only two age groups, children under 6 years of age and those 6 to 14, were distinguished. These studies reported that the use of formal day care centers in 1965 and 1970 was relatively minor even for children under 6 years old. Most children were cared for in their own homes.

Mode of Child Care Reported in 1979

Some 14.5 percent of all the households interviewed in 1979 had children under the age of 12 and either a working mother or a single working parent. These were asked:

> How is your (youngest) child taken care of during work hours?
>
> (If in school) What about after school or when school is closed?
>
> About how many hours a week is your (youngest) child taken care of (not counting time in regular school)?

Additional questions addressed the care of all the children during work hours, the cost in time or money, whether the government paid for any of it, and days lost from work because the child-care arrangements broke down. Many respondents could mention more than one method of care and two methods were coded, with the highest priority given to formal, paid methods like day-care centers or babysitters and the lowest priority to considering the public schools as child care.

Table 16.1 presents the distributions across the child-care methods and shows how they vary according to various family characteristics. A majority of the methods were informal ones, with the type of arrangement varying with the age of the youngest child. Only one-tenth of the families used day-care centers or nursery schools, but for those with two to five year olds that doubled to one-fifth. The most common method of child care, particularly for the younger children, was the paid babysitter, who could be a relative, friend, or neighbor; but a surprisingly large proportion reported that the husband and/or wife cared for the child by splitting shifts or working at home, even when the child was very young. Children under two seldom went to day-care centers or nursery schools, in part, no doubt, because they are rarely accepted in such facilities at that age.

444

Table 16.1 (page 1 of 3)

1979 METHOD OF CHILD CARE OF YOUNGEST CHILD BY VARIOUS FAMILY CHARACTERISTICS[a]
(For 1,273 families with a child under age 12 and a working wife or unmarried working parent.)

Family Characteristic	Number of Cases	Percentage Using Child Care Method for Youngest Child						
		Day Care Center/ Nursery School	Babysitter/ Friend/ Neighbor	Head and/or Wife Split Shifts[b]	Relatives/ Siblings Over 12/"Each Other"	Relatives Not in Household[c]	Child Taking Care of Self	Public School
Age of Youngest Child								
Less than 2	281	5	37	30	7	29	0	0
2-5	513	20	38	24	8	22	2	7
6-11	479	4	25	29	20	1	8	48
Number of Children under Age 18								
1	506	14	36	19	5	23	5	28
2	430	9	33	32	12	17	5	31
3	200	5	23	36	31	12	4	23
4 or more	137	5	16	30	33	16	5	20
Race								
White	616	11	33	30	13	16	5	27
Black	607	7	23	20	17	31	5	25
Other	43	8	33	18	16	19	0	19

Table 16.1 (page 2 of 3)

Family Characteristic	Number of Cases	Day Care Center/ Nursery School	Babysitter/ Friend/ Neighbor	Head and/or Wife Split Shifts[b]	Relatives/ Siblings Over 12/"Each Other"	Relatives Not in Household[c]	Child Taking Care of Self	Public School
Age of Household Head								
20-24	168	13	36	19	9	35	0	3
25-29	341	11	42	17	4	29	4	17
30-34	332	13	38	31	6	17	4	25
35-39	172	9	25	31	26	14	7	41
40-44	93	7	25	36	22	6	3	32
45 or more	152	4	10	30	32	8	10	36
Education of Household Head								
0-5 grades	33	2	24	21	31	20	4	33
6-8 grades	80	3	14	31	31	19	5	30
9-11 grades	285	6	25	27	18	23	3	20
High school	310	12	38	25	11	23	5	22
High school plus nonacademic training	200	9	32	24	10	22	9	28
Some college	208	10	35	28	14	15	2	32
College degree	110	16	29	34	16	10	6	27
Advanced or professional degree	39	18	35	38	5	6	5	28

Percentage Using Child Care Method for Youngest Child

Table 16.1 (page 3 of 3)

Family Characteristic	Number of Cases	Percentage Using Child Care Method for Youngest Child						
		Day Care Center/Nursery School	Babysitter/Friend/Neighbor	Head and/or Wife Split Shifts[b]	Relatives/Siblings Over 12/"Each Other"	Relatives Not in Household[c]	Child Taking Care of Self	Public School
Family Income/Needs Decile								
Lowest	127	5	12	16	26	32	11	22
2	133	8	24	33	14	23	3	15
3	155	9	25	31	14	23	2	26
4	159	5	28	29	14	30	3	23
5	157	6	27	25	19	20	5	27
6	127	11	32	27	15	14	3	24
7	145	10	34	32	16	15	4	30
8	119	18	44	29	9	10	6	24
9	97	12	39	26	3	14	7	26
Highest	54	15	47	22	6	6	5	46
All	1273	10.0	31.4	27.6	13.9	18.7	4.6	26.0

[a] Two methods could be reported, so the figures in each row can sum to more than 100 percent.
[b] Includes working at home arrangements.
[c] Includes situations where it was unclear whether the relative was in the household.

Some families with older children relied entirely on the public schools as their method of child care, and a substantial number used the schools in combination with some other child-care arrangement. Once the youngest child was of school age, the public schools predominated as the method of care, with nearly half the parents of school-age children relying on the schools for at least part of the child care during their working hours.

When there was more than one child in the family, the use of paid methods like day care centers and babysitters dropped off and increasing reliance was placed on children taking care of one another. Parents with two or more children were also most likely to report splitting their work hours so one of them was home to care for the children.

Blacks were nearly twice as likely to rely on relatives outside the household and were less likely to rely on babysitters or on splitting shifts. More black families with children had a single parent who worked, so there was less chance to rely on split shifts, though the same code did include a few parents who worked at home.

The age of the family head was of course related to the number of children and the age of the youngest child, but the parental age patterns for child care methods are of interest in themselves. Table 16.1 shows that the young parents relied heavily on relatives living nearby. Somewhat older parents relied more on babysitters. At somewhat later ages, heavy reliance was placed on the husband and wife splitting their paid work shifts to cover the time when the children were not in school. Finally, older parents relied more heavily on older siblings caring for younger ones, still with a secondary reliance on the schools.

Parents' education reflected both income (ability to pay) and perhaps preferences for specific qualities in child care. The more education the parents had, the more they relied on day-care centers, nursery schools, or paid babysitters and the less they used relatives or older siblings. Indeed, at the highest levels of education, split shifts became more important particularly as a secondary method. The results were the same when families were ranked according to their income/needs ratios. With increasing affluence, the use of day-care centers and paid babysitters also increased.

Breakdowns of Arrangements

Without restricting the discussion to the youngest child only, a general question was asked about breakdown problems:

In the past year, how many days did someone have to stay home from work
to take care of the child/children because these arrangements broke down?
The vast majority reported no days lost. This does not mean that arrangements
never broke down, but that people managed to cope with the system and get to work
most of the time. No one primary mode for the youngest child's care appeared to
be associated with more frequent breakdowns, except perhaps relying on older
siblings to care for younger ones (Table 16.2). Nor was there much relation
between the total cost of child care and its reliability. If anything, loss of
work days was somewhat more frequent for those reporting the smallest and the
largest costs (Table 16.3). The few who reported that the government paid for
part or all of their child care were the most likely to have to stay home from
work because the arrangements broke down.

The striking thing here is the small number of days actually lost from work
because of breakdown in child care. The arrangements surely broke down far more
frequently than that, but apparently people managed to scramble around for
alternative arrangements rather than lose work. Employers' discrimination
against working mothers on the assumption that their attendance will suffer is
clearly unjustified.

We made a flexible search for subgroups who lost more than the usual number
of days from work because their child care provisions broke down (Figure 16.1).
Where the wife or single parent was working less than 500 hours, as might be
expected, less time was lost from work for child care reasons. As we said
earlier, a small group who reported that the government paid for some or all of
their child care had much more frequent breakdowns. Government-subsidized
centers may well be stricter about refusing sick children, or they may be newer
and less well organized, or they may serve clients with fewer alternative or
emergency arrangements. For the remainder it was those families where the wife
or single parent worked full time, 1,500 hours or more in 1978, who reported the
smallest number of days lost from work.

Table 16.4 shows, for the three main groups of Figure 16.1, the differential
effect of the age of the youngest child or the number of children in the family
on days lost due to breakdown. When there were few or young children, breakdown
time losses were more frequent when the wife or employed single parent was
working less than full time, but the greatest loss of work time was among full-
time employed parents with more or older children.

Perhaps when parents work only part time, they can afford to miss a day, and
do so when the child is younger and more vulnerable. On the other hand, when

Table 16.2

DAYS LOST FROM WORK BECAUSE OF BREAKDOWN IN CHILD-CARE ARRANGEMENTS, BY METHOD OF CHILD CARE
(For 1,273 families with a child under age 12 and a working wife or unmarried working parent.)

Days Lost From Work[a]	Child-Care Method for Youngest Child							
	Day Care Center/ Nursery School	Babysitter/ Friend/ Neighbor	Head and/or Wife Split Shifts[b]	Relatives/ Siblings Over 12/"Each Other"	Relatives Not in Household[c]	Child Taking Care of Self	Public School	All Methods
Never	76	75	82	79	82	79	74	78
1-2 times	13	14	6	8	7	1	15	10
3-4 times	1	3	1	2	3	1	6	2
5-9 times	6	4	5	4	6	7	3	5
10 or more	3	3	6	8	2	12	3	6
	99	99	100	101	100	100	101	101
Percentage of Sample	10.0	31.4	27.6	13.9	18.7	4.6	26.0	100
Number of cases	158	343	248	143	279	34	36	1273

[a] The question was: In the past year, how many days did someone have to stay home from work to take care of the child/children because these arrangements broke down?
[b] Includes working at home arrangements.
[c] Includes situations where it was unclear whether the relative was in the household.

Table 16.3

DAYS LOST FROM WORK, BY COST PER WEEK OF THE CHILD-CARE AND
WHETHER GOVERNMENT PAID FOR PART OR ALL OF THE CARE
(For 1,273 families with a child under age 12 and a
working wife or unmarried working parent.)

Days Lost From Work	Cost Per Week (Dollars)						Whether Government Paid for Care	
	0	1-9	10-19	20-39	40-79	80+	Yes	No
0	80	71	83	74	74	71	59	79
1-2	6	20	10	13	18	0	13	10
3-4	2	3	3	3	0	1	2	3
5-9	4	2	3	6	5	18	8	5
10 or more	8	4	3	3	3	10	18	3
	100	100	102	99	100	100	100	100
Percentage of Sample	53	5	11	25	5	1	2	93

mothers or single parents are working practically full time, it may be simply
more difficult to find alternative arrangements to care for older children than
for infants, and more difficult for multiple children than for one or two.

Hours Per Week of Care

Extensive hours of child care were concentrated among the more formal
methods: day care, paid babysitter, or relatives outside the household
(Table 16.5). Dividing the care between husband and wife with split shifts, of
course, was associated with very few hours of child care per week. There was
very little association between the hours of care required and the work hours of
the wife or single parent, or between the number of children and the total hours
of care, so those tables are omitted. The single-child family, if anything, was
more likely to report 32 or more hours a week of child care. And of course, the
younger the child, the more extensive the child care.

Figure 16.1

DAYS LOST FROM WORK IN 1978 BECAUSE CHILD-CARE ARRANGEMENTS BROKE DOWN

(For 1,273 families with a child under age 12 and a working wife or unmarried working parent.)

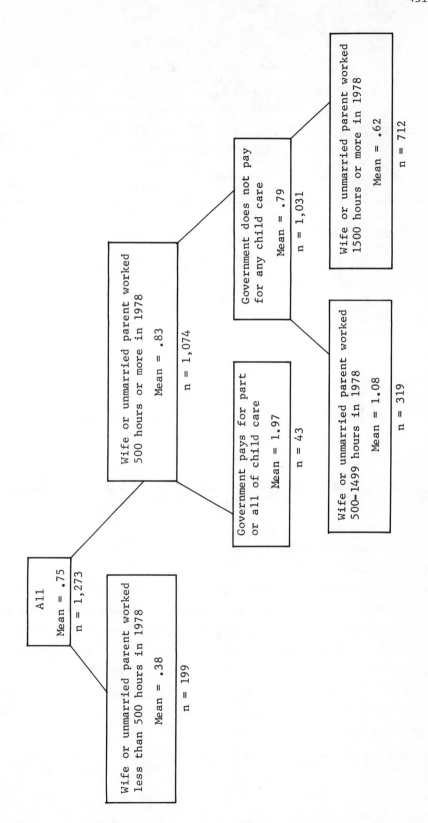

Table 16.4

DAYS LOST FROM WORK IN 1978 BECAUSE
CHILD-CARE ARRANGEMENTS BROKE DOWN
(For 1,273 families with a child under age 12 and a
working wife or unmarried working parent.)

| | Hours Worked by Wife or Unmarried Parent in 1978 | | |
	Less than 500	500-1499[a]	1500 or More[a]
Age of Youngest Child			
Less than 2	.82	.93	.36
2-5	.38	.71	1.15
6-11	.10	.51	1.39
Number of Children			
1	.45	.67	1.02
2	.42	.67	.76
3	.22	.63	1.78
4 or more	.27	.08	1.71
Percentage of Sample	17.7	30.3	52.1

[a]Excludes a few households where government paid for part or all of it.

Cost of Care

Cost of care, of course, was associated with the method of care.
Table 16.6, which compares the primary method used with the total cost, shows,
however, that even when husband and wife split shifts, there was an occasional
report of some other cost. Nearly half of those relying on relatives reported
paying at least something for child care. An impressive range of costs exists,
with more than half of the families reporting no cost at all, but more than one
in 20 reporting spending more than $40 a week on child care. For the types of
care that are paid for, the most common amount seemed to be about $30 a week, or
$1,500 a year--no small item in any budget.

Table 16.5

PERCENTAGE DISTRIBUTION OF HOURS OF CHILD CARE BY
TYPE OF CARE OR AGE OF CHILD
(For 1,273 families with a child under age 12 and a
working wife or unmarried working parent.)

Subgroup Category	Hours of Child Care Per Week						
	Less than 1	1-3	4-7	8-15	16-31	32 or More	All
Primary Method of Child Care							
Day care center/nursery school	0	0	3	19	23	55	100
Babysitter/friend/ neighbor	1	3	13	21	23	40	101
Head and/or wife split shifts[a]	68	5	2	9	12	3	99
Relatives/siblings over 12/ "each other"	26	5	19	15	27	8	100
Relatives not in household[b]	2	2	10	17	30	39	100
Age of Youngest Child							
Less than 2	17	2	3	6	29	43	100
2-5	16	1	3	9	25	47	101
5-11	38	5	14	22	16	4	99
Percentage of Sample	26.8	3.2	8.3	14.7	21.5	25.5	100

[a] Includes working at home arrangements.
[b] Includes situations where it was unclear whether the relative was in the household.

Families with many children were more likely to report no cost at all and were also less likely to report extensive cost. They were relying more on split-shifts and on older siblings for care. The work hours of the wife or single parent had little to do with cost of taking care of the children; however, the age of the youngest child had a major effect. Younger children need more hours per week of care, so it is understandable that the younger the child the greater the child-care costs.

Table 16.6

PERCENTAGE DISTRIBUTION OF COST OF CHILD CARE
FOR VARIOUS SUBGROUP CATEGORIES
(For 1,273 families with a child under age 12 and a
working wife or unmarried working parent.)

Subgroup Category	Cost of Child Care Per Week (in Dollars)						
	0	1-9	10-19	20-37	40-79	80 or More	All
Primary Method of Child Care							
Daycare center/ nursery school	12	4	17	58	10	0	101
Babysitter/friend/ neighbor	7	10	24	47	10	1	99
Head and/or wife split shifts[a]	94	3	1	2	0	0	100
Relatives/sibling over 12/ "each other"	93	1	0	6	0	0	100
Relatives not in household[b]	52	5	13	30	1	0	101
Number of Children Under 18							
1	44	5	17	32	3	0	101
2	52	6	7	27	7	1	100
3	59	5	19	14	2	0	99
4 or more	76	2	7	12	3	0	100
Age of Youngest Child							
Less than 2	44	3	8	36	7	2	100
2-5	35	4	13	43	5	0	100
5-11	70	6	11	10	3	0	100
Percentage of Sample	53	5	11	26	5	0	100

[a]Includes working at home arrangements.
[b]Includes situations where it was unclear whether the relative was in the household.

SUMMARY

There are life-cycle patterns in child care, revealed when one looks at the age of the youngest child and the number of children. Families tend to start with babysitters or arrange care by the nuclear family itself, later move to day-care centers, and then rely more on older siblings and the school system. Most keep the costs down by relying on family members and informal methods. Loss of time from work because of breakdown in child-care arrangements is rare and, clearly, discrimination against working parents on the assumption that their attendance would be less dependable is prejudicial. On the other hand, difficulties in securing good child care apparently persist. From the point of view of a society investing in its next generation, the absence of growth in the use of well-organized day-care centers may reflect a major problem, and the lack of any trend toward an increased use of such facilities indicates that the problem is not being solved.

References

ABT Associates. National Day Care Study: Preliminary Findings and Implications. Cambridge, Mass.: ABT Associates, 1978.

Dickinson, Katherine. "Child Care." In Five Thousand American Families-- Patterns of Economic Progress, Vol. III, edited by Greg J. Duncan and James N. Morgan. Ann Arbor: Institute for Social Research, 1975.

Duncan, Greg J., and Hill, C. Russell. "Modal Choice in Child Care Arrangements." In Five Thousand American Families--Patterns of Economic Progress Vol, III, edited by Greg J. Duncan and James N. Morgan. Ann Arbor: Institute for Social Research, 1975.

_____. "The Child Care Choice of Working Mothers." In Five Thousand American Families--Patterns in Economic Progress, Vol. V, edited by Greg J. Duncan and James N. Morgan. Ann Arbor: Institute for Social Research, 1977.

Hofferth, Sandra L. "Daycare in the Next Decade." Journal of Marriage and the Family (August 1979): 649-58.

Kamerman, Sheila. Managing Work and Family New York, Free Press, 1980.

Low, Seth, and Spindler, Pearl G. Child Care Arrangements of Working Mothers in the United States. Washington, D.C.: U.S. Childrens Bureau and W.W. Women´s Bureau, 1968.

Presser, Harriet B., and Baldwin, Wendy. "Child Care as a Constraint on Employment: Prevalence, Correlates, and Bearing on the Work and Fertility Nexus." American Journal of Sociology 85 (March 1980): 1202-13.

456

Schultze, C; Fried, E; Rivlin, A.; and Teeters, Nancy. Setting National
    Priorities: The 1973 Budget. Washington, D.C.: Brookings, 1973.

Westinghouse Learning Corporation and Westat Research Inc. "Day Care
    Survey-1970; Summary Report and Basic Analysis." Report prepared for
    Evaluation Division, Office of Economic Opportunity. Washington, D.C.: OEO,
    1971.

Chapter 17

SOME ILLUSTRATIVE DESIGN EFFECTS: PROPER SAMPLING
ERRORS VERSUS SIMPLE RANDOM SAMPLE ASSUMPTIONS

Martha S. Hill

INTRODUCTION

Because of the tremendous monetary expense of interviewing the entire population, surveys other than the decennial census rely on samples of the population as their data source. Quite efficient probability sampling techniques have evolved to derive a sample much smaller in size than the whole population but still expected to be representative of it. The techniques used in sample selection often involve departure from simple random sampling (SRS) when such randomization is quite expensive. From an analysis standpoint, though such samples remain representative probability samples, there are costs associated with this departure from SRS. One such cost, which we focus on here, is the introduction of additional sampling error per interview (though not per dollar).

Estimates vary from sample to sample of the same population, so in analysis of survey data it is generally desirable to obtain a good notion of their reliability. Reliability is measured in terms of sampling variation, or "sampling errors." Many standard statistical computer programs provide measures of sampling errors, but these measures assume the use of a simple random sample. The measures of reliability derived from such programs can be deceptive when the sample is not a simple random one.

The sample used in the Panel Study of Income Dynamics departs in several instances from a simple random sample. It consists, in fact, of two samples which could overlap--a 1967 Census sample comprised of one subgroup of particular interest to the study (the poor), combined with a 1968 Survey Research Center (SRC) cross-sectional sample. The Census portion of the sample was restricted to original Census sample members in the lower ranges of income relative to needs who were under age 65, who resided in a selected subset of the Census sampling areas, and who had signed a release of their information (approximately three quarters signed). In addition, both portions of the sample involved stratification (selections from partitions, or strata, of the population) and

457

clustering (where primary sampling unit areas are selected, then areas within each of them are designated, and so on, ending with several addresses along selected blocks). All of these aspects of the sample design involve departure from simple random sampling and may have differing effects on the degree to which standard sampling errors depart from actual sampling errors. Stratification, for example, reduces the DEFT (the square root of the design effect, which is the ratio of the actual sampling variance to the SRS sampling variance), whereas clustering raises it.[1] The reduction in the DEFT from stratification is greatest when the strata are most dissimilar; the increase in the DEFT from clustering is least when the individuals within the cluster are most dissimilar, with the degree of similarity varying from a characteristic such as race of respondent which is likely to be the same for all the addresses in a block to characteristics such as height or month of birth which may have no geographic clustering at all.

ANALYSIS

There are several ways to estimate proper sampling errors, and these methods vary depending on the parameter for which the sampling error is being calculated. The Survey Research Center's OSIRIS computer package currently offers two separate programs for calculating proper sampling errors and design effects-- PSALMS and REPERR. PSALMS uses standard "collapsed stratum" methods for estimating sampling errors for means and proportions, and similar techniques combined with hand calculations can be used in estimating actual sampling errors for Multiple Classification Analysis (MCA) statistics. More complex methods of calculating sampling errors are required for regression statistics. REPERR is the OSIRIS program designed to calculate sampling errors for these estimates.

The calculation of sampling errors is somewhat cumbersome and expensive, so that, as a practical matter, it cannot be done for every parameter one investigates. While the design effect need not be the same for each estimate, general purpose tables illustrating the range of sampling errors and design effects by type of statistic--mean, proportion, regression coefficient, etc.--can be helpful in assessing the extent to which actual sampling errors are likely to differ from standardly computed sampling errors. The first volume of this series (Volume I, Appendix B) described Panel Study sampling errors for percentages, means, and MCA coefficients. Sampling errors for regression statistics were not

[1] See Lansing and Morgan (1971), pp. 71-75, and Kish (1965).

examined at that time because a computer program for such analysis was not
available. REPERR, mentioned above, is such a program and we use it in the
analysis presented in this chapter to enlarge the range of estimates for which
design effects have been calculated.

REPERR uses repeated replication techniques, with the replications being
created using one of three methods: balanced half-sample, jackknife, or user-
specified replications. Once the replications are created, sampling errors are
computed for the regression statistics by examining the departure or variation of
the calculated replication estimates from the total sample estimates. The larger
the number of replicates, the greater the precision of the variance estimates.

The differing techniques for creating the replicates have been described in
detail by Kish and Frankel (1968) and by McCarthy (1966) and more briefly in the
OSIRIS IV manual (1980). All rely on classifying the geographically defined
primary sampling units (PSUs), created when the sample was first selected, into a
set of mutually exclusive and exhaustive units knows as Sampling Error Computing
Units (SECUs) and then classifying these SECUs into subsets known as strata
which, again, are mutually exclusive and exhaustive. In the case of the balanced
set of half-samples which was used for the analysis in this chapter, each stratum
contains exactly two SECUs and half-sample replications are created by selecting
one of the two SECUs from each stratum. Balancing, which reduces the number of
replications needed for calculating the sampling errors, is accomplished by
selecting certain of the half-samples for the replicates with minimum
duplication. For the Panel Study a variable which divides the sample into 64
separate SECUs was created and will be added to the cross-year family/individual
tapes beginning with the 13th wave so that users will be able to calculate
sampling errors of interest to them. This variable readily allows the creation
of 32 strata pairs. For the analysis reported below, 32 replicates or
independent half-samples were created for the computation of sampling errors and
design effects.

Many of the recent Panel Study analyses of labor force issues have looked
separately at the four primary race/sex subgroups--white men, white women, black
men, and black women. Since time constraints have limited our present analysis
of regression sampling errors to one basic investigation, we chose to examine
these subgroups and the relation of their characteristics to wages. This
sample--like that examined by Corcoran, Datcher, and Duncan (1980) in Volume VIII
of this series--is comprised of household heads or wives who were employed and
under age 45 in 1978 and who worked more than 250 hours in 1977. For each of the

four race/sex subgroups in this sample, we regressed the natural logarithm of
hourly earnings (annual earnings/annual work hours) on a small set of explanatory
variables--education, experience, region, and city size. These explanatory
variables, typically used in wage analyses, form the base for the Corcoran,
Datcher, and Duncan investigation of the additional wage effects of information
and influence networks in labor markets.

The REPERR results are presented in Tables 17.1 through 17.3. The first
table shows the ratios (DEFT) of true sampling error estimates to those which
assume simple random sampling for the regression statistics; these include
regression coefficients, the multiple R^2s, and the means of the variables used in
the analysis (one--whether south--is a dichotomous variable). The second table
examines the implications for interpreting the regression results in more detail.
The third table provides detailed information on the means, which we do not
discuss but are presented for the interested reader.

As Table 17.1 shows, there were substantial differences in design effects
across the four demographic groups, ranging from relatively small effects for
white men to substantial ones for black women, with both groups of blacks having
larger design effects than the corresponding groups of whites. The design
effects tended to be larger for means than for regression coefficients or R^2s,
with a few exceptions (compare the design effects for means and coefficients for
the years with present employer variables and the fraction of experience full
time variable). There were large differences across the variables in design
effects for given estimates, but these differences were not systematic across the
demographic groups.

The levels of the design effects indicate that, while adjustments for design
effects tend to be smaller for regression coefficients than means, even for
regression coefficients one should increase the simple-random-sampling error
estimates by anywhere from one-fourth to three-fourths, with the higher
adjustment for minorities.

Viewing the results of the sample design adjustments in terms of the
interpretational impact for the hourly earnings regression results (Table 17.2),
we see that only a few of the coefficients underwent changes in terms of the
significance levels customarily used in interpreting results. These changes were
confined to the minority groups, who had the largest design effects. Of the
coefficients that were significant at the .01 level assuming simple random
sampling, all but three remained significant at that level when design effects
were incorporated. The three exceptions were, for black men, city size and for

black women, both fraction of full time work experience and whether they resided in the south. But even these exceptions remained significant at either the .05 or .10 level. The more serious effects were for coefficients significant at only the .05 level assuming simple random sampling. Of the three such coefficients, two dropped to insignificance. These two were also for a minority group--black men--whereas the one remaining significant at the .05 level was for a non-minority group--white women.

Table 17.1 (page 1 of 2)

RATIOS OF ACTUAL SAMPLING ERROR TO SRS[a] SAMPLING ERROR (DEFT) IN
REGRESSION ANALYSIS WITH HOURLY EARNINGS AS THE DEPENDENT VARIABLE
(For race/sex subgroups of household heads and wives employed and under
45 years of age in 1978 and working at least 250 hours in 1977.)

Variable	White Males	White Females	Black Males	Black Females
DEFT For Regression Coefficients[b]				
Years of schooling	1.51	1.04	1.52	1.37
Pre-employer experience	1.14	1.12	1.58	2.06
Pre-employer experience squared	1.12	1.10	1.65	2.04
Years with present employer	1.08	1.17	2.10	2.43
Years with present employer squared	0.95	1.34	2.18	2.39
Fraction of experience full time	1.50	1.13	1.89	1.61
Whether south	1.32	1.52	1.85	1.68
Ln city size	1.22	1.27	1.66	1.53
DEFT For Multiple R Squared (R^2)				
	1.10	1.06	1.87	1.50

Table 17.1 (page 2 of 2)

Variable	White Males	White Females	Black Males	Black Females
DEFT For Means				
Years of schooling	1.66	1.60	1.75	2.48
Pre-employer experience	1.16	1.22	2.27	2.19
Pre-employer experience squared	1.25	1.15	2.53	2.24
Years with present employer	1.52	1.10	2.00	1.80
Years with present employer squared	1.39	1.08	2.21	2.02
Fraction of experience full time	1.36	1.08	1.53	2.10
Whether south	1.68	1.66	2.10	2.51
Ln city size	1.79	1.48	1.99	2.37
Ln hourly earnings	1.44	1.40	1.84	1.87
Sample size	1,509	1,048	693	639

[a] SRS stands for simple random sampling, which is assumed in the usual methods of calculating sampling errors.
[b] This is the unstandardized coefficient.

Table 17.2

REGRESSION COEFFICIENTS AND CORRESPONDING SIGNIFICANCE LEVELS BASED ON ACTUAL STANDARD ERROR AND SRS[a] STANDARD ERROR IN REGRESSION ANALYSIS WITH HOURLY EARNINGS AS DEPENDENT VARIABLE

(For race/sex subgroups of household heads and wives employed and under 45 years of age in 1978 and working at least 250 hours in 1977.)

	White Males			White Females			Black Males			Black Females		
		Significance			Significance			Significance			Significance	
Explanatory Variables	Coefficient	Actual	SRS	Coefficient	Actual	SRS	Coefficient	Actual	SRS	Coefficient	Actual	SRS
Years of schooling	.057	**	**	.088	**	**	.089	**	**	.074	**	**
Pre-employer experience	.016	**	**	.029	**	**	.001	@	@	.006	@	@
Pre-employer experience squared	.0001	@	@	-.0012	*	*	.0010	@	*	.0003	@	@
Years with present employer	.064	**	**	.099	**	**	.083	**	**	.114	**	**
Years with present employer squared	-.0017	**	**	-.0036	**	**	-.0027	**	**	-.0052	**	**
Fraction of experience full time	.272	**	**	.208	**	**	.047	@	@	.230	*	**
Whether south	-.098	**	**	-.012	@	@	-.080	@	*	-.136	*	**
Ln city size	.041	**	**	.051	**	**	.028	+	**	.045	**	**
R² (adjusted)	.304	**	**	.335	**	**	.318	**	**	.351	**	**
Sample size	1,509			1,048			693			639		

**Significant at .01 level.
*Significant at .05 level.
+Significant at .10 level.
@Not significant at .10 level or higher.
[a]SRS stands for simple random sampling, which is assumed in the usual methods for calculating sampling errors.

Table 17.3

MEANS AND STANDARD DEVIATIONS, ACTUAL AND SRS[a], FOR VARIABLES IN HOURLY EARNINGS REGRESSIONS
(For race/sex subgroups of household heads and wives employed and under 45 years of age in 1978 and working at least 250 hours in 1977.)

Variable	White Males			White Females			Black Males			Black Females		
		Standard Deviation			Standard Deviation			Standard Deviation			Standard Deviation	
	Mean	Actual	SRS	Mean	Actual	SRS	Mean	Actual	SRS	Mean	Actual	SRS
Years of schooling	13.12	0.11	0.07	13.00	0.12	0.07	11.84	0.15	0.08	12.00	0.19	0.08
Pre-employer experience	6.48	0.17	0.15	5.45	0.18	0.14	5.99	0.46	0.20	5.88	0.46	0.21
Pre-employer experience squared	75.59	3.85	3.08	51.51	2.86	2.49	64.68	9.78	3.86	63.28	9.17	4.10
Years with present employer	5.58	0.21	0.14	3.85	0.14	0.13	5.37	0.41	0.20	4.14	0.31	0.16
Years with present employer squared	58.93	3.49	2.51	32.70	2.47	2.28	57.52	9.24	4.18	33.88	5.34	2.64
Fraction of experience full time	0.87	0.01	0.01	0.73	0.01	0.01	0.88	0.01	0.01	0.78	0.02	0.01
Whether south	0.28	0.02	0.01	0.29	0.02	0.01	0.57	0.04	0.02	0.56	0.05	0.02
Ln city size	11.68	0.08	0.05	11.74	0.08	0.06	12.22	0.15	0.07	12.21	0.17	0.07
Ln hourly earnings	1.82	0.02	0.01	1.40	0.02	0.02	1.56	0.04	0.02	1.31	0.04	0.02
Sample size	1,509			1,048			693			639		

[a]SRS stands for simple random sampling, which is assumed in the usual methods for calculating sampling errors.

SUMMARY

There are design effects associated with the Panel Study data that generally lead to a net increase in the real sampling error relative to the simple random sampling one. Significance tests with large samples, however, are relatively robust, particularly for regression findings significant at the .01 level or higher. In general, the use of three standard deviations rather than two for conservative significance tests appears called for, particularly when dealing with highly clustered subsamples such as blacks, the poor, or black women workers.

References

Corcoran, Mary; Datcher, Linda; and Duncan, Greg. "Information and Influence Networks in Labor Markets." In Five Thousand American Families—Patterns of Economic Progress, edited by Greg J. Duncan and James N. Morgan. Ann Arbor: Institute for Social Research, The University of Michigan, 1980.

Lansing, John B., and Morgan, James N. Economic Survey Methods. Ann Arbor: Institute for Social Research, The University of Michigan, 1971.

Kish, Leslie. Survey Sampling. New York: John Wiley and Sons, Inc., 1965.

Kish, Leslie, and Frankel, Martin R. "Balanced Repeated Replications for Standard Errors." Journal of the American Statistical Association (September 1970): 1071-93.

McCarthy, P.J. Replication: An Approach to the Analysis of Data from Complex Surveys. Public Health Service, Series 2 No. 14, Washington, D.C., 1966.

OSIRIS IV User's Manual, Sixth Edition. Ann Arbor: Institute for Social Research, The University of Michigan, February 1980.

Chapter 18

THE CHARACTERISTICS OF HOUSING DEMAND
IN THE 1970s: A RESEARCH NOTE

Sandra J. Newman and Michael Ponza

INTRODUCTION

In recent years, substantial progress has been made toward understanding the characteristics of housing demand (Quigley, 1979). This progress can be attributed in part to a greater emphasis on developing a more realistic view of the behavior of households in housing markets. The development and maturation of several rich, systematic, time-series data bases such as the Annual Housing Survey, the Experimental Housing Allowance Program data, and the Panel Study of Income Dynamics (PSID), have facilitated these advances by translating and testing concepts with careful empirical measurement. As a source of information about changes over time in the housing behavior of individuals and families in the nation, the last of these data sets remains unique because it is based on a national sample and has followed all members of original sample families each year since 1968.

The present research, still in progress, is being undertaken very much in the spirit of this empirical exploration. The Panel Study data are used to address several questions about the status and decisions of housing consumers over approximately the last decade. The 1970s have been marked by three major changes: substantial shifts in the demographic composition of the nation's population (particularly family formation and size); fluctuations in several supply-side characteristics of housing markets; and the pervasiveness of a number of factors exogenous to housing markets, such as economy-wide inflation, recession, and unemployment. Thus, there is an opportunity to investigate whether these structural shifts are revealed in changes in various attributes of housing demand.

Four sets of research questions are being addressed in two topic areas: residential mobility and housing deprivation. The purpose of this Note is to report the results of our preliminary descriptive analysis of each question.

467

Basic and dramatic patterns are shown in graph form within the text. Appendix tables contain the large majority of the individual estimates.

RESIDENTIAL MOBILITY

The Pattern of Annual Mobility Rates, 1968-1979

There appears to have been a small but fairly steady increase in the residential mobility rates of families over the period 1968-1979.[1] In 1968, somewhat less than one-fifth of family heads reported a change in residence from the previous year. By 1979, this fraction had increased to approximately one-quarter.[2]

Is the overall pattern of annual mobility rates for the total population reproduced for subgroups of the population?

The general increase in mobility rates over the period applies not only to the population as a whole but also to a large number of subgroups, including

---

[1] Moves were reported within one year after they were undertaken. Moves made between 1968 and 1969 were reported in the 1969 interview, those occurring between 1969 and 1970 were reported in the 1970 interview, and so on. Thus, the maximum number of moves coded over the 12-year period is 11 moves.

[2] There are two meaningful ways to calculate the annual mobility rates of families with the Panel Study data: to look at the fraction of family heads who reported a move in each of the 11 years (1969-1979), or to look at the fraction of individuals who appear in the 1979 data set and count their reported mobility for each year in which they headed a family. (The weight adjustment for nonresponse among the latter group provides distributions that represent cross-section estimates of annual mobility rates of families.) Estimates from each method produced almost identical annual rates. The actual point estimates discussed in the text and reported in the appendix tables were derived from the latter method, however.

Estimates from the Current Population Survey covering part of the decade are at odds with these estimates from the Panel Study. However, the CPS estimates are based on individuals while the Panel Study estimates are based on families. Finding an increasing rate of family mobility and a decreasing rate of individual mobility is plausible under the condition of declining family size and/or growing incidence of family splits--trends that have been clearly documented over the decade.

owners and renters, whites and blacks,[3] poor and non-poor,[4] male and female single-person households, and married couples in which the wife does not work, works part-time, or works full-time. There are, of course, sizable differences in the initial levels of mobility between each class within a subgroup; renters, for example, began the period more than three times as likely to move than owners. Since our interest is in changes over time, the more important question is whether the gap between classes of a subgroup has widened or narrowed over the decade.

The relationship between owners and renters was the most stable among those examined (Figure 18.1). Also relatively stable was the relationship between the mobility rates of male and female single-person households: the former moved at or near twice the rate of the latter (Figure 18.2). While poor families were always more likely to report a move over the 11-year period than were non-poor families, the gap between them narrowed and widened in an erratic fashion, dropping at one point to less than one percentage point and widening at another to more than 13 percentage points.

Among married couples distinguished by the working status of the wife (wife works full time, up to half time, or doesn't work), there was very little difference between mobility rates of up to half-time versus full-time working wives (Figure 18.3). The major distinction, then, was between working and non-working wives, and the gap appears to have widened over time: couples with non-working wives moved more often than those with working wives.

The differences between black and white mobility rates were seldom more than a few percentage points and any difference may be within the range of sampling

---

[3]Other races were excluded from the calculations due to small sample sizes.

[4]The following adjustments were made to the Panel Study's annual needs standard in classifying an individual or head or household as "poor":
1. the needs standard was multiplied by .80 to make it comparable with the Census Bureau definition of poverty;
2. 1967 dollars were converted into current dollars using the CPI;
3. the needs standard value for farmers was multiplied by .85 (since the original estimates were not adjusted for the fact that some people are farmers);
4. an adjustment in the food needs values for elderly women were adjusted downward since as originally coded they overstated these needs; and
5. if the needs standard was less than $2,000, we adjusted it to equal $2,000.

Family income was then divided by this adjusted needs standard. If the resulting ratio was less than one, we considered the family or individual to be poor.

470

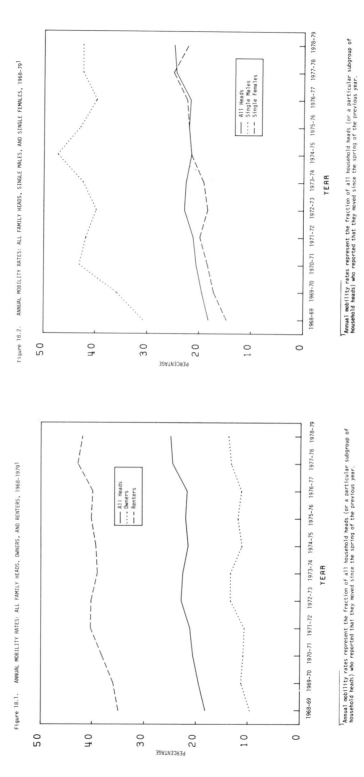

Figure 18.1. ANNUAL MOBILITY RATES: ALL FAMILY HEADS, OWNERS, AND RENTERS, 1968-1979[1]

[1]Annual mobility rates represent the fraction of all household heads (or a particular subgroup of household heads) who reported that they moved since the spring of the previous year.

Figure 18.2. ANNUAL MOBILITY RATES: ALL FAMILY HEADS, SINGLE MALES, AND SINGLE FEMALES, 1968-79[1]

[1]Annual mobility rates represent the fraction of all household heads (or a particular subgroup of household heads) who reported that they moved since the spring of the previous year.

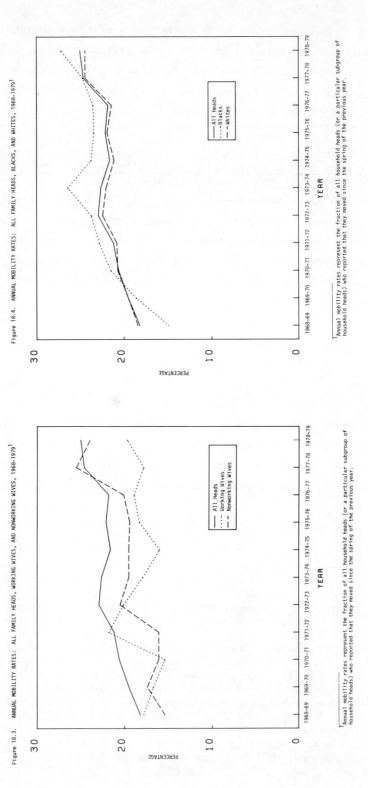

471

Figure 18.4. ANNUAL MOBILITY RATES: ALL FAMILY HEADS, BLACKS, AND WHITES, 1968-1979[1]

All Heads
Blacks
Whites

PERCENTAGE

1968-69 1969-70 1970-71 1971-72 1972-73 1973-74 1974-75 1975-76 1976-77 1977-78 1978-79

YEAR

[1]Annual mobility rates represent the fraction of all household heads (or a particular subgroup of household heads) who reported that they moved since the spring of the previous year.

Figure 18.3. ANNUAL MOBILITY RATES: ALL FAMILY HEADS, WORKING WIVES, AND NONWORKING WIVES, 1968-1979[1]

All Heads
Working Wives
Nonworking Wives

PERCENTAGE

1968-69 1969-70 1970-71 1971-72 1972-73 1973-74 1974-75 1975-76 1976-77 1977-78 1978-79

YEAR

[1]Annual mobility rates represent the fraction of all household heads (or a particular subgroup of household heads) who reported that they moved since the spring of the previous year.

error. A note of caution should be added here: a shift in position among the two racial subgroups may have occurred over the period. In the earliest years of the study, whites were somewhat more likely to move than blacks, but this relationship was reversed in the early seventies and remained fairly stable through the end of the decade (Figure 18.4).

Is the overall pattern of annual mobility rates for all types of mobility reproduced for each main type of mobility: productive moves, consumptive moves, and involuntary moves?

This question parallels the previous one but shifts the focus from patterns in the mobility rates of demographic subgroups to the reason moves are undertaken. Both consumptive and involuntary moves increased quite steadily over the period; productive moves were somewhat more erratic, but by the end of the period, the rate of productive moves was essentially the same as at the beginning (Figure 18.5). In all cases, however, the year-to-year differentials were small and may be within the range of sampling error. In general, consumptive moves were at least twice as frequent as productive moves and about four times more frequent than moves undertaken for involuntary reasons.

The dominance of moves for consumption reasons makes them a particularly important type of mobility to examine. One reasonable set of hypotheses regarding motivations for upgrading the housing bundle concern actual, or imminent, increases in family size. However, in view of the increased attractiveness of homeownership, and particularly the investment opportunities in the ownership market, the importance of growing families in such moves might have declined.

Initial distributions of the fraction of all consumptive moves made by families who experienced an increase in family size over the 11-year period show

---

[5] Productive moves are those undertaken for job-related reasons (e.g., to take another job, job transfer, etc.).

Consumptive moves are undertaken for housing-related reasons (e.g., to buy/rent a bigger or smaller housing unit, live in a better neighborhood, etc.).

Involuntary moves are undertaken for reasons that are beyond the control of the mover. Included here are by-product or derivative moves, such as moves occasioned by the death of a family member, separation, divorce, health problems, or forced by fire or natural disaster. Also included are displacement moves such as those resulting from sale or reoccupation of the property by the landlord, demolition or condemnation of the unit, etc. Other involuntary moves that are more ambiguous are those resulting from eviction.

Cases not accounted for by these three categories were either moves made for ambiguous reasons, or they represent missing data.

Figure 18.5. ANNUAL MOBILITY RATES: ALL FAMILY MOVES AND TYPES OF MOVES. 1968-1979[1]

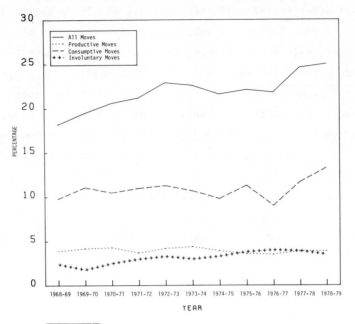

[1]Annual mobility rates represent the fraction of household heads who reported that they moved since the spring of the previous year.

this fraction to be consistently small over the decade, never exceeding 20 percent. This fraction was also always lower than the proportion of families whose moves were associated with decreases or, even more dramatically, no changes in family size. This hierarchy did not change much over the decade, increasing only marginally with time: the largest fraction of families who undertook consumptive moves were those who did not experience family size changes.

These initial distributions may be misleading, however, because they include at least one identifiable subset of consumptive moves for which the coding of changes in family size is ambiguous. Children who split-off from their parental families are likely to report their moves as consumptive moves. However, the Panel Study would generally code these moves as decreases in parental family size, since the number of family members with whom the child shared a housing unit in time t versus time t+1 would be compared. But viewed from the perspective of the splitoff´s newly formed household, one could argue that coding an increase is more appropriate since the household did not exist in time t but

did exist with, say, one member in time t+1. Since we viewed this situation to
be sufficiently ambiguous, the distributions were recalculated for only those
families headed by the same persons between time t and time t+1. A somewhat
different pattern emerged from this second distribution: the fraction of these
families whose consumptive moves were associated with family size increases was
between two and three times greater than those experiencing decreases in family
size. Again, however, the fraction of families whose consumptive moves were not
associated with any changes in family size, whether increases or decreases,
remained dominant. This general pattern applies both to the full sample of
stable headed families and to the racial and economic subgroups.

It may be, of course, that families make consumptive moves in anticipation
or preparation for planned increases in family size, or they may wait for a while
after their family has expanded before making a consumptive move. Since we have
measured only family size increases that occurred over the same period as that in
which the move took place (i.e., spring of year t to spring of year t+1), moves
of the latter type were not accounted for. In future work, we plan to test each
of these alternative notions.

Blacks and whites experienced very similar rates of consumptive mobility
over the decade, but blacks were less likely to make productive moves and more
likely to be forced to move in each year. The difference in level of productive
moves between races was roughly constant over the period, but the gap between
black and white rates of involuntary moves seems to have grown slightly. A
similar observation applies to mobility patterns for poor and non-poor families:
the tendency for the poor to suffer higher involuntary mobility rates has become
more marked over the decade of the 1970s (Figures 18.6, 18.7, and 18.8).

Since splitting-off from a parental family is generally synonymous with
changing one's residence, our analysis addressed a different mobility question
with respect to this group: What fraction of all moves in each year were
undertaken by individuals who left their parental families? The same question
was asked of "splitups," i.e., husbands and wives who divorced. In each case,
these respective fractions were higher at the end of the decade than at its
outset, but the distributions were not smooth. Splitoffs accounted for roughly
11 percent of all moves between 1968 and 1969 and about 17 percent between 1978
and 1979. Splitups began the period at about 2 percent; by 1977-78, the fraction
was 6.1 percent.

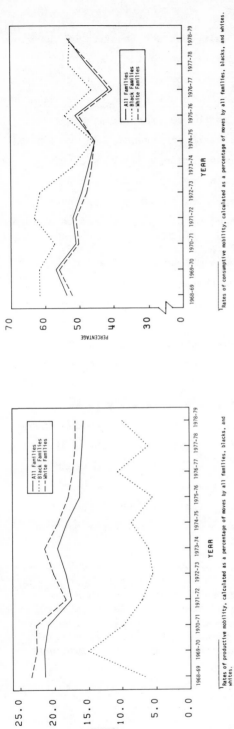

Figure 18.6. ANNUAL RATES OF PRODUCTIVE MOVES: ALL FAMILIES AND BY RACE, 1968-1979[1]

[1]Rates of productive mobility, calculated as a percentage of moves by all families, blacks, and whites.

Figure 18.7. ANNUAL RATES OF CONSUMPTIVE MOVES: ALL FAMILIES AND BY RACE, 1968-79[1]

[1]Rates of consumptive mobility, calculated as a percentage of moves by all families, blacks, and whites.

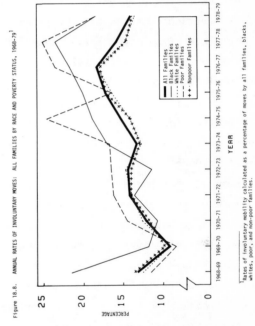

Figure 18.8. ANNUAL RATES OF INVOLUNTARY MOVES: ALL FAMILIES BY RACE AND POVERTY STATUS, 1968-79[1]

[1]Rates of involuntary mobility calculated as a percentage of moves by all families, blacks, whites, poor, and non-poor families.

The Pattern of Repeat Moves, 1968-1979

Residential moves are predicted to occur only when the benefits of changing locations are greater than the full costs of moving, which include leaving the current location as well as a wide range of transaction costs. Since these costs are generally substantial (and especially so for homeowners), we might expect any single family to move infrequently. Findings to the contrary might suggest either substantial and frequent shifts in tastes and preferences, job location, income, or other basic demand attributes, or less rational and less careful location choices than are presumed by economic theory.

Before deciding which interpretation is appropriate, we need to investigate whether there is a problem. Some basic evidence on this question can be gathered from the incidence and pattern of repeat moves.

The rate of multiple moves among individuals who have remained in the sample over the decade was substantial. More than two-thirds of all movers made repeat moves over the decade. That is, more than two-thirds of individuals who moved at least once over the decade actually moved more than once. Further, nearly one-third of individuals who moved more than once over the period changed residences five or more times. (This fraction is about equal to the fraction of movers who moved only once.)

Even if the "bad decision" interpretation were prematurely attached to this high rate of multiple moves, the high transaction costs of moving would argue against repeat moves occurring very often in consecutive years. The empirical evidence generally supports this argument: it is unlikely that a move in one year is followed immediately by another move in the next year. For most repeat movers between 1968 and 1978, more than one year separated each of their moves. A small fraction of individuals experienced two moves in a row but almost none made more than two moves in sequential years.[6]

---

[6]Repeat mobility consists of return moves (a move back to a location where the individual previously lived) and forward moves (a repeat move to a new location). DaVanzo and Morrison (1978) suggested that, of those individuals who do make short interval _return_ moves (about one year), the initial move of the sequence appears to be one that is carelessly planned. Furthermore, economic hardship plays an important role in both the original move and the subsequent return.

Have racial and economic subgroups in the population
experienced substantially different rates of repeat mobility?

Although blacks were more likely than whites to move at least once over the
decade, they were no more likely to be chronic movers nor to move in immediate
succession when they did make more than one move.

There were, however, considerable differences in the rates of repeat moves
across economic classes. Individuals who had ever been part of the poverty
population experienced multiple move rates that were nearly 20 percentage points
greater than those who were never poor. The fraction of "ever-poor" who have
made five or more moves over the decade was more than twice as large as the rate
for the never-poor (Figure 18.9).

Figure 18.9.   PATTERN OF REPEAT MOVES BY ALL INDIVIDUALS, RACIAL AND POVERTY STATUS[1]

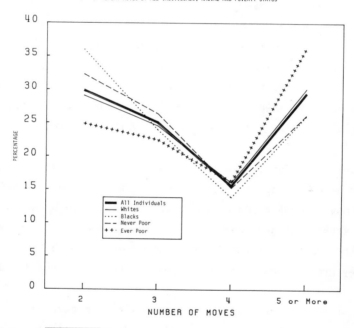

[1]Percentage distribution based on total number of individuals who moved at least once over the period.

The ever-poor were also more likely to make multiple moves in rapid
succession than the never-poor. This difference is quite small for two moves,
but it grew larger for three or more moves.

Has the rate of repeat mobility changed over the decade?

Since the probability of experiencing more than one move is directly related to the number of years an individual is part of the sample, we approached the question of change over time by arbitrarily dividing the 11-year period into two equal periods, 1969-1974 and 1974-1979, and compared the rates of repeat moves by individuals who were continuously in the sample in each of the two periods.

There were no substantial differences in the rate or pattern of repeat mobility between the first and second halves of the decade. One-quarter of all individuals moved at least twice during each five-year period, and the fraction undertaking between two and five moves, consecutive or not, was nearly identical over the two periods. This absence of difference persisted for all individuals and for racial and poverty status subgroups.

The Pattern of Return Moves, 1968-1979

Another set of evidence regarding the success or failure of moves is whether one or more moves is followed by a return move to the community in which the individual grew up.[7] Viewed from this perspective, return moves are a subset of repeat moves. A very different perspective is also possible: return moves may gauge the strength of family and community ties which some argue are weakening over time.

The fraction of all families who made moves "home" was very small, never reaching even as high as 5 percent in any year. The year-to-year differences in rates of return moves among heads of families over the decade have also been small. To the extent that any change has occurred, however, it appears to be a positive one: the fraction of family heads who moved back to the state and county where they grew up was somewhat larger at the end of the decade than at its outset.

Regardless of one's perspective on the meaning of return moves, this information alone may not have any practical significance since the move home may have been followed by another move away. Since those who made their return moves in the earliest years of the decade have had a longer time to move again, the best data on long-term adjustment is derived from them. The estimates of post-return moves are dramatic: nearly all family heads who moved home between 1968 and 1973 moved again at some subsequent time. Although the case counts are very

---

[7]That is, the state and county in which the family head spent most of his or her time while growing up.

low, it appears that the likelihood of a move home followed by a subsequent move to some location outside the home county increased with time.

HOUSING DEPRIVATION

The happy fact that, according to traditional physical measures of housing adequacy, there has been substantial progress in upgrading the housing conditions of American families does not eliminate all worry about the housing situation of the population. It says nothing directly about the distribution of improvements in housing conditions across a range of subgroups in the population nor about the persistence of inadequate housing conditions when they do occur. And, by definition, it does not address the possibly more basic question of whether the meaning of adequacy has changed over time.

Our initial look at the first two of these questions focused on two concepts of housing adequacy. The first, crowding, was measured in two ways: (1) the traditional measure of persons per room, with families living in housing units with more than one person per room designated as "crowded"; and (2) a measure of room requirements, with families having fewer rooms than required considered "crowded."[8] Since the latter measure takes family composition into account as well as family size, the measures are not strictly comparable. It is generally the case, however, that for mid-size and larger families (e.g., a couple with children) the persons per room measure is more restrictive, while for very small family sizes (including single-person households) the required rooms measure yields higher estimates of crowding. The second concept is housing cost burden, or affordability. The widely adopted rule of thumb of more than 25 percent of income allocated to housing costs is adopted as the indicator of excessive burden.[9] Crowding represents the more traditional standard of adequacy, while affordability reflects more recent concerns that inadequate housing has changed from a problem of physical inadequacy to excessive cost (Frieden, et al., 1977).

---

[8] In computing required rooms, a base of two rooms (exclusive of bathrooms) was allowed for head and spouse or for a single head. One additional room was allocated for each single person age 18 or older, one room for a married couple other than the head and spouse, and one room for every two children of the same sex under age 18. Children under age 10 were paired regardless of sex if this reduced the room requirement.

[9] The housing cost/income variable uses a combined contract rent and annual house value variable for the numerator and total family income for the denominator.

Trends in Housing Deprivation, 1968-1978[10]

By either measure of crowding, the fraction of families living in crowded conditions has declined over the decade. Thus, by this standard of physical adequacy, the housing conditions of the nation have improved. Over the same period, however, affordability has become a greater problem: between 1968 and 1978, there has been a fairly steady increase in the fraction of families allocating more than 25 percent of their incomes to housing costs. In 1968, less than one-fifth of families exceeded this "rule of thumb" category; by 1978, the fraction was very nearly one-quarter.

Has this pattern of change in housing conditions of the population as a whole been reproduced across different subgroups in the population?

A parallel pattern of decline in crowded conditions was detected across families distinguished by race, housing tenure status, poverty status, and sex of head of families with children. Disregarding initial level, each of the dichotomous classes of each subgroup experienced roughly a two-to-threefold decrease in the incidence of crowding over the decade as measured by the persons per room ratio. This decline was less dramatic but still observable for the required rooms measure. The importance of family size and composition (and possibly the characteristics of the housing stock) is probably responsible for the difference between measures.

The pattern of change in the fraction of families with different attributes who had heavy housing cost burdens over the decade also generally conformed to the pattern observed for all families taken together. Of all subgroups examined, however, blacks experienced the least change in affordability over time.[11]

Conclusions about the stability of the gap between classes of each subgroup of families classified as crowded vary greatly, depending on the measure of crowding used. Using the persons per room measure, the distance between classes has remained stable, except among blacks and whites: among blacks the incidence of crowding was roughly three times higher than among whites in 1968 and about

---

[10]Eleven years of the Panel Study have been used in the analysis of housing deprivation. Some deprivation variables such as crowding are reported in a particular year and pertain to that year. Income, however, is reported in one year and pertains to the previous year. Thus, since we could not construct a housing cost to income variable for 1979 (because the denominator would be derived from the 1980 interview), we terminated the period of analysis with 1978.

[11]These subgroups include race, housing tenure, poverty status, sex of family head with children, splitoffs, and splitups.

five times higher at the end of the 1970s. When family composition is accounted for under the required rooms measure, however, the gap does not appear to have widened. The required rooms measure also indicates that the gap in crowding between the poor and the non-poor may have lessened over the decade, although the year-to-year pattern was somewhat erratic.

Is housing deprivation a long-term status?

Somewhat more than 30 percent of the individuals who were in the panel sample all 11 years lived in housing units with more than one person per room at least once over the period. This figure is closer to one-fifth for the required rooms measure, probably because average family size, though decreasing, did not fall below 2.5 over the period. Since the required rooms measure is less restrictive for larger families, and particularly so for non-single person families, it produces a smaller incidence rate of crowding. The corresponding fraction for the affordability measure is 54.5 percent. Thus, more than half of all individuals who were members of panel families over the entire period 1968-1979 experienced housing cost burdens between 1969 and 1978 that exceeded the 25 percent ratio of costs to income at least once. Stated another way, over this period, an individual was more likely to have experienced heavy burdens at least once than not at all.

The gap within subgroups of families with high housing cost burdens has been remarkably stable. What may be the most dramatic information in these comparisons is the absolute size of the poverty population that is classified as excessively burdened by housing costs. Although the pattern is somewhat erratic, this fraction has never fallen below 50 percent over the decade and in a number of years has risen to nearly 60 percent.

How often did panel individuals experience housing deprivation, and how persistent were these problems over time?

From a family welfare standpoint, what may be more important than whether a family has ever experienced crowding or excessive cost burden is how often these problems are experienced and how persistent they are when they do occur.

The frequency pattern for all measures of deprivation is generally the same: an individual who experienced crowding or an excessive housing cost burden at any point over the decade was likely to have experienced it more than once. In fact, a fairly sizable fraction of individuals experienced each of these housing problems five or more times.

The persistence of each status was also roughly similar. Even though a substantial proportion of panel individuals could be classified by our measures as inadequately housed multiple times during the study period, it was less likely that these multiple occurrences were experienced in successive years, and particularly so after two occurrences in a row. This general pattern notwithstanding, there were still some individuals who were crowded or burdened by high housing cost to income ratios for more than four or even five consecutive years.

Were there differences among subgroups in the frequency or persistence of housing problems?

For both crowding measures, whites and never-poor individuals were indistinguishable from the population as a whole in terms of the number of years in crowded housing over the panel period. In contrast, more than half of the blacks and individuals who were ever poor in the 11 years had lived in housing units with more than one person per room; the corresponding fractions for these subgroups using the generally less restrictive required rooms measure were more than half for blacks and somewhat less than half for the ever-poor. The most dramatic differences among groups were concentrated at the higher frequency ranges. For each measure of crowding, blacks and the ever-poor had twice the probability of being crowded five or more times over the period compared to the population as a whole. This probability is magnified if the residual category rather than the total population is used as the basis for comparison (i.e., whites and never-poor). Blacks, for example, were about six times as likely to suffer a deficit of "required" rooms five or more times over the period compared to whites.

These same subgroups were also much more likely to suffer persistent crowding in their housing units than either the total population or their respective counterparts. More than one-fifth of blacks and nearly one-fifth of those ever in poverty lived in homes for five or more consecutive years that contained more persons than rooms. The corresponding figure for the total population was 8.6 percent; for whites and the never-poor, 6.5 percent and 5.2 percent, respectively. The parallel rates of crowding using the required rooms measure were much lower, but the pattern was the same.

As for the annual rates of excessive burden, we observed only modest differences between blacks and whites in either the frequency or persistence of housing affordability problems. More than half of the total sample of individuals, of whites, and of blacks experienced high cost burdens at least once over the period, and multiple occurrences of excessive burdens--whether consecutive or not--were also experienced by roughly equal proportions of individuals in each group.

The disparities between the poverty-status classes were much more dramatic. More than three-fourths of individuals who were poor at least once in the 11 years also experienced excessive housing cost burdens at least once. The fraction for those never-poor was somewhat less than one-half--a proportion that was lower than for the population as a whole. Ever-poor individuals were also somewhat more likely to experience high cost burdens five or more times over the period than either those never poor or than all individuals.

Compared to crowding problems, affordability problems were more likely to be suffered intermittently. Unfortunately, crowding problems seem to be fairly persistent, particularly for blacks and the ever-poor.

References

DaVanzo, Julie, and Morrison, Peter. "Dynamics of Return Migration: Descriptive Findings from a Longitudinal Study," Rand Paper Series P-5913. Santa Monica, California: Rand Corporation, March 1978.

Frieden, Bernard, et al. The Nation's Housing: 1975-1985. Cambridge, Massachusetts: Joint Center for Urban Studies, 1977.

Quigley, John. "What Have We Learned about Urban Housing Markets?" In Current Issues in Urban Economics, edited by Peter Mieszkowski and Mahlon Straszheim. Baltimore: The Johns Hopkins University Press, 1979.

Appendix to Chapter 18

Table A18.1

ANNUAL RATES OF RESIDENTIAL MOBILITY, 1968-1979[a],[b]
(Percentage Distribution)

Subgroup	1968-69[c]	1969-70	1970-71	1971-72	1972-73	1973-74	1974-75	1975-76	1976-77	1977-78	1978-79
All heads of households	18.2	19.5	20.6	21.2	22.9	22.6	21.6	22.1	21.8	24.6	25.0
Housing Status[d]											
Homeowners	9.6	11.3	10.9	10.7	13.4	13.4	11.2	12.0	11.3	13.3	13.8
Renters	34.9	35.9	38.1	40.3	40.2	39.0	39.3	40.2	39.9	42.8	41.9
Race of Head											
White	18.4	19.5	20.7	20.8	22.4	22.0	21.1	21.9	21.4	24.4	24.4
Black	14.9	18.6	21.5	22.8	23.7	26.4	23.3	23.4	23.5	24.7	27.2
Poverty Status											
Not poor	17.6	19.4	20.5	20.7	22.2	21.7	20.5	21.0	21.2	23.9	24.6
Poor	23.5	20.3	22.1	26.6	31.6	34.2	34.1	34.1	28.5	31.9	29.3
Single-Person Household											
Male	30.8	35.9	43.1	41.8	39.8	42.4	47.3	42.9	39.8	42.5	42.5
Female	14.7	17.2	18.4	19.9	18.4	19.2	21.6	22.1	22.5	25.1	22.3
Work Status of Wife[e]											
Non-working	15.4	17.4	16.1	16.1	20.5	19.5	19.5	19.4	20.1	25.5	23.9
Works up to half time	18.0	17.0	19.3	19.8	23.4	22.8	18.7	19.8	16.9	19.0	20.7
Works full time	17.8	16.7	15.4	21.8	20.1	17.9	16.0	18.3	18.9	17.8	19.7

[a]For number of observations, see Table A18.5.

[b]Data presented in this table were derived from the 1979 merged family-individual tape. The distributions represent the fraction of individuals who appeared in the 1979 data set who headed households in each year and who reported that they had moved since the spring of the previous year. Family weights were applied to adjust for nonresponse, yielding distributions that were representative cross-section estimates of annual mobility rates of families. (A single-person household constitutes a "family" in the PSID.)

[c]Respondents were asked whether they had moved since the spring of the previous year. Thus, for each pair of years listed in the columns of this table, the second year is the year of the interview in which the move was reported; the pair of years indicates that the move took place sometime between the spring of the first and the time of the interview in the second year listed. Subgroup status (e.g., poverty status, single-person household) refers to status in the first year of each pair of years.

[d]Those who neither own nor rent were excluded from the estimates due to low sample sizes.

[e]Up to half time means 1 to 1,499 hours per year. Full time means 1,500 or more hours per year. In all of these cases, the husband works full time.

Table A18.2

ANNUAL RATES OF RESIDENTIAL MOBILITY FOR CONSUMPTIVE REASONS, 1968-1979[a,b]

(Percentage Distribution)

Subgroup	1968-69[c]	1969-70	1970-71	1971-72	1972-73	1973-74	1974-75	1975-76	1976-77	1977-78	1978-79
All heads of households	53.8	56.9	51.0	51.9	49.3	47.3	45.4	51.1	41.3	47.6	53.2
Housing Status[d]											
Homeowners	56.3	54.9	59.6	53.3	49.3	48.5	42.9	50.1	42.5	43.6	59.8
Renters	55.3	60.2	47.5	52.6	52.7	49.2	50.1	53.7	43.6	51.6	54.2
Race of Head											
White	52.2	55.9	50.2	51.0	47.8	46.4	45.5	50.1	40.2	46.7	53.3
Black	61.7	61.8	57.2	63.2	61.6	51.9	45.9	54.2	46.4	53.0	52.6
Poverty Status											
Not poor	55.1	57.2	51.2	53.1	49.5	48.4	47.3	53.1	42.9	49.7	54.2
Poor	43.8	54.2	-50.7	44.0	48.7	38.3	32.6	37.8	28.7	31.3	45.7
Single-Person Household											
Male	32.5	37.0	34.3	45.7	38.9	36.6	35.9	42.1	31.6	45.9	40.5
Female	40.8	65.1	32.6	49.7	45.7	41.1	39.8	45.3	37.3	41.4	46.3
Work Status of Wife[e]											
Non-working	56.5	58.0	49.1	45.3	43.4	43.6	42.1	44.3	36.8	41.1	48.5
Works up to half time	56.7	60.0	62.2	64.6	55.1	50.9	50.3	60.1	53.8	52.6	61.8
Works full time	68.5	68.9	61.7	66.5	73.6	65.9	65.0	73.5	60.8	70.8	63.4

[a]For number of observations, see Table A18.5.

[b]Data presented in this table were derived from the 1979 merged family-individual tape. The distributions represent the number of individuals who appear in the 1979 data set who headed households in each year and who reported that they had moved for consumptive reasons since the spring of the previous year, expressed as a fraction of all heads who moved for any reason. In other words, the table provides estimates of the fraction of all moves that are consumptive moves.

[c]Respondents were asked whether they had moved since the spring of the previous year. Thus, for each pair of years listed in the columns of this table, the second year is the year of the interview in which the move was reported; the pair of years indicates that the move took place sometime between the spring of the first and the time of the interview in the second year listed. Subgroup status (e.g., poverty status, single-person household) refers to status in the first year of each pair of years.

[d]Those who neither own nor rent were excluded from the estimates due to low sample sizes.

[e]Up to half time means 1 to 1,499 hours per year. Full time means 1,500 or more hours per year. In all of these cases, the husband works full time.

Table A18.3

ANNUAL RATES OF RESIDENTIAL MOBILITY FOR PRODUCTIVE REASONS, 1968-1979[a,b]

(Percentage Distribution)

Subgroup	1968-69[c]	1969-70	1970-71	1971-72	1972-73	1973-74	1974-75	1975-76	1976-77	1977-78	1978-79
All heads of households	21.4	21.5	20.9	17.5	18.3	19.5	18.1	16.2	16.1	15.8	15.6
Housing Status[d]											
Homeowners	17.7	23.0	19.3	18.7	19.4	22.4	19.6	16.7	17.7	16.5	18.9
Renters	20.1	18.1	20.5	17.4	15.9	16.4	16.5	15.7	15.2	14.9	13.4
Race of Head											
White	23.4	22.6	22.7	18.3	20.1	21.4	19.4	17.9	17.2	16.8	16.8
Black	6.7	15.1	9.8	7.0	5.5	6.1	8.6	5.5	10.6	6.1	9.9
Poverty Status											
Not poor	20.5	21.6	22.0	17.4	18.5	19.8	20.0	16.2	16.5	15.8	16.2
Poor	28.5	18.2	12.2	15.8	16.1	17.0	6.5	18.2	15.1	14.1	11.6
Single-Person Household											
Male	37.7	37.0	23.7	24.4	20.9	27.1	16.7	23.1	20.6	21.0	17.6
Female	19.0	18.6	29.3	15.6	15.2	18.2	16.2	11.8	13.7	13.1	13.4
Work Status of Wife[e]											
Non-working	25.3	22.4	26.1	21.1	25.9	21.0	21.0	15.9	22.4	17.2	19.6
Works up to half time	27.2	23.5	19.7	19.2	23.1	21.5	27.3	25.2	21.9	25.7	20.2
Works full time	7.3	16.8	16.2	18.8	11.4	16.8	18.1	10.4	12.2	13.5	23.3

[a]For number of observations, see Table A18.5.

[b]Data presented in this table were derived from the 1979 merged family-individual tape. The distributions represent the number of individuals who appear in the 1979 data set who headed households in each year and who reported that they had moved for productive reasons since the spring of the previous year, expressed as a fraction of all heads who moved for any reason. In other words, the table provides estimates of the fraction of all moves that are productive moves.

[c]Respondents were asked whether they had moved since the spring of the previous year. Thus, for each pair of years listed in the columns of this table, the second year is the year of the interview in which the move was reported; the pair of years indicates that the move took place sometime between the spring of the first and the time of the interview in the second year listed. Subgroup status (e.g., poverty status, single-person household) refers to status in the first year of each pair of years.

[d]Those who neither own nor rent were excluded from the estimates due to low sample sizes.

[e]Up to half time means 1 to 1,499 hours per year. Full time means 1,500 or more hours per year. In all of these cases, the husband works full time.

Table A18.4

ANNUAL RATES OF RESIDENTIAL MOBILITY FOR INVOLUNTARY REASONS, 1968-1979[a],[b]

(Percentage Distribution)

Subgroup	1968-69[c]	1969-70	1970-71	1971-72	1972-73	1973-74	1974-75	1975-76	1976-77	1977-78	1978-79
All heads of households	13.2	9.2	12.1	14.2	14.4	13.3	15.3	17.2	18.3	15.8	14.0
Housing Status[d]											
Homeowners	9.4	6.2	5.5	8.4	11.2	10.4	14.3	16.7	16.8	14.2	12.1
Renters	15.2	12.3	16.3	16.9	15.7	14.4	15.3	17.4	18.3	16.1	14.3
Race of Head											
White	12.5	9.2	12.6	13.9	14.7	12.7	14.2	16.4	18.2	14.7	13.5
Black	21.5	11.8	10.7	13.6	11.4	17.0	18.9	20.1	21.7	23.5	18.4
Poverty Status											
Not poor	13.6	9.8	11.7	14.0	14.0	12.9	14.1	17.1	17.9	14.6	13.8
Poor	11.5	8.4	14.5	16.2	16.5	16.7	24.6	16.4	23.5	25.1	18.4
Single-Person Household											
Male	12.7	7.2	20.9	14.4	13.6	9.4	14.6	18.4	21.6	13.4	19.5
Female	13.6	11.6	12.0	17.6	18.5	16.7	19.9	17.6	17.8	16.3	15.2
Work Status of Wife[e]											
Non-working	9.7	8.0	13.7	14.3	14.1	14.4	23.1	27.3	18.9	18.4	17.9
Works up to half time	13.3	10.0	5.7	10.6	12.0	12.3	8.0	5.0	8.2	6.8	7.2
Works full time	15.2	7.8	11.0	6.4	2.0	7.8	4.4	4.9	7.4	6.7	6.1

[a]For number of observations, see Table A18.5.

[b]Data presented in this table were derived from the 1979 merged family-individual tape. The distributions represent the number of individuals who appear in the 1979 data set who headed households in each year and who reported that they had moved for involuntary reasons since the spring of the previous year, expressed as a fraction of all heads who moved for any reason. In other words, the table provides estimates of the fraction of all moves that are involuntary moves.

[c]Respondents were asked whether they had moved since the spring of the previous year. Thus, for each pair of years listed in the columns of this table, the second year is the year of the interview in which the move was reported; the pair of years indicates that the move took place sometime between the spring of the first and the time of the interview in the second year listed. Subgroup status (e.g., poverty status, single-person household) refers to status in the first year of each pair of years.

[d]Those who neither own nor rent were excluded from the estimates due to low sample sizes.

[e]Up to half time means 1 to 1,499 hours per year. Full time means 1,500 or more hours per year. In all of these cases, the husband works full time.

Table A18.5

NUMBER OF OBSERVATIONS (UNWEIGHTED) FOR TABLES A18.1-A18.4

Subgroup	1968-69	1969-70	1970-71	1971-72	1972-73	1973-74	1974-75	1975-76	1976-77	1977-78	1978-79
All household heads	3,162	3,426	3,685	3,966	4,282	4,617	4,960	5,313	5,656	6,009	6,455
Housing Status											
Homeowners	1,628	1,805	1,923	2,091	2,307	2,521	2,652	2,843	2,976	3,157	3,424
Renters	1,374	1,447	1,557	1,661	1,751	1,851	2,053	2,181	2,358	2,521	2,652
Race of Head											
White	2,007	2,184	2,339	2,510	2,698	2,889	3,074	3,275	3,453	3,629	3,841
Black	1,054	1,134	1,234	1,336	1,453	1,585	1,724	1,868	2,016	2,177	2,391
Poverty Status											
Not poor	2,551	2,838	3,050	3,326	3,664	3,978	4,293	4,555	4,852	5,177	5,597
Poor	611	588	635	640	618	639	667	758	804	832	858
Single-Person Household											
Male	128	136	178	214	250	284	351	398	457	505	570
Female	285	315	366	401	421	477	523	583	646	696	747
Work Status of Wife											
Non-working	884	874	902	900	1,038	1,064	1,070	1,004	1,070	1,106	1,093
Works up to half time	501	554	550	586	615	718	704	744	738	803	829
Works full time	354	431	430	495	520	599	623	656	775	822	992

Table A18.6

INCIDENCE OF REPEAT MOBILITY, 1968-1979[a]

(Percentage Distribution)

Period: 1968-79

Frequency	All Individuals		Whites		Blacks		Never Poor		Ever Poor	
	NC[b]	C[c]	NC	C	NC	C	NC	C	NC	C
Never[d]	54.5	88.2	55.3	87.9	52.5	89.4	58.7	89.2	42.1	84.8
2 moves	13.6	7.4	13.0	7.5	17.1	7.0	13.3	7.0	14.4	8.7
3 moves	11.4	2.3	11.0	2.2	11.4	2.2	10.9	2.0	13.0	3.2
4 moves	7.1	0.8	7.2	0.9	6.6	0.4	6.3	0.8	9.4	1.1
5 or more moves[e]	13.4	1.3	13.5	1.5	12.4	1.0	10.8	1.0	21.1	2.2
Ever	45.5	11.8	44.7	12.1	47.5	10.6	41.3	10.8	57.9	15.2
Repeat movers/All movers	68.1		68.3		65.2		65.9		73.4	
(Total N)										

Period: 1969-1974 and 1974-1979

	Period: 1969-1974										1974-1979									
Frequency	All Individuals		Whites		Blacks		Never Poor		Ever Poor		All Individuals		Whites		Blacks		Never Poor		Ever Poor	
	NC[b]	C[c]	NC	C	NC	C	NC	C	NC	C	NC	C	NC	C	NC	C	NC	C	NC	C
Never[d]	75.8	86.4	76.0	86.6	76.5	87.4	77.8	87.7	66.3	80.0	74.9	86.6	75.0	86.8	75.9	86.8	77.2	88.1	63.2	78.7
2 moves	13.0	7.7	12.5	7.5	14.1	7.6	12.1	7.3	17.1	9.9	12.8	7.5	12.8	7.2	11.3	6.2	12.3	7.1	15.0	9.8
3 moves	6.6	3.1	6.5	2.9	5.7	3.4	6.0	2.8	9.4	4.7	7.3	2.7	7.2	2.6	7.8	3.7	6.5	2.3	11.3	4.8
4 moves	3.8	2.0	4.0	2.1	3.1	1.1	3.5	1.6	5.4	3.6	3.9	2.0	3.9	2.0	3.9	2.2	3.3	1.7	7.1	3.4
5 or more moves[e]	0.9	0.9	1.0	0.9	0.5	0.5	0.7	0.7	1.8	1.8	1.2	1.1	1.1	1.1	1.1	1.1	0.7	0.7	3.4	3.4
Ever	24.2	13.6	24.0	13.4	23.5	12.6	22.2	12.3	33.7	20.0	25.1	13.4	25.0	13.2	24.1	13.2	22.8	11.9	36.8	21.3
Repeat movers/All movers	50.0		51.5		41.7		48.7		54.2		52.9		53.3		50.0		51.1		59.8	
(Total N)																				

[a] Calculations based on all individuals who were in the panel during the period 1968-1979.

[b] NC = Not necessarily in consecutive years.

[c] C = Consecutive years.

[d] "Never" includes non-movers as well as those who moved only once over the period.

[e] For the two periods 1969-1974 and 1974-1979, "5 or more" has a maximum value of 5.

Table A18.7

FAMILIES WITH MORE THAN ONE PERSON PER ROOM, 1968-1978[a,b]
(Percentage Distribution)

Subgroup	1968	1969	1970	1971	1972	1973	1974	1975	1976	1977	1978
All heads of households	10.1	10.1	8.5	7.4	7.0	5.7	5.5	5.1	4.7	4.0	3.6
Whites	8.2	8.1	6.4	5.5	5.1	3.9	3.8	3.8	3.2	2.6	2.3
Blacks	24.7	24.0	20.9	18.8	16.3	14.9	14.4	11.9	13.4	11.5	10.6
Homeowners	8.5	8.3	7.0	6.3	5.9	4.7	4.5	4.2	4.0	3.4	2.8
Renters	13.2	13.9	11.1	9.2	9.3	7.6	7.0	7.0	6.0	5.0	5.1
Poor	27.8	20.4	19.6	22.2	19.4	16.0	16.1	14.9	14.6	11.4	9.7
Not poor	8.3	9.1	7.4	6.1	6.1	5.0	4.6	4.3	3.8	3.3	3.1
Male heads with children	17.9	18.7	15.8	14.1	13.3	11.3	11.1	10.4	10.0	9.1	7.8
Female heads with children	18.7	16.1	15.2	15.3	16.1	13.1	13.8	13.6	12.4	8.6	9.2

[a]For number of observations, see Table A18.10.

[b]Data presented in this table were derived from the 1979 merged family-individual tape. The distributions represent the fraction of individuals who appear in the 1979 data set who headed households in each year and who were classified as having more than one person per room in their dwelling unit.

Table A18.8

FAMILIES WITH FEWER ROOMS THAN REQUIRED, 1968-1978[a,b,c]

(Percentage Distribution)

Subgroup	1968	1969	1970	1971	1972	1973	1974	1975	1976	1977	1978
All heads of households	5.4	5.5	4.7	4.7	4.5	4.4	4.7	4.2	4.2	4.6	4.1
Whites	3.8	4.0	3.4	3.2	2.9	3.1	3.2	2.9	2.8	3.3	2.9
Blacks	16.7	16.2	15.2	14.8	14.7	12.7	13.9	11.4	13.6	13.3	11.4
Homeowners	2.3	2.8	2.0	1.7	2.1	1.5	1.9	1.7	1.7	1.6	1.2
Renters	10.8	9.5	8.6	9.1	8.4	9.1	8.6	7.5	6.6	8.3	7.5
Poor	22.4	17.7	13.5	19.9	14.8	18.9	17.6	14.5	15.4	15.2	11.9
Not poor	3.7	4.3	3.9	3.4	3.7	3.4	3.7	3.3	3.2	3.6	3.4
Male heads with children	5.6	5.9	4.4	4.1	3.8	3.8	4.0	3.6	3.5	3.5	2.7
Female heads with children	14.2	15.4	14.2	15.6	16.3	14.0	16.2	13.8	13.0	11.9	12.5

[a]For number of observations, see Table A18.10.

[b]Data presented in this table were derived from the 1979 merged family-individual tape. The distributions represent the fraction of individuals who appear in the 1979 data set who headed households in each year and who were classified as having fewer rooms than required by their family composition and size.

[c]In computing required rooms, a base of two rooms (exclusive of bathrooms) was allowed for head and spouse or for a single head. One additional room was allocated for each single person age eighteen or older, one room for a married couple other than the head and spouse, and one room for every two children of the same sex under age eighteen. Children under age ten were paired regardless of sex if this reduced the room requirement.

Table A18.9

FAMILIES WITH HOUSING COST TO INCOME RATIO OF MORE THAN 25 PERCENT, 1968-1978[a,b]

(Percentage Distribution)

Subgroup	1968	1969	1970	1971	1972	1973	1974	1975	1976	1977	1978
All heads of households	16.7	16.0	17.5	17.4	18.2	19.2	20.0	21.6	22.4	23.1	24.9
Whites	16.4	15.9	17.5	17.2	18.0	18.8	19.7	21.5	22.4	22.9	25.3
Blacks	20.9	17.6	19.6	19.8	20.5	22.1	21.8	21.9	22.1	24.6	22.7
Homeowners	19.6	18.9	20.2	19.9	19.7	21.3	22.8	24.8	25.3	25.7	29.3
Renters	12.8	11.9	14.3	14.5	17.5	17.5	17.0	18.5	20.4	21.8	21.0
Poor	47.8	49.5	55.8	55.9	57.2	51.1	50.3	54.8	58.2	57.3	53.0
Not poor	13.6	12.8	13.8	14.0	15.2	17.0	17.7	18.7	19.3	20.2	22.5
Male heads with children	7.5	7.7	8.8	8.0	9.3	8.5	10.6	12.0	12.1	12.2	14.1
Female heads with children	30.7	24.0	24.3	26.8	26.8	22.2	28.7	29.1	29.9	32.2	35.0

[a]For number of observations, see Table A18.10.

[b]Data presented in this table were derived from the 1979 merged family-individual tape. The distributions represent the fraction of individuals who appear in the 1979 data set who headed households in each year and who were classified as excessively burdened by housing costs.

Table A18.10

NUMBER OF OBSERVATIONS (UNWEIGHTED) FOR TABLES A18.6-A18.8

Subgroup	1968	1969	1970	1971	1972	1973	1974	1975	1976	1977	1978
All heads of households	3,013	3,162	3,426	3,685	3,966	4,282	4,617	4,960	5,313	5,656	6,009
Whites	1,935	2,040	2,185	2,340	2,510	2,698	2,889	3,074	3,275	3,453	3,629
Blacks	1,002	1,047	1,092	1,233	1,336	1,453	1,585	1,724	1,868	2,016	2,177
Homeowners	1,544	1,649	1,766	1,911	2,103	2,276	2,435	2,598	2,753	2,934	3,133
Renters	1,320	1,350	1,469	1,573	1,652	1,767	1,940	2,085	2,249	2,398	2,510
Poor	576	531	564	560	553	563	614	684	816	756	777
Not poor	2,437	2,631	2,862	3,125	3,413	3,719	4,003	4,276	4,587	4,900	5,232
Male heads with children	1,467	1,505	1,560	1,602	1,698	1,786	1,883	1,988	2,109	2,238	2,364
Female heads with children	498	517	542	574	605	623	640	697	718	766	776

Table A18.11

PERSISTENCE OF HOUSING DEPRIVATION: MORE THAN ONE PERSON PER ROOM, 1968-1978[a]

(Percentage Distribution)

Frequency	All Heads of Households		Whites		Blacks		Ever Poor		Never Poor		Female Head with Children		Male Head with Children	
	NC[b]	C[c]	NC	C	NC	C	NC	C	NC	C	NC	C	NC	C
Never	68.5	68.5	72.8	72.8	41.1	41.1	45.4	45.4	76.4	76.4	30.3	30.3	54.5	54.5
1 year	8.0	14.2	8.0	13.0	8.9	23.0	9.3	20.8	7.6	11.9	12.3	32.1	9.5	17.6
2 years	3.8	4.7	3.5	4.0	5.0	8.4	5.2	7.4	3.3	3.8	6.6	10.0	4.5	5.7
3 years	2.5	1.7	2.3	1.5	4.5	3.2	4.0	2.9	2.0	1.2	6.4	2.5	3.2	2.7
4 years	3.3	2.4	2.8	2.0	6.2	4.0	6.0	5.2	2.3	1.4	3.8	2.0	4.6	3.7
5 or more years	13.9	8.6	10.5	6.5	34.2	20.3	30.0	18.3	8.5	5.2	40.6	23.2	23.6	15.9
Ever	31.5	31.5	37.2	37.2	58.9	58.9	54.6	54.6	23.6	23.6	69.7	69.7	45.5	45.5
(Total N)														

[a]Calculations based on all individuals who were in the panel during the period 1968-1979.

[b]NC = Not necessarily in consecutive years.

[c]C = Consecutive years in status.

Table A18.12

PERSISTENCE OF HOUSING DEPRIVATION: FEWER ROOMS THAN REQUIRED, 1968-1978[a]

(Percentage Distribution)

Frequency	All Heads of Households		Whites		Blacks		Ever Poor		Never Poor		Female Head with Children		Male Head with Children	
	NC[b]	C[c]	NC	C	NC	C	NC	C	NC	C	NC	C	NC	C
Never	78.4	78.4	83.4	83.4	48.0	48.0	53.6	53.6	87.0	87.0	37.1	37.1	79.7	79.7
1 year	8.4	13.8	7.5	11.1	13.9	29.3	13.6	28.1	6.5	8.8	8.3	27.9	6.6	11.0
2 years	3.9	3.6	3.3	2.8	7.4	7.9	7.9	7.1	2.6	2.4	11.5	11.6	3.2	3.6
3 years	2.3	1.3	1.7	0.8	5.7	4.1	5.4	2.9	1.2	0.7	8.7	5.4	2.0	1.3
4 years	1.4	0.6	0.8	0.3	5.0	2.3	3.6	1.9	0.7	0.2	2.1	2.2	1.5	0.9
5 or more years	5.7	2.3	3.2	1.5	20.0	8.3	16.0	6.4	2.1	0.8	32.4	15.7	7.1	3.5
Ever	21.6	21.6	16.6	16.6	52.0	52.0	46.4	46.4	13.0	13.0	62.9	62.9	20.3	20.3
(Total N)														

[a]Calculations based on all individuals who were in the panel during the period 1968-1979.

[b]NC = Not necessarily in consecutive years.

[c]C = Consecutive years in status.

Table A18.13

PERSISTENCE OF HOUSING DEPRIVATION: EXCESSIVE HOUSING COST BURDENS,[a] 1968-1978[b]

(Percentage Distribution)

Frequency	All Heads of Households		Whites		Blacks		Ever Poor		Never Poor		Female Head with Children		Male Head with Children	
	NC[c]	C[d]	NC	C	NC	C	NC	C	NC	C	NC	C	NC	C
Never	45.5	45.5	45.9	45.9	43.8	43.8	24.1	24.1	52.9	52.9	26.0	26.0	61.1	61.1
1 year	18.6	37.7	18.7	37.3	18.1	40.3	20.1	50.7	18.0	33.3	17.6	54.5	13.4	27.6
2 years	10.2	6.9	10.0	6.8	11.2	7.5	14.1	10.2	8.9	5.8	12.3	7.8	7.8	4.2
3 years	7.3	3.3	7.0	3.2	8.7	3.4	11.3	5.4	5.9	2.5	11.6	6.3	5.7	3.1
4 years	4.8	1.7	4.8	1.9	4.1	0.5	6.5	2.3	4.1	1.5	8.9	0.7	3.6	1.5
5 or more years	13.6	5.0	13.4	4.8	14.2	4.4	23.8	7.3	10.2	4.1	23.6	4.6	8.4	2.5
Ever	54.5	54.5	54.1	54.1	56.2	56.2	75.9	75.9	47.1	47.1	74.0	74.0	38.9	38.9
(Total N)														

[a]More than 25 percent of income spent on housing costs.

[b]Calculations based on all individuals who were in the panel during the period, 1968-1979.

[c]NC = Not necessarily in consecutive years.

[d]C = Consecutive years in status.

Chapter 19

SUMMARY OF OTHER RESEARCH

Abowd, John M., and Ashenfelter, Orley. Anticipated Unemployment, Temporary Layoffs and Compensating Wage Differentials.

Abowd, John M., and Ashenfelter, Orley. Unemployment and Compensating Wage Differentials.

Abowd, John M., and Farber, Henry S. Job Queues and the Union Status of Workers.

Ashenfelter, Orley, and Ham, John. Education, Unemployment, and Earnings.

Bremer, Frederick C. The Measurement of Income Inequality for Public Policy Analysis.

Cohen, Alan. The Impact of Inflation on Nominal Wage Rates.

Cohen, Alan. Economics, Marital Instability, Race.

Cohn, Richard. The Effect of Employment Status Change on Self Attitudes.

Cramer, James C. Fertility and Female Employment: Problems of Causal Direction.

DaVanzo, Julie, and Kobrin, Frances. Work in Progress.

Freeman, Richard B. The Exit-Voice Tradeoff in the Labor Market: Unionism, Job Tenure, Quits, and Separations.

Hall, Robert E., and Mishkin, Frederic S. The Sensitivity of Consumption to Transitory Income: Estimates from Panel Data on Households.

Hampton, Robert L. Husband´s Characteristics and Marital Disruption in Black Families.

Hanushek, Eric A., and Quigley, John M. Life-cycle Earning Capacity and the OJT Investment Model.

Hanushek, Eric A., and Quigley, John M. Implicit Investment Profiles and Intertemporal Adjustments of Relative Wages.

Harris, Richard J. The Rewards of Migration for Income Change and Income Attainment: 1968-1973.

Harris, Richard J., and Hedderson, John. A Method to Analyze the Effects of Wife´s Income on Family Income Inequality.

498

Hausman, Jerry A., and Taylor, William E. Panel Data and Unobservable Individual Effects.

Hofferth, Sandra L. The Consequences of Remaining Childless or Having Only One Child: An Analysis of Selected Outcomes for Husbands and Wives.

Hunt, Janet C., and Kiker, B. F. The Effect of Fertility on the Time-Use of Working Wives.

Kim, Joochul. Characteristics of Migrants within the Framework of Current Migration Direction in the United States: Some Evidence from Micro-Data Analysis.

Lillydahl, Jane H., and Singell, Larry D. Measuring Equality through the Life Cycle.

Madden, Janice Fanning. Urban Land Use and the Growth of Two-Earner Households.

Mincer, Jacob, and Linda Leighton. Effect of Minimum Wages on Human Capital Formation.

Moen, Phyllis. Family Impacts of the 1975 Recession: Duration of Unemployment.

Onaka, J. L. A Multiple-Attribute Housing Consumption Disequilibrium Model of Intra-Metropolitan Residential Mobility.

Polachek, Solomon W. Secular Changes in Female Job Aspirations.

Wigle, Randall. The Theory of the Allocation of Time Reconsidered.

Wolf, Douglas A. Income in Labor Supply and Family Stability: An Empirical Analysis of Marital Dissolution.

ANTICIPATED UNEMPLOYMENT, TEMPORARY LAYOFFS AND
COMPENSATING WAGE DIFFERENTIALS
John M. Abowd, University of Chicago
Orley Ashenfelter, Princeton University
(Working Paper No. 137, Industrial Relations
Section, Princeton University, June 1980.)

This paper models the competitive equilibrium wage rate when employment offers vary according to the amount of anticipated unemployment and unemployment risk. Abowd and Ashenfelter used Panel Study data to construct a model of anticipated unemployment and unemployment variance which depends on personal employment history, industry, and economy-wide factors. Compensating wage differentials ranging from less than 1 percent to more than 14 percent were estimated for a two-digit industry classification over the years 1970 to 1975.

UNEMPLOYMENT AND COMPENSATING WAGE DIFFERENTIALS
John M. Abowd, University of Chicago
Orley Ashenfelter, Princeton University
(Report No. 7923, Center for Mathematical Studies in
Business and Economics, University of Chicago, June 1979.)

This paper considers the issue of whether or not the market wages received by individuals who expect to be underemployed or temporarily laid off in the course of their employment reflect the appropriate compensating differentials. The model implies that individuals who accept employment under these circumstances will receive a certainty equivalent compensating differential proportional to the squared expected extent of unemployment and a risk compensation proportional to the squared coefficient of variation of hours of work. The factor of proportionality for the certainty equivalent compensation is the inverse of the compensated labor supply elasticity in the absence of employment constraints. The risk factor is the relative risk aversion parameter defined over hours of work randomness. The model allows for the existence of an unemployment insurance system, and it is estimated using Panel Study data for the period 1970-1975. The authors found significant compensating differentials of 5 percent to 20 percent in the hourly wage of the typical constrained worker. This result is consistent with the labor contract theory of temporary layoff unemployment.

JOB QUEUES AND THE UNION STATUS OF WORKERS
John M. Abowd, University of Chicago
Henry S. Farber, M.I.T.
(Report No. 8017, Center for Mathematical Studies in
Business and Economics, University of Chicago, May 1980.)

Abowd and Ferber have developed a model of the determination of the union status of workers which allows for the possibility of queueing for union jobs. The empirical results derived using a Panel Study sample, are unsupportive of the queueing hypothesis. The no-queue model can be rejected using a likelihood ratio test. This suggest that a simple probit or logit model for union status is misspecified because it is not based on any consistent behavioral theory.

An important implication of the model is that, because most new entrants to the labor market prefer union jobs but cannot get them, and because accrual of nonunion seniority makes workers progressively less likely to desire union jobs, the union status of workers is largely determined by their success in being selected from the queue early in their working life.

EDUCATION, UNEMPLOYMENT, AND EARNINGS
Orley Ashenfelter, Princeton University
John Ham, University of Toronto
(Published in Journal of Political Economy, 87 (1979): 99-116.)

Using data on adult male workers, we first investigate the incremental effect of one year of schooling on unemployed hours and use this calculation to explain the difference in the proportional effects of schooling on earnings and wages. Schooling apparently reduced unemployed hours by reducing the incidence of unemployment spells, but it does not significantly affect their duration. We next test whether unemployed hours represent real constraints on worker behavior. To do this we develop and estimate life-cycle models of labor supply for workers with and without spells of unemployment, using longitudinal data. The results imply that perhaps three-quarters of the unemployed hours of male workers are part of the offer to sell labor.

THE MEASUREMENT OF INCOME INEQUALITY FOR PUBLIC POLICY ANALYSIS
Frederick C. Bremer, Columbia
(Ph.D. Thesis, Columbia University, 1980.)

Census data has generally shown that income inequality has not changed since World War II. This study compares the Census Money Income definition with other income definitions closer to economic theory to determine whether this conclusion is dependent upon the narrow government income definition.

Using a sample consisting of all individuals in families where the head is 35 years old in 1967, empirical tests were made with 12 income definitions ranging from Census Money Income (which considers only cash received) to Economic Income (which modifies Census Money Income by deducting taxes, adding several forms of in-kind government transfers and imputed income, and adjusting income for family size and geographical differences in the cost of living).

The results of the empirical analysis revealed that the government definition of income consistently showed a more pessimistic appraisal of the change in income inequality in the United States during the 1967-1975 period. Under each of the 12 definitions of income, inequality was found to have increased during the period studied. Using the Atkinson inequality measure, the government definition indicated an increase in inequality of 20 percent, while the definition closest to economic theory showed an increase of only 5 percent.

The ratio of female- to male-headed family income was about 50 percent higher using the Economic Income definition than with Census Money Income, although neither measure showed any significant change during the 1967-1975 period. Nonwhite families were found to have the same level of relative income under both definitions (about half the income of white-headed families), but the Census Money Income definition showed a 12.5 percent drop in this ratio between 1967 and 1975, while the Economic Income definition showed a 2.5 percent increase in the ratio. Income inequality by family size showed an insignificant drop using Census Money Income, but a substantial drop using the Economic Income definition. Results of the tests using a sample consisting only of children always differed significantly from results using the full sample.

THE IMPACT OF INFLATION ON NOMINAL WAGE RATES
Alan Cohen, U.S. Department of Health and Human Services

Cohen is planning an analysis of the impact of inflation on nominal real wages. There are periods during the panel when different rates of inflation occurred, and a pooled sample can be constructed of individual changes in each of several three-year periods. Explanatory variables then include both individual characteristics and behavior and aggregate changes in the price level and in other macroeconomic variables.

ECONOMICS, MARITAL INSTABILITY, RACE
Alan Cohen, U.S. Department of Health and Human Services
(Ph.D. Thesis, University of Wisconsin at Madison, 1979.)

THE EFFECT OF EMPLOYMENT STATUS CHANGE ON SELF ATTITUDES
Richard Cohn, Duke University
(Published in Social Psychology 41 (1978): 81-93.)

This article is based on Richard Cohn's dissertation, "The Consequences of Unemployment on Evaluations of Self." (Ph.D. Thesis, University of Michigan at Ann Arbor, 1977.)

FERTILITY AND FEMALE EMPLOYMENT: PROBLEMS OF CAUSAL DIRECTION
James C. Cramer, University of California at Davis
(Published in American Sociological Review, 45 (April 1980): 167-90.)

Using Panel Study data, Cramer discusses methodological problems, multicollinearity, misspecification, difference between attitudes, intentions, and behavior, and static versus dynamic models. He concludes that dominant effects are from fertility to employment in the short run and from employment to fertility in the long run.

WORK IN PROGRESS
Julie DaVanzo, Rand Corporation
Frances Kobrin, Brown University

Julie DaVanzo and Frances Kobrin are working on a NICHD-funded project to Rand on the Process by which children separate from the parental household and assume residentially separate adult roles. The study will include a description of the nestleaving process--relating leaving home, completing school, beginning work, establishing a household, marrying, and becoming parents. In addition, the analysis will examine the determinants and consequences of varying sequences and timing in the nestleaving process.

THE EXIT-VOICE TRADEOFF IN THE LABOR MARKET:
UNIONISM, JOB TENURE, QUITS, AND SEPARATIONS
Richard B. Freeman, Harvard University
(Published in Quarterly Journal of Economics, 94 (June 1980): 643-674.)

This article uses the Panel Study data, among other sets, to test the theory that grievance machinery is an alternative to quitting, holding fixed the monopoly wage effect.

THE SENSITIVITY OF CONSUMPTION TO TRANSITORY INCOME:
ESTIMATES FROM PANEL DATA ON HOUSEHOLDS
Robert E. Hall, Stanford University
Frederic S. Mishkin, University of Chicago
(Working Paper No. 505, National Bureau of Economic Research,
July 1980.)

Hall and Mishkin investigated the stochastic relation between income and consumption (specifically, consumption of food) within a panel of about 2,000 households. Their major findings are:

1. Consumption responds much more strongly to permanent than to transitory movements of income.

2. The response to transitory income is nonetheless clearly positive.

3. A simple test, independent of the model of consumption, rejects a central implication of the/pure life cycle/permanent income hypothesis.

4. The observed covariation of income and consumption is compatible with pure life cycle/permanent income behavior on the part of 80 percent of families and simple proportionality of consumption and income among the remaining 20 percent.

As a general matter, their findings support the view that families respond differently to different sources of income variations. In particular, temporary income tax policies have smaller effects on consumption than do other, more permanent changes in income of the same magnitude.

HUSBAND'S CHARACTERISTICS AND MARITAL DISRUPTION IN BLACK FAMILIES
Robert L. Hampton, Connecticut College
(Published in The Sociological Quarterly, 20 (Spring 1979): 255-66.)

Throughout the 1960s and the 1970s, a great deal of scholarly and popular literature has addressed the status of blacks in American society, some of it concerned with the stability of black family life. This paper, concerned with the relationship between husband's characteristics and marital disruption, focuses on 575 intact black families and identifies several factors associated with disruption. Although the husband's age is the strongest bivariate predictor of marital disruption, the husband's income is the most important predictor; and the husband's employment problems and religiosity are also strong predictors. A causal model of marital disruption shows that education, employment, and age at marriage influence marital disruption through their influence on income. Only age, income, and religiosity had a significant direct effect.

LIFE-CYCLE EARNING CAPACITY AND THE OJT INVESTMENT MODEL
Eric A. Hanushek, University of Rochester
John M. Quigley, University of California, Berkeley
(Discussion Paper No. 7904, Public Policy Program,
University of Rochester, March 1980.)

The OJT investment model, while commonly accepted as an explanation of significant variation in life-cycle earning capacity, has been tested only in quite indirect ways--subject to important untestable assumptions in the absence of investment data. This paper generalizes and extends the basic OJT model and then subjects it to a series of fairly exacting tests. The empirical analysis, considering the pattern of earnings growth for different race, sex, and schooling groups, provides only limited support for common specifications of investment patterns and raises questions about the usefulness of the theory.

IMPLICIT INVESTMENT PROFILES AND INTERTEMPORAL
ADJUSTMENTS OF RELATIVE WAGES
Eric A. Hanushek, University of Rochester
John M. Quigley, University of California, Berkeley
(Published in American Economic Review, 68 (March 1978): 67-79.)

This paper begins by extending the model of human capital accumulation to distinguish between the effects of labor market experience and aging on observed earnings profiles, to incorporate other individual differences explicitly, and to incorporate shortrun dynamics. On this basis, the implied postschool investment profiles are then estimated, and the impact of aggregate economic conditions on earnings profiles is considered.

For both black and white males within any schooling class, the theory of postschool investment explains roughly 25 percent of the variation in productivity; 45 percent is "explained" by other systematic (but unmeasured qualities) of individual workers (e.g., "motivation") or their work histories (e.g., "good luck"), and about 30 percent is completely unexplained. The

intertemporal shifts in the earnings profiles are explained by GNP growth, price
changes, and terms relating to specific race and schooling classes.

THE REWARDS OF MIGRATION FOR INCOME CHANGE AND
INCOME ATTAINMENT: 1968-1973
Richard J. Harris, University of Southern California
(Forthcoming in Social Science Quarterly)

An abstract of this research appeared in "Summary of Other Research," Five
Thousand American Families, Vol. 8.

A METHOD TO ANALYZE THE EFFECTS OF WIFE'S INCOME ON
FAMILY INCOME INEQUALITY
Richard J. Harris, University of Southern California
John J. Hedderson, University of Texas at El Paso

Harris and Hedderson have developed to evaluate the effects of wife's income
on family income inequality and those effects are examined between 1967 and 1976,
employing data from the Panel Study. The coefficient of variation is employed as
a measure of family income inequality. Results indicate that income inequality
increased substantially between 1967 and 1976 for U.S. families, but this
increase was not due to the effects of wife's income. There have been
substantial differences in the effects of wife's income for black and white
families. In general, a movement toward greater equality of earnings between
husbands and wives would tend to promote less family income inequality.

PANEL DATA AND UNOBSERVABLE INDIVIDUAL EFFECTS
Jerry A. Hausman, M.I.T.
William E. Taylor, Bell Laboratories

An important purpose in pooling time series and cross section data is to
control for individual-specific unobservable effects which may be correlated with
other explanatory variables: for example, latent ability in measuring returns to
schooling in earnings equations or managerial ability in measuring returns to
scale in firm cost functions. Using instrumental variables and the time-
invariant characteristics of the latent variable, they derived: (1) a test for
the presence of this effect and for the over-identifying restrictions we use;
(2) necessary and sufficient conditions for identification of all the parameters
in the model; and (3) the asymptotically efficient instrumental variable
estimator and conditions under which it differs from the within-groups
estimators. They calculated efficient estimates of a wage equation from the
Panel Study data which indicate substantial differences from within-groups and
Balestra-Nerlove estimates--particularly a significantly higher estimate of the
returns to schooling.

THE CONSEQUENCES OF REMAINING CHILDLESS OR HAVING ONLY ONE CHILD:
AN ANALYSIS OF SELECTED OUTCOMES FOR HUSBANDS AND WIVES
Sandra L. Hofferth, The Urban Institute

The goal of this research project funded by the National Institute of Child
Health and Human Development is to assess the consequences for couples and ever-
married individuals of having smaller families, specifically, having no children
or one child versus having two or more children. The outcomes of interest
include the economic well-being of the family; time availability; schooling,
training, and work experience of husbands and wives; geographic mobility; marital
stability; and health. Besides the particular number of children, a focus of
this research will be the timing of the births within the marital cycle. This is
an especially important issue because of the increased incidence of delayed
childbearing. Having three children in rapid succession 10 or 15 years after
marriage may have no effect at all on the well-being of families, whereas having
three children with the first five years may have numerous economic and social
consequences damaging both to the marriage and to the well-being of the family.
Since it is expected that the particular consequences of different family sizes
for couples and ever-married individuals will depend on their stage in the
marital cycle (and their age), the outcomes of interest will be examined among
couples and individuals who are comparable in terms of length of time since first
marriage. Finally, the impact of adding a child to the family will be examined
among couples at different stages in the marital cycle. The policy implications
of the outcomes associated with smaller families and the timing of childbearing
will be discussed.

THE EFFECT OF FERTILITY ON THE TIME-USE OF WORKING WIVES
Janet C. Hunt, University of Georgia
B. F. Kiker, University of South Carolina
(Forthcoming in Journal of Consumer Research.)

By applying data from the Panel Study of Income Dynamics to a household
utility maximization model, Hunt and Kiker have found that number and presence of
young children tend to increase while "quality" of children tends to decrease the
time wives devote to household production (including childcare).

Quality of children, proxied by expectations that they will get a college
education is treated as endogenous, but expected number of children or the
current number or the age of the youngest child are not. The wife's time in
market work and in housework-childcare are then treated as a function of
"expected quality."

CHARACTERISTICS OF MIGRANTS WITHIN THE FRAMEWORK OF CURRENT MIGRATION
DIRECTION IN THE UNITED STATES: SOME EVIDENCE FROM MICRO-DATA ANALYSIS
Joochul Kim, Arizona State University
(Published in Policy Sciences, 12 (1980): 355-378.)

In recent years, there has been growing interest in the phenomenon of an
apparent population distribution reversal in the United States. This paper
examines the characteristics of migrants participating in such moves between 1969
and 1977, based on data from the Panel Study of Income Dynamics. The data show
that the amount of ruralward migration outweighs that of urbanward migration.
While the ruralward migration was particularly prevalent in the Northeast, the
direction of migration in the South was predominantly urbanward. Ruralward
migrants appeared to be young single people and young married people without
children, as well as stable families. The "most ruralward" migrants tended to be
from the most highly urban environments. This new pattern of migration is
independent of both "white suburban flight" and the "sun-belt" phenomenon. The
findings suggest an important societal reorganization towards a newer "post-
industrial" and less urban population distribution.

MEASURING EQUALITY THROUGH THE LIFE CYCLE
Jane H. Lillydahl, University of Colorado
Larry D. Singell, University of Colorado
(Paper presented American Economic Association
meetings Denver, Colorado September 5, 1980.)

This paper presents updated findings, to 1977, of the Morgan-Baerwaldt
estimates of intra-family transfers.

URBAN LAND USE AND THE GROWTH OF TWO-EARNER HOUSEHOLDS
Janice Fanning Madden, University of Pennsylvania
(Published in American Economic Review 70 (May 1980) 191-97.)

This article uses the 1976 wave of the Panel Study of Income Dynamics to
examine distance to work, house size, and amenities for men and for women
earners.

There are four primary empirical findings in this study:

1. Two-earner, husband-wife households behave as one-earner, husband-wife
households in their choice of housing location, house size, and house quality;
that is, the observed differences are fully explained by fertility, income, and
job characteristics.

2. Unmarried individuals live closer to their jobs, purchase smaller and
higher quality housing units than married persons, other things being equal.

3. Households with children trade off house quality for larger housing units.

4. While married women earners with children reside in more suburbanized locations than other earners, their commuting behavior implies that their workplaces are substantially more suburbanized than that of other earners.

EFFECT OF MINIMUM WAGES ON HUMAN CAPITAL FORMATION
Jacob Mincer, Columbia University
Linda Leighton, Queens College
(Working Paper No. 441, National Bureau of Economic Research, Cambridge.)

FAMILY IMPACTS OF THE 1975 RECESSION: DURATION OF UNEMPLOYMENT
Phyllis Moen, Cornell University
(Published in Journal of Marriage and the Family 41 (August 1979): 562-572.)

Using data from Panel Study of Income Dynamics, this study examines the likelihood of extended joblessness for breadwinners who were unemployed during the recession of 1975. Both husband-wife and female-headed families with children under 18 are included in the analysis. Using log-linear techniques, several factors were found to increase the probability of unemployment lasting 15 weeks or more. A contextual variable, the county unemployment rate, was negatively related to extended joblessness: the "hard-core" unemployed have trouble getting re-employed even under favorable economic conditions. Women who head families are more likely to be unemployed for an extended period than are male breadwinners. Family heads with young children (under six) are more likely to be unemployed 15 weeks or more than are breadwinners of families at later stages of the life cycle. Policy considerations to lessen the potential for prolonged joblessness of breadwinners are discussed.

A MULTIPLE-ATTRIBUTE HOUSING CONSUMPTION DISEQUILIBRIUM
MODEL OF INTRA-METROPOLITAN RESIDENTIAL MOBILITY
J. L. Onaka, University of California
(Ph.D. Dissertation, School of Architecture and Urban Planning, UCLA.)

This paper reexamines the disequilibrium model of intrametropolitan residential mobility proposed by Goodman (1974) and Hanushek and Quigley (1978). The paper retains the assumption that a household maximizes utility defined over vectors of housing attributes and non-housing goods, subject to a budget constraint. The utility loss associated with the consumption of a non-optimal bundle of housing attributes is assumed monotonically related to the probability of moving. Unlike the earlier approaches, however, the proposed model incorporates the theory of hedonic prices developed by Rosen (1974) and Ellickson (1977) to specify a structural equation for the loss of household utility on multiple attributes of housing consumption. Parameters of the equation are estimated by stepwise logistic regression for the ´best´ combination of interaction terms, which are used to infer the marginal willingness-to-pay for housing attributes by different population subgroups. The model provides a significant fit to data from the Panel Study of Income Dynamics, correctly classifying 80 percent of sample cases as movers or stayers.

SECULAR CHANGES IN FEMALE JOB ASPIRATIONS
Solomon W. Polachek, Duke University
(Published in Retirement Policy in an Aging Society, 87, edited by
Robert L. Clark, Durham, NC: Duke University Press, 1980.)

This article uses both NLS and PSID to show different atrophy from intermittent employment in different occupations, and different total participation in those occupations.

THE THEORY OF THE ALLOCATION OF TIME RECONSIDERED
Randall Wigle, The University of Western Ontario

This paper considers a few of the estimation and data problems involved in the estimation of individual labour supply and hours equations. The major part of the paper evaluates the estimation techniques in Reuben Gronau´s paper (Journal of Political Economy, December 1977). A "replication" is performed which does not support the original hypothesis about the significance of unearned income in the theoretical section. Further estimates are presently being computed.

INCOME IN LABOR SUPPLY AND FAMILY STABILITY: AN
EMPIRICAL ANALYSIS OF MARITAL DISSOLUTION
Douglas A. Wolf, Economics Office of Income Security
Policy, Department of Health, Education, and Welfare
(Ph.D. Thesis, University of Pennsylvania, 1977.)

Appendix A

1979 QUESTIONNAIRE

Although the questionnaire, codes, and study procedures are described each year in a separate documentation volume, we reproduce the 1979 questionnaire in this appendix for readers without access to these volumes.

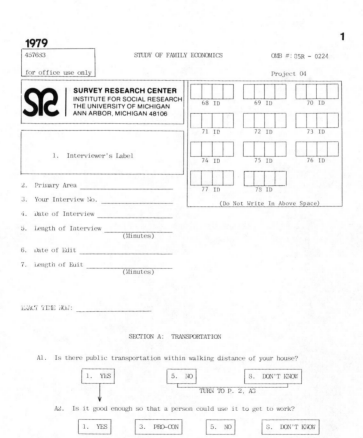

3

A9. During 1978 did you (or anyone else in the family here) do any of your own repair work on your car(s) or truck(s)?

1. YES

5. NO → TURN TO P. 4, SECTION B

A10. We would like a rough idea of how much time you spent and how much money you saved doing your repair work. What kinds of things did you do?

_____

_____

_____

_____

A11. About how much time did that take altogether? _____ HOURS IN 1978

A12. About how much do you think you saved doing this last year? $_____ SAVED IN 1978

→ TURN TO P. 4, SECTION B

A13. Was it more than $100?

DON'T KNOW

YES

NO

A14. Was it more than $200 you saved?

YES

NO → TURN TO P. 4, SECTION B

A15. About how much did you save? $_____

A16. Was it more than $50 you saved?

YES → TURN TO P. 4, SECTION B

NO

A17. Was it more than $25?

YES

NO

A3. Is your house inside the city limits?

1. YES

5. NO

9. NA; DON'T KNOW GO TO A6

A4. About how far are you from the center of that city?

1. LESS THAN 5 MILES
2. 5 - 14.9 MILES
3. 15 - 29.9 MILES
4. 30 - 49.9 MILES
5. 50 OR MORE MILES

A5. About how far are you from the center of the nearest city?

1. LESS THAN 5 MILES
2. 5 - 14.9 MILES
3. 15 - 29.9 MILES
4. 30 - 49.9 MILES
5. 50 OR MORE MILES

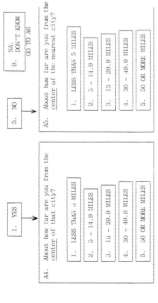

A6. Do you (or anyone else in the family here) own a car or truck?

1. YES

5. NO → TURN TO P. 4, SECTION B

A7. How many cars and trucks do you (and your family living here) own?

_____

A8. During the last year, about how many miles did you (and your family) drive in your (car(s)/and truck(s))?

_____

2

5

SECTION B: HOUSING

B1. How many rooms do you have for your family (not counting bathrooms)?

B2. Do you live in a one-family house, a two-family house, an apartment, a mobile home, or what?

1. ONE-FAMILY 3. APARTMENT 7. OTHER (SPECIFY): _____

2. TWO-FAMILY 4. MOBILE HOME

B3. Do you own the (home/apartment), pay rent, or what?

1. OWNS OR IS BUYING 5. PAYS RENT 8. NEITHER OWNS NOR RENTS

→ TURN TO P. 5, B12 TURN TO P. 5, B17

B4. About how much did heat, electricity and water cost you last year?

$ _____ UTILITIES IN 1978

B5. Could you tell me what the present value of your (house/apartment/farm) is— I mean about what would it bring if you sold it today?

$ _____ HOUSE VALUE

B6. Do you have a mortgage on this property?

1. YES 5. NO ——→ GO TO B11

	1st MORTGAGE	2nd MORTGAGE
B7. About how much is the remaining principal on this mortgage?	$ _____	$ _____
B8. How much are your monthly mort-gage payments?	$ _____	$ _____
B9. About how many more years will you have to pay on it?	_____	_____

B10. Do you also have a second mortgage?

1. YES 5. NO ——→ GO TO B11

ASK B7-B9 FOR SECOND MORTGAGE

B11. About how much are your total yearly property taxes including city, county and school taxes?

$ _____ PROPERTY TAX PER YEAR

TURN TO P. 6, B21

IF R PAYS RENT

B12. About how much rent do you pay a month?

$ _____ RENT PER MONTH

B13. Is this (house/apartment) rented fully furnished?

1. YES 5. NO

B14. Do you pay for heat, electricity, or water yourself?

1. YES 5. NO ——→ TURN TO P. 6, B21

B15. About how much did they cost you altogether last year?

$ _____ UTILITIES IN 1978

B16. Is heating included in your monthly rent?

1. YES 5. NO

TURN TO P. 6, B21

IF R NEITHER OWNS NOR RENTS

B17. How is that? _____

B18. How much would it rent for if it were rented?

$ _____ PER _____
AMOUNT MONTH, YEAR

B19. Do you pay for heat, electricity or water yourself?

YES NO ——→ TURN TO P. 6, B21

B20. About how much did they cost you altogether last year?

$ _____ UTILITIES IN 1978

4

B21. Have you (HEAD) moved any time since the spring of 1978?

1. YES   5. NO ──→ GO TO B24

B22. What month was that? (MOST RECENT MOVE)

_____ MONTH

B23. Why did you (HEAD) move?

_____

_____

B24. Do you think you might move in the next couple of years?

1. YES, MIGHT OR MAYBE   5. NO   8. DON'T KNOW

└─→ TURN TO P. 7, B27

B25. Would you say you definitely will move, probably will move, or are you more uncertain?

1. DEFINITELY   2. PROBABLY   3. MORE UNCERTAIN

B26. Why might you move?

_____

_____

_____

B27. Did you (or your family) do any work (yourself/yourselves) on your (house/apartment) during 1978? I mean repairs or remodelling.

1. YES   5. NO ──→ TURN TO P. 8, SECTION C

B28. We would like a rough idea of how much time you spent and how much money you saved. What did you do?

_____

_____

_____

B29. About how much time did that take? _____ HOURS IN 1978

B30. About how much do you think you saved by doing it yourself?

$ _____ SAVED IN 1978

TURN TO P. 8, SECTION C

B31. Was it more than $100?

DON'T KNOW   YES   NO ──→ TURN TO P. 8, SECTION C

B32. Was it more than $200?

YES   NO ──→ TURN TO P. 8, SECTION C

B33. About how much do you think you saved?

$ _____

B34. Was it more than $50?

YES ──→ TURN TO P. 8, SECTION C   NO

B35. Was it more than $25?

YES   NO

9

C6. What is your main occupation? What sort of work do you do?

OCC ☐☐   IND ☐☐

_____

C7. Tell me a little more about what you do.

_____

C8. What kind of business or industry is that in?

_____

C9. How long have you had your present position?

_____ MONTHS   OR   _____ YEARS   MOS ☐☐

C10. INTERVIEWER CHECKPOINT

☐ A. HEAD HAS HAD PRESENT POSITION LESS THAN ONE YEAR

☐ B. HEAD HAS HAD PRESENT POSITION ONE YEAR OR MORE. TURN TO P. 10, C16

C11. What month did you start this job?

_____

C12. What happened to the job you had before--did the company go out of business, were you laid off, promoted, were you not working, or what?

_____ | 5. NO PREVIOUS JOB |
                                      TURN TO P. 10, C16

C13. On the whole, would you say your present job is better or worse than the one you had before?

| 1. BETTER | | 5. WORSE | | 3. SAME | → TURN TO P. 10, C16

C14. Why is it (better/worse)?

_____

C15. Does your present job pay more than the one you had before?

| 1. YES, MORE | | 5. NO, SAME OR LESS |

8

SECTION C: EMPLOYMENT OF HEAD

C1. We would like to know about what you do--are you (HEAD) working now, looking for work, retired, a student, (a housewife), or what?

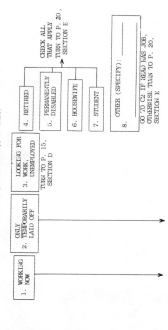

| 1. WORKING NOW | | 2. ONLY TEMPORARILY LAID OFF | | 3. LOOKING FOR WORK, UNEMPLOYED | TURN TO P. 15, SECTION D

| 4. RETIRED | | 5. PERMANENTLY DISABLED | | 6. HOUSEWIFE | | 7. STUDENT | CHECK ALL THAT APPLY TURN TO P. 20, SECTION E

8. OTHER (SPECIFY): _____

GO TO C2 IF HEAD HAS JOB, OTHERWISE TURN TO P. 20, SECTION E

C2. Do you work for someone else, yourself, or what?

| 1. SOMEONE ELSE | | 2. BOTH SOMEONE ELSE AND SELF | | 3. SELF ONLY | TURN TO P. 9, C6

C3. (In your work for someone else,) do you work for the federal, state, or local government?

| 1. YES | | 5. NO |

C4. Is your current job covered by a union contract?

| 1. YES | | 5. NO | → TURN TO P. 9, C6

C5. Do you belong to that labor union?

| 1. YES | | 5. NO |

C16. Did you miss any work in 1978 because someone else in the family was sick?

1. YES → 5. NO → GO TO C18

C17. How much work did you miss?

_____ DAYS   _____ WEEKS   _____ MONTHS

C18. Did you miss any work in 1978 because you were sick?

1. YES → 5. NO → GO TO C20

C19. How much work did you miss?

_____ DAYS   _____ WEEKS   _____ MONTHS

C20. Did you take any vacation or time off during 1978?

1. YES → 5. NO → GO TO C22

C21. How much vacation or time off did you take?

_____ DAYS   _____ WEEKS   _____ MONTHS

C22. Did you miss any work in 1978 because you were on strike?

1. YES → 5. NO → TURN TO P. 11, C24

C23. How much work did you miss?

_____ DAYS   _____ WEEKS   _____ MONTHS

C24. Did you miss any work in 1978 because you were unemployed or temporarily laid off?

1. YES → 5. NO → GO TO C26

C25. How much work did you miss?

_____ DAYS   _____ WEEKS   _____ MONTHS

C26. Then, how many weeks did you actually work on your main job in 1978?

_____ WEEKS IN 1978

C27. And, on the average, how many hours a week did you work on your main job in 1978?

_____ HOURS PER WEEK IN 1978

C28. Did you work any overtime which isn't included in that?

1. YES → 5. NO → TURN TO P. 12, C30

C29. How many hours did that overtime amount to in 1978?

_____ HOURS IN 1978

C30. Are you salaried, paid by the hour, or what?

1. SALARIED   3. PAID BY HOUR   7. OTHER

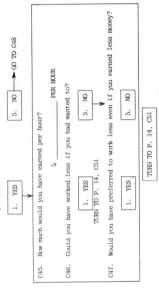

C31. How much is your salary?
$____ PER ____
MONTH, YEAR

C32. If you were to work more hours than usual during some week, would you get paid for those extra hours of work?
1. YES   5. NO → GO TO C36

C33. About how much would you make per hour for those extra hours?
$____ PER HOUR
TIME AND A HALF
DOUBLE TIME
REG
OT

C34. What is your hourly wage rate for your regular work time?
$____ PER HOUR

C35. What is your hourly wage rate for over-time?
$____ PER HOUR
TIME AND A HALF
DOUBLE TIME
REG
OT

C36. How is that?
____

C37. If you worked an extra hour, how much would you earn for that hour?
$____

C38. Did you have any extra jobs or other ways of making money in addition to your main job in 1978?
1. YES
5. NO   C44
TURN TO P. 13, C44

OCC

C39. What did you do?
____

C40. Anything else?
____

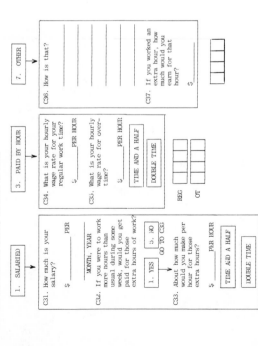

C41. About how much did you make per hour at this?
$____ PER HOUR

C42. And how many weeks did you work on your extra job(s) in 1978?
____ WEEKS IN 1978

C43. On the average, how many hours a week did you work on your extra job(s)?
____ HOURS PER WEEK IN 1978

C44. Was there more work available (on your job/any of your jobs) so that you could have worked more if you had wanted to?
1. YES
5. NO → GO TO C48

C45. How much would you have earned per hour?
$____ PER HOUR

C46. Could you have worked less if you had wanted to?
1. YES → TURN TO P. 14, C51
5. NO

C47. Would you have preferred to work less even if you earned less money?
1. YES
5. NO
TURN TO P. 14, C51

C48. Would you have liked to work more if you could have found more work?
1. YES → TURN TO P. 14, C51
5. NO

C49. Could you have worked less if you had wanted to?
1. YES → TURN TO P. 14, C51
5. NO

C50. Would you have preferred to work less even if you earned less money?
1. YES
5. NO

SECTION D: HEAD LOOKING FOR WORK, UNEMPLOYED IN C1

D1. What kind of job are you looking for?

_____

D2. How much would you expect to earn?

$ _____ PER _____

D3. Will you have to get any training to qualify?

1. YES   5. NO   8. DON'T KNOW

D4. Have you been doing anything in the last four weeks to find a job?

1. YES   5. NO → GO TO D6

D5. How many places have you been to in the last four weeks to find out about a job?

0. NONE   1. ONE   2. TWO   3. THREE   4. FOUR   5. FIVE OR MORE   8. DON'T KNOW

D6. Are there jobs available around here that just aren't worth taking?

1. YES   5. NO → TURN TO P. 16, D8

D7. How much do they pay?

$ _____ PER _____

C51. About how much time does it take you to get to work each day, door to door?

____ HOURS ____ MINUTES   00. NONE → GO TO C54

C52. About how many miles is it to where you work?

_____ ONE WAY

C53. Do you use public transportation to get to work, (drive with your wife), have a car pool, drive by yourself, walk, or what?

1. PUBLIC TRANS-PORTATION   2. DRIVE WITH WIFE   3. CAR POOL   4. DRIVE BY SELF   5. WALK

7. OTHER (SPECIFY): _____

C54. Have you been thinking about getting a new job, or will you keep the job you have now?

1. THINKING ABOUT GETTING A NEW JOB   5. KEEP JOB HAVE NOW → GO TO C56

C55. Have you been doing anything in particular about it?

1. YES   5. NO

C56. Would you be willing to move to another community if you could earn more money there?

1. YES   2. MAYBE   3. DEPENDS   5. NO →

TURN TO P. 22, SECTION F

C57. Why is that? _____

TURN TO P. 22, SECTION F

D8. Would you be willing to move to another community if you could get a good job there?

1. YES, MAYBE, OR DEPENDS → D9. How much would a job have to pay for you to be willing to move?

$ _____ PER _____

5. NO → D10. Why is that?

_____

D11. How long have you been looking for work? _____ WKS

D12. Have you ever had a job?

1. YES

5. NO → TURN TO P. 22, SECTION F

D13. What sort of work did you do on your last job? What was your occupation?

_____

D14. What kind of business or industry was that in?

_____   OCC   IND

D15. What happened to that job—did the company go out of business, were you laid off, or what?

_____

D16. When did you last work?

_____

D26. Did you miss any work in 1978 because you were unemployed or temporarily laid off?

1. YES →

5. NO → GO TO D28

D27. How much work did you miss?

___ DAYS   ___ WEEKS   ___ MONTHS

D28. Then, how many weeks did you actually work on your job in 1978?

___ WEEKS IN 1978

D29. And, on average, how many hours a week did you work when you worked?

___ HOURS PER WEEK IN 1978

D30. On your last job, how much time did it take you to get to work each day, door to door?

___ HOURS   ___ MINUTES   ONE WAY

00. NONE → TURN TO P. 22, SECTION F

D31. About how many miles was it to where you worked?

___ ONE WAY

D32. Did you use public transportation to get to work, (drive with your wife,) have a car pool, drive by yourself, walk, or what?

1. PUBLIC TRANS-PORTATION   2. DRIVE WITH WIFE   3. CAR POOL   4. DRIVE BY SELF   5. WALK

7. OTHER (SPECIFY): _____

TURN TO P. 22, SECTION F

D17. INTERVIEWER CHECKPOINT

A. HEAD WORKED IN 1978 OR 1979 [ ]

B. HEAD DID NOT WORK IN 1978 OR 1979 → TURN TO P. 22, SECTION F [ ]

D18. Did you take any vacation or time off during 1978?

1. YES →

5. NO → GO TO D20

D19. How much vacation or time off did you take?

___ DAYS   ___ WEEKS   ___ MONTHS

D20. Did you miss any work in 1978 because someone else in the family was sick?

1. YES →

5. NO → GO TO D22

D21. How much work did you miss?

___ DAYS   ___ WEEKS   ___ MONTHS

D22. Did you miss any work in 1978 because you were sick?

1. YES →

5. NO → GO TO D24

D23. How much work did you miss?

___ DAYS   ___ WEEKS   ___ MONTHS

D24. Did you miss any work in 1978 because you were on strike?

1. YES →

5. NO → TURN TO P. 19, D26

D25. How much work did you miss?

___ DAYS   ___ WEEKS   ___ MONTHS

SECTION E: HEAD IS RETIRED, HOUSEWIFE, STUDENT, PERMANENTLY DISABLED IN C1

E1. INTERVIEWER CHECKPOINT
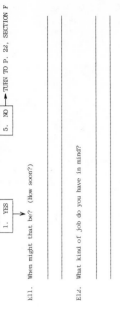
1. HEAD IS RETIRED
5. HEAD IS PERMANENTLY DISABLED, HOUSEWIFE, STUDENT, OR OTHER → GO TO E3

E2. In what year did you retire?

E3. During 1978, did you do any work for money?
1. YES
5. NO TURN TO P. 21, E10

E4. What kind of work did you do? What was your occupation?

OCC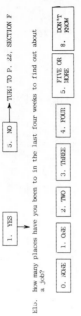

E5. What kind of business or industry was that in?

IND

E6. How many weeks did you work last year? _____ WEEKS IN 1978

E7. About how many hours a week did you work? _____ HOURS PER WEEK IN 1978

E8. Are you still working?
1. YES TURN TO P. 21, E10
5. NO

E9. What happened to that job--did the company go out of business, were you laid off, or what?

E10. Are you thinking of getting (a/another) job in the future?
1. YES
5. NO → TURN TO P. 22, SECTION F

E11. When might that be? (How soon?)

E12. What kind of job do you have in mind?

E13. Would you have to get any training to qualify?
1. YES   5. NO   8. DON'T KNOW

E14. Have you been doing anything in the last four weeks to find a job?
1. YES
5. NO → TURN TO P. 22, SECTION F

E15. How many places have you been to in the last four weeks to find out about a job?

0. NONE   1. ONE   2. TWO   3. THREE   4. FOUR   5. FIVE OR MORE   8. DON'T KNOW

SECTION F

F7. What is your (wife's/friend's) main occupation? What sort of work does she do?

OCC ☐☐   IND ☐☐

F8. Tell me a little more about what she does.

_____

F9. What kind of business or industry is that in?

_____

F10. How long has your (wife/friend) had her present position?

_____ MONTHS   OR   _____ YEARS

F11. INTERVIEWER CHECKPOINT

☐ A. WIFE HAS HAD PRESENT POSITION LESS THAN ONE YEAR

☐ B. WIFE HAS HAD PRESENT POSITION ONE YEAR OR MORE ──→ TURN TO P. 24, F14

F12. What month did she start this job?   MOS ☐☐

_____

F13. What happened to the job she had before--did the company go out of business, was she laid off, promoted, not working, or what?

_____

5. NO PREVIOUS JOB

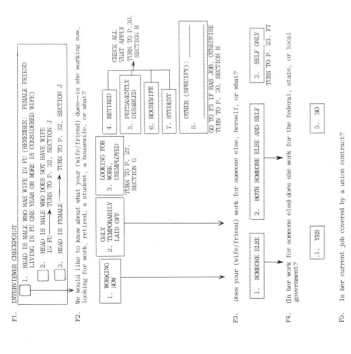

SECTION F

F1. INTERVIEWER CHECKPOINT

☐ 1. HEAD IS MALE WHO HAS WIFE IN FU (REMEMBER: FEMALE FRIEND LIVING IN FU ONE YEAR OR MORE IS CONSIDERED WIFE)

☐ 2. HEAD IS MALE WHO DOES NOT HAVE WIFE IN FU ──→ TURN TO P. 32, SECTION J

☐ 3. HEAD IS FEMALE ──→ TURN TO P. 32, SECTION J

F2. We would like to know about what your (wife/friend) does--is she working now, looking for work, retired, a student, a housewife, or what?

1. WORKING NOW

2. ONLY TEMPORARILY LAID OFF

3. LOOKING FOR WORK, UNEMPLOYED → TURN TO P. 27, SECTION G

4. RETIRED
5. PERMANENTLY DISABLED
6. HOUSEWIFE
7. STUDENT
8. OTHER (SPECIFY): _____

CHECK ALL THAT APPLY → TURN TO P. 30, SECTION H

GO TO F3 IF HAS JOB, OTHERWISE TURN TO P. 30, SECTION H

F3. Does your (wife/friend) work for someone else, herself, or what?

1. SOMEONE ELSE   2. BOTH SOMEONE ELSE AND SELF   3. SELF ONLY → TURN TO P. 23, F7

F4. (In her work for someone else) does she work for the federal, state, or local government?

1. YES   5. NO

F5. Is her current job covered by a union contract?

1. YES   5. NO ──→ TURN TO P. 23, F7

F6. Does she belong to that labor union?

1. YES   5. NO

F14. Did your (wife/friend) miss any work in 1978 because you or someone else in the family was sick?

1. YES

5. NO → GO TO F16

F15. How much work did she miss?

_____ DAYS   _____ WEEKS   _____ MONTHS

F16. Did your (wife/friend) miss any work in 1978 because she was sick?

1. YES

5. NO → GO TO F18

F17. How much work did she miss?

_____ DAYS   _____ WEEKS   _____ MONTHS

F18. Did your (wife/friend) take any vacation or time off during 1978?

1. YES

5. NO → GO TO F20

F19. How much vacation or time off did she take?

_____ DAYS   _____ WEEKS   _____ MONTHS

F20. Did your (wife/friend) miss any work in 1978 because she was on strike?

1. YES

5. NO → GO TO F22

F21. How much work did she miss?

_____ DAYS   _____ WEEKS   _____ MONTHS

F22. Did your (wife/friend) miss any work in 1978 because she was unemployed or temporarily laid off?

1. YES

5. NO → TURN TO P. 25, F24

F23. How much work did she miss?

_____ DAYS   _____ WEEKS   _____ MONTHS

F24. Then, how many weeks did your (wife/friend) actually work on her main job in 1978?

_____ WEEKS IN 1978

F25. And, on the average, how many hours a week did your (wife/friend) work on her main job in 1978?

_____ HOURS PER WEEK IN 1978

F26. Did your (wife/friend) work any overtime which isn't included in that?

1. YES

5. NO → GO TO F28

F27. How many hours did that overtime amount to in 1978?

_____ HOURS IN 1978

F28. Is your (wife/friend) salaried, paid by the hour, or what?

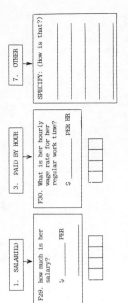

1. SALARIED

F29. How much is her salary?

$_____ PER _____

3. PAID BY HOUR

F30. What is her hourly wage rate for her regular work time?

$_____ PER HR

7. OTHER

SPECIFY: (How is that?)

SECTION G: WIFE/FRIEND LOOKING FOR WORK, UNEMPLOYED IN F2

OCC ☐☐

G1. What kind of job is your (wife/friend) looking for?

_____

G2. Has she been doing anything in the last four weeks to find a job?

| 1. YES | 5. NO → GO TO G4 |

G3. How many places has your (wife/friend) been to in the last four weeks to find out about a job?

| 0. NONE | 1. ONE | 2. TWO | 3. THREE | 4. FOUR | 5. FIVE OR MORE |

WKS ☐☐

G4. How long has she been looking for work?

_____

G5. Has your (wife/friend) ever had a job?

| 1. YES | 5. NO → TURN TO P. 32, SECTION J |

G6. What sort of work did your (wife/friend) do on her last job? (What was her occupation?)

OCC ☐☐

_____

G7. What kind of business or industry was that in?

IND ☐☐

_____

G8. What happened to that job--did the company go out of business, was she laid off, or what?

_____

G9. When did your (wife/friend) last work?

_____

F31. Did your (wife/friend) have any extra jobs or other ways of making money in addition to her main job in 1978?

OCC ☐☐

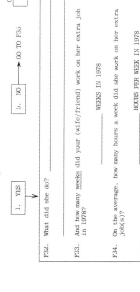

| 1. YES | 5. NO → GO TO F35 |

F32. What did she do?

_____

F33. And how many weeks did your (wife/friend) work on her extra job in 1978?

_____ WEEKS IN 1978

F34. On the average, how many hours a week did she work on her extra job(s)?

_____ HOURS PER WEEK IN 1978

F35. About how much time does it take your (wife/friend) to get to work each day, door to door?

_____ HOURS _____ MINUTES ONE WAY

| 00. NONE → TURN TO P. 32, SECTION J |

F36. About how many miles is it to where your (wife/friend) works?

_____ ONE WAY

F37. Does she use public transportation to get to work, drive with you, have a car pool, drive by herself, walk, or what?

| 1. PUBLIC TRANS-PORTATION | 2. DRIVE WITH HEAD | 3. CAR POOL | 4. DRIVE BY SELF | 5. WALK |

7. OTHER (SPECIFY): _____

TURN TO P. 32, SECTION J

28

G10. INTERVIEWER CHECKPOINT

☐ A. WIFE WORKED IN 1978 OR 1979

☐ B. WIFE DID NOT WORK IN 1978 OR 1979 → TURN TO P. 32, SECTION J

G11. Did your (wife/friend) take any vacation or time off during 1978?

1. YES   5. NO → GO TO G13

G12. How much vacation or time off did she take?

___ DAYS   ___ WEEKS   ___ MONTHS

G13. Did your (wife/friend) miss any work in 1978 because you or someone else in the family was sick?

1. YES   5. NO → GO TO G15

G14. How much work did she miss?

___ DAYS   ___ WEEKS   ___ MONTHS

G15. Did your (wife/friend) miss any work in 1978 because she was sick?

1. YES   5. NO → GO TO G17

G16. How much work did she miss?

___ DAYS   ___ WEEKS   ___ MONTHS

G17. Did your (wife/friend) miss any work in 1978 because she was on strike?

1. YES   5. NO → TURN TO P. 29, G19

G18. How much work did she miss?

___ DAYS   ___ WEEKS   ___ MONTHS

29

G19. Did your (wife/friend) miss any work in 1978 because she was unemployed or temporarily laid off?

1. YES   5. NO → GO TO G21

G20. How much work did she miss?

___ DAYS   ___ WEEKS   ___ MONTHS

G21. Then, how many weeks did she actually work on her job in 1978?

___ WEEKS IN 1978

G22. And, on average, how many hours a week did she work when she worked?

___ HOURS PER WEEK IN 1978

G23. On her last job, how much time did it take her to get to work each day, door to door?

___ HOURS   ___ MINUTES   ONE WAY

00. NONE → TURN TO P. 32, SECTION J

G24. About how many miles was it to where she worked?

___ ONE WAY

G25. Did your (wife/friend) use public transportation to get to work, drive with you, have a car pool, drive by herself, or what?

1. PUBLIC TRANSPORTATION   2. DRIVE WITH HEAD   3. CAR POOL   4. DRIVE BY SELF   5. WALK

7. OTHER (SPECIFY): ___

TURN TO P. 32, SECTION J

H10. Is your (wife/friend) thinking of getting (a/another) job in the future?

[1. YES] → [5. NO] → TURN TO P. 32, SECTION J

H11. has your (wife/friend) been doing anything in the last four weeks to find a job?

[1. YES] → [5. NO] → TURN TO P. 32, SECTION J

H12. How many places has your (wife/friend) been to in the last four weeks to find out about a job?

[0. NONE] [1. ONE] [2. TWO] [3. THREE] [4. FOUR] [5. FIVE OR MORE] [8. DON'T KNOW]

SECTION H: WIFE/FRIEND IS RETIRED, HOUSEWIFE, STUDENT, PERMANENTLY DISABLED IN F2

H1. INTERVIEWER CHECKPOINT

[1.] WIFE IS RETIRED

[3.] WIFE IS PERMANENTLY DISABLED, HOUSEWIFE, STUDENT OR OTHER ──→ GO TO H3

H2. In what year did your (wife/friend) retire?

H3. During 1978, did your (wife/friend) do any work for money?

[1. YES] →

[5. NO] → TURN TO P. 31, H10

H4. What kind of work did she do? What was her occupation?

OCC [ ][ ]

IND [ ][ ]

H5. What kind of business or industry was that in?

H6. How many weeks did your (wife/friend) work last year?

_____ WEEKS IN 1978

H7. About how many hours a week did your (wife/friend) work?

_____ HOURS PER WEEK IN 1978

H8. Is she still working?

[1. YES] → TURN TO P. 31, H10

[5. NO] →

H9. What happened to that job—did the company go out of business, was she laid off, or what?

_____

_____

33

SECTION J: HOUSEWORK, FOOD, AND CHILDCARE

J1. Are you (HEAD) married, widowed, divorced, separated, or single?

| 1. MARRIED | 2. SINGLE | 3. WIDOWED | 4. DIVORCED | 5. SEPARATED |

GO TO J4   GO TO J4

J2. Were you ever married?

1. YES

5. NO → GO TO J4

J3. What happened to your last marriage—were you widowed, divorced, separated, or what?

| 3. WIDOWED | 4. DIVORCED | 5. SEPARATED | 7. OTHER (SPECIFY): |

J4. INTERVIEWER CHECKPOINT

1. HEAD IS MALE WHO HAS WIFE IN FU (REMEMBER: FEMALE FRIEND LIVING IN FU ONE YEAR OR MORE IS CONSIDERED WIFE.)

2. HEAD IS MALE WHO DOES NOT HAVE WIFE IN FU → GO TO J6

3. HEAD IS FEMALE → GO TO J6

J5. About how much time does your (wife/friend) spend on housework in an average week—I mean time spent cooking, cleaning and doing other work around the house?

_____ HOURS PER WEEK

J6. About how much time do you (HEAD) spend on housework in an average week? (I mean time spent cooking, cleaning, and doing other work around the house?)

_____ HOURS PER WEEK

32

J7. INTERVIEWER CHECKPOINT

A. ANY OTHER PEOPLE LIVE WITH HEAD (AND WIFE) IN FU, INCLUDING CHILDREN

B. HEAD (AND WIFE) LIVE ALONE IN FU → TURN TO P. 34, J12

J8. Does anyone else here in the household help with the housework?

1. YES

5. NO → TURN TO P. 34, J12

J9. Who is that? (LIST RELATIONSHIP TO HEAD AND AGE FOR EACH PERSON IN COLUMN J9 AND ASK J10 FOR EACH.)

J9

J10. About how much time does (he/she) spend on housework in an average week?

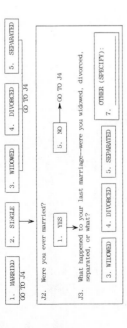

| RELATIONSHIP TO HEAD | AGE | SEQ # |

J11. Anyone else? (LIST IN J9 AND ASK J10 FOR EACH PERSON.)

J21. How much do you (or anyone else in your family) spend on food that you use at home in an average week?

$ _____ PER _____ WEEK, MONTH
AMOUNT

J22. Do you have any food delivered to the door which isn't included in that?

YES / NO → GO TO J24

J23. How much do you spend on that food?

$ _____ PER _____ WEEK, MONTH
AMOUNT

J24. About how much do you (and everyone else in your family) spend eating out, not counting meals at work or at school?

$ _____ PER _____ WEEK, MONTH
AMOUNT

J25. Now we would like to know about last year. Did you (or anyone else in your family) use government food stamps at any time in 1978?

YES / NO → TURN TO P. 36, J29

J26. How much did you pay for the stamps in 1978?

$ _____ PER _____ WEEK, MONTH
AMOUNT

J27. How much food could you buy with the stamps in 1978?

$ _____ PER _____ WEEK, MONTH
AMOUNT

J28. For how many months did you use food stamps in 1978?

_____ MONTHS

J12. Did you (or anyone else now living in your family) receive or buy government food stamps last month?

YES / NO → TURN TO P. 35, J21

J13. For how many members of your family were stamps issued?

J14. How much did you pay for the stamps?

$ _____ PER _____ WEEK, MONTH
AMOUNT

J15. How much food could you buy with the stamps?

$ _____ PER _____ WEEK, MONTH
AMOUNT

J16. In addition to what you spent on food stamps, did you (or anyone else in your family) spend any money on food that you use at home?

YES / NO → GO TO J18

J17. How much? $ _____ PER _____ WEEK, MONTH
AMOUNT

J18. Do you have any food delivered to the door which isn't included in that?

YES / NO → GO TO J20

J19. How much do you spend on that food?

$ _____ PER _____ WEEK, MONTH
AMOUNT

J20. About how much do you (or anyone else in your family) spend eating out, not counting meals at work or at school?

$ _____ PER _____ WEEK, MONTH
AMOUNT

TURN TO P. 35, J25

J36. INTERVIEWER CHECKPOINT

1. ☐ CHILDREN UNDER AGE 12 LIVING IN FU

5. ☐ NO CHILDREN UNDER 12 IN FU → TURN TO P. 39, SECTION K

J37. INTERVIEWER CHECKPOINT

1. ☐ HEAD IS WORKING FEMALE

2. ☐ HEAD IS MALE, WIFE IS WORKING

3. ☐ HEAD IS MALE, NO WIFE

4. ☐ HEAD IS MALE, WIFE IS NOT WORKING → TURN TO P. 39, SECTION K

5. ☐ HEAD IS FEMALE WHO IS NOT WORKING → TURN TO P. 39, SECTION K

J38. How is your (youngest) child taken care of during work hours?

_____

_____

(IF IN SCHOOL)
J39. What about after school or when school is closed?

_____

_____

J40. How many hours a week is your (youngest) child taken care of (not counting time in regular school)?

_____ HOURS PER WEEK

J29. Did you (or anyone else in your family) raise any of your own food during 1978, or do any canning or freezing?

1. YES

5. NO → TURN TO P. 37, J36

J30. How much do you think you saved doing this last year?

$_____
TURN TO P. 37, J36

DON'T KNOW

NO

J31. Was it more than $100?

YES

NO → TURN TO P. 37, J36

J32. Was it more than $200?

YES

NO → TURN TO P. 37, J36

J33. About how much did you save?

$_____

J34. Was it more than $50?

YES → TURN TO P. 37, J36

NO

J35. Was it more than $25?

YES

NO

SECTION K: INCOME

To get an accurate financial picture of people all over the country, we need to know the income of all the families that we interview.

K1. INTERVIEWER CHECKPOINT

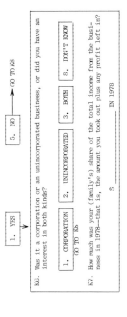

- [ ] 1. HEAD IS FARMER, OR RANCHER
- [ ] 5. HEAD IS NOT A FARMER OR RANCHER → GO TO K5

K2. What were your total receipts from farming in 1978, including soil bank payments and commodity credit loans? $_____ A

K3. What were your total operating expenses, not counting living expenses? $_____ B

K4. That left you a net income from farming of? (A - B =) $_____ A-B

K5. Did you (or anyone else in the family here) own a business at any time in 1978, or have a financial interest in any business enterprise?

1. YES

5. NO → GO TO K8

K6. Was it a corporation or an unincorporated business, or did you have an interest in both kinds?

1. CORPORATION   GO TO K8
2. UNINCORPORATED
3. BOTH
8. DON'T KNOW

K7. How much was your (family's) share of the total income from the business in 1978—that is, the amount you took out plus any profit left in?

$_____ IN 1978

K8. How much did you (HEAD) receive from wages and salaries in 1978, that is, before anything was deducted for taxes or other things?

$_____ IN 1978

J41. (Now, thinking of the care of all your children during work hours)—do you pay money for any of this child care?

1. YES

5. NO → GO TO J43

J42. How much does it cost you?

$_____ PER _____ WEEK, MONTH

$_____ /WK

J43. Did you (or your wife) do something (else) in return for the care?

1. YES

5. NO → GO TO J45

J44. How much time does that take per week?

_____ HOURS PER WEEK

J45. Does the government pay for any of this child care?

1. YES

5. NO

8. DON'T KNOW

J46. In the past year how many days did someone have to stay home from work to take care of the (children/child) because these arrangements broke down?

_____ DAYS PER YEAR

40

K9. In addition to this, did you have any income from bonuses, overtime or commissions?

YES → | NO | → GO TO K11

K10. How much was that? _____ IN 1978

K11. I'm going to be reading you a list of other sources of income you might have. Did you (HEAD) receive any other income in 1978 from professional practice or trade? (FOR EACH "YES" TO K11, ASK K12.)

K12
How much was it? $ _____ PER _____

K13
(IF K12 IS NOT PER YEAR) During how much of 1978 did you get this income? _____

a. PROFESSIONAL PRACTICE OR TRADE — NO | YES

b. from farming or market gardening? — NO | YES

c. roomers or boarders? — NO | YES

d. dividends, interest, rent, trust funds, or royalties? — NO | YES

e. ADC, AFDC — NO | YES

f. Supplemental Security Income (the gold/tan/yellow checks)? — NO | YES

g. other welfare? — NO | YES

41

K14. INTERVIEWER CHECKPOINT

1. ☐ HEAD HAS INCOME FROM ADC, AFDC, SUPPLEMENTAL SECURITY INCOME, OR OTHER WELFARE ("YES" TO K11e, K11f, OR K11g)

2. ☐ HEAD DID NOT HAVE ANY INCOME FROM THESE SOURCES → GO TO K18

K15. Did welfare also help with your rent or other bills?

1. YES | 5. NO → GO TO K18

K16. What did they pay for? _____

(IF RENT)
K17. Was the rent paid directly to the landlord?

1. YES | 5. NO

K18. Did you (HEAD) receive any income in 1978 from social security? (FOR EACH "YES" TO K18, ASK K19.)

K19
How much did you receive in 1978? $ _____ PER _____

K20
(IF K19 IS NOT PER YEAR) During how much of 1978 did you get this income? _____

a. SOCIAL SECURITY? — NO | YES

b. Other retirement pay, pensions or annuities? — NO | YES

c. Unemployment compensation? — NO | YES

d. Workmens compensation? — NO | YES

e. Alimony? — NO | YES

f. Child support? — NO | YES

g. Help from relatives? — NO | YES

h. Anything else? (SPECIFY) — NO | YES

K34. **PRE-LIST** K34 FROM THE PREVIOUS YEAR'S COVER SHEET AND THE COMPUTER LISTING ON THE 1979 COVER SHEET BEFORE THE INTERVIEW

LIST BELOW:

- All persons over 15 years old from the previous year's cover sheet who were living in the household at the time of the 1978 interview.
- All persons over 15 who moved into the FU since the 1978 interview and before January 1, 1979.
- Any persons over 15 who were in the FU at any time during 1978.
- 1978 HEAD OR WIFE WHO MOVED OUT SINCE 1978 INTERVIEW.

UPDATE K34 USING THE ABOVE RULES AFTER THE CURRENT FAMILY COMPOSITION IS OBTAINED.

DO NOT ASK "EXTRA EARNER" SECTION FOR CURRENT HEAD OR WIFE

Relationship to Head	Sex	Age	"✓" Below When Each Extra Earner Completed
1			☐ YES
2			☐ YES
3			☐ YES
4			☐ YES
5			☐ YES
6			☐ YES

K35. INTERVIEWER CHECKPOINT

☐ A. ANY ELIGIBLE PERSONS LISTED ABOVE → ASK AN EXTRA EARNER SECTION K36-K50 FOR EACH PERSON LISTED IN 1 - 6 ABOVE

☐ B. NO ELIGIBLE PERSONS LISTED ABOVE → TURN TO P. 50, K51

K21. Did anyone (else) not living here now help (you/your family) out financially-- I mean give you money, or help with your expenses during 1978?

YES ↓   NO → GO TO K23

K22. How much did that amount to last year? $ _____

K23. INTERVIEWER CHECKPOINT

☐ A. HEAD IS MALE AND HAS WIFE IN FU
☐ B. HEAD IS MALE, DOES NOT HAVE WIFE IN FU → TURN TO P. 43, K34
☐ C. HEAD IS FEMALE → TURN TO P. 43, K34

K24. Did your (wife/friend) have any income during 1978?

YES ↓   NO → TURN TO P. 43, K34

K25. Was any of it earnings from her work?

YES ↓   NO → GO TO K27

K26. How much did she earn from work in 1978 before deductions?
$ _____ IN 1978

K27. Did she receive any unemployment compensation in 1978?

YES ↓   NO → GO TO K29

K28. How much was that? $ _____ IN 1978

K29. Did she receive any Social Security in 1978?

YES ↓   NO → GO TO K31

K30. How much was that? $ _____ IN 1978

K31. Did she have any other income in 1978 such as interest, dividends, or rent?

YES ↓   NO → TURN TO P. 43, K34

K32. What was it from? SOURCE _____ SOURCE _____

K33. How much did that amount to in 1978? $ _____ IN 1978   IN 1978

(DO NOT WRITE IN THIS SPACE)
HEAD TYPE INCOME:

TAXABLE	TRANSFER
L A	

(DO NOT WRITE IN THIS SPACE)
WIFE TYPE INCOME:

TAXABLE	TRANSFER
L A	

FIRST EXTRA EARNER: RELATIONSHIP TO HEAD _____ AGE _____ [ ]

K36. We would like to know about what (INDIVIDUAL) does--is (he/she) working now, looking for work, retired, a student, keeping house, or what? (CHECK ALL THAT APPLY).

1. WORKING NOW
2. ONLY TEMPORARILY LAID OFF
3. LOOKING FOR WORK, UNEMPLOYED
4. RETIRED
5. PERMANENTLY DISABLED

6. KEEPING HOUSE
7. STUDENT
8. OTHER (SPECIFY): _____

K37. During 1978 did (he/she) have a full-time or part-time job (not counting work around the house)?

FULL-TIME JOB

PART-TIME JOB

DID NOT HAVE A JOB
GO TO K42

K38. About how many weeks did (he/she) work last year?
_____ WEEKS IN 1978
DON'T KNOW

K39. During the weeks that (he/she) worked about how many hours did (he/she) usually work per week?
_____ HOURS PER WEEK
DON'T KNOW

K40. What kind of work did (he/she) usually do?

K41. About how much money did (he/she) earn from work last year?
$ _____ IN 1978

K42. Did (he/she) have any (other) income last year?
YES

NO → TURN TO P.45, K45

K43. What was that from?

K44. How much was that last year? $ _____ IN 1978

K45. During 1973 was there any time when (he/she) was laid off or looking for work and could not find a job?

YES

NO
GO TO K47

DON'T KNOW

K46. About how many weeks was that?
_____ WEEKS IN 1973

K47. During 1978 was (he/she) enrolled in school as a full-time or part-time student?

1. FULL-TIME STUDENT
3. PART-TIME STUDENT
5. NOT ENROLLED IN SCHOOL
GO TO K49

K48. How many weeks did (he/she) attend school in 1973?
_____ WEEKS IN 1973
8. DON'T KNOW

K49. What is the highest grade or year of school that (he/she) has completed?
_____ GRADE/YEAR

K50. INTERVIEWER CHECKPOINT

A. MORE THAN 1 EXTRA EARNER LISTED IN K34 → GO TO P. 46, SECOND EXTRA EARNER SECTION

B. ONLY 1 EXTRA EARNER LISTED IN K34 → TURN TO P. 50, K51

TAXABLE   TRANSFER
L   A   [ ][ ]

TX [ ][ ][ ][ ]   WEEKS [ ][ ]

U/EMP [ ][ ][ ]   TR [ ][ ]

46

SECOND EXTRA EARNER: RELATIONSHIP TO HEAD _____ AGE _____ ☐

K36. We would like to know about what (INDIVIDUAL) does--is (he/she) working now, looking for work, retired, a student, keeping house, or what? (CHECK ALL THAT APPLY).

| 1. WORKING NOW | 2. ONLY TEMPORARILY LAID OFF | 3. LOOKING FOR WORK, UNEMPLOYED | 4. RETIRED | 5. PERMANENTLY DISABLED |

| 6. KEEPING HOUSE | 7. STUDENT | 8. OTHER (SPECIFY: _____ |

K37. During 1978 did (he/she) have a full-time or part-time job (not counting work around the house)?

FULL-TIME JOB   PART-TIME JOB   DID NOT HAVE A JOB
                                               GO TO K42

K38. About how many weeks did (he/she) work last year?

_____ WEEKS IN 1978

K39. During the weeks that (he/she) worked about how many hours did (he/she) usua work per week?

_____ HOURS PER WEEK   DON'T KNOW

K40. What kind of work did (he/she) usually do? _____

K41. About how much money did (he/she) earn from work last year?

$ _____ IN 1978

K42. Did (he/she) have any (other) income last year?

YES   NO → TURN TO P. 47 , K45

K43. What was that from? _____

K44. How much was that last year? $ _____ IN 1978

K45. During 1978 was there any time when (he/she) was laid off or could not find a job?

YES   NO   DON'T KNOW
                         GO TO K47

K46. About how many weeks was that?

_____ WEEKS IN 1973

K47. During 1978 was (he/she) enrolled in school as a full-time or part-time student?

| 1. FULL-TIME STUDENT | 3. PART-TIME STUDENT | 5. NOT ENROLLED IN SCHOOL |
                                                    GO TO K49

| | 8. DON'T KNOW |

K48. How many weeks did (he/she) attend school in 1973?

_____ WEEKS IN 1973

K49. What is the highest grade or year of school that (he/she) has completed?

_____ GRADE/YEAR

K50. INTERVIEWER CHECKPOINT

☐ A. MORE THAN 2 EXTRA EARNERS LISTED IN K34 → GO TO P. 48 , THIRD EXTRA EARNER SECTION

☐ B. ONLY 2 EXTRA EARNERS LISTED IN K34 → TURN TO P. 50, K51

TAXABLE   TRANSFER
L   A   ☐

TX ☐ ☐☐☐ ☐   WEIGHT ☐ ☐☐☐☐
UNEMP ☐ ☐☐   TR ☐☐

48

K36. THIRD EXTRA EARNER: RELATIONSHIP TO HEAD _____ AGE _____ ☐☐

K36. We would like to know about what (INDIVIDUAL) does--is (he/she) working now, looking for work, retired, a student, keeping house, or what? (CHECK ALL THAT APPLY).

1. WORKING NOW
2. ONLY TEMPORARILY LAID OFF
3. LOOKING FOR WORK, UNEMPLOYED
4. RETIRED
5. PERMANENTLY DISABLED
6. KEEPING HOUSE
7. STUDENT
8. OTHER (SPECIFY): _____

K37. During 1978 did (he/she) have a full-time or part-time job (not counting work around the house)?

FULL-TIME JOB →
PART-TIME JOB →
DID NOT HAVE A JOB → GO TO K42

K38. About how many weeks did (he/she) work last year?
_____ WEEKS IN 1978
DON'T KNOW

K39. During the weeks that (he/she) worked about how many hours did (he/she) usually work per week?
_____ HOURS PER WEEK
DON'T KNOW

K40. What kind of work did (he/she) usually do? _____

K41. About how much money did (he/she) earn from work last year?
$ _____ IN 1978

K42. Did (he/she) have any (other) income last year?
YES →
NO → TURN TO P. 49, K45

K43. What was that from? _____

K44. How much was that last year? $ _____ IN 1978

49

K45. During 1978 was there any time when (he/she) was laid off or looking for work and could not find a job?
YES →
NO → GO TO K47
DON'T KNOW

K46. About how many weeks was that? _____ WEEKS IN 1978

K47. During 1978 was (he/she) enrolled in school as a full-time or part-time student?
1. FULL-TIME STUDENT →
3. PART-TIME STUDENT →
5. NOT ENROLLED IN SCHOOL → GO TO K49

K48. How many weeks did (he/she) attend school in 1978?
_____ WEEKS IN 1978
8. DON'T KNOW

K49. What is the highest grade or year of school that (he/she) has completed? _____ GRADE/YEAR

K50. INTERVIEWER CHECKPOINT

☐ A. MORE THAN 3 EXTRA EARNERS LISTED IN K34 → USE EXTRA EARNER SUPPLEMENTAL SECTION (BLUE)

☐ B. ONLY 3 EXTRA EARNERS LISTED IN K34 → TURN TO P. 50, K51

TAXABLE TRANSFER
L   A   ☐☐

TX ☐☐☐   WEIGHS ☐☐
UNEMP ☐☐☐   TR ☐☐

K51. Did anyone else living here in 1978 have any income in 1978? (INCLUDING CHILDREN UNDER 16)

YES | NO → GO TO K56

K52. Who was that? (LIST EACH PERSON AND ASK K53 AND K54)

RELATIONSHIP TO HEAD	AGE	K53 What was that from?	K54 About how much was that
___	___	___	___

K55. Did anyone else living here in 1978 have any income in 1978?

YES | NO → GO TO K56

ASK K52 - K54 ABOVE

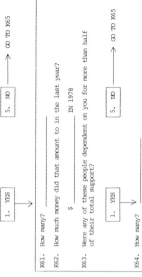

SEQ #

TAXABLE	TRANSFER		TAXABLE	TRANSFER
L A			L A	
TX			TX	
TR			TR	

SEQ #

K56. During the past year, has anyone in the family received medical care which has been or will be paid for by Medicare or Medicaid (Medi-Cal, Medical Assistance, Welfare, Medical Services)?

1. YES | 5. NO → TURN TO P. 51, K58

K57. Which program was it?

1. MEDICARE
2. MEDICAID, MEDI-CAL, MEDICAL ASSISTANCE WELFARE, MEDICAL SERVICES
7. OTHER (SPECIFY): _____
8. DON'T KNOW

K58. Did you get any other money in 1978—like a big settlement from an insurance company, or an inheritance?

1. YES | 5. NO → GO TO K60

K59. How much did that amount to ?
$ _____ IN 1978

K60. Last year did you help support anyone who doesn't live here with you now?

1. YES | 5. NO → GO TO K65

K61. How many?

K62. How much money did that amount to in the last year?
$ _____ IN 1978

K63. Were any of these people dependent on you for more than half of their total support?

1. YES | 5. NO → GO TO K65

K64. How many?

K65. Would you feel you had to help your parents or other relatives (more) if you had more money? _____

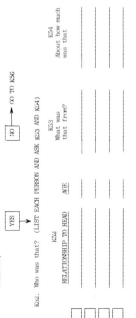
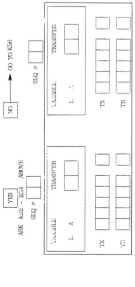

K75. Do you belong to a labor union?

1. YES   5. NO

K76. INTERVIEWER CHECKPOINT

1. ☐ THERE IS A WIFE IN FU

5. ☐ NO WIFE IN FU → GO TO K78

K77. Does your wife belong to a labor union?

1. YES   5. NO

K78. Do you (HEAD) have any physical or nervous condition that limits the type of work or the amount of work you can do?

1. YES   5. NO → TURN TO P. 54, SECTION L

K79. Does it limit your work a lot, somewhat, or just a little?

1. A LOT   3. SOMEWHAT   5. JUST A LITTLE

K66. Do you (or your family) have any savings such as checking or savings accounts or government bonds?

1. YES   5. NO → GO TO K68

K67. Would they amount to as much as two month's income or more?

1. YES (GO TO K69)   5. NO

K68. Was there a time in the last five years when you had as much as two month's income saved up?

1. YES   5. NO

K69. Prices and costs have been rising generally—are there some particular increases that have hit you especially hard?

1. YES   5. NO → GO TO K73

K70. What are they?

K71. Have you been able to do anything about it?

1. YES   5. NO → GO TO K73

K72. What have you done?

K73. Has inflation caused you to change your ideas about retirement?

1. YES   5. NO → TURN TO P. 53, K75

K74. How have they changed?

SECTION M: NEW HEAD

M1. INTERVIEWER CHECKPOINT

☐ 1. HEAD IS A NEW HEAD THIS YEAR

☐ 5. HEAD IS THE SAME HEAD AS IN 1978 → TURN TO P. 3 OF COVER SHEET
   EXACT TIME NOW: ___

M2. Now I have some questions about your (HEAD'S) family and past experiences.
Where did your father and mother grow up? (FROM BIRTH TO 18 YEARS OF AGE.)

ST, CO- FA ☐☐☐ ☐☐☐
Father: _____ _____ _____
                 (STATE IF U.S., COUNTRY IF FOREIGN) (COUNTY OR TOWN)

ST, CO- MA ☐☐☐ ☐☐☐
Mother: _____ _____ _____
                 (STATE IF U.S., COUNTRY IF FOREIGN) (COUNTY OR TOWN)

M3. What was your father's usual occupation when you were growing up?

_____ OCC ☐☐☐

M4. Thinking of your (HEAD'S) first full-time regular job, what did you do?

_____

                    ☐ 0. NEVER WORKED
                       TURN TO P. 56, M6

M5. Have you had a number of different kinds of jobs, or have you mostly worked
in the same occupation you started in, or what?

_____ OCC ☐☐☐

_____

SECTION L: NEW WIFE

L1. INTERVIEWER CHECKPOINT

☐ 1. HEAD HAS NEW WIFE THIS YEAR (REMEMBER: SHE MAY HAVE BEEN
      'FRIEND' LAST YEAR)

☐ 5. HEAD IS FEMALE ──────→ TURN TO P. 55, SECTION M
☐ 5. HEAD IS MALE WITH NO WIFE ──→ TURN TO P. 55, SECTION M
☐ 5. HEAD IS MALE WITH SAME WIFE AS IN 1978 → TURN TO P. 55, SECTION M

L2. How many grades of school did your (wife/friend) finish?

GRADES OF SCHOOL

☐00 ☐01 ☐02 ☐03 ☐04 ☐05 ☐06 ☐07 ☐08 ☐09 ☐10 ☐11 ☐12

COLLEGE

☐13 ☐14 ☐15 ☐16 ☐17+

L3. Did she have any other schooling?

☐ 1. YES   ☐ 5. NO → GO TO L8

L4. What other schooling did she have?

_____

_____

L5. What college was that?

_____

L6. Does she have a college degree?

☐ 1. YES   ☐ 5. NO
                 GO TO L8

L7. Does she have any advanced degrees?

☐ 1. YES   ☐ 5. NO

L8. How much education did your (wife's/friend's) father have? _____

L9. How much education did your (wife's/friend's) mother have? _____

L10. How many years altogether has your (wife/friend) worked for money since she
was 18?

_____ YEARS   ☐ 00. NONE ── TURN TO P. 55, SECTION M

L11. How many of these years did she work full-time for most or all of the year?

_____ YEARS   ☐ ALL ── TURN TO P. 55, SECTION M

L12. During the years that she was not working full-time how much of the time did
she work? (PROBE FOR TIME PERIOD)

☐☐

☐☐

M17. Have you (HEAD) ever moved out of a community where you were living in order to take a job somewhere else?

1. YES
GO TO M19

5. NO →

M18. Have you ever turned down a job because you did not want to move?

1. YES   5. NO

M19. Were your parents poor when you were growing up, pretty well off, or what?
_____

M20. How much education did your (HEAD'S) father have?
_____

(IF LESS THAN 6 GRADES)
M21. Could he read and write?

M22. How much education did your (HEAD'S) mother have?
_____

(IF LESS THAN 6 GRADES)
M23. Could she read and write?

M24. Are you (HEAD) a veteran?

1. YES   5. NO

M25. How many years have you worked since you were 18?
_____ YEARS

M26. How many of these years did you work full-time for most of the year?
_____ YEARS

ALL → TURN TO P. 58, M28
00. NONE → TURN TO P. 58, M28

M27. During the years that you were not working full-time, how much of the time did you work?
_____
_____

M6. Do you (HEAD) have any children who don't live with you?

YES →
NO → GO TO M9

M7. How many? _____ NUMBER

M8. When were they born? _____ YEAR BORN _____ YEAR BORN _____ YEAR BORN

1st
2nd
3rd
BY 25
#

M9. Did you (HEAD) have any children who are not now living?

YES →
NO → GO TO M11

M10. When were they born? _____ YEAR BORN _____ YEAR BORN

M11. How many brothers and sisters did you (HEAD) have?
_____ NUMBER

0. NONE → GO TO M13

M12. Were any of your brothers or sisters older than you?

1. YES   5. NO

M13. Did you (HEAD) grow up on a farm, in a small town, in a large city, or what?

1. FARM   2. SMALL TOWN   3. LARGE CITY   OTHER (SPECIFY): _____

M14. In what state and county was that? (EXAMPLE: ILLINOIS, COOK COUNTY)

_____ STATE _____ COUNTY

ST.
CO- H

(IF DON'T KNOW TO M14)

M15. What was the name of the nearest town? _____ TOWN

M16. What other states or countries have you lived in, including time spent abroad while in the armed forces?
_____

SECTION N: BY OBSERVATION ONLY

N1. Who was respondent (relation to Head)? _____

N2. Number of calls? _____

THUMBNAIL SKETCH: MUST BE FILLED OUT. EXPLAIN FAMILY INTER-RELATIONSHIPS SUCH AS WHO IS DEPENDENT UPON WHOM—AND PLEASE DO NOT EVER USE NAMES IN QUESTIONNAIRE (THIS IS A CARDINAL RULE FOR INTER-VIEWERS.)

M28. How many grades of school did you (HEAD) finish?

GRADES OF SCHOOL

| 00 | 01 | 02 | 03 | 04 | 05 | 06 | 07 | 08 | 09 | 10 | 11 | 12 |

COLLEGE

| 13 | 14 | 15 | 16 | 17+ |

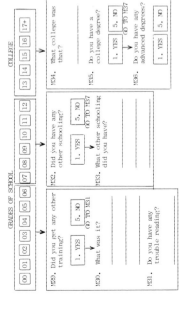

M29. Did you get any other training?
1. YES | 5. NO GO TO M31

M30. What was it? _____

M31. Do you have any trouble reading? _____

M32. Did you have any other schooling?
1. YES | 5. NO GO TO M37

M33. What other schooling did you have? _____

M34. What college was that? _____

M35. Do you have a college degree?
1. YES | 5. NO GO TO M37

M36. Do you have any advanced degrees?
1. YES | 5. NO

M37. Now we would like to ask for your religious preference. This involves a right that is protected by the United States Constitution. You are under no obligation to answer these questions, and, if for any reason, you decide you do not wish to answer them, we will accept and respect your decision. The information requested is important to us, and we hope you will decide to answer them.

May we record your religious preference?

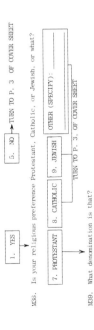

1. YES

5. NO → TURN TO P. 3 OF COVER SHEET

M38. Is your religious preference Protestant, Catholic, or Jewish, or what?

7. PROTESTANT | 8. CATHOLIC | 9. JEWISH | OTHER (SPECIFY): _____

TURN TO P. 3 OF COVER SHEET

M39. What denomination is that? _____

TURN TO P. 3 OF COVER SHEET

EXACT TIME NOW: _____